This is the first specific, large-scale study of conduct in warfare and the nature of chivalry in the Anglo-Norman period.

The extent to which the knighthood consciously sought to limit the extent of fatalities among its members is explored through a study of notions of a brotherhood in arms, the actualities of combat and the effectiveness of armour, the treatment of prisoners, and the workings of ransom. Were there 'laws of war' in operation in the eleventh and twelfth centuries and, if so, were they binding? How far did notions of honour affect knights' actions in war itself? Conduct in war against an opposing suzerain such as the Capetian king is contrasted to behaviour in situations of rebellion and of civil war.

A study of aristocratic violence towards churches in war, and of the mechanisms of ravaging, examines the behaviour of the knighthood to the other *ordines* of society, the Church and the peasantry. An overall context is provided by an examination of the behaviour in war of the Scots and the mercenary *routiers*, both accused of perpetrating 'atrocities'.

WAR AND CHIVALRY

WAR AND CHIVALRY

THE CONDUCT AND PERCEPTION OF WAR IN ENGLAND AND NORMANDY, 1066–1217

MATTHEW STRICKLAND
University of Glasgow

CAMBRIDGE
UNIVERSITY PRESS

Published by the Press Syndicate of the University of Cambridge
The Pitt Building, Trumpington Street, Cambridge CB2 1RP
40 West 20th Street, New York, NY 10011-4211, USA
10 Stamford Road, Oakleigh, Melbourne 3166, Australia

First published 1996

Printed in Great Britain at the University Press, Cambridge

A catalogue record for this book is available from the British Library

Library of Congress cataloguing in publication data

Strickland, Matthew, 1962–
War and chivalry: the conduct and perception of war in England
and Normandy, 1066–1217 / Matthew Strickland.
p.   cm.
Includes bibliographical references and index.
ISBN 0 521 44392 X (hc)
1. Great Britain–History, Military–1066–1485. 2. England–
Civilization–Medieval period, 1066–1485. 3. Great Britain–
History–Angevin period, 1154–1216. 4. Great Britain–History–
Norman period, 1066–1154. 5. Knights and knighthood–France–
Normandy. 6. Normandy (France)–History, Military. 7. Knights and
knighthood–England. 8. Normans–England–History. 9. Chivalry.
I. Title.   II. Series.
DA60.S77   1996
942.02–dc20   95-44002 CIP

ISBN 0 521 44392 X

To my Mother and Father

CONTENTS

─────

List of illustrations   *page* xii
List of maps   xiv
Preface   xv
List of abbreviations   xvii

1   INTRODUCTION: THE CONQUEST AND CHIVALRY   1
    Through a glass darkly: chivalry and the sources   7
    Veracity or wishful thinking? The problem of Orderic Vitalis   12
    The scope of the enquiry   16
    The nature of chivalry   19

2   A 'LAW OF ARMS'?   31
    Legnano, Bonet and the laws of war   31
    Ius, lex or *mos*? Positive law, custom and military regulations   34
    Authority and enforceability   46

3   A CHRISTIAN CHIVALRY? WAR, PIETY AND SACRILEGE   55
    'Dieux aide!': the invocation of divine aid in battle   58
    The knights' war and the Church's peace: ecclesiastical attempts
        to limit the nature of war   70
    'Non militia sed malitia': clerical reportage of knightly violence
        against churches   75
    The plundering of churches: sacrilege or military expediency?   78
        The violation of sanctuary   78
        The plundering of churches   81
        Tenserie: the long-term exploitation of ecclesiastical resources   84
    Damage and destruction of churches in war   86

The psychology of destruction   90
'Pro restauratione dampnorum': deed and atonement   91

4   HONOUR, SHAME AND REPUTATION   98
    Prowess in arms: the vocabulary of honour   98
    Tourneys, boasting and war: the sustaining and augmenting of
        honour   104
    The price of glory? Individual honour and corporate discipline 113
    Cowardice, shame and dishonour   117
    Ruse, guile and the limitations of honour as a coercive force 124

5   CONDUCT IN BATTLE: A BROTHERHOOD IN ARMS?   132
    The changing face of war   133
    Feud and civil war   138
    Milites and the militia   142
    The impact of the tournament   149
    Restraint from killing in battle   153

6   THE LIMITS OF CHIVALRY AND THE REALITIES OF
        BATTLE   159
    Adding insult to injury: the taunting and abuse of opponents 160
    Killing in battle   162
    The effectiveness of armour   169
    The treatment of infantry   176

7   RANSOM AND THE TREATMENT OF PRISONERS   183
    Ransom: the financial incentive for clemency   183
    Ransom and feudal custom   186
    The value of ransoms   193
    The treatment of prisoners   196

8   RESPITE, RESISTANCE AND HONOURABLE SURRENDER:
        CONVENTIONS OF SIEGE WARFARE   204
    The role of the castle in war   204
    Conditional respite: the fusion of honour and pragmatism   208
    No surrender? Heroism, vassalic loyalty and the limits of
        resistance   212
    Clemency, franchise and reputation: the treatment of enemy
        garrisons   218
    The right of storm   222
    Faint-hearted defence: cowardice or treachery?   224

9   REBELLION, TREASON AND THE PUNISHMENT OF
       REVOLT   230
    Treason, rebellion and divided allegiance   231
    The punishment of rebellion   240
    Clemency or expediency? The limitations of royal action   247

10 WAR AGAINST THE LAND: RAVAGING AND ATTRITION   258
    Foraging: the command of local resources   260
    War against the land: economic attrition   268
    Killing of the peasantry   270
    The effects of ravaging: problems of evidence   273
    Ravaging as intimidation and political control   277
    The antithesis of chivalry?   281

11 TOTAL WAR? THE SCOTS AND THE ROUTIERS   291
    The reporting of atrocity: propaganda or truth?   294
    The constituents of atrocity   304
       Indiscriminate slaughter   304
       The enslavement of prisoners   313
       Sacrilege   317
    The extent of royal complicity   320
    Indiscipline and the control of ravaging   323

CONCLUSION   330

Bibliography   341
Index   366

ILLUSTRATIONS

———

1 The death of Harold at Hastings, 1066, from the Bayeux *page* 6
  Tapestry (by special permission of the City of Bayeux).
2 Abraham receiving communion from Melchizedek, from the
  interior of the west front, Reims cathedral, mid-thirteenth
  century (James Austin).   61
3 A mid-twelfth-century sword, inlaid with the letters BOAC
  (Glasgow Museums and Art Galleries).   63
4 English bishops bless the royal forces who engage Louis's fleet
  at the battle of Sandwich, 1217 (Matthew Paris, *Chronica majora*,
  Corpus Christi College, Cambridge, MS 16, f. 52r).   69
5 A sinful knight is pitchforked into Hell, from the tympanum of
  Sainte Foi, Conques, Aveyron (James Austin).   93
6 The battle of Bouvines, 1214, from the *Chronica majora* of
  Matthew Paris (Corpus Christi College, Cambridge,
  MS 16, f. 37r).   105
7 Following a skirmish, knights lead off bound prisoners and
  livestock, from the Maciejowski Bible (Pierpont Morgan
  Library, M. 638, f. 24v, detail).   172
8 An enemy camp is surprised, from the Maciejowski Bible
  (Pierpont Morgan Library, M. 638, f. 3v, detail).   177
9 A Norman knight dispatches an Anglo-Saxon ceorl, from the
  Bayeux Tapestry (by special permission of the City of Bayeux).   178
10 Siege warfare, from the Maciejowski Bible (Pierpont Morgan
  Library, M. 638, f. 23v, detail).   206
11 Conan, count of Brittany, surrenders the castle of Dinan to
  Duke William in 1064, from the Bayeux Tapestry (by special
  permission of the City of Bayeux).   217

12 The execution of the garrison of Bedford, 1224, from the
    Chronica majora of Matthew Paris (Corpus Christi College,
    Cambridge, MS 16, f. 60r).   243
13 Norman soldiers forage for food and slaughter captured
    livestock, from the Bayeux Tapestry (by special permission of
    the City of Bayeux).   262
14 A woman and her child flee from a house being torched by
    Norman troops, from the Bayeux Tapestry (by special
    permission of the City of Bayeux).   272
15 Tartar atrocities from the *Chronica majora* of Matthew Paris
    (Corpus Christi College, Cambridge, MS 16, f. 166r).   297
16 Decapitated captives from the tenth-century Sveno stone at
    Forres, Moray (T. E. Gray).   308
17 The oppression of John's subjects by his agents from the
    Chronica majora of Matthew Paris (Corpus Christi College,
    Cambridge, MS 16, f. 166r).   313

The author would like to thank the following for their permission to repro-
duce illustrations:
Musée de la Tapisserie, Centre Guillaume le Conquérant, Bayeux, 1, 9, 11,
13, 14; the Master and Fellows of Corpus Christi College, Cambridge, 4, 6,
12, 15, 17; the Pierpont Morgan Library, New York, 7, 8, 10; James Austin,
2, 5; T. E. Gray, 16; Glasgow Museums and Art Galleries, 3; and R. Ewart
Oakshott for the figure accompanying Plate 3.

MAPS

———

1 The Duchy of Normandy   *page* xxiii
2 Twelfth-century France   xxiv
3 Anglo-Norman England   xxv

PREFACE

———

The ability both to give and to heed good counsel ranked high among the many chivalric qualities expected of the *prudhomme*. If this book is far from being *sans reproche*, then the fault is mine alone, for in its preparation, as in so much else, I have benefitted enormously from the help and advice of many friends and colleagues. A brief preface such as this can do them scant justice.

I owe a particular debt to Jim Holt, who provided incisive comment and constructive advice at every stage during the long metamorphosis from thesis to book, and who encouraged me to keep faith with a broad thematic and conceptual treatment of Anglo-Norman chivalry. Two others deserve special thanks. Bill Zajac has given unstintingly of his wide knowledge, above all on the crusades, and over many years has helped to hone my thoughts concerning conduct in medieval warfare. John Hudson cast the expert eye of an Anglo-Norman legist over the text, and made invaluable suggestions for its improvement.

I have been saved from numerous infelicities of style and content by the efforts of Archie Duncan, John Gillingham, Richard Barber, Jackie Hill, Rachel Neaman, Lesley Abrams, Andrew Roach, Stuart Airlie and Simon Ball, all of whom read all or part of the book in its various stages. Michael Kennedy has been as generous with his erudition on the twelfth century as with access to his fine collection of books.

Warm thanks are equally due to Marjorie Chibnall, John Hatcher, Martin Brett, Rosamond McKitterick and Barrie Dobson for their support and advice. And while the emphasis of this study falls mainly post-Conquest, the influence of Simon Keynes, David Dumville, Ray Page and Peter Clemoes of the Anglo-Saxon Norse and Celtic Department at Cambridge may, I hope, still be glimpsed in some of the following pages.

If the acknowledgement of formative influences is one of the pleasures of a first book, it is equally a great sadness that Vivien Fisher, who instilled in me an abiding interest in Anglo-Norman history, Allen Brown, who offered me much encouragement in the early stages of my thesis, and Lewis Warren, who examined it with gentle rigour, did not live to see the completion of this work.

The Master and Fellows of Fitzwilliam College, Cambridge, generously awarded me a visiting scholarship, allowing me to make final revisions of the text in the most convivial of atmospheres. Robert Hardy has not only borne the long delay of our joint enterprise on the medieval longbow with great *franchise*, but as with Chaucer's Franklin, 'it snewed in his hous of mete and drinke'. Thanks are also due to David Luscombe for his careful editing, and to William Davies of Cambridge University Press for his patient sufferance.

Last, but far from least, I would like to thank my parents, John and Elizabeth, for their unfailing support in this as in so much else. My debt to them is unbounded, and it is to them that I dedicate this book.

ABBREVIATIONS

AM	*Annales monastici*, ed. H. R. Luard, 5 vols. (Rolls Series, 1864–9).
Ambroise	*L'Estoire de la Guerre Sainte par Ambroise*, ed. G. Paris (Paris, 1897); tr. M. J. Hubert and J. L. La Monte as *The Crusade of Richard the Lion-Heart by Ambroise* (Columbia, 1941, repr. New York, 1976).
ASC	*The Anglo-Saxon Chronicle*, tr. in *English Historical Documents*, I (500–1042), ed. D. Whitelock (2nd edn, London, 1979), for annals up to 1042, and *English Historical Documents*, II (1042–1189), ed. D. C. Douglas (2nd edn, London, 1981) for annals 1042–1144.
Beha-ad-Din	Beha-ad-Din (Ibn Shaddad), *The Life of Saladin*, tr. C. L. Conder (Palestine Pilgrims' Text Society, XIII, London, 1897).
BT	*The Bayeux Tapestry. The Complete Tapestry in Colour with an Introduction and Commentary*, ed. D. M. Wilson (London, 1985).
Carmen	*The Carmen de Hastingae Proelio of Guy, Bishop of Amiens*, ed. and tr. C. Morton and H. Muntz (Oxford, 1972).
Chronica de Hida	*Chronica de Hida*, in *Liber monasterii de Hyda*, ed. E. Edwards (Rolls Series, 1886).
Chronicle of Melrose	*The Chronicle of Melrose*, ed. A. O. and M. O. Anderson (Studies in Economics and Political Science, London, 1936).

Chronicles and Memorials	*Chronicles and Memorials of the reigns of Stephen, Henry II, and Richard I,* ed. R. Howlett, 4 vols. (Rolls Series, 1884–90).
Chronicon universale	*Chronicon universale anonymi Laudenensis,* ed. A. Cartellieri and W. Stechele (Leipzig and Paris, 1909).
Chroniques des comtes d'Anjou	*Chroniques des comtes d'Anjou et des seigneurs d'Amboise,* ed. L. Halphen and R. Pourpardin (Paris, 1913).
Coggeshall	*Radulphi de Coggeshall Chronicon Anglicanum,* ed. J. Stevenson (Rolls Series, 1875).
Devizes	*Richard of Devizes, Chronicon,* ed. and tr. J. Appleby (London, 1963).
Diceto	*Radulphi de Diceto decani Lundoniensis opera historica,* ed. W. Stubbs, 2 vols. (Rolls Series, 1876).
Diplomatic Documents	*Diplomatic Documents Preserved in the Public Record Office,* I, (1101–1272), ed. P. Chaplais (London, 1964).
Documents of the Baronial Movement	*Documents of the Baronial Movement of Reform and Rebellion 1258–1267,* selected by R. E. Treharne, ed. I. J. Saunders (Oxford, 1973).
Ducange	Ducange, *Glossarium mediae et infimae latinitatis,* ed. L. Favre, 10 vols. (Niort, 1883–7).
Eadmer	*Eadmeri historia novorum in Anglia,* ed. M. Rule (Rolls Series, 1884).
EHR	*English Historical Review.*
Expugnatio	Gerald of Wales, *Expugnatio Hibernica,* ed. A. B. Scott and F. X. Martin (Dublin, 1978).
Foedera	*Foedera, conventiones, litterae et cujuscunque generis acta publica,* ed. T. Rymer, new edn, vol. 1, part 1, ed. A. Clarke and F. Holbrooke (Record Commission, 1816).
Foliot	*The Letters and Charters of Gilbert Foliot,* ed. A. Morey and C. N. L. Brooke (Cambridge, 1967).
FW	Florence of Worcester, *Chronicon ex chronicis,* 2 vols., ed. B. Thorpe (London, 1848–9).
Gervase	*The Historical Works of Gervase of Canterbury,* ed. W. Stubbs, 2 vols. (Rolls Series, 1879–80).
GF	*Ottonis et Rahewini Gesta Friderici Imperatoris,* ed. G. Waitz and B. von Simson, *MGH, SS,* xlvi (repr., Hannover, 1922).

GFr	*Gesta Francorum et aliorum Hierosolimitanorum*, ed. R. Hill (London, 1962).
GH	*Gesta regis Henrici secundi Benedicti Abbatis*, ed. W. Stubbs, 2 vols. (Rolls Series, 1867).
GR	William of Malmesbury, *De gestis regum Anglorum*, ed. W. Stubbs, 2 vols. (Rolls Series, 1887–9).
GS	*Gesta Stephani*, ed. and tr. K. R. Potter, with an introduction by R. H. C. Davis (Oxford, 1973).
Guibert	*Self and Society in Medieval France: The Memoirs of Abbot Guibert of Nogent*, tr. J. F. Benton (New York, 1972).
HGM	*L'Histoire de Guillaume le Maréchal*, ed. P. Meyer, 3 vols. (Société de l'histoire de France, Paris, 1891–1901).
HH	Henry of Huntingdon, *Historia Anglorum*, ed. T. Arnold (Rolls Series, 1879).
Histoire des ducs	*Histoire des ducs de Normandie et des rois d'Angleterre*, ed. F. Michel (Société de l'histoire de France, Paris, 1840).
HN	William of Malmesbury, *Historia Novella*, ed. K. R. Potter (Nelson's Medieval Texts, London, 1955).
Howden	*Chronica Rogeri de Hovedene*, ed. W. Stubbs, 4 vols. (Rolls Series, 1868–71).
Itinerarium	*Itinerarium perigrinorum et gesta regis Ricardi*, ed. W. Stubbs, *Chronicles and Memorials of the reign of Richard I*, 2 vols. (Rolls Series, 1864), I.
JF	*Jordan Fantosme's Chronicle*, ed. and tr. R. C. Johnston (Oxford, 1981).
JH	*Historia Johannis, prioris Haugustadensis ecclesiae*, ed. J. Raine, *The Priory of Hexham, its Chroniclers, Endowments and Annals*, 2 vols. (Surtees Society, XLIV, Durham, 1868), I, pp. 107–72.
Joinville	Jean, sire de Joinville, *Histoire de Saint Louis*, ed. M. N. de Wailly (Société de l'histoire de France, Paris, 1868).
JW	*The Chronicle of John of Worcester, 1118–40*, ed. J. R. H. Weaver (Oxford, 1908).
Mansi	*Sacrorum conciliorum nova et amplissima collectio*, ed. J. D. Mansi (Florence, Venice and Paris, 1759 ff.).

Map	Walter Map, *De nugis curialium*, ed. and tr. M. R. James (Oxford, 1983).
MC	Magna Carta, ed. and tr. in J. C. Holt, *Magna Carta* (2nd edn, Cambridge 1992), pp. 448–73.
MGH SS	*Scriptores Rerum Germanicarum in usum scholarum ex Monumentis Germanicae Historicis separatim editi.*
Migne, *PL*	*Patrologia cursus completus, series latina*, ed. J. P. Migne *et al.*, 221 vols. in 222 with supplements (Paris, 1878–1974).
MP	*Matthaei Parisiensis, monachi sancti Albani, Chronica majora*, ed. H. R. Luard, 7 vols. (Rolls Series, 1872–3).
Niermeyer	J. F. Niermeyer, *Mediae Latinitatis Lexicon Minus* (Leiden, 1976).
Orderic	*The Ecclesiastical History of Orderic Vitalis*, ed. and tr. M. Chibnall, 6 vols. (Oxford, 1969–80).
Relatio	*Relatio venerabilis Aelredi, abbatis Rievallensis, de Standardo*, ed. R. Howlett in *Chronicles and Memorials*, III (Rolls Series, 1886), pp. 181–99.
RH	Richard of Hexham, *De gestis regis Stephani et de bello Standardii*, ed. J. Raine, *The Priory of Hexham, its Chroniclers, Endowments and Annals*, 2 vols. (Surtees Society, XLIV, Durham, 1868), I, pp. 63–106.
RHC	*Recueil des historiens des croisades*, 16 vols. (Paris, 1841–1906).
Occ.	*Historiens occidentaux.*
Or.	*Historiens orientaux.*
RHF	*Recueil des historiens des Gaules et de la France*, ed. M. Bouquet *et al.*, nouv. édn, ed. L. Delisle, 24 vols. (Paris, 1869–1904).
Rigord	Rigord: *Gesta Philippi Augusti*, in *Oeuvres de Rigord et Guillaume le Breton, historiens de Philippe Auguste*, ed. H-F. Delaborde, 2 vols. (Paris, 1882–5), I.
Rot. de Lib.	*Rotuli de Liberate ac de missis et Praestitis*, ed. T. Duffus Hardy (Record Commission, 1844).
Rot. Lit. Claus.	*Rotuli litterarum clausarum in turri Londinensi asservati*, ed. T. Duffus Hardy (Record Commission, 1833–4).
Rot. Litt. Pat.	*Rotuli litterarum patentium in turri Londinensi asservati*, ed. T. Duffus Hardy, vol. I (Record Commission, 1835).

Rot. Norm.	*Rotuli Normanniae in turri Londinensi asservati*, ed. T. D. Hardy, 1 (Record Commission, 1835).
Rot. de Ob. et Fin.	*Rotuli de oblatis et finibus in turri Londinensi asservati*, ed. T. Duffus Hardy, 2 vols. (Record Commission, 1835).
RRAN	*Regesta regum Anglo-Normannorum*, vol. I, ed. H. W. C. Davis (Oxford, 1913); vol. II, ed. C. Johnson and H. A. Cronne (Oxford, 1956); vols. III and IV, ed. H. A. Cronne and R. H. C. Davis (Oxford, 1968–9).
RRS	*Regesta Regum Scottorum*, vols. I and II, ed. G. W. S. Barrow (Edinburgh, 1960, 1971).
SD	*Simeon of Durham: Symeonis monachi opera omnia*, ed. T. Arnold, 2 vols. (Rolls Series, 1885).
Select Charters	*Select Charters and other Illustrations of English Constitutional History from the earliest times to the reign of Edward the First*, ed. W. Stubbs (9th edn, revised by H. W. C. Davis, Oxford, 1913).
Song of Dermot	*The Song of Dermot and the Earl*, ed. and tr. G. H. Orpen (London, 1892).
Song of Roland	*The Song of Roland: An Analytical Edition*, ed. and tr. G. J. Brault (University Park, Pennsylvania and London, 1978).
TCWAAS	*Transactions of the Cumberland and Westmorland Archaeological and Antiquarian Society.*
TLP	*Anthology of Troubadour Lyric Poetry*, ed. and tr. A. R. Press (Edinburgh, 1971).
Torigny	*The Chronicle of Roger of Torigni*, ed. R. Howlett in *Chronicles of the Reigns of Stephen, Henry II and Richard*, IV.
TRHS	*Transactions of the Royal Historical Society.*
Usamah	*An Arab-Syrian Gentleman and Warrior in the Period of the Crusades. The Memoirs of Usamah ibn Munqidh*, tr. P. K. Hitti (New York, 1929).
Vigeois	*Chronica Gaufredi coenobitae monasterii sancti Martialis Lemovicensis ac prioris Vosiensis coenobii, RHF*, XII, pp. 421–50 (1060–1182), XVIII, pp. 211–23 (1183–4).
Vita Ailredi	*Walter Daniel, The Life of Ailred of Rievaulx*, ed. and tr. F. M. Powicke (London, 1950).
Vita Herluini	*Vita Domni Herluini Abbatis Beccensis*, in J.

	Armitage Robinson, *Gilbert Crispin, Abbot of Westminster: A Study of the Abbey under Norman Rule* (Cambridge, 1911)
WB, *Gesta*	William le Breton, *Gesta Philippi Augusti* in *Oeuvres de Rigord et Guillaume le Breton, historiens de Philippe Auguste*, ed. H-F. Delaborde, 2 vols. (Paris, 1882–5), I, pp. 168–333.
Philippidos	William le Breton, *Philippidos*, ibid., II, pp. 1–385.
WC	*Memoriale fratris Walteri de Coventria*, ed. W. Stubbs, 2 vols. (Rolls Series, 1872–3).
WJ	Guillaume de Jumièges, *Gesta Normannorum ducum*, ed. J. Marx (Société de l'histoire de Normandie, 1914).
WN	William of Newburgh, *Historia Rerum Anglicarum, Chronicles and Memorials* (Rolls Series, 1884), I, and II, pp. 409–53.
WP	*Guillaume de Poitiers: Histoire de Guillaume le Conquérant*, ed. R. Foreville (Paris, 1952).
WT	William of Tyre: *Willelmi Tyrensis archiepiscopi chronicon*, ed. R. B. C. Huygens (*Corpus Christianorum Continuatio Medievalis*.

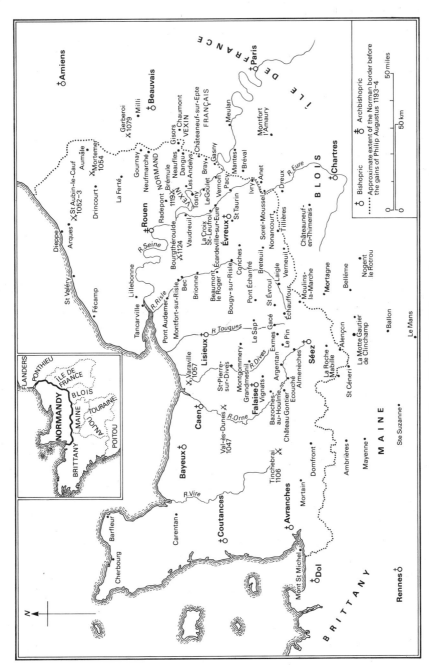

Map 1 The Duchy of Normandy

Map 2 Twelfth-century France

Key (on map):
- — — Approximate boundaries of the territorial principalities
- —— Approximate extent of Plantagenet dominions (with overlordship claimed over Toulouse and the Quercy)

Cherbourg
Rouen
Bouvines ✕ 1214
Coucy
Soissons
Bayeux
Coutances
Caen
R. Seine
VEXIN
ÎLE DE FRANCE
Paris
CHAMPAGNE
NORMANDY
Falaise
Chartres
Troyes
Dol
Le Puiset
Sens
Rennes
MAINE
Ballon
BLOIS
Orléans
BRITTANY
Roche-au-Moine
Le Mans
Fréteval
Vendôme
Mayet
Angers
Tours
Blois
R. Loire
ANJOU
TOURAINE
Saumur
Nantes
Fontevrault
Chinon
Loches
Thouars
Mirebeau ✕ 1202
BERRY
Vouvant
POITOU
Poitiers
La Rochelle
ANGOULÊME
LA MARCHE
Grandmont
SAINTONGE
Gorre
Limoges
AUVERGNE
Saintes
Châlus
Aixe
AQUITAINE
Angoulême
LIMOUSIN
Hautefort
Vigeois
Bordeaux
PÉRIGORD
Martel
Sarlat
R. Dordogne
Rocamadour
AGENAIS
QUERCY
R. Garonne
GASCONY
Albi
Toulouse
BÉARN
TOULOUSE
LANGUEDOC
N

100 miles
150 km

Map 3 Anglo-Norman England

INTRODUCTION: THE CONQUEST AND CHIVALRY

Shortly after his victory at Hastings on 14 October 1066, Duke William of Normandy marched on the Anglo-Saxon burgh at Dover, determined to secure control of this vital port. On his arrival, the Anglo-Saxon defenders, demoralized by the defeat of their army and the death of their king on Senlac ridge, decided to capitulate at once, despite the natural strength of the site which they were holding. As they were in the process of yielding, however, some Norman troops eager for booty set fire to the place. 'The duke', noted his biographer William of Poitiers, 'not wishing those to suffer who had begun negotiations with him to surrender, paid for the rebuilding of the houses and made good the other losses; and he would have severely punished those who had started the fire if their numbers and base condition had not prevented their detection'.[1]

Though only a minor event in the Norman subjugation of south-east England in 1066, this incident at Dover is of considerable significance. Victorious in the field and at the head of a powerful army, William could easily have overwhelmed such localized pockets of Anglo-Saxon resistance. Yet the duke clearly believed that in attacking a garrison in the process of surrender his men had committed a grave wrong for which they deserved punishment and for which the townsmen deserved recompense. In turn, the culprits themselves had been motivated by the assumption that if the enemy fortifications fell by storm, they had the right to plunder at will,[2] and therefore had precipitated an assault so that a negotiated surrender would not cheat them of booty. Conduct in war was clearly not a wholly arbitrary affair.

---

[1] *Guillaume de Poitiers: Histoire de Guillaume le Conquérant* (WP), ed. R. Foreville (Paris, 1952), pp. 210–13.
[2] On this 'right of storm' see below, pp. 222–4.

   The same considerations are visible two years later in William's treatment of the rebellious citizens of Exeter, who had refused to perform
homage to the new Norman king. On the approach of William's army, a
delegation came out to beg for peace and to offer hostages. Fearing the
severity of William's retribution, however, the townsmen changed their
minds and decided to offer resistance. Infuriated by such a *volte face*, William
had one of the hostages blinded in front of the defenders. Nevertheless, it
was only when, after repeated assaults, the Normans had begun to mine the
walls that the leading citizens and clergy came out bearing their books and
treasures and threw themselves on the king's mercy. William pardoned their
resistance, 'refrained from seizing their goods and posted a strong and
trustworthy guard at the gate, so that the rank and file of the army could
not break in and loot the city'.[3] Once a formal act of submission had been
performed, the citizens were now under the king's peace and were to be
protected from pillage, even if this meant keeping his own men, again
hungry for booty, back by force.
   In both these instances, William's propriety and clemency had been
inspired by the desire to show himself as a powerful yet merciful ruler,
thereby encouraging other erstwhile opponents to capitulate without fear
of reprisal and to accept him as King Edward's legitimate heir. The fate of
those who did not yield or who put themselves beyond his mercy had been
graphically demonstrated in 1051, when he had had the garrison of a castle
across the river from Alençon mutilated by cutting off their hands and
feet.[4] Yet William's behaviour at Dover, Exeter and Alençon was also
clearly conditioned by his awareness of and adherence to a series of
notions concerning conduct in war. And he evidently believed such
notions applied equally to his Anglo-Saxon opponents – who were also

---

[3] *The Ecclesiastical History of Orderic Vitalis*, (Orderic), ed. and tr. M. Chibnall, 6 vols., (Oxford, 1969–80),
II, pp. 212–15. Orderic here bases his narrative on the lost portion of William of Poitiers's *Gesta
Guillelmi*. Cf. the *Anglo-Saxon Chronicle* (*ASC*), 'D', s.a. 1067 (*recte* 1068); *English Historical Documents*
(*EHD*), Vol. 1 (c. 500–1042), ed. Whitelock (2nd edn, London, 1979) for annals from the inception of
the *Chronicle* to 1042, and *English Historical Documents*, Vol. II (1042–1189), ed. D. C. Douglas (2nd edn,
London, 1981) for annals from 1042–1144. For an excellent discussion of the context of the siege of
Exeter see J. O. Prestwich, 'Military Intelligence under the Norman and Angevin Kings', *Law and
Government in Medieval England and Normandy. Essays in Honour of Sir James Holt*, ed. G. Garnett and J.
Hudson (Cambridge, 1994), pp. 4–8.
[4] *Guillaume de Jumièges, Gesta Normannorum docum* (WJ), ed. J. Marx, (Société de l'Histoire de Normandie,
1914), p. 171; and for a full critical study of this text, see the introduction to *The Gesta Normannorum
Ducum of William of Jumièges, Orderic Vitalis and Robert of Torigny*, ed. and tr. E. M. C. van Houts, 2 vols.
(Oxford, 1992–95), 1. pp. xix ff. Marx's edition of Jumièges has been used here, however, as only the
first volume of Dr van Houts's work, extending to the death of Duke Richard I in 996, was available
at the time of writing. William was roused to such brutality because, according to Orderic's interpola-
tion, the defenders had beaten hides at him and shouted 'Tanner!', alluding to the allegation that his
mother Herleve had been a tanner's daughter (WJ, p. 171). The date of this incident is either 1051 or
possibly 1048 (R. A. Brown, *The Norman Conquest* (London, 1984), p. 11, n. 10).

now his subjects – as to his enemies in the feudal warfare of North-West France.

Whether the Anglo-Saxons themselves had a body of custom regulating the conduct of siege prior to 1066 is uncertain. For although castles *per se* were a Norman import into England, larger communal fortifications or *burghs* had played a significant defensive and indeed offensive role in the Alfredian wars, the 'Reconquest' of the Danelaw and the later invasions of Svein and Cnut.[5] The investment of such fortresses was often a lengthy process lending itself to negotiation and pragmatic compromise, and it may be that the laconic entries of the *Anglo-Saxon Chronicle* hide incidents similar to those at Dover and Exeter at an earlier date. What is more certain, however, is that the Conquest marked a profound change in warriors' conduct in battle itself.[6] To the Anglo-Saxons, accustomed to fighting essentially defensive wars to safeguard the *patria* against a foreign invader, who up to the early eleventh century had usually been pagan Vikings, pitched battle habitually entailed the wholesale slaughter of the defeated force. The annihilation of Harald Hardraada and his Norwegians at Stamford Bridge in 1066 had been a grim, if timely, reminder to William and his men of the fate which awaited them if they suffered defeat at the hands of King Harold.[7] For once, William of Poitiers was not indulging in empty rhetoric when he has Duke William rally his fleeing troops at Hastings with the exhortation that they must either conquer or die.[8]

By contrast, the conventions of ransom and the sparing of knightly opponents in battle, which appear to be essentially Frankish in origin, are visible in the Norman duchy by 1066, though by no means as a universal usage.[9] Yet at Hastings both the Normans' perception of their enemy and a desperate military situation combined to render such notions of restraint both impractical and undesirable. In strategic terms, the Normans, with

---

[5] A detailed and specifically military study of the strategic use of Anglo-Saxon communal defences is still lacking, but for burghs in general see: C. A. R. Radford, 'The Pre-Conquest Boroughs of England, 9th–11th Centuries', *Proceedings of the British Academy*, 64 (1980 for 1978), pp. 131–53; *idem.*, 'The Later Pre-Conquest Boroughs and Their Defences', *Medieval Archaeology*, 14 (1970), pp. 83–103; M. Biddle and D. Hill, 'Late Saxon Planned Towns', *Antiquaries Journal*, 51 (1971), pp. 70–85; M. Biddle, 'Towns', *The Archaeology of Anglo-Saxon England*, ed. D. M. Wilson (London, 1976), pp. 99–150; and J. Dyer, 'Earthworks of the Danelaw Frontier', *Archaeology and the Landscape*, ed. P. J. Fowler (London, 1972), pp. 222–36. For the offensive use of burghs by Edward the Elder and his sister Aethelflaed, see *ASC* (all versions), *s.a.* 903–14; *ASC* 'A', *s.a.* 915–20; and *ASC* 'B', *s.a.* 902–24; and for a good general account, F. M. Stenton, *Anglo-Saxon England* (3rd edn, Oxford, 1971), pp. 319–63.
[6] For a fuller discussion of what follows see M. J. Strickland, 'Slaughter, Slavery or Ransom? The Impact of the Conquest on Conduct in Warfare', *England in the Eleventh Century. Proceedings of the 1990 Harlaxton Symposium*, ed. C. Hicks (Harlaxton Medieval Studies, Vol. II, Stamford, 1992), pp. 41–59.
[7] *ASC* 'C' and 'D', *s.a.* 1066; Strickland, 'Slaughter, Slavery or Ransom?', p. 46 and n. 21.
[8] WP, pp. 190–1, and cf. the similar sentiments expressed in William's harangue to his men before the battle (*ibid.*, pp. 182–3).
[9] Strickland, 'Slaughter, Slavery or Ransom?', pp. 41–5, 56–8; below, pp. 133–4, 138–9.

only a limited beach-head and their backs to a sea in which a hostile fleet
was operating, needed a speedy and decisive victory: hence William's decision to risk all on a pre-emptive strike against Harold.[10] If, moreover, fear of
the consequences of defeat outweighed the anticipation of rich pickings,
William could bolster the morale of his army by stressing that they fought a
just war under a papal banner against a perjured usurper.[11]

When the Normans finally gained their hard-won victory, the ensuing
slaughter of the routed Saxons was due less to the 'otherness' of the
enemy[12] than to the realization that effective conquest would be greatly
facilitated by the extirpation of the Anglo-Saxon royal family and as many
of the warrior elite as could be killed *in situ*. There was no question of
sparing Harold or his brothers Gyrth and Leofwine for ransom. No
mention is made of prisoners, and among the slain ranked several leading
Anglo-Saxon ecclesiastics. Such considerations meant that Hastings was to
stand *sui generis* as a bitterly fought war of conquest, where the Normans
themselves neither gave nor expected quarter. For most of William's army,
the battle would be the largest, and certainly the most sanguinary engagement in which they would ever fight.[13]

Even in such circumstances, however, notions of honourable behaviour
might find some place. Writing considerably after the event, William of
Malmesbury believed that Duke William had deprived a Norman knight of
his belt of knighthood for gashing King Harold's thigh as he lay prostrate
on the battlefield.[14] Certainly, twelfth-century sources indicate that the
attacking of a disadvantaged opponent was regarded as shameful,[15] and the

[10] R. A. Brown, 'The Battle of Hastings', *Proceedings of the Battle Conference*, 3 (1980), pp. 8–10; J.
Gillingham, 'William the Bastard at War', in *Studies in Medieval History Presented to R. Allen Brown*, ed. C.
Harper-Bill, C. J. Holdsworth and J. L. Nelson (Woodbridge, 1989), pp. 157–8. Both articles are
reprinted in M. J. Strickland (ed.), *Anglo-Norman Warfare* (Woodbridge, 1992), pp. 161–81, and pp.
143–60, and it is this pagination which has been used for subsequent references.
[11] For the papal banner at Hastings see WP, pp. 154–5, 184–5; Orderic, II, pp. 142–3 and n. 2 (cf. p. 59, n.
4); *The Bayeux Tapestry. The Complete Tapestry in Colour with an Introduction and Commentary by D. M. Wilson*
(*BT*), (London, 1985), pl. 68; but also the doubts cogently expressed by C. Morton, 'Pope Alexander
II and the Norman Conquest', *Latomus*, 34 (1975), pp. 362–82. For the context of such papal grants, I.
S. Robinson, *The Papacy, 1073–1198* (Cambridge, 1990), pp. 324–5; and *idem.*, 'Gregory VII and the
Soldiers of Christ', *History*, 57 (1973), pp. 169–92.
[12] To highlight the courage of the Normans and to further his comparison of Duke William to Caesar,
William of Poitiers stressed that the Saxons, with their strident trumpets and unnerving war-cries,
appeared to be barbaric and terrifying (WP, pp. 186–7). He was echoed in this belief by William of
Malmesbury (William of Malmesbury, *De gestis regum Anglorum* (*GR*), ed. W. Stubbs, 2 vols., (Rolls
Series, 1887–9), II, pp. 301, 305). Yet while Orderic also remarks on the 'otherness' of Anglo-Saxon
dress and coiffure in Norman eyes (Orderic, II, pp. 198–9), there had been much contact between the
two countries not least in the reign of Edward the Confessor, and the Normans cannot have been
surprised by the nature of the enemy they encountered in 1066. The dress and equipment, if not the
hairstyles, of both Saxons and Normans on the Bayeux Tapestry, moreover, is near identical (N. P.
Brooks and H. E. Walker, 'The Authority and Interpretation of the Bayeux Tapestry', *Proceedings of
the Battle Conference*, 1 (1978), pp. 1–34.   [13] Strickland, 'Slaughter, Slavery or Ransom?', pp. 55–9.
[14] *GR*, II, p. 303.   [15] Below, p. 154.

tradition is lent some support by the Bayeux Tapestry which seems to depict just such an act (Plate 1).[16] For all the retrospective and politically expedient vilification of Harold as a tyrannical usurper by the Norman apologists, it is not impossible that Duke William's own sense of honour had been offended by the treatment of an opponent on whom he had personally bestowed arms and whom he knew to be a brave warrior.[17] Nevertheless, if Malmesbury's story has any validity, William can only have been troubled at the manner of Harold's demise, not his actual slaying.[18] The *Chanson de Guillaume*, part of a cycle of chansons featuring the legendary exploits of the Carolingian warrior William count of Orange,

[16] *BT*, pl. 24. For a discussion of the divergent accounts of Harold's death see G. H. White, 'The Battle of Hastings and the Death of Harold', in *The Complete Peerage*, ed. G. E. Cokayne, revised by V. Gibbs, H. E. Doubleday and Lord Howard de Walden, 12 vols. in 13 (London, 1910–57), xii, Pt. 1. Appendix L; *The Carmen de Hastingae Proelio of Guy, Bishop of Amiens (Carmen)*, ed. and tr. C. Morton and H. Muntz (Oxford, 1972), pp. 116–20; and Brown, 'The Battle of Hastings', pp. 17–18. For a recent reassessment of the *Carmen*, whose date and authenticity have been much disputed, see E. M. C. van Houts, 'Latin Poetry and the Anglo-Norman Court, 1066–1135: The *Carmen de Hastingae Proelio*', *Journal of Medieval History*, 15 (1989), pp. 39–62. The *Carmen* has Harold slain by Duke William and three companions, one of whom, Giffard, hews off his thigh (*coxa*) and carries the limb away, a remark that has led to the suggestion that 'thigh' may be a euphemism for genitals (*Carmen*, pp. 34–7, and p. 37, n. 1; cf. D. J. Bernstein, 'The Blinding of Harold and the Meaning of the Bayeux Tapestry', *Anglo-Norman Studies*, 5 (1982), pp. 40–64; and *idem.*, *The Mystery of the Bayeux Tapestry* (London, 1986), p. 160, and pp. 144–61 for the possible symbolism of Harold's blinding and death in the Tapestry). If this is so, Harold's fate compares closely to that of Simon de Montfort, whose body – as that of a traitor – was mutilated following the battle of Evesham, 1265. His head, hands and genitals were cut off and sent as trophies to the wife of his bitter enemy, Roger Mortimer (M. Prestwich, *Edward I* (London, 1988), p. 51).

[17] *BT*, pl. 71; J. Flori, *L'essor de la chevalerie, XIe–XIIe siècles* (Geneva, 1986), pp. 66–8; below, p. 25.

[18] Sources disagree as to William's treatment of Harold's body following the battle. William of Poitiers, followed by Orderic, says that although William allowed the rest of the English freedom to bury their dead, the duke refused the offer of Harold's mother, Gytha, to redeem it for its weight in gold. Rather, he ordered William Malet to bury Harold's corpse by the sea shore as a mocking gesture 'to leave him as the keeper of the shore and sea which he had so recently sought to defend in his insanity' (WP, pp. 204–5, 208–9; Orderic, ii, pp. 178–9). The *Carmen* adds that William Malet was deputed to this task as being 'part Norman, part English' and Harold's comrade (*compater*) (*Carmen*, pp. 36–9, and p. 38, n. 1; cf. pp. xliii–v). The editors of the *Carmen* are surely mistaken, however, in seeing Harold's interment as a Scandinavian funeral echoing pagan practice; for although Harold's mutilated body is wrapped in purple cloth, the duke here also angrily rejects Gytha's offer, and the stone raised above Harold's cliff-top grave bears an epitaph echoing the mocking comment recorded by Poitiers.

William of Malmesbury, however, believed William had restored Harold's body to Gytha without charge and that it was buried directly at his foundation at Waltham abbey, a tradition followed later by Wace and the Waltham Chronicle (*GR*, ii, pp. 306–7; *Le Roman de Rou de Wace*, ed. A. J. Holden, 3 vols. (Société des anciens textes français, Paris, 1970–3), 11. 8967–70; *The Waltham Chronicle*, ed. L. Watkiss and M. Chibnall (Oxford, 1994), pp. 50–7). To reconcile divergent traditions, Freeman suggested that after its initial burial, Harold's body was removed to Waltham (E. A. Freeman, *A History of the Norman Conquest of England*, 6 vols. (Oxford, 1870–9), iii, pp. 514 ff. and Appendix MM; cf. R. A. Brown, *The Normans and the Norman Conquest* (London, 1969), p. 175). The editors of the new edition of the Waltham Chronicle, however, make a strong case for the authenticity of the tradition that William allowed Harold Christian burial directly, granting his body, identified by his mistress Edith Swan-neck, to two canons of Waltham, refusing the ten marks of gold they offered for it. The chronicler also believed that William had intended to include Harold among the list of those prayed for by the monks of his new foundation at Battle (*Waltham Chronicle*, p. xliiii–xlvi). I am most grateful to Dr Chibnall for her assistance on this point.

1 Harold's death from the Bayeux Tapestry. Spanned by the legend 'Here Harold was slain', two scenes show the king, accompanied by his standard bearer, being wounded in the eye by an arrow, then being attacked by a Norman horseman. This latter scene corresponds closely to the tradition preserved by William of Malmesbury that a knight gashed Harold's thigh as he lay prostrate, but was stripped of his belt of knighthood by the Conqueror for such a dishonourable act. In the lower margin, the dead are plundered for their valuable hauberks, while shields and swords are collected. Would the missing portion of the Tapestry have shown the ultimate fate of Harold's body? (By special permission of the City of Bayeux.)

offers an instructive parallel. Here William upbraids his nephew Guy for beheading the injured Saracen king Desramed as he struggles on the ground; 'Vile wretch, how dare you attack a crippled man. You will be blamed for this in the high court.' Guy, however, responds with a ruthlessly pragmatic reply, with which Harold's slayers at Hastings would doubtless have fully concurred: 'I have never heard such a thing. Even if he had not got a foot to walk on, he still had eyes to see and genitals to beget children. He would have had himself carried back to his country and we would have seen Desramed's heirs coming thence to work evil in this land. One should free oneself completely.' 'Nephew', admits William, 'you speak very wisely.

You have a child's body but a warrior's sense. After my death you will hold my lands.'[19]

Duke William's victory at Hastings on 14 October 1066 marked the dominance in England of a new warrior aristocracy. It is with the perceptions of war of this aristocracy and with the nature and operation of custom and convention in warfare from the Conquest to the defeat of Louis of France's invasion of England in 1217 that this book is concerned.[20]

THROUGH A GLASS DARKLY: CHIVALRY AND THE SOURCES

Fundamental limitations in the nature and availability of the sources confront the study of the warrior aristocracy's conduct and perception of war in the eleventh and twelfth centuries. First, while there is an abundance of Latin chronicles and other ecclesiastically produced material such as letters, didactic tracts and conciliar legislation, the limited extent of literacy in a predominantly oral lay culture has resulted in a relative paucity of sources emanating from a secular milieu. Second, much of this material that is extant is of a literary nature, not simply the legendary or quasi-historical chansons de geste, but also the more overtly 'factual' poems such as the *Histoire de Guillaume le Maréchal*.[21] Consequently, their form and content pose peculiar problems of interpretation. Thirdly, as a result of these considerations, one is forced to a disproportionate extent to approach the

[19] J. Walthelet-Willem, *Recherches sur la chanson de Guillaume. Etudes accompagnés d'une édition (William of Orange)*, 2 vols. (Paris, 1975), II, 11. 1961–78. Walthelet-Willem's edition contains the two main manuscript variants in parallel, accompanied by a modern French translation, but for an English translation I have followed G. Price, *William Count of Orange. Four Old French Epics* (London, 1975), p. 170. For notes and further references on both the historical William and the legendary figure, who by the end of the eleventh century had become a popular military saint, see Orderic, III, pp. 216–27. William's deeds were among those employed by Gerold, chaplain to Hugh d'Avranches, earl of Chester, to instruct the knights of Hugh's *familia*, while Orderic, referring to the chanson of William by the jongleurs, preferred to insert a more edifying hagiographic *vita* in his own *Ecclesiastical History* (*ibid.*, pp. 216–27). The chanson cycle itself is discussed in detail by J. Frappier, *Les chansons de geste du cycle de Guillaume d'Orange*, 3 vols. (Paris, 1955–83).

[20] The geographic scope is primarily the Anglo-Norman *regnum* and the Angevin 'empire', though the paucity of sources for Aquitaine and the southern provinces naturally leads to a greater emphasis on England and northern France. Since Anglo-Norman and Frankish concepts of behaviour in war remained fundamentally unchanged by their contact with the Turks, Egyptians and Arabs in Outremer, I have felt it legitimate to include, where pertinent, material from crusading sources, which are frequently qualitatively, as well as quantitatively, richer than those available for the study of warfare and chivalry in Western Europe in this period.

A comparative study of Frankish and German chivalry and knighthood is another book, and by one better qualified for the task, but for Germany see, *inter alia*, J. Bumke, *Studien zum Ritterbegriff im 12. und 13. Jahrhundert* (Heidelberg, 1977), tr. W. T. H. and E. Jackson as *The Concept of Knighthood in the Middle Ages* (New York, 1982); and B. Arnold, *German Knighthood, 1050–1300* (Oxford, 1985).

[21] *L'Histoire de Guillaume le Maréchal*, (*HGM*), ed. P. Meyer, 3 vols. (Société de l'histoire de France, 1891–1901).

actions and mentality of a warrior nobility through the distorting lens of clerical writers. Whether secular clergy or religious, such authors belonged to a social group which was itself forbidden the use of arms, which had long harboured grave theological reservations about the value of the *militia saecularis* in the Christian world order, and which all too frequently was the victim of knightly aggression and despoliation.

Of these difficulties, the first is the most acute. Just as the vast majority of wall paintings, tapestries, carving and other plastic arts which would have done so much to enrich our understanding of the warriors' thought-world have been lost to us for the Anglo-Norman period, leaving only the bare shells of extant castles or churches, so the bulk of the poems and songs, particularly those of a non-fictional nature relating to specific polit-ical or military events that must have been in circulation through the halls of the Anglo-Norman nobility, are irretrievably lost, glimpsed if at all only in fragments or as fleeting references. We may well regard the *Histoire de Guillaume le Maréchal*, hailed as the first biography of a non-royal, non-saintly secular aristocrat, as an isolated innovation.[22] Yet the survival of works such as Jordan Fantosme's *Chronicle*, a vernacular Anglo-Norman poem dealing with the 'great war' of 1173–4 and written shortly afterwards as a didactic courtly praise poem,[23] or *The Song of Dermot and the Earl* recounting the Norman invasion of Ireland and the deeds of Earl Richard de Clare,[24] leaves little doubt as to the wealth of such material that must once have existed in a society obsessed with honour and reputation.[25] For such works, usually designed to be recited orally, were the principal vehicle by which a lord's valour and feats of arms could be bruited abroad, main-taining and enlarging his reputation in the eyes of his peers.[26]

We are, it is true, fortunate in those vernacular texts surviving. The *Histoire de Guillaume le Maréchal* is effectively the *sine qua non* for the study of warfare, the tournament and knightly values in the later twelfth century, without which our knowledge would be irreparably diminished. But just as the isolated survival of *Beowulf* gives one pause as to the wealth of Anglo-

[22] D. Crouch, *William Marshal: Court, Career and Chivalry in the Angevin Empire, 1147–1219* (London and New York, 1990), pp. ix, 1–2.
[23] *Jordan Fantosme's Chronicle* (JF), ed. and tr. R. C. Johnston (Oxford, 1981). For an extended discussion of the nature of Jordan's poem and his perceptions of chivalry see M. J. Strickland, 'Arms and the Men: War, Loyalty and Lordship in Jordan Fantosme's *Chronicle*', in *Medieval Knighthood IV. Papers from the Fifth Strawberry Hill Conference*, ed. C. Harper-Bill and R. Harvey (Woodbridge, 1992), pp. 187–220.
[24] *The Song of Dermot and the Earl*, ed. G. H. Orpen (London, 1892).
[25] For a valuable contextual survey of vernacular French literature in Anglo-Norman England see I. Short, 'Patrons and Polyglots: French Literature in Twelfth Century England', *Anglo-Norman Studies*, 14 (1991), pp. 229–49; while for a perceptive study of knightly audiences and patronage see G. Duby, 'The Culture of the Knightly Class: Audience and Patronage', *Renaissance and Renewal in the Twelfth Century*, ed. R. L. Benson and G. Constable (Oxford, 1982), pp. 248–62.   [26] Below, pp. 99–102.

Saxon epic poetry that has been lost to us, so the very diversity in form, scope and content of 'factual' vernacular poetry emphasizes the limitations of the extant corpus. Thus, for instance, the poet of the *Estoire de la Guerre Sainte*, a vivid eye-witness account in verse of the Third Crusade, cannot have been the only minstrel present in the host, nor the only survivor to recount the epic events such as the siege of Acre or the battles of Arsuf and Jaffa that would have spellbound audiences back in England, Normandy or Aquitaine.[27] Unlike the peasantry, visible only as victims through monastic chronicles or the ecclesiastical legislation that sought to provide them with a degree of protection, the knights themselves are by no means silent. But their voices are few and rarely speak to us directly. For while the early thirteenth-century *Histoire des Ducs de Normandie* marks the emergence of vernacular prose chronicles,[28] there is nothing comparable – not even the *Histoire de Guillaume le Maréchal* – to approach the immediacy of personal expression found in Joinville's *Life of St Louis*.[29]

The complex problems of interpretation raised by the literary conventions, hyperbole and formulaic construction of the chansons de geste have long been recognized. Not without reason does Flori preface his semantic examination of the chansons by a caveat:

> Ces sources littéraires nous donnent de la réalité une image déformée, parfois idéalisée, et il serait périlleux de les interroger pour tenter de résoudre les grands problèmes qui divisent encore sur ce point les meilleurs historiens de notre temps: signification sociale de la chevalerie, rapports chevalerie-noblesse, chevalerie-féodalité, et autres problèmes délicats.[30]

Because in many respects their representation of warfare is clearly considerably distanced from reality, the use of chansons has been consciously restricted in this study. Yet while it would be dangerous to take chansons like the *Song of Roland* as accurate reflections of the forms of combat or of the actualities of chivalric behaviour, they nevertheless are of great value as extended expressions of ideals of chivalry.[31] The blows of Roland and

---

[27] *L'Estoire de la Guerre Sainte par Ambroise*, ed. G. Paris (Paris, 1871); cf. below, p. 27, n. 113.

[28] *Histoire des Ducs de Normandie et des Rois d'Angleterre*, ed. F. Michel (Société de l'histoire de France, 1840).

[29] Jean, sire de Joinville, *Histoire de Saint Louis* (Joinville), ed. M. N. de Wailly (Société de l'Histoire de France, 1868); tr. M. R. B. Shaw as *The Life of St Louis*, in idem., *Joinville and Villehardouin: Chronicles of the Crusades*, (Harmondsworth, 1963).

[30] Flori, 'La notion de chevalerie dans les chansons de geste du XIIe siècle. Etude historique du vocabulaire', *Le Moyen Age*, 81 (1975), pp. 211–40, 407–45, at p. 211.

[31] Cf. G. F. Jones, *The Ethos of the Song of Roland* (Baltimore, 1963); and J. Bédier, *La Chanson de Roland commentée* (Paris, 1927). For this most famous of chansons G. J. Brault, *The Song of Roland: An Analytical Edition* (*The Song of Roland*), 2 vols. (University Park, Pennsylvania and London, 1978), provides a standard text, translation and extensive commentary, though for English translations I have followed G. Burgess, *The Song of Roland* (Harmondsworth, 1990). The latter provides as an appendix the majority

Oliver may be superhuman, cleaving horse and rider in half, but their value system of prowess, courage, loyalty and largesse was one to which contemporary knightly audiences aspired.[32] By holding up models for knights to emulate, moreover, such literature, at once both epic and didactic, served to blur the distinctions between ideal and reality. According to William of Malmesbury, the Normans advanced to battle at Hastings singing a song about Roland.[33] Equally, the author of the *Itinerarium perigrinorum* could regard Richard I as superior even to Roland because he was seen to epitomize the chivalric ideal.[34]

Concentration here on conduct in war itself means that we are less troubled by the problems inherent in using the overtly ficticious Arthurian romance, with its blend of the contemporary and the fantastic, than is Keen for the study of the broader social context of chivalry.[35] Chrétien de Troyes has not been wholly ignored in this study, but his is a world almost totally divorced from the realities of siege, the battlefield or feudal warfare, where the tournament has replaced pitched battle and a lover's loyalty to his lady has supplanted the crucial bonds between lord and man.[36]

Less obviously, but no less importantly, these caveats concerning the use of literary sources for concepts of chivalry and warfare must be applied equally to the more sober vernacular poems such as the *Histoire de Guillaume le Maréchal* or the *Estoire de la Guerre Sainte*. For such texts cannot be seen merely as versified chronicles providing unadored historical narrative.[37] They too are essentially literature for a courtly milieu and an audience which would not have recognized any meaningful distinction between liter-

---

of the French text, based on the edition of F. Whitehead, *La Chanson de Roland* (Oxford, 1942; 2nd edn, 1946). Cf. C. R. Dodwell, 'The Bayeux Tapestry and French Secular Epic', *The Burlington Magazine*, 107 (1966), pp. 549–60; and D. C. Douglas, 'The Song of Roland and the Norman Conquest of England', *French Studies*, 14 (1960), pp. 99–116.

For chivalry in the chansons see in particular Flori, 'La notion de chevalerie dans les chansons de geste', pp. 211–45; W. M. Hackett, 'Knights and Knighthood in *Girart de Roussillon*', *The Ideals and Practice of Medieval Knighthood II. Papers of the Third Strawberry Hill Conference, 1986*, ed. C. Harper-Bill and R. Harvey (Boydell, 1988), pp. 40–5; and L. Paterson, 'Knights and the Concept of Knighthood in Twelfth-century Occitan Epic', *Forum for Modern Language Studies*, 17 (1981), pp. 115–30, reprinted in *Knighthood in Medieval Literature*, ed. W. H. Jackson (Woodbridge, 1981), pp. 23–38.

[32] J. Benton, '"Nostre Franceis n'unt talent de fuir": The *Song of Roland* and the Enculturation of a Warrior Class', *Olifant*, 6 (1979), pp. 237–49.   [33] *GR*, II, p. 302.

[34] *Itinerarium perigrinorum et gesta regis Ricardi, (Itinerarium)*, ed. W. Stubbs (Rolls Series, 1864), p. 422.

[35] Keen, *Chivalry*, pp. 2–3.

[36] J. Flori, 'Pour une histoire de la chevalerie: l'adoubement chez Chrétien de Troyes', *Romania*, 100 (1979), pp. 21–53. For valuable comparative studies see W. H. Jackson, 'Aspects of Knighthood in Hartmann's Adaptations of Chrétien's Romances and in the Social Context', and M. H. Jones, 'Chrétien, Hartmann and the Knight as Fighting Man: On Hartmann's Chivalric Adaptation of *Eric and Enide*', both in *Chrétien de Troyes and the German Middle Ages*, ed. M. H. Jones and R. Wiseby (Cambridge and London, 1993), pp. 37–55, 85–109. On Chrétien himself see L. T. Topsfield, *Chrétien de Troyes* (Cambridge, 1984).

[37] Strickland, 'Arms and the Men', pp. 189–93; A. Lodge, 'Literature and History in the *Chronicle* of Jordan Fantosme', *French Studies*, 44 (1990), pp. 257–70.

ary and more overtly 'historical' works. The *estoires* furnished by Jordan or Ambroise were 'serious entertainments',[38] which amused, diverted, exhorted and instructed through the medium of actual events. As a result, despite their largely factual content, their form and style is heavily influenced by the dictates of literary convention and current poetic trends. Thus, for example, it has been argued that the author of the *Histoire de Guillaume le Maréchal*, writing in the 1220s, was influenced in his portrayal of tournaments and the role of courtly women by the romances of Chrétien de Troyes,[39] while elements of Jordan Fantosme's *Chronicle* echo or parody epic convention.[40] Equally, questions of authorship, purpose, patronage, sources of information and inherent bias must be carefully considered. Thus before accepting the *Histoire de Guillaume le Maréchal*'s claim that William was 'the best knight in the world' and regarding his deeds as a model for chivalric behaviour, it is clearly important to bear in mind that the work was commissioned by William's family and drew heavily on the reminiscences of both William himself and one of his own knights, John d'Earley.[41] Nevertheless, with careful handling, even quasi-historical texts such as Wace's *Roman de Brut* and *Roman de Rou* which blend contemporary observation with legendary material can be made to yield much of value concerning the nature and conduct of war.[42]

Such vernacular literary sources can be supplemented by documentary material such as charters, *conventiones*, and records of royal government like the Pipe, Close, Patent and Fine Rolls which, although almost exclusively drafted in Latin by clerics, can furnish considerable if often more oblique evidence concerning behaviour in war. In particular, the series of *conventiones* or treaties between Anglo-Norman magnates provide pragmatic, working assumptions about conventions governing the inception of war.[43]

---

[38] To borrow the title of N. F. Partner's valuable study of twelfth-century chronicle writing, *Serious Entertainments: The Writing of History in Twelfth Century England* (Chicago and London, 1977).

[39] L. D. Benson, 'The Tournament in the Romances of Chretien de Troyes and *L'Histoire de Guillaume le Maréchal*', *Chivalric Literature: Essays on Relations between literature and Life in the Middle Ages*, ed. L. D. Benson and J. Leyerle (Kalamazoo, 1981), pp. 1–24; cf. U. T. Holmes, Jr, 'The Arthurian Tradition and Lambert d'Ardres', *Speculum*, 25 (1950), pp. 100–3.

[40] Strickland, 'Arms and the Men', p. 190 and n. 13.

[41] See Meyer's introduction in *HGM*, iii, pp. 1–19; Crouch, *William Marshal*, pp. 5–8; and for a perceptive review of historians' approaches to the *Histoire*, see Gillingham, 'War and Chivalry in the History of William the Marshal', pp. 251–63.

[42] On Wace see M. Bennet, 'Poetry as History? The *Roman de Rou* of Wace as a Source for the Norman Conquest', *Anglo-Norman Studies*, 5 (1982), pp. 1–39; and *idem.*, 'Wace and Warfare', *Anglo-Norman Studies*, 11 (1988), pp. 37–58, reprinted in Strickland, *Anglo-Norman Warfare*, pp. 230–50.

[43] Of particular importance are the indentures drawn up between the kings of England and the counts of Flanders for the provision of Flemish knights (*Diplomatic Documents Preserved in the Public Record Office, I (1101–1272) (Diplomatic Documents)*, ed. P. Chaplais (London, 1964), pp. 1–12; and see F. L. Ganshof, 'Note sur le premier traité Anglo-Flamand de Douvres', *Revue du Nord*, 40 (1958), pp. 245–57; J. O. Prestwich, 'The Military Household of the Norman Kings', *EHR*, 96 (1981), pp. 1–37,

Nevertheless, the bulk of material concerning the actual prosecution of war, such as the course of sieges, the granting of truces or respites, and the outcome of battles is furnished by contemporary Latin chroniclers. The richness, variety and volume of Latin narrative sources for England and Normandy between the Conquest and the death of Richard I, scarcely equalled in the Middle Ages, allows a considerable degree of empirical study concerning aspects of conduct in war. Yet one must always view the motivation ascribed to knights with great caution and be aware of the clerical bias inherent in such works. Clerics not only harboured considerable theological reservations about the spilling of blood, but were also acutely aware of the stark reality of widespread knightly violence to church lands and property during time of war. Thus even when, from the later eleventh century, ecclesiastical thinkers began to develop a more positive view of the role of knighthood as a vocation which, if properly directed in the service of the Church, might lead to salvation in its own right, the majority of chroniclers still regarded the activities of the warriors with fear and suspicion. The question of clerical bias is explored here through an examination of ecclesiastics' reaction to noble aggression,[44] and through their relating of 'atrocities'. For accusations of sacrilege, the destruction of churches and the slaying of priests formed an integral element of tales of atrocity imputed to both the Scots and the mercenary *routiers* by ecclesiastical chroniclers.[45]

VERACITY OR WISHFUL THINKING? THE PROBLEM OF ORDERIC VITALIS

The problems inherent in such sources for the study of chivalry and the nature of ecclesiastical perceptions of the knighthood may be considered

reprinted in Strickland, *Anglo-Norman Warfare*, pp. 93–127, at pp. 100–1. Equally significant is the treaty between Rannulf de Gernons, earl of Chester and Robert de Beaumont, earl of Leicester, drawn up sometime between 1148 and 1153. Subsequent references to this famous *conventio* cite the pagination of the text edited in Stenton, *English Feudalism*, Appendix, document no, 48, pp. 286–8, followed by that of his translation at pp. 250–3. See also the treaties between Robert earl of Gloucester and Miles, earl of Hereford (1141 x 1143), (edited by R. H. C. Davis, 'Treaty between William Earl of Gloucester and Roger Earl of Hereford', in *A Medieval Miscellany for D. M. Stenton*, ed. P. M. Barnes and C. F. Slade (London, 1962), pp. 145–6; and more recently in *Earldom of Gloucester Charters*, ed. R. B. Patterson (Oxford, 1973), no. 95, pp. 95–6); the renewal of this agreement (1147 x 1150) by the sons of the two men (Davis, 'Treaty between William Earl of Gloucester and Roger Earl of Hereford', pp. 144–5; *Earldom of Gloucester Charters*, no. 96, p. 97); and that between Earl Roger of Hereford and William de Braose, his brother-in-law (1148 x 1154) (printed as an appendix by Z. N. and C. N. L. Brooke, 'Hereford Cathedral Dignitaries in the Twelfth Century – Supplement', *Cambridge Historical Review*, 8 (1944–46), p. 185). For the nature of the *conventio* in general see E. King, 'Dispute Settlement in Anglo-Norman England', *Anglo-Norman Studies*, 14 (1991), pp. 115–30; and D. Crouch, 'A Norman "Conventio" and Bonds of Lordship in the Middle Ages', *Law and Government*, pp. 299–234.   [44] Below, pp. 70–7.   [45] Below, pp. 294–300.

through the case study of Orderic Vitalis's *Ecclesiastical History*, the single most important chronicle source for contemporary warfare and chivalry in the later eleventh and first half of the twelfth century.[46] At first sight, Orderic's statements in relation to conduct in war appear as the unambiguous observations of a well-informed contemporary, and have frequently been unquestioningly accepted as such. Yet how far is Orderic's interpretation of knightly observance a valid reflection of the realities of lay conduct? Or rather, as a religious, is he attempting through his writings to propagate a clerical *ideal* of behaviour and motivation?

Interpreting the significance of Orderic's remarks on knightly behaviour assumes a particular importance given that his *Ecclesiastical History* well antedates the influential statements of John of Salisbury and Stephen of Fougères concerning the function and conduct expected of the knightly *ordo*.[47] Unlike these overt polemicists, however, Orderic presents his own perception of knightly conduct as an integral part of a detailed historical narrative, so that personal opinion appears as authoritative statement of fact. The *Ecclesiastical History* constantly reveals Orderic to be a well-informed, perceptive chronicler, acutely aware of the many unpalatable realities of his world. Yet he was moved by this very awareness to use his work as a vehicle to promote his own heartfelt notions as to the ordering and behaviour of society, views which naturally were heavily influenced by his monastic vocation.[48]

Thus, for example, the necessity of a strong ruler to combat the lawlessness and centrifugality of the Norman baronage, ensuring peace to the peasantry and the Church, is a constant *lietmotif*. It lies behind Orderic's explanation for the restraint from killing at the battle of Brémule, 1119,

---

[46] In addition to the valuable introductions to her edition of Orderic's *Ecclesiastical History*, see M. Chibnall, 'Feudal Society in Orderic Vitalis', *Anglo-Norman Studies*, 1 (1978), 35–48; idem., *The World of Orderic Vitalis* (London, 1984); and P. Rousset, 'La description du monde chevaleresque chez Orderic Vital', *Le Moyen Age*, 75 (1969), pp. 427–44.

[47] Orderic's work stops in 1141, the year of his presumed death. Book XII, which contains his comments on Brémule, was probably written between 1136 and 1137 (Orderic, vi, pp. xvii–xviii). John of Salisbury's remarks on knighthood occur principally in his *Policraticus* of 1159; *Ioannis Saresberiensis episcopi Carnotensis Policratici sive De nugis curialium et vestigiis philosophorum libri VIII*, (*Policraticus*) ed. C. C. J. Webb, 2 vols. (Oxford, 1909); tr. J. Dickinson, *The Statesman's Book of John of Salisbury* (New York, 1927). Stephen of Fougères' *Livre des Manières*, c. 1185, is edited by J. Kremer in *Ausgaben und Abhandlung aus dem Gebiete der romanischen Philologie*, 39 (Marburg, 1887), pp. 119–43, and by R. A. Lodge, *Le Livre des manières* (Geneva, 1979), while an extract with a facing translation is given by M. Switten, '*Chevalier* in Twelfth-Century French and Occitan Literature', *The Study of Chivalry: Resources and Approaches*, ed. H. H. D. Chickering and T. H. Seiler (W. Michigan University, 1988), pp. 403–47, at pp. 442–7. See below, pp. 55–6.

[48] For Orderic's monastic background see Chibnall, *The World of Orderic Vitalis*, while C. Holdsworth, 'Ideas and Reality: Some Attempts to Control and Defuse War in the Twelfth Century', *The Church and War*, ed. W. J. Sheils (*Studies in Church History*, 20, Oxford, 1983), pp. 59–78, provides a good general discussion of Orderic's perception of the regulation of war.

which he regarded as a triumph for Henry I and the forces of peace over
the Norman rebels and their French accomplices. As Henry I's apologist,
Orderic was careful to portray the king's forces closely adhering to the
Augustinian precepts of the just war. At Tinchebrai, 1106, Henry reluc-
tantly fights against his brother Robert not out of any greed for power and
conquest but to save the Norman church from the forces of anarchy.[49] So
at Brémule, Orderic again stresses the right intent of Henry's knights. To
the victors, it was enough simply to receive God's confirmation of the
justice of their war: 'As Christian soldiers, they did not thirst for the blood
of their brothers, but rejoiced in a just victory given by God, for the good
of holy Church and the peace of the faithful.'[50] Since they fight in a limited
war of defence, not out of hatred but in a spirit of Christian charity, God
blesses their enterprise with victory.

Clearly, however, such statements reflect the ideals of Orderic, not nec-
essarily the beliefs of the knights themselves. Orderic drew on both classical and ecclesiastical concepts of virtuous conduct in warfare and applied
them to contemporary knighthood, thereby prefiguring elements of both
John of Salisbury's *Policraticus* and Stephen of Fougères's *Livre des Manières*.
Hence anticipating John of Salisbury, and possibly drawing on Vegetius's
De re militari,[51] he contrasts the indiscipline of knights with the order of the
Roman army. Describing the acts of plunder and sacrilege carried out by
the invading Angevin army in 1136, he notes:

> The magnates who ought to have led separate squadrons in a properly levied
> army, were, unless I am mistaken, unaware of the strictness of discipline
> practised by the Romans in military matters, and did not conduct their
> knightly quarrels with restraint as lords should (*nec ipsas haerorum more militares
> inimicicias modeste disponebant*). Consequently all of them, to the best of my
> belief, sullied their reputations with atrocious crimes, showing no respect to

---

[49] Orderic, VI, pp. 86–7, for the speech put into Henry I's mouth before Tinchebrai. For the concept of
right intent see F. H. Russell, *The Just War in the Middle Ages* (Cambridge, 1975, repr. 1979), pp. 16 ff.
[50] Orderic, VI, pp. 240–1. The effect of Orderic's monastic vocation on his concepts of war is well
expressed by Dr Chibnall: '. . . the deeds of heroism in battle, praised in the vernacular chansons of
the day, which Orderic knew so well even when he criticized them, might be directed toward the
service of Christ in a different sphere. In his writing the more violent feelings of the chansons were
softened by a Christian morality. The sheer joy of battle, the deliberate cruelty, of vernacular epic was
replaced by a constant reminder of the will of God, the duties of the true Christian, the terrible consequences of sin. Orderic wrote not only for the knightly converts who had been brought up on epic
songs, but also for secular knights, in the hope of moderating their brutality and directing their
swords to the service of God. So he recorded both the deeds of knights and the theory, at least, of
chivalry as it was cherished by the Church' (Chibnall, 'Feudal Society in Orderic Vitalis', p. 36).
[51] Orderic, VI, p. 472, n. 1; *ibid.*, I. p. 19, n. 10, and p. 38, where Dr Chibnall notes that a copy of Vegetius
existed at both Bec and Saint-Evroul, and ascribes its popularity in monastic libraries to its ready
interpretation as an allegory of the war of the monk against sin. For Vegetius in general, see below,
p. 38, n. 38. Particular passages of the *Policraticus* drawing on classical military models are Book VI,
chapters 2–4, 5 and 7, while on discipline see especially chapters 11–12.

principle and, by every kind of wickedness, endangering body and soul, so that they appeared loathsome to God and man alike.[52]

The occasion of an attack on Saint-Evroul itself shows how much Orderic's perception of correct conduct was shaped by his own monastic status and by membership of an element of society which, being especially vulnerable to the effects of war, could only benefit by the propagation of notions of behavioural restraint. In 1136, a local brigand, Robert Blouet, and his men had raided Saint-Evroul, and 'instead of overunning the lands of warlike knights, tried to carry off without warning the herds that were peacefully grazing in the fields belonging to the monks'.[53] The raiders were caught and hanged by the townsfolk, but this deed brought down upon them reprisal from the men of Richer de Laigle, among whose ranks Blouet had been numbered. Descending on the town, they ill-treated the monks and burnt eighty-four houses, prompting Orderic to assert the dishonourable nature of this conduct: 'Warfare of this kind, where men took up arms against helpless monks and their tenants and tried to avenge evil oppressors out to commit every kind of crime, rightly brought discredit on the would-be avengers.'[54]

Though the men of Laigle had grown 'wealthy and proud with the spoils of Saint-Evroul', Orderic portrays them as henceforth suffering consistent setbacks as divine punishment for their sacrilege:

> Deservedly the men, who had fought against unarmed, simple folk and had not spared them out of fear of God, afterwards found valiant and warlike champions when they did not seek them, and often heard from the knights they encountered such mocking and derisive words as these: 'Come on, knights! We are not cowled and tonsured monks, but knights in armour challenging you to battle. We are your brothers in arms (*socii vestri*); you should see what we can do!'[55]

Given the circumstances of the account – an attack on the author's own monastery – it is not surprising that Orderic vilifies the men of Laigle, and attributes their demise to the simple cause and effect of sacrilege followed by divine retribution.[56] It is clear, however, from the numerous accounts of the pillaging and burning of monasteries and churches – often in the pages of Orderic himself – that it was wishful thinking on his part to believe these sacrilegious knights had somehow been set apart and taunted by their fellow knights as the exception to the norm of behaviour towards churches in war.[57] Orderic must have been only too well aware how common such

---

[52] Orderic, VI, pp. 472–3.   [53] *Ibid.*, pp. 458–61.   [54] *Ibid.*, pp. 460–1.   [55] *Ibid.*, pp. 462–3.
[56] For the use of such a topos, see below, pp. 76–7.   [57] Below, pp. 78–97.

conduct was, even among the most distinguished knights and leading magnates. Yet he still felt the need to express his own feelings through created
speeches attributed to other knights. Such are the considerations that must
inform our use of Orderic who remains, nonetheless, the *sine qua non* for
the study of Anglo-Norman knighthood up to the 1140s.

THE SCOPE OF THE ENQUIRY

Our focus here will not be primarily on strategy and tactics *per se*, nor on logistics and the organization of armies, though, as we shall see, the nature of
forces and methods of combat were intimately connected with modes of
behaviour. Nevertheless, the anatomy of medieval warfare affords an
obvious structure in which to explore behaviour during hostilities and the
working of those conventions arising from it. In the eleventh and twelfth
centuries, as indeed throughout the Middle Ages, hostilities comprised of
three principal elements, closely if not inseparably connected: battle, whether
this be small-scale skirmishing or major engagements; siege, since castle-
based warfare dominated warfare; and 'ravaging', that is the infliction of economic attrition against an opponent's lands. An examination of the knights'
behaviour, in both ideal and actuality, in relation to each of these main elements of warfare, thus forms the core of the book and a fulcrum for a series
of comparative studies. These consider the treatment in war both of noble
opponents and of the other *ordines* of society, the clergy (*oratores*) and the
peasantry (*laboratores*),[58] who were the main victims of knightly aggression.
Hostilities within the context of baronial revolt are explored to determine the
extent to which chivalric conventions continued to operate in relation to
rebellious vassals or were overriden by the need to suppress and punish political discontent. A final dimension seeks to contextualize all such conduct by a
study of the nature of 'atrocity', approached through the behaviour in war of
the Scots and the bands of mercenary *routiers*, both regarded by Anglo-
Norman observers as the habitual perpetrators of sacrilege and slaughter.

The emphasis throughout this book is on conduct in war itself. This is in
an attempt to redress the tendency to divorce, or at least to distance, the
study of eleventh- and twelfth-century chivalry from the actualities of
warfare. The experience of war, for so long marginalized as merely 'military
history', has generally been restricted to analysis of battles and campaigns
or to the structure of armies,[59] whilst chivalry and its associated institutions

---

[58] Cf. G. Duby, *Le trois ordres ou l'imaginaire du féodalisme* (Paris, 1978), tr. A. Goldhammer as *The Three
Orders. Feudal Society Imagined* (Chicago and London, 1980).
[59] See in particular the perceptive discussion by J. Keegan, *The Face of Battle* (Harmondsworth, 1976,
repr. 1984), pp. 13–77; cf. Strickland, *Anglo-Norman Warfare*, pp. xii–xiii.

have been studied – with honourable exceptions[60] – primarily as a developing social phenomenon. Hence much recent scholarship on chivalry has focused on the changing status of knighthood, the significance of rituals of dubbing, the tournament, heraldry, the growth of courtly love and the impact of Arthurian romance, notions of nobility, and on ecclesiastical attitudes to war. All these go far to enhancing our knowledge of knighthood and its cultural milieu, but it is a milieu largely at a remove from the field of battle.

Such approaches are in themselves inherently valid. I would contend, however, that a study of the *mentalité* of a warrior elite must be centred on war itself. Warfare was the *raison d'être* of the Anglo-Norman aristocracy, and the ultimate justification for its social dominance in a world profoundly influenced by the resonances of war.[61] Not without reason does the great battle of Bouvines in 1214 form the epicentre of Duby's study of French society in the early thirteenth century.[62] It is, moreover, in behaviour in war that the essence of chivalry and its most fundamental manifestations lie. Thus, for example, while the enormous importance of the tournament for training, the fostering of a sense of professional solidarity and the development of corporate notions of conduct among the knighthood have rightly been highlighted,[63] it was in actual combat where the constituent elements of the warriors' value system, such as courage, prowess and loyalty, mattered most and were tested *in extremis*. It was here that conventions seeking to mitigate the nature of aggression between knightly combatants, such as ransom, truce and conditional respite, were conceived and developed as a practical response to the actualities of warfare. It is through the aims, limitations and workings of such conventions that one can approach most closely the knighthood's own perceptions concerning warfare and the essence of chivalry.

[60] Most notably F. Verbruggen, *De Krijgskunst in West-Europa in de Middeleeuwen (IXe tot begin XIVe eeuw)* (Brussels, 1954), tr. S. C. M. Southern and S. Willard as *The Art of Warfare in Western Europe During the Middle Ages, From the Eighth Century to 1340* (Amsterdam and New York, 1976); and more recently the work of John Gillingham, particularly *Richard the Lionheart* (London, 2nd edn, 1989); *idem.*, 'Richard I and the Science of War in the Middle Ages', in *War and Government in the Middle Ages*, ed. J. Gillingham and J. C. Holt (Woodbridge, 1984), pp. 78–91; and *idem.*, 'War and Chivalry in the *History of William the Marshal*', *Thirteenth Century England. Proceedings of the Newcastle upon Tyne Conference II, 1987*, ed. P. R. Coss and S. D. Lloyd (Woodbridge, 1988), pp. 1–14, both of the latter articles being reprinted in Strickland, *Anglo-Norman Warfare*, pp. 194–207, 251–263. [61] Strickland, *Anglo-Norman Warfare*, pp. ix–xii.

[62] G. Duby, *Le dimanche de Bouvines* (Paris, 1973), tr. C. Tihanyi as *The Legend of Bouvines. War, Religion and Culture in the Middle Ages* (Cambridge, 1990).

[63] R. Barber, *The Knight and Chivalry* (London, 1970, repr. 1974), pp. 159–92; M. Keen, *Chivalry* (New Haven and London, 1984), pp. 83–101; M. Parisse, 'Le tournoi en France, des origines à la fin du XIIIe siècle', in *Das ritterliche Turnier im Mittelalter*, ed. J. Fleckenstein (Göttingen, 1985), pp. 175–211; J. R. V. Barker, *The Tournament in England, 1100–1400* (Woodbridge, 1986); R. Barber and J. Barker, *Tournaments. Jousts, Chivalry and Pageants in the Middle Ages* (Woodbridge, 1989).

Equally, while it is possible to study ecclesiastical thinking concerning the just war and the nature of Christian knighthood in a theological vacuum, the actual behaviour of the knighthood in war, not least towards the possessions of the Church, provides a vital yardstick for assessing the impact of such ideas in practice. The perplexing disparity between aristocratic benefaction towards the Church in time of peace and of violence against it in time of war is thereby thrown into still sharper relief.[64] And nowhere is the interface of chivalry and Christianity more tangible and more cogently expressed than by those notions of *Ritterfrömigkeit* – knightly piety – visible on the battlefield itself.[65]

Clearly, a study which examines *developing* concepts of chivalrous behaviour primarily through the actualities of combat which helped to forge them is little troubled by considerations of supposed decadence and decline which have been a fundamental concern of historians of late medieval chivalry. Thus the work of Maurice Keen and Malcolm Vale[66] has sought to demonstrate the continuing social, political and military validity of the late medieval cult of chivalry. Both have striven to refute the contention, raised by Huizinga and fostered by Kilgour,[67] that chivalric culture had degenerated into merely 'a thing of forms and words and ceremonies which provided a means whereby the well-born could relieve the bloodiness of life by decking their activities with a tinsel gloss borrowed from romance'.[68]

Nevertheless, a detailed exposition of the realities of eleventh- and twelfth-century warfare further disproves the supposed contrast between

[64] See, for example, C. Erdmann, *Die Entstehung des Kreuzzuggedankens* (Stuttgart, 1935), tr. M. W. Baldwin and W. Goffart as *The Origin of the Idea of Crusade* (Princeton, 1977); H. E. J. Cowdrey, 'The Peace and Truce of God in the Eleventh Century', *Past and Present*, 46 (1970), pp. 42–67; Russell, *The Just War in the Middle Ages*; Holdsworth, 'Ideas and Reality', pp. 59–78; E. Hehl, *Kirche und Krieg im 12. Jahrhundert. Studien zu kanonischem Recht und politischer Wirklichkeit* (Stuttgart, 1980); J. A. Brundage, *Medieval Canon Law and the Crusader* (Wisconsin, 1969); *idem.*, 'Holy War and the Medieval Lawyers', *The Holy War*, ed. T. Murphy (Columbus, Ohio, 1976), pp. 99–140; and *idem.* 'The Limits of the War-Making Power: The Contribution of Medieval Canonists', *Peace in a Nuclear Age: The Bishop's Pastoral Letter in Perspective*, ed. C. J. Reid, jr (Washington, 1986), pp. 69–85, both these latter articles being reprinted (with original pagination) in Brundage's collected papers, *The Crusades, Holy War and Canon Law* (Aldershot, 1991).   [65] Below, pp. 58–68.
[66] M. H. Keen, *The Laws of War in the Late Middle Ages* (Oxford, 1965); *idem.*, 'Chivalry, Nobility and the Man-at-Arms', *War, Literature and Politics in the Late Middle Ages*, ed. C. T. Allmand (Liverpool, 1976), pp. 32–45; *idem.*, 'Huizinga, Kilgour and the Decline of Chivalry', *Medievalia et Humanistica*, new ser., 8 (1977), pp. 1–20; *idem.*, 'Chaucer's Knight, the Aristocracy and the Crusades', *English Court and Culture in the Late Middle Ages*, ed. V. J. Scattergood (London, 1983), pp. 47–61; M. Vale, *War and Chivalry. Warfare and Aristocratic Culture in England, France, and Burgundy at the End of the Middle Ages* (Georgia, 1981). This theme remains the dominant *leitmotif* in Keen's seminal monograph on chivalry, *Chivalry* (New Haven and London, 1984).
[67] J. Huizinga, *The Waning of the Middle Ages* (London, 1927, repr. 1985); R. L. Kilgour, *The Decline of Chivalry* (Cambridge, Mass., 1937); cf. A. B. Ferguson, *The Indian Summer of English Chivalry. Studies in the Decline and Transformation of Chivalric Idealism* (Durham, North Carolina, 1960).
[68] Keen, *Chivalry*, p. 3.

the decadence of late medieval chivalry and a 'golden age' of the High Middle Ages which Keen has rightly highlighted as being integral to the arguments of Huizinga and Kilgour.[69] Not only was contemporary criticism of knighthood a *topos* equally prevalent in the eleventh and twelfth as in the fourteenth and fifteenth centuries,[70] but the mechanisms of war, at the heart of which lay the *chevauchée* and methods of economic attrition, the extent of brutality, and its conscious limitation by chivalric convention, remained fundamentally unchanged. To argue for 'an earlier period of vigour, a period when reality approached more closely to an ascetic ideal' epitomized by the fusion of chivalry and religion in the military orders such as the Templars and Hospitallers,[71] is not simply to overestimate the chivalric significance of the military orders.[72] Crucially, it is also to ignore the fact that the tensions between ideals of conduct and actual behaviour in war itself were present *ab initio* in the Anglo-Norman period, if not indeed existing as a universal paradox within the culture of any warrior aristocracy.

THE NATURE OF CHIVALRY

Any work which makes extensive use of the term chivalry and its related vocabulary must attempt the difficult task of proffering a definition of this concept. As Maurice Keen notes, however, chivalry 'remains a word elusive of definition, tonal rather than precise in its implications', which 'could and did mean different things to different people at different times'.[73] Nevertheless, with such caveats in mind, Keen ventures a valid working definition:

> Chivalry cannot be divorced from the martial world of the mounted warrior: it cannot be divorced from aristocracy, because knights commonly were men of high lineage: and from the middle of the twelfth century on it very frequently carries ethical or religious overtones.[74]

In many respects, these considerations hold true for the Anglo-Norman era, though they call for an element of qualification. Thus while it is certain that the nobility was predominantly a warrior aristocracy and that many

---

[69] Keen, 'Huizinga, Kilgour and the Decline of Chivalry', pp. 5–6.
[70] Flori, *L'essor de la chevalerie*, pp. 331–6, gives several examples of such earlier, predominantly ecclesiastical, criticism.
[71] Keen, 'Huizinga, Kilgour and the Decline of Chivalry', pp. 4–5, summarizing Kilgour.
[72] Keen, *Chivalry*, p. 50.
[73] *Ibid.*, p. 2; *idem.*, 'Huizinga, Kilgour and the Decline of Chivalry', p. 1.
[74] Keen, *Chivalry*, p. 2. Cf. *idem.*, 'Huizinga, Kilgour and the Decline of Chivalry', p. 2; 'Perhaps . . . chivalry can be broadly defined as the ethos of a Christian and martial nobility, together with the mystique associated with that ethos.'

men of high birth could style themselves *milites* from at least the mid-eleventh century,[75] we should also note that much recent continental scholarship on the social origins of knighthood has stressed both the humble origins of the *milites* as a class and the relatively modest social position they had achieved by c. 1100.[76]

Marc Bloch has propounded the classic theory concerning the origins of knighthood, whereby the old Carolingian nobility was subsumed into and replaced by a rising class of non-noble, professional warriors who, by the mid-eleventh century, had come to form a 'new aristocracy'.[77] The demonstration, however, that many of the eleventh-century Frankish aristocracy can be traced back to noble Carolingian families[78] has led to a far-reaching reassessment of the status and social development of the class of retainers who served the existing aristocracy in a specifically military function as mounted warriors. The growing importance of these horse-troopers, known in Latin chronicles and charters as *milites* and as *cnihtas* – knights – by the Anglo-Saxons following the Conquest,[79] has been seen as an essential index of the nature and pace of change in the 'feudal transformation' of the eleventh century. By c. 1000, the *milites* were forming a recognizable social group visible in almost every area of France and northern Spain, a phenomenon inextricably linked

[75] See, for example, P. van Luyn, 'Les *milites* de la France du XIe siècle', *Le Moyen Age*, 77 (1971), pp. 1–51, 193–238; G. Duby, *La Société aux XIe et XIIe siècles dans la région mâconnaise* (repr. Ecole des Hautes Etudes, 1982); *idem.*, 'La diffusion du titre chevaleresque sur le versant méditerranéen de la Chrétienté latine', *La Noblesse au Moyen Age*, ed. P. Contamine (Paris, 1976), pp. 39–70; *idem.*, 'The Origins of Knighthood' and 'Lineage, Nobility and Knighthood: the Mâconnais in the Twelfth Century – a Revision', both in G. Duby, *The Chivalrous Society*, tr. C. Postan (London, 1977), pp. 158–170 and pp. 59–80 at pp. 75–9. Cf. Keen, 'Huizinga, Kilgour and the Decline of Chivalry', p. 2, who rightly notes that the collective noun '*chevalerie* (or militia) carried social overtones over and beyond a purely military connotation'.

[76] The most detailed guide to the extensive French literature is by Flori, *L'essor de la chevalerie*, especially pp. 119–90, with briefer resumés by T. Hunt, 'The Emergence of the Knight in France and England, 1000–1200', in *Knighthood in Medieval Literature*, ed. W. H. Jackson (Woodbridge, 1981), pp. 1–22 and J. P. Poly and E. Bournazel, *The Feudal Transformation, 900–1200* (New York, 1991). Synopses and valuable comment are provided by D. Crouch, *The Image of Aristocracy in Britain, 1000–1300* (London and New York, 1992), pp. 120–63, and P. Coss, *The Knight in Medieval England, 1000–1400* (Stroud, 1993), pp. 5–29.

[77] M. Bloch, *La Société Féodale*, 2 vols. (1939–40), tr. L. A. Manyon as *Feudal Society* (2nd edn, 1962), pp. 283–93; Douglas, *William the Conqueror*, pp. 83–104; D. Bates, *Normandy Before 1066* (London, 1982), pp. 106–11.

[78] L. Genicot, 'La noblesse au moyen age dans l'ancienne Francie; continuité, rupture ou évolution?', *Comparative Studies in Society and History*, 5 (1962), pp. 52–9; *idem.*, 'Recent Research on the Medieval Nobility', *The Medieval Nobility*, ed. T. Reuter (New York, Oxford and Amsterdam, 1978), pp. 17–36; L. Musset, 'L'aristocratie normande au XIe siècle', *La Noblesse au Moyen Age*, pp. 85–94; G. Duby, 'Lineage, Nobility and Knighthood', *The Chivalrous Society*, pp. 59–80; *idem.* 'Une enquête à poursuivre: la noblesse dans la France médiévale', *Revue historique*, 226 (1961), pp. 1–22; J. Martindale, 'The French Aristocracy in the Early Middle Ages: A Reappraisal', *Past and Present*, 75 (1977), pp. 5–45. Cf. Bates, *Normandy Before 1066*, p. 111: 'Knighthood failed to transform the Norman aristocracy before 1066. Indeed, the survival of a Carolingian terminology is very much an argument against the fundamental re-organization of the Norman aristocracy at any stage of its eleventh century history.'

[79] Van Luyn, 'Les *milites* dans la France', pp. 5–51, 193–238; F. M. Stenton, *The First Century of English Feudalism* (2nd edn, Oxford, 1961), pp. 132–7. For the Anglo-Saxon use of the term *miles* see R. P. Abels, *Lordship and Military Obligation in Anglo-Saxon England* (Berkeley, 1988), pp. 132–45.

to the proliferation of castles, the creation of castellanries and the increasing annexation by local seigneurs of formerly public powers of taxation and jurisdiction from the late tenth and early eleventh centuries.[80]

Duby's celebrated study of the Mâconnais had shown how, from the late tenth century, the term *miles* first replaced terms of vassalic servitude such as *vassus* and *fidelis*, then gradually became adopted as a designation of rank by the aristocracy, finally being assumed by even the greatest lords.[81] An initially subordinate but rising warrior class had aspired, through their specialist military skills, to enter the ranks of the aristocracy and had, by c. 1050, achieved the integration of knighthood with nobility. The Mâconnais, however, now appears to be precocious in regard to such a fusion. While undeniable as a broad development throughout the eleventh century, the social elevation of the *milites* as a coherent class was far slower elsewhere than the Burgundian evidence would suggest. Almost invariably of humble, often peasant, origin, the *milites* were still by the end of the eleventh century a social group distinct from and subordinate to the older aristocracy in terms of lineage, rank and wealth.

Though in some areas knights were approaching a *petite noblesse* by c. 1100, and aspired to higher status by means of their value as professional cavalrymen, they remained essentially the armed followers of castellans or other lords, who were well aware of the social inferiority of these *parvenus de la guerre*.[82] In England at the time of Domesday, for example, it has been argued that the majority of *milites* were only moderate freeholders, whose holdings of single fees or fractions of fees scarcely raised them above the economic status of well-to-do peasants.[83] Harvey's use of Domesday, however, has been criticized.[84] Not least, it is important to realise that Domesday Book marked only a *stage* in a process of sub-enfeoffment of vassals by tenants-in-chief which, as the *cartae baronum* of 1166 reveal, was largely complete by 1135, but had only recently begun by 1086.

Even accepting Harvey's general findings 'that many (perhaps very many) knights were indeed poor knights',[85] it is nonetheless misleading to assess social status principally by wealth, and particularly by landed wealth.

---

[80] Poly and Bouznazel, *The Feudal Transformation*, pp. 25–34, 97–113; G. Duby, *Le Moyen Age, 987–1460* (Paris, 1987), tr. J. Vale as *France in the Middle Ages, 987–1460* (London, 1991), pp. 55–64.

[81] Duby, *La Société dans la région mâconnaise; idem.*, 'The Origins of Knighthood' and 'Lineage, Nobility and Knighthood: the Mâconnais in the Twelfth Century – a Revision', *The Chivalrous Society*, pp. 158–70 and pp. 75–9. Cf. *idem.*, 'La diffusion du titre chevaleresque', pp. 39–70.

[82] Flori, *L'essor de la chevalerie*, pp. 119–41; Crouch, *The Image of Aristocracy*, pp. 120–63; and Coss, *The Knight in Medieval England*, pp. 5–29.

[83] S. Harvey, 'The Knight and the Knight's Fee in England', *Past and Present*, 49 (1970), pp. 133–73.

[84] R. A. Brown, 'The Status of the Norman Knight', *War and Government*, pp. 18–32, and reprinted in Strickland, *Anglo-Norman Warfare*, pp. 128–42, at pp. 130–5; D. F. Fleming, 'Landholding by Milites in Domesday Book', *Anglo-Norman Studies*, 13 (1990), pp. 83–98.

[85] Crouch, *The Image of Aristocracy*, p. 128.

Many younger sons of noble families, whose chances of gaining an inheritance were slight, took honourable service in the royal or honorial *familia*. William the Marshal is but a prominent example of a household knight who for much of his early career remained landless, yet clearly enjoyed considerable status and prestige through his skill in arms. The crucial point is that the essence of knighthood lay in *function*, not in relative material wealth. The greatest lords adopted the style *miles*, not as a designation of rank but in recognition of a shared sense of *function* as elite mounted warriors.[86] Though there would always be a distinction in rank, pedigree and wealth between an honorial lord and the more lowly knights in his *familia* or *mesnie*, they were all *chevaliers*, united by their social function as *bellatores*, those who fought. Far less of a gulf existed between such men than between the warriors with their costly arms and war horses and the *rustici*, the agricultural classes, who as *inermes* did not fight.[87] The use of a more general label such as the later designation *homines ad arma*, which in the fifteenth century embraced a number of social categories from squire to knight banneret, might circumvent the ambiguities of the terms knight and *miles*. But I would contend that the profession of arms and membership of the *militia* carried an elevated social status, and that in war contemporaries saw the crucial divide not between lords and their knights, but between the *milites* and the *pedites*.[88] It is with these considerations in mind that the terms knight and knighthood have been used throughout this book.

It has been argued that in terms of the broader social manifestations of chivalry, it was only the twelfth century that saw the fusion of the knights as a class of warrior retainers and the nobility.[89] Such a view fails to recognize that the aristocracy itself had always been a warrior elite from at least the times of the Merovingians. The existing nobility did not become militarized in the eleventh century and come to adopt the new values of the socially ascendant body of *milites*. A study of the actualities of war strongly suggests that in terms of shared concepts of behaviour in combat and of custom and usage on the battlefield, such an amalgamation had occurred far earlier. Rather, lords and their men shared common methods of combat and a common martial culture, which to be sure was to be refined and developed during the twelfth century, but which, it could well be argued, is visible in its essentials as far back as at least the ninth century.[90]

---

[86] Below, pp. 142–9.   [87] Brown, 'The Status of the Norman Knight', pp. 134–40.   [88] Below, pp. 176–81.
[89] For an extended treatment of this thesis, epitomized in his title, see Flori, *L'essor de la chevalerie, passim*.
[90] J. Nelson, 'Ninth-Century Knighthood: the Evidence of Nithard', *Studies in Medieval History*, pp. 255–66; see too the important study by K. Leyser, 'Early Medieval Canon Law and the Beginnings of Knighthood', *Communications and Power in Medieval Europe. The Carolingian and Ottonian Centuries*, ed. T. Reuter (London, 1994), pp. 51–72.

This brings us to a second qualification of Keen's definition. In a literal sense, it is undoubtedly right to link chivalry with the mounted warrior. The words *cheval*, *chevalier* and chivalry are cognate, while the term *chevalerie* could, particularly in the twelfth century, simply be used as the collective noun for a group of mounted warriors.[91] The man on horseback was indeed elevated both physically and socially.[92] But we should be cautious about regarding concepts of chivalry solely as the preserve of those who *fought* as cavalry. While cavalry remained an integral, if not the predominant arm in most Anglo-Norman armies, the propensity of knights to dismount to fight on foot in battles such as Tinchebrai, 1106, Brémule, 1119, Bourgthéroulde, 1124, the Standard, 1138 and Lincoln, 1141, should warn us against too rigid an association between the knight and the charge with the couched lance.[93]

This caveat is more germane, however, in regard to Anglo-Saxon and Viking warriors, who used horses for rapid mobility in war and regarded costly mounts as symbols of status,[94] but once at the field of battle generally – though not universally – dismounted to fight on foot.[95] For few would deny that many of the martial values inherent in eleventh- and twelfth-century Frankish chivalry were equally prominent in the ethos of the warrior visible in epics such as *Beowulf* or the sagas, and even glimpsed as early as Tacitus's *Germania*.[96] The thought-worlds of the *Battle of Maldon* and

[91] For the developing sense of the word *chevalier* see Flori, 'La notion de chevalerie dans les chansons de geste', pp. 211–44, 407–45; and Switten, '*Chevalier* in Twelfth-Century French and Occitan Literature', pp. 403–47.   [92] Crouch, *The Image of Aristocracy*, p. 124.

[93] C. W. Hollister, *Anglo-Saxon Military Institutions on the Eve of the Norman Conquest* (Oxford, 1962), pp. 131–2; J. Bradbury, 'Battles in England and Normandy, 1066–1154', *Anglo-Norman Studies*, 6 (1983), pp. 1–12, reprinted in Strickland, *Anglo-Norman Warfare*, pp. 182–93.

[94] G. R. Owen-Crocker, 'Hawks and Horse-Trappings: the Insignia of Rank', *The Battle of Maldon, AD 991*, ed. D. Scragg (Oxford, 1991), pp. 220–37, especially pp. 229–37, and p. 229 where the gnomic *Maxims*, I. 62 is cited: '*Eorl sceal on eos boge*' – 'a nobleman ought to be on a horse's back'; J. Graham-Campbell, 'Anglo-Scandinavian Equestrian Equipment in Eleventh-Century England', *Anglo-Norman Studies*, 14 (1991), pp. 77–90.

[95] Hollister, *Anglo-Saxon Military Institutions*, pp. 132–40; R. H. C. Davis, 'Did the Anglo-Saxons have Warhorses?', *Weapons and Warfare in Anglo-Saxon England*, ed. S. C. Hawkes (Oxford University Committee for Archaeology Monograph no. 21, Oxford, 1989), pp. 141–4; R. Abels, 'English Tactics, Strategy and Military Organization in the Late Tenth Century', *The Battle of Maldon*, pp. 143–55; N. J. Higham, 'Cavalry in Early Bernicia?', *Northern History*, 27 (1991), pp. 236–41; C. Cessford, 'Cavalry in Early Bernicia: A Reply', *Northern History*, 29 (1993), pp. 185–7; N. Hooper, 'The Aberlemno Stone and Cavalry in Anglo-Saxon England', *Northern History*, 29 (1993), pp. 188–96.

[96] G. N. Garmonsway, 'Anglo-Saxon Heroic Attitudes', *Franciplegius: Medieval and Linguistic Studies in Honour of F. P. Magoun*, ed. J. B. Bessinger, Jr and R. P. Creed (New York and London, 1965), pp. 139–46; P. Foote and D. M. Wilson, *The Viking Achievement: The Society and Culture of Early Medieval Scandinavia* (London, 1972), pp. 100–8, 283–5, and cf. pp. 319–69; R. Woolf, 'The Ideal of Men Dying with their Lord in the *Germenia* and in *The Battle of Maldon*', *Anglo-Saxon England*, 5 (1976), pp. 63–81; K. O. O'Keefe, 'Heroic Values and Christian Ethics', *The Cambridge Companion to Old English Literature*, ed. M. Godden and M. Lapidge (Cambridge, 1991), pp. 107–25; R. Frank, 'The Ideal of Men Dying with their Lord in *The Battle of Maldon*: Anachronism or *Nouvelle Vague*', in *People and Places in Northern Europe, 500–1600*, ed. I. Wood (Woodbridge, 1991), pp. 95–106.

the *Song of Roland*, while by no means identical, are very close. Both proclaim ideas of courage and prowess in arms, of loyalty to one's lord and comrades, of largesse and gift-giving. Both celebrate Christian warriors fighting the heathen for their lords, faith and *patria*.[97] And whether we choose to view the *ofermod* and *desmesure* that unites Byrhtnoth and Roland as sinful pride or heroic resignation to fate,[98] this epic *topos* reflects, as we shall see, the very real tensions between the dictates of honour and military sagacity.[99]

Seen in this light, chivalry is not a peculiarly Frankish phenomenon (though in origin several of its dependent institutions clearly are) but rather just one label for the ethos of any warrior aristocracy sharing timeless martial values. Huizinga had noted how 'a conception of military life resembling that of medieval chivalry is found nearly everywhere, notably with the Hindus of the *Mahabharata* and in Japan. Warlike aristocracies need an ideal form of manly perfection.'[100] This concept is still more cogently expressed by Malcolm Vale:

> There is too much that can never be known about the motives which have led men to wage war, and to adopt (or to reject) certain codes of behaviour towards their comrades and their enemies. Yet there can be no doubt that the ideal qualities of chivalry – honour, loyalty, courage, generosity – have fulfilled a fundamental human need, felt especially among warrior elites whose social function has been to fight. Chivalry was often no more, and no less, than the sentiment of honour in its medieval guise . . . among warrior classes, it possesses a universal and, perhaps, an eternal validity.[101]

---

[97] Cf. G. Clark, 'The Hero of Maldon: *Vir pius et strenuus*', *Speculum*, 54 (1979), pp. 257–82; and J. E. Cross, 'Oswald and Byrhtnoth: A Christian Saint and a Hero who is Christian', *English Studies*, 46 (1965), pp. 93–109. C. Clark, 'Byrhtnoth and Roland: A Comparison', *Neophilologus*, 51 (1967), pp. 288–93 is far too dismissive of the element of Christian conflict against the heathen in *Maldon*. For an excellent discussion of Anglo-Saxon concepts of the just war and defence of the *patria* against the Vikings see J. E. Cross, 'The Ethic of War in Old English', *England Before the Conquest*, ed. P. Clemoes and K. Hughes (Cambridge, 1971), pp. 269–82.

[98] Much literary ink has been spilt by critics over the moral and even tactical validity of Byrhtnoth's decision to allow the Vikings across the causeway from Northey island to do battle in 991, and of Roland's comparable decision not to summon the aid of Charlemagne by blowing his horn, the *olifant*, but *inter alia* see J. R. R. Tolkein, 'Homecoming of Beorntnoth Beorhthelm's Son', *Essays and Studies*, n.s. 6 (1953), pp. 1–18, at pp. 13–18; F. Whitehead, '*Ofermod* et desmesure', *Cahiers de civilisation médiévale*, 3 (1960), pp. 115–7; H. Gneuss, 'The Battle of Maldon 89: Byrhtnoth's *Ofermod* Once Again', *Studies in Philology*, 73 (1976), pp. 117–37; W. W. Kibler, 'Roland's Pride', *Symposium*, 26 (1972), pp. 147–60; L. S. Crist, 'A propos de la desmesure dans la Chanson de Roland: quelques propos (démesurés?)', *Olifant*, 4 (1974), pp. 10–20. Cf. D. Evans, 'Old English and Old French Epics: Some Analogues', *Guillaume d'Orange and the Chanson de Geste*, ed. W. van Emden and P. E. Bennet (Reading, 1984), pp. 23–31.   [99] Below, pp. 113–17.

[100] Huizinga, *The Waning of the Middle Ages*, p. 77. Yet while aspiration to a noble life, 'pure and beautiful', acted as a constant cultural dynamic, for Huizinga it was always 'at the same time a cloak for a whole world of violence and self interest'. For the universality of the heroic ethos in literature see, for example, H. M. Chadwick, *The Heroic Age* (Cambridge, 1912); G. Dumezil, *The Stakes of the Warrior* (Berkeley, 1983); and R. Frank, '*The Battle of Maldon* and Heroic Literature', in *The Battle of Maldon*, pp. 196–207.   [101] Vale, *War and Chivalry*, p. 1.

Consequently, the outward expression of such martial values could span cultural divides. Thus Harold Godwineson could be invested with arms by Duke William following his bravery in rescuing Norman troops from the quicksands of the river Couesnon near Mont St Michel in 1064 during a Norman expedition against Conan II of Brittany.[102] Though here the act was pregnant with the symbolism of political submission which Harold could subsequently be vilified by Norman propagandists for breaching, he must have been fully aware of the resonances of lord–man bonding which the receipt of arms entailed in Anglo-Scandinavian as much as in Norman society.[103] Indeed, the act of a Norman bestowing arms upon an Anglo-Saxon may not have been without precedent. It seems very likely that the *aethelings* Edward and Alfred, brought up in exile at the Norman court, were given martial training, and knighting would have been the natural conclusion to such apprenticeship.[104] If we can believe Orderic, sometime after 1052 Edward himself, already half-Norman by birth, belted to knighthood the young Robert of Rhuddlan, then serving as his squire (*armiger*).[105]

If close cultural and political ties between Normandy and Anglo-Saxon England made for the ready interchange of such ritual, it is more striking to find the same phenomenon visible between peoples far more profoundly distinct in terms of race and religion. A vernacular poem, the *Ordene de Chevalerie*, c. 1250, provides a fictional account of how, in order to gain his

---

[102] *BT*, plates 19, 24. On the receipt of arms and dubbing see J. Flori, 'Les origines de l'adoubment chevaleresque; étude des remises d'armes dans les croniques et annales latines du IXe au XIIIe siècle', *Traditio*, 35 (1979), pp. 209–72; *idem*. 'Sémantique et société médiévale: le verb *adouber* et son évolution au XIIe siècle', *Annales*, 31 (1976), pp. 915–40; *idem., L'essor de la chevalerie*, p. 118.

[103] Thus the skald Sigvat received a sword on entering St Olaf's guard in 1016 (L. M. Larson, *The King's Household in England Before the Norman Conquest* (Wisconsin, 1904), p. 162 and n. 87); and cf. *Beowulf*, ed. and tr. M. Swanton (Manchester, 1978), 11. 2601–46. The Anglo-Saxon *heriot*, or death duty, paid by thegns to the king in the form of horses, weapons and armour, was intimately linked to the practice of bestowing arms upon warriors entering a lord's retinue; see N. P. Brooks, 'Arms, Status and Warfare in Late Anglo-Saxon England', *Ethelred the Unready*, ed. D. Hill (British Archaeological Reports, British Series, 59 (Oxford, 1978), pp. 81–103 and especially pp. 81–9). Cf. Keen, *Chivalry*, pp. 66–9.

It is worth noting in this context that according to the *Waltham Chronicle*, written 1177 x 1189, the Anglo-Scandinavian noble Tofi the Proud had belted the Holy Rood of Waltham with the sword with which he was first made a *miles* ('quo primo fuerat accintus miles') (*Waltham Chronicle*, pp. 22–3). While this latter phrase is almost certainly anachronistic, the propensity to dress such crucifixes with crowns, belts and other precious items, makes the act itself inherently plausible, and would accord well with the image of a militant Christ portrayed in the *The Dream of the Rood* (cf. C. R. Dodwell, *Anglo-Saxon Art: A New Perspective* (Manchester, 1982), pp. 119–21). Conversely, the *Gesta Herewardi*'s dubious statement that Hereward received his sword-belt from Abbot Brand of Peterbrough according to English custom ('et eum militari gladio et baltheo Anglico more praecingeret'), seems to reflect contemporary, and predominantly clerical, thinking about the ritual (*Gesta Herewardi incliti exulis et militis*, in *Geffrei Gaimar, L'Estoire des Engles*, ed. T. D. Harris and C. T. Martin, 2 vols. (Rolls Series, 1888), I. p. 268). Our knowledge of the actual rituals involved in the bestowal of arms by Anglo-Saxon lords remains scanty.

[104] F. Barlow, *Edward the Confessor* (London, 1970), pp. 39–42.

[105] Orderic, IV, pp. 136–7, 'ab illo [ie Edward] cingulum militiae accepit'; Barlow, *Edward the Confessor*, p. 191.

liberty from Saracen captivity, Hugh of Tiberias had to instruct Saladin in the ritual of dubbing a Christian knight and to explain the symbolism of the constituent elements of the ceremony.[106] In this guise, the story is but a product of the Frankish mind-set. It illustrates nevertheless the extent to which by the mid-thirteenth century Saladin had come to be regarded in Western eyes as a chivalrous opponent and the epitome of the noble pagan.[107] And whether or not the author of the *Ordene* was aware of it, there existed factual precedents for such an act.

It is just possible that Saladin himself may have been knighted when a young commander by the Frankish lord Humphrey of Toron, who significantly was accused of too great a familiarity with the Muslim leader.[108] Certainly the author of an eye-witness account of the siege of Acre, who was probably an English chaplain of the Templars, believed this to be the case when he sketched out Saladin's earlier career.[109] Even if this incident was romantic invention – and corroborating evidence is lacking – it is nevertheless striking that a crusader and contemporary could envisage such an event as a possibility, and that the theme of Saladin being dubbed by a great Christian lord had begun to circulate even before his death in 1193.

With an analogous dubbing we are perhaps on firmer ground. Throughout the Third Crusade, Richard I had enjoyed close and near-constant diplomatic relations with Saladin's brother Al-Adil (known to the Latins as Safadin), since Saladin himself would not treat with Richard in person while the two rulers were at war.[110] A friendship born of mutual respect had grown between the two men and at Acre, on Palm Sunday 1192, Richard 'in great state girded with the belt of knighthood (*insignavit magnifice cingulo militiae*) Safadin's son who had been sent there for this purpose'.[111] The bestowal of arms on Al-Adil's son was a highly symbolic gesture; the

---

[106] Keen, *Chivalry*, pp. 6–8.

[107] For Saladin's image in later medieval romance see S. Lane Poole, *Saladin and the Fall of the Kingdom of Jerusalem* (London, 1901), pp. 377–401.

[108] For this criticism, see *Willelmi Tyrensis archiepiscopi chronicon* (WT), ed. R. B. Huygens (*Corpus Christianorum Continuatio Medievalis*, LXIII, 1986), Bk XXI, c. 31, p. 973; tr. E. A. Babcock and A. C. Krey as *William of Tyre: Deeds Done Beyond the Sea*, 2 vols. (New York, 1943, repr. 1976), II, p. 410. If Humphrey did belt Saladin to knighthood, the most likely occasion was following the siege of Alexandria, when Saladin spent time in the Christian camp on conclusion of peace and was honourably received (WT, Bk XIX, c. 31, p. 907–8; trans. Babcock and Krey, p. 342).

[109] *Itinerarium*, p. 9; 'cum iam aestas robustior officium militare deposceret ad Enfridum de Turone, illustrem Palaestinae principem paludanus accessit, et Francorum ritu cingulum militiae ab ipso suscepit'. For the authorship of this tract, which prefaces the *Itinerarium perigrinorum et gesta regis Ricardi* in the Rolls Series text but was a separate text composed 1191 x 1192, see the introduction to *Das Itinerarium Perigrinorum. Eine zeitgenossiche englische Chronik zum dritten Kreuzzug in ursprunglicher Gestalt*, ed. H. E. Meyer (*Schriften der Monumenta Germaniae Historia*, 18, Stuttgart, 1962). Meyer labels this text, called the *Itinerarium Perigrinorum*, as *IP1*.

[110] Beha-ad-din (Ibn Shaddad), *The Life of Saladin*, (Beha-ad-din), tr. C. L. Conder (Palestine Pilgrims' Text Society, XIII, London, 1897), p. 252.   [111] *Itinerarium*, p. 325.

resonances of overlordship which it conferred on the grantor both reflected and reinforced a proposed alliance. A compliment was paid to Al-Adil, while the young man gained the associative honour of being knighted by so great a warrior as Richard.[112]

Al-Adil showed himself capable of reciprocating chivalrous gestures. When, in August 1192, Richard's tiny force was hard pressed in the defence of Jaffa, and the knights were suffering from an acute shortage of horses,[113] Al-Adil sent Richard two fine Arab chargers on which to continue the fight, 'as a token of his admiration of his valour'.[114] That such gestures could take place reflected essential similarities between the respective warrior aristocracies in their concepts of a martial ethos and of honour. The memoirs of the Syrian emir Usamah ibn Munqidh reveal a delight in feats of arms lovingly described, in horses and weaponry, a passion for hunting, notions of lordship and vassalage and a sense of companionship in arms that might as readily have come from the *Histoire de Guillaume le Maréchal*.[115]

Above all, in the age before the massed deployment of effective field artillery and hand-held firearms, warriors' experience of combat must have been broadly similar. Despite significant differences in tactics and organization of armies, the nature of hand-to-hand combat with a limited range of weapons such as spear, sword, axe and mace ensured that fighting retained an essential element of personal contact between members of the military

---

[112] A generation later in 1227, Frederick II knighted the Egyptian emir, Fakhr-ad-Din, ambassador of Al-Adil's son, al-Kamil, sultan of Egypt: T. M. Van Cleve, *The Emperor Frederick II of Hohenstaufen* (Oxford, 1972), p. 203. Joinville noted that subsequently 'On his banner, which was barred, he bore on one bar the arms of the Emperor who had knighted him' (Joinville, p. 70; tr. Shaw, p. 214).

[113] Ambroise, 11. 11339–40; *Itinerarium*, p. 413, where it is noted that the Franks had been reduced to only fifteen horses, several of which were not destriers. For subsequent translations of Ambroise I have used the verse translation *The Crusade of Richard Lion-Heart by Ambroise*, (Ambroise), tr. M. J. Hubert and J. L. La Monte (Columbia, 1941, repr. New York, 1976). The relationship between this vernacular *Estoire* and the very close but not exact Latin prose version, the *Itinerarium regis Ricardi*, is complex and in dispute. It appears that either the *Itinerarium* was a rendering of Ambroise's poem into Latin with certain new information, or (less probably) that both texts were based on a lost vernacular original, possibly in prose. Since neither is an absolute copy of the other, each provides some independent material (J. G. Edwards, 'The *Itinerarium Regis Ricardi* and the *Estoire de la Guerre Sainte*', *Historical Essays in Honour of James Tait*, ed. J. G. Edwards, V. H. Galbraith and E. F. Jacob (Manchester, 1933), pp. 59–77; Ambroise, pp. 3–18). Consequently, references here will cite the line numbering of Ambroise (the same in both Paris's text and the translation of Hubert and La Monte), followed by the text of the *Itinerarium*, except where the *Itinerarium* is to be preferred, where it will be cited first.

[114] Ambroise, 11. 11544–64; *Itinerarium*, p. 419. For the differing, though more romanticized and untrustworthy versions of this story by Ernoul and the *Estoire d'Eracles*, in which the horses are trained to refuse the rider's commands and bring Richard helpless back to the Muslim camp, see M. R. Morgan, *The Chronicle of Ernoul and the Continuations of William of Tyre* (Oxford, 1973), pp. 73–6; and *idem.*, *La Continuation de Guillaume de Tyre (1184–1197)*, (Paris, 1982), pp. 146–7.

[115] *An Arab-Syrian Gentleman and Warrior in the Period of the Crusades: Memoirs of Usamah Ibn-Munqidh*, (Usamah), trans. P. K. Hitti (New York, 1924).

elite. And when confronted with the actuality of war and the threat of death, the warrior's appeal to divine aid and protection, his response to those within his group, the loyalty felt towards his lord and companions, the need to suppress fear and display courage through prowess in arms, must have been a near-universal experience.[116] As Jean de Bueil expressed it in *Le Jouvencel*:

> It is a joyous thing, is war . . . You love your comrade so in war. When you see that your quarrel is just and that you are fighting well, tears rise to your eye. A great sweet feeling of loyalty and pity fills your heart on seeing your friend so valiantly exposing his body to execute and accomplish the command of the Creator.[117]

To Huizinga, such words 'show us the very core of courage; man, in the excitement of danger, stepping out of his narrow egotism, the ineffable feeling, the rapture of fidelity and sacrifice – in short, the primitive and spontaneous asceticism, which is at the bottom of the chivalrous ideal'.[118]

By these broader criteria, chivalry and Christianity, the third major component suggested by Keen, are not necessarily inseparable. Thus, for example, while the paucity and ambiguity of source material makes it difficult to assess the impact of pagan beliefs on their conduct of war, it seems clear that in other respects than the religious, the martial values of the Vikings prior to their conversion differed but little from their Anglo-Saxon and Frankish counterparts.[119] Even in the poem *Beowulf*, almost certainly written in a Christian milieu but echoing folk-memories of the pre-conversion migration period, the influence of Christianity – quite unlike *Maldon* and still less like *Roland* – does not significantly impinge on the heroic ethos ascribed to the Danes and Geats.[120]

Nevertheless, to highlight certain basic values common to warrior elites is by no means to deny important distinguishing features between these elites. Nor is it to minimize the influence of significant cultural or religious determinants in the expression of a particular martial ethos. Several features central to the chivalric culture of knighthood were peculiar to Western Europe, heavily if not predominantly derivative of French culture;

---

[116] For perceptive discussions of these psychological dimensions in relation to medieval warfare see Keegan, *The Face of Battle*, pp. 78–116, which takes the battle of Agincourt, 1415, as a case study; and Verbruggen, *The Art of War*, pp. 39–71, and pp. 150 ff.

[117] Jean de Bueil, *Le Jouvencel*, ed. C. Favre and L. Lecestre, 2 vols. (Paris, 1887–9), II, pp. 20–1, and quoted by Huizinga, *The Waning of the Middle Ages*, p. 73.   [118] *The Waning of the Middle Ages*, pp. 73–4.

[119] H. R. Ellis Davidson, *Myths and Symbols in Pagan Europe* (Syracuse, 1988), pp. 69–78.

[120] See, for example, T. A. Shippey, *Old English Verse* (London, 1972), esp. ch. 2, 'The Argument of Courage: Beowulf and Other Heroic Poetry', pp. 17–52; M. D. Cherniss, *Ingeld and Christ: Heroic Concepts and Values in Old English Poetry* (Mouton, 1972); M. A. Parker, *Beowulf and Christianity* (New York, 1987).

the tournament, the development of blazon and the role of heralds, the pervasive influence of Arthurian romance, and even the military and later the secular orders of chivalry. Equally, while most if not all warrior cultures contained a religious dimension, often linked to the need for supernatural protection and divine assistance in war, this element might vary greatly in its form and expression between organized belief systems; the influence of Islam among Arab and Turkish warriors, for instance, differed markedly in its manifestations from that of Zen Bhuddism in the *bushido* of the samurai.[121]

Keen is thus undoubtedly right to equate the chivalry of medieval Europe with Christianity, in that concepts of knighthood were profoundly influenced by its distinctive dictates. So profound were these influences, indeed, that the very spiritual legitimacy and social function of the warriors as a distinct class could be subject to the changing interpretations of a hierarchical clergy who were themselves forbidden the use of arms, and who in the course of the later eleventh century had moved from regarding the knight's *metier* as intrinsically sinful to directing his aggression to meritorious holy war.

Here we should note again, however, that there had been a strong Christian flavour to the warfare waged by the Germanic peoples virtually *ab initio* following their respective conversions, particularly (though far from exclusively) when the enemy were heathen Frisians, Saxons, Slavs, Avars, Magyars, Vikings or Arabs. The Christian dimension to the ethos of the warriors was thus no novel construct of the eleventh century, born of the attempts of the Gregorian reformers to harness knights to the service of the papacy as *milites sancti Petri* and of the crusade ideology promulgated by Urban II at Clermont in 1095. To be sure, the eleventh and twelfth centuries witnessed profound developments; in the growth of military saint cults; in concepts of holy war transforming into papally preached crusades; in clerical perceptions of the role and legitimacy of the *bellatores* in Christian society; and in the fusion of knighthood and monasticism in the military orders such as the Templars and Hospitallers. Yet the God of Clovis and Oswald of Northumbria had been a God of battles, and his aid and that of his saints was perceived as crucial for the attainment of victory long before Duke William carried relics and the papal banner into battle at Hastings, with the war-cry 'Dieu aie!' on the lips of his knights.[122]

Nonetheless, a common adherence to Christianity by no means guaran-

---

[121] On *bushido*, Zen and the Japanese warrior ethic see, *inter alia*, R. Storry, *The Way of the Samurai* (London, 1978), pp. 43–62; and T. Cleary, *The Japanese Art of War* (Boston and London, 1992).
[122] Below, pp. 64–5.

teed a uniformity of conduct in war. For whereas vital cohesive factors such as courage, loyalty and generosity achieved near universality when operating *within* the warrior group, be it Anglo-Saxon *comitatus*, Norse *hird*, Celtic *teulu* or Anglo-Norman *mesnie*, assumptions concerning race and class might result in considerable divergence in behaviour in regard to the treatment of the *external* enemy, whether on the battlefield or as prisoners. It is here, in the vital area of conduct towards defeated or disarmed opponents, that the universality of a 'chivalric' ethic breaks down.[123] The Conquest, as we have suggested, saw conventions of ransom replace the habitual killing of noble opponents, though non-noble combatants continued to be butchered out of hand by the victors.[124] In their Celtic neighbours, moreover, the Normans encountered peoples who had little concept of the 'non-combatant', who still enslaved captives and whose time-honoured methods of war included wholesale killing. We may say, indeed, that the propensity to spare rather than slaughter adversaries of a similar rank, and the practice of redeeming rather than selling captives into slavery, marked a crucial development in the nature of Anglo-Norman chivalry.[125]

'Chivalry', Keen has noted, 'is a word that came to denote the code and culture of a martial estate which regarded war as its hereditary profession'.[126] It is with the reality of that code in late eleventh- and twelfth-century England and Normandy and with the conduct of the martial estate in war itself that this book is concerned.

---

[123] A study of the widely varying perceptions of conduct towards prisoners in World War II, for example, would amply bear this out. Racial preconceptions resulted in a marked polarity of behaviour by the Germans towards prisoners on the Western and Eastern fronts, while Japanese atrocities towards prisoners of war stemmed largely from the belief that for soldiers to surrender was an act of shame that forfeited the right to humane, still less honourable treatment.

[124] Above, pp. 3–7; Strickland, 'Slaughter, Slavery or Ransom?', pp. 41–59; below, pp. 176–81.

[125] These themes have been further explored by J. Gillingham, 'Conquering the Barbarians: War and Chivalry in Twelfth-Century Britain', *Haskins Society Journal*, 4 (1993), pp. 57–65; and *idem.*, '1066 and the Introduction of Chivalry into England', *Law and Government*, pp. 31–55.

[126] Keen, *Chivalry*, p. 239.

2

A 'LAW OF ARMS'?

In offering compensation to the defenders of Dover in 1066 and in protecting the citizens of Exeter in 1068 once they had formally submitted, William I had clearly believed he was acting with propriety.[1] But was he conscious of some form of a *ius belli*, of a 'law of arms' or 'laws of war' in some well-defined or even codified form? Or were his actions simply dictated by a series of customs, a loose collection of gradually accumulated *mores* concerning correct conduct in war that had become operational among the knighthood of Normandy and France? What, indeed, did 'custom' and 'convention' mean in this context? Were such conventions binding in any judicial sense, or did men observe them merely because of the pragmatic military benefits which they frequently entailed? How widespread, indeed, was adherence to these usages, and how far were knights constrained by the dictates of honour, shame and reputation?

To set such questions in perspective and to help define our terms of reference, it is instructive to compare the nature of the 'laws of war' in the fourteenth and fifteenth centuries, a period in which conventions regulating war were coming to be increasingly enunciated and defined.

LEGNANO, BONET AND THE LAWS OF WAR

In the introduction to his *Laws of War in the Later Middle Ages* Maurice Keen quotes the words attributed by Froissart to two French knights attempting to surrender to John of Gaunt and the earl of Cambridge at the siege of Limoges in 1370, despite the express command of the Black Prince not to give quarter: 'My lords, we are yours: you have vanquished us. Act therefore

---

[1] Above, pp. 1–2.

according to the law of arms.'[2] Clearly, Froissart, the French nobles in question and the English lords who accepted their surrender had a well-defined concept of behaviour that could be labelled by a highly informed secular observer as a 'droit d'armes'.

The title of Keen's book, indeed, suggests a tangible and precise phenomenon, which Keen regards as 'some sort of prototype of the Geneva convention, a branch of international law governing the conduct of war'.[3] He suggests that the development of war during the fourteenth century into what amounted, particularly to those warring in France, to 'a large scale commercial venture' acted as a dynamic for the elaboration, definition and, most important, the enforcement of the laws of war: 'If one was going to make a living out of the profits of war, as these men did, one needed to be sure that one's enemies were going to observe the rules of the game, and that if they did not, there would be ways of forcing them to do so.'[4]

The Hundred Years War, hitherto unparalleled in the Middle Ages in its extent, duration and international nature, offered the catalyst for the increasing formulation and development of such rules of conduct, reflected by the production of tracts concerned specifically with the ethical and juridical aspects of warfare. Most influential among these was John of Legnano's *Tractatus de bello, de represaliis et de duello*, and its subsequent reworking into the vernacular by Honoré Bonet as *L'arbre des batailles*.[5] The concept of the 'law of arms' or *ius armorum* encapsulated by these legists was a complex theological, philosophical and customary amalgam:

> The legitimacy of warfare in general was . . . regarded as established by divine and natural law [the *ius divinum* and the *ius naturale*]. The principles governing the conduct of human war were to be inferred from their rules; these principles were called the *ius gentium*. In wars between states or kingdoms which were part of the Roman people, the canon and civil laws, which equally had their origin in divine and natural law, added a further series of

---

[2] Keen, *Laws of War*, p. 1. For a discussion, however, of Froissart's reliability concerning this incident see R. Barber, *Edward, Prince of Wales and Aquitaine* (London, 1978), pp. 225–6.

[3] Keen, *Laws of War*, p. 2. For Keen the existence of, and international adherence to, a clearly defined law of arms is crucial to underpinning one of his central contentions, namely that chivalric conduct, for all its complexity of interpretation and definition, can be seen to have been integral to the waging of war itself, and not simply – as argued by Huizinga – an elaborate, but highly artificial set of trappings which served simply as a veneer to disguise the greed and brutality of the knighthood. Speaking of the relationship of the 'law of arms' to chivalric ideals he notes: 'The demands of such a law would necessarily fall short of the highest possible standards, for it is in the nature of law that its rules are formal, not ideal. Even a formal minimum of chivalrous conduct, however, would if judicially enforceable add meaning to the "chivalry" of the fourteenth and fifteenth centuries, which some have considered to be no more than an anachronistic pose' (*ibid.*, p. 3).   [4] *Ibid.*, p. 4.

[5] John of Legnano, *Tractatus de bello, de represaliis et de duello*, ed. T. E. Holland, tr. J. L. Brierly (Oxford, 1917); Honoré Bonet, *L'arbre des batailles*, ed. E. Nys (Brussels, 1883), tr. G. W. Coopland, *The Tree of Battles* (Liverpool, 1975).

specific rules to the principles of the *ius gentium*. These two laws formed the essential basis of the law of arms . . . To these laws must be added a further body of customary rules, observed from old times by soldiers in pursuit of their calling.[6]

Yet while these scholastic concepts formed the basis on which lawyers of the later Middle Ages might prosecute actual cases arising from war in the courts, Keen rightly points out that such abstract theorizing on the nature of law would have meant little to the soldier. To him, the *ius militare* meant the 'law of chivalry', 'not so much a professional law . . . as the law of a certain privileged class, whose hereditary occupation was fighting'.[7] The binding force of agreements in war, whether they were indentures with an ally such as a lord or comrade, or truces, safe-conducts and ransom arrangements with an enemy, was thus less 'the sanctity of all voluntary pacts' according to the *ius gentium* as a lawyer might argue, but rather the knight's oath on his honour of knighthood.[8]

Soldiers, argues Keen, adhered to the rules laid down by Bonet and later by Christine de Pisan in her largely derivative work, the *Livre des Fays d'Armes et de Chevalerie*, 'because they thought of them as the laws of the ancient and honourable order of knighthood'.[9] Yet since in consulting Bonet's *The Tree of Battles*, soldiers were effectively referring to the civil law of John of Legnano in a simplified, vernacular form, the law of arms achieved a universal validity.[10]

Nevertheless, it has been argued that the 'laws of war', as expounded by Bonet and based on written canon and civil law, differ radically from the unwritten *droit d'armes* observed by the contemporary knighthood. Bonet's work, intended to enhance the power of the civil authority over the volatile *hommes d'armes* operating in France, subjugates the personal rights of the soldier to the 'public good', and is more concerned with immunity from seizure and ransom than with the actual workings of the profits of war.[11] This stands in marked contrast to the concept of the law of arms expressed by Geoffrey de Charny in his *Demandes*, a series of questions concerning rulings of the *droit d'armes* on jousts, the tourney and war, put to the members of King John II's Order of the Star, of which Charny became a member in 1352. From the *Demandes*, the contemporary law of arms appears 'a matter of military custom and usage', concerned above all with

[6] Keen, *Laws of War*, p. 17.   [7] *Ibid.*   [8] *Ibid.*, pp. 19–20.   [9] *Ibid.*, p. 22.
[10] *Ibid.*; 'the law of arms . . . was respected indifferently in all places, because it was founded in rules which all lawyers knew, and at the same time appealed to the social and professional pride which bound together all who bore arms'.
[11] N. A. R. Wright, 'The Tree of Battles of Honoré Bouvet and the Laws of War', *War, Literature and Politics in the Late Middle Ages*, ed. C. T. Allmand (Liverpool, 1976), pp. 12–31.

issues of booty and ransom.[12] Uncodified, it was not positive written law but was found 'in the everyday practices and customs of gens d'armes as interpreted by eminent members of their own professions: old knights, military officers, and heralds'.[13]

But what then of the later eleventh and twelfth centuries? Can we speak of a 'law of arms' or 'laws of war' in the Anglo-Norman and Angevin kingdoms? For the word 'law' carries a weight and precision which may not be wholly applicable to the conventions operating in the warfare of this earlier period. Was there, indeed, 'a *formal* minimum of humane and rational behaviour'[14] that was defined, regulated and enforced?

IUS, *LEX* OR *MOS*? POSITIVE LAW, CUSTOM AND MILITARY REGULATIONS

Canon law, evolving rapidly during the later eleventh and twelfth centuries, was much concerned with the nature of the 'just war', not only expounding criteria for the legitimate inception and prosecution of war, the *ius ad bellum*,[15] but also attempting to regulate the nature of war itself by a *ius in bello*.[16] Thus the Peace of God attempted to protect clergy and agricultural labourers as non-combatants, the Truce of God aimed to circumscribe the extent of warfare between knights themselves, and successive Lateran councils forbade the use of the crossbow and the employment of *routiers*.[17] Yet while rulers might clearly be anxious to fulfil the criteria of the *ius ad bellum* to secure legitimacy for aggression and conquest – Duke William, for example, bearing a papal banner at Hastings and sanctioning a penitential edict laid upon his army by the legate, Ermenfrid of Sion[18] – the impact of an ecclesiastically sponsored *ius in bello* on the warriors themselves may be judged to have been far less significant.

While there is evidence that some commanders might abstain from hostilities in respect for Sundays or other festivals in accordance with the Truce of God, such instances are limited, and in the majority of warfare, the knights seem to have paid scant heed to the Church's strictures on conduct. The prohibition on crossbows and *routiers* was flagrantly and

---

[12] *Ibid.*, pp. 19–21.   [13] *Ibid.*, p. 21; cf Keen, *Laws of War*, pp. 15 and 245.
[14] Keen, *Laws of War*, p. 3 (my italics).   [15] Russell, *The Just War, passim.*
[16] See, for example, Cowdrey, 'The Peace and Truce of God in the Eleventh Century', pp. 42–67; Holdsworth, 'Attempts to Control and Defuse War', pp. 59–78; and Hehl, *Kirche und Krieg im 12. Jahrhundert.*   [17] Below, pp. 70–3.
[18] H. E. J. Cowdrey, 'Bishop Ermenfrid of Sion and the Penitential Ordinance Following the Battle of Hastings', *Journal of Ecclesiastical History*, 20 (1969), pp. 225–42. By contrast, at the council of Rheims in 1119, Louis VI appealed to Pope Calixtus against Henry I's seizure of Normandy as being unjust, while as Henry's apologist, Orderic Vitalis was at great pains to portray his invasion of 1105–6 as a just war (Orderic, VI, pp. 256–7, 61–9, 86–9, and 88 n. 1).

consistently ignored, while the persons and property of both churchmen and peasantry remained prime targets in despite of the injunctions of the Peace of God.[19] Significantly, even though the Book of Deuteronomy (20: 1–20) sets out specific rules for behaviour in war, the first time these are apparently cited concerning medieval war is the *Gesta Henrici Quinti*, a retrospective tract designed to demonstrate the justice of Henry V's war against France and to win the support of the Emperor Sigismund.[20] In short, the creation of and adherence to conventions concerning ransom, truce or respites had little or nothing to do with the dictates of canon law.

The influence of Roman civil law appears to have been still less. Those sections of the *Corpus Iuris Civilis* dealing with military issues were largely concerned with internal affairs of the Roman army,[21] while, as Ullman has remarked of the Justinian code as a whole, 'very few legal details were directly applicable to conditions in medieval Europe, and these could be applied only after the appropriate scholarly interpretation'.[22] While the Investiture Contest had, moreover, provided a fundamental catalyst for the study of Roman law, the jurists of the twelfth century concentrated their efforts essentially on the theory and practice of government; it is hard in this period to discern a John of Legnano, concerned with expounding the 'laws of war'. Had chroniclers like Roger of Howden and William of Newburgh been familiar with such a *ius*, one would have expected to find them inveighing against its violation by Louis VII in 1173, for example, or the Young King in 1183,[23] but they do not.

Very occasionally, Anglo-Norman or Angevin chroniclers use the term *lex* or *ius* in connection with the conduct of warfare. Hence Henry of Huntingdon says that, after the battle of Lincoln in 1141, the town was given over to pillage 'hostili lege', while Diceto speaks of a respite given by Louis VII to the citizens of Verneuil 'lege proposita'.[24] Vigeois records how the 1183 revolt in Aquitaine ended when Richard besieged Bertran de Born's castle of Hautefort, and took it 'iure praelii',[25] while the English author of the *Itinerarium* has Saladin's advisors urge the sultan to allow the

---

[19] Below, pp. 71–3, 78–91, 268–73.

[20] *Gesta Henrici Quinti*, ed. and tr. F. Taylor and J. S. Roskell (Oxford, 1975), pp. xxiii–xxxi, 34 and n. 3, 48, 154.   [21] *Ibid.*, p. 16.

[22] W. Ullman, *Law and Politics in the Middle Ages. An Introduction to the Sources of Medieval Political Ideas* (London, 1975), p. 55, and cf. p. 78. For Roman law in Anglo-Norman England see P. Stein, 'Vacarius and the Civil Law', in *Church and Government in the Middle Ages*, ed. C. N. L. Brooke, D. E. Luscombe *et al.* (Cambridge, 1976), pp. 119–38.   [23] Below, pp. 50, 52.

[24] Henry of Huntingdon, *Historia Anglorum* (HH), ed. T. Arnold (Rolls Series, 1879), p. 275; *Radulphi de Diceto decani Lundoniensis opera historica* (Diceto), ed. W. Stubbs, 2. vols. (Rolls Series, 1876), I. p. 374.

[25] *Chronica Gaufredi coenobitae monasterii sancti Martialis Lemovicensis ac prioris Vosiensis coenobii* (Vigeois), *Recueil des historiens des Gaules et de la France (RHF)*, 24 vols., ed. M. Bouquet *et al.* (nouv. edn, ed. L. Delisle, Paris, 1869–1904), XVIII, p. 218. It is significant that when in his *Gesta Friderici* Rahewin referred to Frederick Barbarossa acting 'in accordance with the laws of war' (*se omnia iure belli*

Muslim garrison of Acre to surrender in 1191 lest they should all be put to death 'jure belli' if the city fell to the crusaders by storm.[26] The author of the *Gesta Stephani*, employing a less accurate noun than *jus* or *lex*, noted how the garrison of Bedford castle were permitted honourable egress following the siege of 1137–8 'sub militari . . . conditione'.[27] Nowhere, however, do these authors state the nature or provenance of such 'laws' and it is highly improbable that they allude to Roman law or, indeed, any codified legislation concerning conduct in war. Rather, the context, divergence of vocabulary and extreme rarity of occurrence of such phrases strongly suggest that they were intended simply as tags to imply custom or usage.

Where we encounter a more tangible expression of prescriptive law is in legislation concerning the internal organization of contemporary military forces. Almost in their entirety, however, these deal simply with practical matters of pay, service and internal discipline, and do not attempt to regulate behaviour or define ethics towards opponents. There exist, for example, a number of codes governing Anglo-Danish and Scandinavian military households of the early eleventh century, of which the most important is the *Lex castrensis*, preserved in a late twelfth-century form by the chronicler Sveno but generally accepted as reflecting regulations governing the housecarls of King Cnut.[28] This deals with questions of pay and food allowances, terms of service, placement and precedence at table and the competence of the military household's court or *Huskarlesteffne* over issues such as the division of land and plunder or quarrels between

---

gesturum) at the siege of Crema in 1159, he lifted the passage verbatim from the description of the siege of Jerusalem by Titus in Josephus's *Jewish Wars* (*Ottonis et Rahewini gesta Friderici imperatoris* (*GF*), ed. G. Waitz and B. von Simson (*Scriptores rerum germanicarum in usum scholarum ex Monumentis Germanicae Historicis seperatim editi* (*MGH, SS*), XLVI (Hannover, 1912)), pp. 293–4; cf Josephus 6:6.3). While Rahewin might well have wished to portray Frederick as a second Titus, and while Frederick's own behaviour was undoubtedly affected by his imperial title, it seems unlikely that either biographer or emperor was consciously citing Roman law to justify his treatment of the rebellious citizens. The passage is translated and discussed in *The Deeds of Frederick Barbarossa by Otto of Freising and his continuator, Rahewin,* tr. C. C. Mierow (New York, 1953), pp. 284–5 and p. 284, n. 182, where the discrepancy between Frederick's actual conduct and the contents of the passage borrowed from Josephus is noted. Rahewin had earlier employed the phrase 'the rights of war' (*leges belli*) (*GF*, p. 293, tr. Mierow, p. 284), but once again this was taken directly from Josephus (6:6.2).

[26] *Itinerarium*, p. 231. Similarly the *Chronica de gestis consulum Andegavorum* records how the garrison of Saumur surrendered to Fulk Nerra '*sub lege deditionis*' (*Chroniques des Comtes d'Anjou et des Seigneurs d'Amboise* (*Chroniques des Comtes d'Anjou*), ed. L. Halphen and R. Pourpardin (Paris, 1913)), p. 53.

[27] *Gesta Stephani* (*GS*), ed. and tr. K. R. Potter, with new introduction and notes by R. H. C. Davis (Oxford, 1976), pp. 50–1.

[28] For a summary of the contents of the *Lex castrensis* and a critique of its authenticity see Larson, *King's Household,* pp. 158 ff and Hollister, *Anglo-Saxon Military Institutions,* pp. 12–15. The text is published in *Scriptores rerum Danicarum,* ed. J. Langebek (Copenhagen, 1772–1834), III, pp. 139–64. Larson, *King's Household,* pp. 154–6, also discusses the regulations governing the semi-legendary warrior brotherhood of the Jomsvikings, as set out in the *Jomsvikinga Saga* (*Jomsvikinga Saga,* ed. and tr. N. F. Blake (London, 1962), pp. 17–18, and p. 17, n. 3), but displays insufficient caution in dealing with the saga material, now recognized to be fraught with problems of dating and interpretation.

members. Questions of conduct are restricted to behaviour towards other guild members or towards their lord: anyone who slew a comrade was to be declared an outcast or *niðing*, and to suffer execution or exile, while treason to the king merited death and confiscation of all property.[29] Doubtless common assumptions as to the appropriate treatment of opponents or prisoners rendered further codification unnecessary. Camp regulations concerning armies as a whole might be similarly promulgated, such as Frederick Barbarossa's *Lex castrensis*.[30]

It is difficult to assess the extent to which such legislation represented the creation of new regulations or merely reflected the codification of existing custom. In certain instances, the *ad hoc* nature of royal decree is apparent. Roger of Howden, for example, preserves Richard's written edict governing behaviour on board the fleet bound for the Holy Land in 1190,[31] a specific response to the exceptional nature of a crusade expedition, during which the maintainence of cohesion and discipline became still more acute. What, however, of the ruling proclaimed by Richard before his assault on Messina in 1190 that any common soldier who ran away was to lose a foot, while a knight was to lose his belt – the symbol of his rank and military function?[32] Were such punishments of Richard's own devising, or were they but the formal expression of penalties habitually inflicted on deserters? That the loss of the *cingulum militiae* prescribed here distantly echoes William of Malmesbury's story of the knight demoted by William I for gashing Harold's thigh at Hastings[33] may suggest a customary form of

---

[29] Larson, *King's Household*, pp. 150–60, and p. 160, n. 76. On the housecarls themselves see N. Hooper, 'The Housecarls in England in the Eleventh Century', *Anglo-Norman Studies*, 7 (1984), pp. 161–76. See also *Saxo Grammaticus*, ed. K. Christianson (British Archaeological Reports, International Series, 84) 1, x, pp. 37–44. [30] *GF*, pp. 199–202.

[31] *GH*, II, pp. 110–11, where Howden refers to the text not as an assize (*assisa*) but simply as a *carta*. At Messina in October 1190, Richard and Philip jointly promulgated a further set of the disciplinary measures, including the regulation of bread sales established 'by the lord king of England and the constables, justiciars and marshals of the army of the king of England' (*ibid.*, pp. 129–32). The hybrid force that embarked for crusade at Dartmouth in 1147 and which ended up aiding in the Christian capture of Lisbon had been bound by similar ordinances, designed to preserve internal discipline and aid the cohesion of a racially divergent army composed chiefly of Germans, Flemings and English (*De expugnatione Lyxbonensis: The Conquest of Lisbon*, ed. and tr. C. W. David (New York, 1936), pp. 56–7). For a discussion of this 1147 legislation, and the suggestion that it was in part inspired by the *leges pacis* found in Flemish and neighbouring French and German municipal charters, *ibid.*, p. 57, n. 5. David also cites references for the *leges in exercitu servandae*, also promulgated at Dartmouth, before the 1217 expedition of Counts George of Weid and William of Holland, though once again, these are concerned primarily with the maintenance of peace, not behaviour during the prosecution of war (*ibid.*).

[32] *Chronicon Richardi Divinensis de tempore regis Ricardi primi* (Devizes), ed. and tr. J. Appleby (London 1963), p. 22: 'Sit lex servate sine remedio. Pedes pleno pede fugiens pedem perdat. Miles privitur cingulo.'

[33] Above pp. 4–6. Conversely, however, the subsequent injunction ascribed by Devizes to Richard I that 'Each man shall have the booty he gets' would seem to be at odds with known custom dealing with the division of spoil (Devizes, p. 22; below, pp. 187–8).

discipline for members of the knightly class, while equally there are analogies for the mutilation of offenders of common rank. Thus during John's punitive expedition against his baronial opponents in northern England in 1216 one Thomas, the son of Robert, 'lost his hand in the war by the judgement of the marshal of the army for a cow which he stole from a churchyard'.[34]

This latter vignette from the rolls of the justices in eyre is a reminder that while army regulations might occasionally be codified, as with Barbarossa's *Lex castrensis*, the majority of military discipline, whether in accordance with existing custom or the *verbum regis*, remained unwritten. For while the twelfth century witnessed the increased study of Roman civil law and important moves toward the codification of canon law, such a process was less true for customary law. The tract *Glanvill*, written 1187 × 1189, is precocious in this respect and is essentially procedural: written prescription of secular norms was not to become common until the thirteenth century.

As a result, the nature of military regulations and their operation is all but lost to us save for sporadic and laconic references. Hence according to William of Poitiers, Duke William forbade looting while his army of invasion lay at St Valéry waiting for a favourable wind in 1066,[35] while Orderic recounts how in 1136, during an invasion of Normandy, Geoffrey of Anjou sent a herald through his army to prohibit the seizure of any ecclesiastical goods.[36] Published orally by heralds throughout the army, such regulations were doubtless enforced by the verbal command of officers such as the marshal or constable.[37]

Such disciplinary measures, however, were far removed from the specific ethical and juridical tracts of the fourteenth century on conduct in war itself. The *Epitoma rei militaris* of Vegetius, well known throughout the Middle Ages, was a manual of tactics and strategy, not of ethics.[38] Sections

---

[34] *Rolls of the Justices in Eyre for Yorkshire, 1218–19*, ed. D. M. Stenton (*Selden Society*, 56, 1937), no. 851, pp. 310–11.

[35] WP, pp. 150–3: 'All looting was forbidden and 50,000 men [*sic*] were fed at his own expense while contrary winds delayed them for a month at the mouth of the Dives. Such was his moderation and prudence: he made generous provision both for his own knights and those from other parts, and would not allow anyone to pillage anything. The sheep and cattle of the neighbouring peasantry were safely pastured either in the meadow or in the open country. The crops awaited untouched the sickle of the harvester and were neither arrogantly ridden down by horsemen nor cut by foragers. Weak or unarmed, any man might ride where he would, singing on his horse, without trembling at the sight of soldiers.' Cf. B. S. Bachrach, 'Some Observations on the Military Administration of the Norman Conquest', *Anglo-Norman Studies*, 8 (1985), pp. 1–26.   [36] Orderic, VI, pp. 470–3.

[37] Cf. M. Keen, 'The Jurisdiction and Origins of the Constable's Court', *War and Government*, pp. 159–69.

[38] *Flavius Vegetius Renatus, Epitoma rei militari*, ed. and tr. L. F. Stelton (New York, 1990). For the use of Vegetius see B. Bachrach, 'The Practical Use of Vegetius' *De Re Militari* in the Early Middle Ages', *The Historian*, 47 (1985), pp. 239–55; P. Contamine, *La guerre au moyen âge* (Paris, 1980), tr. M. Jones as *War in the Middle Ages* (Oxford, 1984), pp. 210–12, and further bibliography there cited, and Orderic, VI, p. 472, n. 1.

of the *Consuetudines et judicie* of 1091 forbid certain acts of hostility in the context of private war within the Norman duchy – for example the burning of mills, or the seizure of horses and arms after an affray – but these cannot be viewed as a coherent ethical code, being simply a ducal attempt to curb the profusion of local conflict by striking at its chief manifestations.[39] Similarly, Henry II's *Assize of Arms* of 1181, and its reissue in 1242, is concerned solely with the provision of armour and weapons according to a sliding scale of wealth, and wholly ignores any statement of the expected conduct of troops once in arms.[40] Even the first expansive secular legislation pertaining to military behaviour, which formed part of the *Siete Partidas* of Alphonso X the Wise, of Castile, compiled c. 1250, is chiefly concerned not with moral issues, but with the more pragmatic consideration of regulating the division of spoil.[41]

If we seek for a twelfth-century equivalent of the *Tractatus de bello* or *L'arbre des batailles* we shall be disappointed. None is extant and given, as we have seen, the heavy reliance of these tracts on Roman law, it seems improbable that any was composed at this earlier date. It is only in the rules of the military orders that one approaches an extensive codification of behaviour, but, due to their monastic nature, these were primarily concerned with the regulation of communal and spiritual life. The *Rule of the Temple* in addition deals in some detail with tactics, questions of booty and of discipline in camp, on the march or in battle, but again these clauses aim essentially at internal cohesion and there is no attempt to regulate the actual conduct in war toward the enemy.[42]

It thus appears difficult for the eleventh and twelfth centuries to speak of a 'law of arms' governing the nature of conduct between protagonists in the sense of an enunciated, written corpus resting on an amalgam of canon, civil and customary law, as Keen is able to do for the fourteenth and fifteenth

---

[39] This important document was edited by C. H. Haskins, 'The Norman "*Consuetudines et Justicie*" of William the Conqueror', *EHR*, 1st ser., 89 (1908), pp. 502–8, then reprinted in Haskins, *Norman Institutions*, Appendix D, to which all subsequent references are made.

[40] *GH*, 1. p. 278; *Foedera, conventiones, litterae et cujuscunque generis acta publica* (*Foedera*), ed. T. Rymer, new edn, vol. 1, pt 1. ed. A. Clarke and F. Holbrooke (Record Commission, London, 1816), p. 281. Both Assizes are also printed in *Select Charters and Other Illustrations of English Constitutional History* (*Select Charters*), ed. W. Stubbs (9th edn, revised by H. W. C. Davis, Oxford, 1913), pp. 183–4, 362–5.

[41] *Alfonso the Wise, King of Castile, Las Siete Partidas*, ed. G. Lopez (Paris, 1861), II, Titles xxiii–xxx, pp. 243–350; tr. S. P. Scott, *Las Siete Partidas* (Chicago, 1931), pp. 439–526.

[42] *La Règle du Temple*, ed. H. de Curzon (Paris, 1886), tr. J. M. Upton-Ward as *The Rule of the Templars* (*The Rule of the Temple*), (Woodbridge, 1992), particularly cc. 148–68. On the military aspects of the *Rule* see M. Bennett, 'La Règle du Temple; or, How To Deliver a Cavalry Charge', *Studies in Medieval History*, pp. 7–20 and reprinted as an appendix to Upton-Ward's translation of the *Rule*.

If the Hospitallers had similar enactments for military discipline in the field, which seems most likely, they have not survived among the corpus of regulations for the order (*The Rule, Statutes and Customs of the Hospitallers, 1099–1310*, tr. E. J. King (London, 1934)).

centuries. Yet this is not to deny the existence of a powerful body of custom relating to behaviour in war. If the term *lex* is rarely employed, that of *mos* ('custom') occurs more frequently in contemporary narratives relating to aspects of conduct in war. Orderic, for example, noted how Rufus had insisted that the vanquished rebels at Rochester in 1088 should be forced to leave the city to a fanfare of royal trumpets, 'as is customary when an enemy is defeated and a stronghold captured by force (*sicut moris est dum hostes vincuntur et per vim oppidum capitur*)'.[43] William of Malmesbury likewise refers to 'escort (*conductus*) which it is not the custom of honourable knights to refuse any one (*negare laudabilium militum mos non est*), even their bitterest enemy'.[44] When Robert of Gloucester besieged Stephen's forces in Wareham in 1142, the garrison 'asked for a truce that, as is customary with those people (*sicut moris est illorum hominum*), they might beg aid from the king'.[45]

Appeal to custom, indeed, and specifically to that of the *diffidatio* or renunciation of feudal homage, was central to Malmesbury's attempts to portray his patron Robert of Gloucester as something more than an unprincipled opportunist.[46] To legitimize his desertion of Stephen for Matilda in 1138, the earl 'sent representatives and abandoned friendship and faith in the traditional way, also renouncing homage (*more maiorum amicitiam et fidem interdixit, homagiam etiam abdicato*)'.[47] Similarly, Malmesbury's claim that Stephen had failed to defy Rannulf of Chester – once again '*more maiorum*' – before laying siege to Lincoln castle in 1141 was an integral part of his justification for the defeat and capture of the king in the ensuing battle.[48] In practice, it is highly unlikely whether rulers such as Stephen, who were not

[43] Orderic, IV, pp. 132–3.

[44] *The Historia Novella by William of Malmesbury (HN)*, ed. and tr. K. R. Potter (London, 1955), p. 35.

[45] *Ibid.*, p. 75.

[46] On William's bias see R. B. Patterson, 'William of Malmesbury's Robert of Gloucester: A Re-evaluation of the Historia Novella', *American Historical Review*, 70 (1964–5), pp. 983–97; J. W. Leedom, 'William of Malmesbury and Robert of Gloucester Reconsidered', *Albion*, 6 (1974), pp. 251–62; D. Crouch, 'Robert Earl of Gloucester and the Daughter of Zelophehad', *Journal of Medieval History*, 11 (1985), pp. 227–43; R. M. Thomson, *William of Malmesbury* (Woodbridge, 1987), pp. 34–6.

[47] *HN*, p. 23. On the diffidation in general see F. Pollock and F. W. Maitland, *The History of the English Law Before the Time of Edward I.* 2 vols. (2nd edn, Cambridge, 1898), I. p. 303, and cf., II, p. 505; below, pp. 231–5. While Malmesbury's interpretation of the *diffidatio* is certainly suspect, the defiance was not, as Gillingham has recently claimed, 'a new practice first recorded in 1138' essentially coined by Malmesbury (Gillingham, 'The Introduction of Chivalry', pp. 48–9). According to the *De injusta vexatione*, William of St Calais informed Rufus that when in 1088 he presented Ralph Paynell, the sheriff of Yorkshire, with a royal writ giving him safe conduct to come to court, Ralph not only denied him peace, 'but on your behalf he defied me (*de parte vestra me diffidavit*)' (Simeon of Durham, *Symeonis monachi opera omnia*, (SD), ed. T. Arnold, 2 vols. (Rolls Series, 1885), I. 173). Orderic records how, in 1119, Reginald of Bailleul came to Henry I at Falaise and renounced his fealty (*fidelitatem reliquit*) (Orderic, VI, pp. 214–15). This, it might be argued, occurred in Normandy, but Geoffrey Gaimar (writing c. 1140s) was well enough acquainted with the process of defiance for him to have Beorn Butsecarl defy King Osbryht (*le defiat*) for raping his wife, with the words: 'Jo te defi, et tut te rent; De tei nel voil tenir nient. Jameis de tei ren ne tendrai, ton homage ci te rendrai' (Gaimar, II. 2682–6).

[48] *HN*, p. 47.

merely feudal suzerains but anointed kings, felt any obligation to defy erst-while vassals before attacking them. Equally, the punishment which kings attempted to mete out to rebellious subjects during or after the suppression of revolt strongly suggests that the process of *diffidatio* failed to ameliorate the legal position of insurgents in any significant way.[49]

Nevertheless, the *conventio* drawn up some time between 1148 and 1153 between Rannulf, earl of Chester, and Robert, earl of Leicester, pre-supposes the defiance as a formal declaration of hostilities. Neither earl may 'for any cause or chance lay snares' for the other unless he has defied him fifteen days in advance ('nisi eum difidaverit quindecim dies ante').[50] Guile and ruse in warfare were thereafter considered perfectly legitimate,[51] but there was mutual concern to avoid falling victim by surprise to a dam-aging 'first strike' by the potential adversary. If, as Malmesbury protested, Rannulf had been taken unawares by Stephen at Lincoln in 1141 – and it was not to be for the last time[52] – then the earl wanted to make sure that such an occurrence would not happen again at the hands of the earl of Leicester. Similarly, on his departure from Acre in 1191, Philip Augustus was made to swear that he would both abstain from attacking Richard's lands in the latter's absence, and that he would also give Richard forty days' warning after his return before commencing hostilities.[53]

Custom regulating the inception of war is particularly prominent in the Anglo-Norman treaties or *conventiones*, couched as binding treaties either in anticipation of imminent war or at a time of ongoing hostilities. Close attention was paid to questions of military service and vassalic obligation in situations of divided loyalties, while some even sought to restrict the aid brought to a liege lord.[54] Allies in a potential conflict might be defined or limited. Thus the Leicester–Chester *conventio* circumscribes the aid Robert may afford Simon de Senlis, earl of Northampton, and that which Rannulf may give Robert de Ferrers, earl of Derby,[55] while in the *compositio amoris* between William, earl of Gloucester and Roger, earl of Hereford, drawn up between 1147 and 1150, both men pledge to bring aid to the other against all men except the person of their lord, Henry Plantagenet. Earl William goes on to state that in particular he will aid Roger to disinherit Gilbert de Lacy.[56] This feud is further reflected in Earl Roger's treaty with

---

[49] Below, pp. 240–7. [50] Stenton, *English Feudalism*, pp. 287, 251–2. [51] Below, pp. 128–31.
[52] When, in 1146, Rannulf came to Stephen's court, he was suddenly seized, imprisoned and not released until he had yielded up castles demanded by the king (*GS*, pp. 196–9).
[53] Ambroise, 11. 5305–28; *Itinerarium*, p. 238. [54] Below, pp. 236–8.
[55] Stenton, *English Feudalism*, pp. 287, 252.
[56] *Earldom of Gloucester Charters*, no. 96, p. 97. For the background to this enmity against Gilbert de Lacy see *ibid.*, no. 6 and n., p. 35, and Davis, 'The Treaty between William, Earl of Gloucester and Roger, Earl of Hereford', pp. 140–1.

his brother-in-law, William de Braose, ratified in the presence of Bishop Gilbert Foliot, in which Roger pledges to aid William to gain and defend disputed lands and not to make peace or truce (*nec pacem nec treuias*) with Gilbert de Lacy.[57]

Such a fear that an erstwhile ally might make peace before the aims of the other partner had been realised was an important concern, commonly voiced in such treaties. In the earlier *confederatio amoris* between Robert earl of Gloucester and Miles earl of Hereford (1141 × 1143), Robert promised that if Miles should go to war (*guerreare*) against anyone attacking him, he would aid Miles and that he himself would not make any peace or truce (*pacem ne trewias*) detrimental to the earl of Hereford.[58] In 1173, at a great council in Paris where Louis VII had assembled his nobles, all swore to aid the Young King and his brothers in their war against Henry II, but in return the Plantagenet princes had to give oaths and sureties that they would neither abandon the king of France, nor make peace with their father without the consent of Louis and his barons.[59] Louis's fears that Henry would try to isolate his sons from their allies and conclude a peace with them before the coalition could profit from the war were amply justified. In September 1173, after a series of military successes, Henry offered his sons reasonable terms for peace. They were made to reject them, however, by the French king and his nobles.[60] Significantly, when the war finally ended in 1174, Henry was sure to make the Young King surrender all the charters and sealed agreements into which he had entered with his father's enemies.[61]

Just as there was a fundamental need to mark the transition from a state of peace to a state of war by some tangible process lest the two conditions become irrevocably blurred, so custom attempted to regulate, even ritualize, the onset of actual fighting once hostilities had commenced. If the *diffidatio* in its strict feudal sense of renunciation of homage might have an important, if ambiguous, role in the declaration of war, the issue to an enemy of a defiance or challenge (*cembellum*) to single or group combat was commonplace. Thus Gilbert Crispin, the biographer of Herluin of Bec, believed that during the reign of Duke Robert the Magnificent (1027–35), Herluin's powerful lord, Gilbert de Brionne, 'in order to advertise his strength, advised his enemies by messenger of what he proposed to do and

[57] Brooke and Brooke, 'Hereford Cathederal Dignitaries', p. 185.
[58] *Earldom of Gloucester Charters*, no. 95, p. 95.   [59] *GH*, I. p. 44.   [60] *Ibid.*, p. 59.
[61] *Ibid.*, pp. 77, 83. Similarly, when, in July 1216, Alexander, king of Scots, did homage to Prince Louis in London, Louis and the English barons swore 'upon the holy gospels that they would never enter into any agreement for peace or truce with the king of England unless the king of Scotland were included' (*Chronicle of Melrose*, ed. A. O. and M. O. Anderson (London, 1936), p. 63).

when, not just beforehand, but several days in advance'.[62] The Norman *Consuetudines et justicie* of 1091 equally regarded such challenges as an integral element of private warfare, forbidding anyone to carry a banner, wear a hauberk, sound a horn or send a challenge (*cembellum*) when seeking out an ememy or exercising distraint.[63] William of Poitiers relates how, at the siege of Domfront (c. 1049 × 51), Geoffrey Martel, count of Anjou, announced to the Norman duke's men that 'he would be at Domfront the next morning to arouse William's watch with his trumpets' and gave them notice of his arms and the horse he would be riding, while they replied with a similar challenge.[64] The challenge fulfilled a variety of functions. It not only sought to establish a fixed time and place for combat, and so avoid the uncertainties of ambush and surprise attack, but was a public assertion of a lord's power and aggressive intent, an act of bravado and of intimidation.[65] Indeed, rather than the prelude to inevitable conflict, challenges might more frequently serve as a deliberate means of *avoiding* battle, designed merely to call the enemy's tactical bluff. At Domfront, for example, Martel in fact withdrew without battle, judging the tactical circumstances unfavourable.[66] At Verneuil in August 1173, Henry II succeeded in raising the siege of this vital frontier fortress without bloodshed by issuing a formal challenge to Louis VII, who, as Henry must have guessed, beat a hasty retreat.[67] Conversely in 1194, Philip sent word to Richard, encamped at Vendôme, telling him to expect a hostile attack that same day, but instead attempted unsuccessfully to slip away while Richard's men made ready. Instead, Richard managed to overtake his rearguard the following day in the woods near Fréteval and came within an ace of capturing Philip himself.[68]

Nevertheless, such instances of pre-emptive challenges only serve to reinforce the contention that the majority of commanders were anxious to avoid pitched battle whenever possible, due to the enormous strategic, political and physical risks which it entailed.[69] The same desire to avoid heavy loss of life led to occasional attempts to determine the outcome of battle by the combat of champions in either single or group combat in the

---

[62] *Vita domni Herluini abbatis Beccensis* (*Vita Herluini*), in J. A. Robinson, *Gilbert Crispin, Abbot of Westminster: A Study of the Abbey under Norman Rule*, (Cambridge, 1911), p. 88. Crispin was writing with considerable hindsight, c. 1107–9.

[63] C. H. Haskins, *Norman Institutions* (Harvard, 1918), p. 283. For the term *cimbellum/cembellum* see J. F. Niermeyer, *Mediae latinitatis lexicon minus* (Niermeyer), (Leiden, 1976), p. 179.   [64] WP, pp. 38–40.

[65] Duby, *William Marshal*, p. 64.   [66] Gillingham, 'William the Bastard at War', pp. 152–3.

[67] Diceto, I. p. 375; WN, pp. 174–5. Cf. below, pp. 126–7.

[68] Howden, III, pp. 255–6; Diceto, II, p. 117; WN, p. 419; Rigord, p. 129; WB, *Philippidos*, Bk. IV, 11. 530–68.

[69] See, for example, Gillingham, 'Richard I and the Science of War', pp. 197–9; *idem.*, 'William the Bastard at War', pp. 145–8. The idea is now so commonplace that it may safely be said to have moved from revisionism to orthodoxy.

form of a judicial duel.[70] At Antioch in 1098, for example, the Franks offered the Turks limited combat between five, ten, twenty or a hundred warriors on each side to decide possession of the land.[71] According to Suger, in 1109 Louis VI proposed to determine possession of Gisors and Bray by single combat *lege duelli*, and Jordan Fantosme believed that in 1173 William the Lion made a similar proposal to Henry II concerning his claim to Northumberland.[72] In all these cases, however, the challenge was made by the party that was militarily disadvantaged, and was rejected outright by their more powerful adversaries. If Duke William did offer Harold single combat before Hastings, as William of Poitiers claimed, he can hardly have expected Harold to have accepted.[73] In such situations, the challenge was but a mechanism for gaining the moral high ground, for postponing actual battle and gaining time for further negotiation.[74] Once transferred from a seigneurial court to a situation of war between two princes, the judicial duel became untenable because of 'the obvious impossibility of securing guarantees that the issue would be regarded as a verdict'.[75]

Contemporaries, then, were conscious of a number of usages regulating the conduct of war and believed many of them to be of long standing. Though their origins are obscure, many of the conventions such as those governing truce, ransom and the prosecution of siege which we shall explore subsequently, were hardly innovations in the eleventh century when they emerge from the more plentiful and detailed sources. Such conventions, moreover, were far more than merely 'local customary rules concerning war, such as the ancient law of the Marches'.[76] They enjoyed a wide currency both within and between the territorial principalities of eleventh- and twelfth-century France, and in the Anglo-Norman *regnum*.

[70] For an extended discussion of trial by battle outside the context of war see R. Bartlett, *Trial by Fire and Water* (Oxford, 1986), pp. 103–26; and for early examples of the judicial duel in Europe, M. W. Bloomfield, 'Beowulf, Byrhtnoth and the Judgment of God: Trial by Combat in Anglo-Saxon England', *Speculum*, 44 (1969), pp. 545–59.

[71] *Fulcheri cartonensis historia Hierosolymitana*, (Fulcher), ed. H. Hagenmayer, (Heidelberg, 1913), Bk 1 c. xxi, pp. 247–8; tr. F. R. Ryan as *Fulcher of Chartres: A History of the Expedition to Jerusalem, 1095–1127*, (University of Tennesse, 1976 edn), p. 103. (Subsequent references cite Hagenmeyer's text followed by Ryan's translation.) The offer of battle by a limited number of champions is also noted by Albert of Aachen (*Alberti Aquensis historia Hierosolymitana, RHC, Historiens occidentaux*, (*Occ*), 5 vols. (1841–95), IV, c. 45, pp. 420–1). This detail is not recorded by the two authors present at Antioch, but both mention the challenge to combat by the Christian army (*Gesta Francorum et aliorum Hierosolimitanorum*, (*GFr*), ed. R. Hill, (London, 1962), pp. 66–7; Raymond d'Aguiliers, *Historia francorum qui ceperunt Iherusalem*, ed. J. H. Hill, (Philadelphia, 1968), p. 79).

[72] *Vie de Louis VI le Gros* (Suger), ed. H. Waquet (Paris, 1929), pp. 106–10; tr. R. C. Cusimano and J. Moorhead as *The Deeds of Louis the Fat* (Washington, 1992), pp. 72–4; JF, 11. 334–5.

[73] *WP*, pp. 176–181; *EHD*, II, p. 224.

[74] The question of single combat and judicial duel is explored further in M. J. Strickland, 'Challenge, Single Combat and Judicial Duel in Early Medieval Warfare', in *Armies, Chivalry and Warfare in Medieval Britain. Proceedings of the 1995 Harlaxton Symposium*, ed. M. J. Strickland (Stamford, forthcoming).

[75] F. M. Powicke, *The Loss of Normandy. Studies in the History of the Angevin Empire* (2nd edn, 1961), p. 242.

[76] Keen, *Laws of War*, p. 7.

Aspects of such customs might cross cultural as well as political barriers. We have already noted William I's compensation of the townsmen of Dover in 1066 and his treatment of Exeter in 1068, suggesting that he regarded conventions of behaviour in war as applying equally to his Anglo-Saxon subjects. Recognition of such 'international' notions of conduct can be seen more clearly still in Frankish–Muslim relations in Outremer. Here, despite the racial and religious divergence between Muslims and Franks, the essential similarity of the opposing warrior elites in many respects, the dominance in warfare of siege, the protracted nature of which offered ample scope for negotiations, and the precarious balance of forces, all helped to foster adherence to shared customs concerning the prosecution of war. The chronic shortage of Frankish manpower in the Latin principalities (save during the main expeditions from Europe) resulted in a political and military *status quo* which necessitated near-constant diplomatic intercourse with the Muslims. The resulting importance of truces and respites led in certain instances to appeals against breaches of mutually accepted conduct to the king of Jerusalem or to the Muslim sultan.[77]

Custom itself might well have the force of law,[78] while aspects of warfare had a profoundly legal dimension. 'Law in a feudal society', wrote Powicke,

> was inseparable from force, but was not obscured by it: they were informed by the theory of contract which informed all feudal relations . . . Force was never absent, yet was never uncontrolled. In civil procedure we find the elements of war, such as the duel, and the hue and cry; and in war, we find constant applications of legal theory. War was a great lawsuit. The truce was very like an essoin, a treaty was drawn up on the lines of a final concord, the hostage was a surety, service in the field was the counterpart of suit of court. The closeness of the analogy between the field of battle and the law court is seen in the judicial combat. Trial by battle was a possible incident in all negotiations.[79]

The periods of fifteen and forty days that recur in truces, respites, the formal declaration of war and the establishment of a *status quo ante bellum*, were standard legal terms. Thus, for example, the peace treaty of 1174 between Henry II and his sons stipulated that both parties were to hold the

---

[77] See, for example, Usamah, pp. 93–4, and Abu Shama, *Le Livre Des Deux Jardins, Recueil des historiens des Croisades (RHC), Historiens orientaux (Or)*, 5 vols., (1872–1906), IV, pp. 133–4. The regulation of behaviour in war between Christians and Muslims is dealt with in detail by W. G. Zajac in his PhD thesis 'The Laws of War and Siege Warfare on the Crusades and in the Latin East, 1095–1193', currently in preparation.

[78] See S. Reynolds, *Kingdoms and Communities in Western Europe, 900–1300* (Oxford, 1984), especially chapter 1, 'Collective Activity in Traditional Law, 900–1100'; *ibid.*, p. 15, 'unwritten custom formed the bedrock of law all over western Europe'. [79] Powicke, *Loss of Normandy*, p. 242.

lands and castles of which they had had possession fifteen days before the war, and that all castles that had been fortified against Henry during the war should be reduced to their condition fifteen days before its outbreak.[80] In 1173, William the Lion granted Roger de Stuteville a respite for forty days, while this period occurs repeatedly in the indentures between the king of England and the count of Flanders.[81]

Yet here we must draw a distinction between customary law or *consue-tudines,* and the forms of action described by writers such as Malmesbury and Orderic which were hardly analogous to national, regional or tribal customary law. Grants of truces, for example, or respite to a besieged garrison were essentially expressions of honourable behaviour which might be expected from warriors and which had entered a common currency of chivalric conduct. Yet were such actions binding? Was there any sense in which such military customs could be enforced, and if so, by whom?

AUTHORITY AND ENFORCEABILITY

The notion of *enforceability* is central to Keen's definition of the 'law of arms' in the later Middle Ages, noting as he does that 'no legal system has any true authority unless it can be enforced in practice'.[82] By the mid-fourteenth century, a knight who sought redress from an opponent concerning, for example, default on ransom payment could prosecute his case according to the law of arms expounded by Legnano and Bonet in permanent courts of a sovereign specially designated for the purpose, presided over either by his Constable, as in English-held Aquitaine, or by his Marshal, as in Burgundy, Anjou and Brittany, or by both, as in the English Court of Chivalry.[83] Other than this, he might seek redress from a royal lieutenant such as the Seneschal of Aquitaine, the Captain of Calais or the Warden of the Marches, or appeal to the court of the king himself.[84]

Yet in the eleventh and twelfth centuries, such mechanisms for appeal are hard if not impossible to discern. The High Court of Chivalry, for example, seems only to have sat on a regular basis from the reign of

---

[80] *GH,* I. pp. 77–8, and cf. *ibid.,* I. pp. 81–3. Equally, in the Leicester–Chester *conventio,* the sureties of each earl were to surrender their pledges if either party did not amend any violation within fifteen days (Stenton, *English Feudalism,* pp. 287–8, 251–3).

[81] JF, II. 500–1, 510–11, 519; *Diplomatic Documents,* I. nos, 1, 2 and 3, pp. 1–12. For forty days as a legal period see *Magna Carta,* clauses 7, 14 and 61 (J. C. Holt, *Magna Carta* (2nd edn, Cambridge, 1992), pp. 318–19, 320–1, 334–45. All references to Magna Carta (*MC*) cite the edition and translation supplied by Holt, *Magna Carta,* Appendix 6, pp. 448–73).

[82] Keen, *Laws of War,* p. 4, 'an enforceable code of chivalrous laws, acknowledged by all soldiers regardless of allegiance'; *ibid.,* p. 23.

[83] Keen, *Laws of War,* p. 27. The kings of France had courts of both the Constable and the Marshal of France.   [84] Keen, *Laws of War,* pp. 26–30.

Edward III.[85] Earlier, we can glimpse the constable or marshal enforcing discipline *within* an army, but the sources fail to show them hearing specific appeals of an international nature lodged by actual or erstwhile opponents. The reason for such an absence is that by the end of the twelfth century there was as yet no 'law of arms' that had the character of international law. This could only come into being once customary, canon and civil law had achieved greater fusion. Without the law of arms, there could be no courts with special competence to deal with cases arising from it.

A legislation universal to Christendom was, of course, furnished by canon law, important elements of which concerned war. Yet the appeals we find being made to the papal *curia* or other ecclesiastical courts are not based on the infringment of a coherent code, a *ius armorum*, dealing with such matters as ransom or the violation of truces. Rather, appeals deal only with those areas where warfare and ecclesiastical concerns overlapped. Hence when the supporters of Amaury de Montfort raised the issue of Henry I's burning of Evreux before the Council of Reims in 1119, they were not impleading the king for acting in contravention of a given law of arms, but rather accusing Bishop Audoin for having authorized the torching of his own episcopal city.[86] Likewise, when Richard appealed to the pope over his capture and imprisonment by Leopold of Austria and the Emperor Henry VI, it was because at the time of his seizure Richard should have enjoyed the protection afforded by the Church to a crusader and pilgrim.[87] When in turn, Philip, the warrior bishop of Beauvais, petitioned the pope for his release from lengthy and harsh captivity following his seizure by Richard I at the castle of Milli in 1197, it was on the grounds that Richard was holding an ecclesiastic prisoner, not that the refusal to ransom him was contrary to a 'law of arms'. The pope's response – that he would only request, not demand, Philip's release – was equally dependent on an essentially ecclesiastical stricture: Philip had been caught in combat when in flagrant violation of the canonical prohibition on the bearing of arms by churchmen.[88]

[85] G. D. Squibb, *The High Court of Chivalry* (Oxford, 1959), pp. 15–16; Keen, *Laws of War*, p. 27.
[86] Orderic, VI, pp. 256–7.
[87] E. Bridney, *La condition juridique des croisés et le privelège de la croix* (Paris, 1900), pp. 120–35; *Selected Letters of Pope Innocent III Concerning England, 1198–1216 (Letters of Innocent III)*, ed. and tr. C. R. Cheney and W. H. Semple (London, 1953), pp. 3–8; J. A. Brundage, 'The Crusade of Richard I: Two Canonical *Quaestiones*', *Speculum*, 38 (1963), pp. 443–52, reprinted in *idem., The Crusades, Holy War and Canon Law* (Aldershot, 1991); and below, p. 50. n. 97.
[88] *Chronica Rogeri de Hovedene* (Howden), ed. W. Stubbs, 4 vols. (Rolls Series, 1868–71), IV, pp. 16, 21–4 (including a forged letter of rebuke from Pope Celestine); William of Newburgh, *Historia rerum Anglicarum* (WN), in *Chronicles and Memorials of the Reigns of Stephen, Henry II and Richard I*. ed. R. Howlett, 4 vols. (Rolls Series, 1884–90), II, pp. 493–4. The legality of Philip's capture was discussed in detail by Master Nicholas de Laigle in his *Quaestiones Londinienses*, in which he argued that as a

This is not to say, however, that the concept of appeal concerning violation of customary behaviour was completely absent. As in the later law of
arms, an appeal might be made to the lord of a defaulting opponent. The
Histoire de Guillaume Le Maréchal records how at a tournament in 1179, held
in the Eure valley between Anet and Sorrel-Moussel, William the Marshal
captured two horses from a group of French knights seeking refuge in an
old motte, but while he was dismounted and thus disadvantaged, two other
French knights whom he recognized seized the horses that were now
William's prize and made off. After the tourney was ended, the Marshal laid
his complaint before William des Barres, whose nephew had been one of
the offending knights. Shocked by such a breach of expected conduct, des
Barres ordered his nephew to restore the horse or leave his household.
Similarly, the lord of the other knight commanded his vassal to return the
charger to the Marshal.[89]

Here there was clearly a mutual recognition that an accepted – if unwritten – code had been violated, and that it was within the competence of a
lord to order redress arising from such violations from a miscreant vassal.
This incident, however, took place not in war itself but in the artificial
conditions of the tournament. In a sport which was fought primarily for
financial gain achieved through ransoms and the seizure of horses and
arms,[90] it was clearly imperative to clarify rules governing such issues and to
ensure adherence to them by all participants. The desire to ensure profit
was thus a powerful catalyst for the crystallization of rules of conduct.

The relative safety of the tournament, moreover, meant that the moni-
toring of these ground rules was far easier than on the field of battle.
Indeed, it was primarily as the guardians, interpreters and enforcers of
these rules, coupled with their expertise in blazon, that heralds would rise
to prominence from the thirteenth century.[91] In the 1170s, however, such
formalization was still distant: the settlement between the Marshal and the
lords of the two *juvenes* was a personal one, based not on a *judicially* enforceable code but merely on mutually accepted conventions implemented
through a shared sense of honourable conduct.

That it was honour rather than any binding power of law which proved

crusader enjoying the special protection of the Holy See, Richard had a right to take action against
any impeding him from this task. By taking part in battle, the bishop had not only brought his capture
upon himself and renounced the protection afforded by the Church to unarmed clergy, but he also
deserved to be defrocked for causing the death of many (Brundage, 'Two Canonical *Quaestiones*', pp.
445–7, 448–50; and on Philip's capture see also W. Ullman, *Medieval Papalism: The Political Theories of the
Medieval Canonists* (London, 1949), pp. 191–3, 200–1).

[89] *HGM*, 11. 3881–90, 3919–86, 4075–284. The incident is cited in detail by S. Painter, *William the
Marshal: Knight Errant, Baron and Regent of England* (Johns Hopkins, 1933), pp. 41–3.

[90] Keen, *Chivalry*, p. 85.   [91] *Ibid.*, pp. 125 ff.

the overriding factor in adherence to custom between warriors is still more forcefully illustrated by an incident from the reign of Stephen. In 1146, Philip, the son of Robert of Gloucester, (who nevertheless was currently fighting for Stephen), seized Reginald earl of Cornwall and many of his knights 'when Reginald was relying on a truce with the king (*regiis induciis fretum*)' and had been on his way from the Empress to discuss peace terms. According to the *Gesta Stephani*, Stephen was incensed at such conduct 'because this capture took place without the king's knowledge, or rather because Philip had ventured on an unlawful capture when a truce for peace and safe-conduct had been granted by both sides'.[92] As a result Philip at length 'gave the man up and appeased the king's resentment'.[93] Stephen's reaction could hardly have been in response to a formal appeal by either Reginald or Matilda to the *curia regis*, for the Angevins were disputing Stephen's very claim to the throne. Equally, Reginald's capture had been 'illicit' only in the sense that it violated both Stephen's highly developed sense of personal honour,[94] and a prior agreement which for the purposes of negotiation it was essential should remain inviolate. If safe conduct during parleys was consistently violated, both parties ran the risk of rendering unworkable the very mechanisms by which warfare might be postponed or brought to a conclusion.

It might, however, be argued that because of the disputed nature of authority – and hence the lack of effective appeal – Stephen's reign stands sui generis. Certainly, the appearance of ecclesiastics as guarantors in the *conventio* between the earls of Leicester and Chester strongly suggests the ineffectiveness of any higher secular tribunal to adjudicate on such issues.[95] The efficacy of the treaty between the two earls ultimately rested on the pledges held by the two bishops, and on the abstract notion of Bishop Robert de Chesney's 'Christianity'.

Yet even outside the peculiarities of Stephen's reign, appeals made to the court of a liege lord concerning breaches of conduct are rare. In part this was due to the problematical nature of the available sources of higher

[92] 'Pacis et securitatis ex utraque parte datis induciis ad illicitam Philippus proruit captionem', (*GS*, pp. 186–7). [93] *Ibid.*
[94] Stephen's chivalric nature overrode military and political pragmatism on several crucial occasions, leading to profound repercussions both for the authority of his own kingship and for the future of the house of Blois. Among these may be cited his magnanimous, but fatally over-generous treatment of the garrison of Exeter in 1136 (*GS*, pp. 41–3), his escort under safe-conduct of Matilda from Arundel to Bristol in 1139 (*HN*, p. 35), and his payment of Henry of Anjou's passage home after his disastrous expedition of 1147 (*GS*, pp. 206–7). Such behaviour extended to battle. Despite the fact that David I showed himself a consistent and formidable enemy to Stephen, the latter rescued his son, Earl Henry, from capture at the hands of the enemy during the siege of Ludlow castle, 1139, only a year after Henry had figured prominently in the battle of the Standard against the English forces (HH, p. 265). [95] Stenton, *English Feudalism*, pp. 288, 253.

authority. Appeal might be made to the papacy, as we have noted, against violations of those precepts of canon law germane to warfare, but the papacy's powers of de facto intervention were severely circumscribed. When in early 1192 Philip planned to invade the Norman Vexin while Richard was in Palestine, he was prevented from so doing not by papal admonition but by the refusal of his own nobles to attack the lands of an absent crusader.[96] Similarly, while Richard could claim that his war against Philip from 1194 was a just one, seeking only the recovery of lands illicitly seized during his captivity in Germany, there was little the intervention of the papacy could do in practical terms to speed the restoration of his territories.[97]

Political actualities equally militated against the viability of the notional framework for appeal afforded by ties of overlordship between the Capetians and the territorial principalities of France. The politically fraught context of Plantagenet–Capetian relations ensured that suzerains were seldom disinterested parties, while it would have been scarcely conceivable for the peers of France to have sat in judgement on their own king following an appeal, say, by Henry II concerning Louis VII's breach of safe conduct to the citizens of Verneuil in 1173, though technically Louis was his liege lord.[98] Even if an appeal was made, enforcement of redress might be difficult if not impossible.

Such considerations are well illustrated by a major dispute which arose in 1188 between Richard as count of Poitou and Count Raymond of Toulouse. Raymond had, according to Howden, seized some Aquitainian

---

[96] *Gesta regis Henrici secundi Benedicti abbatis* (*GH*), ed. W. Stubbs, 2 vols. (Rolls Series, 1867), II, pp. 236–7. At Messina in March, 1191, Philip had vowed not to attack Richard's lands, until forty days after his return (*ibid.*, II, pp. 184–5; *Itinerarium*, p. 238; WN, p. 357; and *Letters of Pope Innocent III*, p. 7). For a perceptive assessment of the nature of Philip's vow see Gillingham, *Richard the Lionheart*, p. 179. When Philip had visited the Pope on his return from Palestine in October 1191, Celestine III had refused his request for permission to attack Richard's lands in order to right injuries he had sustained during the expedition. The pope indeed, had forbidden any assault on Richard's lands under pain of anathema, but Philip had ignored this (*GH*, II, p. 229).

[97] For all his criticism of a war between two Christian kings that delayed a fresh crusade, William of Newburgh admitted that Richard fought a just war (WN, pp. 455–6). On Richard's position in regard to Philip's hostilities see Brundage, *Canon Law and the Crusader*, pp. 167–8. In 1193, Celestine III had threatened to excommunicate the Emperor unless Richard was released, but the sentence was only carried out against Leopold of Austria, whose lands were also laid under interdict (Howden, III, p. 208; Diceto, II, p. 119). There was a general feeling, in the Angevin lands at least, that the pope had displayed insufficient speed and vigour in attempting to secure Richard's release; see B. A. Lees, 'The Letters of Queen Eleanor to Pope Celestine', *EHR*, 21 (1906), pp. 78–93; and the poem complaining about the inactivity of the pope and kings edited in C. L. Kingsford, 'Some Political Poems of the Twelfth Century', *EHR*, 5 (1890), pp. 311–26 at pp. 320–1. Richard continued to appeal to the papacy long after his release, asking Innocent III to compel both Leopold's son, Frederick, and Henry VI's brother, Philip of Swabia, to restore the ransom money. Yet although the pope promised intervention, there is no indication that any compensation was forthcoming, despite the fact that Duke Leopold, stricken with guilt on his death-bed, had given orders to this effect (*Letters of Innocent III*, pp. 4–5). [98] *GH*, I. pp. 50–55, and below, pp. 126–7.

merchants in his territories, some of whom he blinded and castrated, others he imprisoned. Richard responded by retaliatory raids, during which he captured one of Raymond's leading counsellors, Peter Seillan, and holding this man responsible both for the assault on the merchants and for earlier injuries, Richard had him straitly confined and refused to ransom him. Unable to procure Seillan's release by payment, Raymond then seized two of Henry II's household knights who were returning from Compostela, and attempted to negotiate an exchange. Richard indignantly refused to trade Seillan or to ransom the knights, as they had been seized in flagrant violation of the protection afforded by the Church to pilgrims.

Despite this breach of canon law, however, there is no mention of an appeal by Richard or Henry to the pope, or of the intervention of any churchmen. Rather, it was the hapless knights themselves who appealed not to the *curia* but to King Philip, doubtless judging him to be the best source of effective intervention. Yet the French king's attempts at arbitration were in vain, his request that Henry's household knights should be released 'not out of love for the king of England or of Count Richard his son, but on account of reverence and love for the blessed apostle James',[99] being refused by Raymond unless his own counsellor was released. Though their nominal overlord, Philip was powerless to enforce a settlement between the two warring counts.

Richard's response was to launch a full-scale invasion of the Quercy, whereupon Raymond appealed to Philip, and Philip in turn complained to Henry II as Richard's father and lord, demanding that he ensured Richard made restitution.[100] When Henry disclaimed any responsibility for his son's actions, Philip invaded Berry, justifying his attack as a reprisal for Richard's attack on Toulouse, despite Richard's insistence that he had done no harm to the count of Toulouse without the King of France's permission, particularly since Raymond had claimed to be exempt from the 'truce and peace' established between Philip and the Plantagenets in 1187. It was clear, however, that Philip was merely using hostilities in the Toulousin as an excuse for blatant aggression against the Angevin heartlands, for despite representations from some of Henry's leading *familiares*, Philip merely intensified his campaign and, in a symbolic act, cut down the great elm tree at Gisors which had been the site of previous peace conferences.[101] Appeal over legalities had become irrelevant, and Henry threatened to renounce his homage to Philip and hold him as a mortal enemy.[102]

The inherent prejudices of the court of an erstwhile enemy and the difficulties of enforcing any judicial decisions were not, however, the principal

---

[99] *GH*, ii, pp. 34–5.   [100] *Ibid.*, pp. 35–6.   [101] *Ibid.*, pp. 40, 45–6.   [102] *Ibid.*, p. 46.

reasons for lack of appeal concerning breaches of conduct in the eleventh and twelfth centuries; analogous problems did not deter men from prosecuting cases arising from the *ius armorum* in the fourteenth and fifteenth centuries.[103] Rather, what was lacking in this period was the concept itself of such an international, enforceable *ius* for the regulation of conduct. Warriors of the eleventh and twelfth centuries did not regard the breach of convention and customary usage as a violation of law. An incident occurring during the hostilities of 1188 discussed above is revealing. The great French knight William des Barres had been captured by Richard near Mantes and put under parole (*per fidem positus fuit*). While his captors were preoccupied, however, William made good his escape on a squire's rouncey.[104] Here was a case of breach of pledge which in the fourteenth century might well have been brought to court according to the law of arms. Yet there is no record of Richard impleading des Barres for defrauding his captor of ransom; the only binding force on William had been his word of honour, and there was no formal means of redress for his act of bad faith.[105]

Still more telling is lack of any appeal against forms of warfare that were assuming extreme manifestations during the bitter internecine strife of 1183 between Henry II's sons. Geoffrey and the Young King attacked and wounded men sent by their father to establish peace to whom they had given safe conduct,[106] while Richard ordered the immediate beheading of all those of his brothers' supporters who were captured, irrespective of rank.[107] This last was an act with few parallels within the context of warfare between members of the Anglo-Norman or Frankish aristocracy, and in violation of customary behaviour concerning the treatment of prisoners.[108] Howden, however, notes the fact laconically, and Geoffrey of Vigeois confirms that it was no idle threat. In February 1183, Richard defeated the forces of Aimar, viscount of Limoges, and the mercenary leader Raymond Brennus in battle at Gorre. The leading insurgents escaped, but those who were captured were dragged to Aixe, where

---

[103] Keen, *Laws of War*, pp. 23–59.   [104] *GH*, II, p. 46.
[105] This incident does not seem to have dented William's high chivalric reputation, though it may go far to explain the deep hostility displayed towards him by Richard at Messina in 1191, when a mock-joust turned into a bitter wrangle (below, p. 101).
[106] *GH*, I. p. 298. In 1183, the younger Henry and Geoffrey were guilty of several successive breaches of acceptable conduct. The rebellious brothers had acquiesced to two successive attempts by the men of Limoges to shoot at Henry II with arrows, which had come close to killing him (*GH*, I. p. 296). Subsequently, after the Young King had pleaded for and gained his father's clemency for the citizens, the royal envoys sent to collect hostages for their good behaviour were attacked and seriously wounded. He then allowed some of his father's men, though sent 'cum treuga', to be killed in his presence. A few days later, Geoffrey asked his father to send him Oliver fitz Ernis and Jerome de Montreuil 'in treuga', but on their arrival the former was cast into the river and the latter wounded (*ibid.*, pp. 298–9).   [107] *GH*, I. p. 293.   [108] Below, pp. 199–203.

some were drowned in the Vienne, some beheaded and about eighty blinded.[109]

Similarly, though Philip Augustus might be outraged when in 1194 the Normans under the command of Prince John beheaded the French knights they had captured at Evreux,[110] he could hardly lodge a complaint with Richard concerning his brother's behaviour or seek to discipline John in any way. The act might grossly exceed the expected conduct of a knight, but Philip clearly recognised that such matters, not having the status of law, were outside the competence of both his or any other ruler's court. If Froissart believed that the French knights at Limoges in 1370 could appeal to a law of arms to avoid death, it seems that Richard's opponents in Aquitaine in 1183 and those of John in Normandy in 1194 could not.

To sum up, it does not seem possible regarding Anglo-Norman and Angevin warfare to speak of 'laws of war' or of a 'law of arms' in a precise juridical sense, as Keen is able for the fourteenth and fifteenth centuries. The formative influences of Roman law had not as yet fused with custom to produce an international *ius armorum* which could be enunciated by legists such as John of Legnano and Honoré Bonet, or enforced in specific courts empowered for the purpose. Nevertheless, one can point to a body of uncodified custom, practices which Bonet could later call *bonnes coutumes* or *coustumes et usaiges du monde*,[111] concerned both to regulate the profits of war and to mitigate the full rigours of conflict. Save where men violated specific disciplinary regulations issued by their commander, such convention and customary behaviour seems to have been in no judicial sense compulsory, lacking the force of law. The granting and maintenance of truces or respite to besieged garrisons, for example, depended ultimately on the volition of the besieging commander.[112] Similarly, while widespread, the custom of taking opponents for ransom rather than slaying them was anything but obligatory, its operation often being subject to a complex blend of military, political and personal considerations.[113] Yet by frequent repetition and their innate practical value in the prosecution of war these customs had become generally accepted, though not wholly universal, usage.

[109] Vigeois, *RHF*, XVIII, p. 213. The severity of their punishment may be attributable in part to Richard's own temperament and partly to the large mercenary element in the defeated force, which was composed amongst others of Basques. For the treatment of mercenaries in and following battle see below, pp. 179–80.

[110] Rigord, *Gesta Philippi Augusti* (Rigord), ed. H.-F. Delaborde in *Oeuvres de Rigord et de Guillaume le Breton, historiens de Philippe Auguste*, 2 vols. (Paris, 1882–5), I. p. 127.

[111] Wright, 'The *Tree of Battles* of Honoré Bouvet', p. 23.   [112] Below, pp. 218–20.

[113] Below, pp. 162–9.

The application and observation of such usages depended on two principal factors. The first was the pragmatic advantages to be gained in military terms, which will be examined below in relation to the conventions themselves. The second was the dictates of honour and reputation. But before turning to this concept of honour, so central to the self-perception of the knighthood, we must first ask to what extent behaviour in war was regulated or constrained by the religious dimensions of chivalry and by the dictates of the Church.

3

A CHRISTIAN CHIVALRY? WAR, PIETY
AND SACRILEGE

Today the military discipline which Vegetius Renatus and many others taught has utterly vanished . . . Once soldiers bound themselves by oath that they would stand up for the state, that they would not flee from the battle-line, and that they would give up their lives for the public interest. Now the young knights receive their swords from the altar and thereby they profess that they are the sons of the Church and that they have taken up the sword for the honour of the priesthood, the protection of the poor, for the punishment of malefactors, and for the liberation of the homeland. But matters are very different; for immediately they have been girt with the belt of knighthood they at once rise up against the anointed of the Lord and rage violently against the patrimony of the Crucified. They despoil and rob the subject poor of Christ, and miserably oppress the wretched without mercy . . .[1]

So wrote Peter of Blois, inveighing against what he regarded as the pride, decadence and rapacity of the knighthood and their persecution of the clergy. Though the First Crusade had gone far to rehabilitate the social validity of the *bellatores* in the eyes of the Church,[2] it seemed to ecclesiastical *literati* like Peter of Blois, John of Salisbury and Stephen of Fougères, acquainted with classical precedents for military discipline and service to

---

[1] *Petri Blesensis archidiaconi opera omnia*, ed. J. A. Giles, 4 vols. (Oxford, 1846–7), I. no. 94, p. 292; the letter is also printed in *Patrologia cursus completus, series latina*, (Migne, *PL*), ed. J. P. Migne, 221 vols. (Paris, 1844–65), CCVII, no. 94, cols. 293–7. For Peter of Blois see R. W. Southern, 'Peter of Blois. A Twelfth Century Humanist?', idem., *Medieval Humanism and Other Essays* (Oxford, 1970), pp. 105–32.

[2] For these developments and further bibliography see, *inter alia*, Erdmann, *The Origin of the Idea of Crusade*; Flori, *L'essor de chevalerie*, especially pp. 164–90; and J. Riley-Smith, *The First Crusade and the Idea of Crusading* (London, 1986); M. Bull, *Knightly Piety and the Lay Response to the First Crusade. The Limousin and Gascony, c. 970–1130* (Oxford, 1993).

the state, that contemporary knighthood had become the very antithesis of its divinely ordained function.[3] The proper task of the *bellatores* was not simply to defend and extend the frontiers of Christendom against external pagan enemies, but within it to protect the poor, the helpless and, above all, Holy Church.[4]

Yet the pages of numerous chronicles and charters abound in notices of the seizure or pillaging of ecclesiastical lands, the violation of sanctuary, the despoliation and even destruction of churches, and assaults on clerics and the religious. The knighthood, moreover, had paid scant heed to the Church's attempts to create and enforce a *ius in bello*.[5] While the call to crusade against external enemies had met with an enthusiastic response, ecclesiastical efforts to restrict the extent and nature of warfare within Christendom through the Peace and Truce of God had enjoyed only a limited effect. The canonical prohibition of the crossbow, of the employment of *routiers*, and of the tournament, was largely ignored.[6]

Yet paradoxically, religious belief and the prosecution of warfare were inextricably fused. The assistance of God and his saints might be sought in a number of ways; acts of benefaction or restitution prior to campaign or battle; spiritual purification before combat; the use of relics, hallowed banners and war-cries in battle itself; and always, supporting and reinforcing such measures, by the prayers and intercessions of clergy and the religious.[7]

To what extent, then, did the moral dictates of Christianity affect the conduct of the knighthood in war itself? How did knights reconcile belief

---

[3] C. Morris, 'Equestris Ordo; Chivalry as a Vocation in the Twelfth Century', *Religious Motivation: Biographical and Sociological Problems for the Church Historian*, ed. D. Baker (*Studies in Church History*, XV, Oxford, 1978), pp. 87–96; J. Flori, 'L'idéologie politique de l'Eglise au XIIe siècle: Bernard de Clairvaux, Jean de Salisbury, Géroh de Reichersberg', *Conscience et Liberté*, 1, 1978, pp. 29–37; *idem.*, 'La chevalerie selon Jean de Salisbury', *Revue d'Histoire Ecclésiastique*, 77, 1982, pp. 35–77; and *idem.*, *L'essor de chevalerie*, pp. 280–9. For comment on Stephen of Fougères' *Livre des Manières*, c. 1185, see Keen, *Chivalry*, p. 4; S. Painter, 'The Ideas of Chivalry', *Feudalism and Liberty*, ed. F. A. Cazel, Jr (Baltimore, 1961), pp. 94–6; *idem.*, *French Chivalry*, pp. 72–3, where he assumes a far more cautious position as to the reliance of Stephen on John of Salisbury's *Policraticus*, and Flori, *L'essor de chevalerie*, pp. 315–9. Cf. the comments by Jacques de Vitry in his sermon 'Ad proceres et milites', quoted in A. Luchaire, *La société française au temps de Philippe Auguste* (Paris, 1090), tr. E. B. Krehbiel as *Social France at the Time of Philip Augustus* (London, 1912; repr. New York, 1967), pp. 254–5.

[4] Thus, for example, in his *Policraticus* of 1159, John of Salisbury defines the knighthood's function as being to: 'defend the Church, to assail infidelity, to venerate the priesthood, to protect the poor from injuries, to pacify the province, to pour out their blood for their brothers ... and if need be lay down their lives ... The high praises of God are in their throats and two edged swords in their hands ... that they may execute the judgement that is committed to them to execute; wherein each follows not his own will, but the deliberate decision of God, the angels and men, in accordance with equity and public utility' (*Policraticus*, II, p. 23).

[5] An excellent survey of the Church and war as seen through the work of Orderic Vitalis is furnished by Holdsworth, 'Ideal and Reality', pp. 59–78; see also Brundage, 'The Limits of War-Making Power', pp. 69–86.   [6] Below, pp. 70–5.   [7] Contamine, *War in the Middle Ages*, pp. 296–302.

and benefaction with widespread violence towards the temporal possessions of the Church in time of war? Did the nature of war make sacrilege
and the destruction of churches inevitable? Or rather was there a profound dichotomy between the chivalric ethos and the teachings of the
Church?

The relationship between the nobility and the Church, and the effects of
Christianity and ecclesiastical precepts on the knighthood's corporate identity and individual behaviour, were complex and multifaceted. To regard
'the Church' in this respect as a monolithic institution, moreover, is misleading. Noble scions in abbey or chapter, clerks in a seigneurial household
or local parish clergy would have widely differing perceptions of the social
legitimacy of warriors, of the spiritual dimensions knighthood and, indeed,
of certain concepts of Christianity itself than the reformers of the
Gregorian curia or of Cîteaux.

Equally, the Christianity of the knights was not a superficial veneer pre-
cariously grafted by churchmen onto a fundamentally hostile warrior aristocracy. Peter of Blois's own description of the ceremony of belting to
knighthood, with the receipt of arms from the altar and the oath to defend
Holy Church, shows the extent to which the knightly *ordo* had by the later
twelfth century become deeply imbued with Christian ideology and
symbolism. Yet concepts of holy war for the faith and *patria* against the
heathen, the blessing of weapons and banners, the use of relics in battle
and the burgeoning cults of the military saints had been integral aspects of
the warriors' ethos long before Urban II preached the First Crusade at
Clermont in 1095.[8]

Vernacular literature abounds with forthright statements of deep,
unself-conscious faith. Knightly piety may not have conformed to the
ideals of men like Bernard of Clairvaux, but it was no less intense for that.
In the chansons, dying heroes such as Vivien in the *Chanson de Guillaume* are
given lengthy *credos* and an attitude of uncompromising hostility toward the
infidel, epitomized in Roland's stark statement that 'The pagans are wrong
and the Christians are right!'[9] Nowhere, indeed, is the ready absorption of
militant Christianity into the martial values of the warrior aristocracy more
readily apparent than in *The Song of Roland*.

Keen has, however, rightly cautioned against allowing the crusading
dimension of knighthood to dominate or precondition our perceptions
of 'religious chivalry'.[10] As a secular aristocracy, the knighthood fully

---

[8] Keen, *Chivalry*, pp. 44–50; Flori, *L'essor de la chevalerie*, pp. 81–118.
[9] Keen, *Chivalry*, pp. 51–63; *Song of Roland*, 1. 1015.   [10] Keen, *Chivalry*, pp. 44–5.

indulged in all the conventional expressions of religious devotion, such as pilgrimage, almsgiving and benefaction.[11] Orderic noted how the knights of Maule would come to the cloister to join in discourse with the monks,[12] and recent scholarship has emphasized the complex and multifaceted interdependence between knightly patrons and monastic foundations: the role played by a monastic house in the prestige and status of the founder and his kin, the reception as oblates of younger sons for whom there was little provision, and of patrons as *conversi*; the death-bed assumption of the habit *ad succurendum* by old or sick knights; economic transactions; the role of the monastery as a focus for honorial solidarity and corporate expression through the gifts of vassals; and the expansion of specific orders through family patronage or that of certain governmental classes.[13]

As Leyser has so aptly commented, 'the very term *militia saecularis* must teach us how deeply rooted, quintessential and inescapable war was in the societies, the economies, the politics and the world picture itself of early medieval Europe'.[14] Monastic liturgy and clerical writings mirrored the militaristic world of the knight in its expression and self-conception.[15] Ecclesiastical texts abound with metaphors of the war against sin drawn from contemporary warfare.[16] Monasteries were seen as spiritual castles protecting the kingdom and duchy, with their inmates engaged in a constant battle against the devil and the forces of evil.[17] And nowhere was knightly piety so visible as in battle and on campaign.

DIEUX AIDE! : THE INVOCATION OF DIVINE AID IN BATTLE

War confronted warriors with the imminent prospect of serious injury or death.[18] For while, as we shall see, chivalric conventions such as ransom

---

[11] C. Harper-Bill, 'The Piety of the Anglo-Norman Knightly Class', *Anglo-Norman Studies*, 2 (1979), pp. 63–77.   [12] Orderic, III, pp. 206–7.

[13] Harper-Bill, 'The Piety of the Anglo-Norman Knightly Class', pp. 63–77; E. Mason, 'Timeo Barones et Donas Ferentes', *Religious Motivation*, pp. 87–96; R. Mortimer, 'Religious and Secular Motives for Some English Monastic Foundations', *Religious Motivation*, pp. 77–86.

[14] K. Leyser, 'Early Medieval Warfare', in *idem., Communications and Power in Medieval Europe: The Carolingian and Ottonian Centuries*, ed. T. Reuter (London, 1994), p. 50.

[15] See B. H. Rosenwein, 'Feudal War and Monastic Peace: Cluniac Liturgy as Ritual Aggression', *Viator*, 2 (1971), pp. 129–57; Holdsworth, 'Ideas and Reality', pp. 76–78.

[16] Harper-Bill, 'The Piety of the Anglo-Norman Knightly Class', pp. 65, 75–6; Chibnall, 'Feudal Society in Orderic Vitalis', p. 36; *idem., The World of Orderic Vitalis*, pp. 142–3; R. W. Southern, *St Anselm and his Biographer* (Cambridge 1962), p. 109; Contamine, *War in the Middle Ages*, pp. 296–7.

[17] Speaking of the monasteries in the duchy, Orderic noted: 'These are the fortresses by which Normandy is guarded; in these men learn to fight against devils and the sins of the flesh' (Orderic, IV, pp. 92–3). Cf. Chibnall, 'Feudal Society in Orderic Vitalis', p. 36.

[18] Verbruggen, *Warfare in Western Europe*, pp. 39–41.

undoubtedly lessened the extent of killing, knightly combat still remained fraught with danger. To take the chansons de geste at face value and regard the knights as latterday possessors of the *furor teutonicus*, scorning death and revelling in a martial ecstasy, is to mistake the nature of chivalry and the warriors' psychology.[19] Rather, much of the *raison d'être* of the heroic or chivalric ethos was to bolster men's courage against the natural feelings of panic and terror in battle. Such secular ideals of bravery, loyalty and steadfastness were, however, crucially reinforced by the invocation of divine aid in battle. To the knights, God was essentially a God of Battles, the Old Testament Lord of Hosts whose aid was vital to ensure both personal safety and corporate victory in war.

Men regarded battle as a judicial duel on a grand scale, in which God would grant victory to the side whose cause was most just.[20] Fulk le Rechin, count of Anjou, was not simply engaging in empty rhetoric when he ascribed the victory of Fulk Nerra over Odo of Blois at Pontlevoy, 1016, and his own triumph over his brother Geoffrey in 1067 as being won *Dei gratia*.[21] For though in the castle-based warfare of the eleventh and twelfth centuries, sieges and skirmishes were commonplace, the great set-piece battle (*praelium campestre*) was rare indeed. Most commanders eschewed pitched battle wherever possible, even if they possessed superior numbers. Not only were the military and political consequences of defeat potentially catastrophic, but the difficulties of communications once troops were committed, the imponderables of morale and enemy resistance, the chance death of a leader that might bring disaster, all conspired to make the final outcome uncertain and a matter of divine judgement.[22] Even some Anglo-Saxons shared the view of William I's apologists that Hastings had been God's vindication of his rightful claim in trial by battle.[23] Eadmer recorded without any hint of disagreement that

> of that battle the French who took part in it do to this day declare that, although fortune swayed now on this side and that, yet of the Normans so many were slain or put to flight that the victory which they had is truly and without doubt to be attributed to nothing else than the miraculous

---

[19] Cf. L. Gautier, *Chevalerie* (2nd edn, Paris, 1900), ed. J. Levron and tr. C. D. Dunning as *Chivalry* (London, 1965, repr, 1989), p. 56: 'The old barbaric leaven of the German forest was still working beneath the coat of mail. In their eyes, the spectacle of a gory sword or armour was a charming sight: a fine lance thrust transported them to the seventh heaven of delight.'

[20] See also below, pp. 61–2.

[21] *Fragmentum historiae Andegavensis*, in *Chroniques des comtes d'Anjou et des seigneurs d'Amboise*, ed. L. Halphen and R. Poupardin (Paris, 1913), p. 237; Gillingham, 'William the Bastard at War', p. 149.

[22] Above, p. 43 and n. 69.

[23] Thus the *Anglo-Saxon Chronicle*, 'D', *s.a.* 1066, noted that the Normans won the battle of Hastings 'even as God granted it to them because of the sins of the people'.

intervention of God, who by so punishing Harold's wicked perjury shewed that He is not a God that hath any pleasure in wickedness.[24]

If God was to intervene thus in the affairs of men, it was clearly vital for knights, both corporately and individually, to expiate any sins which might forfeit divine aid in their hour of need. Grants of land or quitclaims in disputes with churches were offered as pre-emptive measures before embarking on a particularly perilous voyage or expedition to gain the benison of the religious rather than their malediction.[25] Such restitution was but the other side of the coin from benefaction in the hope of future spiritual aid in war, and frequently the two were inseparable. Thus before his departure for Spain, Ralph de Conches sought pardon for his part in the burning of the town of Saint-Evroul when in league with Arnold d'Echauffour, and promised many further gifts, which he pledged on the high altar, if he came back unharmed.[26] Similarly, the undoubted danger entailed by the attempted conquest of England, for example, led Roger de Montgomery to quitclaim land at Givervilla to La-Trinité-du-Mont, Rouen, when Duke William 'was about to cross the sea with his fleet'.[27] Immediately prior to the battle of Tinchebrai in 1106, Henry I 'vowed to God' to restore the church of Saint-Pierre-sur-Dive which he had burnt, lest God avenge an act of sacrilege by depriving Henry of victory in battle.[28]

Prayer, the taking of mass and confession were essential elements of pre-battle preparation, to safeguard one's soul irrespective of the outcome.[29] Further acts of purification, however, might be undertaken. Before the battle of the Standard in 1138, three days of prayer, fasting and almsgiving were enjoined upon the Anglo-Norman army, which included local levies led by their parish priests.[30] The emphasis here on spiritual warfare against the invad-

---

[24] *Eadmeri historia novorum in Anglia* (Eadmer), ed. M. Rule (Rolls Series, 1884), p. 9; tr. G. Bosanquet, *Eadmer's History of Recent Events in England* (London, 1964), p. 9.

[25] For settlements and grants before crusade, see *Calander of Documents Preserved in France Illustrative of the History of Great Britain and Ireland*, ed. J. H. Round (London, 1899), p. 401; Riley-Smith, *The First Crusade and the Idea of Crusading*, pp. 36–8; L. and J. Riley-Smith, *The Crusades: Idea and Reality* (London 1981), pp. 156–7.   [26] Orderic, III, pp. 124–7.

[27] *Recueil des actes des ducs de Normandie (911–1066)* (Fauroux), ed. M. Fauroux (Caen, 1961), no. 233, pp. 448–9; *Regesta regum Anglo-Normannorum (RRAN)*, ed. H. W. C. Davis, C. Johnson, H. A. Cronne and R. H. C. Davis, 3 vols. (Oxford, 1913–69), I, no. 3, p. 1; cf. *ibid.*, I, no. 71, p. 19.

[28] Orderic, VI, pp. 88–9. Chibnall, *ibid.*, VI, p. 88, n. 3, draws attention to the charter by which Henry fulfilled this promise.

[29] Contamine, *War in the Middle Ages*, pp. 298–301; Orderic, V, pp. 108–9, 110–11, 138–9, 164–5; VI, pp. 544–5.

[30] Richard of Hexham, *De gestis regis Stephani et de bello Standardi* (RH), ed. J. Raine, *The Priory of Hexham, its Chroniclers, Endowments and Annals*, 2 vols (Surtees Society, 44, 1868), I. pp. 86–7; John of Hexham, *Historia Johannis, prioris Haugustadensis ecclesiae* (JH), *ibid.*, p. 119; *Relatio*, p. 182. Similarly at the siege of Bréval in 1092, Philip I's forces included priests and their parishioners with holy banners (Orderic, IV, pp. 288–9). Louis the Fat's bishops 'set up the communities of the people in France, so that the priests might accompany the king to battle or siege, carrying banners and leading all their parishioners' (Orderic, VI, pp. 156–7, and cf. pp. 244–5).

2 Confession, absolution and the hearing of Mass were vital preliminaries before
most engagements. Here a knight receives communion from a priest (thought to
represent Abraham and Melchizedek) from the interior of the west front of Reims
cathedral (c. 1240–60). Such an image of the pious warrior conforms to the clerical
ideal of the knights as protectors – and servants – of the Church (James Austin).

ing Scots was doubtless heightened by the fact that in the absence of King Stephen, Archbishop Thurstan of York had overall command of the English army. Yet forces led by kings or other rulers could undergo similar rituals in the hope of obtaining God's favour in battle.[31] Galbert of Bruges records how before the battle of Axspoele in Flanders, 1128, William Clito and his knights cut their hair in the church at Ouenburg as an offering for victory, received penance for their sins, then, having removed their armour, shirts and secular garb, vowed to God to be advocates for the poor and the Church.[32]

Such forthright and public expressions of piety blended propitiation with valuable political theatre. It was this inseparable fusion of motives that in 1105 led Henry I, shrewdly aware of the value of ecclesiastical sanction for his invasion of the Norman duchy, to allow Bishop Serlo of Séez to cut his hair and that of his magnates in the church in Carentan. The bishop had preached a sermon against the lax morals of the time, outwardly manifested in effeminate dress and long locks, so that his cropping of the king was a symbolic recognition of Henry as the harbinger of peace and righteous living to the disordered and corrupt duchy of his brother Robert.[33]

In battle itself, divine aid might be invoked by the carrying of relics or hallowed banners into combat, by war-cries which called upon God or individual saints, and by religious inscriptions on weapons and armour. Unlike the later plate armour of the fourteenth to sixteenth centuries, mail armour did not lend itself to the etching or embossing of religious scenes or motifs.[34] None of the very few helmets surviving from the eleventh or twelfth centuries bears invocations, common on the brow of many later bascinets, although the practice is visible as early as the eighth-century Coppergate helmet (c. 750–775).[35] Few real swords contained relics in the

---

[31] Cf. K. Leyser, 'Ritual, Ceremony and Gesture: Ottonian Germany', *The Carolingian and Ottonian Centuries*, pp. 204–5, 'fasting did not mean that the warriors ate and drank nothing, it meant in fact only that they did not eat and drink too much, as was all too often their habit. They were thus fitter for action. Drunkenness could have helped to overcome fear and anxiety, but it also incapacitated or at least reduced fighting skills ...' The Franks fasted for three days before engaging with Kerbogha at Antioch in 1098, a resourceful way of turning famine into a morale-boosting exercise (Orderic, v, pp. 108–9, and cf. vi, pp. 400–1).

[32] Galbert of Bruges, *De vita et martyrio beati Caroli boni Flandriae comitis; vita altera*, Migne, *PL*, CLXVI, col. 1038; his knights repeated Clito's vow 'ut deinceps pauperum foret advocatus et ecclesiarum Dei'.

[33] For a general discussion of fashion and morals in the reigns of Rufus and Henry, see F. Barlow, *William Rufus* (London, 1983), pp. 104–8.

[34] For depictions of saints, the crucifixion and other religious scenes on late medieval armour see Vale, *War and Chivalry*, p. 110.

[35] The inscription reads 'IN NOMINE DNI IHV SCS SPS DI ET OMNIBUS DECEMUS AMEN OSHERE XPI' – which has been rendered 'In the name of our Lord Jesus, the Holy Spirit, God the Father, and with all we pray. Amen', followed by the personal name Oshere and XRI, the first three letters of Christ in Greek: D. Tweddle, *The Coppergate Helmet* (York, 1984), pp. 17–18. The helm traditionally associated with St Wenceslas has a stylized crucifix superimposed above the nasal. The dating of both the helmet and the applied detail is disputed, though a tenth- or eleventh-century date seems probable (C. Blair, *European Arms and Armour London*, 1958, repr. 1979; S. Coupland, 'Carolingian Arms and Armour in the Ninth Century', *Viator*, 21 (1990), pp. 29–50 at 32–3; *BT*, p. 233).

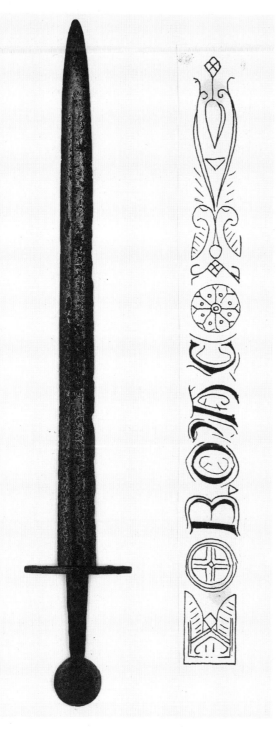

3 A mid-twelfth-century sword inlaid with the letters ʙᴏᴀᴄ, which may stand for the invocation 'Beati Omnipotentesque (sunt) Angeli [or Armati] Christi'. The circles may be talismanic as well as decorative, possibly alluding to the Trinity, but the meaning of such symbols, as with many other inscriptions, is still imperfectly understood. The sword, whose place of manufacture is uncertain (?Italy), was found in a kitchen in Northumbria. The detail of the inscription, which occurs repeatedly on both sides of the blade, is reproduced by kind permission of R. Ewart Oakeshott (Glasgow Museums and Art Galleries).

manner of Roland's Durendal,[36] but religious inscriptions such as 'In Nomine Domini', 'Sancta Maria', 'Benedictus Deus' were very common on sword blades or, more rarely, on their hilts[37] Many of these are garbled and imperfectly understood (as they may well have been to their owners) but seem to have possessed talismanic qualities.[38] Though the resonances of the sword as a magic weapon with its own personality were less vibrant by the eleventh century than they had been in the heroic world of *Beowulf*, swords still had names and could be regarded as possessing, or at least transmitting, supernatural power.[39]

War-cries fused a direct appeal for divine assistance with the practical and psychological value of a rallying cry. Since many countries had their own distinctive war cry – 'Dieux aide' in the case of the Normans, 'Mountjoie! St Denis!' in that of the French – group solidarity was further reinforced by such regional or national associations.[40] When in 1098, for example, Helias of Maine attacked Robert de Bellême's forces on the river Riolt in the Sonnois, he invoked St Julian, the tutelary saint of Le Mans and the county of Maine.[41] By contrast, during the Third Crusade, Richard I used the war-cry 'God and the Holy Sepulchre aid us!'.[42] The same cry was raised each evening on the march by the whole host to maintain morale and to remind constantly this hybrid and dissension-torn army of their common goal.[43]

The Song of Dermot and the Earl neatly encapsulates the vital role which

[36] *The Song of Roland*, ll. 2344–50. The dying hero, having failed to break his sword to prevent it from falling into pagan hands, addresses it: 'O, Durendal, how fair and sacred you are! In the golden hilt there are many relics: Saint Peter's tooth and some of Saint Basil's blood; some hair from the head of my lord St Denis and a part of the raiment of the Blessed Virgin. It is not right for pagans to possess you: you must be wielded by Christians.'

The sword said to be Durendal was stolen by the Young King when he plundered Rocamadour in 1183, but on no firmer evidence than 'local tradition' (K. Norgate, *England under the Angevin Kings*, 2 vols. (London, 1887), II, p. 227). For a sword possibly containing relics see R. Ewart Oakeshott, *Records of the Medieval Sword* (Boydell, 1991), p. 185.

[37] *Ibid.*, pp. 260, and for but a few of many examples *ibid.*, pp. 28–9, 35, 38–9, 58–9 ('In Nomine Domine'), 52 ('Jesus, Maria'), 55 (Sanctus Petrus Benedicat), 84, 86; I. Pierce, 'The Development of the Medieval Sword, c. 850–1300', *The Ideals and Practice of Medieval Knighthood*, III, ed. C. Harper-Bill and R. Harvey (Boydell, 1990), pp. 142, 149, 156; cf. R. Ewart Oakeshott, *The Sword in the Age of Chivalry*, pp. 139–43. The so-called sword of St Maurice, c. 1050–1120, probably redecorated for the coronation of Otto IV in 1198, bears on hilt, 'Christus Vincit, Cristus Reinat, Christus Inperat' (sic) (Oakeshott, *Records of the Medieval Sword*, p. 56).

[38] Oakeshott, *Records of the Medieval Sword*, pp. 31, 46, 63, 81, and Appendix B, pp. 253–60, which deals with a sword bearing the letters BOAC four times, which Oakeshott suggests might be rendered '*Beati Omnipotentesque Angeli Christi*' – 'Blessed and Omnipotent [are] the Angels of Christ'. Above plate 3.

[39] H. Ellis Davidson, *The Sword in Anglo-Saxon England, Its Archaeology and Literature* (Oxford, 1962, repr. Boydell, 1994), p. 104 f.; and E. Mason, 'The Hero's Invincible Weapon: An Aspect of Angevin Propaganda', *The Ideals and Practice of Medieval Knighthood*, III, pp. 121–38, for valuable remarks on the use of swords reputed to be those of legendary characters.

[40] Orderic, V, pp. 362–3 ('Dieux aide'); VI, pp. 216–17 ('Montjoie'); Wace, l. 8236 ('Deu aie!').

[41] Orderic, V, pp. 226–7.   [42] Ambroise, ll. 5893–904; *Itinerarium*, p. 270.   [43] *Itinerarium*, p. 253.

knights believed patron saints played in guarding both their lives and their honour. It describes how during the Norman attack on Limerick, Melier fitz Henry was the first to cross a difficult ford:

> When the knight had crossed over, 'St David!' he shouted loud and clear. For he was his lord under the Lord God the Creator. And the knight with great affection invoked St David night and day that he might aid him in doing deeds of valour; that he should give him strength and praise and renown against all his enemies. Often he invoked St David, that he should not leave him in forgetfulness, but give him might and vigour in the midst of his enemies that day.[44]

Melier had been born at St David's, but he was not alone among his colleagues to call upon this powerful protector, a striking example of cultural assimilation that had taken place among the Marchers.[45]

In the great war of 1173–4, the rebel forces against Henry II attempted to harness the aid of the recently martyred Thomas Becket to their cause.[46] The seemingly miraculous correlation, however, between Henry's public act of atonement at Becket's tomb on 12–13 July 1174, and William the Lion's capture by English forces at Alnwick, convinced many contemporaries that Becket had become reconciled with the king and was supporting him against his enemies.[47] William the Lion certainly believed so. When he came to build the royal abbey of Arbroath, he dedicated it to St Thomas.[48]

The aid of saints could be summoned by the more tangible means of hallowed banners and relics. At the Standard in 1138, Archbishop Thurstan had ordered the collection of saints' banners from the most important religious houses in the north of England, including those of Cuthbert from Durham, Wilfrid from Ripon and John from Beverley, while he sent the banner of St Peter from York and his own archepiscopal cross. These were hoisted from a ship's mast, at the top of which was secured a pyx containing the consecrated host, thereby forming the standard which gave the battle its name.[49] Strongly reminiscent of the *carrochio* of the Italian city-states – war-carts bearing religious insignia and painted with images of the saints – this assembly of hallowed banners acted not only as a visible

[44] *Song of Dermot*, 11. 3424–55.
[45] St David is also invoked by Maurice de Prendergast and others, *ibid.*, 11. 744–53; Crouch, *The Image of Aristocracy*, p. 324.
[46] The hymn *Novus miles sequitur* invokes the help of St Thomas on behalf of the earl of Leicester and the Young King; S. D. Stevens, *Music in Honour of St Thomas* (Sevenoaks, 1973), pp. 10–11; A. Duggan, 'The Cult of St Thomas Becket in the Thirteenth Century', *St Thomas Cantilupe, Bishop of Hereford. Essays in His Honour*, ed. M. Jancey (Hereford, 1982), p. 32 and n. 73.
[47] See Strickland, 'Arms and the Men', pp. 205–6, for full references.
[48] *Early Sources for Scottish History*, tr. A. O. Anderson, 2 vols. (Edinburgh, 1922, repr. Stamford, 1990), II, p. 298.   [49] RH, pp. 87, 90–1; JH, p. 119; *Relatio*, pp. 188–9.

rallying point in battle for the Anglo-Norman forces, but as a spiritual powerhouse.[50] In his *Relatio de Standardo*, Ailred of Rievaulx puts a striking speech into the mouth of Walter Espec, one of the leading Anglo-Norman commanders, in which he tells the army that the saints are fighting alongside them against the sacrilegious Scots, and that even Christ himself is present with shield and arms.[51] In a similar manner, William le Breton believed that the French had been aided at Bouvines, 1214, by St Denis and St Germain, the latter being so preoccupied in the battle that he neglected to defend his church at Auxerre from sack by robbers.[52]

The French war-cry 'Mountjoie! St Denis!', indeed, reflected the dual origin of the famous Oriflamme banner borne into battle by the kings of France. Two originally separate standards, a royal banner known as *Mountjoie* and the banner of the abbey of St Denis, had fused by the later twelfth century into the Oriflamme, kept at the abbey of St Denis and ritually taken from the high altar when the Capetian kings went to war.[53] Louis VII and Philip Augustus took the banner on the Second and Third Crusade respectively, while Philip also bore the Oriflamme at Bouvines.[54] A similar practice was followed by Henry III who kept the royal war banner, a dragon worked on red samite with eyes of sapphires and a fiery tongue, at Westminster, taking it out against the Welsh in 1257 and against forces of De Montfort in 1264.[55] In the twelfth century, the Angevins had shown a predilection for the protection of St Edmund. In 1173, the royalist forces

---

[50] A similar wheeled flagpole, called the Standard and which bore Richard's banner and formed the rallying point for Richard's army in 1191, is described in detail by the *Itinerarium*, pp. 249–50.

[51] *Relatio*, pp. 188–9. On Ailred's account of the Standard see D. Baker, 'Ailred of Rievaulx and Walter Espec', *The Haskins Society Journal*, ed. R. B. Patterson, 1 (1989), pp. 91–8; J. Bleise, 'Aelred of Rievaulx's Rhetoric and Morale at the Battle of the Standard, 1138', *Albion*, 20 (1988), pp. 543–56; idem., 'The Battle Rhetoric of Aelred of Rievaulx', *The Haskins Society Journal*, 1 (1989), pp. 99–107; idem., 'Rhetoric and Moral: A Study of Battle Orations from the Central Middle Ages', *Journal of Medieval History*, 15 (1989), pp. 201–26.

[52] WB, *Gesta*, p. 178; *Phillipidos*, Bk xi, 11. 32–9, p. 319; Bk xii, 11. 764–803, pp. 378–9. At Worcester in 1139, the citizens commended themselves to the protection of Mary, Oswald and Wulfstan, and as the forces of Robert of Gloucester attacked the city, the monks put on albs and processed outside the church with the relics of St Oswald (*The Chronicle of John of Worcester 1118–1140*, (JW), ed. J. R. H. Weaver (Oxford 1908), pp. 56–7). For German parallels see F. Graus, 'Der Heilige als Schlachtenhelfer', *Festschrift für Helmut Beumann*, ed. K.-U. Jäschke and R. Wenskus (Sigmaringen, 1977), pp. 330–48.

[53] G. M. Spiegel, 'The Cult of St Denis and Capetian Kingship', *Journal of Medieval History*, 1 (1975), pp. 43–69 at pp. 58–9. For the Oriflamme in the fourteenth and fifteenth centuries see P. Contamine, *Guerre, état et société a la fin du moyen Age. Etudes sur les armées des rois de France, 1337–1494* (Paris, 1972), pp. 671–3.

[54] Odo of Deuil, *De profectione Ludovici VII in Orientem*, ed. and tr. V. G. Berry (Columbia, 1948), p. 16; WB, *Gesta*, pp. 178, 272, 284; *Philippidos*, Bk xi, 11. 20–39, p. 318–9, Bk xii, 11. 41–50, p. 350, where William le Breton notes that the Oriflamme triumphed over Otto's Imperial standard of a dragon surmounted by an eagle.

[55] F. M. Powicke, *Henry III and the Lord Edward* (Oxford, 1947, repr. 1966), p. 459 and n. 4; D. Carpenter, *The Battles of Lewes and Evesham 1264/5* (University of Keele, 1987), p. 14.

under the justiciar Richard de Lucy carried the banner of St Edmund at their head in the battle of Fornham against the rebel forces of the earl of Leicester.[56] Richard I, who had gone on pilgrimage to Bury St Edmunds in 1189 prior to departing on crusade, sent back to the abbey as a thank offering the richly wrought imperial banner he had taken in battle from Isaac, ruler of Cyprus, in 1191.[57]

Most potent of all means of securing divine aid was the bearing of relics themselves into battle. According to William of Poitiers, Duke William wore the relics on which Harold had sworn allegiance to him around his neck at Hastings.[58] If so, they may well have been housed in a small shrine akin to the Brechbennoch or reliquary of St Columba which accompanied the Scottish kings to war.[59] In Capetian France, the relics of St Denis were displayed on the altar during times of danger, while masses were said and prayers were offered for the victory of the army. This occurred, for example, in 1124 when there was the threat of a German invasion, and in 1191 to ensure the safety of Philip Augustus and the success of the crusade.[60] Relics themselves might be a target of seizure in warfare, as in 1055, when the forces of Aelfgar of Mercia and Griffith ap Llewelyn took away the relics from Hereford minster during their sack of the city.[61] In 1197, Richard I burnt the port of St Valéry and carried off the saint's relics.[62]

Relics linked to Christ himself were naturally regarded as the most efficacious. The 'lance of St Maurice', containing a nail believed to be from the True Cross, was carried by Otto I at his great victory over the Magyars at the Lech.[63] The invention at Antioch during the First Crusade of a still more potent lance, the Holy Lance with which Christ's side was pierced at the crucifixion, was a crucial boost to the morale of the Christian army.[64] Conversely, the capture of the True Cross by Saladin's army at Hattin in

---

[56] *GH*, I, p. 61; JF, II. 1026–9, where Jordan has the earl of Arundel exclaim, 'Let us go and strike them for the honour of God and St Edmund who is a true martyr!'

[57] Howden, III, p. 16; Coggeshall, p. 97; *GH*, II, p. 164.   [58] WP, pp. 180–2.

[59] F. C. Eeles, 'The Monymusk Reliquary or Brechbennoch of St Columba', *Proceedings of the Society of Antiquaries of Scotland*, 68 (1934), pp. 433–8; *Regesta regum Scottorum* (*RRS*), II, ed. G. W. S. Barrow (Edinburgh, 1971), p. 57 and no. 499, by which William the Lion granted Arbroath Abbey custody of the Brechbennoch and land for its support at Forglen in Banffshire, on condition that army service is performed for the land and that the reliquary is brought to the army.

[60] *Suger, Vie de Louis VI le Gros* (Suger), ed. H. Waquet (Paris, 1929), p. 228; tr. R. Cusimano and J. Moorhead, *Suger, The Deeds of Louis the Fat* (Washington, 1992), p. 131; Rigord, pp. 113–14. On his return from Outremer in 1192, Philip had given thanks to St Denis and laid a fine silk pall on the altar (Rigord, p. 118).   [61] *ASC*, 'C', *s.a.* 1055.   [62] Howden IV, p. 19; Diceto, II, p. 152.

[63] K. Leyser, 'The Battle of the Lech, 955', *History*, 50 (1965), pp. 1–25, reprinted in *idem., Medieval Germany and Its Neighbours* (London, 1982), pp. 43–68, at p. 66.

[64] C. Morris, 'Policy and Visions: the Case of the Holy Lance at Antioch', in *War and Government*, pp. 33–45; cf. S. Runciman, 'The Holy Lance found at Antioch', *Analecta Bollandiana*, 68 (1950), pp. 197–209.

1187 deprived the kings of Jerusalem of their most potent source of spiritual and psychological aid in war and was a great blow to Christendom.[65]

Armies might assume the sign of the cross not simply in battles against the Muslims or other pagans, but in conflicts in Europe. The allied army ranged against Philip Augustus at Bouvines bore crosses on their surcoats in 1214, as did the royalist forces under William the Marshal in the campaign of 1217.[66] In January 1217, the legate Guala had granted royalist supporters remission for their sins 'as if they were fighting against pagans', and prior to the battle of Lincoln both the Marshal and the legate reminded the royalists that they fought against excommunicated men.[67] In a conscious inversion of the claim by the rebel leader Robert fitz Walter to be 'Marshal of the army of God', the royalist commander Philip d'Albini was called 'dux milicie Christi' – 'leader of the army of Christ'.[68] The leading role played by papal legates as supporters of the royal cause in the campaigns of 1215–17 and 1265–6 had made the use of such spiritual warfare a prominent feature of the campaigns.[69]

All such manifestations of religion and piety sought to aid warriors in the successful fulfilment of their *metier*. The need to bolster morale and courage, and actively to seek supernatural aid to achieve victory led to a natural and necessary elision of *spiritualia* and *militaria*. Likewise, there were pressing political, as well as moral, reasons for rulers to be highly conscious of the dictates of the *ius ad bellum* to justify acts of war and legitimize conquests.[70] Yet when the Church hierarchy attempted to curb the activities of the knighthood by legislating on the nature of war itself, they were imposing an artificial set of restrictions which often ran counter not only to pragmatic military dictates but also, in the case of the prohibition of the tournament, to integral aspects of the chivalric ethos.

---

[65] Cf. the comments of Ibn al-Athir and Imad al-Din, F. Gabrielli, *Arab Historians of the Crusades* (London, 1969), pp. 122, 136–7.

[66] Duby, *The Legend of Bouvines*, p. 117; D. Carpenter, *The Minority of Henry III* (London, 1990), pp. 28, 36.

[67] *Memoriale fratris Walteri de Coventria* (WC), ed. W. Stubbs, 2 vols. (Rolls Series, 1872–3), II, pp. 235–6; Carpenter, *The Minority of Henry III*, p. 28. Similarly, before the siege of Bedford commenced in 1224, Archbishop Langton and his bishops excommunicated William de Bréauté and his garrison, even though William invoked letters of papal protection for a crusader on behalf of Fawkes's castle (WC, p. 265; for the siege, see Carpenter, *The Minority of Henry III*, pp. 360–7).

[68] *Patent Rolls of Henry III . . . 1216–1225* (1901), p. 108.

[69] See S. D. Lloyd, '"Political Crusades" in England c. 1215–17 and c. 1263–5', *Crusade and Settlement: Papers Read at the First Conference of the Society for the Study of the Crusades and the Latin East*, ed. P. W. Edbury (Cardiff, 1985), pp. 113–20; and N. Housely, 'Crusades Against Christians; Their Origin and Early Development', *ibid.*, pp. 17–36; C. J. Tyerman, *England and the Crusades, 1095–1588* (Chicago, 1988), pp. 137–40.

[70] Holdsworth, 'Ideas and Reality', pp. 64–8; Brundage, 'The Limits of War-Making Power', pp. 74–5.

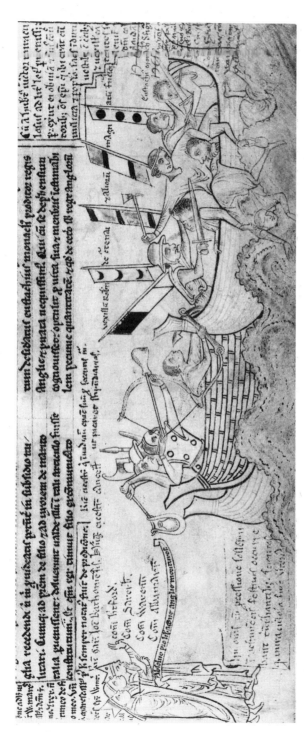

4 'I absolve those who are about to die for the liberation of England', runs the caption given by Matthew Paris to the English bishops who bless the royal forces engaging Louis's fleet at the battle of Sandwich, 1217. The English shoot bags of quick-lime to blind the French, who are then dispatched. Sea battles appear to have been particularly sanguinary, and at Sandwich, even the lives of the French nobles were in danger at the hands of the English serjeants. On the far right, the French fleet's commander, Eustace the Monk, is summarily beheaded as a renegade (Corpus Christi College, Cambridge, MS 16, f. 52 r).

THE KNIGHTS' WAR AND THE CHURCH'S PEACE: ECCLESIASTICAL ATTEMPTS TO LIMIT THE NATURE OF WAR

The decline of effective Frankish kingship from the late ninth century had resulted in the fragmentation of effective peace-keeping authority and incessant aristocratic feuding. The violence and depredations caused by such endemic local warfare had, by the last quarter of the tenth century, forced the higher clergy to assume a conceptual militancy by which they attempted to redefine the nature and scope of warfare. Originating in southern France from the 980s, the Peace of God was a complex social, religious and political phenomenon.[71] At its core, however, was the attempt by ecclesiastical councils to give to the two unarmed *ordines* of society, the clergy and the peasantry, limited, though by no means absolute protection from violence. It is clear, however, that despite the repeated prohibitions by Peace councils, the peasantry remained the principal target of knightly aggression. Nor could it be otherwise. For ravaging and economic warfare, which involved the burning of crops and villages and even the killing of husbandmen themselves, was, as we shall see, so integral an aspect of medieval warfare that any attempt by the Church to designate the peasantry as effective non-combatants was doomed to failure.[72] Equally, the same considerations deeply compromised any concept of immunity of the persons and property of the Church from attack and despoliation in time of war.[73]

Given this, the subsequent development from the 1020s of the Truce of God,[74] which sought to prohibit warfare between the knighthood itself during holy periods, on certain religious feasts and between specific days of the week, was bound to meet with widespread violation.[75] While there are

---

[71] Cowdrey, 'The Peace and Truce of God in the Eleventh Century', pp. 42–67; G. Duby, 'The Laity and the Peace of God', in *idem.*, *The Chivalrous Society*, pp. 123–33; *The Peace of God. Social Violence and Religious Response in France around the Year 1000*, ed. T. Head and R. Landes (Ithaca and London, 1992). For the reissue of the Peace and Truce by the Third Lateran Council (1179) and discussion of the canons *Treugas autem* and *Innovamus*, see Brundage, 'The Limits of War-Making Power', pp. 76–7.

[72] Below, pp. 258–90.   [73] Below, pp. 78–91.

[74] For early expressions of these limitations see the Councils of Toulouges (Elne), 1027, and Narbonne, 1054; J. D. Mansi (continued by J. B. Martin and L. Petit), *Sacrorum conciliorum nova et amplissima collectio* (Mansi), (Florcence, Venice, Paris and Leipzig, 1759–1927), XIX, cols. 483, 827–8. See also Orderic's account of the Councils of Lillebonne, 1080, Rouen, 1096 and Clermont, 1095 (Orderic, III, pp. 26–7; V, p. 13–14, 20–1). Bibliography on the extensive literature on the Peace and Truce is provided by Cowdrey, 'The Peace and Truce of God in the Eleventh Century' and Contamine, *War in the Middle Ages*, pp. 357–9, but see, *inter alia*, M. de Bouard, 'Sur les origines de la trève de Dieu en Normandie', *Annales de Normandie*, 9 (1957), pp. 179–89; and A. Grabois, 'De la Trève de Dieu à la paix de roi. Étude sur la transformation du mouvement du paix au XIIe siècle', *Mélanges offerts à René Crozet*, ed. P. Gallais and Y.-J. Riou, 2 vols. (Poitiers, 1966), I, pp. 585–96.

[75] Orderic, IV, pp. 235–6; V, pp. 24–5; VI, pp. 250–1, 460–1; WN, p. 460 (Richard and Philip fighting during Advent, 1195); Holdsworth, 'Ideas and Reality', pp. 69–71.

instances of warriors refraining from combat on Sundays and various religious festivals, these would appear to be very much the exception.[76] Easter was seen less as a brake to the prosecution of hostilities as the beginning of the campaigning season.[77] And while the dates of the frequent truces which interrupted the rhythm of warfare were calculated by saints' feast days, their inception and conclusion were predominantly matters of political and military expediency. The Church was not committed to a total ban on war, not did it espouse pacifism, except for the clergy.[78] The Truce of God had been not so naive as to attempt to prohibit knightly warfare in its entirety. Yet its restrictions, permitting fighting only from Monday morning to Wednesday evening, were wholly unrealistic.[79] For though the forces of kings and princes were exempt from its restrictions in order to enforce peace, refraining from fighting on Sundays or certain feasts would have played havoc with the effectiveness of a campaign and further compromised the effectiveness of the feudal host. Bitter local feuding was still less likely to abide by restrictions that might give an unscrupulous opponent tactical or strategic advantages.

Nevertheless, in theoretical terms, the importance of the Truce was that it marked a crucial change from more passive notions of self-protection and regulation of the martial activities of the knighthood towards the *oratores* and *laboratores* alone, to direct ecclesiastical interference in the scope of warfare between the *bellatores* themselves. From such attempted limitations of the incidence of war, it was only a short step to legislating on actual methods of fighting. Yet here again, canonical prohibition on the use of the crossbow and the employment of the itinerant bands of mercenary *routiers*, notorious for their cruelty and sacrilege, foundered on the practical dictates of war.[80]

---

[76] Orderic, v, pp. 258–9; vi, pp. 182–3, 540–1.

[77] Thus Bertran de Born's famous paean to the joys of war begins 'Well am I pleased by the gay Eastertide which makes leaves and flowers come . . . and I'm pleased when over the fields I see tents and pavilions pitched and I'm greatly cheered when I see lined up on the plain horsemen and horses, armed' (*Be.m platz lo gais temps de pascor, TLP*, pp. 158–9: Gouiran, *L'Amour et la Guerre*, pp. 732–5). Cf. *Rassa tan creis e monta e poia, TLP*, pp. 158–9, 'let the count [Richard] seek them [the lands of Aimar of Limoges] from him by force, and let us see him here soon at Eastertide!'; Gouiran, *L'Amour et la Guerre*, pp. 18–21.

[78] Brundage, 'The Limits of War-Making Power', p. 73; Holdsworth, 'Idea and Reality', p. 61, 'one does not find in Orderic any commendation of Christian pacifism, indeed it is hard to find within orthodox circles in the twelfth century'.

[79] The Truce, as laid out in the Council of Rouen, 1096, limited war 'from Septuagesima Sunday until dawn on the Monday after the octave of Pentecost, and from sunset on the Wednesday before Advent until the octave of Epiphany, and in every week throughout the year from sunset on Wednesday until dawn on Monday, and on all the feasts of St Mary with their vigils, and on all the feasts of the apostles with their vigils' (Orderic, v, pp. 20–1).

[80] For a study of the Church's attitudes to war, including the prohibition of the *routiers* and the crossbow, seen largely from the canonical standpoint, see Hehl, *Kirche und Krieg im 12. Jahrhundert*.

Clerics were indeed correct in recognizing the lethal qualities of the crossbow, which claimed many knightly and even royal victims in the eleventh and twelfth centuries.[81] Yet the crossbow was far from an innovation at the time of its ban by the Second Lateran Council,[82] and it is important to note that the canon also forbids the use of ordinary bows.[83] Churchmen were not outlawing the crossbow as a deadly novelty, but, as an extension of the Peace and Truce, they were seeking to prohibit all missile weapons which could inflict such casualties among Christian warriors. It was, however, this very effectiveness that caused commanders utterly to ignore this ban. Archers and crossbowmen continued to form an integral element of Anglo-Norman and Angevin armies, playing a key role in both battle and siege warfare.[84] Richard I and Philip Augustus, moreover, did not scruple to use crossbows themselves, not simply against the infidel in Outremer but against fellow Christians.[85]

Pragmatic military considerations similarly led to the uninterrupted use of the *routiers* by European rulers in the teeth of canonical prohibition by the Third Lateran Council. The professionalism of *routier* bands, which were in effect small standing armies, and their loyalty (if paid) in situations of rebellion, made such troops invaluable to Plantagenets and Capetians alike, and captains such as Mercadier and Cadoc stood high in royal favour.[86] Kings were acutely aware of the grave social disruption caused by such bands once they had been dismissed from employment, yet they were more than ready to unleash the *routiers* against their opponents; the terror inspired by their unsavoury reputation could only heighten their effectiveness. In short, the practical

---

[81] Below, p. 175.

[82] The crossbow had been known since at least the tenth century, and was illustrated in the Codex of Haimo of Auxerre (E. Harmuth, 'Die Armbrustbilder des Haimo von Auxerre', *Waffen- und Kostümkunde*, 12 (1970), pp. 127–30). It was in widespread use by the mid-eleventh century (*Carmen*, Appendix C, pp. 112–15, for collected references). The comments of P. Fournier, 'La prohibition par la deuxième concile de Latran d'armes jugées trop meutrières', *Revue générale de Droit international public*, 33 (1916), pp. 471–9, should be treated with caution as a nationalistic attempt to demonstrate that the French kings alone adhered to the Lateran's ban, until forced to adopt the weapons in response to its deployment by the Angevins – an uncritical acceptance of William le Breton's propaganda.

[83] *Decrees of the Ecumenical Councils*, ed. N. P. Tanner from the text of G. Alberigo *et al.*, 2 vols. (Georgetown, 1990), I, pp. 200–1, canon 18: 'Artem illam mortiferam et Deo odibilem balistariorum et sagittariorum adversus christianos et catholicos exerceri, de cetero sub anathemate prohibemus'; Contamine, *War in the Middle Ages*, p. 71, has been one of the few commentators to recognize that the prohibition covers bows as well.　　　[84] J. Bradbury, *The Medieval Archer* (Woodbridge, 1985), pp. 39–57.

[85] For Richard's use of the crossbow, see below, p. 100, n. 13. He personally shot a knight in the rebel garrison of Nottingham in 1194, but Howden does not specify whether this was with a crossbow or bow (GH, II, p. 239). Among other complaints laid before Innocent III by English ambassadors was that at the siege of Messina in 1191, Philip had not only failed to support Richard but had personally shot three of his knights with a crossbow (*Letters of Innocent III*, pp. 6–7).　　　[86] Below, p. 322 and n. 148.

dictates of warfare led the knighthood largely to ignore any conciliar pronouncement concerning a *ius in bello* that hindered the effective prosecution of hostilities.

Yet just as *Ritterfrömmigkeit* saw some of its most profound expressions in time of war, so the warrior aristocracy was fundamentally interconnected with the personnel and institutions of the Church. Monasticism remained essentially aristocratic, the majority of the higher clergy were drawn from the nobility, and churchmen played leading roles in secular administration. Ecclesiastical lands yielded military service, while many prelates held important castles. Some bishops were great castle-builders and might, as in the case of Gundulf of Rochester, even be military architects.[87] Though militant ecclesiastics, who violated canon law by the bearing of arms, were comparatively rare,[88] many powerful churchmen retained sizeable bodies of household knights and it was not uncommon for them to lead forces to the host or to direct military operations.[89] Church reformers and canonists found such close involvement with the *negotium saecularis* distressing, but the effective separation of secular and spiritual remained a practical impossibility given the extent of the Church's resources in land and literate personnel.

Given these interconnections, we should not posit a fundamental or irreconcilable hostility between the knighthood as warriors and the *oratores*, for the clergy and religious were a widely diverse group. Rather, the knights' rejection of elements of a *ius in bello* represent flashpoints between the often unrealistic idealism of ecclesiastical reformers and both the practical dictates of military professionalism and the chivalric ethos which it bred. Perhaps the most glaring clash of respective values comes in the attempt of the Council of Clermont, 1130, to forbid the tournament, in which, it was claimed, knights risked their lives and souls for mere vainglory.[90] Though in reality many clergy, particularly in England, adopted a far more tolerant attitude, recognizing the need for training and its enormous popularity among the knighthood, more vociferous critics saw the tournament as leading to mortal sin through pride, anger, envy and – because of feasting and the

---

[87] M. Ruud, 'Monks in the World: The Case of Gundulf of Rochester', *Anglo-Norman Studies*, 11 (1988), p. 248. The Le Poer bishops and Henry of Blois, bishop of Winchester were but prominent examples of bishops as castle-builders (*GS*, pp. 72–5: HN, pp. 25–8 (Roger of Salisbury and his nephews); *GS*, pp. 126–7 and n. 2 (Henry of Blois; cf. M. Biddle, 'Wolvesey: the *domus quasi palatium* of Henry de Blois in Winchester', *Château Gaillard*, 3 (1966), pp. 28–36)).

[88] According to Orderic, Odo of Bayeux and Geoffrey of Coutances bore arms and were certainly among William's leading commanders (Orderic, II, pp. 172–3, 204–5, 228–9, 266–7; IV, pp. 114–17; cf. *BT*, pl. 67). Henry of Blois was very much to the fore in military affairs, and the *Gesta Stephani* complained that he was not alone among his episcopal colleagues in bearing arms (*GS*, pp. 128–31, 144–5, 156–7). For the French warrior prelate, Philip of Beauvais, see above, p. 47 and n. 88.

[89] Holdsworth, 'Ideas and Reality', pp. 63–4.

[90] Mansi, XXI, col. 429 (Clermont, 1130, canon 9), cols. 460–1 (Reims, 1131, canon 12).

presence of women – gluttony and lust.[91] Yet it was exactly these aspects, viewed in a very different light, that ensured the enormous popularity of the tournament among the knights. It was the ideal arena to train for battle in the mêlée, to win glory and ransoms, to attract patronage of lords and the favour of ladies, and to meet one's brothers in arms.[92] As William of Newburgh perceptively commented,

> although such a solemn assembly of knights is forbidden by authority under a heavy censure, yet the fervour of those youths, who in their vanity seek glory in arms and who rejoice in the fervour of kings, who desire to have expert soldiers, has treated with contempt the provisions of this ecclesiastical decree, even to the present day.[93]

Barker has shown, however, that while ignoring the canonical prohibition, knights would pray, take communion and make votive offerings before the tournament just as before real battle, while such gatherings might serve as recruiting grounds for the crusade rather than, as clerical critics alleged, distractions from it.[94]

Resistance by the knighthood to clerical interference in matters deemed the preserve of warriors was thus far from incompatible with profound expressions of Christian belief. Keen has likewise shown that although the ceremony of dubbing remained resolutely secular in many of its aspects and that attempts by the priesthood to monopolize its rituals were strongly and successfully resisted, nevertheless the knighthood were highly conscious of a developed religious symbolism inherent in these rituals, as emphatically demonstrated by the early thirteenth-century tract the *Ordene de Chevalerie*.[95]

These considerations are epitomized by the conduct of William the Marshal, who had established his career by his excellence in the tournament. William had been on pilgrimage to Cologne and the Holy Land, and on his death-bed assumed the mantle of the Templars.[96] Yet the Marshal would have fiercely rejected the accusations of Bernard of Clairvaux in his tract 'In Praise of the New Chivalry' (1128 × 1136) that in contrast to the Templars, the wordly knighthood fought only for 'the irrational movements of anger, or the appetite for empty glory, or the desire for some sort of worldly possession', thereby jeopardizing their souls in unjust wars whether they killed or were killed. A barbed pun epitomized Bernard's view

---

[91] Barker, *The Tournament in England*, pp. 70–5; cf. also N. Denholm-Young, 'The Tournament in the Thirteenth Century', *Studies Presented to F. Powicke*, ed. R. W. Hunt, W. A. Pantin and R. W. Southern (Oxford, 1948) pp. 204–68; especially pp. 243–9.   [92] Below, pp. 149–53.   [93] WN, p. 423.
[94] Barker, *The Tournament in England*, pp. 74–83.   [95] Keen, *Chivalry*, pp. 6–8, 64–6, 71–7.
[96] HGM, 11. 6171–92, 7275–88, 18351–66.

of a decadent secular knighthood: 'I cannot call it a militia but a malice (. . . *saecularis . . . non dico militiae, sed malitiae*)'.[97] Yet William, the 'flower of chivalry', had not been moved to renounce the *militia secularis* which had brought him so much honour and success until extreme old age. Even on his death-bed, the Marshal kept a firm sense of priorities. When his clerk, Philip, advised William to sell his costly wardrobe of robes and use the money to assist his salvation, the Marshal rounded on him:

> Be silent, mischievous man! You have not the heart of a gentleman, and I have had too much of your advice. Pentecost is at hand, and my knights ought to have their new robes. This will be the last time that I will supply them, yet you seek to prevent me from doing it.[98]

The duties of good lordship were not to be overridden by the importuning of mere clerks. Pride and self-confidence in the validity of the profession of arms may well have been augmented by the crusades, but it was by no means created by it, nor did it remain dependent upon it.[99]

Tension was inevitable between the warrior aristocracy's self-perception and the theocratic views concerning the correct behaviour and function of the knighthood espoused by ecclesiastical theorists like John of Salisbury, Peter of Blois and Stephen of Fougères. For drawing on and elaborating the pronouncements of Gregory VII and his apologists Bonizo of Sutri and Anselm of Lucca, their views on chivalry were not only visibly much removed from the realities of *de facto* warfare, but were dominated by and subsumed into the wider Gregorian dogmas concerning the supremacy of ecclesiastical over lay society, of *sacerdotia* over *regnum*, of the papacy over kings and emperors.[100] The clerical ideal, moreover, clashed all too frequently with the actual conduct of the knights, and nowhere more starkly than in their treatment of the temporal possessions of the Church in time of war.

NON MILITIA SED MALITIA : CLERICAL REPORTAGE OF KNIGHTLY VIOLENCE AGAINST CHURCHES

The plundering of churches, their use as fortifications or their outright destruction in war naturally achieved great prominence in sources that were predominantly ecclesiastical in origin and even in some that were

---

[97] *De Laude novae militiae, Sancti Bernardi opera,* III: *Tractatus et opuscula,* ed. J. Leclercq and H. M. Rochais (Rome, 1963), p. 216: 'Quis igitur finis fructusve saecularis huius, non dico militiae, sed malitiae, si et accisor letaliter peccat, et occisus aeternaliter perit?'.

[98] *HGM,* 11. 18685–706; and see below, pp. 96–7.   [99] Below, pp. 142–9.

[100] Robinson, 'Gregory VII and the Soldiers of Christ', pp. 169–92.

not. Most chroniclers could furnish instances of the desecration of their own or neighbouring houses in times of warfare, and it is from these impassioned, localized and often highly coloured descriptions that the majority of evidence for lay behaviour towards the temporal possessions of the Church must be drawn.[101] The limitations of such material are readily apparent. Monastic or clerical writers naturally felt it incumbent upon themselves to record such sacrilege, thereby revenging themselves on the perpetrators by branding them as delinquents for posterity. As part of the same cathartic process, they also sought to provide a didactic warning by showing the inexorable vengeance of God to have overtaken the guilty. Thus Henry of Huntingdon regarded the deaths of both Geoffrey de Mandeville and Robert Marmion as divine punishment for the crime of expelling monks and fortifying holy places.[102] The *Gesta Stephani* likewise saw in the death of one of Robert of Gloucester's sons and the fatal hunting accident of Miles of Hereford clear retribution for the desecration of the convent at Wilton.[103] To emphasize the magnitude of their requital, such men were portrayed as dying excommunicate or unshriven.

Acts of sacrilege, moreover, provided effective moral ammunition to chroniclers engaged in partisan propaganda. Hence William of Malmesbury asserted that one of the justifications for Robert of Gloucester's attack on Stephen at Lincoln in 1141 was that the king had turned the cathedral into a castle.[104] And in stark contrast to Henry of Blois, who had not scrupled to destroy numerous churches by firing his own episcopal city of Winchester, Earl Robert 'though he was hard-pressed by daily battles between the king's men and his own and his success was not proportionate to his expectations, still he always thought he must refrain from burning churches . . .'[105] Gloucester was in fact equally guilty of sacrilege, breach of sanctuary and church burning, and it is fortunate that the *Gesta Stephani* exists as a corrective to Malmesbury. In turn, it fulminates against the earl's violation of sanctuary at Wilton.[106]

---

[101] Instances of chroniclers recording the violation of their own houses are plentiful. Thus Orderic could report the attack on Saint-Evroul by the men of Richer de Laigle (Orderic, VI, pp. 458–63); Ralph of Coggeshall the plundering by Savaric de Mauleon of Coggeshall (Coggeshall, p. 177); Geoffrey of Vigeois the Young King's despoliation of St Martial at Limoges (Vigeois, *RHF*, XVIII, pp. 216–17); William of Malmesbury the threats of Robert fitz Hubert (*HN* p. 43); the author of the *Gesta Stephani* the ill treatment of the bishop of Bath by Gilbert de Lacy (*GS*, pp. 58–63); Gilbert Foliot the exactions of William Beauchamp (Foliot, no. 3 p. 38); and Wendover the extortion of protection money from St Albans by Prince Louis, Fawkes de Bréauté and French *routiers* in turn (MP, III, pp. 8–9, 12, 16).

[102] HH, pp. 277–8. Marmion is struck down outside the very monastery at Coventry he had profaned, while at Ramsey, retribution falls not only on Geoffrey but also upon his captains of horse and foot, and upon Arnulf, his son, who suffers capture and exile.

[103] *GS*, pp. 148–9, 160–1; cf. *HN*, pp. 43–4.   [104] *HN*, p. 48.   [105] *Ibid.*, p. 60.   [106] *GS*, pp. 146–9.

In attempting to impugn the morality of the enemy, moreover, an author might be careful to omit any indications that such breaches of sanctuary had occurred because of armed resistance by knights from within churches. A greater effect of outrage was achieved by portraying sacrilegious aggressors attacking passive fugitives. Hence William of Malmesbury, hostile to Stephen's leading mercenary captain Willam of Ypres, relates how Wherwell abbey was burnt by him 'on the grounds that some of the Empress' adherents had taken refuge in it'.[107] The *Gesta Stephani*, however, while deploring this act of sacrilege, was quick to stress that the Empress's men were using it not as sanctuary but as a fortification.[108]

Invaluable though such material was for highlighting the moral supremacy of a patron, the indignation and moral horror at the violation of ecclesiastical immunities might in the eyes of some clergy override loyalty to a secular cause. Even though a firm supporter of Stephen, the author of the *Gesta Stephani* felt the need sharply to censure the king for fortifying a church as one of two siege-castles to contain Wallingford. When both siege-works were seized by an Angevin relief force under Miles of Hereford, he attributed this set-back to divine retribution for Stephen's sacrilegious deed.[109] The ruler existed not to commit acts of sacrilege, but to suppress the lawless and ungodly men who did; the whole mechanism of the Peace and Truce of God had developed precisely because of a hiatus in effective royal authority. Thus central to the arguments used by Orderic to justify Henry I's seizure of Normandy in 1105–6 was the fact that Robert Curthose had failed in his primary duty of defending the Norman church from the depredations of his nobility.[110] Conversely, Ralph of Diceto was at great pains to vindicate Henry II for expelling by force those of Richard's men who had violated the great church at Saintes by turning it into a fortress during the rebellion of 1173–4.[111]

Yet while reflecting a reaction to lay violence doubtless common to many of the clergy and further disseminated through these very writings, few if any clerical writers ventured to give any realistic appraisal of the motive of warriors in attacking churches, or demonstrating an appreciation of the logistical or tactical necessities underlying the perpetration of such acts.

---

[107] *HN*, p. 60.
[108] *GS*, pp. 132–3, and cf. pp. 130–3, where the *Gesta* notes that the Angevins had agreed to build a castle for a garrison of 300 knights at Wherwell abbey to give better defence against royalist attackers and to bring supplies into Winchester. The divergent accounts of the fighting around Wherwell are discussed by Meyer, *HGM*, III, p. 5, n. 2.   [109] *GS*, pp. 94–5.   [110] Orderic, VI, pp. 61–5, 86–7.
[111] Diceto, I, p. 380.

THE PLUNDERING OF CHURCHES: SACRILEGE OR MILITARY
EXPEDIENCY?

The violation of sanctuary

Notwithstanding their frequent use as banks,[112] the material wealth possessed by many churches, with their plate, crucifixes and reliquaries
adorned with precious metals and gems, made them extremely vulnerable
to despoliation in an age when booty was seen by knights and common soldiers alike as a necessary supplement to wages.[113] In time of war, moreover,
churches might become crowded with the goods of the local population
seeking protection for themselves and their chattels.[114] As a potent symbol
for the malaise of Normandy under Robert Curthose, Orderic described
how in 1105, when Bishop Serlo of Séez came to celebrate the Easter mass
for Henry I at Carentan, the church was so full 'of peasants' chests and
various tools and gear of all kinds' that the king and his men had to sit on
boxes at the back of the church.[115] In 1139, expecting an attack from
Robert of Gloucester's forces, the citizens of Worcester carried so many of
their possessions into the church that John of Worcester complained, no
doubt with some exaggeration, that it was being turned into 'a warehouse
for furniture' and that the monks hardly had room to celebrate the divine
service for the mass of chests and sacks.[116]

In theory, rights of sanctuary extended beyond a church itself to its
atrium or churchyard and adjoining cemetery. Such an area might provide
refuge for a sizeable body of people, who might remain there for considerable periods.[117] The Council of Lillebonne, 1080, ruled that refugees might
build habitations for themselves in cemeteries in frontier regions (*in*

---

[112] When, for example, Geoffrey de Mandeville attacked Cambridge in 1144, he broke into the
churches and plundered 'their ornaments and the wealth that the townsmen had laid up in them',
stripped the shrines of churches in the area and took 'anything deposited for safety in their treasuries' (*GS*, pp. 164–5; and cf. *The Chronicle of Jocelin of Brakelond* (Brakelond), ed. and tr. H. E. Butler
(London, 1949), p. 10). Even royal treasuries and archives may have originally been deposited in
monasteries (L. M. Larson, *The King's Household in England before the Norman Conquest* (Madison, 1904),
pp. 130–3; and J. Le Patourel, *Normandy and England, 1066–1144* (Stenton Lecture 1970, University of
Reading, 1971), p. 14, n. 35, noting that ducal records and cash had been deposited in monasteries in
Gascony as late as the thirteenth century.
[113] For a valuable comparison to what follows see A. T. Lucas, 'The Plundering and Burning of
Churches in Ireland, 7th to 16th Century', *North Munster Studies*, (1967), pp. 172–229.
[114] In 1215, the Fourth Lateran Council forbade the holding of markets, fairs or stalls in a church
'unless by reason of hostile invasion, sudden fire or other reasons it should be necessary to store
them [goods] there' (*Ecumenical Councils*, 1, p. 244, canon 19).   [115] Orderic, vi, pp. 60–3.
[116] JW, p. 56.
[117] In 1059, a bull of Nicholas II established the extent of such cemeteries as a circuit round the church
sixty paces in width for major churches and thirty paces for lesser churches and chapels (Mansi, xix,
col. 873). For a discussion of this role of cemeteries, see L. Musset, 'Cimiterium ad refugium tantum
vivorum non ad sepulturam mortuorum', *Revue du Moyen Age Latin*, 4 (1948), pp. 56–60.

marchiis) in time of war and live in this outer sanctuary for safety, provided they left following the cessation of hostilities.[118] In practice, however, unscrupulous clergy might amerce refugees for the benefit of this protection which was all too ineffectual.[119] For such an additional concentration of moveables made churches a still more tempting target for knights, who frequently did not scruple to seize these goods and even the peasants themselves for ransom.

Occasionally warriors might observe sanctuary. Orderic noted with approval how Richer de Laigle spared the peasants of Gacé, who on being attacked by his knights, threw themselves at the foot of a wooden crucifix at the side of a road:

> At the sight Richer was moved by the fear of God, and for sweet love of his Saviour dutifully respected his cross . . . So the honourable man, in awe of his Creator, spared about one hundred villagers, from whom he might have extorted a great price if he had been so irreverent as to capture them.[120]

Nevertheless, the fact that Orderic records the incident as 'something that deserves to be remembered forever' strongly suggests that in his act of clemency, Richer was proving himself to be the exception.[121]

If, moreover, a tidy sum could be made from ransoming groups of peasants, then it is not surprising to find that sanctuary was often violated in order to seize knightly fugitives for their far larger ransoms. As both a royalist and an ecclesiastic, the author of the *Gesta Stephani* was predictably outraged when, after defeating Stephen's forces at Wilton in 1143, Robert of Gloucester dragged the fugitive royalists out from sanctuary at the nunnery of St Etheldreda. Yet it was natural that the earl should seek to seize as many of the king's supporters as he could in order further to weaken Stephen's position.[122] Again, there were honourable exceptions.[123] Nevertheless, few knights were prepared to forgo either the financial or political advantage accruing from the seizure of valuables from churches or

---

[118] *Layettes du Trésor des Chartes*, ed. M. A. Teulet and M. J. De Laborde, 3 vols. (Paris, 1866–75), I, no. 22, p. 26, c. XI; Orderic, III, pp. 28–31 and p. 29, n. 5.

[119] Thus the Council of Lillebonne laid down that bishops should have no right to amercements from refugees other than those enjoyed before they fled to the sanctuary (Orderic, III, pp. 28–31). For instances of episcopal abuse of sanctuary see *Layettes de Trésor des Chartes*, III, no. 4663, p. 571; Musset, 'Cimiterium ad refugium', p. 58.   [120] Orderic, VI, pp. 250–1.

[121] Holdsworth, 'Ideas and Reality', p. 70.

[122] GS, pp. 146–9. For the violation of sanctuary even in peacetime for political reasons see the *cause célèbre* of Hubert de Burgh, seized first from Brentwood chapel in 1232, then from Devizes church the following year despite vocal clerical opposition (MP, III, pp. 227–230, 249–50; Powicke, *Henry III and the Lord Edward*, pp. 82–3, 139–40).

[123] When in 1119, for example, the French took by surprise the Norman garrison of Andely, King Louis allowed Henry I's natural son Richard and his knights, who had fled to the church, to depart freely 'out of reverence for the Virgin Mother who bore the Saviour of the world, whose church he had resorted to in faith to obtain her help' (Orderic, VI, pp. 216–19).

the taking prisoner of those who had sought sanctuary within them, simply for the sake of ecclesiastical precept.

Breach of sanctuary, however, was in violation of canon law. Appeal could thus be made to the church courts against those who infringed it, unlike instances of the disregard for secular custom in war for which there was as yet no established source of legal redress. A valuable insight into this process is furnished by a group of Gilbert Foliot's letters, dealing with several alleged violations of sanctuary by Roger, earl of Hereford. In 1150, Ralph of Worcester had appealed first to Gilbert as bishop of Hereford, then to Archbishop Theobald in his capacity as papal legate, against Roger, whom he accused of violating sanctuary by seizing some of Ralph's knights in the abbey of Evesham.[124] Similarly, Gilbert de Lacy had earlier lodged a case with Foliot against the earl of Hereford, alleging he had taken prisoner four of Gilbert's knights by violating the protection of a cemetery and church.[125] In both instances, Roger's political opponents were invoking the authority of the Church against him, both to discredit him as a sacrilegious brigand and to obtain the release of their men without ransom.

Roger of Hereford's response to Gilbert de Lacy's suit is revealing. He claimed that he had taken the knights not in, but outside the cemetery, 'and on this account had legitimately held them to ransom'. Indeed, far from committing sacrilege himself, he had captured de Lacy's knights in the act of seizing the church in question, and had accordingly treated them as excommunicated men, since they had violated the peace of the Church by attempting this act of aggression during the holy Ember days following Pentecost. He had, moreover, appealed to Archbishop Theobald, thereby considerably delaying the case. Roger was turning the very mechanisms of appeal against his accusers.[126]

The two cases once more underline the great importance of ransom as the overriding motive for the violation of sanctuary. Although Foliot assumed the Church was empowered to release the captives from the earl of Hereford's custody, he was nonetheless concerned to ensure that if the case against the earl was not proven, the prisoners, whose release Foliot had commanded in order for them to attend the trial, would be returned to Roger.[127] All parties clearly regarded the taking of knights for ransom outside any protection of sanctuary as a fully legitimate act, and despite his

---

[124] The Letters and Charters of Gilbert Foliot (Foliot), ed. C. N. L. Brooke and A. Morely (Cambridge, 1967), no. 93, pp. 127–30. For the dating of this and other letters dealing with Roger's alleged offences (nos. 94–6) see Foliot, no. 93, pp. 128–9. For Gilbert see C. N. L. Brooke and A. Morely, Gilbert Foliot and his Letters (Cambridge, 1965).   [125] Foliot, nos. 94, 95, pp. 130–3.   [126] Ibid., no. 96, p. 134.
[127] Foliot, no. 94, p. 131.

suspicion of Roger,[128] Foliot was careful not to prejudice his rights in this matter.

The plundering of churches

If considerations of ransom led knights to violate the sanctuary of churches and their cemeteries, the riches of the churches themselves were a standing temptation which few could resist in times of unrest. Indeed, the habitual and ubiquitous looting of churches themselves in time of war forms one of the most striking features of medieval warfare and directly challenges any assumptions that the Christian element in chivalry acted as an effective restraint on the conduct of the warriors.

At times, such behaviour could be the result of indiscipline. According to Orderic, during the Angevin offensive against Normandy in 1136, troops destroyed churches and attacked priests 'as pagans do', with the common stipendary knights (*gregarii milites*) being the worst offenders.[129] Petitioned by priests Geoffrey of Anjou and his commanders 'sent a herald to Le Sap to command the whole army not to desecrate holy things, but there were reckless looters in that great mob who paid no attention to the commands of the magnates'.[130]

To outraged ecclesiastics like Orderic and William of Malmesbury, it was mercenaries who loomed large as undisciplined plunderers of churches, and employment of such impious brigands was another stick with which clerical propagandists could beat the antagonists of a patron.[131] That there was considerable validity in such complaints is suggested by the repeated correlation between acts of despoliation and the employment of mercenaries. Invaluable because of their military professionalism and dependability in situations of revolt, mercenaries not only exacerbated the cost of war but also ensured the ubiquity of men ready to catch the nearest way to ensure or supplement their wages.

The sack of the nunnery at Wilton was carried out in part by Robert fitz Hildebrand, an Angevin mercenary leader, while Geoffrey de Mandeville had in his pay a large force of *gregarii milites* when he carried out

---

[128] Roger's alleged violation of Leominster is mentioned without further detail in Foliot, no. 96, p. 135.

[129] Orderic, VI, pp. 470–3. For *milites gregarii* see *ibid.*, VI, p. 350, n. 1; M. Chibnall, 'Mercenaries and the *Familia Regis* under Henry I', *History*, 62 (1977), pp. 15–23, reprinted in Strickland, *Anglo-Norman Warfare*, pp. 84–92, at pp. 88–9.   [130] Orderic, VI, pp. 470–3.

[131] Thus William of Malmesbury described the Flemish and Breton mercenaries who flocked to Stephen in 1136 as 'a class of men full of greed and violence, who cared nothing for breaking into churchyards or robbing churches; moreover, they not only rode down members of the religious orders, but even dragged them off into captivity' (*HN*, p. 17; cf. *ASC*, 'E', *s.a.* 1102).

his depredations in Cambridgeshire in 1144.[132] Savaric de Mauleon, who though he commanded units of John's mercenaries was himself no mere *routier* captain but a leading Poitevin noble and a troubadour of repute, plundered Tilty abbey during the celebration of mass on Christmas Day itself, 1215, and on 1 January repeated this sacrilege at Coggeshall.[133]

Yet while stipendiary troops were doubtless difficult to discipline, the stripping of churches was widely practised by both lay and ecclesiastical magnates, and was sanctioned by commanders of the highest rank. In 1136, Roger de Tosny failed to take the castle of La Croix-St-Leufroi, but 'burnt the monks' bourg, attacked the church, carried off the fugitives hiding in the enclosed monastic buildings, and seized the treasures of both monks and refugees'.[134] Robert, abbot of Saint-Pierre-sur-Dives, turned the abbey he had purchased off Robert Curthose into a fortress during the disturbances of 1106, garrisoned it with knights and sold the church ornaments to pay his men.[135] William of Malmesbury similarly accuses Henry of Blois of stripping the great crucifix given by Cnut to the New Minster, which had fallen when his men fired the town, and of using the great wealth gained thereby to pay the *milites gregarii*, who, notes the *Gesta Stephani*, he had hired 'at very great expense'.[136]

The direct relationship between the ruthless mulct of ecclesiastical wealth and the need for ready cash to retain the service of such troops is forcefully illustrated by the movements of the Young King and his brother Geoffrey in the Limousin during the revolt against their father and Richard in 1183. The Young King, notorious for his prodigality, lavished money on the Brabançon and Basque *routiers* in his service, fearing lest they desert to his father for the promise of a higher wage.[137] Such profligacy soon exhausted the 'loan' of 20,000 shillings he had obtained from the citizens of Limoges, and the Young King was quickly forced to turn to the richly endowed religious houses of the area.

The first victim was St Martial in Limoges, whose monks were expelled while Henry's men stripped gold and silver from statues and reliquaries and took vessels and cash from the monastic treasury. Geoffrey of Vigeois provides a doleful inventory of his abbey's losses, remarking bitterly that while the Young King gave a sealed chirograph promising the repayment of the wealth thus 'borrowed', his agents deliberately undervalued the amount

[132] *GS*, pp. 148–9, 152–3, 164–5.

[133] Coggeshall, p. 177. On Savaric see H. J. Chaytor, *Savaric de Mauléon, Baron and Troubador* (Cambridge, 1939).   [134] Orderic, VI, pp. 474–5.   [135] *Ibid.*, VI, pp. 74–5.

[136] *HN*, pp. 59–60; *GS*, pp. 128–9. Malmesbury noted that the cross yielded 'more than five hundred marks of silver ... and thirty of gold, and they helped to provide largesse for the knights' (*HN*, pp. 59–60). 'Florence' of Worcester confirms its enormous value (FW, II, pp. 135–6).

[137] Vigeois, *RHF*, XVIII, p. 216.

taken.[138] Even this proved insufficient to keep his forces in the field, and young Henry repeated such sacrilege at Grandmont, where he stole a costly pyx given by his father, and at other churches in the Angoumois, including the monastery of La Couronne. It was little wonder, therefore, that when he fell ill shortly after having despoiled the tomb of St Amadour at Rocamadour,[139] the chroniclers were swift to point up the correlation between his fatal sickness and his recent sacrilege.

One must, however, set such despoliation in context. Ecclesiastics themselves might not be averse to plundering the wealth of their own churches or those of others. The Conquest itself had witnessed the wholesale stripping of Anglo-Saxon religious houses, often enough by their new Norman incumbents.[140] Likewise, the need of lords for ready cash in return for pledges of land with which to embark on the First Crusade led to the spoliation by certan bishops of valuables from churches under their jurisdiction.[141]

Despite their sacred associations, moreover, reliquaries and church fittings were frequently the last resort of a financially desperate community.[142] The fate of Ely, forced to strip many of its statues and reliquaries to buy the goodwill of the king following its support for the rebels of 1071, cannot have been an isolated one in the political upheavals of the 1060s and 1070s, while ecclesiastics were forced to strip reliquaries, melt down chalices, crucifixes and book covers to meet the taxation entailed by Rufus when Robert Curthose pawned the duchy to him in 1096.[143] In exceptional circumstances, churchmen were even prepared to sanction despoliation by laymen. During the punitive sack of Lincoln by royalist forces in 1217, the papal legate explicity authorized the pillaging of the cathedral and other churches, because their clergy were excommunicate for having sided with the baronial rebels and Prince Louis.[144]

Some commanders might stop short of actual pillage, but instead demanded protection money from religious houses. During a foray into

---

[138] *Ibid.*, p. 217; Howden (*GH*, I, p. 299) ascribes the spoliation to Geoffrey, but as prior of St Martial, Vigeois must be regarded as the more authoritative in placing responsibility for the extortion squarely upon the Young King.   [139] Howden, II, p. 278.
[140] The evidence is discussed by C. R. Dodwell, *Anglo-Saxon Art: A New Perspective* (Manchester University Press 1982), pp. 216–18. Cf. Orderic, IV, pp. 42–3, where Odo of Bayeux is accused of stripping English churches of their ornaments.
[141] Riley-Smith, *The First Crusade and the Idea of Crusading*, p. 44 and examples cited on pp. 174–5, n. 55.
[142] Jocelin of Brakelond recorded how even in peacetime the monks of Bury had considered utilizing the gold- and silver-covered statues of St John and the Virgin and even stripping the feretory of St Edmund itself in order to pay the papacy for a privilege of exemption from a legatine visitation by Archbishop Richard (Brakelond, p. 5; cf *GH*, I. p. 106).
[143] *Liber Eliensis*, ed. E. O. Blake (Camden Third Series, XCII, London, 1962), pp. 194–5; Eadmer, pp. 74–5; William of Malmesbury, *De gestis pontificum Anglorum*, ed. N. Hamilton (Rolls Series, 1870), p. 432; *GR*, II, pp. 371–2.   [144] MP, III, p. 23; below, pp. 280–1.

Normandy in 1137, Geoffrey of Anjou accepted 110 marks from the monks of Dives to prevent themselves from sharing the fate of Bazoches-au-Houlme, which he had burnt together with its church containing sixteen people. Similarly the monks of Fécamp bought his protection for the town of Argences for a sum of 100 marks.[145] The following year saw King David of Scotland receiving 27 marks from the monastery at Tynemouth to spare it from pillage, and it is unlikely that the monks of Hexham received their charter of immunity during the same campaign without some payment.[146]

Nowhere is this process more starkly or more eloquently revealed than in the extensive but matter-of-fact list of protection payments and losses incurred during the war of 1215–17, written out by William of Trumpington, abbot of St Albans and copied by Matthew Paris into his *Gesta abbatum*. According to William, 'the total of money lost and of ransoms paid during the war [to protect] Abbot William and his mens' manors, and those of Dom Martin the cellarer', was £2,555.[147] Numerous small payments in money, horses and other goods to safe-guard the town of St Albans, the abbey and its outlying manors had been paid not only to Prince Louis of France but also to John's commanders Fawkes de Bréauté and Engelard de Cigogné, and to a host of local lords who, irrespective of political affiliation, had been able to threaten sufficient force to extract protection money.[148] Instead of suffering a single act of despoliation, the abbey was being spared by all protagonists so that it could be repeatedly milked for bribes and 'gifts' to avoid destruction.

Tenserie: *the long-term exploitation of ecclesiastical resources*

Both the plundering of the moveable wealth of churches and the extortion of protection money were *ad hoc*, short term means of finance resorted to by commanders of itinerant forces. In periods of sustained hostilities,

---

[145] Orderic, vi, pp. 482–3.   [146] RH, pp. 80–1; below, p. 324.

[147] *Gesta abbatum monasterii sancti Albani*, ed. H. T. Riley, 3 vols. (Rolls Series, 1867), i, pp. 297–8; *Chronicles of Matthew Paris: Monastic Life in the Thirteenth Century*, ed. and tr. R. Vaughn (New York and Glouchester, 1984), pp. 58–9. In addition, the abbot swore that the abbey had lost in one year at least one hundred draught, sumpter, cart and riding horses, as well as carts, asses, pigs and much timber (*ibid.*, p. 259; tr., p. 38). It was little wonder that the St Albans chroniclers Roger of Wendover and Matthew Paris vilified Fawkes de Bréauté and rejoiced in his final downfall.

[148] The hapless Abbot William of St Albans had been the victim of such extortion twice within two months, first at the hands of Prince Louis in December 1216, then in January by Fawkes de Bréauté, who demanded three hundred pounds of silver to prevent the burning of both the monastery and the town, while in April 1217, St Albans was actually pillaged by Louis's *routiers* (MP, iii, pp. 8–9, 12, 16).

however, local seigneurs attempted to meet the great cost of warfare by appropriating ecclesiastical rents and labour through exactions known collectively as *tenserie*.[149] The author of the *Gesta Stephani*, again stressing the hire of stipendiary knights as the chief cause of expense to lords, made a direct link between the exhaustion of moveable plunder and the instigation of *tenserie*.[150] Its principal features were forced labour for the construction or maintenance of castles, and the exaction of money and supplies to support the *milites* who garrisoned them.

Thus Orderic recounts how, confronted by Giroie's new castle of Montaigu, Robert de Bellême 'compelled all the peasants on his own and his neighbours lands to forced labour (*ad angariam*) to pull it down'. He further forced the men of Saint Evroul 'to help in the work on his own castles, seizing the possessions of any who defaulted, and even cruelly threatened to destroy the abbey itself unless they would be subject to him in all things as their lord'.[151] Bellême was far from alone in such actions. The process was widespread, and closely linked to the breakdown of royal or ducal authority, becoming visible in Normandy under Robert Curthose and in England during Stephen's reign from the 1140s. Among the catalogue of depredations and exactions suffered by the nuns of Holy Trinity, Caen, during the rule of Duke Robert, the future Henry I himself is accused of forcing their tenants to work on his castles.[152] When, in 1143, Miles of Hereford 'needed a great deal of money for the hire of knights he had assembled against the king, he compelled the churches he had brought under the yoke of his lordship to pay unprecedented levies'.[153] By 1144, John fitz Gilbert, William the Marshal's father, was but one of several prominent magnates exacting similar services.[154] The nature of these exactions, suffered among others by the abbeys of Ramsey, Abingdon and Gloucester, were detailed by Gilbert Foliot in a letter asking Simon, bishop

---

[149] For a general discussion of *tenserie*, see the comments of J. H. Round and P. Toynbee in *The Academy*, 1001 (1891), pp. 37–8, and more fully in J. H. Round, *Geoffrey de Mandeville* (London, 1892), pp. 215, 414–16. In a letter written to Archbishop Theobald and his bishops in 1144 at the request of Nigel, bishop of Ely, Pope Lucius complained that Ely had been ransacked and that certain lords were despoiling villages and men, and oppressing them with unjust labour and exactions 'sub nomine tensarium' (W. Holtzmann, *Papsturkunden in England*, (Abhandlung der Gesellschaft der Wissenschaften zu Gottingen, Philologisch-Historische Klasse, Dritte Folge, no. 14, Berlin 1935), II: 1, no. 40, p. 188). The legatine council of London in 1151 decreed that the church and its possessions should be free 'ab operationibus et exactionibus quas vulgo tenserias sive tallagias vocant' (*Councils and Synods with Other Documents Relating to the English Church*, ed. D. Whitelock, M. Brett and C. N. L. Brooke (Oxford, 1981), I: ii, p. 823 and n. 4).   [150] *GS*, pp. 154–5.

[151] Orderic, IV, pp. 296–7.   [152] Haskins, *Norman Institutions*, p. 66.   [153] *GS*, pp. 158–9.

[154] *Ibid.*, pp. 168–9. The accusations of the *Gesta Stephani* are confirmed by a letter of pope Eugenius to four English prelates in 1147, naming John the Marshal, together with William Martel, Hugh de Bolbec and William de Beauchamp, among those accused of plundering the lands of Abingdon and of exacting forced labour for castle-building (*Chronicon monasterii de Abingdon*, ed. J. Stevenson (Rolls Series, 1858), II, p. 200).

of Worcester, to excommunicate William Beauchamp for his oppression of Gloucester abbey.[155]

The imposition of such *tenserie* has been seen as one manifestation of the establishment or extension of the rights of lay advocacy, whereby patrons exploited troubled times to extend their power over religious houses in their locality.[156] Equally, it is possible that in demanding forced labour on castles, lords may have been attempting to extend or usurp pre-existing feudal obligations owed in respect of 'castle-work (*operatio castelli*)'.[157]

DAMAGE AND DESTRUCTION OF CHURCHES IN WAR

Given both their extent and vulnerability, it was inevitable that the landed holdings of ecclesiastical foundations should suffer loss during hostilities, even when they were not deliberate targets. Such damage might involve lands, crops and livestock being caught up in the foraging by an army for supplies or in the laying waste of a hostile countryside during siege or a chevauchée. Monasteries might own extensive granaries which could be utilized by a commander to feed his men or destroyed to deprive the enemy of supplies.[158] During times of siege, the fabric of churches might be stripped for the needs of defence or assault.[159] Referring to the great siege of Baldwin de Redvers's garrison in Exeter in 1136, Stephen granted lands to the cathedral church at Exeter 'in compensation for the damage which I did to the aforesaid church during the siege'.[160] Similarly, in 1153 Henry Plantagenet made grants to St Paul's, Bedford 'in compensation for destruction and losses' presumably incurred during his siege of the town that year.[161]

---

[155] Foliot, no. 3, p. 38, and cf. no. 27, pp. 67–8. Beauchamp had taken wheat destined for the brothers' use, exacted monthly cash payments for the provision of his men, forced the abbey's men to plough and sow land at both the autumn and spring sowing, and requisitioned (*angariare*) innumerable services. The chronicle of Ramsey abbey states that it was burdened by *tenserie* during the unrest of Stephen's reign, while the *Gesta Stephani* notes that the Flemings Henry de Caldret and his brother Ralph imposed burdens and forced labours on church lands in Gloucestershire, including Gloucester abbey (*Historia Ramesiensis*, ed. W. D. Macray in *Chronicon abbatiae Ramesiensis* (Rolls Series, 1886), p. 334; *GS*, pp. 188–9).

For further details on such exactions, and a stimulating discussion of the relationship between lay lords and church communities in general during Stephen's reign, see E. King, 'The Anarchy of Stephen's Reign', *TRHS*, 5th ser., 34 (1984), pp. 133–53.

[156] Mason, '*Timeo Barones et Dona Ferentes*', pp. 63–4; cf. King, 'The Anarchy of Stephen's Reign', p. 137.

[157] Stenton, *English Feudalism*, pp. 171, 175–6.

[158] Hence in his campaign in East Anglia in 1216, John systematically destroyed the granaries of Bury St Edmunds and Crowland, (*Matthei Parisiensis monachi Sancti Albani historia Anglorum, sive, ut vulgo dicitur, historia minor*, (MP, *Historia Anglorum*), ed. F. Madden, 3 vols. (Rolls Series, 1866), II, pp. 188–9).

[159] In 1183, for example, when the citizens of Limoges took up arms against Henry II and Richard, they seized wood from six or more churches to build ramparts and towers (Vigeois, *RHF*, XXVIII, p. 214).

[160] *RRAN*, III, no. 285, p. 107. [161] *Ibid.*, no. 81, p. 32.

The proximity of some castles to churches or conventual buildings greatly increased the risk of damage by direct involvement in the fighting.[162] Churches themselves were frequently converted into makeshift castles. As Cronne has noted:

> in an age of timber and wattle-and-daub building, when stone houses were still uncommon and a great many of the castles were of a motte-and-bailey type, a stone-built church was always a potential and sometimes an actual strongpoint. A military commander neglected it at his peril in the course of any operations in its neighbourhood.[163]

Despite the limitations of their size, parish churches were of some military value for both defence and offence. Hence the Empress fortified the tower of Bampton as an outpost for her vital base at Oxford, while Stephen fortified a church as one of two siege-castles to contain Brian fitz Count at Wallingford.[164] Such practices, however, were hardly an innovation caused by the troubles of the 'anarchy'. The stone towers of some Anglo-Saxon churches, particularly when associated with thegnly residences, may well have been designed with defence in mind as much as the symbolism of lordship.[165] And in southern France, defensive features were integral to the design of many parish churches and larger ecclesiastical buildings, not only in the thirteenth and fourteenth centuries, but sometimes considerably earlier.[166] Nevertheless, although it was naturally more economic in time and labour resources to occupy a church rather than throw up a motte, even rudimentary siege-castles, let alone the more complex examples of motte-and-bailey castles, probably offered greater all-round protection than parish churches, which, despite their construction in stone, were still highly vulnerable to attack by fire. Their conversion into fortifications was an expedient usually dictated by haste.

---

[162] At Malmesbury, for example, Roger, bishop of Salisbury 'had begun a castle actually in the church-yard, hardly a stone's throw from the abbey'. As a result the abbey was caught up in the fighting that ensued in 1144–5, and prompted Gilbert Foliot to complain bitterly to Eugenius III that the church was being turned into a battleground (*HN*, p. 25; *GS*, pp. 170–1, 178–9; Foliot, no. 35, pp. 74–5). Writing once more to Eugenius, Foliot informed the pope of the plight of Reading abbey, attacked by both factions in the civil war as it lay on the political border (Foliot, no. 85, p. 120).

[163] Cronne, *The Reign of King Stephen*, p. 2.

[164] *GS*, pp. 138–9, 92–5. Gilbert Foliot also complained to Bishop Simon of Worcester that the church of St Mary, Slaughter, had been turned into a castle and was the scene of fighting (Foliot, no. 5, p. 40).

[165] See A. Williams, 'A Bell-house and a Burgh-geat: Lordly Residences in England before the Norman Conquest', in *Ideals and Practice of Medieval Knighthood*, 4 (1992), pp. 221–40; and D. F. Renn, 'Burghgeat and Gonfanon: Two Sidelights from the Bayeux Tapestry', *Anglo-Norman Studies*, 16 (1993), pp. 177–98, especially pp. 178–86.

[166] On fortified churches in France see R. Rey, *Les vielles églises fortifiées du midi de la France* (Paris, 1925); P. Barbier, *La France féodal, 1: Chateaux forts et églises fortifiées* (Paris, 1968); G. Fournier, *Le château dans la France médiévale. Essai de sociologie et monumentale* (Paris, 1978), pp. 201–9.

Cathedrals or large conventual buildings, by virtue of their size and strength of construction, offered a far more significant defence, even though in England or Normandy there were few buildings comparable to the castle-like structures in southern France such as the cathedral at Albi.[167] Their towers might be large enough to mount engines on, while they could accommodate sizeable numbers of troops. Thus Geoffrey de Mandeville occupied Ramsey abbey in 1144 and Robert Marmion Coventry, while the great church at Saintes constituted a major element of Richard's defences against his father in 1174.[168] Such buildings were of particular tactical effectiveness when used as siege-castles against the existing castle in a city, which might often be in close proximity. In 1141, Stephen had used Lincoln cathedral as a fortified base during his siege of Rannulf of Chester's castle only yards away, while the year previously, Geoffrey Talbot had expelled the monks from Hereford cathedral, garrisoned it and, placing engines on the tower, threw up a motte in the churchyard to besiege the royal castle.[169]

The common tactic of firing suburbs or even towns themselves to drive off attackers made the burning of churches a frequent, if often unintentional, occurrence.[170] The death of two anchorites burned during William the Conqueror's attack on Mantes in 1087, and the infamous burning of the church at Vitry in which 1,300 people perished during Louis VII's war against Theobald of Champagne, appear to have been the accidental result of firing other buildings.[171] Yet though not seeking the deliberate destruction of churches *per se* in such instances, commanders must have been fully aware that many ecclesiastical buildings – and possibly their occupants – might perish in these blazes.

Military expediency, however, overrode such considerations. Where a garrison held a castle or citadel against a hostile force or populace who controlled the town or city in which it was situated, the indiscriminate use of fire was often the last resort of the beleaguered. Hence in 1099, the hard pressed Norman garrison of the citadel at Le Mans fired molten dross from their engines into the town, which set alight the roofs of the houses

---

[167] The most prominent example of a fortified church in England from this period is furnished by Lincoln cathedral; R. Gem, 'Lincoln Minster: *Ecclesia Pulchra, Ecclesia Fortis*', *Medieval Art and Architecture at Lincoln Cathedral* (British Archaeological Association Conference Transactions, 8, 1986 for 1982), pp. 9–28.

[168] HH, p. 277: *GS*, pp. 164–5: *Historia Ramesiensis*, pp. 329–32; Round, *Geoffrey de Mandeville*, pp. 209–11; Dicto, I. p. 380.

[169] *HN*, p. 48; *GS*, pp. 108–11; JW, p. 58, n. 4. The siege of Hereford is also the subject of two letters of Gilbert Foliot (Foliot, nos. 1 and 2, pp. 33–7).

[170] For the use of fire in general see J. F. Fino, 'Le feu et ses usages militaires', *Gladius*, 8 (1970), pp. 15–30; Contamine, *War in the Middle Ages*, p. 244, n. 15; Gillingham, 'Richard I and the Science of War', p. 85; below, pp. 265–6.

[171] Orderic, IV, pp. 78–9; ASC, 'E', *s.a.* 1087, p. 163; and for Vitry, see *RHF*, XII, p. 472; *RHF*, XIII, p. 272.

and quickly reduced the whole city to ashes.[172] Similarly, when besieged by Matilda's forces in Winchester castle in 1141, Henry of Blois's garrison flung out firebrands into the town, whose citizens were firm supporters of the Empress. The whole town was burnt, including Hyde abbey (the New Minster), the nunnery of St Mary's and over forty churches.[173] Henry was not only abbot of Glastonbury and the bishop of Winchester but a papal legate and a man renowned for his cultural patronage. Yet he was also a competent soldier, who did not scruple to burn his great episcopal city at a moment of grave strategic and political crisis.

Sometimes, moreover, the firing of towns was not adopted simply as a final expediency, but as a calculated policy of aggression to inflict total destruction. When, in 1105, Henry I set fire to Bayeux, burning the town, its churches and many men, it was a deliberate act of terrorism designed to break further resistance to his occupation of the duchy.[174] The same action was employed by Henry against Evreux in 1119, to strike at the principal base of one of the leading rebels Amaury de Montfort, even though the king was fully aware of, and – if Orderic may be believed – deeply concerned about, the destruction to ecclesiastical property that would ensue.[175]

There are numerous instances of the premeditated firing of individual churches, even when people were sheltering inside. In describing Robert de Bellême's ravaging of the Hiemois in 1102, Orderic noted that 'many villages were depopulated and churches burnt to the ground with the people who had fled to take refuge in them', while he has Serlo, bishop of Séez accuse Bellême of burning the church of Tournay in his diocese with forty-five men and women in it.[176] Despite Orderic's hostility to Bellême, it is clear that in his treatment of churches he was far from the exception. When in 1140, for example, Robert of Gloucester took Nottingham, the citizens everywhere fled into churches; some were captured, others killed, but many were burnt alive in those very churches.[177] In 1136, Waleran de Meulan and his brother Robert attacked the village of Bougy-sur-Risle, 'and at the suggestion of the earl of Leicester set fire to the houses round about and burnt the beautiful church of St Mary Magdalene with the men and women in it'.[178] In the same war, Roger de Tosny burnt down the church of St Stephen at Vaudreuil.[179] Magnates, it seems, did not scruple to burn considerable numbers of people as an end in itself. If in these instances there was

---

[172] Orderic, v, pp. 254–5.   [173] HN, p. 59; GS, pp. 130–1; FW, ii, p. 133.

[174] Orderic, vi, pp. 78–9; Serlo of Bayeux, De capta Bajocensium civitate, in The Anglo-Latin Satirical Poets and Epigrammatists, ed. T. Wright, 2 vols. (London, 1892), ii, pp. 241–51.

[175] Orderic, vi, pp. 228–9, and below, p. 94.

[176] Orderic, vi, pp. 32–3, 62–3. When supporters of Duke Robert occupied the nunnery of Almenèches as a base against him, Bellême burnt the place to the ground (ibid., vi, pp. 34–5).

[177] Gervase, i. p. 122.   [178] Orderic, vi, pp. 464–5.   [179] Ibid., vi, pp. 474–7; cf. HN, p. 43.

an absence of continued opposition, the incineration of those seeking sanctuary in churches must be seen as one of the ultimate expressions of total war. Such conduct is among the sharpest indications of the short-term ineffectuality of concepts of moral restraint and ecclesiastical strictures on the behaviour of knights in war.

THE PSYCHOLOGY OF DESTRUCTION

The destruction of churches, however, was not necessarily insensate. Religious foundations, which often served as the necropolis of a noble family, might be deliberately targeted precisely because they were tangible symbols of an opponent's status and prestige. If we place in the context of war Orderic's well-known statement that the Norman aristocracy vied with each other to build bigger and more richly endowed monasteries, one reason for the widespread sacking and burning of religious establishments becomes more intelligible.[180] As with the destruction of castles or manor houses, assaults on churches marked not simply the negation of an immense investment of capital and labour but a psychological blow which highlighted a lord's inability to defend his own. Such motivation is graphically described in the chanson *Raoul de Cambrai*. Attacking the lands of the sons of Herbert, Raoul gives the following order to his nobles concerning the church at Origny:

> Quickly take up arms without delay: there are to be 400 of you, each on a good horse, and you must reach Origny before nightfall. Pitch my tent in the middle of the church and my packhorses will stand in its porches; prepare my food in the crypts, my sparrow-hawks can perch on the golden crosses, and prepare a magnificent bed for me to sleep on in front of the altar; I will use the crucifix as a back rest and my squires can make free with the nuns. I want to destroy the place utterly, because it is well loved by Herbert's sons.[181]

Religious houses might be burnt as a means of reprisal in war or of punishment for revolt. In 1194, for example, Philip Augustus set fire to the great church of St Taurin and destroyed other churches in Evreux as part of his reprisal against the citizens for Count John's slaying of the French garrison.[182] John himself ordered the burning of the monasteries of Crowland and Ely during his campaign in East Anglia in 1216.[183] As with his destruction of the lands of Bury St Edmunds immediately prior to marching

---

[180] Orderic, II, pp. 10–11.   [181] *Raoul de Cambrai*, ed. and tr. S. Kay (Oxford, 1992), ll. 1055–67.
[182] Rigord, I. p. 127; WN, p. 418; MP, II, p. 479.
[183] MP, *Historia Anglorum*, II, pp. 173, 189–90. In the event his commands were not implemented. Ely was saved from the flames kindled by Fawkes de Bréauté and Savaric de Mauleon by the efforts of the prior, and Savaric spared Crowland.

against Crowland, John sought to punish these houses, with their influential saint cults, for supporting the rebels both politically and spiritually. These measures also struck vicariously at rebel lords who were the patrons of these houses; at the same time as burning the crops of Crowland in Holland, John destroyed the buildings and grain of Conan son of Ellis, a notable patron of Crowland and other fenland houses.[184] Church burning was thus but an extension, albeit an extreme one, both of the process of ravaging carried out against an opponent's lands, which formed the basis of contemporary warfare, and of the implementation of royal *ira et malevolentia* against recalcitrant subjects.[185]

PRO RESTAURATIONE DAMPNORUM : DEED AND ATONEMENT

The violation of sanctuary, the spoliation and burning of churches, and the immolation of refugees were not deeds restricted to a minority of tyrant lords, but a commonplace, fully indulged in even by kings and the greatest magnates. Yet as we have seen, the majority of knights were not impious brigands, but men capable of displaying a profound piety, not least in time of war. Even the *routiers* usually stopped short of killing priests and clergy.[186] How, then, could knights reconcile such acts of blatant aggression against the Church with their own faith, with their belief in the efficacy of saintly assistance in battle, and with ecclesiastical precept?

Just as some knights observed sanctuary, others showed the reluctance they felt at the robbing or destruction of churches by accepting bribes or protection money in lieu. Savaric de Mauleon refrained from burning Crowland when confronted by a procession of barefoot monks bearing an image of the Virgin, church regalia and a bribe of 50 marks.[187] When, in *Raoul de Cambrai*, Raoul's men are turned from their mission of desecration by the church bells of Origny, they excuse their inaction: "'Do not be hard on us, lord, for God the Redeemer's sake! We are not Jews or executioners,

---

[184] Conan was an important tenant of the honour of Richmond, holding five knight's fees, of which two were formed by holdings at Whaplode and Holbeach. It is uncertain whether he was with the rebel barons at Stamford in 1215, but John clearly regarded Conan as an enemy by 1216, a conviction no doubt strengthened by his close association with Richmond; K. Major, 'Conan the Son of Ellis, an Early Inhabitant of Holbeach', *Associated Architectural Societies Reports and Papers*, 42 (1934), pp. 1–28. John's attack on this area represented the devastation of lands reclaimed from the fen by Crowland, Spalding and local lay lords; cf. H. E. Hallam, 'The New Lands of Elloe: A Study of Early Reclamation in Lincolnshire', *University of Leicester: Department of English Local History, Occasional Papers*, 6 (1954), pp. 1–42.   [185] Below, pp. 277–81.   [186] Below, pp. 319–20.

[187] According to Paris, John only pacified his anger at this failure by supervising in person the burning of the abbey's crops garnered in Holland (MP, *Historia Anglorum*, II, p. 173, 189–90).

to destroy holy relics.'"[188] Yet equally one must be cautious of the numerous *exempla* of vengeful saints who inspire terror in erring knights, when such were the products of manifest bias and a deeply vested interest in demonstrating the efficacy of a patron saint. In battle, men's fear and the desire for supernatural protection may have heightened belief in direct saintly intervention, but in less pressing circumstances, knights clearly felt able to desecrate the shrines of saints or destroy churches with impunity from immediate reprisal.[189]

To risk the anger of God or his saints in the after-life was, however, a very different matter. Ecclesiastics were quick to emphasize the contrast between the abuse of power in this world and the requital God would demand in the next for sins committed. Thus Gilbert Foliot, writing in response to some unknown demand by his uncle William de Chesney, followed his notification of a 'gift' of fifteen marks by a salutary *memento mori*: not only would William's glory turn to dust and another possess his castles, but at Judgement Day, he would be overwhelmed by the cries of widows, paupers and others he had oppressed.[190] Mechanisms of atonement were, however, readily available. In the very same letter of admonition, Gilbert confirmed that William had secured entry into the confraternity of Foliot's monastery.[191] Likewise, in a grant and confirmation to St John of Pontefract, making good damage inflicted during a feud with Henry de Lacy, Gilbert de Gant stated that the monks had absolved him from his excommunication which they had brought about, and had taken him into the full confraternity of their order.[192] These lords had clearly not scrupled to despoil monasteries when need arose, but equally were carefully looking to their future salvation.

Grants of land or rents to injured religious houses in atonement for violence were very common, and the close of Stephen's reign witnessed a spate of such restorative endowments. Gilbert de Gant's grant of the revenues of a ferry across the Humber to Pontefract priory was 'for the great damage, brought about by my sins, which I did to the aforesaid church and

---

[188] *Raoul de Cambrai*, ll. 1090–2. Raoul is temporarily moved to spare Origny by a procession of the nuns, each bearing her psalter (*ibid.*, ll. 1123–9).

[189] For alleged indifference to tutelary saints see WN, pp. 45–6, 48; HH, p. 277; and *Historia Ramesiensis*, pp. 330–1. Matthew Paris records a mocking jingle attributed to de Mandeville's followers, referring to his plundering of St Benedict's at Ramsey and its daughter house at St Ives: 'I ne mai a live, for Benoit ne for Ive' (*Historia Anglorum*, i. p. 271, n. 3).   [190] Foliot, no. 20, p. 55.

[191] Foliot, no. 20, pp. 54–5 and 55, n. 1. Gilbert notes, 'For if you help us in temporal matters, we shall not deny you our spiritual intercession. Every day when the Son is sacrificed to the Father, there your memory will be brought to mind amongst us all.'

[192] *Cartulary of St John of Pontefract (c. 1090–1258)*, ed. R. Holmes, 2 vols. (Yorkshire Archaeological Society Record Series, 25, 1899; 30, 1902), ii, no. 399, p. 521; no. 400, p. 521, 'et susceperunt me in pleniarum fraternitatem ecclesie sue et totius ordinis sui'.

5 The Church's warning to erring *milites*. A detail from the tympanum of Sainte Foi, Conques (Aveyron), c. 1124, shows devils pitchforking a knight into Hell to join the ranks of the damned (James Austin).

to the monks in the war between myself and Henry de Lacy', while he similarly compensated Norwich priory for his depredations at Lynn.[193] William de Roumare gave half a carucate in Sibsey to Crowland abbey 'for the absolution of my son William, whose household laid violent hands on the same abbey in the time of war'.[194] Similar grants were made by Rannulf of Chester and others.[195] William of Aumâle had not scrupled to drive out the canons regular from Bridlington, but later, noted William of Newburgh approvingly, 'he repented in the hope of divine mercy. He bestowed generous and repeated alms on the poor, and atoned for his transgression by building considerable monasteries.'[196]

---

[193] *Ibid.*, II, no. 399, pp. 520–1; Stenton, *English Feudalism*, p. 244.

[194] *Documents illustrative of the Social and Economic History of the Danelaw*, ed. F. M. Stenton (London, 1920), no. 516, p. 357.

[195] Rannulf of Chester gave thirty librates of land to the cathedral of Lincoln in 1153 to make good the losses suffered by the cathedral, probably during the campaign of 1149 (*RRAN*, III, no. 491, p. 183 and no. 492, pp. 183–4); cf. *The Registrum Antiquissimum of the Cathedral Church of Lincoln*, (*Registrum Antiquissimum*), ed. C. W. Foster and K. Major, 10 vols. (Lincoln Record Society, 1931–00), II, no. 316, p. 7; and *ibid.* no. 324, pp. 16–17, for a grant to Lincoln made by Robert of Leicester for damages inflicted by himself and his men. Cf. Stenton, *English Feudalism*, p. 244.

[196] WN, pp. 47, 48. He thus 'obtained mercy rather than judgement at Almighty God's hands, for he was preserved for repentance and atonement'.

Although crude and essentially mechanical, repentance was immediately quantifiable. The belief that current sins could be readily expiated by a future foundation or grants must have led to but momentary hesitation on the part of many knights before bowing to the practical dictates of war. Should secular demands force a resumption of acts of violence toward the churches, moreover, the process could simply be repeated. The words attributed by Orderic to Henry I, seeking permission from Bishop Audoin of Evreux to set fire to the city to drive out the rebel forces of Amaury de Montfort in 1119, gets us close to this mind-set: 'If heaven grants a victory through a conflagration, then with God's help the damage to the church shall be repaired, because we will gladly give large sums from our treasure so that the houses of God may be built, as I believe, better than before.'[197]

Strongly partisan to Henry I, Orderic is naturally eager to show him concerned for the ultimate welfare of Holy Church, ready to seek the advice and permission of the bishop, and to be ready with recompense. Yet this mentality of material remuneration as recompense and justification is closely paralleled by an account almost a century earlier. Describing how the church of St Florent at Saumur was burnt when Fulk Nerra fired the town in 1026, the abbey's hostile chronicler has Fulk exclaim very similar sentiments: 'St Florent, leave it to burn! I will build you a more beautiful residence at Angers.'[198] Divine anger could be assuaged or deflected by pre-emptive promises not only of restoration but of increased endowment and more lavish rebuilding.

As a result, this practice was not necessarily condemned by the religious houses involved. As Emma Mason has written:

> They bemoaned the persecution they endured in time of civil war, but could then overwhelm the offenders with fears of the consequences. In the event, a house might not merely recoup its losses, but also add substantially to its estates, like Nostell, Pontefract and Leominster.[199]

As far as atonement for war damage was concerned, moreover, the question for knights was less *if* but *when*. If many waited until the dictates of war has passed, lest appropriated church resources were still needed for military purposes, or lest further damage or encroachment might necessitate another act of recompense, sickness or the immediacy of death were

---

[197] Orderic, VI, pp. 228–9. According to Orderic, Audoin blamed Amaury for the burning of Evreux at the papal consistory court held at Reims in 1119, but in turn was accused of culpability by one of Amaury's clerks (*ibid.*, VI, pp. 260–1).

[198] *Historia Sancti Florentii Salmurensis*, in *Chroniques des Eglises d'Anjou*, ed. P. Marchegay and E. Mabille (Paris, 1896), pp. 277–8. For other acts of sacrilege by Fulk Nerra, see Halphen, *Le comté d'Anjou*, pp. 129–30.

[199] Mason, 'Timeo Barones et Donas Ferentes', p. 67; cf. Cronne, *The Reign of King Stephen*, p. 3.

powerful stimulants to restitution. William I, for example, was quick to make reparation to the churches burnt in Mantes in 1087 when he knew himself to be dying.[200] Nothing could highlight more sharply the contrast between the willingness to despoil ecclesiastical property when in good health and sudden repentence when sick than the end of the Young King in 1183. Knowing that he was dying, Henry imposed a severe penance upon himself, begging the forgiveness of the saints whose shrines he had so recently injured. He entrusted vicariously to William Marshal his vow of pilgrimage to Jerusalem, then confessing his sins, he finally received absolution and the viaticum.[201] In some instances, reparation might even be posthumous. The abbey of Ramsey, for example, desecrated in 1144 by Geoffrey de Mandeville who was killed in that year, had to wait until 1163 for compensation from his son. This was despite the fact that in the interim, the earl's body had been denied Christian burial.[202] Nevertheless the grant did finally occur.

More efficacious acts of atonement could supplement these grants of restitution. Sins might be expiated by pilgrimage or crusade.[203] A stipulated period fighting in the Holy Land, enjoined as penance by successive Lateran Councils, might even atone for so heinous a crime as the murder of Becket.[204] And if pilgrimage itself might do little to guarantee against recurrent acts of violence, it was a mechanism of repentance that could be readily repeated.[205]

The frequency with which knights entered monasteries as *conversi* at the end of their active military careers or assumed the habit *ad succurendum* on their death- or sickbeds leaves no doubt as to the immense importance

---

[200] Orderic, IV, pp. 80–1. When William Rufus fell ill in 1093 and believed himself to be dying, the fears of Hell led not simply to a promise of atonement for his personal sins, but to a pledge to correct governmental abuses, including his extensive exploitation of the Church (Barlow, *William Rufus*, pp. 299–300); cf. the charter of restitution, 1109 x 1114, made on his sickbed by Nigel d'Aubigny when troubled by fears of hell (D. E. Greenaway, *Charters of the Honour of Mowbray* (London, 1972), no. 4).

[201] *HGM*, 11. 6891–911; *GH*, i. pp. 300–2; Howden, ii, pp. 278–9; Thomas Agnellus, *De morte et sepultura Henrici regis junioris*, ed. J. Stevenson, in *Radulphi de Coggeshall chronicon Anglicanum* (Rolls Series, 1875).

[202] Geoffrey's restitution is recorded in a charter of Thomas Becket, 1163, printed in C. R. Cheney, *English Bishop's Chanceries, 1100–1250* (Manchester, 1950), p. 154, and translated *EHD*, ii, no. 167, p. 836.

[203] William X of Aquitaine, for example, 'felt repentance for the harm he knew he had recently done in Normandy and set out on a pilgrimage to St James', while William of Dover, 'repenting of the woes and the sufferings that he had pitilessly brought on the people' went on pilgrimage to Jerusalem before dying in battle against the Muslims (Orderic, vi, pp. 480–3; *GS*, pp. 178–9).

[204] Thus the Second Lateran Council imposed crusading in the Holy Land or Spain as penance for incendiaries (Mansi, xxi, col. 531, canon 18). For the judgement on the murderers of Becket, Barlow, *Thomas Becket*, p. 258.

[205] The pilgrimages of Fulk Nerra, undertaken after respective acts of brutality, in 1002–3 (or 1003–4), 1008 or 1009, and 1039–40, provide a vivid, if perhaps extreme example of this phenomenon; L. Halphen, *Le comté d'Anjou au XIe siècle* (Paris, 1906), p. 130 and Appendix ii, pp. 213–18.

attached to this the greatest and usually most final act of atonement.[206] It is indicative that of the two protagonists involved in the case concerning breach of sanctuary brought before Gilbert Foliot, Roger of Hereford became a monk, while Gilbert de Lacy took the mantle of the Templars.[207] William the Marshal similarly became a Templar on his deathbed, an action he had long planned, but went on to augment this by obtaining further spiritual benefits.[208] He endowed the abbey of Nutley with fifty marks, and an equivalent sum to each abbey in his 'lands beyond the sea'. He was rewarded by the news that he had been received into the benefits of the Arrouaisian order, whose chapter general had instructed all its chapters to pray for his soul.[209] Finally, he obtained a plenary absolution of all sins duly confessed from his colleague in government, the papal legate Pandulf.[210] The Marshal may well have died with the thought that if such an armoury of atonement and satisfaction did not save him from the snares of Hell, then few of his order would ever gain salvation.

Yet even *in extremis*, William was aware but unrepentant of a discrepancy between his martial lifestyle and the teachings of the Church. When one of his knights, Henry fitz Gerold, expressed concern about reconciling a life in arms with the Church's teaching that salvation was unobtainable unless a man had returned everything he had taken from others, the Marshal replied:

> Henry, listen to me a while. The clerks are too hard on us. They shave us too closely. I have captured five hundred knights and have appropriated their arms, horses and their entire equipment. If for this reason the kingdom of God is closed to me, I can do nothing about it, for I cannot return my booty. I can do no more for God than give myself to him, repenting of all my sins. Unless the clergy desire my damnation, they must ask no more. But their teaching is false – else no one could be saved.[211]

William's preparations for death epitomize the phenomenon of knightly piety and Christian chivalry. Yet his words show that it was a piety which

---

[206] Harper Bill, 'The Piety of the Anglo-Norman Knightly Class', pp. 69–72.

[207] For Roger's adoption of the habit see Davis, 'The Treaty between William, Earl of Gloucester and Roger, Earl of Hereford', p. 142; *Historia et cartularium monasterii sancti Petri Gloucestriae*, ed. W. H. Hart (Rolls Series, 1863), I, p. 331. For Gilbert becoming a Templar, W. E. Wightman, *The Lacy Family in England and Normandy, 1066–1194* (Oxford, 1966), p. 189; H. M. Colvin, 'Holme Lacy: An Episcopal Manor and its Tenants in the Twelfth and Thirteenth Century', *Medieval Studies Presented to Rose Graham*, ed. V. Ruffer and A. J. Taylor (Oxford, 1950), p. 18.

[208] *HGM*, ll. 18377–8. William had obtained the Templars' cloak, as well as other rich furnishings for his funeral, during his pilgrimage to the Holy Land in 1183 (ll. 18355–66). For a detailed account of William's last days, see Painter, *William Marshal*, pp. 279–89; and Duby, *William Marshal*, pp. 3–21.

[209] *HGM*, ll. 18653–70. For William's earlier endowments of religious houses, see Painter, *William Marshal*, p. 282; Crouch, *William Marshal*, pp. 65–6, 188–94, 130–2.   [210] *HGM*, ll. 18939–54.

[211] *Ibid.*, ll. 18480–96.

could be at odds with ecclesiastical teaching over pragmatic aspects of warfare and the knight's profession. Unlike the conventions developed by the knighthood itself to regulate behaviour in war, born from and reinforced by mutual advantage and self-preservation, the knights stood to gain little temporal profit from adherence to the moral dictates of the Church. Indeed, they might stand to lose much in financial and military terms.

To fulfil their own function adequately, moreover, the temporal *militia* frequently had recourse to the exploitation and plundering of the spiritual. Paradoxically, although the knighthood indulged in profound expressions of piety on the battlefield, the fiscal and tactical demands of contemporary warfare created a situation that was in effect the very antithesis of the clerical ideal of chivalry. And ironically, it was the very accessbility of means of atonement and retrospective compensation that perpetuated the warriors' readiness to commit short-term acts of sacrilege for the dictates of military expediency. We must conclude that concepts of Christian morality and the precepts of the Church concerning a *ius in bello* were singularly unsuccessful in restraining the conduct of the warriors. Far more effective were secular notions of honour and reputation, and it is to these crucial concepts that we now must turn.

4

HONOUR, SHAME AND REPUTATION

PROWESS IN ARMS: THE VOCABULARY OF HONOUR

Hear ye, true and loyal knights! At a time when, to preserve our reputation, to defend ourselves, our wives, our children, our friends and our land, to win great honour, for the peace of Holy Church which our enemies have broken, to be pardoned of our sins, we support the burden of arms, beware that there is amongst you no coward! . . . We should be soft indeed if we did not take vengeance upon those who have come from France to rob us of our heritage. They desire our destruction. For God's sake, let us make a great effort, for, if we are victorious, we shall have increased our glory and defended our freedom and that of our lineage . . .[1]

Thus the author of the *Histoire de Guillaume le Maréchal* has William exhort the royalist army to resist the invading army of Prince Louis of France prior to the battle of Lincoln in 1217. The Marshal's priorities are most revealing: the safeguarding of reputation heads the list before defence of family, *patria* and Holy Church, the reward of victory is glory as much as safety from conquest.

Although in medieval society concepts of morality and behavioural restraint were heavily influenced by the dynamic of guilt, enforced through the Church's teaching on sin, penance and atonement,[2] the warrior aristocracy was equally if not more constrained in its conduct by considerations of honour and shame. Nothing was more esteemed than honour, a quality

---

[1] *HGM*, 11. 16,137–52. The translation here is from *English Historical Documents, III, 1189–1327*, ed. H. Rothwell (London, 1975), p. 87, which is an English rendering (only for the years 1216–19) of Meyer's précis in *HGM*, vol. III.

[2] See in general, J. Delumeau, *La Péché et la Peur* (Paris, 1983), tr. E. Nicholson as *Sin and Fear: The Emergence of a Western Guilt Culture, 13th–18th Centuries* (New York, 1990).

defined by Julian Pitt-Rivers as 'the value of a person in his own eyes, but also in the eyes of his society. It is his estimation of his own worth, his *claim* to pride, but it is also the acknowledgement of that claim, his excellence recognized by society, his *right* to pride.'[3] Notions of honour, reputation and shame dominate the secular literature of the period, whether the fictitious chansons and romances, or the more historically based poetic narratives such as the *Histoire de Guillaume le Maréchal,* Jordan Fantosme's *Chronicle* or Ambroise's *L'Estoire de la Guerre Sainte.* The whole of the *Histoire de Guillaume le Maréchal,* indeed, is at once both a biography of William Marshal and a *speculum militis* – an extended tract on the nature of honour and reputation, seen through the career of a man whom the author sought to portray as the embodiment of honour and chivalric values. So too the chief purpose of Jordan Fantosme's praise poem was to laud the bravery and constancy of Henry II's loyal and victorious supporters in the war of 1173–4, and by so doing both to preserve and to enhance their knightly reputations.[4]

To be regarded as a *prudhomme,* as one of *les preux,*[5] a man needed to display a number of qualities: loyalty to one's lord and kin, sagacity of counsel in war and diplomacy, largesse, particularly to one's vassals or companions in arms, *franchise* or a greatness of spirit, piety and, increasingly from the twelfth century, *courtoisie,* the ability to conduct oneself correctly before ladies and in courtly circles.[6] Yet above all, a knight's reputation, honour and pride rested on his *prouesse* – prowess in combat and on the performance of feats of arms. The concept was epitomized by Geoffrey de Charny, the renowned fourteenth-century French knight and author of the *Livre de Chevalerie*: 'Qui plus fait, miex vault' – 'he who achieves more is the more worthy.'[7] For this was a world where warriors still strove, as their Frankish, Viking and Anglo-Saxon forbears had done, to win 'undying glory by the sword's

[3] J. Pitt-Rivers, 'Honour and Social Status', in *Honour and Shame. The Values of Mediterranean Society,* ed. J. G. Peristiany (London, 1965), p. 21, also quoted by J. Barnie, *War in Medieval Society. Social Values and the Hundred Years War, 1337–99* (London, 1974), p. 75. Compare Huizinga's statement concerning honour, 'this strange mixture of conscience and egotism'; 'the source of the chivalrous idea is pride aspiring to beauty, and formalized pride gives rise to a conception of honour, which is the pole of noble life' (*Waning of the Middle Ages,* p. 67).   [4] Strickland, 'Arms and the Men', pp. 198–204.
[5] Keen, *Chivalry,* pp. 8, 56, 98; S. Painter, *French Chivalry* (Baltimore, 1940). p. 29: 'To call a nobleman a *preudome,* a man of prowess, was to pay him the highest compliment known to the Middle Ages.'
[6] For a good general discussion of these virtues, see Painter, *French Chivalry,* pp. 29 ff. Cf. S. North, 'The Ideal Knight as Presented in Some French Narrative Poems, c. 1090–c. 1240: An Outline Sketch', *The Ideals and Practice of Medieval Knighthood. Papers from the First and Second Strawberry Hill Conferences,* ed. C. Harper-Bill and R. Harvey (Woodbridge, 1986), pp. 111–32.
[7] For Charny, who was killed at the battle of Poitiers in 1356, carrying the Oriflamme banner, see Keen, *Chivalry,* pp. 12–15, and for his *dictum,* p. 21. The *Livre de Chevalerie,* a longer prose version of his earlier verse *Livre,* is edited by K. de Lettenhove, *Oeuvres de Froissart,* 28 vols. (Brussels, 1867–77), I, pt iii, pp. 463–533.

edge',[8] to achieve lasting 'word-fame' – *lof, dom, los* – by feats of arms.[9] Honour and military prowess were inseparable; or put more bluntly by Pitt-Rivers, 'the ultimate vindication of honour lies in physical violence'.[10]

Numerous texts, not least the *Song of Roland*, serve to illustrate this fundamental connection between physical valour and reputation. Let us, however, take but one, the *Histoire de la Guerre Sainte*, a Norman-French poem attributed to the *jongleur* Ambroise describing the course of the Third Crusade.[11] For although concerned with warfare in Outremer, Ambroise's poem is second only in value to the *Histoire de Guillaume le Maréchal* in revealing secular perceptions of Frankish chivalry in the later twelfth century. Unsurprisingly, it is the feats of arms of King Richard I which dominate the narrative. This is not simply because Richard was both king and, after the departure of Philip Augustus from Acre in July 1191, the effective leader of the Third Crusade. Rather, it is because the author is consistently struck by Richard's sheer physical prowess. Whether leading the charge mounted on his swift Cyprian charger or jumping ashore from his galley to relieve Jaffa, whether on a foray or in the thick of battle, Richard is portrayed as always the first into the attack, vanquishing all his adversaries and scything a path of death through the Turks.[12] As an individual warrior the king is peerless, be it with lance, sword or even crossbow.[13] Richard is greater than Antaeus, Achilles, Alexander and Judas Maccabeus, a warrior 'to whom Roland himself cannot be compared'.[14]

Indeed, the *Estoire* strikingly demonstrates the extent to which Richard's martial reputation was a lynch-pin in his successful practice of kingship. Richard's personal prowess was underpinned by great military skill as a strategist, a tactician and as a commander of men, qualities which were visible long before the Third Crusade.[15] Yet it is clear that

---

[8] The phrase is found in the Old English poem *The Battle of Brunanburgh*; 'King Aethelstan, the lord of warriors, patron of heroes, and his brother too, Prince Edmund, won themselves eternal glory in battle with the edges of their swords (*ealdorlange tir geslogon aet saecce sweorda ecgum*) round Brunanburgh' (R. Harmer, *A Choice of Anglo-Saxon Verse* (London, 1970), pp. 42–3 for text and translation).

[9] As the ninth-century Viking poem the *Havamal* (*The Words of the High One*) puts it, 'Wealth dies, kinsmen die, a man himself must likewise die; but word-fame never dies, for him who achieves it well' (M. Magnusson, *Vikings!* (London, 1980), p. 15). For very similar sentiments by Welsh and Irish court poets see J. E. Caerwyn Williams, 'The Court Poet in Medieval Ireland', *Proceedings of the British Academy*, 57 (1971), pp. 93–4.   [10] Pitt-Rivers, 'Honour and Social Status', p. 29.

[11] Above, p. 27, n. 113.

[12] See, for example, Ambroise, 11. 5,791–99; 11. 6,469–90; 11. 6,602–10; 11. 7,147–76; 11. 7,327–59; 11. 11,127–85; *Itinerarium*, pp. 251, 270, 273–4, 288, 293–4, 408–9.

[13] For the king's skill as a marksman see Ambroise, 11. 4,931–40, 4,967–72; *Itinerarium*, pp. 225–6. Cf. Howden, III, p. 239.   [14] *Itinerarium*, pp. 421–2.

[15] Gillingham, 'Richard I and the Science of War', pp. 194–207; *idem.*, *Richard the Lionheart*, esp. pp. 286–7; *idem.*, 'The Unromantic Death of Richard I', *Speculum* 54 (1979), pp. 18–41; and cf. J. O. Prestwich, 'Richard Coeur de Lion: *Rex Bellicosus*', in *Riccardo Cuor di Leone Nella Storia e Nella Leggenda* (Accademia Nazionale dei Lincei, Rome, 1981), pp. 1–15.

Richard not only led from the front, but assiduously cultivated an aura of personal invincibility by constant acts of daring. Again and again we hear of Richard leading raids and reconnaissances against the Turks, relentlessly pursuing their forces, sometimes for miles. Richard repeatedly came to the rescue of his men when beleaguered in battle or siege, saving them from capture or death. This was a high-risk strategy of leadership. As his despairing counsellors constantly reminded him, his death would deprive the crusade of its head and frustrate the entire enterpirse;[16] in 1191 alone, Richard was wounded at least once and came very close to being captured.[17] In 1199, it was to be this reckless bravado and contempt for danger that led to his being mortally wounded at Chaluz Chabrol.[18]

Yet there was method in such madness, for the psychological effects of this calculated bravery were tangible. By constantly putting his own life in jeopardy, Richard not only showed he was sharing the dangers of his fellow crusaders to the full, but he also heightened their morale and inspired them to imitate his daring. Here was a man worth fighting for, who would rescue them from peril and who seemed unvanquishable. Richard's prowess, moreover, helped dispel his own men's fear of Saladin's forces and in turn struck fear into the Turks. Nowhere is this more clearly seen that in his remarkable relief and defence of Jaffa in August 1192, against considerable odds, which culminated in his issuing a challenge of single combat to the Turkish army which none dared accept.[19]

Conversely, when rumours began to circulate that his crusading zeal had been dulled by his unseemly rapport with Saladin's brother, Al-Adil, Richard countered such criticism by bringing back from forays the severed heads of Turks attached to his bridle, to symbolize his commitment to war against the infidel.[20]

How much his martial reputation mattered to Richard was shown by the king's implacable hostility towards William des Barres after the king had failed to worst the French champion in an impromptu joust fought with canes whilst in Sicily in 1191 en route for the Holy Land.[21] Significantly, however, it was des Barres's outstanding bravery in countering a dangerous Turkish assault on the rearguard during the march from Acre to Caesarea that brought about his reconciliation with Richard.[22]

---

[16] Ambroise, ll. 7,147–76, 7,326–48; *Itinerarium*, pp. 288, 293–4.
[17] Ambroise, ll. 6,059–66, 7,079–146; *Itinerarium*, pp. 258, 286–8.
[18] K. Norgate, *Richard the Lion Heart* (London, 1924), pp. 325–7; Gillingham, *Richard the Lionheart*, pp. 9–23.
[19] Ambroise, ll. 11,106–652; *Itinerarium*, pp. 407–24, and for the challenge, Beha-ad-Din, p. 300.
[20] *Itinerarium*, p. 297.   [21] *GH*, ii, pp. 155–7.   [22] Ambroise, ll. 5,800–6; *Itinerarium*, p. 251.

Yet it is not only Richard who is singled out for praise in the *Estoire*. The course of Ambroise's narrative is studded with references to the prowess of other warriors who distinguished themselves by their bravery in arms, and whose fame was thereby assured for posterity; Alberic Clements, the French marshal, who died storming a breach at Acre when the ladder carrying the men following his bold assault collapsed, leaving him to be surrounded and slain by the Turks;[23] Everard, one of the bishop of Salisbury's serjeants, who, having his right hand cut off in a skirmish, without flinching seized his sword in his left hand and carried on fighting;[24] James de Avesnes, the much-mourned crusade leader who fell at Arsuf, surrounded by the bodies of Turks he had slain;[25] Robert, earl of Leicester, of whom 'it is truly said that no man so young and of so small stature ever performed such splendid feats of arms';[26] Andrew de Chauvigni, who among other deeds slew a formidable Turkish emir;[27] William des Barres,[28] the Capetian counterpart to William the Marshal, and many others.

Ambroise's whole narrative, indeed, gives a vivid impression of an overwhelmingly masculine, aristocratic and martial milieu in which a man's standing rested directly on his feats of arms in war. Such deeds invited both praise and emulation, as knights strove to gain increased honour and to outshine each other in deeds of prowess. 'I recognize you, brother', Roland tells his companion Oliver after the latter has cleaved a pagan lord clean in half, 'For such blows the Emperor loves us.'[29] Though subject to epic exaggeration, these lovingly described blows of lance and sword, with which the *Song of Roland* is replete, accurately reflect the fascination of a knightly audience with individual deeds of arms. That such an interest was the common preserve of any warrior aristocracy is suggested by the equally enthusiastic and detailed descriptions of lance and sword blows furnished by the Syrian noble Usamah.[30]

A man might further enhance his reputation by combining prowess with other virtues. The distribution of arms and horses won in battle to fellow warriors not only showed valour but largesse, while in turn such gifts served as a lasting reminder to the recipients of the prowess of the

---

[23] Ambroise, ll. 4,887–907; *Itinerarium*, pp. 223–4.   [24] Ambroise, ll. 5,776–84; *Itinerarium*, pp. 250–1.

[25] Ambroise, ll. 6,631–734; *Itinerarium*, pp. 275–7.

[26] Ambroise, ll. 7,479–596; *Itinerarium*, pp. 300–2. As internal evidence suggests that Ambroise was a Norman from the region of Evreux, he may well have had connections with Earl Robert of Leicester, who was lord of Pacy and Breteuil, and who receives frequent mention in the narrative (Edwards, 'The *Itinerarium Regis Ricardi*', pp. 68–9).

[27] Ambroise, ll. 7,274–80, 7,571–82; *Itinerarium*, pp. 292, 302.

[28] Ambroise, ll. 6,594–601, *Itinerarium*, p. 273, for William's prowess in rescuing comrades hemmed in by the Turks at Arsuf. For William II des Barres, see the notes given by Meyer, *HGM*, III, p. 32, n. 1.

[29] *Song of Roland*, ll. 1376–77.   [30] Usamah, pp. 70–8, 146–7.

grantor.[31] Equally, the sparing of a vanquished foe displayed magnanimity or *franchise*.[32] Most lauded of all, however, were those who were prepared to place the life of their lord before their own in situations of conflict.[33] Thus in 1191, William des Préaux rescued Richard from capture when heavily outnumbered in a Turkish ambush by crying out that he was the king. Thus deceived into believing he was 'Melek Richard', the Turks seized William and made off, allowing Richard himself to reach safety.[34]

A more common way to rescue one's lord was to provide him with one's own mount should he become unhorsed in battle. Such an act involved great risk for the vassal, for it put him at a considerable disadvantage in combat and prevented him from flight. In 1119, Henry I's captain Ralph the Red was immediately captured by the French after he had given his own horse to Richard, the king's natural son, whose own mount had just been slain. For this deed, however, 'the loyal Ralph was approved and honoured by the king', who speedily had him released in exchange for Walo de Trie, and 'from that time was counted one of the king's greatest and closest friends'.[35] Given the danger involved, it was little wonder that some were reluctant to make such a sacrifice. When, at Hastings, Duke William's horse was slain under him, he signalled to a knight from Maine to give him his horse, but the latter, fully realizing the dangers, refused. To gain his mount, William had to seize him by the nasal of his helmet and drag him from the saddle. Later, however, when William lost this second horse, Eustace of Boulogne 'hastened to be held first to the duke's aid and became a foot-soldier so that he might depart mounted'. 'There was a certain knight', adds the *Carmen*, 'whom the count had reared; what Eustace had done for his commander, that man did for him'.[36] Such was vassalic propriety at its finest.

---

[31] Thus, for example, at the siege of Breteuil in 1119 the Norman commander Ralph de Gael 'brought down many distinguished champions that day, and when the knights had been unhorsed he generously gave their horses to his needy comrades, so earning high and enduring praise for the chivalrous qualities that distinguished him among the most eminent warriors' (Orderic, VI, pp. 246–7). Ganelon says of Roland that the Franks 'love him so much they will not fail him. So much gold and silver does he bestow on them, mules and war-horses, silks and arms' (*Song of Roland*, 11. 396–9).

[32] Above, pp. 153–4; cf. Bertan de Born's remark, 'The lion's custom appeals to me, who is not cruel to a creature once overcome, but who is proud in the face of pride' (*Ar ve la cointeda sazos*, TLP, pp. 166–7; Gouiran, *L'amour et la guerre*, pp. 713–20).

[33] 'For his lord a vassal must suffer great hardship and endure both great heat and great cold: he must also part with flesh and blood', is a common refrain in the *Song of Roland* (eg. 11. 1010–12, 1117–19).

[34] Ambroise, 11. 7,086–146; *Itinerarium*, pp. 287–9. Prior to leaving Outremer, Richard himself 'performed a noble deed, like a most loyal man and true' by exchanging ten noble Saracen prisoners for William (Ambroise, 11. 12,263–69; *Itinerarium*, p. 440).   [35] Orderic, VI, pp. 220–1.

[36] *Carmen*, pp. 32–35. Similarly, Robert of Newburgh earned the fulsome praise of the *Itinerarium* for giving up his horse to the earl of Leicester during a fierce skirmish in December 1191, near Ramlah (Ambroise, 11. 7,523–30; and for additional praise, *Itinerarium*, p. 301).

Some men, indeed, paid the ultimate price for such loyalty,[37] though they might be recompensed with lasting fame. The *Anglo-Saxon Chronicle* proudly noted that it was whilst bringing William I a new mount that Toki, son of Wigod, was killed by a crossbow bolt at Gerberoi in 1079.[38] At Bouvines, 1214, Philip Augustus was saved from certain death by the sacrifice of one of his knights, who threw himself between the king and the sword of Renaud of Boulogne, receiving the fatal blow himself.[39]

Equally, to merit esteem a lord had to be speedy to succour his vassals in their need. 'Who could relate his great worth?', says Ganelon of Charlemagne, 'God has made so much valour shine forth from him that he would rather die than forsake his men.'[40] The sentiment applied equally to Richard I, who, as we have noted, was constantly rescuing his men from danger in battle, skirmish or ambush on the Third Crusade. When on one occasion his advisers counselled him to abandon a force under the earl of Leicester and the count of St Pol surrounded by the Turks, lest in attempting a rescue he himself would be captured, the author of the *Itinerarium* has Richard angrily reply;

> When I sent my loved comrades out to war it was with the promise of bring-ing them aid. And if I fail to do this, so far as I can, I shall deceive those who trusted to me. And should they meet with death in my absence – which I pray may never happen – never more will I bear the name of king.[41]

The ability to protect his vassals *in extremis* was an integral element of a lord's reputation and, as we shall see, his duty to bring succour to men besieged was a fundamental concept in the formation of conventions of siege and notions of honourable surrender.[42]

TOURNEYS, BOASTING AND WAR: THE SUSTAINING AND AUGMENTING OF HONOUR

The pursuit of honour was fiercely competitive. As a result, there was con-stant pressure on a knight continually to reaffirm his prowess and replenish

---

[37] Thus a sergeant who gave Baldwin de Carron his horse during a fierce skirmish with Turks in June 1192, lost his head for his pains (Ambroise, 11. 10,021–29; *Itinerarium*, p. 374).

[38] ASC, 'D', *s.a.* 1079.

[39] *Matthaei Parisiensis, monachi sancti Albani, chronica majora* (MP), ed. H. R. Luard, 7 vols. (Rolls Series, 1872–3), II, p. 580; and for Matthew Paris's drawing of this event see Plate 6, and S. Lewis, *The Art of Matthew Paris in the Chronica Majora* (University of Califoria and Aldershot, 1987), p. 185.

[40] *Song of Roland*, 11. 534–6.

[41] Thus the *Itinerarium*, pp. 293–4, enlarging on Ambroise, 11. 7,332–348. The psychological importance of the king's presence among his forces is discussed further in M. J. Strickland, 'Against the Lord's Anointed: Aspects of Warfare and Baronial Rebellion in England and Normandy, 1066–1265', *Law and Government*, pp. 61–7.   [42] Below, pp. 212–18.

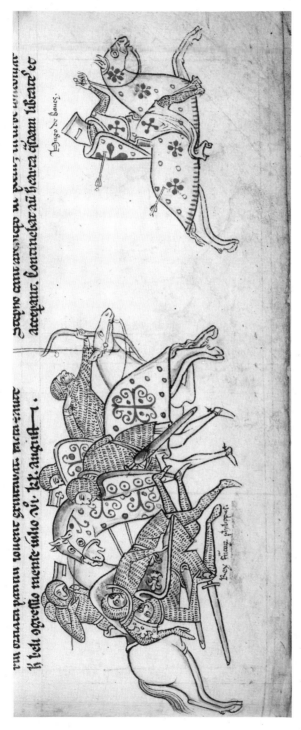

6 Bravery and honour or cowardice and shame? Matthew Paris's illustration of the battle of Bouvines, 1214, contrasts the bravery of one of Philip Augustus's knights, who saves the prostrate king from the attack of Renaud de Dammartin by interposing his own body, with the cowardly flight of John's mercenary captain, Hugh de Boves (Corpus Christi College, Cambridge, MS 16, f. 37r).

his store of honour by new feats of daring. Such an imperative was particularly acute for the younger warriors, anxious to prove their prowess. 'Long
inactivity shames a young man' noted the *Histoire de Guillaume le Maréchal*[43]
In Chrétien's *Cligés* the young Alexander, wishing to set out for the court of
Arthur 'in order to learn honour and win fame and glory' tells his father:
'Many high-born men through indolence have forfeited great fame they
might have had, had they set off through the world. Idleness and glory do
not go well together, it seems to me; a noble man who sits and waits gains
nothing.'[44] In *Erec*, the hero tarnishes his martial reputation and earns
reproach for tarrying too long in the joys of the marriage-bed because 'ne
s'acordent pas bien ansamble repos et los'.[45] To the St Albans chroniclers,
John's similar dalliance with his young wife Isabelle was a major reason for
his failure to defend Normandy in 1202–4.[46] As Philippe de Navarre,
writing contemporaneously with the author of the *Histoire de Guillaume le
Maréchal*, advised in his *Les Quatre Ages de l'Homme*:

> In his youth a man should use without laziness or delay his prowess, his
> valour, and the vigour of his body for the honour and profit of himself and
> of his dependants; for he who passes his youth without exploit may have
> cause for great shame and grief. The young nobleman, knight or man at arms
> should work to acquire honour, to be renowned for valour, and to have tem-
> poral possessions, riches and heritages on which he can live honourably . . .[47]

In a masterly discussion of aristocratic 'youth', Duby has shown how the
juventus – young men, either first-born sons chafing to inherit their father's
fief, or younger sons eager to win lands or an heiress – were the 'spearhead
of feudal aggression'.[48] It was the desire to achieve glory through feats of
arms, and the material rewards concomitant to martial success, that led

[43] *HGM*, 1. 2402.
[44] *Les Romans de Chrétien de Troyes, II: Cligés*, ed. A. Micha (Paris, 1957), 11. 152–8; *Chrétien de Troyes, Arthurian Romances* (Chrétien, *Arthurian Romances*), tr. G. S. Burgess (Harmondsworth, 1991), pp. 124–5.
[45] *Les Romans de Chrétien de Troyes, I: Erec et Enide*, ed. M. Roques (Paris, 1953), 11. 2430–64; Chrétien, *Arthurian Romances*, p. 67. For a discussion of this behaviour that makes Erec *recreant* see G. S. Burgess, *Chrétien de Troyes: Erec et Enide* (London, 1984), p. 49; N. Bradley-Cromey, 'The *Recreantise* Episode in Chretien's *Erec et Enide*', *The Study of Chivalry*, pp. 449–71; Jones, 'Chrétien, Hartmann and the Knight as Fighting Man', pp. 87–90.
  Although Erec's martial fevour has been dulled, the poet is nevertheless anxious to stress that the hero remains a generous lord, for 'still he continued to provide his knights with arms, clothing and with déniers. Whenever there was a tournament he sent them there, most richly apparelled and equipped. He gave them fresh chargers to tourney and joust with, regardless of the cost' (*Eric et Enide*, 11. 2445–54; Chrétien, *Arthurian Romances*, p. 67). By contrast, Yvain deserts his bride for adventure and renown.   [46] W. L. Warren, *King John* (London, 1964), pp. 87–8.
[47] *Les Quatres Ages de l'Homme*, ed. M. de Fréville (*Société des Anciens Textes Français*, Paris, 1888), pp. 38–9, and quoted by Painter, *William Marshal*, p. 30.
[48] 'Youth in Aristocratic Society' in Duby, *The Chivalrous Society*, pp. 115–16.

these young knights to clamour for hostilities against other principalities or to support the rebellions of royal cadets like Robert Curthose or the young Henry Plantagenet.

War, indeed, might be portrayed by contemporaries as the policy of the young and inexperienced. Jordan Fantosme recalls the reaction of the young knights at the Scottish court when William the Lion received Henry II's forthright rejection of his demands for the restoration of Northumbria:

> Then you should have heard the knights, those young and untutored men (*la gent jeufne et salvage*), swearing mighty oaths and making a show of boldness: 'If you do not make war on this king who treats you with such curtness, you are not fit to hold lands and overlordships, rather should you serve Maud's son in bondage.'[49]

Equally, once war had commenced, it was frequently the younger men who urged the joining of battle, in opposition to older and wiser counsel that warned against the hazards of a full-scale engagement. Thus on seeing the strong defensive position adopted by Odo Borleng and a unit of Henry I's *familia regis* at Bourgthéroulde in 1124, the experienced Amaury de Montfort cautioned against an engagement. The young Waleran of Meulan, however, 'anxious to prove his knighthood, exulted boyishly as if he had already defeated them', and battle was joined with disastrous results.[50] At a council of war before the battle of Lincoln, 1141, the older nobles who advised Stephen to garrison the city then withdraw to muster a larger force, were derided by the younger men as 'battle-shy boys (*pueros imbelles*)'.[51] Acutely conscious of his own honour and 'not wishing his glory to be stained by the opprobrium of flight',[52] Stephen was swayed by such taunts to offer battle despite unfavourable circumstances.[53]

In the absence of real warfare or rebellion, the opportunity to perform feats of arms and win the acclaim of one's knightly peers was afforded by the tournament. Following the war of 1173–4, for example, the Young King, chafing at the *ennui* of his enforced inactivity in England, finally gained his father's permission to cross to France. Here, under the patronage

---

[49] JF, 11. 378–82. For a discussion of these 'gent jeufne et salvage', see Strickland, 'Arms and the Men', pp. 210–16.   [50] Orderic, VI, pp. 350–1.

[51] *Historia Johannis, prioris Haugustadensis ecclesiae* (JH), ed. J. Raine in *The Priory of Hexham, its Chroniclers, Endowments and Annals*, 2 vols. (Surtees Society, 44, 1868), I, p. 134.   [52] *GS*, p. 112.

[53] See the perceptive comments of R. H. C. Davis, *King Stephen* (3rd edn, London, 1990), p. 49: 'For Stephen, the situation must have been agonizingly similar to that from which his father had run away at Antioch. Knowing, as he must have done, that to refuse battle would mean being labelled as his father's son, instead of grandson of the Conqueror, it is not surprising that he disregarded the odds against him and decided to fight.'

of the count of Flanders, he indulged his desire for glory to the full in a constant round of tournaments. As Ralph of Diceto noted:

> Young King Henry, the king's son, left England and passed three years in
> tournaments, spending a lot of money. While he was rushing all over France
> he put aside the royal majesty and was transformed from a king into a knight,
> carrying off victory in various meetings. His popularity made him famous;
> the old king was happier counting up and admiring his victories, and
> although the Young King was still under age, his father restored in full his
> possessions which he had taken away. Thus occupied with knightly matters
> until no glory was lacking to him, he sailed from Wissant and was received
> with honour by the king his father . . .[54]

Yet such feats, as the Young King must have been all too well aware,
faded into insignificance in comparison with the hard-won victories in
real warfare of his younger brother Richard. The young count of Poitou
was fast earning a reputation as a skilful commander and a formidable
besieger in the incessant hostilities against rebel lords in Aquitaine.
The acid-tongued Bertran de Born was not slow to draw the contrast
when he noted scornfully; 'Mariner [the Young King], you have lands and
titles, but we've changed lords – a jouster for a fine warrior [i.e.
Richard].'[55]

Nevertheless, what is striking is the extent to which the Young King
could create a considerable chivalric reputation for himself by means of
the tournament circuit, despite his conspicuously inglorious failures in
war itself. For all his earlier taunts, Bertran de Born marked young Henry's
death in 1183 with a *planh* or lament in which he praised the Young King as
'the best king who ever bore a shield, the most audacious, the best jouster',
the head and father of 'youth' (*de joven*), whose equal was unknown before
or since Roland.[56] A similar *planh*, possibly also by de Born, declared that
Merit and Youth (*Pretz et Jovens*) were left grieving, because death had
'robbed the world of the best knight there was of any nation (*il melhor
chavalier as tout al mon*)', 'the most valiant of the worthy (*lo plus valens dels
pros*)'. The poet implored God, as a gracious and just lord, to set the Young

---

[54] Diceto, I, p. 428.

[55] The *canso* 'Rassa, tan creis e monta e poia', stanza 6; *TLP*, pp. 158–9; Gouiran, *L'amour et la guerre*, pp.
13–35 for text and full critical apparatus. John Gillingham, in correspondence to the author, has
rightly pointed out that Press (*TLP*, p. 154), in his introduction to Born's poems, has confused
Bertran's attributions; a comparison of the two brothers' activities from 1174 onwards makes it clear
that it is the Young King and not Richard who 'is mentioned as the lord who prefers tourneys to war'.
The fact that Born's comment is addressed to the Young King himself (to whom Born gives the
name *Mariniers*) makes the jibe all the more biting.

[56] *Mon chan fenis ab dol et ab maltraire*, ll. 45–6 (Gouiran, *L'amour et la guerre*, pp. 242–3, and pp. 237–45 for
critical discussion). Cf. the similar sentiments of Robert of Torigny (Torigny, p. 305).

King 'among his honoured companions (*ab onratz companhos*)' in Paradise.[57]

Such a reputation had been created above all by the Young King's largesse to his knights in the tourney. The Young King, noted the *Histoire*, had revived chivalry when it was almost dead. By retaining the best knights in his service, by giving young men horses, arms, money and lands, he had set an example to the great men who hitherto had done nothing for such *juvenes*. He had been the standard-bearer of chivalry, who had released *largesse* from its prison and given laughter and joy back to the world. After his death, bemoaned the trouvère, the great had once more imprisoned chivalry and largesse, so that tournament and the life of the knight-errant had given way to mere games.[58]

Equally, for much of his career the reputation of William the Marshal rested primarily on his skill in the tourney, not in battle.[59] The Marshal's detractors, indeed, claimed that William had inflated his standing by means of a herald, Henry le Norreis, who followed him around at tournaments crying 'God aid the Marshal!'[60] It was this ability to gain glory (as well as valuable ransoms) in an environment that was not only considerably less dangerous than real war but also in which deeds of prowess could be recorded and savoured, that accounted for the immense popularity of the tournament.[61]

If Richard won glory in war and the Young King glory in the tournament, their youngest brother John failed to gain acclaim in either.[62] It is

---

[57] *Si tuit li dol e.lh plor e.lh marrimen*, *TLP*, pp. 168–71. For a critical text and full discussion of the problems of attribution see Gouiran, *L'amour et la guerre*, pp. 255–67, who is inclined to include it among Born's *oeuvre*.   [58] *HGM*, ll. 2637–92. Cf. ll. 3643–8, 6985–88.

[59] Before the war of 1173, William had only taken part in two hostile engagements, a minor clash at Drincourt in 1167 and a skirmish at Lusignan in 1168 in which he was wounded and his uncle, Patrick earl of Salisbury, was slain. The feats of arms which led him to be appointed 'tutor' to the Young King and later to be awarded the honour of knighting him, were thus performed almost wholly in the tournament (Painter, *William Marshal*, pp. 19–29; cf. Gillingham, 'War and Chivalry', p. 12).

[60] *HGM*, ll. 52,221–234, and cf. ll. 5,891–892, 6,220–236. For the origin and function of heralds see Keen, *Chivalry*, pp. 134–42.   [61] Below, pp. 149–53.

[62] For the important subject of royal participation in the tournament, principally in relation to the later Middle Ages, see J. Barker and M. Keen, 'The Medieval English Kings and the Tournament', *Das Ritterliche Turnier*, pp. 212–28. Although *a priori* it would seem likely that Richard participated in tournaments as training for war, the sources are scant indeed to support the claim here that 'Richard himself was a celebrated habitué of the tournament' (*ibid.*, p. 215), I have found no direct evidence of his involvement in tournaments – in striking contrast to the material available for the Young King – either as count of Poitou or, after 1189, as king of England, save for the impromptu joust with canes at Messina alone cited by Barker and Keen in support of their contention (above, p. 101; and cf. p. 108, n. 55). One gains the impression that Richard was mainly preoccupied with the realities of war and crusade, although he certainly approved of tournaments, licensing them in England in 1194 in order to provide revenue for the crown, internal order and training for warfare 'so that the French should not be able to upbraid the knights of England with rudeness and lack of skill' (WN, pp. 422–3; Howden, III, p. 268; *Foedera, conventiones, litterae et cujuscunque generis acta publica (Foedera)*, ed. T. Rymer, new edn, ed. A. Clarke and F. Holbrooke (Record Commission, 1816), I, p. 65).

significant that while Geoffrey Plantagenet was killed in a tournament,[63] as a young man John was conspicuous by his absence from hastiludes, let alone real warfare. Though John was by no means militarily inept, he had to wait for the engagement at Mirebeau in 1202 for his first major triumph, and what prestige this accrued quickly evaporated with unduly harsh treatment of his prisoners[64] and his catastrophic loss of Normandy by 1204. To men who had witnessed the fiasco of John's expedition to Ireland and the humiliating peace treaty of Le Goulet, the epithet of 'Softsword' coined by some of John's detractors seemed to have much justification.[65]

While the virtues of humility and modesty ranked high among the Christian values urged by the Church, they could have little place in such a secular, aristocratic milieu where men strove to court esteem.[66] If William the Marshal's achievements were proclaimed by a herald, then such self-praise was merely following a long-established tradition. Warriors might proclaim their courage and steadfastness at the outbreak of a war in the counsel chamber, or before and during battle itself.[67] Orderic noted how, at the siege of Breteuil in 1119, a Flemish champion who had vanquished Ralph the Red and Luke of La Barre 'boasted proudly as he led away their horses'.[68] It was generally prior to a campaign or an engagement, however, that saw the almost ritual bandying of vows and great boasts about deeds men would perform when battle came. In the *Song of Roland*, Charlemagne, mourning the death of his nephew Roland, recalls that

> Once I was at a solemn festival at Aix and my valiant knights boasted of great battles and violent struggles; I heard Roland make a claim: never would he die on foreign soil without advancing beyond his men and his peers. His head would be turned towards the enemies' land, and he would end his days as a conqueror.[69]

Similarly, in the *Chanson de Guillaume* William tells his dying nephew Vivien that 'It is but a short time since you were knighted. You swore then an oath

[63] He was slain at Paris in 1186, (*GH*, I, pp. 350, 361).   [64] Below, p. 197.
[65] *The Historical Works of Gervase of Canterbury*, (Gervase), ed. W. Stubbs, 2 vols. (*RS*, 1879–90), II, pp. 92–3.
[66] For a striking expression of the conflict between the knight's obsession with reputation and glory and Christian precepts see the remarkable confessional tract written by Henry of Grosmont, first duke of Lancaster (1310–61). One of the many sins to which he confessed was vainglory. Striving 'to be held best in this world', he had augmented his own reputation at the expense of others, and had boasted and lied in order to increase his honour and standing (*Le Livre de Seyntz Medicines*, ed. E. J. Arnould (Oxford, 1940), ANTS 2, pp. 66ff: K. Fowler, *The King's Lieutenant. Henry of Grosmont, First Duke of Lancaster, 1310–1361* (London, 1969); Barnie, *War in Medieval Society*, pp. 61–5.
[67] Cf above, p. 107; below, p. 111.   [68] Orderic, VI, pp. 246–7.
[69] *Song of Roland*, ll. 2860–67. For ritual boasting in Ottonian Germany, 'astonishingly frequent in the histories of the tenth century' see Leyser, 'Ritual, Ceremony and Gesture', pp. 205–6; and *idem*., 'Early Medieval Warfare', *The Carolingian and Ottonian Centuries*, pp. 42–3.

to the Lord God that you would never flee on the field of battle and you did not break your word to God.'[70]

It was of just such boasts that the Anglo-Saxon thegn Aelfwine reminds his companions during their struggle to the death at Maldon in 991, following the death of their lord, Ealdorman Byrhtnoth: 'Remember the words we uttered many a time over the mead, when on the bench, heroes in hall, we made our boast (*beot ahofon*) about hard strife. Now it may be proved which of us is bold!'[71]

In part, such vows sought to bolster men's courage and to act as an incentive to bravery in battle, lest a man should incur ignominy by failing to live up to his earlier boastings. Here the connection between war, oral poetry and literature becomes intimate. For it was the role of the poet not only to record feats of valour, but to measure men's words against their deeds. Just as bravery won praise, so cowardice received censure, not simply for the moment but, by the act of recording, for perpetuity.[72] Poets, indeed, had long accompanied armies into battle to exhort, to witness and to praise. William of Malmesbury believed the Normans advanced at Hastings to a *cantilena* about Roland, while the deeds of the jongleur or *histrio* Taillefer became a key element in later Norman tradition concerning the battle.[73] If Ambroise and Jordan Fantosme were, as they claimed, eye-witnesses of the campaigns they recorded and the deeds of the nobles they praised, they were in this very much the heirs of the earlier Celtic bards, the Anglo-Saxon *scops* or Scandinavian *skalds*, even if they did not enjoy their predecessors' more elevated social position.[74] From the thirteenth century, this important

[70] *Chanson de Guillaume*, 11, 896–905. Among the vows taken by members of the fourteenth-century French Order of the Star was that they would not flee further than four 'arpents' before standing their ground till they were either killed or taken captive (D'A. J. D. Boulton, *The Knights of the Crown. The Monarchical Orders of Knighthood in Later Medieval Europe* (Woodbridge, 1987), p. 181).

[71] *Battle of Maldon*, 11. 212–15. The poet notes approvingly that with Offa, another of Byrhtnoth's thegns, was eventually slain, 'yet he had compassed what he had promised his chief, as he bandied vows with his generous lord in days gone by (*swa he beotode aer wid his beahgifan*), that they should both ride home to the town unhurt or fall among the host, perish of wounds on the field. He lay, as befits a thegn, at his lord's side' (*ibid.*, 11. 289–94).   [72] Below, pp. 119–24.

[73] For other examples of minstrels in battle see E. Faral, *Les jongleurs en France au Moyen Age* (Paris, 1971), pp. 55–7; Contamine, *War in the Middle Ages*, p. 253 and n. 9; and cf. Dodwell, 'The Bayeux Tapestry and French Secular Epic', pp. 549–60, for the influence of the mentalité of the chansons on the composition of the Tapestry. For Taillefer, see *Carmen*, pp. 81–3.

[74] For a comparative discussion of these court poets and extensive further bibliography see Caerwyn Williams, 'The Court Poet in Medieval Ireland', especially pp. 88–94, 99–100, 130. According to several sagas, the epic Norse poem *Bjarkamal* was recited before the battle of Stiklestadir in 1030, though the dating of this poem, and thus the veracity of this incident, has been hotly debated (Frank, 'The Ideal of Men Dying with their Lord', pp. 97–8). The suggestion of Klaus von See, however, that the incident was merely borrowed by four sagas from William of Malmesbury's mention of the *cantilena* of Roland at Hastings seems somewhat implausible (K. von See, 'Hastings, Stiklastadir und Langemarck: Zur Uberlierieung vom Vortrag heroischer Lieder auf dem Schlachtfeld', *Germanisch-romanische Monatsschrift*, 57 (1976), pp. 1–13, and reprinted in K. von See, *Edda, Saga Skaldendichtung: Aufsatze zur skandinavischen Literatur des Mittealters* (Heidelberg, 1981), pp. 259–71).

role as recorders, guardians and remembrancers of honour was to be subsumed by the developing class of heralds, who significantly had earlier been
closely associated, if not synonymous, with minstrels and jongleurs.[75] Their
very *raison d'être*, indeed, lay in the crucial need to perpetuate deeds of
valour and glory in an aristocratic culture dominated by concepts of reputation.

The all too natural discrepancy between fine words and actual deeds was
a favourite theme of such contemporary writers and jongleurs. Thus the
Histoire de Guillaume le Maréchal noted that, in 1216, Prince Louis's French
routiers

> were boasting foolishly that England was theirs and that the English, having
> no right to the land, could only evacuate it. These boasts had no effect. Later
> I saw eaten by dogs a hundred of them whom the English slew between
> Winchester and Romsey. That was how they kept the land.[76]

Similarly, Ambroise, no doubt echoing similar vauntings among the Franks,
has Saladin upbraid his emirs and household 'that was wont so pridefully to
boast and vaunt' for their defeat at Arsuf: 'Where are those threatening
words, those blows of maces and of swords, which, blustering, ye said
would be dealt when ye met the enemy? Where is the fulsome talk and
prattle of rich conquest and mighty battle?'[77]

By contrast, men faced with the terrors of battle might take heart from
the prospect of achieving glory. If we are to believe William le Breton, at
the battle of Bouvines, the Flemish knight Baldwin de Buridan called upon
his fellows to think of their lady loves and the tournament.[78] At the battle
of Mansourah, 1250, where the Franks were heavily pressed, Joinville
recalled how the count of Soissons had sought to encourage him and other
knights by the thought of recounting brave feats in days to come:

> The good Comte de Soissons, hard put to it as we were at that moment, still
> made a joke of it and said to me gaily, 'By God's Bonnet' – that was his
> favourite oath – 'we shall talk of this day yet, you and I, sitting at home with
> our ladies!'[79]

---

[75] Keen, *Chivalry*, pp. 93–4, 134–41.

[76] *HGM*, ll. 15102–13; *EHD*, III, p. 81. Cf. JF, ll. 459–66; and *Maldon*, ll. 198–201, where, speaking of
the cowardly flight of Godric from the battlefield, the Maldon poet remarked; 'It was as Offa had
told them on the field when he held a council, that many were speaking proudly there, who later
would not stand firm in time of need.'

[77] Ambroise, ll. 6,769–778; *Itinerarium*, p. 278. The *Chanson d'Aspremont*, ll. 3675–84 (quoted by
Verbruggen, *Art of Warfare*, p. 46), has an analogous scenario with the Saracen Eaumons reproaching
his own men for their lack of courage despite their earlier boastings.

[78] WB, *Gesta*, p. 177. As Duby points out, however, William may well have been attempting to demonstrate 'that the enemy side is that of frivolity' (*The Legend of Bouvines*, p. 14).

[79] Joinville, p. 86; tr. Shaw, p. 225.

Nowhere, however, are the incentives of glory more cogently expressed than in the advice, 'true and good', given by John d'Earley to his lord William the Marshal, when the latter, burdened by the gravity of the situation he had inherited as regent in 1216, confided his deep anxieties to his trusted knights:

> Yes, you have undertaken a task that must be carried through at all costs. But when we reach the end, I tell you that, even putting things at their worst, only great honour can come of it. Let us suppose that all your supporters go over to Louis, that they surrender to him all the castles, to the point that you can find no refuge anywhere in England, and that pursued by Louis you are obliged to quit the country and seek refuge in Ireland: that will still be a great honour. And as the worst possible outcome is so honourable, the most propitious will bring you both great honour and great joy. No man will ever have earned such glory on earth.[80]

John d'Earley's counsel almost approaches a secular catechism, echoing the rewards of spiritual faith. Even in adversity, courage would bring honour: in victory, it would bring glory.

THE PRICE OF GLORY? INDIVIDUAL HONOUR AND CORPORATE DISCIPLINE

Given that the performance of deeds of prowess was essential in forming and sustaining a knight's standing in the eyes of his peers and of society, it was natural that in time of hostilities warriors were greatly concerned about where they were placed in the ranks of an army, both on the march and in the battle line itself. To strike the first blow was considered a great honour, and might be eagerly sought by knights as a boon from the commander. Thus, almost certainly echoing Frankish practice, the *Song of Roland* has the nephew of the Saracen emir Marsile ask his uncle for the privilege of being the first to attack Roland, and receives a gauntlet from Marsile in token of this commission.[81] Likewise, when the Franks arrange their battle lines prior to Charlemagne's battle against Baligant, the lord of the Breton contingent 'gives orders to Count Nevelon, to Tedbald of Reims and the Marquis Otton: "Lead my men; I present you with this honour."'[82]

Possession of such an honour might be hotly disputed, and we generally learn of these prerogatives only when arguments occurred over precedent. In a period when armies were frequently composed of hybrid forces,

---

[80] *HGM*, 11. 15655–85; *EHD*, III, p. 84.
[81] *Song of Roland*, 11, 860–77. Similarly, before the great battle between Charlemagne and the emir Baligant, the emir's son Malpramis likewise asks for the first blow (*ibid.*, 1. 3200).
[82] *Song of Roland*, 11. 3052–9.

disputes over questions of rank and honour could threaten to sow discord at the very time when it was essential to ensure cohesion and high morale in the face of the enemy. When, at Northallerton in 1138, King David I of Scotland was drawing up his ranks prior to the battle of the Standard, a bitter dispute broke out between the Galwegians and David's Anglo-Normans over who was to attack first. Well aware that the majority of his native troops were ill-equipped and possessed virtually no defensive armour, David had intended to place his knights and archers in the front rank, so that, in the words of Ailred of Rievaulx, 'armed men should attack armed men, and knights engage with knights and arrows resist arrows'.[83] The Galwegians, however, claimed that the right to strike the first blow was their prerogative, and when David tried to uphold his initial decision, a fierce quarrel erupted between the native earl of Strathearn, Malisse, and Alan de Percy. Fearful lest the Galwegians mutinied or set upon the Anglo-Normans, David yielded to their demands with disastrous results. The unprotected tribesmen were mown down by the English bowmen and their rout precipitated a general panic and flight among the Scots army.[84]

According to the *Histoire de Guillaume le Maréchal*, a similar dispute threatened to divide the royalist army assembled by the Marshal to march against the French force besieging Lincoln in 1217. On their march north

> the Normans in the army sought out the young Marshal [William's son] and said to him, 'My lord, you were born in Normandy. You know that the Normans have the right of striking the first blows in battle; do not let the tradition die out.' But the earl of Chester declared that if he did not command the front line, he would not take part in the action. The Marshal and his men, to avoid a quarrel, granted what he asked, without prejudicing the Norman's right (*salve la dreiture as Normanz*).[85]

Such questions of precedence applied not only to battle formations themselves but to the order of march. Roland is enraged when his uncle Ganelon nominates him to command the rearguard of Charlemagne's army on its retreat from Spain,[86] because he regarded his natural place as in the vanguard, which usually came to grips with the enemy first. Nevertheless, Roland's honour will not allow him to refuse the post, and in token of the command, Charlemagne invests him with a

---

[83] *Relatio*, pp. 189–90. On the poor armament of the native Scottish and Galwegian troops, and the significant military imbalance between Scottish and Anglo-Norman forces see M. J. Strickland, 'Securing the North: Invasion and the Strategy of Defence in Twelfth-Century Anglo-Scottish Warfare', *Anglo-Norman Studies*, 12 (1989), pp. 177–98, reprinted in Strickland, *Anglo-Norman Warfare*, pp. 208–29, especially pp. 221 ff.   [84] *Relatio*, pp. 189–91, 196–7.
[85] *HGM*, ll. 16204–24; *EHD*, III, p. 87.   [86] *Song of Roland*, ll. 740–82.

bow.[87] In Outremer, by contrast, the Turkish tactics of constantly harassing the rear of crusading armies made command of the rearguard as tacti-
cally vital as it was dangerous.[88] As a result, the rear was often entrusted to
the military orders, the Templars and Hospitallers being regarded as possessing both greater discipline and military skill than other crusading
forces.[89]

Questions of honour, however, were no less jealously guarded in this
theatre of war, where religious zeal might fuel the desire to display
prowess. Nowhere, indeed, was the clash between the desire for individual
glory and the need for corporate discipline in an army more acute than in
campaigns in Outremer. Against the fast, highly mobile Turkish horse-
archers and skirmishers, commanders such as Richard I and Louis IX were
well aware that safety lay only in cohesion and well-dressed ranks. Turkish
tactics, conversely, involved continually harassing the knights in order to
provoke them into breaking ranks and charging. When this happened, the
swift Turkish cavalry would flee from the Frankish charge until its impetus
was spent before turning to surround the now hopelessly vulnerable
knights.[90]

In such situations the Frankish knights' sense of individual honour put
them at a grave disadvantage and threatened to frustrate the military skill of
generals like Richard I. For though recent historiography has rightly been at
pains to stress the skill, caution and professionalism of eleventh- and
twelfth-century armies and the great reluctance of commanders to engage
in pitched battle, it is nevertheless important to recognize that a powerful
dichotomy often existed between individuals' desire for glory and the dictates of military discipline. Particularly in Outremer, many were unable to
subjugate personal or corporate pride to tactical wisdom, for to suffer
attack seemingly without retaliation – particularly when it entailed the loss
of valuable destriers to Turkish arrows – was deemed to be a deep affront
and a matter of great shame. Thus at the battle of Arsuf in 1191, the constant assaults of Saladin's troops on the Hospitallers forming the rear of
the crusaders' army prompted the Master of the Hospital to beg King
Richard for permission to attack:

[87] *Ibid.*, 11. 766–70, 780–2. The *Song of Roland* is full of references to the investment of such commands
by the gift of a glove, staff, or, in this instance, a bow. The ambassador to Saragossa is to receive a
glove and staff, and it is taken as an ill omen when Ganelon drops the staff (*ibid.*, 11. 246, 268, 319–35,
340–1, 761–70). The angel Gabriel receives Roland's glove as a token of the surrendering of his soul
to God (*ibid.*, 11. 2373–96; below, p. 187, n. 22).
[88] For Turkish tactics see R. C. Smail, *Crusading Warfare, 1097–1193* (Cambridge, 1956), pp. 77–83; cf. C.
Marshall, *Warfare in the Latin East, 1192–1291* (Cambridge, 1992).
[89] *Ibid.*, p. 80 and n. 4, and pp. 5, 127; A. Forey, *The Military Orders From the Twelfth to the Early Fourteenth
Centuries* (London, 1992), pp. 83–90.   [90] Smail, *Crusading Warfare*, pp. 77–83.

Lord king, we are grievously beset and are likely to be branded with eternal shame as men who dare not strike in their own defence. Each one of us is losing his own horse for nothing, and why should we put up with it any longer?[91]

Richard, however, was awaiting the crucial moment when the main body of the Turkish army became sufficiently engaged for the Frankish charge to have its full impact, and told the Master to endure the harassment for a while longer. But the inability to strike back proved too much. 'There was no leader or count', notes the author of the *Itinerarium*,

> who did not blush for very shame, saying one to the other, 'Why do we not give reins to our horses? Alas! Alas! We shall be convicted of cowardly sloth for evermore, and deservedly too. To whom has such a thing ever happened before? Never has shame of so dark a dye been inflicted upon so great an army. Unless we charge them speedily we shall earn ourselves everlasting ignominy; and the longer we delay, the greater will be our disgrace.'[92]

Two knights, the Marshal of the Hospitallers and Baldwin de Carron, broke prematurely from the ranks, which precipitated a general charge.[93] By swift action Richard was able to turn a potential disaster into a significant victory. But as the author of the *Itinerarium* notes reprovingly, if the king's original plan 'had only been carried out the whole body of the Turks would have been cut off and routed; but thanks to the over-haste of these two knights, the order was not observed to the great disadvantage of the common weal'.[94]

Though, by the standards of other contemporary forces, the military orders were, by virtue of the strict rule imposed upon the brothers, generally better disciplined in battle or on a fighting march, it is nevertheless significant that many of the recorded instances of knights breaking ranks against orders involve Hospitallers or Templars.[95] In part, this was because,

---

[91] *Itinerarium*, p. 267; Ambroise, 11. 6,386–88.   [92] *Itinerarium*, p. 268; Ambroise, 11. 6,393–402.

[93] Ambroise, 11. 6,421–60; *Itinerarium*, p. 268.

[94] *Itinerarium*, p. 269: Ambroise, 11. 6,403–20. On the battle of Arsuf see Smail, *Crusading Warfare*, pp. 161–5; Verbruggen, *Art of War*, pp. 210–20; Gillingham, *Richard the Lionheart*, pp. 188–91.

[95] The inherent tension between military discipline and the desire to achieve personal honour by feats of arms is epitomized by a vignette from the Third Crusade. During a Turkish attack on the Christian camp at Beit-Nuba in June 1192, a Hospitaller, Robert de Bruges, against orders not to engage in single combat, broke ranks and transfixed a prominent opponent with his lance, thereby achieving, says Ambroise, 'a brave feat of rare address, had he not broken discipline. His prowess was to blame therein.' He was at once rebuked by the Master of the Hospital, but was spared from punishment when several nobles begged the Master to pardon his offence 'for his great prowess' sake, the which had led him on to break the rule' (Ambroise, 11. 9,908–46; *Itinerarium*, pp. 371–2). Both Ambroise and the nobles recognized Robert's transgression, yet admired his bravery and skill at arms.

Cf. a very similar occurrence to that at Arsuf, occurring near Damietta in 1249, involving the marshal of the Templars, Renaud de Vichiers (Joinville, pp. 65–6; tr. Shaw, p. 211).

for all the severity of the Rule, many brother knights found it hard if not impossible to suppress the most basic values of the 'worldly chivalry' denounced by St Bernard.[96] Their arms might now be plain, void of decorations, their regimen and diet austere, but notions of prowess, glory and reputation died hard among men who were still a fighting elite. Their zeal was further fired by the assurance of salvation if they should perish in battle.[97] On several occasions, their pride and the thirst for honour, exacerbated by the orders' aggressive military self-confidence, threw caution and military pragmatism to the wind with catastrophic results.[98]

At Arsuf, it had been the fear of reproach for cowardice that had led Baldwin de Carron and the Hospitaller marshal to break ranks, and such a concern was widely shared. 'Better be dead than called a coward', noted the chanson *Elie de Saint-Gilles*.[99] Jordan Fantosme well expresses such sentiments in his description of the counsel of war of the group of Anglo-Norman planning an attack on the William the Lion as he lay before the castle of Alnwick in 1174. 'Shame on him who refuses!' Odinel d'Umfraville is made to say, 'I shall be the very first to strike a blow, if such be God's pleasure.' And in a forthright equation of landholding with military prowess, Bernard de Balliol adds, 'He who is not bold and resolute now does not deserve to have a fief or anything belonging thereto.'[100] Just as the grant of a fief might be the reward for valour, so in Jordan Fantosme's world of ideals continued possession of it had to be constantly justified by further acts of bravery in war.

COWARDICE, SHAME AND DISHONOUR

If feats of arms won honour and glory, then conversely failure in war, timidity and worst of all cowardice incurred the stigma of shame and

---

[96] The desire by brother knights to achieve personal glory was a temptation well understood by the *Rule of the Temple* itself; *Rule of the Temple*, c. 242–3, 611–15, pp. 75–6, 157–8.

[97] This view is expressed most cogently by St Bernard in his address to the Templars, *De laude novae militiae*, p. 217. For contemporary Christian and Muslim views about the bravery and skill of the military orders see Forey, *The Military Orders*, pp. 83–6.

[98] At Ascalon in 1157, the Templars actually held back other Christian forces from exploiting a breach in the walls, so that forty of their brethren might win the glory of seizing the fortress. Instead, they were cut to pieces and the success of the siege jeoparized (WT, Bk XVII, c. 27, pp. 798–9; tr. Babcock and Krey, p. 227). At Cresson in 1187, the Templars suffered very heavy lossess after the desire for glory had led the Grand Master, Gerard de Ridefort, to attack a vastly superior Muslim force (Forey, *The Military Orders*, p. 87).

As Louis IX's army was advancing into Egypt from Damietta in 1249, the Templars, 'thinking they would be shamed if they let the comte d'Artois ahead of them', rushed into an ambush at Mansourah, where the Franks suffered appalling casualities. Artois, Raoul de Coucy and 300 knights were killed while the Templars lost 280 mounted men-at-arms (Joinville, pp. 77–8; tr. Shaw, pp. 218–19).   [99] Quoted by Verbruggen, *Art of War*, p. 56.   [100] JF, 11. 1736–7; cf WN, p. 184.

dishonour. The greatest opprobrium was reserved for those guilty of head-long flight, and cowardice in the face of the enemy might be physically pun-ished. The laws of Cnut prescribed death and total forfeiture for any who by fleeing from battle deserted their lord or comrades, and this stricture was reiterated by the *Leges Henrici Primi*.[101] Richard of Devizes noted that at Messina, Richard I decreed that any knight who fled was to lose his belt of knighthood, while any foot soldier was to lose a foot.[102]

But as grievous as physical punishment was the irreparable damage that the slur of cowardice could have upon a man's honour and reputa-tion. When faced in 1213 with a French invasion, John ordered a general muster of all freemen at Dover, to be obeyed on pain of servitude and of incurring the name of *culvertagium*, a phrase of uncertain derivation but clearly echoing the Anglo-Scandinavian *nithing*.[103] A mark of the greatest shame, this term of ignominy was pronounced against those who, like Svein Godwinson, had utterly violated acceptable norms of behaviour.[104] That it was used to stigmatize those who failed to perform military service is suggested by the *Anglo-Saxon Chronicle*'s statement that in the face of the rebellion of 1088, Rufus summoned to the army everyone, both French and English, 'who was not a *nithing*'.[105] Nor was it only in war that a man might incur the shameful brand of cowardice. 'Glanvill' notes how in trial by battle, 'the vanquished champion is liable to a penalty of

---

[101] II Cnut 77, *EHD*, I, p. 466; *Leges Henrici Primi*, ed. L. J. Downer (Oxford, 1972), c. 13:12, and cf. 10:1, which lists 'qui in bello campali vel navali fugerit' amongst pleas of the crown.

[102] Devizes, p. 22.

[103] MP, II, p. 539; 'et quod nullus remaneat qui arma portare possit, sub nomine culvertagii et perpetuae servitutis'. Wendover is here citing a royal writ in full. Earlier that same year, he noted that Philip Augustus summoned his forces to muster at Rouen for an invasion of England 'sub nomine cul-vertagii . . . ne crimine laesae majestatis damnum exhaeredationis incurrere viderentur', to which Matthew Paris adds 'vulgariter sub nomine felonis' (MP, II, p. 537). The exact meaning and etymol-ogy of the word is uncertain. Du Cange, who quotes the above two passages as his main source for the word (*Glossarium mediae et infimae latinitatis* (*Glossarium*), ed. L. Favre, 10 vols. (Niort), III, p. 697), rejects the suggestion of Selden, Twysden and others that it derives from *culum vertere*, or to take flight, and believes 'sub nomine culvertagii' to equate with 'sub poena confiscationis'. Latham (*Revised Medieval Latin Word-List*, p. 95), equates *culvertagium* with *colibertus*, and gives one meaning as 'reduction to status of a freed serf', a suggestion that would fit in well with the 'et perpetuae sevi-tutis' of John's writ. It clearly was a label of great ignominy, and the vernacular French 'cuivert, culvert, cuvert' means a traitor, or one guilty of treason, infamy or perjury (*Glossarium*, pp. 696–7).

[104] Following the treacherous murder of his cousin Beorn, 'the king and all the *here* [army] declared Swein a *nithing*' (*ASC*, 'C', *s.a.* 1046). The term seems to have been Scandinavian in origin. Sveno's *Lex Castrensis* relates that if any housecarl slew a brother member, he should be tried by the *huskar-lasteffne* and, if found guilty, be exiled and given the 'nithing-name' (Larson, *The King's Household*, pp. 165–6; but see the important revision of Larson's findings by Hooper, 'Housecarls in England', especially pp. 162–4, for a further discussion of the term *nithing*). In Iceland, if an opponent failed to attend the duel or *holmgang*, the challenger might proclaim the '*nithing* name' against him three times and erect a 'pole of scorn', carved with scenes of his alleged cowardice and/or sexual perversions (M. Ciklamini, 'The Old Icelandic Duel', *Scandinavian Studies*, 35 (1963), pp. 175–94).

[105] *ASC*, 'C', *s.a.* 1088; cf. *GR*, II, p. 362, which renders *nithing* as *nequam*.

sixty shillings for crying craven (*nomine recreantise*), and shall also lose his law'.[106]

In most cases, however, the brand of cowardice was imputed by far less official means. When forced in 1192 to retreat a second time from within sight of Jerusalem, the French crusaders under the duke of Burgundy vented their bitterness by singing insulting songs about the king of England. Richard replied in kind, composing the verses in person.[107] Derisory ballads were sung about the 'brave' defence of the key Norman fortress of Vaudreuil, surrendered to Philip Augustus without a blow in 1203,[108] while men scoffed at the rapid and near-bloodless defeat of the French and baronial forces at the 'fair of Lincoln' in 1217.[109] This was a predominantly oral culture, and such verses must have been the chief vehicle for reproach as much as praise. The written word, however, could ensure lasting opprobrium for the cowardly. Irrespective of their political affiliations, chroniclers fulminated at Stephen's earls who broke and fled at Lincoln in 1141, leaving the king and a group of more steadfast nobles to fight on until they were overwhelmed.[110] Roger of Wendover was careful to record the ignominious flight of the commander of John's mercenaries, Hugh de Boves, at Bouvines, while Matthew Paris even illustrated the event.[111] The author of the *Itinerarium* did not spare to record the fact that, at the battle of Arsuf in 1191, the count of Dreux and his men 'were stamped with indelible infamy' for failing to go to the rescue of the prominent crusader James of Avesnes, who as a result was surrounded and slain.[112]

Authors were well aware of this power to preserve enduring shame. Speaking of a raid by a large body of horsemen on Bamburgh castle during the Scots invasion of Northumbria in 1174, Jordan notes; 'I am well acquainted with the baron who took them there as their leader; I shall refrain from naming him, because his reputation suffered there.'[113] Joinville similarly avoids naming names when speaking of the cowardly flight of many at Mansourah: 'I could tell you their names, but shall refrain from

[106] *Glanvill*, II, 3, p. 25. 'Glanvill' explains that the Grand Assize has been granted to the people by the king so they might avoid 'unexpected and untimely death, or at least the reproach of the perpetual disgrace which follows that distressed and shameful word which sounds so dishonourably from the mouth of the vanquished' (*ibid.*, p. 28).   [107] Ambroise, 11. 10,651–64; *Itinerarium*, pp. 395–6.
[108] Coggeshall, pp. 143–4.
[109] MP, III, p. 24. The term *nundinae* used here by Wendover was also applied to the tournament. John of Hexham similarly records how the English called the battle of the Standard in 1138 'Baggamoor', in derision of the Scots' rout which had left so much equipment strewn on the battlefield (JH, p. 120).
[110] *HN*, p. 49; *GS*, pp. 112–13; Orderic, VI, pp. 542–5.
[111] MP, II, p. 580; WB, *Gesta*, p. 287; Lewis, *The Art of Matthew Paris*, p. 185; above, illustration 6.
[112] *Itinerarium*, p. 276; Ambroise, 11. 6,651–658, notes that this failure 'caused much talk' and 'so many censured this neglect, that I cannot their views reject'.   [113] JF, 11. 1153–5.

doing so because they are now dead.'[114] Others chose not to exercise such discretion. Roger of Howden was deliberately explicit when he came to record the cowardly actions of Louis VII at Verneuil in 1173,[115] while Angevin chronicles were fulsome in their denunciation of Philip Augustus's decision to abandon the Third Crusade after the fall of Acre in 1191.[116]

Whatever the fear knights actually experienced in combat,[117] the desire to avoid being thus branded with cowardice was a powerful stimulus to stand fast. At Roncevalles, it is Roland's pride that prevents him from blowing his horn to summon aid from Charlemagne. 'That', he tells Oliver, 'would be an act of folly; throughout the fair land of France I would lose my good name'.[118] Instead, he exhorts the Franks: 'Now let each man take care to strike great blows, so that no one can sing a shameful song about us.'[119] Nor were such sentiments restricted to the epic world of the chansons. When, for example, the baronial force sent to occupy Rochester castle in 1215 found it unprovisioned, many wished to abandon it, but their commander William d'Albini, 'exhorting and continually animating the minds of his companions to deeds of valour, said that it was not right for knights to desert, lest, what would be a great disgrace to them, they should subsequently be called deserter knights'.[120] Similarly, confronted with Louis's demand to surrender Dover in 1216, the castellan, Hubert de Burgh, took council with the garrison, but they were all unanimous in refusing to surrender it to Louis 'lest they might be branded with treachery for a cowardly submission'.[121]

Naturally, however, military pragmatism frequently demanded retreat or strategic withdrawal. The *Rule* of the Temple allowed the brothers to leave the field of battle without reproach if no Christian banner was left flying as a rallying point.[122] Nevertheless, withdrawal in the face of the enemy ran the risk of incurring the stigma of shame and cowardice. Describing events on the Anglo-Scottish border in 1173, Jordan Fantosme has a messenger

---

[114] Joinville, p. 87; tr. Shaw, p. 226.

[115] *GH*, I, p. 55: 'In order that these events may be kept in memory, it is as well to know that this flight of the king of France took place on the fifth day of the week, upon the vigil of St Laurence, to the praise and glory of our Lord Jesus Christ, who by punishing the crime of perfidy so speedily avenged the indignity done to his martyr.'

[116] Ambroise, ll. 5,245–88; *Itinerarium*, pp. 236–7; *GH*, II, pp. 182–3; Devizes, p. 48. According to Howden at least, his barons, bitterly shamed, in vain begged their lord not to bring the reputation of the French into disrepute by this indecorous act (*GH*, II, pp. 182–3).

[117] For an excellent discussion of fear in medieval warfare see Verbruggen, *Art of War*, pp. 39–52, and cf. Contamine, *War in the Middle Ages*, pp. 250–9.

[118] *Song of Roland*, ll. 1053–4.   [119] *Ibid.*, ll. 1013–14.

[120] *Chronica Rogeri de Wendover liber qui dicitur Flores Historiarum* (Wendover), ed. H. G. Hewlett, 3 vols. (*RS*, 1886–9), II, p. 146. Matthew Paris considerably shortens this passage (MP, II, p. 621).

[121] MP, III, p. 5.   [122] *Rule of the Temple*, c. 421.

tell William the Lion that unless he withdraws from the siege of Carlisle, he will be routed and put to shame by the stronger force of the English justi-ciar Richard de Lucy:

> Look to yourselves by the Divine majesty, lest you be shamed and dis-honoured . . . Take my advice – it is the best that can be given to you – betake yourself to the safety of Roxburgh! If you tarry longer here, a mocking song will be sung of you. Thibault de Balesgué did not trounce the French as badly as you will be trounced by the hardened soldiers from the south if you and they clash in battle.[123]

Though William the Lion wanted to stay and fight, his counsellers urged a rapid withdrawal 'if he wanted to preserve his reputation henceforth', prompting Jordan to remark contemptuously;

> None of his men drew rein. In great haste they came to Roxburgh whence they had previously set forth. Not a single man of his army that had been before Carlisle but scurried in arrant cowardice (*par mult grant lasché*) without any attack being launched on them, any challenge given or any hurt inflicted.[124]

Jordan's scathing words highlight an acute dilemma faced by William the Lion. Ever since William's grandfather David I had been raised in the court of Henry I as an Anglo-Norman baron, the Scots kings, increas-ingly surrounding themselves with Franco-Norman counsellors, had sought to emulate the customs and institutions south of the Tweed. To Henry of Huntingdon and Ailred of Rievaulx, Earl Henry, William's father, had been a model prince and a dashing knight. William himself, who had accompanied his brother Malcolm IV on Henry II's Toulouse expedition in 1159 and who later took an enthusiastic part in the tourna-ment circuit of northern France, regarded himself first and foremost as an Anglo-Norman knight.[125] Yet this desire to appear as a leading expo-nent of knighthood, closely reflected as we shall see in his conduct in war,[126] was gravely compromised by the nature of the military forces at his disposal.

The Scottish army, composed largely of unarmoured Scots and Galwegian infantry and bolstered by only a handful of knights, was inca-pable of meeting an English army on equal terms in the open field, as the battle of the Standard in 1138 had so graphically shown. Raiding, the studied avoidance of battle and rapid withdrawal from superior Anglo-Norman field armies were the tactics which best suited the

---

[123] JF, 11.724–35.   [124] *Ibid.*, 11.752–8.
[125] Strickland, 'Arms and the Men', pp. 208–13; below, pp. 150, 155–6, 326–9.   [126] Below, pp. 219–20.

Scottish forces.[127] But in such a strategy, there was no glory, no chance for feats of arms and individual deeds of prowess. A policy of non-engagement, though sound in military terms, ran the risk of the commander being labelled a coward. Conversely, however, standing one's ground risked almost inevitable defeat and, as William found to his cost, the concomitant shame of imprisonment and a humiliating peace settlement. Speaking of William's capture at Alnwick in 1174, Jordan noted, 'No member of his house was ever put to such shame (*ne fust si avilé*)!'[128]

The effects of acts of cowardice on a man's standing in society are sharply revealed by the case of Count Stephen of Blois and the 'rope dancers' of Antioch, who had fled the Christian camp there in 1098 when Kerbogha laid siege to the city. Orderic notes that Stephen 'was an object of contempt to almost everyone, and was continually reproached because he had fled disgracefully from the siege of Antioch, deserting his glorious comrades who were sharing in the agonies of Christ'.[129] The subsequent success of those who took Jerusalem only served to highlight the indignity of the flight of Stephen and his colleagues. Although he completed a pilgrimage to Jerusalem in 1102, and died fighting at Ramla, he never fully recovered from the ignominy.[130] William the Carpenter and Peter the Hermit, who had deserted the Christian camp earlier on the First Crusade, were caught by Tancred, brought back and exposed to the anger of Bohemond and the contumely of all.[131]

A moment's panic brought about the disgrace and total ruin of Henry of Essex, a noble who, noted Jocelin of Brakelond, had been 'accounted a man of high renown among the first in the realm, for he was of illustrious birth, conspicuous in feats of arms, the King's standard bearer, and feared by all'.[132] In 1157, when Henry II's army was ambushed in the pass of Coleshill near Harwarden during an expedition into Wales, Henry of Essex, believing the king to have been slain, 'lowered the royal standard, which should have served to rally the army's courage, and took flight, proclaiming the king's death to all he met'.[133] For this cowardice, and the crime of 'imagining' the king's death, Henry was accused of treason by Robert de Montfort in 1163, and defeated in trial by combat. Though Henry II

---

[127] Strickland, 'Securing the North', pp. 190–8.   [128] JF, 11. 1708.   [129] Orderic, v, pp. 324–5.

[130] Davis, *King Stephen*, pp. 3–4; J. Brundage, 'An Errant Crusader: Stephen of Blois', *Traditio*, 16 (1960), pp. 380–95, reprinted in *idem., The Crusades, Holy War and Canon Law*. When Pope Paschal threatened to excommunicate all who had not fulfilled their crusading vows, Stephen 'was driven to embark on another crusade as much by fear as by shame' (Orderic, v, pp. 324–5).

[131] *Gesta Francorum et aliorum Hierosolimitanorum (GFr)*, ed. and tr. R. Hill (Oxford, 1962), p. 33.

[132] Brakelond, p. 69.   [133] WN, p. 108.

commuted the death sentence, he confiscated his extensive inheritance and ordered Henry to enter the monastery at Reading.[134]

A man might not simply bring infamy upon himself by such cowardice. Roland refuses to flee or summon Charlemagne to his aid at Roncevalles, for to lose face thereby would sully not only his own reputation, but that of his kin and of France: 'God forbid that my kinsmen should incur reproach because of me or that the fair land of France should fall into disrepute.'[135] How acute such fear of tarnishing the family name might be is strikingly revealed by Joinville. At Mansourah in 1250, he and his men were surrounded in a ruined house by an overwhelming number of Turks. Though terribly wounded, his knights put up a fierce resistance for which 'they were afterward highly praised by all men of good standing in the army, both those who witnessed their bravery and those who heard of it later'.[136] One of them, Erard de Siverey, whose nose had just been cut off by a blow, came to Joinville and said: 'My lord, if you think that neither I or my heirs will incur reproach for it, I will go and fetch you help from the Comte d'Anjou, whom I see in the fields over there.' Joinville, much more of a pragmatist than Roland, replied; 'My dear man, it seems to me you would win great honour for yourself if you went for help to save our lives; your own, by the way, is in great danger.' 'I spoke truly', adds Joinville, 'for he died of his wound'. Erard then 'consulted the other knights who were there, and they all gave him the same advice as I had given him'.[137]

Fear of bringing disrepute upon one's kin was a universal concern. Orderic has Ralph, vicomte of Beaumont, express similar anxieties when, in 1098, he sought a truce from William Rufus who had invaded Maine. Ralph asked for a cessation of hostilities while he journeyed to Le Mans to learn the orders of the regency council: 'This I propose my lord king, by the advice of my oldest councillors, because if I should be the first to give in without a blow and the first to desert my peers and enter into a peace I would certainly leave a legacy of shame and dishonour to all my descendants.'[138] Rufus, highly conscious of questions of honour, readily agreed.

Honour, or conversely shame, was thus seen as hereditary; men might bask in the reflected glory of ancestors or bear the stigma of their dishonour.[139] Men such as William Rufus, Ralph de Beaumont or the poet of the *Song of Roland* would have fully appreciated the desire to uphold and, by

---

[134] The fullest account of the incident is given by Brakelond, pp. 68–71. Cf. Gervase, I, 165; Diceto, I, p. 310; and WN, p. 108. [135] *Song of Roland*, 11. 1062–4. [136] Joinville, p. 79; tr. Shaw, p. 221.
[137] Joinville, p. 80; tr. Shaw, p. 221. [138] Orderic, v, pp. 240–1.
[139] Henry III used William the Marshal's supposed connivance with Philip and Prince Louis in 1216–17 to taunt Gilbert Marshal in 1241 (F. M. Powicke, *Henry III and the Lord Edward*, 2 vols. (Oxford, 1947, repr. 1966 as a single volume), p. 18).

noble deeds in war, to augment a family's honour, strikingly expressed by the Maldon poet. Among the speeches of mutual exhortation given to Byrhtnoth's warriors as they fight to the finish, is that of Aelfwine, son of Aelfric:

> I will make known my lineage to all, how I was born in Mercia of a great race. Ealhelm was my grandfather called, a wise ealdorman, happy in the world's goods. Thegns shall have no cause to reproach me among my people that I was ready to forsake this action and seek my home, now that my lord lies low, cut down in battle.[140]

Whether we choose to regard the Norman conquest as heralding a 'military revolution' with the introduction of cavalry and castle-based warfare, or as a fusion of Frankish and Anglo-Scandinavian methods of warfare, whereby Anglo-Norman knights might regularly dismount to fight on foot,[141] what is clear is that in fundamental respects the knighthood's concepts of reputation, loyalty and honour were but little removed from those of their Anglo-Scandinavian predecessors.

RUSE, GUILE AND THE LIMITATIONS OF HONOUR AS A COERCIVE FORCE

Honour and reputation thus lay at the heart of the self-perception of the knighthood, and it is within this context that adherence to conventions of conduct in war must be placed. Acts of magnanimity such as the granting of a respite to a beleaguered garrison, the granting of free egress with horses and arms to valiant defenders or the freeing of prisoners, augmented a man's reputation and standing in the eyes of his peers.[142] In turn, the fact that such actions brought praise and heightened esteem acted as a powerful incentive for their emulation by others, thereby creating and maintaining a currency of conduct that was deemed honourable and worthy. Conversely, violation of such notions might incur dishonour and stigmatization.

Nevertheless, there were significant limitations on the coercive powers of honour and shame. Given the abstract nature of such notions, there was liable to be considerable divergence from the standard set by those warriors like Rufus, Richard I or William Marshal, regarded as the epitome of knightly virtue, but who *ipso facto* were the exception. Notions of chivalry,

---

[140] *The Battle of Maldon*, ll. 216–23; and cf. ll. 249–53.
[141] Cf D. R. Cook, 'The Norman Military Revolution in England', *Proceedings of the Battle Conference*, I (1978), pp. 94–102; Hollister, *Anglo-Saxon Military Institutions*, pp. 127 ff.; and above, p. 23.
[142] Below, pp. 203, 210–11, 218–21.

like religious precepts, offered a model, a standard to which men might aspire, but of which many fell short.[143] Despite drawing on established concepts, honour was ultimately a personal issue, with acceptance or rejection of convention being governed by the conscience and self-esteem of the individual.

If, moreover, men like William Rufus or William the Marshal stood at one end of the spectrum of decorous conduct, there were men like Thomas de Marle, lord of Coucy, or Robert de Bellême who stood at the other, notorious for their flagrant disregard for convention and their sadistic treatment of prisoners.[144] Yet even here, the boundaries of accepted conduct might be blurred. The shame incurred by a resounding defeat or by cowardice and flight from the face of the enemy was manifest and universally recognized. But what of acts of brutality, particularly if executed by a warrior successful against the enemy? What indeed constituted brutality or atrocity in the eyes of contemporaries? These are crucial themes to which we shall return.[145]

For the moment, however, the complex, even contradictory nature of contemporary knightly values may be suggested by the fact that despite his notorious cruelty and maltreatment of prisoners, Robert de Bellême's prowess was undeniable and acknowledged even by his most vociferous critics. A fine soldier and an expert in fortification and siege warfare,[146] Robert served as Rufus's principal, and highly successful, commander in Maine. That Rufus, the epitome of late-eleventh-century chivalry, could hold Robert is such esteem says much about men's attitudes to conduct.[147] Bellême might receive general censure for his excesses, but no one disputed his competence as a warrior, his undeniable value in war.

In many instances, as we shall see in the following chapters, there was a happy and far from accidental correlation between honourable conduct in war and pragmatic self-interest. Yet this was not always the case, and if some lords were prepared to sacrifice tactical, strategic or political advantage for questions of honour and adherence to chivalric conduct, others were equally prepared to violate such norms for military advantage. Two incidents that occurred during the 'great war' of 1173–4 may serve to reveal the complex and often paradoxical relationship that might exist between

---

[143] Cf. Huizinga, *Waning of the Middle Ages*, p. 67: 'The conception of chivalry as a sublime form of secular life might be defined as an aesthetic ideal assuming the appearance of an ethical ideal . . . Chivalry, however, will always fall short of this ethical function. Its earthly origin draws it down.'
[144] Below, pp. 199–200.   [145] Below, pp. 281–320.   [146] Orderic, IV, pp. xxxiv, 228–30.
[147] For William Rufus's chivalry see William of Malmesbury, *GR*, II, pp. 359, 365–6; Gaimar, *Estoire des Engles*, II. 5924–5, 5965–74; F. Barlow, *William Rufus* (1983), pp. 23–5, 100, 396–7; and below, pp. 149, 203. 221. 254.

accepted usage, notions of honourable conduct and tactical realism. Significantly, both occur during the two most important sieges of the war, those of Verneuil 1173 and Rouen 1174.

In July 1173, Louis VII closely invested the key Norman border town of Verneuil which boasted a powerful castle and a town comprised of a number of fortified 'burghs', each separated from the other by its own walls and a water-filled moat.[148] After a month's investment, Louis's army had made no headway against the citadel, but the 'great burgh' or the 'Queen's burgh' had been cut off from support and its inhabitants, comprising many of the poor and sick, had been reduced to dire straits by hunger and disease. On report of their plight, Louis offered the burgh a truce of three days in which to seek aid from Henry II.[149] The townspeople gave hostages and pledged to surrender if relief was not forthcoming by 9 August, the vigil of St Lawrence, who appropriately – or so it seemed – was Louis's patron saint.[150] Louis in turn pledged that on surrender their hostages would be freely restored and that no harm would come to the citizens.[151] Despite Henry II's proximity, a respite of only three days was remarkably short; as the outcome of events was to show, Louis intended that the prospect of relief should be as slight as possible.

On receiving the messengers from the beleaguered burgh, Henry II rapidly gathered his forces and on 8 August drew up his army at Breteuil and challenged the French to battle.[152] Believing that by offering battle he had relieved the town before the expiry of the respite, Henry agreed to peace talks set for 9 August and gave the French a truce till the morrow. But the French had deceived Henry in order to buy time. For on 9 August, instead of meeting him to parley, Louis fired the great burgh, seized the townspeople, their chattels and their hostages and retreated precipitously into France. It seems that the citizens had surrendered, ignorant of Henry's negotiations and believing that relief was not forthcoming. Alerted to the French king's trickery by the smoke rising from Verneuil, Henry gave pursuit, killed many stragglers and overran the French camp, gaining much booty.[153]

Whether Louis's guile was premeditated from the granting of the respite or was merely the panicked response to Henry II's rapid arrival is unclear.

---

[148] *GH*, I, p. 50; Torigny, p. 257; Diceto, I, p. 374, who calls the besieged burgh the 'Queen's burgh' and notes that it was one of seven in the town. See also M. F. Salet, 'Verneuil', *Congrès Archéologique de France*, III (1953), especially pp. 407–11, 418–22. For the strategic aims of the coalition against Henry II and a good general account of the campaigns of 1173–4, see Warren, *Henry II*, pp. 121–36 and J. Boussard, *Le Gouvernment d'Henri II Plantagenêt* (Paris, 1961), pp. 471–88.

[149] For the convention of respite see below, pp. 208–12.

[150] *GH*, I, pp. 50, 55; Diceto, I, p. 374; WN, pp. 192–3.   [151] *GH*, I, p. 50; Diceto, I, pp. 374–5.

[152] *GH*, I, p. 51; Diceto, I, p. 375; WN, pp. 174–5.   [153] *GH*, I, pp. 54–5; Diceto, I, p. 375; WN, p. 175.

The events at Verneuil nevertheless demonstrate how tactical expediency might triumph over considerations of honour. Nevertheless, to a considerable extent Louis's actions had themselves been conditioned by established convention. His manipulation of the mechanism of parley was intended to keep Henry II away from Verneuil long enough for the townsfolk to believe that Henry had failed to relieve them, so that Louis could take the burgh according to the strict letter of convention. Equally, even though he set a deliberately short respite to frustrate their chances of rescue, the French king had accepted the citizens' request to seek relief. There was no legal compulsion for a commander to accept such proffers, and Louis might well have starved the occupants of the great burgh into unconditional surrender or have taken the weakened defenders by storm.

Yet if we are to believe the Angevin chroniclers, and unfortunately there is little by way of corrective from Capetian sources, Louis once again breached a respite granted on his sworn oath to the citizens of Rouen, exactly a year after he sullied his reputation at Verneuil. The principal account, provided by William of Newburgh some twenty years after the event, invites caution with its invented speeches and classical quotation. Had he been familiar with the details of Louis's duplicity at Verneuil, one might be tempted to dismiss this as just one more story of French perfidy. But Newburgh shows no knowledge of the violation of the respite in 1173,[154] and his description of the siege of Rouen is so detailed it suggests access to an eye-witness report.

In July 1174, Louis, the Young King and Philip of Flanders had invested Rouen. As the citizens controlled the crossing of the Seine and could easily be resupplied, blockade was impossible, leaving direct assault as the besiegers' only option.[155] The citizens conducted a fierce defence and the attackers had made little headway by the time the feast of St Lawrence, 10 August, again approached. Perhaps to offer satisfaction to his patron for the debacle at Verneuil, Louis ordered a day's respite to celebrate the festival of Lawrence, 'whom he was accustomed especially and devoutly to venerate'.[156] This was not a conditional respite, for control of the Seine meant the citizens could summon aid whenever they wished. Nevertheless, they celebrated with jousts and dancing 'as much out of joy at the day as to irritate the enemy'.[157]

This was too much for many of the army's commanders. They had watched with impotent anger as the city was revictualled, and now their king, whose military acumen was less evident than his piety, had granted a respite to an enemy who had repeatedly repelled them, and who now

[154] *Ibid.*, pp. 173–5.   [155] WN, pp. 190–1.   [156] *Ibid.*, p. 191.   [157] *Ibid.*, p. 192.

seemed to mock them by their festivities. It was against this mounting sense of frustration that Philip of Flanders approached Louis and suggested that while the citizens were preoccupied, off-guard and with many of them outside the city on the far bank, the allies should launch a surprise attack. They could thus gain their chief objective at a blow.[158]

According to Newburgh, Louis at first indignantly refused: 'Far be it from me to blemish my kingly honour with such a stain, for you know that I have granted the city repose for this day out of reverence to the most blessed Lawrence.' But his army leaders 'with familiar boldness reproved his mildness' and finally winning the king over, they launched a clandestine assault on the town.[159] Their movements, however, were spotted, the alarm raised, and the attackers repulsed after fierce fighting. Defeated and discredited, Louis tried to shift the blame onto Philip of Flanders. But the stain of this treachery fell principally on the person of the king.[160]

What Angevin observers found so heinous about Louis's conduct at Verneuil and Rouen (and why to his discredit they related these events in detail) was not so much its sacrilegious quality, but the fact that Louis had violated sworn agreements of respite and truce that he had entered into of his own volition. We have already noted King Stephen's angry reaction to a violation of safe conduct,[161] and here the same thinking prompted such opprobrium against the French king. For in violating such central conventions of war, Louis was threatening to undermine the very mechanisms by which aggression could be contained and which sought to regulate siege to the mutual benefit of the combatants.[162]

Where no prior agreement was involved, however, surprise and guile might be considered perfectly legitimate.[163] Low cunning was not itself dishonourable; what brought shame was perjury of an oath promising to abstain from such acts. The case of Count Philip of Flanders is instructive. The *Histoire de Guillaume le Maréchal* records how in tournaments Count Philip and his knights developed the ruse of waiting on the sidelines until the opposing teams were tired and disorganized, then rushing in and taking many of the fatigued knights prisoner.[164] Yet far from condemning Philip's ruse in the tournament – of which young Henry and the Marshal were erstwhile victims – the *Histoire* proudly notes that it was on the advice of

---

[158] By way of justification, Newburgh has Philip add, 'Who asks if it be valour or deceit in an enemy?' (*ibid.*, p. 193). Gerald of Wales uses the same quote, taken from the *Aeneid*, II, 1. 390, in his *Topographica Hibernica* to describe the pragmatic attitude of the Irish to perfidy in war (Gerald of Wales, *Opera Omnia*, ed. J. F. Dimock and G. F. Warner, 8 vols. (Rolls Series, 1861–91), v, p. 166.
[159] WN, pp. 192–3.   [160] *Ibid.*, pp. 193–4.   [161] Above, p. 49.   [162] Below, pp. 208–12.
[163] Cf. Leyser, 'Early Medieval Warfare, p. 42; '*dolus* and *astutia*, craft and cunning, were admired qualities in a commander'.   [164] HGM, 11. 2715–41.

William himself that the Young King's *mesnie* adopted this tactic and henceforth employed it regularly, thereby greatly improving their fortunes in the
tourney.[165]

Philip, indeed, was regarded as one of the leading exponents of chivalry,
and whatever his real part in the affair at Rouen in 1174,[166] it clearly did little
to dent his high reputation. Chrétien de Troyes dedicated his last, unfin-
ished work, *Perceval* or the *Conte du Graal*, to him,[167] and shortly after 1183
Walter Map could write that 'of all the princes of these days, except our
own king, he is the mightiest in arms and in the art of ruling'.[168] Although
he had been a leading opponent of Henry II in the war of 1173–4, Philip
thereafter acted as the chivalric patron of the Young King and his knights,
bestowing costly arms and equipment on the profligate prince and his
retinue.[169] Map recalls how the younger Henry, not yet twenty 'offered
himself alone and a foreigner to Philip, count of Flanders, to learn of him
(if worthy) the art of chivalry, and chose him out for his lord'.[170] The
Histoire calls him 'li proz, qui par son sens sormontot toz cels qui estoient a
son tens', while Jordan Fantosme portrays him as 'le noble guerreur', an
experienced commander who advocates ravaging as the most effective
means of waging war.[171]

If cunning was applauded in the tournament, guile and surprise were
acknowledged as fundamental and ubiquitous aspects of war itself and –
save where they violated truces or other pre-arranged conventions – were
often praised as an integral element in the successful prosecution of
warfare. In the *conventio* between the earls of Chester and Leicester, it was
agreed that neither should lay traps or snares for the other except after a
defiance fifteen days before.[172] The implication was that thereafter such
behaviour was perfectly acceptable. The *Histoire de Guillaume le Maréchal* saw
no cause to censure John fitz Gilbert, the Marshal's father, for a ruse
whereby he ambushed and slew many of Earl Patrick of Salisbury's knights
when they were unprepared.[173] The approbation suggested by the inclusion
of this anecdote is still more pronounced in the *Histoire*'s subsequent relation of how in 1188 William the Marshal advised Henry II to pretend to
disband his army, wait till the opposing French forces had dispersed, then
to ravage Philip II's lands unhindered. Far from being considered 'unchival-
rous', his counsel was greeted with favour and applauded by Henry as '*mult*

---

[165] *Ibid.*, ll. 2742–72.
[166] William of Newburgh adds a cautious 'it is said' when ascribing to him the instigation of treachery
at Rouen (WN, p. 192).   [167] *Le Conte du Graal*, ll, 1–68; Chrétien, *Arthurian Romances*, pp. 381–2.
[168] Walter Map, *De nugis curialium* (Map), ed. and tr. M. R. James (Oxford, 1983), pp. 278–9.
[169] *HGM*, ll. 2443–96.   [170] Map, pp. 278–9.
[171] *HGM*, ll. 2715–17; JF, ll. 439–52, and see below, p. 266–7.   [172] Above, p. 41.
[173] For the incident in detail see *HGM*, ll. 283–354; and Painter, *William Marshal*, pp. 8–9.

courteis.[174] As Gillingham notes, 'the well organized chevauchée was one which took the enemy by surprise'.[175]

In battle, surprise or ruse might be a key factor in gaining victory. The Normans' use of the 'feigned flight' at Hastings, which proved decisive, is but the most celebrated example of a widespread and highly successful tactic, employed, for example, by the Normans at St Aubin-le-Cauf near Arques in 1052–3, near Messina in 1060, and by Count Robert of Flanders at Cassel in 1071.[176] In siege warfare, moreover, the strength of many castles made trickery one of the most favoured and effective methods of attempting to gain possession.[177] The sources abound with references to castles seized by ruse, and it is no coincidence that Louis's two acts of guile discussed above occurred during sieges of extremely strong fortifications. At Verneuil and Rouen, violation of respite appears as a desperate last effort to gain an impregnable site of key strategic importance. Equally, Philip Augustus only gained the great Norman fortress of Gisors by the defection of its castellan in 1194,[178] and the Angevins were never able to regain it.

The extent to which subterfuge was employed in warfare is well illustrated by the campaigns of 1118–19 fought principally in Normandy between Henry I and Louis VI, who lent powerful French support to William Clito and a disaffected element of the Norman baronage. In 1118, Henry I was diverted from besieging Laigle when William de Tancarville tricked him into retiring to meet a fictitious assault on Rouen, while in 1119, Gilbert, castellan of Tillières, fell upon the French forces of William de Chaumont in an ambush, taking many valuable prisoners.[179] In 1118, Louis had effected entry to the cell of St Ouen at Gasny, which he proceeded to fortify, having disguised himself and his knights as monks.[180]

The following year, Ascelin son of Andrew, at odds with the archbishop of Rouen, promised to help Louis seize the archiepiscopal vill of Andely. Intruding some French warriors into the place by night., Ascelin hid them in his storehouse under some straw. When next day Louis arrived outside the gates, 'the men hidden under the straw suddenly burst out and, shouting out the royal battle-cry of the English with the people, ran to the castle; but once inside they changed their shouts to the French "Montjoie"'. The bewildered garrison were quickly overwhelmed and Louis seized the town.[181] Conversely, following the defeat of the French forces at Brémule

[174] *HGM*, ll. 7782–852; Gillingham, 'War and Chivalry', pp. 5–6.　　[175] *Ibid.*, p. 6.
[176] Brown, 'The Battle of Hastings', pp. 14, 16.　　[177] Below, p. 206.
[178] Howden, III, p. 206; Gillingham, *Richard the Lionheart*, pp. 231–2.
[179] Orderic, VI, pp. 198–9, 248–9.　　[180] *Ibid.*, VI, pp. 184–5.　　[181] *Ibid.*, VI, 216–19.

the same year, 'Peter of Maule and some of the other fugitives threw away their cognizances to avoid recognition and, cunningly mixing with the pursuers, shouted out the war cry of the victors, proclaiming the greatness of King Henry and his men with feigned praises.'[182]

In demonstrating the repeated use of guile in almost every aspect of warfare, the campaigns of 1118–19 are unrepresentative only in the extent of the detailed description furnished by Orderic. Few if any of these acts accured reproach or shame. Nor, as we shall see, were the still more fundamental mechanisms of ravaging and economic attrition regarded as in any sense dishonourable, even though by its very nature such destruction struck at the most defenceless elements of society.[183]

Such considerations should warn us against anachronistic assumptions about the nature of chivalry. They equally reveal that while concepts of honour and shame were of the profoundest importance to the self-perception of the knighthood, the ambiguities inherent in this value system meant that concepts of honour could not alone ensure adherence to conventions of behaviour in war. Pragmatism, self-interest and even profit were the powerful dynamics that frequently lay behind the development and acceptance of such usages.

---

[182] *Ibid.*, VI, pp. 242–43. A similar ruse was remployed by Earl Henry, son of David I, and his knights to escape from the battle of the Standard in 1138 (*Relatio*, p. 198).   [183] Below, pp. 281–90.

5

CONDUCT IN BATTLE: A BROTHERHOOD IN ARMS?

In 1119, the forces of Henry I, king of England and duke of Normandy, decisively defeated the army of Louis VI of France at Brémule in the Norman Vexin. The battle had been hard fought, and Henry himself had come close to being slain when a leading Norman rebel, William Crispin, succeeded in breaking through the ranks and striking the king on the helmet.[1] Yet despite the fierce fighting, only three knights out of the nine hundred or so who were engaged were killed. This marked lack of fatalities prompted the chronicler Orderic Vitalis to proffer an explanation:

> They were all clad in mail and spared each other on both sides, out of fear of God and fellowship in arms (*notitiaque contubernii*); they were more concerned to capture than to kill the fugitives. As Christian soldiers, they did not thirst for the blood of their brothers, but rejoiced in a just victory given by God, for the good of holy Church and the peace of the faithful.[2]

These themes again occur in his earlier description of Rufus's campaign of 1098 in the Vexin, during which the English king launched a concerted attack against Chaumont, one of the chief French fortresses in this much disputed border area:

> The garrison of distinguished knights defended their walls vigorously, but never forgot their duty to God or respect for humanity. They took care out of chivalry to spare the bodies of the attackers (*insilentium corporibus provide benigniterque pepercerunt*) and turned the full force of their anger against the costly chargers of their enemies. So they killed seven hundred horses of

---

[1] Orderic, vi, pp. 238–9; HH, p. 241; *Chronica de Hida*, in *Liber monaserii de Hyda*, ed. E. Edwards (Rolls Series, 1886), p. 318.
[2] Orderic, vi, pp. 240–1. For earlier discussions of Orderic's views of chivalry see Rousset, 'La description du monde chevaleresque chez Oderic Vital', pp. 427–44; Flori, *L'essor de chevalerie*, pp. 271–4.

great value with arrows and darts; the dogs and birds of France were gorged to repletion on their bodies. In consequence, many who had crossed the Epte as proud knights on their foaming horses returned home with the king as foot soldiers.[3]

Orderic is thus suggesting that the conduct of fighting between Anglo-Norman and Capetian forces at least from the late eleventh century was regulated by ethical considerations composed principally of two inter-related concepts: respect for – or fear of – God, and a sense of profes-sional solidarity, of a brotherhood in arms. To these ideals he adds the more pragmatic considerations of extensive protection by mail armour, and a desire to capture, not kill, the enemy, though in this context Orderic refrains from mentioning ransom as an underlying motive for such clemency. We have noted the extent to which Orderic's statements on the nature of chivalry were influenced by his monastic vocation and his desire to promote an ethos of Christian chivalry.[4] We need, then, to ask how correct was Orderic in his assumptions concerning restraint from killing in battle? Were fatalities consciously limited, and if so, to what extent and for what reasons?

THE CHANGING FACE OF WAR

It had been habitual among Anglo-Saxon and Viking warriors deliberately to slay, not to spare, opposing warriors. Considerations of loyalty and revenge, of fighting to the death for one's lord, and of defending one's homeland and faith against the invader all combined to ensure that the majority of engagements between or among Anglo-Saxon and Viking forces were bitterly fought and sanguinary, resulting in strikingly high numbers of casualties among the nobility and even royalty. While the Vikings were wont to hold kingdoms and communities to corporate ransom, only individuals of the highest rank might be spared, although as many were put to the sword. In battle or in raiding, it was the norm for the enemy's menfolk to be peremptorily slain, and for their women and chil-dren to be enslaved. Thus even when the Anglo-Saxons or Vikings spared captives from death, they were doomed to slavery, seldom if ever to be ran-somed back to their lords or kin.[5]

By contrast, the sparing of warriors in or following battle for substantial payment in cash, arms or even strategic sites seems to have had its origins in

---

[3] *Ibid.*, v, pp. 218–19.   [4] Above, pp. 12–16.

[5] For a fuller discussion of Anglo-Saxon and Viking practice in regard to ransom and the question of sparing of enemy warriors in battle see Strickland, 'Slaughter, Slavery or Ransom?', pp. 41–59; cf. Gillingham, 'The Introduction of Chivalry into England', pp. 31–55.

Frankish warfare.[6] By the mid-eleventh century at the latest, it had become a well-established, though by no means a mandatory practice in France. Thus the treaty between Hugh, lord of Lusignan and Count William V of Aquitaine, drawn up in the first quarter of the eleventh century, already assumes the ransoming of captured knights as the norm of conduct. Certainly, it was a norm that might be violated: the treaty reveals that Hugh's opponent Geoffrey de Thouars had mutilated some of his knights, while in reprisal Hugh had refused to ransom some of Geoffrey's men that he had captured.[7] Yet both these actions were clearly viewed as an infringement of expected behaviour in regard to knightly opponents. Evidence from the Norman duchy points in the same direction. William of Poitiers, for example, recounts how Duke William, when serving in the feudal host of the king of France c. 1050, slipped away from his own contingent in search of combat. Coming across a group of enemy knights, he charged them and unhorsed one of them with his lance, taking care, Poitiers notes, not to run him through. By the time the duke's retinue found their lord, he was leading seven knights captive.[8]

A number of factors account for this changing pattern of conduct. The disintegration of the West Frankish kingdom and the rise of the territorial principalities profoundly affected the nature of war at both a strategic and tactical level.[9] While campaigns in late Anglo-Saxon England had remained highly mobile with extensive use of sea power, in Normandy and France the kind of warfare waged by Rollo and other Viking chiefs operating from the Seine or Loire in the late ninth and early tenth centuries was but a distant memory by the time of Duke William's majority. The warhorse had replaced the longship as the principal weapon of offence. Yet as castles proliferated from the first decades of the eleventh century,[10] war became increasingly dominated by siege, hampering wars of movement and diminishing the opportunities for rapid, successful invasion within France itself.[11] The campaigns of Fulk Nerra, riveting his hold on the enlarged boundaries of Anjou by the erection and defence of a chain of castles, had

---

[6] Strickland, 'Slaughter, Slavery or Ransom?', p. 51, for some earlier Frankish examples of ransom.

[7] J. Martindale, 'Conventum inter Guillelmum Aquitanorum comes et Hugonem Chiliarchum', EHR, 84 (1969), pp. 528–48; below, pp. 201–2.   [8] WP, pp. 24–7.

[9] For good general surveys of this period of 'feudal transformation' see, inter alia, E. M. Hallam, Capetian France (London, 1980); J. Dunbabin, France in the Making, 843–1180 (Oxford, 1985); and J. P. Poly and E. Bournazel, The Feudal Transformation, 900–1200 (New York, 1991).

[10] For castles in Normandy see J. Yver, 'Les chateux forts en Normandie jusqu'au milieu du XIIe siècle. Contribution a l'étude du pouvoir ducal', Bulletin de la Société des Antiquaires de Normandie, 55 (1955–6), pp. 28–115. Cf. A. Debord, 'The Castellan Revolution and the Peace of God in Aquitaine', The Peace of God. Social Violence and Religious Response in France around the Year 1000, ed. T. Head and R. Landes (Ithaca and London, 1992), pp. 135–64.

[11] J. Bradbury, The Medieval Siege (Woodbridge, 1992), pp. 48–66; Gillingham, 'William the Bastard at War', provides an excellent case study of such warfare.

epitomized the new way in war.[12] It was no coincidence that several of Duke William's more serious reverses, namely Dol, 1076, Gerberoy, 1079, and St Suzanne, c. 1084, resulted from the unsuccessful investment of castles.

The tendency to strategic stalemate fostered by castle-based warfare was furthered by the limited forces available to the emergent political entities such as Normandy, Anjou or Blois-Chartres, which, as the constantly shifting network of alliances and the often inconclusive nature of campaigns suggest, were generally evenly matched.[13] The great hostings against external enemies such as the Frisians, Saxons, Avars and Lombards that had characterized Frankish warfare in the eighth and early ninth centuries, or the large-scale campaigns fought between the grandsons of Charlemagne and their heirs,[14] had given way to endemic but small-scale fighting.[15] Whether or not we accept the figure of c. 7,000 men for Duke William's invasion army of 1066, there is no doubt that it was considered exceptionally large, that it could only be mustered by drawing on warriors from many parts of France, and that it could not be maintained long at such a strength.[16] Even after his annexation of England, William could do no more than hold the boundaries of his duchy once the revival of Anjou and the Capetian kingdom restored the balance of power and ended the exceptional political circumstances that had permitted the invasion attempt.[17]

Only in Southern Italy, Sicily, Britain and Ireland, where the Normans and Franks normally enjoyed a technological superiority against enemies

---

[12] B. S. Bachrach, 'Fortifications and Military Tactics: Fulk Nerra's Strongholds circa 1000', *Technology and Culture*, 20 (1979), pp. 531–49; *idem.*, 'The Angevin Strategy of Castle Building in the Reign of Fulk Nerra, 987–1040', *American Historical Review*, 88 (1983), pp. 533–60.

[13] For such changing alliances in relation to Normandy see Bates, *Normandy Before 1066*, pp. 65–85; and for the nature of contemporary field armies see B. Bachrach, 'Angevin Campaign Forces in the Reign of Fulk Nerra, Count of the Angevins, 987–1040', *Francia*, 11 (1), (1989), pp. 67–84.

[14] J. F. Verbruggen, 'L'armée et la strategie de Charlemagne', in *Karl der Grosse. Lebenswerk und Nachleben, I: Personlichkeit und Geschichte* (Dusseldorf, 1965), pp. 420–36; *idem.*, 'L'art militaire dans l'Empire carolingien', *Revue belge d'histoire militaire* (1979), pp. 299–310 and (1980), pp. 343–412; F. L. Ganshof, 'L'armée sous les Carolingiens', *Ordinamenti militari in Occidente nell'alto Medievo*, 2 vols. (Settimane di Studio del Centro Italiano di studi sull'alto Medioevo, Spoleto, 1968), 1, pp. 109–30; *idem.*, 'A propos de la cavalerie dans les armées de Charlemagne', *Académie des Inscriptions et Belles-Lettres. Comptes rendus des séances* (1952), pp. 531–6; C. R. Bowlus and G. M. Schwatz, 'Warfare and Society in the Carolingian Ostmark', *Austrian History Yearbook*, 14 (1978), pp. 3–30; K. F. Drew, 'The Carolingian Military Frontier in Italy', *Traditio*, 20 (1964), pp. 437–47; S. Lebecq, 'Francs contre Frisons (VIe–VIIIe siècle), in *Actes du Cie Congres national des Sociétés savantes, Lille, 1976: Section de philologie et d'histoire jusqu'a 1610: La Guerre et la paix* (Paris, 1978), pp. 53–71. Cf. Leyser, 'Early Medieval Warfare', pp. 29–50.

[15] See J. France, 'La guerre dans la France féodale à la fin du IXe et au Xe siècle', *Revue belge d'histoire militaire*, 33 (1979), pp. 177–98.

[16] Douglas, *William the Conqueror*, p. 198 and n. 4; B. S. Bachrach, 'The Administration of the Norman Conquest', *Anglo-Norman Studies*, 8 (1986), pp. 1–25, argues for the possibility of up to 14,000 'effectives' in the Franco-Norman army.   [17] Douglas, *William the Conqueror*, pp. 227–44.

lacking heavy cavalry and castles,[18] were there opportunities for the levying of great tribute or for the seizure of booty on the kind of scale witnessed earlier by the Carolingians or Vikings at the apogee of their power.[19] As the opportunities for extensive plunder and tribute diminished with the contraction in both the geographical and logistical scale of operations, so other means had to be found for making war pay for itself.[20] The convention of ransom at once satisfied the desire of the knighthood both for self-preservation and for financial gain. In turn, as the incidence of private war became increasingly curtailed in the territorial principalities of Northern France from the early twelfth century, so the growing institution of the tournament sought to provide at once martial training, an outlet for aggression and a significant and regular source of financial gain through ransoms. Thus, for example, Galbert of Bruges records how Charles the Good, count of Flanders (d. 1127):

> undertook chivalric exploits for the honour of his land and the training of his knights in the lands of the counts or princes of Normandy or France, sometimes even beyond the kingdom of France, and there with two hundred knights on horseback he engaged in tourneys, in this way enhancing his own fame and the power and glory of his county.[21]

Such a situation would have been hard to conceive of in the northern France of the mid-eleventh century. Duke William of Normandy and his young aristocratic companions such as Roger de Montgomery and William FitzOsbern had gained their military training in real warfare against the count of Anjou, the Capetian king and internal rebels.[22]

Still more importantly, the nature of the enemy had changed. For while the Franks still confronted the infidel in Outremer, Spain and Sicily, the conversion of the Scandinavian kingdoms and the cultural assimilation of Viking settlements in Normandy ensured that within Western Frankia, warriors were no longer fighting pagan opponents.[23] Warfare between the

---

[18] For an important discussion of the link between the Frankish 'aristocratic diaspora' and the diffusion of military technology see R. Bartlett, 'Technique militaire et pouvoir politique, 900–1300', *Annales: écomonies, sociétés, civilizations*, 41 (1986), pp. 1135–59; and *idem., The Making of Europe. Conquest, Colonization and Cultural Change, 950–1350* (London, 1993), pp. 60–84.

[19] For Frankish spoils of war see T. Reuter, 'Plunder and Tribute in the Carolingian Empire', *TRHS*, 35 (1985), pp. 75–94; and *idem.*, 'The End of Carolingian Military Expansion', in *Charlemagne's Heir: New Perspectives on the Reign of Louis the Pious*, ed. P. Goodman and R. Collins (Oxford, 1990), pp. 391–405.

[20] Cf below, pp. 183–6.

[21] Galbert of Bruges, *The Murder of Charles the Good*, tr. J. B. Ross (New York, 1960), p. 96.

[22] Douglas, *William the Conqueror*, pp. 53–76.

[23] In regard to East Frankia and the Ottonian *Reich*, however, the nature of warfare might not only differ in form, but on the Ostmark the enemy remained largely pagan. For Ottonian warfare see K. Leyser, 'Henry I and the Beginnings of the Saxon Empire', *EHR*, 83 (1968), pp. 1–32, reprinted in Leyser, *Medieval Germany and its Neighbours*, pp. 11–42; and *idem.*, 'The Battle at the Lech, 955', pp. 43–68.

territorial principalities was thus void of the religious dimension which in earlier conflicts between the Franks and the Frisians, Saxons, Avars and Vikings, and between the Anglo Saxons and the Vikings, had lent the fighting a profound intensity and bitterness.[24] To the practical strategic limitations of warfare and the absence of religious hatred was added the extension and reinforcement of pre-existing notions of a common profession of arms, a knightly *militia*.[25] The forces of opposing castellans were not alien invaders but men of a similar cultural, linguistic and military background. In the rapidly shifting political climate of eleventh- and twelfth-century France, moreover, today's enemy might well prove to be tomorrow's ally. Such factors could only be reinforced by the development of cognizances and blazon during the twelfth century, for the adoption of heraldry not only facilitated recognition in battle, but strengthened the knighthood's perception of common membership of an armigerous elite.[26] Given the changing circumstances of warfare and these potential constraints, warriors had greater reason, as well as manifest self-interest, to strive to capture their noble opponents alive rather than merely butcher them out of hand on the field.

The extent to which these developments could affect the conduct of war is nowhere more strikingly revealed than by Orderic's account of the siege of the Norman garrison of Le Mans by Count Helias of Maine in 1100. Though one must keep in mind the caveats regarding Orderic's didactic purpose, his description is a detailed one which inspires considerable confidence. Despite the high political stakes involved in the taking of the capital, and the fact that its Norman garrison had burned down the city the previous year, the relations between Count Helias and the Normans whom he besieged in the citadel were not only chivalrous, but even tinged with humour:

---

[24] One may note in this context that the decision of Count Helias of Maine to regard his war of defence against William Rufus in 1096 as a crusade was very much an exception (Orderic, v, pp. 228–33).   [25] Below, pp. 142–58.

[26] In the eleventh century, Franco-Norman knights bore zoomorphic or geometric devices on their shields, such as those represented on the Bayeux Tapestry, though recognition might still depend on distinctive equipment or mounts (cf. WP, pp. 38–40; Orderic, iv, pp. 232–3). By the early twelfth century, 'proto-heraldic' shields such as those illustrated in Stephen Harding's bible (c. 1109) were beginning to conform to rules of blazon concerning the position of colours and metals, but as with earlier devices these lacked the crucial requirement of true heraldry in that they were not yet hereditary. On this important subject see P. Gras, 'Aux origines de l'héraldique', *Bibliotheque de l'École des Chartes*, 109 (1951), pp. 198–208; A. Ailes, 'Heraldry in Twelfth-Century England', *England in the Twelfth Century. Proceedings of the 1988 Harlaxton Symposium*, ed. D. Williams (Woodbridge, 1990), pp. 1–16; *idem.*, 'The Knight, Heraldry and Armour: The Role of Recognition and the Origins of Heraldry', in *Medieval Knighthood*, iv, ed. C. Harper-Bill and R. Harvey (Woodbridge, 1992), pp. 1–21; and Crouch, *The Beaumont Twins*, pp. 211–12 for the role of Waleran of Meulan in the development of hereditary arms, a process beginning in the middle decades of the twelfth century.

Daily the two sides held parleys and threatened each other, but jokes were often mixed with the threats. They gave Count Helias the privilege whenever he wished of putting on a white tunic and in this way having safe passage to the defenders of the citadel (*sic ad eos qui turrim custodiebant tutius accederet*). Since he trusted the good faith of the men he knew to be both valiant and honourable (*probissimos et legales*), he often visited the enemy wearing the distinctive white garment and never feared to remain alone for long conferences with them. Besieged and besiegers alike passed their time in jocular abuse and played many tricks on each other in a far from malevolent spirit, so that the men of those parts will speak of them in days to come with wonder and delight.[27]

On the death of Rufus, the garrison had been placed in a grave dilemma as to which of his surviving brothers, Robert Curthose or Henry I, they should regard as their lord and from whom they should hold Le Mans. They sent missives to both rulers, seeking their aid against Helias, but neither was in a position to proffer relief.[28] Finally, after receiving permission to surrender from Robert and Henry, the garrison came to terms with Helias and yielded up the citadel: 'After peace had been made the valiant garrison came out with their arms and all their belongings and were received by the counts [Helias of Maine and Fulk of Anjou] not as vanquished foes but as faithful friends (*nec ut hostes devicti sed ut fideles amici*).'[29]

It would be misleading, however, to suggest that by 1100 all warfare was conducted in this spirit and with such restraint. For while of undeniable significance, the effect on conduct in war of notions of ransom and of a brotherhood in arms were, as we shall see, subject to many important qualfications. The most immediate contrast is afforded by the bitter and sanguinary forms of war resulting from the feud and private warfare.

FEUD AND CIVIL WAR

If confessional factors in warfare within Frankia had largely been marginalized by the early eleventh century, feuding between rival aristocratic families was endemic in the majority of the territorial principalities. Fierce competition for limited landed resources led to sanguinary struggles, particularly during periods of ducal or comital weakness. In Normandy, the period between the accession of Duke Robert the Magnificent in 1035 to the re-establishment of effective authority by William the Bastard in the

---

[27] Orderic, v, pp. 302–3.

[28] *Ibid.* Here Orderic once more adds his own view of a lofty motive underlying their conduct, but he was clearly recalling an incident still vivid in the memory of contemporaries when Orderic was writing.   [29] *Ibid.*, v, pp. 306–7.

1050s witnessed particularly vicious and extended feuding between leading Norman families, each vying for local supremacy.[30]

The brutal, ruthless nature of this kind of warfare, with its own self-perpetuating dynamic of vengeance, is powerfully conveyed in the chanson *Raoul de Cambrai*,[31] and it was such violence that had given rise to the Peace and Truce of God. Casualties could be high even though hostilities might be no more than small-scale skirmishes. Orderic believed it was the great dangers inherent in such warfare that had led Robert de Grandmesnil to abandon the world:

> He often called to mind the perils of earthly warfare (*pericula saecularis militiae*) endured by his father and many like him who had met the death they had intended for others while bravely attacking their enemies. For on one occasion his father Robert fought with Roger of Tosny against Roger of Beaumont, and in that conflict Roger together with his sons Elbert and Elinant were slain, and Robert received a mortal wound in his bowels. He was carried home and survived three weeks . . . Deeply moved by this tragedy, Robert set his mind on fighting in better warfare.[32]

A strong impression of how deadly such conflicts could be is furnished by the numerous examples of private warfare in the duchy during the rule of Robert Curthose, when feuding, held in temporary abeyance under the Conqueror, once again became widespread. Twenty knights were killed and many wounded in one day's skirmish during Robert de Bellême's siege of Courcy in 1091.[33] Though Orderic had noted how at the siege of Chaumont the French forces had directed their arrows and javelins not at the Normans but at their horses, there are many incidents of deliberate killing by missile weapons. When Robert de Bellême besieged Gilbert de Laigle in Exmes castle, the defenders killed and wounded many of the attackers with stones and other weapons.[34] During the siege of Brionne, Gilbert of Le Pin, commander of the ducal besieging force, was fatally wounded in the head by a spear thrown from the battlements, while at the siege of Conches in 1090, Richard de Montfort was killed by a missile.[35]

Stephen's reign marked a reversion to localized feuding and private war, in addition to the large-scale engagements such as Lincoln, Winchester and Wilton fought between the protagonists for the throne. In 1141, John fitz Gilbert held off the victorious royalist forces on the river Test at Wherwell to cover Matilda's flight from her disastrous rout at Winchester.

---

[30] Douglas, *William the Conqueror*, p. 42; E. Searle, *Predatory Kinship and the Creation of Norman Power, 840–1066* (Berkley, 1988), pp. 179–98.   [31] *Raoul de Cambrai*, ed. and tr. S. Kay (Oxford, 1992).
[32] Orderic, II, pp. 40–1.   [33] *Ibid.*, IV, pp. 234–5.   [34] *Ibid.*, IV, pp. 200–1.
[35] *Ibid.*, IV, pp. 210–11, 214–15.

John's force was outnumbered, and some of his knights were killed, while
William of Ypres's men tried unsuccessfully to burn John and a companion alive in the church at Wherwell.[36] Later, John in his turn ambushed the
force of Earl Patrick of Salisbury which was on its way to attack John's
castle of Ludgershall. Not expecting attack, Patrick's knights had not put
on their hauberks or helmets, and many of the earl's best men were
killed.[37]

Nevertheless, while warfare in the context of feud might well provoke
acts of savagery, these were essentially specific and limited responses to the
demands of vendetta.[38] The feud was far from being arbitrary or insensate.
As a form of dispute settlement, albeit an extreme form, it was nonetheless
subject to control, regulation and, ultimately, to princely suppression.[39]
Even in local feuding, moreover, ransom not killing might be intended.
Orderic records how the powerful lord Gilbert de Laigle was surprised
without his armour at Moulins-la-Marche, and was pursued by a group of
enemy knights 'wishing to take him alive'. As he was trying to outstrip them
on his horse, a lance thrown by one of the knights pierced his side, and he
died the same day 'to the great grief even of those who had done the
deed'.[40] Geoffrey, count of Mortagne, 'considering that his men had committed a serious crime and had sown the seeds of terrible troubles for his
land by murdering such a warlike baron, made peace with his nephew,
Gilbert of Laigle, and gave him his daughter Juliana in marriage'.[41] In this
instance, reaction to an accidental killing of a great lord served to forge new
bonds of alliance between former enemies.

If feud served to add a viciousness to some aristocratic conflicts, then
conversely family alliance and the ties of marriage, kinship and lordship
might exercise potent constraints on warriors' actions in war. In situations
of civil war within the Anglo-Norman *regnum*, for example, casualties were
kept to a minimum by the dictates of kinship and blood. Though the
Anglo-Norman baronage was split in its support for Henry I and Robert
Curthose, the social homogeneity of the combatants at the battle of
Tinchebrai in 1106 ensured a minimum of casualties. The account of the
priest of Fécamp, referring only to noble casualties, states that Henry I lost

---

[36] *HGM*, 11. 200–65; above, p. 77.
[37] *HGM*, 11. 283–354. Earl Patrick's own death, however, at the hands of the Lusignans in 1167, seems
to have been the cause for regret and censure. See below, p. 154.   [38] Below, pp. 200–1.
[39] On the feud see Searle, *Predatory Kinship*, esp. pp. 179–92; S. D. White, 'Feuding and Peace-making in
the Touraine Around the Year 1100', *Traditio*, 42 (1986), pp. 195–263. Cf. W. I. Miller, *Blood-Taking and
Peace Making: Feud, Law and Society in Saga Iceland* (Chicago and London, 1990), esp. pp. 179–220; and
The Settlement of Disputes in Early Medieval Europe, ed. W. Davies and P. Fouracre (Cambridge, 1986).
For limitations of the feud see J. Yver, 'L'interdiction de la guerre privée dans les tres ancien droit
normand', *Travaux de la Semaine de droit normand tenue à Guernesey du 26 au 30 Mai, 1927* (Caen, 1928), pp.
307–47.   [40] Orderic, IV, pp. 200–1.   [41] *Ibid.*, IV, pp. 202–3.

only two men while but one was wounded.[42] Those knights and nobles of Robert's army who could not escape were almost all taken, not slain, although there seems to have been heavy losses among the ducal infantry.[43]

Speaking of Henry I's war in 1118 against the followers of William Clito, Orderic noted: 'This was indeed more than a civil war, and ties of blood bound together brothers and friends and kinsmen who were fighting on both sides, so that neither wished to harm the other.'[44] At Bourgthéroulde, 1124, no known casualties were sustained, for Odo Borleng and the knights of the *familia regis* had their archers deliberately shoot at the horses of the rebel Norman lords led by Amaury de Montfort and Waleran de Meulan, not at their riders.[45] It would have been inconceivable for knights of the royal *familia* to have deliberately killed such great lords, and Amaury and Waleran were taken alive with eighty of their knights.[46] Likewise at Lincoln in 1217, the presence of many of their relatives among the baronial rebels who were with the French force led Fawkes de Bréauté to order his cross-bowmen to shoot at the horses of the barons and the French.[47] Though their destriers were 'mown down and killed like pigs', there were very few casualties in this engagement.[48] The royalists, moreover, only gave a half-hearted pursuit in order to allow friends and relatives to escape.[49]

Though in Stephen's reign localized feuding might be bloody, it is significant that the larger battles were marked by a general absence of killing

---

[42] The text of this letter was printed by H. W. C. Davis, 'A Contemporary Account of the Battle of Tinchebrai', *EHR*, 24 (1909), pp. 728–32, and received important correction by C. W. David, *Robert Curthose* (Harvard, 1920), Appendix F, p. 247. Eadmer includes a letter sent by Henry to Anselm following Tinchebrai, in which the king notes that 'by the mercy of God the victory was ours and that without any great slaughter of our men' (Eadmer, p. 184). The *Chronica de Hida*, p. 307, says Henry won a 'victoria pene sine sanguine'. Both these statements seem to adjudge the battle by noble casualties alone. Those taken prisoner at Tinchebrai included Duke Robert, William Count of Mortain, Robert de Stuteville, William Crispin and William de Ferrières (Orderic, VI, pp. 90–1; *Chronica de Hida*, p. 307; HH, p. 236; WJ, pp. 283–4). Henry I told Anselm that in addition, 400 knights and 10,000 foot were taken prisoner, though this latter estimate must almost certainly be a gross exaggeration (Eadmer, p. 184).

[43] Orderic states that Helias of Maine's cavalry cut down 225 ducal footsoldiers in their first charge, while Henry I could write that 'of those killed with the sword there is no reckoning' (Orderic, VI, pp. 90–1; Eadmer, p. 184).   [44] Orderic, VI, pp. 200–1.

[45] Orderic, VI, pp. 350–1. In Robert of Torigny's interpolations in William of Jumièges, he notes that the royalist archers fired against the unshielded right sides of the charging knights (WJ, p. 295). The complete absence of known fatalities, however, strongly militates against the knights being the actual targets.   [46] Orderic, VI, pp. 350–1.

[47] MP, III, p. 21. The *Histoire de Guillaume le Maréchal* attributes these instructions to Peter des Roches, bishop of Winchester, who prior to the battle advised the crossbowmen 'to marshal themselves in an extended line in order to kill the horses of the French as they charged' (*HGM*, 11. 16314–24).

[48] MP, III, p. 21. Wendover makes a similar jibe to that of Orderic about Rufus's unhorsed knights returning from Chaumont as mere infantry, for he notes of the royalist crossbowmen that 'in a twinkling of an eye, they made them – knights and barons – into a large force of foot soldiers'. According to Wendover, only three combatants were slain at Lincoln: the count of Perche, Reginald Croc, a knight of Fawkes's household, and an unnamed serjeant from the baronial forces, who, as an excommunicate, was buried outside the city at a crossroads (*ibid.*).   [49] MP, III, p. 22.

among the knights. Although some royalists were killed in the battle of Lincoln in 1141, the victorious Angevins took 'a vast throng of prisoners'.[50] After their victory at Winchester the same year, the royalists captured Robert of Gloucester 'with almost all his force', with each of the victors returning home 'with countless captives'.[51] William Martel and his men who valiantly covered the king's retreat from Wilton in 1143 were taken, not slain.[52] It was only on the rarest of occasions in such a context that the mechanisms of capture and ransom were consciously suspended by the combatants. Nevertheless, the context of civil war inevitably raised pressing problems of divided allegiance and made rebels of many erstwhile vassals. Powerful constraints often prevented rulers from inflicting severe punishment upon baronial insurgents, but where circumstances allowed, kings were not beyond mutilating or hanging rebel garrisons.[53] Yet because rebellion was regarded as 'proditio et infidelitas', a violation of the sacrosanct bonds of homage and fealty, the treatment afforded knights in the context of revolt must stand *sui generis*.

But what of warfare between sovereign principalities, where the constraints imposed by kinship might be less forceful than in warfare within the Anglo-Norman *regnum*? Orderic's accounts of the fighting at Chaumont, 1098, and Brémule, 1119, suggest that the desire to limit casualties could be extended to such external warfare. Was he correct in this assumption, and if so, what motivation lay behind such restraint? Was the conduct of warriors dictated in any way by a sense of belonging to a brotherhood of arms, the 'notitia contubernii' spoken of by Orderic? Or was the principal cause underlying the deliberate preservation of life merely a question of economics, with clemency only a means to securing rich ransoms?

To answer such questions, we must first examine the extent to which knights perceived themselves as belonging to a professional class, an *ordo equestris* or *militia*. This in turn raises the issue of how far such notions were developed and disseminated by the important mechanism of the tournament. We shall then turn to the manifestations and limitations of notions of a brotherhood in arms in battle.

MILITES AND THE MILITIA

The eleventh century witnessed an increased adoption by men of landed resources of the term *miles*. Beginning in the 970s, examples multiply incrementally from c. 1050 to the early twelfth century and mark a concomitant rise in the status of the *milites*. Yet as we have noted, it seems that by c. 1100,

---

[50] *GS*, pp. 112–3.   [51] *Ibid.*, pp. 132–3, 136–7.   [52] *Ibid.*, pp. 146–7.   [53] Below, pp. 241–7.

despite considerable nuances of chronology and of regional variation, knights as a class were only approaching the lower reaches of the aristocracy. The *milites* remained essentially warrior retainers, still distinct from a nobility very much conscious of its superior status, lineage and material wealth.[54]

Nevertheless, the crucial point here is that irrespective of the material or social status of the holder of the title *miles*, it denoted common membership of a *militia*. Men of high birth, not only castellans but also counts and even kings, had assumed the title *miles* not as a title of rank, for qualifying adjectives indicating nobility were frequently added to it.[55] Rather, it was seen as a label denoting *function*, and a function which clearly carried with it connotations of martial prowess. Above all, this function was regarded as that of the warrior, equipped with hauberk, helmet, lance, sword, shield and costly war-horse, who dominated the contemporary battlefield, whether fighting from the saddle or dismounted. Those possessed of both such equipment and the martial virtues associated with their use in war were seen as forming a military elite, a *militia*. As early as the 990s, Richer could write of an *ordo militaris* and regard it as virtually synonymous with an *ordo equestris*. Combatants were now polarized simply between two categories, *milites*, the mounted warriors, and *pedites*, the infantry.[56] There could be no more striking reflection of how this image dominated the aristocracy's self-perception that the prevalence from the late eleventh century of this equestrian image on the seals of Anglo-Norman and French kings and seigneurs alike.[57]

Such a process was well underway by the mid-eleventh century. Norman charters reveal nobles of substance referring to themselves as *milites* as early as 965,[58] and by the mid-eleventh century, members of the greatest Norman families could be so labelled.[59] Gilbert Crispin, himself writing sometime after 1093 but referring to the reign of Duke Robert of Normandy (1027–35), believed that because of Herluin's prowess in arms 'all the chief families in Normandy held him in high esteem, and extolled his knightly prowess'.[60] Before his conversion to the religious life, Herluin

[54] Above, pp. 19–22.
[55] Flori, *L'essor de la chevalerie*, p. 140; Brown, 'The Status of the Norman Knight', pp. 131–2.
[56] Richer, *Histoire de France*, ed. R. Latouche, 2 vols. (Paris, 1937), II, p. 180; Contamine, *War in the Middle Ages*, p. 31.
[57] B. Bedos Rezak, 'The Social Implications of the Art of Chivalry: The Sigillographic Evidence (France, 1050–1250)', in *The Medieval Court of Europe*, ed. E. R. Haymes (Munich, 1986), pp. 1–31; idem., 'Medieval Seals and the Structure of Chivalric Society', *The Study of Chivalry*, pp. 313–72.
[58] *Recueil des actes des ducs de Normandie de 911 à 1066* (Fauroux), ed. M. Fauroux (Caen, 1961), no. 2; Brown, 'The Status of the Norman Knight', pp. 131–2 and examples cited therein.
[59] For examples see Bates, *Normandy Before 1066*, pp. 109–11; Musset, 'L'aristocratie Normande au XIe siècle', in *La Noblesse au Moyen Age*, p. 89.   [60] *Vita Herluini*, p. 87.

was clearly numbered among knights like Richard de Reivers, a 'vir quidam clarus genere seculari milicia deditus', or the Manceaux John of Laval who, like Herluin, abandoned the world aged thirty, in the prime of his martial career, 'when he was still strong and bearing the arms of knighthood, a man born of illustrious lineage'.[61] Bates has even suggested that in Normandy the increased incidence of the label *miles* from the 1040s suggests a relative devaluing or vulgarization of the term. In the duchy, however, the 'the term miles remained pre-eminently one which described function, rather than status'.[62] The clearest proof of this is that King Henry I of France (1031–60) could be termed a *miles accerimus*.[63] Equally, although William of Poitiers does not use the term *miles* itself to describe Duke William of Normandy, he is none the less at pains to portray the young duke in the 1040s and 1050s not simply as a just and pious prince, but as a knight, the flower of the *militia* of Northern France. When as a young man, notes Poitiers, the duke had taken up the arms of knighthood (*arma militaria sumit*), a tremor of fear ran through all of France.[64]

This emphasis on function by no means negated the hierarchy of rank within the nobility itself, which remained as stratified as before in terms of lineage and wealth. But if before 1100 the majority of *milites* as a class had not been admitted into the lower rungs of the aristocracy,[65] a sense had certainly developed that they and their more noble and affluent superiors were in some important sense bonded by a common sharing in the *metier* of the knight and the concomitant institutions of knighthood. As Allen Brown aptly notes, 'at no time were all knights great men, but from an early date all great men were knights'.[66]

But from how early a date? It has been argued, not least by Flori, that it was only the twelfth century that saw the bonding of the knights and the nobility in the shared martial ethos of knighthood.[67] The 'new' technique of the charge with the couched lance and the rise of the tournament, moreover, were the crucial mechanisms of such a fusion.[68] There can be no

---

[61] Fauroux, nos. 147, 137; Brown, 'The Status of the Norman Knight', p. 131.

[62] Bates, *Normandy Before 1066*, pp. 109–11.

[63] M. Bur, *La formation du comté du Champagne, v. 950–1150* (Nancy, 1977), p. 417. William of Poitiers could call Duke William's father-in-law, Baldwin V of Flanders, a *miles* of the Roman Empire (WP, p. 46).

[64] WP, pp. 12–13. Cf. the praise Simon de Crépy, who was effectively Duke William's foster-son, as a knight, *Vita beati Simonis*, Migne, *PL*, CLVI, cols. 1211 ff.

[65] Crouch, *The Image of Aristocracy*, p. 127; cf. Coss, *The Knight in England*, p. 7.

[66] R. A. Brown, *Origins of English Feudalism* (London, 1973), p. 27; Cf. Crouch, *The Image of Aristocracy*, p. 124, 'people in general saw knightliness as an asset, however humble in means the generality of knights may have been. What the knight *was* did not give him much status, but what the knight did gave a man a sort of glamour.'   [67] Flori, *L'essor de la chevalerie*, pp. 233 ff.

[68] D. J. A. Ross, 'L'originalité de "Turoldus": le maniement de la lance', *Cahiers de civilisation médiévale*, 6 (1963), pp. 127–38; J. Flori, 'Encore l'usage de la lance . . . La technique du combat chevaleresque vers l'an 1100', *Calviers de civilisation médiévale*, 31 (1988), pp. 213–40.

doubt that in the course of the twelfth century notions of knighthood underwent elaboration and sophistication.[69] The crusades led to increasing ecclesiastical validation of the *ordo equestris*, while courtly love and the influence of Arthurian romance expanded the social dimensions of chivalry.

Yet there are several major difficulties with the suggestion that the knights and the nobility 'little by little . . . forged a common mentality', not least by means of a revolutionary method of cavalry warfare, still embryonic by 1100, and through the dependent institution of the tournament necessary for its practice.[70] First, the use of the couched lance was not, I would suggest, an innovation haltingly adopted from the second half of the eleventh century. If we are to accept, as we must, the Bayeux Tapestry's depiction of knights using the couched lance alongside companions jabbing overarm or throwing their lances, we must give similar credence to the Carolingian *Psalterium Aureum* of c. 880, which portrays exactly the same combination.[71] This unequivocal depiction of a heavily armed horseman with stirrups and a couched lance echoes earlier capitularies, which prescribe equipment little different from that required of knights by the Assize of Arms of 1181.

Second, irrespective of *how* Frankish horsemen fought in the saddle, lords and their retinues of cavalrymen both fought and trained together from at least the ninth century, if not well before. On this the evidence furnished by Nithard's famous description of the equestrian sports held in 842 between the forces of Louis the German and Charles the Bald is irrefutable.[72] Here too a sense of professional solidarity between members of a warrior elite, similarly equipped and fighting in a like manner, is already clearly visible.

Mock combat, moreover, must have remained as essential a form of training for the *milites* of tenth- and eleventh-century Frankia. The tactical flexibility demonstrated in war by manoeuvres such as the 'feigned retreat' necessitated constant drill and the practice of weapon skills in small groups of the *conroi* or larger units.[73] Though writing c. 1120–2 about events in the 1030s, the biographers of Hugh, abbot of Cluny, believed that as a young man, he had practised handling lance, shield and warhorse and 'all the other idiocies' of cavalry warfare with his companions.[74] Such training would have forged close bonds within and between the knights of seigneurial

---

[69] Flori, *L'essor de la chevalerie*, pp. 181 ff; Brown, 'The Status of the Norman Knight', pp. 140–2.

[70] Coss, *The Knight in Medieval England*, p. 7.

[71] F. Mutherich and J. E. Gaehde, *Carolingian Painting* (London, 1977), p. 46. I hope to explore these themes more fully in a subsequent article.

[72] Nelson, 'Ninth Century Knighthood', p. 260.   [73] Above, p. 130.

[74] Barlow, *William Rufus*, p. 23 and n. 83.

households. While by no means denying the importance of the tournament as a catalyst for many aspects of chivalric culture, the tourney of the twelfth century must in this respect be seen principally as a development of existing practices of cavalry training. We need not posit the *deus ex machina* of the 'invention' of the couched lance to explain the rise of the tournament;[75] social, cultural and political factors would seem far more convincing reasons for the growth of the tourney.

This brings us to our third and most important point. Can we really say that 'within this world the old nobility turned itself increasingly into a military aristocracy'?[76] For what had the Carolingian and later Frankish aristocracy been if not a military elite? Even the most perfunctory perusal of Carolingian sources from the seventh to the tenth century gives the overwhelming impression that the prime function of *nobiles* was fighting and that nobility itself, then as it was always to do throughout the Middle Ages and beyond, carried inseparably with it powerful martial connotations. And as far back as we look, whether it be to Beowulf's retinue, to the Frankish *antrustiones* or *gasindi*, to Alfred's thegns or Byrhtnoth's 'hearthtroop' at Maldon in 991, the military retainers of these lords shared their warrior ethic as much as their way of combat. The nobility, in short, had no need to assimilate the martial culture of the *milites*; it was theirs already.

Nelson, moreover, has shown that many essential aspects of knighthood are clearly visible in Frankia by the middle of the ninth century,[77] and Leyser has done likewise for tenth-century Ottonian Germany. Not only were several great Ottonian lords labelled as *milites* but also there existed a cameraderie between the *commilitones*, or companions in arms, of great nobles and members of the Ottonian house, suggesting 'shared values across whatever social distances which set off the great from their military following'.[78]

Membership of the *militia*, indeed, embraced kings and counts, who were no less anxious than the nobility to portray themselves as warriors. William Rufus and Richard I are but outstanding examples of kings seen to embody the ideals of knighthood. Nowhere, however, is this phenomenon more strikingly revealed than in the case of Henry, eldest son of Henry II. For though the son of a king, and, from 1170 a king in his own right, he was perceived – as he doubtless wished to be – primarily as a knight, 'the most valiant of the worthy'. Contemporaries stressed his attributes of knight-

---

[75] And as Gillingham has rightly noted, in twelfth-century tournaments 'the overwhelming bulk of the fighting was done with mace and sword' (Gillingham, 'Conquering the Barbarians', p. 76, n. 35).
[76] Coss, *The Knight in Medieval England*, p. 5.   [77] Nelson, 'Ninth Century Knighthood', pp. 255–66.
[78] Leyser, 'Henry I and the Beginnings of the Saxon Empire', pp. 40 ff; 'The Beginnings of Knighthood', pp. 53–4.

hood far more than those of regality. He was the fountainhead of *chevalerie*, 'besides whom the most generous were mean', 'the best knight there was of any nation'.[79] So fundamental was this emphasis on knighthood, indeed, that the author of the *Histoire de Guillaume le Maréchal*, anticipating the surprise of his audience, pauses to explain why it was that the young Henry was crowned *before* he was knighted.[80] Howden's detailed description of Richard I's coronation in 1189 shows that a pair of golden spurs had become an important part of the royal regalia.[81] Just as a ruler's investiture with arms had helped to mould the ceremony of belting to knighthood, so now knightly symbolism had penetrated into that of the coronation.

The unusual circumstances of the Young King's own knighting in 1173, described by the *Histoire*, throws much light on concepts of entry into the *militia*. The ceremony whereby the aspiring warrior was girded with the *cingulum militiae* or belt of knighthood was rich in symbolism, carrying with it overtones of investiture with authority, the attainment of majority and the entry of the young man into the warband (*comitatus*), or, in Frankish terms, the household (*mesnie*), of a lord.[82] Almost invariably performed by a social superior, the bestowal of arms, moreover, created a fundamental bond between giver and receiver, with the recipient sharing in the lord's dignity and status by 'associative honour'.[83] The ceremony of knighting might thus act as an overt symbol of political alliance, with strong overtones of overlordship. Young Henry might well have been knighted by his own father, but in 1173, he was in rebellion against him. It was thus expected that he would be knighted by Louis VII, who was not only his father-in-law but also his ally in the 'great war' against Henry II.[84]

Events, however, put paid to such plans. Faced with an imminent attack by Henry II's forces, the Young King's supporters agreed that he should be knighted on the spot before any fighting commenced. Yet despite the fact that several French lords of the highest rank, including Peter de Courtenai, the French king's brother, and Raoul, count of Clermont and constable of France, were present, the Young King was dubbed in the field by William the Marshal, then but a landless household knight owning 'nothing but his chivalry (*sa chevalerie*)'. William had been chosen to bestow this honour upon young Henry because, noted the *Histoire* proudly and with unconcealed partisanship, he was 'the best knight who had ever been'.[85] William's

---

[79] *Si tuit li dol e.lh plor e.lh marrimen*, *TLP*, pp. 168–71; Gouiran, *L'amour et la guerre*, pp. 255–67.

[80] *HGM*, ll. 2112–50; *ibid.*, III, p. 31, n. 2. By contrast, it would seem that the bestowal of arms on earlier Norman princes such as Rufus and Henry predominantly signified investiture with power rather than knighthood itself (Flori, *L'essor de chevalerie*, pp. 56–61).   [81] *GH*, II, p. 81.

[82] Above, p. 25.   [83] Keen, *Chivalry*, pp. 68–9.   [84] *HGM*, ll. 2120.

[85] *Ibid.*, ll. 2079–150; cf. *ibid.*, III, p. 31, n. 2.

prowess, his *function* as a warrior, here overrode considerations of rank or wealth.

William was one of young Henry's *mesnie*, his man by homage, his social inferior. Yet both men, king and batchelor, were warriors, and William was Henry's tutor in arms. Judged in chivalric terms, William was his lord's superior, and the act of dubbing proclaimed this. Little wonder that the honour of knighting Henry II's son earned William the envy of many present.[86] For all the distant echoes of royal or comital investiture inherent in dubbing, the Young King's knighting did not mark any bestowal of regalian authority: he had already been crowned and anointed in 1170. Rather, it marked his entry into a warrior elite and into the *ordo* of knighthood where martial function transcended considerations of wealth and status.

It was this sense of common membership of the *ordo militaris* that allowed John of Marmoutier, writing for Henry II's court, unhesitatingly to portray Count Geoffrey of Anjou, the king's father, as both a knight and the model of chivalric *franchise* and *largesse*. In his *History of Geoffrey, Duke of the Normans and Count of the Angevins*, written c. 1180, John collected, if he did not actually invent, a series of anecdotal incidents, void of any chronological precision, which were designed to illustrate the outstanding qualities of Geoffrey le Bel, and in so doing to serve as a *speculum principis* for his current Angevin patrons. One tale has Geoffrey capture four Poitevin knights in battle, whom he then handed over for custody to Josselin de Tours, the senechal of Anjou. Moved by the subsequent length of their captivity, Josselin contrived to bring about their release. He invited Geoffrey to his castle of Fontaine-Milon, where the captives were held, and treated his lord to a sumptuous feast. He then arranged for the prisoners to come to a window overlooking the route along which the count would walk, and as Geoffrey passed beneath, the prisoners sang verses in praise of the count as they had been instructed to do by Josselin.

Seeing their dirty and unkempt state, Geoffrey was moved to compassion and ordered them to be washed and given fresh clothing before entertaining them to dinner. John's picture of Geoffrey as the epitome of chivalric largesse towards men who were less his erstwhile enemies than his fellow knights was completed by having him grant the prisoners their liberty and bestow costly arms and horses upon them.[87] Irrespective of the veracity of the incident, the remark which John attributes to Geoffrey by way of explanation for his actions is revealing: 'He has an inhuman heart who has no compassion for those of his own profession. Are we not knights? We therefore owe a special compassion to knights in need.'[88]

---

[86] *Ibid.*, 11. 2104–6.   [87] *Chroniques des comtes d'Anjou*, pp. 194–6.   [88] *Ibid.*, p. 196.

Signficantly, very similar sentiments had been attributed by Orderic to William Rufus, when ordering the release on parole of the Angevin and Manceaux knights taken at Ballon in 1098. To his councellors' objections lest the prisoners escape, Rufus is made to reply: 'Far be it from me to believe that a knight would break his sworn word. If he did so, he would be despised forever as an outlaw.'[89] As both this incident and the honourable treatment of the garrison of Le Mans in 1100 indicate, a developed sense of professional empathy is clearly visible by the close of the eleventh century at the latest. It is doubtless only the paucity of sources that conceal earlier manifestations.

This is not to deny that an awareness of a common bond of knighthood was further heightened by both religious and secular influences during the course of the later eleventh and twelfth centuries. Ecclesiastical attempts to redefine the role of the knighthood in Christian society in the wake first of the Gregorian reform then of the First Crusade could only help to sharpen knights' consciousness of membership of an *ordo equestris*.[90] Indeed, such was the confidence and self-esteem of the *militia saecularis* that by the 1180s Chrétien de Troyes could write of Perceval's dubbing that his knightly tutor, Gornemant of Gohort, 'conferred on him the highest order that God had set forth and ordained; that is the order of knighthood which must be maintained without villany'.[91]

From the 1170s, Chrétien's romances played a central role in transforming the contemporary tournament – and by extension chivalric self-perceptions – by instilling it with powerful Arthurian overtones and elements of courtly romance.[92] But what was the influence of the tournament on the formation and dissemination of notions of a brotherhood of arms?

THE IMPACT OF THE TOURNAMENT

The tournament acted as a fundamental catalyst for the development of chivalric institutions. It was probably the tournament rather than war itself

---

[89] Orderic, v, pp. 244–5.

[90] Morris, '*Equestris Ordo*', pp. 87–96; Flori, *L'essor de la chevalerie*, pp. 164–219.

[91] *Le conte du Graal*, ll. 1630–6; Chrétien de Troyes: *Arthurian Romances*, p. 402.

[92] Writing for Henry of Champagne and Philip of Flanders, themselves leading patrons of the tournament, Chrétien took the rough mêlées he observed in reality and, by making them an integral backdrop to his romances, infused them not only with legendary associations with Arthur and his knights, but with heightened theatre, pageantry and eroticism (Keen, *Chivalry*, pp. 84, 91–4; cf. R. S. Loomis, 'Chivalric and Dramatic Imitation of Arthurian Romance', *Medieval Studies in Memory of A. K. Porter*, ed. W. W. Koelher, 2 vols. (Cambridge, Mass., 1939), i, pp. 79–97; and R. H. Cline, 'The Influences of Romances on Tournaments of the Middle Ages', *Speculum*, 20 (1945), pp. 204–11). By the time John the trouvère came to compose the *Histoire de Guillaume le Maréchal* in the early 1220s, he had clearly been influenced by Chrétien and sought to portray William as more than just a fine warrior, but a courtly knight dancing, for example, with the ladies at the tournament at Joingny (Benson, 'Chrétien de Troyes and the *Histoire de Guillaume le Maréchal*', pp. 1–24).

which fostered the growth of heraldry and the concomitant rise of the heralds both as experts on blazon and as *diseurs* or judges of the tourney itself.[93] Arguably the most significant role of the twelfth-century tournament, however, was to bring together knights from different principalities on a frequent basis in an increasingly artificial and controlled environment, the context of which was as much social as martial. Irrespective of the shifting political alliances and animosities of the territorial princes, knights could not only display their prowess and win glory and ransoms, but also become acquainted with their fellows in arms.[94]

This cosmopolitan character is one of the most striking features revealed by the *locus classicus* for the study of the tournament in the second half of the twelfth century, the *Histoire de Guillaume le Maréchal*. In his tourneying career, William the Marshal came to fight alongside English, Normans, Manceaux and Angevins against knights from France, Flanders and Scotland.[95] The fact that teams were frequently formed on 'national' lines or those of pre-existing political divisions meant that in real warfare such as that between Angevin and Capetian rulers, many of the protagonists must have been well known to each other.[96]

William the Lion, king of Scotland, for example, had come to France in 1166 to 'indulge in certain feats of chivalry'.[97] He and his *mesnie* may well have previously encountered in the tournament some of the Anglo-Norman knights who took them captive at Alnwick in 1174 in an equally bloodless engagement.[98] At a tournament held at Le Mans in 1175, William the Marshal himself captured Philip de Valognes, William the Lion's chamberlain.[99] Philip's presence at a tournament only the year after William the Lion's capture and the imposition of the humiliating Treaty of Falaise suggests the tournament's role as a method of political reintergration among the Anglo-Norman aristocracy.

If tournament teams might reflect existing regional or political groupings, the circumstances of the tournament might equally cut across such divisions. The *Histoire* was struck by the international flavour of the Young King's household when enlarged for the tourney, noting that on occasion it contained the pick of young men from France, Flanders and

---

[93] Keen, *Chivalry*, pp. 125–8.

[94] Hence, for example, a tournament held c. 1167 in Maine between Saint-Jamme and Valennes saw Angevins, Manceaux, Poitevins and Bretons ranged against French, Normans and English (*HGM*, ll. 1201–12).

[95] At a tournament between Anet and Sorel-Moussel in 1176, for example, the Young King's *mesnie* included Normans, Bretons, English, Manceaux, Angevins and Poitevins (*HGM*, ll. 2773–96).

[96] Thus, for example, Pierre de Leschans, one of the French knights who had taken William the Marshal's horses at the tournament at Anet, c. 1180, was captured at Gisors by Richard in 1198 (Howden, IV, p. 56; *HGM*, III, p. 47, n. 1).   [97] *Chronicle of Melrose*, p. 37.

[98] Below, pp. 155–6.   [99] *HGM*, ll. 1303–29.

Champagne.[100] Indeed, one gains the overwhelming impression from the *Histoire* of a small, closely knit aristocracy, a community of chivalric interest, formed of men intimately acquainted through diplomacy, the tournament, war and crusade. Many of the names found in its verses form a roll-call of participants on the Third Crusade,[101] another theatre of war where, despite the bickering of their leaders, common adversity and a common religious zeal served to emphasize a brotherhood in arms among a warrior elite politically divided but culturally one. William des Barres, often referred to in the *Histoire* simply as '*le bon Barrois*', was but a prominent example of a French lord very familiar to Angevin knights and greatly respected for his prowess in both the tourney and war.[102]

Serving as an ideal arena for conscious chivalric display, the tournament fostered acts of *largesse* and *franchise*. At a tournament in 1179 between Anet and Sorel-Mousset, for example, William the Marshal came across fifteen French knights besieged in a farmhouse by a larger number of attackers. The French chose to surrender to the Marshal rather than the besiegers who were technically his compatriots, and who were thus deprived of potential ransoms. William then escorted the French knights to safety and released them without ransom.[103]

Not that such behaviour was universal. When at a tournament between Gournay and Resson le Mals in 1169, Baldwin of Hainault joined the French team because they were outnumbered, Philip of Flanders was so enraged that he attacked Baldwin in earnest with considerable loss of life.[104] Nevertheless, though tempers might occasionally flare and the risk of accidental death was always present, the emphasis on profit and prize fighting in the tournament, as we have seen, necessitated the provision of some basic regulations for the taking of ransoms and seizure of horses and arms. The international and essentially non-hostile nature of these war games, moreover, formed a fertile ground for the development, enunciation and propagation of conventions of conduct.[105]

As significantly, the tournament gave warriors ample practice in unhorsing and capturing an opponent, if possible without seriously injuring him, in

---

[100] *Ibid.*, 11. 3583–98; cf. Gerald of Wales, *De principis instructione liber*, ed. G. F. Warner, *Giraldi Cambrensis Opera*, VIII (Rolls Series, 1891), p. 174.

[101] Hence for example Philip of Flanders, Theobald V of Blois, James d'Avesnes and Guy de Chatillion, all of whom died in 1191 on the Third Crusade, had taken part in the tournament at Pleurs in 1177, along with the counts of Clermont and Beaumont and William des Barres (*HGM*, 11. 2909–27; *ibid.*, III, p. 40, ns. 1–8). Similarly, Louis d'Arcelles, one of the French knights who surrendered to William Marshal during the tournament at Anet, died in Outremer in 1191 (*HGM*, 1. 4017; *ibid.*, III, p. 47, n. 3).   [102] On whom see *HGM*, III, p. 32, n. 1; and below, pp. 48, 52, 101.

[103] *Ibid.*, 11. 3997–4074.   [104] Keen, *Chivalry*, p. 85.   [105] Above, p. 48.

order to gain valuable ransoms. At a tournament at Eu in 1177, the *Histoire* claimed that, in one day, the Marshal took ten knights and twelve horses,[106] while according to the Young King's clerk Wigain, William and his tournament partner Roger de Gaugi captured 103 knights in ten months.[107] Techniques of combat practised in the tourney – the attack with the couched lance, sword-play and wrestling an opponent from his mount – were all used in war itself.[108]

A graphic illustration of this is provided by the engagement between Henry III's Poitevin forces and the rebels under the command of Richard Marshal outside Monmouth castle in 1233. Baldwin de Guisnes and his knights made a sustained effort to seize Richard. They slew his horse with their lances, but Richard, 'who was well practiced in the French way of fighting', dragged a knight from his horse and remounted. Baldwin then tore Richard's helmet off with his hands so violently that blood flowed from his nostrils, and grasping the Marshal's horse by the bridle, he attempted to lead it towards the castle.[109] Richard only escaped when Baldwin was shot in the chest by one of the Marshal's crossbowmen. None of Baldwin's men had thought to kill Richard, and it is significant that the wound received by Baldwin himself was inflicted not by a knight, but by a common missileman. That 'the French way of fighting' gave the edge in such close combat was acknowledged by Richard I when he licensed tournaments in England in 1194. One of his principal aims in relaxing the earlier prohibition was in order that English knights might practise their weapon skills and henceforth not be outclassed by their French opponents.[110]

The tournament thus undoubtedly served to reinforce and disseminate the notion of a brotherhood of arms in significant conceptual and practical ways. But it is important to stress that the tournament *eo nomine* did not itself

---

[106] *HGM*, 11. 3372–76. To illustrate the Marshal's prowess, the *Histoire* noted how William had taken one of these horses twice. Having been defeated and had his horse taken by the Marshal, a Flemish knight, Matthew de Walincourt, petitioned the Young King for its return. As a gesture of largesse, Henry ordered William to give it back, which he did. Later that day, the Marshal again defeated Matthew, took his charger but again gave it back to him (*HGM*, 11. 3213–366).

[107] *Ibid.*, 11. 3417–24.

[108] Having 'broken a lance' against his adversary, a knight might then attempt to overpower him physically without endangering his life, either by clubbing him with sword or mace or by wrestling with him till he was overcome. Such wrestling, which might involve attempting to remove the opponent's helmet, is clearly portrayed in the late-thirteenth-century Manesse Codex's vivid depiction of a tournament mêlée (*Codex Manesse. Die Miniaturen der Grosser Heidelberger Liederhandschrift*, ed. I. F. Walther and G. Siebert (Frankfurt, 1988), p. 17). It was resorted to by Richard I and William des Barres during their mock joust at Messina in 1191. Richard tried to wrest William off his horse, but the latter succeeded in clinging stubbornly to his horse's neck, thereby robbing Richard of victory and earning the king's great fury (*GH*, 11, p. 155; above, p. 101).   [109] MP, 111, pp. 255–6.

[110] Howden, 111, p. 268; WN, pp. 422–3.

create such a concept. Significantly, many of Orderic's examples of a practical expression of a brotherhood in arms – the limited nature of the fighting at Chaumont, 1098, Rufus's release on parole of the captive knights at
Ballon, 1098, the honourable treatment of the Norman garrison of Le
Mans – occur before the tournament begins to emerge from the obscurity
of the sources in the first quarter of the twelfth century. And as we have
noted, cavalry exercises and group manoeuvre, which served to foster ideas
of a professional solidarity, were an essential part of warriors' training from
at least the ninth century.

RESTRAINT FROM KILLING IN BATTLE

The most crucial question of all, however, is what impact did such notions
of a brotherhood in arms have in war itself? Outside the comparatively safe
environs of the tournament, did the recognition of common membership
of the *ordo equestris* significantly mitigate the extent of killing?

The author of the *Histoire de Guillaume le Maréchal* certainly believed so.
The *Histoire* gives a powerful and pervading impression of the conscious
and sustained desire to avoid the killing of noble opponents. Such restraint
was not surprisingly much to the fore in the civil war of 1215–17, as it had
been in earlier Anglo-Norman dynastic struggles. But it might also manifest itself in Angevin–Capetian conflicts. When, for instance, the French
launched an attack on the barbican at Gisors in 1188, several *routiers* were
killed or injured by the defending sergeants, but though they lost many
destriers none of the French knights was harmed. William des Barres was
seized by his horse's bridle and detained, but was finally rescued by his
men.[111] At the close of the same campaign, Henry II launched a surprise
chevauchée around Mantes and Bréval after Philip had disbanded his army,
thus taking him completely unawares. The knights he sent out against the
Angevin force were worsted, with several being taken captive and others
injured, but the *Histoire* is explicit that there were no fatalities.[112]

Fighting might be bitter but killing was eschewed whenever possible.
When, at the siege of Milli in 1197, one of the garrison caught a Flemish
knight, Guy de la Bruyère, by the neck with a great fork, he was held there
helpless but was not harmed. Going to his rescue, the Marshal struck down
the constable of the castle, wounding him by a blow which cut through his

---

[111] *HGM*, ll. 7729–62. Howden, seemingly recording a separate incident prior to the events at Gisors,
notes how William des Barres was taken prisoner by Richard in a skirmish near Mantes, but escaped,
despite being on parole (*GH*, ii, p. 46); cf. *Phillipidos*, Bk iii, pp. 431, 487.
[112] *HGM*, ll. 7804–41. Meyer's comment, 'Il n'y a jamais de morts dans ce rencontres' (*HGM*, iii, p. 93,
no. 3), however, needs qualification (below, p. 164–6).

helmet, but then proceeded merely to sit upon his prostrate captive to draw breath.[113] On the rare occasions when knights were slain, the *Histoire* expresses a deep sense of regret. At the battle of Lincoln, 1217, William the Marshal seized the bridle of the count of Perche, unaware that he had just received a fatal lance-wound through the eye slit of his helmet. 'When the Marshal saw him fall', continues the *Histoire*, 'he thought he had simply lost consciousness and ordered William de Montigny to take off his helm. When this was done, they saw that he was dead. It was grievous that he should die in this way.'[114]

The *Histoire*, moreover, regarded the slayer of Earl Patrick of Salisbury, struck in the back when he was without armour and attempting to mount not a war-horse but a palfrey, not only as a traitor, in arms against Henry II in the Lusignan's rebellion of 1167, but as a murderer.[115] As leader of the Poitevin rebels, Geoffrey de Lusignan was held responsible by William the Marshal, but the former felt sufficiently uncomfortable about Patrick's demise to deny these charges strenuously.[116] Indeed, the *Histoire* states explicitly that it was dishonourable to slay a disadvantaged opponent. As Count Richard, lightly armed only in an iron cap and *pourpoint*, led the pursuit of his father from Le Mans in 1189, he encountered the Marshal, fully equipped and covering Henry II's retreat. As William charged at him, the *Histoire* has Richard exclaim, 'By God's legs, Marshal! Do not kill me, for that would not be right (*ce sereit mal*) for I am unarmed.' 'No, let the devil kill you for I shall not', replied William, running Richard's horse through with his lance instead.[117]

In the Arthurian romances of Chrétien de Troyes, written in the 1170s and early 1180s, such behaviour has become part of the knightly creed. When Gornemant instructs the young Perceval in the ways of knighthood, he enjoins on him that 'if you are ever compelled to go into combat with any knight . . . if you gain the upper hand and he is no longer able to defend himself or hold out against you, you must grant him mercy rather than killing him outright'.[118] Chrétien's romances may have influenced the *Histoire*, yet here they afford a striking contrast by portraying combat as far more sanguinary than the engagements described by John the

---

[113] *Ibid.*, 11. 11159–231.
[114] *Ibid.*, 11. 7804–41. It seems, however, if we may trust Roger of Wendover, that the count of Perche was deliberately slain. Surrounded and called upon to surrender, he had refused, saying that he would never yield to the English, who were traitors to their lord. He was thereupon struck through the eye slit of his helm by an irate knight avenging this insult and received his death wound (MP, III, pp. 21–2). According to the *Histoire*, the count of Perche's slayer was an English knight, Reginald Croc, who ironically seems to have been the only other noble casualty in the battle (*HGM*, 11. 16738–42; MP, III, pp. 21–2).   [115] *HGM*, 11. 1629–52.   [116] *Ibid.*, 11. 6455–58.
[117] *Ibid.*, 11. 8803–47.   [118] *Le Conte du Graal*, 11. 1637–45; Chrétien de Troyes. *Arthurian Romances*, p. 402.

trouvère.[119] Drawing heavily as he did upon the descriptions of combat in the chansons, Chrétien does not scruple to have his itinerant heroes such as Erec, Yvain, Gawain and Lancelot slay numerous opponents in single combat, either by running them through with the couched lance or by striking them down with the sword.[120] Only once an adversary has become disadvantaged does Gornemant's injunction come into force.

The surprise and capture of William the Lion at Alnwick, on 13 July 1174, offers a striking contrast to such bloody literary combats. One of the crucial features of this engagement was that the Scots and Galwegians, who formed the bulk of the Scottish army, were absent on foraging raids, leaving the king with only a small, predominantly Anglo-Norman *mesnie* of knights and a mercenary force of Flemings. On learning of the Scots' disposition, a strong force of Anglo-Norman knights, led by Rannulf de Glanville, sallied out from Newcastle and fell upon William's unsuspecting force as he was breakfasting outside Alnwick castle. The Flemish mercenaries were ruthlessly cut down by the English knights.[121] Yet despite a fierce resistance, all of William's Anglo-Normans who spurned flight were captured unharmed.

Jordan Fantosme, who claims to be an eye-witness, describes with obvious enthusiasm the feats of arms of William's own Anglo-Norman knights.[122] For unlike the hated, feared and despised Scots, these lords belonged to the chivalrous, aristocratic society of Jordan's own audience.[123] Indeed, many of the northern English lords in Rannulf de Glanville's force had close connections with the Scottish court and would thus have been familiar with William the Lion's barons and knights.[124] As a result, a conscious effort was made in the fighting at Alnwick not to slay these knights, but simply to unhorse and seize them for ransom.[125]

In Jordan's praise poem, moreover, the ideal of chivalric conduct in war is epitomized not by one of Henry II's *fideles*, but rather by a leading

---

[119] Benson, 'The Tournament in the Romances of Chrétien de Troyes and *L'Histoire de Guillaume le Maréchal*', pp. 1–24.

[120] For the motif of single combat in the chansons see J. Rychner, *La chanson de geste. Essai sur l'art épique des jongleurs* (Geneva and Lille, 1955), pp. 139–46; Jones, 'Chrétien, Hartman and the Knight as Fighting Man', pp. 90–7.   [121] JF, ll. 1796–8, 1807–10. Below, pp. 179–80.

[122] Hence he notes that 'Richard Maluvel performed courageously; he dealt many blows and took many in return. As long as he was on his horse he feared nothing; he had a splendid horse and he was splendidly accoutred, and he himself was bold and chivalrous (*hardiz et pruz*)' (JF, ll. 1872–6). Similarly, William de Mortimer 'sweeps through the ranks like a mad boar. He deals a succession of great blows and takes as good as he gives' (*ibid.*, ll. 1858–9).

[123] For Anglo-Norman attitudes to the Scots, see below, pp. 292–329.

[124] Strickland, 'Arms and the Men', p. 219 and n. 141.

[125] The horses of both William the Lion and Richard Maluvel were slain by lances, while William Mortimer was forced to yield when unhorsed by Bernard de Balliol (JF, ll. 1807, 1782–3,. 1880, 1863–4).

insurgent, Earl David of Huntingdon, younger brother of William the Lion. Describing David's operations from Huntingdon and Leicester against the royalist forces in 1174, Jordan notes:

> And there was no stopping Lord David of Scotland; he carried off so much booty that he was mightily pleased. David fought well in the heart of England (*mult guerria bien*) . . . David was wise as well as nobly born. He defended Holy Church, for it was never his will to do wrong to priest or canon possessed of book learning, or to cause displeasure to any nun from an abbey.[126]

That David had been in arms against Henry II is here all but irrelevant, for nobility, prowess and skill in arms – the qualities of a *prudhomme* – far outweigh considerations of mistaken political allegiance, placing David firmly within the cultural milieu of Jordan's own knightly patrons.[127] It was the same regard for martial distinction that allowed Fantosme to praise the prowess of Roger de Mowbray and Adam de Port as warriors and to exonerate their flight from Alnwick in 1174, despite the fact that they were leading rebels in the war of 1173–4 and were in league with the Scots.[128]

Consideration of an opponent's martial distinction might even override considerations of fealty and vassalic duty. At the battle of Bourgthéroulde, fought in 1124 between a unit of Henry I's household troops and Norman rebels, one of Henry's knights, William de Grandcourt, captured the leading rebel Amaury de Montfort,

> but out of human compassion he took pity on a man of such great valour, knowing for certain that if he were captured he would never or only with great difficulty, get out of the king's clutches. He chose therefore rather to desert the king, abandon his own lands, and go into exile rather than condemn the noble count to perpetual prison.[129]

In this degree of self-sacrifice, William de Grandcourt's actions were clearly exceptional – hence Orderic's emphasis on this incident as the epitome of chivalric conduct. Yet skill in arms and bravery in war were such universally acknowledged values that they might transcend cultural divides. We have seen how despite the intense and ultimately insuperable hostility created between Frank and Muslim by opposing religious convictions, warriors might exchange chivalric gestures and ritual such as gift giving or

---

[126] JF, 11. 1129–31, 1135–8.   [127] Strickland, 'Arms and the Men', pp. 206–13.

[128] JF, 11. 1835–47. Earlier in his poem, Jordan had been careful to censure Mowbray and de Port for their defection, but inseparable from the criticism is an acknowledgement of their prowess as knights: 'They were the best warriors known to man – or rather they had been – but they do not know that God will not tolerate their misguided actions much longer' (*Ibid.*, 11. 1335–7).

[129] Orderic, VI, pp. 350–3.

the bestowal of arms.[130] These actions were but a tangible manifestation of a grudging but consistent recognition of the valour and military professionalism of the enemy. Thus Ibn-al-Althir could praise the desperate bravery of the Frankish knights at Hattin in 1187, and Beha-ad-Din the dogged resilience of their infantry on the march from Acre to Jaffa in 1191.[131] The *Itinerarium*, describing the defenders of Acre in 1191 as men 'of such wonderful valour and warlike excellence', remarked that 'never has there been such a people as these Turks for prowess in war'. 'It was only their superstitious rites', he adds, 'and their pitiful idolatry that had robbed such warriors of their strength'.[132]

This theme is recurrent in crusade sources, and nowhere receives more striking expression than in the reflections of the *Gesta Francorum* on the great but hard-won Christian victory of Dorylaeum in 1098:

> What man, however experienced and learned, would dare to write of the skill and prowess and courage of the Turks, who thought that they would strike terror into the Franks, as they had done into the Arabs and Saracens, Armenians, Syrians and Greeks, by the menace of their arrows? Yet, please God, their men will never be as good as ours. They have a saying that they are of common stock with the Franks, and that no men, except the Franks and themselves, are naturally born to be knights. This is true, and nobody can deny it, that if only they had stood firm in the faith of Christ and holy Christendom . . . you could not find stronger or braver or more skilful soldiers; and yet by God's grace they were beaten by our men.[133]

If such sentiments could be felt despite the religious hatred so evident in *The Song of Roland* and the *Gesta Francorum*, it is easy to see why respect for fellow Christian warriors could result in their honourable treatment as worthy opponents – as long, that is, as they were knights and not common infantrymen.[134] Yet such a recognition of valour did not necessarily prevent the slaying of opponents in combat. In Outremer, both Franks and Muslims were capable of the execution of prisoners and of atrocities.[135] While the Muslims readily acknowledged the prowess of the knights of the military orders, they habitually executed Templars and Hospitallers on

---

[130] Above, pp. 25–7.

[131] *Arab Historians of the Crusades*, tr. F. Gabrielli (New York, 1969), pp. 122–3; Beha-ad-Din, pp. 282–3.

[132] *Itinerarium*, pp. 228, 233.

[133] *GFr*, p. 21. Similarly, the *Song of Roland* could describe leading Saracens in terms echoing the virtues of Christian heroes. King Corsalis 'spoke in the fashion of a good vassal; for all God's gold he would not become a coward', while Margariz of Seville 'is so handsome that the ladies adore him; whenever one sees him, her eyes light up. When she catches sight of him, she becomes all smiles. No pagan is such a good knight' (*Song of Roland*, ll. 887–8, 955–60).

[134] For the treatment afforded common foot soldiers, see below, pp. 176–81.   [135] Below, p. 303.

capture precisely because of their martial qualities.[136] Similarly, admiration for the defenders of Acre in 1191 did not prevent their mass execution by Richard I after the terms of surrender had been unfulfilled.[137]

In the West, the practical effects of the concept of a brotherhood in arms on conduct in war has to be equally qualified. Notions of honour, of respect for knightly adversaries and of ransom did indeed provide warriors with a degree of security, and generally prevented their outright slaughter in the wake of defeat. Yet, as we shall see, a combination of factors ensured that the killing of knights in battle was considerably less of a rarity than implied by Jordan Fantosme or the *Histoire de Guillaume le Maréchal.*

[136] Forey, *The Military Orders*, pp. 83–4.   [137] *GH*, II, pp. 178–9, 187–90.

6

THE LIMITS OF CHIVALRY AND THE REALITIES
OF BATTLE

> He does not leave a good knight alive as far as Baiol, nor treasure nor
> monastery, nor church, nor shrine, nor censer, nor cross, nor sacred vessel;
> everything that he seizes he gives to his companions. He makes so cruel a
> war that he does not lay hands on a man without killing, hanging or
> mutilating him.[1]

Such was the conduct the poet of *Girart de Rousillon*, probably writing in the
1170s, believed possible in *tempus werrae* from the eponymous hero of the
chanson. Here war appears as stark, brutal and pitiless, seemingly unmiti-
gated by any code of behaviour or notions of honour, involving the slaying
or maiming of opponents irrespective of rank. The dynamic for aggression
is material gain, the plundering of religious houses and churches an integral
aspect of waging war. Nothing could be further from Orderic's insistence
on a brotherhood in arms or from Jordan Fantosme's depiction of Earl
David of Huntingdon, who, as the respecter of churches and friend to the
religious in time of war, marked the epitome of chivalric conduct. *Girart de
Rousillon* displays the epic exaggeration common to its genre, but in its
depiction of sacrilege and ravaging it is by no means unrealistic.

Awareness of a brotherhood of arms might, as we have seen, find concrete expression on the battlefield or during siege.[2] Yet such acts might
often be isolated incidents set within the context of a more bitter war, note-
worthy precisely because of the contrast they afforded with the general
tenor of a campaign. There was, for example, a striking disparity between

---

[1] *Girart de Rousillon*, ed. W. M. Hackett, 3 vols. in 2 (Paris, 1953–5), I, 11. 6203–9. The editor tentatively
identifies Baiol as Bayeux (*ibid.*, II, p. 570).   [2] Above, pp. 132–56; and cf. below, p. 208–20.

the jovial relations between Count Helias and the garrison of Le Mans in
1100, and the Normans' earlier campaigns in Maine, waged with utter ruthlessness.[3] As the principal commander in the region during Rufus's
absence, Robert de Bellême had conducted what by contemporary terms
must have appeared to be war in its most extreme form against the supporters of Helias, starving prisoners to death and devastating the land.[4]
Bellême's excesses were notorious, but Rufus himself indulged in wholesale destruction following his retreat from the unsuccessful siege of Mayet
in 1099.[5]

The siege of Mayet itself reveals how closely chivalric gestures and bitter
enmity could be juxtaposed. Despite the fact that Rufus had granted the
garrison a day's respite to observe a Sunday, one of the defenders had
hurled a rock at the king, narrowly missing him but smashing out the brains
of a knight standing close by. 'As the man fell at the king's feet, miserably
slain', noted Orderic, 'long roars of laughter and strident shouts came from
the tower: "See, now the king has fresh meat! Take it to the kitchen to be
served to him for dinner!"'[6] It is significant that Orderic attaches no
censure to the grim humour and conduct of the defenders, but rather
praises their courage and loyalty.[7] Notions of a brotherhood of arms
clearly had their limits.

ADDING INSULT TO INJURY: THE TAUNTING AND ABUSE OF OPPONENTS

If during hostilities the prowess and constancy of an opponent might be
recognized, lauded and even rewarded,[8] the abuse and mockery of an
enemy was equally commonplace. The trading of insults is a prominent
feature of chansons such as *Girart de Rousillon* and *Raoul de Cambrai*, where
protagonists hurl colourful abuse at one another, their mutual denigration
usually focusing on lowly status and questionable paternity. Yet such abuse
was by no means the preserve of epic literature. In 1102, Robert of
Bellême's garrison derided the besieging forces of Robert Curthose as they
retired in confusion.[9] Henry I was mocked by the garrison of Dives in
1106, and the defenders of Exeter castle hurled abuse at Stephen's besieging forces in 1136,[10] while at the siege of Kenilworth in 1266, the garrison

---

[3] Orderic, v, pp. 302–7; above, pp. 137–8.   [4] Orderic, v, pp. 234–5, 242–3.

[5] *Ibid.*, v, pp. 260–1.

[6] *Ibid.*, v, pp. 258–61. Elements of detail weigh against this story being wholly apocryphal. Nor can it
be dismissed merely as anti-Cennomanian propaganda, for Orderic was sympathetic to the cause of
Helias against Rufus's invasion, and was well informed about the war in Maine.

[7] *Ibid.*, v, pp. 258–9.   [8] Below, pp. 218–19.   [9] Orderic, vi, pp. 22–3.

[10] *Ibid.*, vi, pp. 82–3; *GS*, pp. 34–5.

responded to their excommunication by the legate Ottobuono by dressing up a surgeon, Master Philip Porpeis, in a white cape in mimicry of the legate. The rebels' own 'legate' then mockingly excommunicated Henry III, his army, and Ottobuono.[11]

The taunting of attackers, however, might not unnaturally provoke a violent response. Duke William's savage treatment of the garrison of a fortification near Alençon in 1051 was the result of their having taunted him by beating hides over the walls and shouting 'Tanner!' in allusion to the supposedly lowly occupation of his mother, and, by implication, his bastardy.[12] In 1138, some young hotheads in the garrison of Bamburgh, trusting overmuch in a newly built outwork, jeered at the Scots army as it passed. Though the main castle was impregnable, the enraged Scots stormed the barbican and its defenders paid for their raillery with their lives.[13] It was doubtless with such considerations in mind that Jordan Fantosme has the castellan of Wark, Roger de Stuteville, forbid his men to taunt the Scots army of William the Lion as it retreated from a bloody and unsuccessful siege in 1174:

> Make no opprobrious remarks, let us eschew such things, and do not shout and whoop at the men of Scotland . . . I am not forbidding you to disport yourselves and make merry; when you see the king and his whole army far off, proclaim your joy . . .[14]

This ridiculing of an enemy, though itself often the product of fear, can be seen as a mechanism to bolster warriors' own morale by acts of braggadocio and by the belittling of their opponents. In other cases, we find taunting employed as a psychological weapon in an almost ritual combination of boast and formal defiance. Following the defeat of the Franco-Angevin force at Mortemer in 1054, Duke William had a messenger shout the news of the slaughter to the French camp from the top of a tree.[15] Likewise, Henry I instructed his knights to taunt Amaury de Montfort with the burning of his comital town of Evreux in 1119.[16] Enemies could be equally mocked in the literature of victory. In Jordan Fantosme's poem celebrating Henry II's triumph in 1173–4, the corollary of praise for his loyal vassals is the taunting of now vanquished opponents. The rebel earl of Derby is mocked as 'a simple knight, more fitted to kiss and embrace fair ladies than to smite other knights with a war hammer', while William the Lion's failure is parodied in a burlesque incident in which a Scottish catapult at Wark in 1174 misfires and knocks over a knight.[17]

---

[11] *The Metrical Chronicle of Robert of Gloucester*, ed. W. A. Wright, 2 vols. (Rolls Series, 1887), II, p. 772.
[12] WJ, p. 171.   [13] JH, p. 118.   [14] JF, ll. 1293–1301.   [15] WP, pp. 72–3.
[16] Orderic, VI, pp. 230–1.   [17] JF, ll. 947–9, 1242–9.

Nicknames given to siege-castles or siege weapons reveal an earthy and aggressive humour similarly based on derision of the enemy. Hence Rufus's siege-castle built to contain Mowbray's rebel garrison of Bamburgh in 1095 was called 'Malveisin' or, as the *Anglo-Saxon Chronicle* rendered it, 'Yfel nehhbur', 'Bad Neighbour'.[18] At Acre in 1191, Philip Augustus had a stone-engine with the same name, 'Malvoisin', while the Franks nicknamed one of the defenders' engines 'Male Cousine.'[19] A siege-castle built by Henry I's forces at Old Rouen against Count Stephen of Aumâle was named 'Mate-putain' or 'Whore-humbler' in contempt of his wife Hawise, and the great prefabricated castle erected by Richard at the gates first of Messina then of Acre was known as 'Mategriffon' − 'Griffon-killer', in reference to the contemptuous name given to the Sicilian Greeks.[20]

Yet though verbal vilification of an enemy certainly stands in marked contrast to overt expressions of a chivalric brotherhood of arms, taunts and the trading of insults were not fundamentally incompatible with acts of chivalric magnanimity.[21] For like the death-threats commonly made by besiegers to intimidate a garrison but rarely implemented,[22] abuse was an integral part of the psychology of contemporary warfare, intimately connected with mechanisms of boasting and the augmentation or denigration of reputation. Such insults were the necessary, if darker corollary to a culture centred on honour and shame. It was the actualities of battle that posed a far more serious limitation to the effective expression of a brotherhood in arms.

KILLING IN BATTLE

Warfare waged within the Anglo-Norman *regnum* was, as we have seen, polarized between the localized but bitter private war of the feud and the larger scale but restrained engagements in the context of civil war, where the limiting of fatalities was a priority.[23] Orderic's account of the fighting between Capetian and Anglo-Norman forces at Chaumont, 1098, and at the battle of Brémule, 1119, might suggest that war between the territorial princes was closer to the latter form of hostilities, and that it was the feuding element of the internal conflicts that accounted for the high mortality rate.

---

[18] FW, 11, p. 38; *ASC, s.a.* 1095.

[19] Ambroise, 11, 4745–7; for other nicknames see Bradbury, *The Medieval Siege*, p. 268.

[20] Devizes, pp. 25, 43; Ambroise, 11. 937–40; *Itinerarium*, pp. 168, 172–3; *GH*, 11, pp. 138, 150, 162. Orderic, vi, pp. 278–81. Similarly, the forces of Louis VI 'derisively maligned with vulgar names' two siege-castles erected by Henry I outside Gasny (1116 x 1118), calling one 'Ill-placed' (*Malassis*) and the other 'Hare's form' (*Trulla leporis*) (Orderic, vi, pp. 186–7).

[21] Except, that is, in the context of revolt, where insulting the king or duke could be punished as lèse majesty (below, p. 251).   [22] Below, pp. 243–5.   [23] Above, pp. 138–42.

Yet it is important to stress that external warfare could prove equally costly in lives, and that engagements on a far smaller scale than Brémule might lead to many more casualties. In the war of Sainte Suzanne against Hubert, vicomte of Maine, 'Robert of Vieux-Pont and Robert of Ussy and many other famous and much lamented knights were slain', while Richer, son of Engenulf de Laigle, was mortally wounded by an arrow in the face.[24] Indeed, Norman losses in this conflict, which included Matthew de Vitot and Hervey le Breton, William's 'magister militum', were so heavy that the king was finally forced to make peace with Hubert.[25] Similarly, although information is scanty concerning the battles in which Duke William secured control of the Norman duchy, they appear to have been sanguinary affairs. Following the duke's victory at Val-ès-Dunes, many of the rebel forces were slain in pursuit or drowned in the Orne, while the engagements at Mortemer, 1054, and Varaville, 1057, may similarly have involved much carnage.[26]

If such major engagements were infrequent, the numerous small-scale skir-mishes that characterized castle-based warfare were often bloody. Roger of Gloucester, for instance, met his death in combat when Henry I's forces engaged the garrison of Falaise in 1105.[27] In 1119, during the same cam-paign as the battle of Brémule, Henry I's forces attacked the castle of Evreux held against them by a body of distinguished French knights com-manded by Philip and Florus, the sons of Louis VI.[28] The English siege-castle was in turn attacked by Amaury de Montfort who was attempting to bring relief to Evreux. Heavy fighting ensued in which 'neither side would give way to the other, for each burned to be judged the more valiant, and therefore many were killed in daily engagements'.[29] In the same year, many champions were slain in skirmishing outside the walls of Breteuil, while during Louis VI's siege of Châteauneuf-sur-Epte, 'Walter Riblard and the king's troops resisted courageously and, by hurling missiles at the attackers, wounded many of them severely'.[30] The crucial difference between such

---

[24] Orderic, IV, pp. 48–9.   [25] Ibid., IV, pp. 50–3.

[26] For Val-ès-Dunes, WJ, p. 123; WP, pp. 16–18. Poitiers states that the greater part of the rebel forces were slain during a pursuit of several miles, while both authors note that many of those fleeing were drowned in the Orne. Jumièges remarks of Mortemer that a large number of French nobles were slain, while Poitiers adds that the French army was decimated by a terrible carnage (WJ, p. 130; WP, pp. 72–3). Orderic, writing considerably later, believed that 'many were slain on both sides, for each army contained valiant warriors who would fight to the death without thought of yielding' (Orderic, IV, pp. 86–7). Losses are reported to have been heavy at Varaville, and this may well have been so due to the fact that William's forces surprised the French while crossing the Dives (WJ, pp. 131–2; WP, pp. 80–3). In all these engagements, however, it should be noted that the contemporary statements are at best laconic and at worst little more than inflated panegyric that smacks of hyperbole.

[27] Orderic, VI, 78–81.   [28] Ibid., VI, pp. 230–1.   [29] Ibid., VI, pp. 232–3.   [30] Ibid., VI, pp. 246–7.

mêlées and the tourney was that here knights might be deliberately slain, if the opportunity or volition to take opponents prisoner was lacking. For all his concern to show certain elements of the knighthood motivated by Christian restraint Orderic clearly recognized the real nature of many conflicts when, speaking of the death of William, son of Roger de Saint-Laurent, he commented: 'Thus it is that exercise of the fierce arts of war leads to much bloodshed, and the cruel death of fair youths brings sorrow and loss to many.'[31]

These examples of widespread fatalities in war come from the eleventh and the first half of the twelfth century. Given the emphasis in both Jordan Fantosme and the *Histoire de Guillaume le Maréchal* on the absence of killing in combat between knights, can it be argued that the twelfth century witnessed an increasing stress on capture and ransom? The development of the tournament and the cultural elaboration of knighthood might be seen as catalysts for such transformation. Yet attractive though the idea of gradual maturation of chivalric conduct may be, such a chronology must be seriously qualified. In that private war had become far more restricted in Northern France and virtually suppressed in England and Normandy by the later twelfth century, the extent of killing was indeed diminished with the consolidation of the territorial principalities. But warfare between the Angevins and Capetians was not always as unbloody as the *Histoire* might lead us to believe.

Indeed, some contemporaries were of the opinion that the wars of 1194–9 between Richard and Philip were waged with an intense animosity hitherto unseen, which resulted in an escalation of mutilations and the ill-treatment of captured warriors.[32] Howden believed that during his struggle in 1183 to hold Aquitaine against a coalition of rebel barons supported by his brothers Henry and Geoffrey, Richard had ordered that prisoners taken should be beheaded irrespective of rank.[33] In 1194, John had the French garrison of Evreux beheaded.[34] Even within the context of rebellion, such acts find few parallels in the reigns of the Conqueror and his sons. John's accession did nothing to reverse this tendency, as his maltreatment of captives following his signal victory at Mirebeau indicates.[35]

The battle of Bouvines in 1214, which marked the culmination of Angevin–Capetian hostilities, still more strongly suggests that warfare remained as bitter, if not more so, than in Orderic's day. Like Brémule, this was an engagement fought between the French monarch and external

---

[31] *Ibid.*, VI, pp. 232–3.
[32] Howden, iv, p. 54; Rigord, p. 142; below, p. 202. Cf. Powicke, *Loss of Normandy*, p. 128.
[33] *GH*, I, p. 293; above, p. 52.   [34] Rigord, p. 127; below, p. 223.   [35] Below, p. 197.

enemies, which in 1214 comprised the allied forces of Flanders, England, the Empire and other principalities.[36] But in marked contrast to the minimal casualties sustained in 1119, Bouvines was bitterly fought and bloody. Infantry casualties are unknown, but given the nature of the engagement were probably high. The numbers of knights taken or slain, however, are known with some precision and are most revealing. For whereas the French knights captured 131 knights including many of the allied leaders, as many as 169 knights may have been killed.[37] The convention of ransom was thus in operation to a degree, but it is clear that in the heat of battle, knights on both sides did not scruple to slay their opponents. The allied warriors used fine three-edged daggers to penetrate the weak spots in the French knights' armour; Stephen de Longchamp, for example, died after being stabbed through the eye-slit of his helmet.[38]

Bouvines thus furnishes an important corrective to the impression of restraint in knightly warfare portrayed by the near-contemporary *Histoire de Guillaume le Maréchal*, written in the 1220s. The enormous political stakes involved may go far to explaining why the battle was particularly hard fought and sanguinary. Abbot Suger of St Denis had believed that the invasion of the *patria* justified desperate remedies. Speaking of the threatened German invasion in 1124, which in many ways anticipated the Bouvines campaign, he has some of Louis VI's experienced barons advise cutting off the enemy once they had advanced into France. Thereupon the French could

> attack, overthrow and slaughter them without mercy as if they had been Saracens. The unburied bodies of the barbarians would be abandoned to wolves and ravens, to their everlasting shame; and such great slaughter and cruelty would be justified, because the land was being defended.[39]

A similar concept of defence of the *patria* against predominantly heathen invaders had underlain the propensity for Anglo-Saxon armies to slaughter their vanquished opponents,[40] and Suger's words may provide a clue as to why the battles of Mortemer, 1054, and Varaville, 1057, fought as desperate struggles to repel Angevin and French invaders from Normandy, were apparently so bloody. Similarly, Richard's severity in 1183 may be seen as an extreme reaction to the grave political and military crisis which threatened because of the invasion of Aquitaine by his brothers.

Bouvines nonetheless appears as far more representative than Brémule

---

[36] For Bouvines, see Duby, *The Legend of Bouvines*, which gives many of the relevant sources as appendices.   [37] WB, *Gesta*, p. 290; Verbruggen, *The Art of Warfare*, p. 236.
[38] WB, *Gesta*, p. 283, and n. 2.   [39] Suger, p. 222; tr. Cusimano and Moorhead, p. 129.
[40] Above, p. 3.

in demonstrating the risks of battle and the potential limitations of ransom and the concept of a brotherhood in arms. At its most basic level, war was a manifestation of corporate or individual animosity, and it is hardly surprising to find such motivation carried to the logical conclusion of slaying opponents. At Brémule, the rebel Norman lord William Crispin had attempted to slay Henry I, who was saved only by the quality of his mail coif.[41] Howden noted that during Richard's pursuit of Philip at Fréteval in 1194, the king 'came up breathing out threats and slaughter against the men of the king of France, and sought for him that he might slay him or take him alive'.[42] At Bouvines, Philip Augustus would have been slain by Otto's imperial infantry had it not been for his strong right arm and the quality of his armour,[43] while a serious attempt was made on his life by Renaud of Boulogne, who had been disinherited of his county by Philip. Only the heroism of one of his knights, who threw himself in front of the fatal blow, saved Philip's life.[44] Similarly, the French knights who surrounded the Emperor Otto tried unsuccessfully to kill him or force him to surrender.[45]

The desire for self-preservation in the fear and confusion of a battle that hung in the balance, and the surge of aggression needed to carry the day, might lead to instinctive killing. Nor in a hard-fought mêlée might it be practically possible either to surrender or to seize a resisting opponent unharmed, even where there was the volition to do so.[46] The problem is graphically illustrated by the actions of Roger fitz Richard during the battle of Brémule. After his attack on Henry I, William Crispin had in turn been felled by Roger, who 'took him prisoner as he lay prostrate, and, flinging himself over his body prevented the friends who were standing round from killing him on the spot to avenge the king. Many indeed sought his life and Roger had great difficulty in saving him.'[47] Here the determination of the captor to prevent harm to his valuable prisoner was matched by the equally powerful urge by Henry's knights to kill Crispin in revenge for his assault on their lord. At the second battle of Lincoln, 1217, the insults of the count of Perche so enraged one of the English knights, Reginald Croc, that he struck him his death-blow through the eye-slit of his helmet, even though by this stage in the engagement the Franco-baronial army had been routed.[48]

Generally, the taking of prisoners and acts of chivalric largesse, such as William de Grancourt's release of Amaury de Montfort at Bourgthéroulde

---

[41] Orderic, VI, pp. 238–9.   [42] Howden, III, p. 255.   [43] WB, *Gesta*, pp. 282–4; MP, II, p. 580.
[44] MP, II, p. 580; Lewis, *The Art of Matthew Paris*, fig. 106.   [45] MP, II, pp. 580–1; WB, *Gesta*, pp. 283–4.
[46] For a valuable study of behaviour in combat see Keegan, *The Face of Battle*, pp. 97–116, where Agincourt, 1415, is taken as a case study.   [47] Orderic, VI, pp. 238–9.   [48] Above, p. 141.

in 1124,[49] occurred principally once the outcome of the battle had been determined and the enemy forces had broken in flight. The battle of Lincoln, 1141, is instructive in demonstrating the changing tempo of an engagement. In the initial onslaught, many were killed as the charge of Rannulf of Chester and Robert of Gloucester struck Stephen's defensive formation.[50] Once the king's army began to disintegrate, however, many were taken prisoner, though the fighting remained bitter around King Stephen as the Angevin horse attacked the closely formed body of his dismounted knights. Huntingdon says Stephen slew some of his assailants with a great two-handed axe and wounded others, while one of his principal commanders, Baldwin fitz Gilbert, was badly wounded.[51] Nevertheless, now assured of victory, the Angevins clearly made efforts to take the king and the remaining royalists alive. Overall losses were fewer than 100, and far more perished in the ensuing sack of the city.[52]

In a rout most knights would not deliberately slay a noble opponent attempting to escape. Yet there was danger of fugitives being trampled in the panic of flight, or drowned if a river blocked the path of retreat.[53] Many fleeing from the battle of Val-ès-Dunes, 1047, for example, were drowned in the Orne, while Count Robert of Flanders died after being trampled by horses during the flight following a battle between the king of France and Theobald of Blois in the Meaux region in 1111.[54] In 1198, Philip Augustus himself nearly shared the fate of twenty of his knights who were drowned when the bridge over the moat at Gisors broke under the weight of those fleeing from Richard's attack.[55] At Lincoln in 1217, the Franco-baronial forces were fortunate that the royalists did not press home their advantage when their escape was hindered by a narrow turnpike gate.[56]

Escape from battle, however, was not always possible. Although the use of dismounted knights was a highly effective element in Anglo-Norman tactics,[57]

---

[49] Above, p. 156.   [50] Orderic, VI, pp. 542–3; GS, p. 113.   [51] HH, p. 274.

[52] Orderic, VI, pp. 546–7.

[53] Those regarded as renegades, however, might be peremptorily killed. At the siege of Remelard in 1077–8, William I's knights trapped the bandit lord Aymer de Villerai, unhorsed and slew him on the spot before flinging his corpse down outside the tents of Earl Roger de Montgomery (Orderic, II, pp. 360–1). In 1217, Eustace the Monk, who had formerly served the king of England but who now was a leading commander of the French naval forces, was summarily beheaded on being captured during the naval battle off Sandwich between the English and French fleets (HGM, II. 17434–55).

[54] WJ, p. 123; WP, pp. 16–18; Orderic, VI, pp. 160–3.   [55] Howden, IV, p. 58.

[56] MP, III, p. 22. For discussions of the battle of Lincoln see T. F. Tout, 'The Fair of Lincoln and the "Histoire de Guillaume le Maréchal"', EHR, 17 (1903), pp. 240–65; Carpenter, The Minority of Henry III, pp. 37–40.

[57] Dismounted knights were a principal feature of the battles of Tinchebrai, 1106, Brémule, 1119, Bourgthéroulde, 1124, and the Standard, 1138. For a general discussion, see Hollister, Anglo-Saxon Military Institutions, pp. 131–2; idem., The Military Organization of Norman England, pp. 127–8, which largely repeats his previous observations; and Bradbury, 'Battles in England and Normandy, 1066–1154', pp. 11–12.

a knight on foot was at a considerable disadvantage when it came to rapid withdrawal or escape. The hauberk was a very flexible garment and as such did not restrict movement in combat, but its weight seriously hindered flight. According to the *Histoire de Guillaume le Maréchal*, the count of Nantes, a highly respected warrior, always donned his hauberk when on horseback, rather than before mounting which was the usual practice. When asked why, he replied that if the enemy should attack, an armoured knight who was at any distance from his horse was in much greater danger of capture, 'and I have seen many men killed or made prisoner in those circumstances'.[58]

Knights might shed their hauberks for greater mobility in reconnaissance,[59] while in battle they might discard them to facilitate escape if defeated, or if victorious, to speed up pursuit. Ailred of Rievaulx, for example, noted how following the Scots' rout at Northallerton in 1138, many of King David's knights discarded their armour, while at the battle of Axspoele, 1128, William Clito ordered his knights to remove their hauberks for speedier pursuit of the enemy.[60] The inability to escape by knights once dismounted, and hence the necessity to fight more resolutely, was regarded by contemporary observers as a principal reason for drawing up knights on foot.[61] At Bourgthéroulde, on seeing the troops of Henry I's *familia regis* dismount to fight, Amaury de Montfort is made to say: 'See, Odo Borleng and his man have dismounted; you can be sure that he intends to fight resolutely until he has won the day. A mounted soldier who has dismounted with his

---

[58] *HGM*, 11. 2164–88. Few hauberks are extant from before the fifteenth century, and extant shirts are nearly all shorter *haubergeons*, intended to be worn under plate armour. Nevertheless, these give an approximate indication of weight. One of the longer coats, a fourteenth-century Italian example, weighs 31 lb, while a shorter fifteenth-century German coat weighs 20 lb 11 oz (Blair, *European Armour*, Appendix, 'The Weight of Armour', p. 192). Fifteenth-century German examples in the Wallace Collection varied between 13 lb 2½ oz to 19 lb 8 oz, (Sir James Mann, *European Arms and Armour* (*Wallace Collection Catalogues*, London, 1962), i, pp. 1–3). Cf. I. Peirce, 'Arms, Armour and Warfare in the Eleventh Century', *Anglo-Norman Studies*, 10 (1987), p. 240.
  William of Poitiers cites approvingly as an example of Duke William's prowess the story of how, shortly after landing in England, William led a group of knights to reconnoitre, but that the difficulty of the terrain meant they had to return to camp on foot. But 'the duke came back carrying on his shoulder, besides his own hauberk, that of William fitz Osbern, one of his companions. This man was famed for his bodily strength and courage, but it was the duke who relieved him in his necessity of the weight of his armour' (WP, pp. 168–9).

[59] In June 1189, for example, William Marshal and four companions, who had been sent to reconnoitre the advance of Philip and Richard on Le Mans, were careful to avoid the enemy advance guard and to eschew all skirmishing because they were without their hauberks for greater mobility. Conversely, Henry refused to take the Marshal on another reconniasance the next morning because he was already fully armed (*HGM*, 11. 8427–78, 8517–40).

[60] *Relatio*, p. 198, where Ailred praises Earl Henry, the king's son, for enduring the weight of his hauberk until he saw a poor cottager to whom he gave it as alms; Galbert of Bruges, p. 299. Following Henry II's flight from Le Mans in 1189, Richard went in hot pursuit, armed only in an iron cap and gambeson for speed of chase (*HGM*, 11. 8803–7).

[61] HH, p. 235 (Tinchebrai, 1106); Orderic, vi, pp. 350–1 (Bourgthéroulde, 1124); JH, p. 119 (the Standard, 1138).

men will not fly from the field; he will either die or conquer.'[62] There was considerable exaggeration in such sentiments, but the difficulties of flight are revealed in the high instance of capture in those engagements where knights fought on foot, such as Tinchebrai and Lincoln, 1141, or in those where the knights' horses were killed. At Brémule, 'William Crispin and eighty knights charged the Normans, but their horses were quickly killed and they were all surrounded and cut off',[63] while at Lincoln in 1217, 'the party of the barons was greatly weakened, for when the horses fell to the earth slain, their riders were taken prisoners, as there was no one to rescue them'.[64]

THE EFFECTIVENESS OF ARMOUR

Yet if a knight's armour restricted flight, how much protection did it afford in combat? Both Orderic and William le Breton noted in their descriptions of Brémule and Bouvines that the quality of the warriors' armour was a major factor in limiting fatalities.[65] Byzantine and Arab writers were equally struck by the defensive qualities of the Frankish knights' armour,[66] and above all the hauberk, a knee-length coat of mail worn over a padded tunic.[67] Possession of the hauberk, whose enormous cost at once set its wearer apart from the more poorly equipped serjeants and infantry, was regarded as being so integral to the knight's *metier* that *loricati* could be a synonym for knights and a fief referred to as a *feudum loricae* or *fief del haubert*.[68] The *Rule of the Temple* assumed that the protection it offered led to greater resilience in combat; brother serjeants who were without mail could withdraw without permission if wounded or in difficulty, but those 'armed

---

[62] Orderic, VI, pp. 350–1.

[63] *Ibid.*, VI, pp. 238–9. In the same battle, the Normans were also able to capture over one hundred French knights, who Orderic significantly notes 'had been unhorsed' (*ibid.*). Orderic gives the number as 140 knights captured, but the *Chronica de Hida*, p. 318, says only 114. At Bourgethéroulde, Waleran de Meulan, Hugh de Montfort and Hugh de Châteauneuf-en-Thimerais were captured with some eighty other knights when their horses were killed (Orderic, VI, pp. 350–1).   [64] MP, III, p. 21.

[65] Orderic, VI, pp. 240–1; WB, *Phillipidos*, Bk XI, 11. 129–32.

[66] *The Alexiad of Anna Comnena*, tr. E. R. A. Sewter (Harmondsworth, 1969), pp. 415–6; Verbruggen, *The Art of Warfare*, pp. 64–5.

[67] For the defensive equipment of the period see Blair, *European Armour*, pp. 23–36; R. Ewart Oakeshott, *The Archaeology of Weapons. Arms and Armour from Prehistory to the Age of Chivalry* (London, 1960), esp. pp. 175–6; Peirce, 'Arms, Armour and Warfare in the Eleventh Century', pp. 237–57; *idem.*, 'The Knight, his Arms and Armour in the Eleventh and Twelfth Centuries', *The Ideals and Practice of Medieval Knighthood. Papers From the First and Second Strawberry Hill Converences*, ed. C. Harper-Bill and R. Harvey (Woodbridge, 1986), pp. 152–64; *idem.*, 'The Knight, his Arms and Armour, c. 1150–1250', *Anglo-Norman Studies*, 15 (1992), pp. 251–74; D. C. Nicolle, *Arms and Armour of the Crusading Era, 1050–1350*, 2 vols. (New York, 1988).

[68] Stenton, *English Feudalism*, pp. 15–16. Possession of a hauberk was stipulated by the 1181 Assize of Arms for any holding one knight's fee or an income of more than sixteen marks (W. Stubbs, *Select Charters* (9th edn, revised by H. W. C. Davis, Oxford, 1913), p. 183).

in mail should conduct themselves under arms as is given for the knight brothers'.[69]

How valid was such an assumption? Several narrative sources speak of hauberks turning blows from swords and other edged weapons.[70] It seems unlikely that sword thrusts would penetrate mail, for the knightly sword of the eleventh and twelfth centuries was intended primarily as a cutting weapon and its point was rarely pronounced.[71] The wearing of a gambeson or aketon, usually beneath the hauberk, increased protection as well as comfort, for such 'soft armour' was remarkably effective at absorbing blows and lessening bruising.[72] Resistance of armour, however, must have been affected by variables such as the angle of strike, the strength of the assailant, the quality of his blade and that of the hauberk. By contrast, the cutting power of the Danish two-handed axe, the weapon *par excellence* of the Anglo-Scandinavian housecarls but used well into the twelfth century, is repeatedly attested.[73] The *Song of Dermot* notes that during the battle for Dublin in 1171, John 'the Mad' cut off a Norman knight's leg at the thigh with his axe.[74]

As the twelfth century progressed, a greater number of knights gained a greater degree of protection. Leggings of mail, which on the Bayeux Tapestry had been the preserve only of the greatest lords, became more widespread, while the hauberk generally lengthened to cover the forearms and hands in the form of bag-mittens[75] – developments which point to the greater availability of armour and its *falling* cost. Though plate armour only became widespread from the late thirteenth and early fourteenth centuries, some form of solid body armour of iron or hardened leather, worn in addition to the hauberk, may have been in limited use by at least the 1220s if not before.[76]

[69] *Rule of the Temple*, c. 172, p. 61; cf. c. 322, p. 91 for the careful treatment of these costly garments.
[70] At Bouvines, Gerard de Truie attempted to stab the Emperor Otto with his dagger, but it glanced off his hauberk, while Howden recalls how a wealthy London citizen was saved from the knife blow of one of a gang of looters by his hauberk (WB, *Gesta*, pp. 283–4; *GH*, I, pp. 155–6). Similarly, Usamah describes how at the siege of Kafartab, 1115, a Turk dealt a Frankish sergeant a number of blows on his hauberk of 'double linked mail' to absolutely no effect (Usamah, p. 104).
[71] Oakeshott, *The Sword in the Age of Chivalry, passim*; *idem., Records of the Medieval Sword*.
[72] Blair, *European Armour*, pp. 19, 32–5.
[73] WP, pp. 186–8; *BT*, pl. 65; Wace, ll. 8257–80; Peirce, 'Arms, Armour and Warfare in the Eleventh Century', pp. 245–7.   [74] *Song of Dermot*, ll. 2441–8.
[75] Peirce, 'The Knight, his Arms and Armour, c. 1150–1250', pp. 251–5. Some knights, particularly the Normans in Sicily, wore coats of lamellar or scale armour, influenced by eastern fashions (*ibid.*, pl. 3), while the Ostmen at Dublin in 1171 may similarly have worn lamellar (Blair, *European Armour*, p. 37).
[76] According to William le Breton, in a combat between Richard, when still count of Poitou, and William de Barres, both wore in addition to their hauberks plates of worked iron (*fera fabricat patena recocto*) (WB, *Phillipidos*, Bk III, ll. 494–8). If this detail is anachronistic, it is nevertheless a development that must antedate William le Breton's death in 1225. As later sources refer to this form of body armour as a *cuirie*, it would seem that more usually such defences were made of *cuir-bouilli* – leather boiled in oil then dried to achieve considerable hardness (Blair, *European Armour*, pp. 37–9).

On seals, carvings, tombs or illuminations such developments are usually disguised by the surcoat, but Matthew Paris illustrates a number of knights whose surcoats themselves have pronounced, stiffened shoulder protection.[77]

Helmets, particularly when worn over the coif of the hauberk, seem to have afforded reasonable protection against sword cuts.[78] Nevertheless, the design of the helmet, which in the eleventh and through much of the twelfth century was open-faced saved for a nasal protecting the nose, made the face vulnerable to missile wounds.[79] Hugh, earl of Shrewsbury, was slain by bowmen of Magnus of Norway whose arrows struck him in the face,[80] while both Richer de Laigle in the war of Sainte-Suzanne and Geoffrey de Mandeville at the siege of Burwell died after being wounded in the face by an arrow.[81] The introduction first of helmets with more complete face-masks and then of the 'great' helm from the last quarter of the twelfth century improved protection at the expense of ventilation and lightness,[82] but even here arrows, lances or daggers might pierce the eye-slits.

In contrast to narrative accounts commenting on the effectiveness of mail, manuscript illuminations frequently depict swords, axes and hafted weapons cleaving through helmets and hauberks. Chansons and romances are similarly replete with sanguinary engagements where blows of lance and sword pierce armour. Such sources, however, pose considerable problems of verisimilitude. Literary depictions of combat are often stylized, heavily dependent on stock models, such as the attack with the couched lance, and frequently exaggerated.[83] Similar caveats apply to illumination, not least where texts, most notably those of the Old Testament, called for the depiction of carnage in battle. Yet certain manuscripts can be shown to be of considerable accuracy in regard

---

[77] Lewis, *The Art of Matthew Paris*, figs. 112, 171, 234, and pl. xiii. For the development of surcoats see Blair, *European Armour*, pp. 28–9.

[78] At Brémule, Henry I was saved by his mail coif when his helmet was struck by William Crispin's sword, while at the siege of Laigle in 1118, his helmet again prevented injury when he was struck by a stone (Orderic VI, pp. 204–5, 238–9; HH, p. 241; *Chronica de Hida*, p. 318). Baldwin of Flanders would have had his head split during a skirmish in 1119 had it not been for the strength of his helmet (*Chronica de Hida*, p. 315). At a tournament at Pleurs, 1176 x 1180, William the Marshal emerged unscathed despite his helmet having received such a battering that a blacksmith had to remove it for him on an anvil (*HGM*, ll. 3101–3116). If the author of the *Histoire* was not employing anachronistic detail, the incident provides an early reference to the use of the full-faced 'great' helm.

[79] Blair, *European Armour*, pp. 25–7, 28–32.

[80] See the references collected and discussed by E. A. Freeman, *William Rufus* (Oxford, 1882), Appendix, II, pp. 618–24.   [81] Orderic, IV, pp. 48–9; Gervase, I, p. 28; WN, p. 46.

[82] Peirce, 'The Knight, his Arms and Armour, c. 1150–1250', pp. 259–66.

[83] Jones, 'Chrétien, Hartmann and the Knight as Fighting Man', pp. 92–6 and references cited therein; cf. D. M. Legge, '"Osbercs Dublez". The Description of Armour in Twelfth-Century Chansons de Geste', *Société Rencevals. Proceedings of the Fifth International Conference* (Oxford, 1970), pp. 132–42.

7 The face of battle. Probably the work of Parisian artists c. 1250, the Maciejowski Bible follows the normal practice of depicting biblical figures (here Saul defeating the Amalekites and sparing their king, Agag) in contemporary equipment. Its exceptional quality and detail make it an invaluable source for the nature of arms and armour before the introduction of plate. With the exception of the close helms, which appeared in the last decades of the twelfth century, much of the equipment illustrated here had changed little from the eleventh century, and the Amalekites wear the simple conical helmet with nasal identical to those found on the Bayeux Tapestry. Swords and axes are shown cutting through mail. To the right, the victorious knights drive off livestock and bound prisoners (Pierpont Morgan Library, M. 638, f. 24v, detail).

to equipment itself and it would be unwise wholly to reject such evidence.[84]

There have been no controlled scientific tests on the resistance of mail to edged weapons to help resolve these apparent contradictions. Archaeological evidence is regrettably scant as few grave-pits have received detailed scientific investigation and the value of armour ensured that bodies were invariably stripped before burial. Even the findings from the notable exception of the grave-pits from the battle of Wisby in 1361 are subject to many caveats due to the peculiar nature of the battle itself.[85] Nevertheless, examination of over a thousand skeletons graphically revealed the terrible injuries that might be sustained in battle, and the potentially enormous power of axe or sword blows. Blows had in some cases severed legs completely, or had removed large pieces of bone. Most skeletons had received more than one wound, and several crania showed the marks of repeated cuts.[86] Coifs of mail had seemingly been cut through by blows, but the generally poor and fragmented condition of the mail precluded more specific conclusions.[87]

Even if helmets and hauberks prevented penetration of laceration by edged weapons, however, haemorrhaging or brain damage was a constant risk. Count Baldwin of Flanders died following a brain injury sustained when, in a fight against greater odds, his helmet was battered by repeated strokes.[88] In 1106, Robert fitz Hamon received a blow on the temple from a lance 'and losing his faculties, survived a considerable time almost in a state of idiocy', and several days after sustaining a wound in the eyebrow at the siege of Evreux, 1119, Enguerrand de Trie 'went out of his mind and died wretchedly'.[89]

---

[84] The *Maciejowski Bible*, for example, a product of the Paris school c. 1250 and intended for Queen Jeanne of Evreux, furnishes some of the finest pictorial evidence for armour and equipment in the thirteenth century (*A Picture Book of Old Testament Stories of the Thirteenth Century*, ed. S. C. Cockerell (Roxburghe Club, London, 1924)). The quality and detail of its execution suggests a first-hand knowledge by the artist of the construction of weapons and armour and, by extension, their possible performance in battle (*ibid.*, p. 135).

[85] B. Thordeman, *Armour from the Battle of Wisby, 1361*, 2 vols. (Uppsala, 1939). Wisby was an unequal conflict between the royal army of the king of Denmark and a peasant force of Gotlanders, into whose ranks had been pressed every male who could bear arms, including the very young, the old, the crippled and deformed. Most of the Gotlanders were far less well protected than either their attackers or contemporary European knights, and this disparity must have been reflected in the wounds sustained. The skeletons at Wisby, therefore, reflect the effect of weaponry on partially equipped infantry, rather than on fully armoured knights.

[86] Thordeman, *Armour from the Battle of Wisby*, I, pp. 160–209. Wisby was an infantry battle, and the most common injuries were to the legs, almost certainly reflecting an important feature of the Danes' fighting technique. Such leg injuries are unlikely to be representative of wounds sustained in knightly engagements fought on horseback, but may well echo the wounds inflicted in earlier Anglo-Scandinavian battles fought on foot such as Ashingdon, 1016, or Stamford Bridge, 1066.

[87] Thordeman, *Armour from the Battle of Wisby*, I, p. 165. The mail found in the grave-pits is described in some detail (*ibid.*, I, pp. 98–112), but the effects of weapons on the armour is not discussed.

[88] *GR*, II, p. 479.   [89] Orderic, II, p. 475; *ibid.*, VI, pp. 232–5.

Above all, armour was not proof against the charge with the couched lance, the principal form of attack for a knight in the first stages of conflict. Having behind it the weight and momentum of both horse and rider moving at speed, the couched lance was capable of delivering a blow of immense force. The chansons and romances constantly state that such lance blows could pierce shield, hauberk and rider, and in this they are supported by more sober narratives which yield numerous instances of such fatal thrusts. While engaging two knights in single combat during the war of 1090 between Ascelin Goel and William de Breteuil, for example, Amaury de Montfort was struck in the side by one of their lances and died shortly afterwards.[90] At the siege of Le Puiset, Hugh of Le Puiset ran through Anselm de Garlande, the commander of the French army, with his lance, killing him instantly.[91] The Syrian emir Usamah recorded how a lance thrust from one Frankish knight cut three ribs of his opponent, 'and hit with its sharp edge his elbow, cutting it in two, just as a butcher cuts a joint. He died on the spot'.[92] If pierced, moreover, the fractured links of mail might exacerbate or infect the wound. It is again Usamah who records how 'one of our troops, a Kurd named Mayyah, smote a Frankish knight with a lance which made a piece in the link of his coat of chain mail penetrate into his abdomen and killed him'.[93]

Through constant training, a knight had the skill to aim his lance to unhorse or kill as he chose. When in 1189, shortly after William the Marshal had slain Richard's horse to prevent his pursuit of Henry II, the count met William at Fontevrault, he accused the Marshal of trying to kill him, 'and you would have done it if I had not turned your lance aside'. To this the Marshal replied, 'Sire, I had no intention of killing you . . . I am still strong enough to direct my lance. If I had wished, I could have struck your body as I did your horse.'[94] Misjudgements might occur, as the number of accidental fatalities in tournaments bore witness; Geoffrey de Mandeville, for instance, was killed by a Frenchman's lance in a tournament at London in 1216.[95] But in general it seems that if a knight ran another through, it was more a matter of volition than chance and, in such cases, the hauberk offered scant protection.

Equally devastating was missile fire. A hauberk might stop a longbow arrow, depending on the range and the type of arrowhead in use; Henry I and Henry II both owed their lives to this fact.[96] Nevertheless, Gerald of

---

[90] Orderic, IV, pp. 200–1.   [91] *Ibid.*, VI, pp. 158–9.   [92] Usamah, p. 76.   [93] *Ibid.*, p. 77.

[94] *HGM* 11. 9319–36; Painter, *William Marshal*, p. 73.   [95] MP, II, p. 650; WC, II, p. 234.

[96] *GR*, II, p. 477, for an attempted assassination of Henry I by an archer; *GH*, I, p. 296, where Howden notes that an arrow pierced Henry II's surcoat when he was fired at by the defenders of Limoges in 1183. The implication is that it was stopped by his hauberk, as a cloth garment other than pourpoint could not have prevented him being seriously wounded.

Wales adduces striking testimony to the power of the longbow against armour, and there is little doubt that, depending on range, arrows with bodkin heads were capable of piercing mail.[97] Crossbows were still more deadly, having a slower rate of fire but a greater power and velocity. The number of important victims claimed by the crossbow is striking.[98] Contemporaries remarked on the high number of fatalities among the besiegers caused by crossbowmen at the sieges of Rochester, 1215, and Bedford, 1224.[99] Hauberks were clearly of little protection and even if bolt wounds were not instantly fatal, death often followed from shock, loss of blood, or the wound becoming infected.[100] In 1136, Geoffrey Martel, son of Fulk Rechin, was wounded in the arm by a bolt at the siege of Candé, and died the next day, while Matthew of Boulogne died of a wound after a bolt had struck him above the knee at the siege of Drincourt, 1173.[101] The most famous victim of infection following a bolt wound was Richard I, who died of a gangrenous wound some days after a quarrel had pierced his shoulder at the siege of Chaluz, 1199.[102]

Knights' lives were considerably more at risk in engagements where infantry played an important role. It is significant that Brémule, where there were only three knightly casualties, was only a brief engagement fought principally by knights. The increased risk was in part because of the efficacy of the infantry's missile weapons and polearms, but equally because for the common footsoldier, when confronted by a knight, it was a case of kill or be killed. While it seems probable that an infantryman would receive a bounty from his lord on handing over a captured knight, taking a well-armed and mounted knight prisoner was no easy task for men more lightly equipped and thus more vulnerable to blows.

Moreover, the ruthless treatment usually afforded infantrymen by knights made footsoldiers unwilling to forego revenge when they had the

---

[97] Gerald of Wales, *Opera* VI, *Itinerarium Kambriae* Bk 1 c. 4, p. 54: R. Hardy, *Longbow. A Social and Military History* (revised edn, London, 1986), p. 208.

[98] During Henry I's conquest of Normandy, for example, Roger of Gloucester was struck in the head by a crossbow bolt at the siege of Falaise, a fate shared by Eustace de Vesci at the siege of Barnard Castle in 1216 (*GR*, II, p. 475; MP, II, p. 666). During the battle between Richard Marshal and the Poitevin garrison of Monmouth in 1233, the royalist commander, Baldwin de Guisnes, was shot in the chest by one of the Marshal's crossbowmen (MP, III, p. 256).   [99] MP, II, p. 626; *ibid.*, III, p. 85.

[100] For a contemporary view on how to treat arrow and bolt wounds see L. M. Patterson, 'Military Surgery: Knights, Sergeants and Raimon of Avignon's Version of the *Chirurgia* of Roger of Salerno (1180–1209)', *The Ideals and Practice of Medieval Knighthood, II. Papers From the Third Strawberry Hill Conference, 1986*, ed. C. Harper-Bill and R. Hervey (Cambridge, 1988), pp. 117–46, esp. 132–5, 142–3.

[101] Orderic, VI, pp. 76–7; WN, pp. 173–4; Torigny, p. 258.

[102] Coggeshall, p. 95; Howden, IV, p. 82. Cf. J. Gillingham, 'The Unromantic Death of Richard I', *Speculum*, 44 (1979), pp. 18–41. Richard had earlier, however, survived a bolt wound in the knee inflicted on him by the *routier* Cadoc at the siege of Gaillon in 1196 (*RHF*, 24, II, p. 758; WB, *Philippidos*, V, ll. 262–4).

upper hand. When, during the sea battle off Sandwich in 1217, a group of English serjeants seized one of the principal French carracks, it was only with great difficulty that the English knights prevented thirty-two French knights captured on board from being executed by the serjeants.[103] Whether through desire for financial gain, knightly empathy, or fear of establishing a dangerous precedent, the English knights were clearly protecting men of their own rank.

THE TREATMENT OF INFANTRY

The disparity between the treatment of knights and that of the non-noble infantry during battle and particularly following defeat strikingly reveals the limits of chivalric restraint. Whereas the former were frequently taken for ransom, the latter were invariably cut down with great ruthlessness. At the battle of Dol in 1173, fought between the Brabançon mercenaries of Henry II and the rebel forces of Ralph de Fougères, Torigny noted that the vanquished Breton knights fled while the 'plebs' were killed.[104] Similarly, when John, as count of Mortain, defeated Philip, bishop of Beauvais, in 1197, the warrior prelate and his knights were taken captive but a great number of the 'plebs' were slain.[105]

Such conduct mirrored on the battlefield the aggressive disdain shown by the knighthood for the lives of the agricultural *laboratores* and urban artisans during the ravaging of the countryside which formed so integral and ubiquitous a part of warfare.[106] The complete indifference to the fate of footsoldiers is clearly shown by the priest of Fécamp, an eye-witness to the battle of Tinchebrai, 1106, who, remarking on the miraculous fact that King Henry had lost only two knights, could wholly ignore the casualties of the lesser folk.[107] We know from Orderic, however, that the knights of Helias of Maine cut down 225 of the ducal foot in the first charge, and this cannot have been the limit of those infantry slain.[108]

This ruthless killing of infantry, who were generally not regarded as worthy of ransom, highlights an important dichotomy in the attitude of the knighthood. Though significantly underrated by earlier historians such as Oman, it is clear that footsoldiers consistently played a useful supporting

---

[103] *HGM*, 11. 17365–462. Such behaviour may lie behind Wendover's comment that during this battle, the French preferred to throw themselves into the sea than to be taken by the English (MP, III, pp. 27).

[104] Torigny, p. 260. Howden, who listed the numerous knights taken prisoner in the battle, put the slain at 1,500, an estimate which, as with the great majority of chroniclers' figures, can at best only be regarded as a very rough estimate (*GH*, I, p. 56; Howden, II, p. 51).   [105] Howden, IV, p. 16.

[106] Below, pp. 258–90.   [107] C. W. David, *Robert Curthose* (Harvard, 1920), p. 247.

[108] Orderic, VI, pp. 90–1.

8 An enemy camp is surprised, from the Maciejowski Bible. Similar scenes must have occurred at the rout of Louis VII at Verneuil in 1173 or of Philip at Freteval in 1194. Warriors struggle to arm, one attempting to don his hauberk while another, seated, pulls on padded *cuisses*. Several of the infantry wear 'soft' armour in the form of gambesons or aketons, quilted jerkins stuffed with cloth or tow that offered cheap but effective protection (Pierpont Morgan Library, M. 638, f. 3v, detail).

9 A Norman knight dispatching an Anglo-Saxon ceorl, from the Bayeux Tapestry.
While some infantry, particularly serjeants, might be adequately equipped, combat
between heavily armed *milites* and the poorer peasant levies was usually a very
uneven affair in which little quarter was given (by special permission of the City of
Bayeux).

role in both pitched battle and siege warfare.[109] The battles of Hastings, 1066, Alençon, 1118, the Standard, 1138, Lincoln, 1141, Arsuf, 1191 and Bouvines, 1214, to give but prominent examples, clearly demonstrate that the tactical value of infantry began long before the defeat of knightly forces by peasant militias at Courtrai, 1302, Bannockburn, 1314, and Morgarten in 1315.[110] Flemish and Brabançon mercenary infantry were particularly valued, not only for their reliability in times of revolt, but also for their professionalism both in siege warfare and in battle, where their use of massed spears may represent an early version of the pike formation.[111]

Yet it was these very infantrymen, and the mercenary foot in particular, who in circumstances of defeat repeatedly received brutal treatment at the hands of opposing knights. At Fornham, 1173, and Alnwick, 1174, the victorious forces of the justiciar and barons loyal to Henry II took the rebel nobles and knights captive but cut down their Flemish mercenaries.[112] Jordan Fantosme describes how at Fornham, once de Lucy's knights had broken their formation by a charge, it was the local peasantry who finished off the Flemings:

> in all the countryside there was neither villein nor peasant who did not go after the Flemings with fork and flail to destroy them. The knights in armour busied themselves with nothing more than knocking them down and the villeins did the killing: in fifteens, in forties, in hundreds, in thousands they make them fall head over heels into the ditches.[113]

Similarly at Alnwick, 'there was great slaughter of the unfortunate Flemings, the fields were strewn with their bowels torn from their bodies. No more will they cry "Arras!" back in their own country.'[114] Here Jordan reflects the unconcealed disdain of the English lords towards the Flemings: 'Our knights on the English side – better were never seen – have no love for the Flemings who had all but brought disaster on them, and they carry on with the slaying of them.'[115] The same animosity was demonstrated by Philip Augustus at Bouvines in 1214: once victory was assured, he sent

---

[109] J. Beeler, *Warfare in England, 1066–1189* (Ithaca and New York, 1966), esp. pp. 311–17; Verbruggen, *Art of Warfare*, pp. 114–43; Bradbury, *The Medieval Archer*, pp. 39–57. Cf. C. W. C. Oman, *A History of the Art of War in the Middle Ages, 378–1485*, 2 vols. (2nd edn, London, 1924), I, pp. 356–8, and p. 451, where he contrasts the Flemish militias with 'the miserable and ill-equipped horde that generally constituted the infantry of a feudal army'.

[110] Verbruggen, *Art of Warfare*, pp. 99–183. Orderic noted, for example, that at Lincoln in 1141, although Stephen's 'battle' consisted principally of knights, yet 'the enemy were more powerful because of their numerous foot soldiers and the Welshmen' (Orderic, VI, pp. 542–3).

[111] Verbruggen, *Art of Warfare*, pp. 234–6.

[112] For Fornham, Diceto, I, p. 378; Gervase, I, p. 246; *GH*, I, p. 62; *WN*, p. 179; for Alnwick, JF, ll. 1796–98 and for the taking prisoner of knights in this engagement, *ibid.*, ll. 1832–3, 1856–7, 1858–71, 1879–84, 1886–92.   [113] JF, ll. 1080–5.   [114] *Ibid.*, ll. 1796–98.

[115] *Ibid.*, ll. 1808–10.

Thomas de St Valéry to destroy the Flemish mercenaries of Renaud de Dammartin still on the field.[116]

This ruthlessness afforded the Flemings and Brabançons was not to do with their stipendiary status *per se*; the *stipendarii milites* of Robert de Bellême's garrison of Bridgnorth were treated with honour by Henry I in 1101 'because they had served their master as was right'.[117] Rather, these *routiers* were non-knightly, low born and had a highly unsavoury reputation.[118] At Fornham, Alnwick and Bouvines, the fear and hatred bred by their excesses was exacerbated by the sense that they were the instruments of invasion and insurrection, godless violators of the *patria* in the pay of rebels or external enemies. Similarly, disdain for 'barbarian' Celts led to little compunction in cutting down opposing Scots infantry, such as occurred after their rout at the Standard in 1138. The same was true for the Welsh. During Henry II's flight from Le Mans in 1189, 700 of his cavalry manage to escape by crossing a deep ford, but his Welsh and other infantry were massacred by the pursuing forces of Philip and Richard.[119] Following the Norman victory at Baginburn, 1170, over the men of Waterford, the Normans decapitated their Irish prisoners and threw their bodies into the sea.[120]

This same polarity between the recognition of military worth and the desire for reprisal in victory is equally apparent in the knighthood's attitude towards missilemen. Archers and crossbowmen, invaluable as pickets and light infantry, were widely deployed in all forms of warfare. In battle, their volleys might break the impetus of a cavalry charge as at Bourgthéroulde, 1124 and possibly Brémule, 1119, while in siege their covering fire was an integral aspect of attack and defence alike. Crossbowmen in particular were regarded as an elite and were hired precisely because their weapons had the power to penetrate knightly armour. Yet paradoxically, it was hard to reconcile the effectiveness of these troops with those conventions designed and adhered to by the warrior aristocracy to reduce the risks of war to their own class. The phenomenon of consciously shooting horses instead of riders, seen at Chaumont, Brémule, Bourgthéroulde and Lincoln, was an attempt to solve this dilemma of employing lethal weapons without actual harm to the knights themselves.[121] But as the number of knights killed or seriously wounded by arrows or bolts reveals, this was a far from universal policy.[122] It is, moreover, significant that the Church's response to the lethal nature of

---

[116] Verbruggen, *Art of Warfare*, p. 236.   [117] Orderic, vi, pp. 28–9; below, p. 228.
[118] Below, pp. 297–302.   [119] *GH*, ii, p. 68; Howden, ii, pp. 363–4.
[120] Gerald of Wales, *Expugnatio Hibernica*, ed. and tr. A. B. Scott and F. X. Martin (Dublin, 1978), pp. 58–63; and see Gillingham, 'Conquering the Barbarians', esp. pp. 67–8, 83–4.
[121] Above, pp. 133, 141.   [122] Bradbury, *The Medieval Archer*, p. 3.

missile weapons, namely a canonical prohibition of bow and crossbow by the Second Lateran Council, was universally ignored by commanders.[123]

The result of such a paradox could be the bizarre occurrence of lords who themselves had crossbowmen or archers in their pay executing captured missilemen. It was seldom that captured infantry were executed as a deliberate act following hostilities (as opposed to being cut down in battle or a rout), but that bowmen were singled out reflected the sense of outrage that, despite their costly equipment, the knights were highly vulnerable to weapons that were generally the preserve of an inferior class. Hence Henry of Anjou, who was to hire considerable numbers of archers and crossbowmen in his many campaigns, had sixty of Stephen's archers beheaded during the siege of Crowmarsh, 1153.[124] Similarly, while John was persuaded to spare the majority of the garrison of Rochester in 1215, he had the crossbowmen hanged as they had inflicted considerable casualties on his men.[125] Henry III had 315 archers beheaded after his forces had been harassed by archers as they passed through the Weald in 1264.[126]

If we return to Orderic's description of the battle of Brémule in 1119, we must conclude that the marked lack of fatalities in this engagement was exceptional. Though frequently taken as a *locus classicus* for Anglo-Norman chivalric mores, Orderic's stress here on the restraint from killing is less representative of the realities of knightly combat than of his attempts to show Henry I abiding by the Augustinian precepts of right intent in a just war. His own pages reveal that while considerations of kinship, of a shared profession of arms and of ransom resulted in a significant limitation on blood-letting in war, engagements between knights, even in small-scale skirmishing, could be bitterly fought and sanguinary both in internal feuding and in conflicts between the territorial principalities. Armour afforded a considerable degree of protection, but knights were by no means invulnerable. Had Orderic not been in the cloister but fighting in the saddle, he may well have been more circumspect in his remarks concerning the limited extent of risk in battle.

---

[123] Above, p. 72.

[124] Torigny, pp. 173–4. If, as Dr Chibnall plausibly suggests, the commander of Robert de Bellême's garrison of Saint-Céneri, Robert Quarrel, was a crossbowman, this may in part explain his immediate mutilation by order of the enraged Robert Curthose (Orderic, IV, p. 154–5, and p. 154, n. 4).

[125] MP, II, p. 626. It is perhaps significant in this context that of the garrison of Framlingham taken by John's forces in 1216, seven crossbowmen appear not in the Close Roll with the landed or landless knights who had been pardoned, but on the Patent Roll because a safe conduct had been issued to them (Rott. Litt. Pat., I, p. 171; R. A. Brown, 'Framlingham Castle and Bigod, 1154–1216', *Proceedings of the Suffolk Institute of Archaeology*, 25 (1951), pp. 127–48 and reprinted in *idem.*, *Castles, Conquest and Charters. Collected Papers* (Woodbridge, 1989), pp. 187–208, at pp. 206–8.

[126] Carpenter, *The Battles of Lewes and Evesham*, p. 16.

Nevertheless, in the treatment of knightly opponents in defeat or on capture we are undoubtedly in another thought-world from that of the Anglo-Saxons and Vikings. The Anglo-Scandinavian insistence on the habitual, near-systematic slaughter of defeated warriors in and following battle had given way to a greater, though not universal, stress on the capture and ransom of knightly opponents by the Franco-Norman aristocracy. Though the realities of battle imposed significant constraints on the ability to take prisoners, a knight who survived a mêlée and suffered capture could generally assume that his life was not in further danger. In part, as we have seen, this was due to a concept of a brotherhood in arms, the *notitia contubernii* spoken of by Orderic. But Orderic's concern to demonstrate the right intent of Henry I's knights at Brémule led him to omit reference to one the most potent – if not *the* most potent – constraint on the limiting of bloodshed in combat among the nobility, the convention of ransom.

7

RANSOM AND THE TREATMENT
OF PRISONERS

RANSOM: THE FINANCIAL INCENTIVE FOR CLEMENCY

Seizure of booty and the plundering of the dead or those captured on the battlefield is as old as war itself. Plunder, particularly in the form of armour, weapons and high-status goods, was the crucial dynamic behind much of the warfare of the early Middle Ages. A warleader needed a constant source of such spoil to reward his followers and attract new fighters to his banner. In this respect, the world of the Anglo-Norman *mesnie* surrounding lords and kings was little different from that of Frankish, Anglo-Saxon or Viking warbands. The *Histoire de Guillaume le Maréchal* is replete with references to both the capture of valuable hauberks, weapons and destriers and their distribution as acts of largesse. Indeed, one of William's first lessons taught him as a young knight in the household of the chamberlain of Tancarville was the need to exercise financial acumen in war and to make even small-scale engagements pay.[1]

Most knights did not need such encouragement. Because of their great value, the seizure of horses and arms was among warriors' foremost objectives. At the siege of Breteuil in 1119, for example, the Norman commander Ralph de Gael

> brought down many distinguished champions that day, and when the knights had been unhorsed he generously gave their horses to his needy comrades, so earning a high and enduring praise for the chivalrous qualities that distinguished him among the most eminent warriors.[2]

---

[1] See *HGM*, 11. 3214–38 for but one instance of many; *ibid.*, 11. 804–1302 and Painter, *William Marshal*, pp. 21–2. [2] Orderic, VI, pp. 246–7.

183

The Bayeux Tapestry graphically portrays soldiers stripping corpses of their armour amongst the human and material debris of battle.[3] It was precisely because such plundering was recognized as a mechanism for the perpetuation and escalation of private war that the Norman *Consuetudines et justicie* of 1091, which set down customs in operation in the duchy under William the Bastard, prohibited the seizure of horses and armour following an affray.[4] Significantly, the equipment of a defeated opponent was to become the standard form of ransom in the tournament.[5]

Yet though the taking of horses, arms and equipment provided a valuable source of income for knights, the financial gain accrued from the capture and ransoming of a noble captive could be far greater. In 1091, for example, William de Breteuil was vanquished in pitched battle by Ascelin Goel, his own vassal. He had to pay for his ransom 1,000 livres in the money of Dreux, with horses, arms and other goods, and was forced to give Goel both his daughter Isabel in marriage and the powerful castle of Ivry. He was again captured soon afterwards by Ralph de Tosny, his uncle, when he was intercepted on a plundering raid, and was forced to pay 3,000 livres.[6] Substantial sums in ransom payments are equally revealed for the later period by the Close, Patent and Liberate Rolls. Thus in 1203, John ordered that, if possible, the Master of the Temple in England should deliver his favoured captain Gerard d'Athée from the King of France's prison by payment of 2,000 marks,[7] while the Exchequer was ordered to release 700 marks in pennies of the best weight and quality for the ransom of William Briwerre the Younger.[8] The ransom of Roger, constable of Chester, taken prisoner in the same war, was £1,000, while King John demanded £4,000 Angevin for the release of Conan, son of the viscount of Leon, taken at Mirebeau in 1202.[9] Nicholas de Stuteville, captured at the

---

[3] *BT*, pls. 71–2.

[4] The clause (c. 14) runs 'Nulli licuit pro guerra hominem capere vel redimere nec de bello vel conflictu pecuniam portare vel arma vel equum ducere' (Haskins, *Norman Institutions*, p. 284). It is interesting to note that this final clause of the *Consuetudines* follows what is in essence a conclusion to the document (c. 13), as if this ban on the escalation of private war was added as an important afterthought. Barker, *The Tournament in England*, p. 7, n. 14, rightly points out that this clause does not refer to tournaments, but to skirmishes during private war.   [5] Above, pp. 48, 152.

[6] Orderic, IV, pp. 216–17. By contrast, William de Chaumont, the son-in-law of Louis VI, captured in 1119 by Gilbert Crispin, Henry I's castellan of Tillières, was released for the far smaller sum of 200 marks (*ibid.*, VI, pp. 248–9).

[7] *Rotuli litterarum patentium in turri Londinensi asservati* (*Rot. Litt. Pat.*), ed. T. Duffus Hardy (Record Commission, 1835), p. 65a; *Rotuli de oblatis et finibus in turri Londinensi asservati* (*Rot. Ob. et Fin.*), ed. T. Duffus Hardy (Record Commission, 1835), p. 271; cf. also *Rot. Litt. Pat.*, pp. 41b–42a.

[8] *Rot. Ob. et Fin.* p. 271; cf. also *Rot. Litt. Pat.*, pp. 41b–42a.

[9] *Rotuli de Liberate ac de Misis et Praestitis* (*Rot. de Lib.*), ed. T. Duffus Hardy (Record Commission, 1844), p. 103; *Rot. Pat.*, p. 33b.

battle of Lincoln in 1217, was obliged to pay William Marshal the heavy ransom of 1,000 marks.[10]

Indeed, the financial gain provided by ransom served not only as an incentive to spare the lives of enemy knights but also as a crucial dynamic for the continuation of war. Thus, somewhat paradoxically, the convention of ransom at once both limited the execution of warfare itself by the prevention of wholesale killing among the warrior nobility and yet, as one of the principal *raisons d'être* of war for participants of all ranks, acted as an incentive to the prosecution and further escalation of hostilities. Orderic recalls how during warfare on the Vexin frontier in 1097, the French warriors seized a number of knights during a Norman offensive: 'The needy French were encouraged to keep on fighting by the rich ransoms.'[11] As a result of both the wealth and glory they were accruing, 'they attracted distinguished champions and courageous young knights from all parts of France, and by resisting their foes time and time again won valuable rewards for themselves'.[12]

Volatile areas such as the Vexin or Maine where fighting was frequent attracted a fluid body of knights from a wide area, very much as champions were to flock to the great tournaments in northern France in the second half of the twelfth century. Such war zones served as a source of material gain and as arenas for the display of martial prowess. The prolonged hostilities from 1083–5 between William I and Hubert de Sainte-Suzanne, vicomte of Maine, attracted experienced knights (*probati milites*) 'from Aquitaine and Burgundy and other French provinces'.[13] There was constant small-scale fighting between the Norman forces manning a siege-castle in the valley of Beugy and the garrison of Sainte-Suzanne. As at Chaumont, the ability to draw on reserves of experienced champions, who came in what was essentially a mercenary role, led to a more effective resistance, and hence the protraction of hostilities. Orderic describes this phenomenon in operation at Sainte-Suzanne, where as a result of the success of Hubert's garrison

> the castle of Sainte-Suzanne was stocked with booty taken from the defenders of Beugy and each day became better equipped for defence . . . In this way Hubert kept the Normans at bay for three years, growing rich at the expense of his enemies and remaining unvanquished.[14]

Despite the severe casualties suffered by the Normans, ransom was here again the chief dynamic in the protraction of the war, for 'wealthy Norman

---

[10] *Rotuli litterarum clausarum in turri Londinensi asservati* (*Rot. Litt. Claus.*), ed. T. Duffus Hardy (Record Commission, 1833–4), I, p. 600b.   [11] Orderic, v, pp. 216–17.   [12] *Ibid.*   [13] *Ibid.*, IV, pp. 48–9.
[14] *Ibid.*

and English lords were frequently captured and Hubert the vicomte and Robert the Burgundian, whose niece he had married, and their other supporters made an honourable fortune out of the ransoms of these men'.[15] Similarly, at the siege of Courcy in 1091, fought between the men of Hugh de Grandmesnil and Robert de Bellême, 'the garrison captured William de Ferrières, William of Rupierre, and many others and gained much wealth from their ransoms'. In their turn, the besiegers took captive Ivo de Grandmesnil and Richard fitz Goubert.[16] This process can equally be seen in operation in England during the hostilities of Stephen's reign. After the king had taken Faringdon in 1145 in a crucial campaign, he 'enriched his comrades most bountifully from the capture of the knights who had surrendered to him on terms of being held to ransom (*sub redimendi conditione*)'.[17] Revenue from ransom was thus a vital mechanism in the prosecution of war, offering knights an incentive to fight and providing cash with which to hire more knights. Ransom facilitated success in war that in turn bred further success.

It is a significant indication of contemporary attitudes towards the process of ransom that even as a monastic *nutritus*, Orderic could regard wealth so accrued as being gained honourably – 'honorifice'.[18] He again clearly states the honourable nature of gaining wealth by ransom in recounting how Helias, count of Maine, defeated Robert de Bellême in battle and took many Normans prisoner. Alluding to the fact that Robert had built castles on ecclesiastical lands, particularly those of La Couture and St Vincent, Orderic notes: 'The Manceaux received rich ransoms for them, thereby avenging the injuries done to the saints and their own losses.'[19]

RANSOM AND FEUDAL CUSTOM

Despite the obvious prevalence and importance of ransom, information concerning its operation in both customary and *de facto* terms in the eleventh and twelfth centuries is scant indeed compared to the wealth of material for the later Middle Ages.[20] There is nothing comparable, for example, with the type of legal records later emanating from the Court of Chivalry or the Parlement of Paris. Nor is this surprising since there was as yet, in the West, no mechanism of appeal to judicial tribunals concerning secular conventions of war. Evidence for the division of the profits of

---

[15] *Ibid.*   [16] *Ibid.*, pp. 232–3.   [17] *GS*, pp. 182–3.   [18] Orderic, IV, pp. 48–9.
[19] *Ibid.*, V, pp. 226–7.
[20] For a detailed discussion of the theory and practice of ransom in the later Middle Ages see Keen, *Laws of War*, pp. 156–85.

ransoms, and for conditions of surrender, imprisonment and release must be pieced together from haphazard and frequently laconic chronicle references, in part supplemented from the later twelfth century by record material such as the Close, Patent and Fine Rolls, which record a number of ransom payments for the wars of 1202–4 and 1215–17.

Much of this later material, however, is complicated by its relation to situations of revolt, so that the distinction between ransoms demanded for men taken in combat and fines proffered for royal benevolence become indistinguishable and may not reflect conditions in operation between knights of opposing principalities. Thus, for example, John's anger at the perfidy of his trusted servant Gilbert fitz Renfrey, who had sided with the baronial rebels, is reflected both by the extraction of a charter of fealty with punitive clauses for default and in the enormous fine of 20,000 marks demanded of him not simply to ransom his son and two other knights taken prisoner at Rochester in 1215, but to buy off the royal *ira et malevolentia*.[21]

Nevertheless, some principal features of ransom can be discerned, if only in outline. Ransom was as yet a purely personal obligation, based on the act of capture, sometimes accompanied by a parole or oath of surrender,[22] which secured the life of the captive; rights to a ransom and the obligation to pay were only to become heritable from the fourteenth century.[23] By then, it had also become standard practice for the king to take a third part of the profits of ransoms and booty from subordinate commanders, who in turn claimed a similar share from their men. He also enjoyed a prescriptive right to any prisoners of importance, though their actual captors were entitled to an appropriate bounty.[24] Earlier practice, however, is far less clear. Lords naturally laid claim to a share of booty, though customary percentages varied considerably with time, place, conditions of seizure and the status of the commander.[25] Though division by

---

[21] *Rot. Ob. et Fin.*, p. 570.

[22] On the nature of these oaths, see Keen, *Laws of War*, pp. 164–8. By the fourteenth century, it was accepted that to establish his legal right over a prisoner, the captor had to be the first man to seize the captive's right hand and place his own within it, with the gauntlet thereafter serving as a token of his right (*ibid.*, pp. 165–6). In this context, it is striking that 'for his sins', the dying Roland offers his right glove to God. Gabriel takes it from him, and, as Roland joins his hands in the gesture of a supplicant vassal, the archangel and St Michael carry his soul to God (*Song of Roland*, ll. 2365–96). Unvanquished by any mortal enemy, Roland has, in effect, surrendered his soul to God.

[23] Keen, *Laws of War*, pp. 157–9.

[24] D. Hay, 'The Division of the Spoils of War in Fourteenth Century England', *TRHS*, 5th ser., 4 (1954), pp. 91–109.

[25] The complex and important subject of the division of booty is beyond the scope of this present work. The most valuable discussion for eleventh- and twelfth-century practice in the West as well as the Latin East is to be found in W. G. Zajac, 'Captured Property on the First Crusade: A Study on the Late Eleventh Century Laws of War' (unpublished MA thesis, University of Milwaukee, 1986), esp. pp. 104 ff. Cf. also Hay, 'The Division of the Spoils of War', pp. 107–9 and references cited therein.

thirds was an ancient and widespread one, the strict application of the formula of a royal third and thirds of thirds would itself appear to be only a fourteenth-century development.[26]

Evidence for the regulation of profits from ransoms is more scanty, and further research is needed in this important area. It seems certain, however, that, as in later practice,[27] the king or suzerain could by the later eleventh century command the disposal of valuable prisoners. *A priori*, it would have been unacceptable, particularly in situations of revolt or civil war, to allow the automatic release of powerful enemies simply on payment of ransom to individual knights. Thus when Robert de Bellême captured Helias of Maine in an ambush in 1098, he handed him over to Rufus, who ordered him to be kept in honourable captivity.[28] At Tinchebrai, 1106, Robert Curthose had been captured by Henry I's chancellor Waldric, though it was King Henry who determined his fate of perpetual imprisonment,[29] just as Robert of Gloucester was to have Stephen confined to Bristol keep after his capture at Lincoln in 1141 by William de Cahagnes.[30] Similarly, though the warrior bishop Philip of Beauvais had been captured in 1196 by Count John and Mercadier, it was Richard's decision to condemn him to long and harsh captivity.[31]

That this prescriptive right applied not simply to key political figures but to all knightly captives is strongly suggested by a letter of King John to the constable of Radepont in 1203, informing him that he had granted Ralph Archer 'whatever he is able to make from our enemies in the March and that he should have this, saving to us knights and those things which pertain to us'.[32] John was clearly granting away certain profits of war but reserving among other rights (*illis qua ad nos pertinent*) the ransoms of knights as a key exception.[33] This demand was no innovation. Following his suppression of a major revolt in Poitou in 1176, Richard sent the count of Angoulême and other leading prisoners to his father in England,[34] while the *Histoire* records

---

[26] The implication of Hay's argument is that the principle of royal thirds and thirds of thirds for all profits of war developed during the course of the Hundred Years War (*ibid.*). To cite but one example of the division by thirds in the twelfth century, the French under the duke of Burgundy joined Richard I's attack on a great Egyptian caravan in 1192 on condition that they received one third of the booty (Ambroise, ll. 10291–7; *Itinerarium*, p. 384).

[27] Hay, 'The Division of the Spoils of War', pp. 99–102.   [28] Orderic, v, pp. 238–9.

[29] Orderic, vi, pp. 90–1. One wonders whether Waldric's subsequent promotion to bishop of Laon was partly in reward for his service. On Waldric see H. W. C. Davis, 'Waldric the Chancellor of Henry i', *EHR*, 26 (1911), pp. 84–9.   [30] HH, p. 274; *HN*, p. 50; FW, ii, p. 129.

[31] Howden, iv, pp. 16, 21, 23, 71, 94.

[32] *Rot. Litt. Pat.*, p. 24b; 'concessimus Radulpho Archer quicquid ipse lucrari poterit in Marchia super inimicos nostros et quod idem habeat, salvis nobis militibus et illis qua ad nos pertinent'.

[33] The implication is that prisoners of the rank of sergeant and below were at the free disposal of Ralph Archer, though it is unclear whether this was by virtue of royal grant or by the fact that the royal right did not extend to these lesser ranks.   [34] *GH*, i, p. 121.

the surrender of prisoners to the king by the Marshal as an automatic act of a loyal vassal. Thus at Le Mans in 1189, William the Marshal presented Henry II with one of Count Richard's knights, Heimeri Odart, and later gave Richard the castellan of Milli whom he had captured at that castle in 1197.[35]

Sometimes, however, the transfer of important prisoners from captor to king might be difficult to effect. At Tinchebrai, 1106, Henry I and his men had great trouble trying to extract Count William of Mortain, one of Curthose's foremost barons, from the Bretons who had captured him. At Bourgthéroulde, 1124, it was precisely the knowledge that King Henry would never release Amaury de Montfort once in captivity that caused William de Grandcourt, one of Henry's own *familia*, to release his eminent captive on the field of battle.[36]

Such a prescriptive right goes far to explain both the detailed lists supplied in the *Gesta Henrici* of rebels captured in the war of 1173–4,[37] and the appearance in the *Rotuli de oblatis et finibus* of knights of only very minor standing caught in opposition to the king in 1215–16, fining for release and the remittance of royal *malevolentia*. Thus John de Grandmesnil, captured by the serjeants of Berkhampstead and in the king's prison, paid the king 20 marks for his ransom and gave his eldest son as a hostage.[38] John of Orreby offered three palfreys, Saher of Sutton one palfrey, one hawk and 20 marks, Simon fitz Walter 100 marks and his war-horse.[39]

The royal prerogative over captives is most strikingly demonstrated by the ability of rulers to command collective acts of vengeance or clemency in regard to prisoners. Thus in 1183, Richard could order the beheading, irrespective of rank, of any of his brothers' men taken during the internecine warfare in Poitou, and himself supervised the blinding, beheading and drowning of a number of these captives.[40] At Acre in 1191, it was his prescriptive right, shared with Philip Augustus, to all the prisoners captured in the city that permitted him to behead over 2,700 Muslim captives.[41] By

---

[35] *HGM*, ll. 8703–32, 11242–64. Such instances suggest added significance to the fact that when Owain of Gwynedd, who had performed homage to Henry II following the latter's Welsh expedition of 1157, captured a rival prince in 1160, he handed him over to Henry as his suzerain (J. E. Lloyd, *A History of Wales from the Earliest Times to the Edwardian Conquest*, 2 vols. (3rd edn, London, 1939), ii, pp. 499–500).   [36] Orderic, vi, pp. 90–1, 350–3 and above, p. 156.

[37] *GH*, i, pp. 56–8, 62–3. The lists, which pertain only to Henry's victories in Brittany and in Anjou in 1173 (an equivalent record of those prisoners taken by the justiciar at Fornham is not recorded), contain not only the names of leading rebels but also those of their men, some of whom may have been serjeants rather than knights. Howden clearly had access to 'official' lists, doubtless compiled for the purposes of ransom and possibly as a record of those who had violated their homage and fealty.   [38] *Rot. Ob et Fin.*, p. 601.   [39] *Ibid.*, pp. 569, 574, 571.

[40] *GH*, i, p. 293; Vigeois, *RHF*, xviii, p. 213.

[41] *GH*, ii, pp. 185–90; Ambroise, ll. 5526–42; *Itinerarium*, p. 243; Beha-ad-Din, pp. 240 ff. Howden earlier states explicitly that Richard and Philip had divided up all the prisoners taken at Acre between them (*GH*, ii, p. 185).

the same token, Count John had the garrison of Evreux executed in 1194.[42] Similarly, the ability of a commander to refuse the surrender of an enemy garrison and order their deaths, which would deny his own men the profits of ransom, was a vital feature of the right of storm in contemporary siege warfare.[43]

Conversely, the common practice whereby a besieger allowed a defeated garrison freedom to leave a castle without ransom in recognition of their honourable defence again presupposes his right to dispose of actual or potential captives as he saw fit, weighing considerations of franchise against material rewards.[44] Likewise, following battle or campaign, a ruler might free individuals or large numbers of captives. In 1098, Rufus had assumed the right to release on parole the numerous noble Angevin prisoners captured by his garrison at Ballon who were being held in strait confinement.[45] Before Tinchebrai, 1106, as an act of atonement for the violation of sanctuary, Henry I ordered the release of Reginald de Warenne and all those captured in the church of St Pierre-sur-Dives, and following Brémule, 1119, he freed Burchard and Hervey of Gisors.[46]

In the aftermath of his victory in the war of 1173–4, Henry II demonstrated his qualities as a statesman by releasing without ransom the majority of those he had captured in the war, who numbered over 969 knights and greater lords.[47] Such an act of generosity, performed from a position of great strength, was motivated by magnanimity and a desire to achieve conciliation with his rebellious sons and their supporters. More hard-headed pragmatism lay behind the stipulation of the Treaty of Lambeth (or Kingston) in 1217, that all prisoners taken after Prince Louis's first arrival were to be released and ransoms paid only up to those instalments due at the time of the peace settlement.[48] Such terms were due to the desperate need to win over baronial rebels to the minority government and to rid England of Louis as quickly as possible.

Such a system could only work if the king adequately rewarded the original captors. Frequently, he might immediately return the captive to the captor by way of a financial reward and as a recognition of his vassal's prowess. Thus in 1176, Henry II honoured his victorious son by returning to Richard those captives he had taken in the rebellion in Poitou and had presented to his father. In 1197, Richard himself gave William Marshal

---

[42] Rigord, p. 127.   [43] Below, pp. 222–4.   [44] Below, pp. 218–20.

[45] Orderic, v, pp. 244–5. The prisoners taken at Ballon included several high-ranking lords and over 140 knights. These were later exchanged with Norman captives as part of the peace settlement (*ibid.*, pp. 246–7).   [46] Orderic, vi, pp. 88–9, 240–1.

[47] Diceto, i, p. 395. The majority were released on the receipt of hostages or pledges of good behaviour.   [48] Carpenter, *The Minority of Henry III*, pp. 41, 44–9.

back the castellan of Milli as a reward for his valour, saying he would have done so even if the prisoner had been worth a hundred times more.[49] Following his victory at Faringdon, Stephen immediately rewarded his knights from the ransoms taken.[50] King John returned to Gerard de Furnival the valuable prisoner, Conan son of Guiomarc'h, whom he had taken at Mirebeau. The king then bought him back for 400 marks, the sum Gerard owed the king for the purchase of an heiress. The quittance of this debt allowed Gerard to undertake a pilgrimage, while John himself, though rewarding a loyal supporter, stood to make a substantial profit by demanding £4,000 Angevin for the ransom of this captive.[51]

How and when this important seigneural prerogative in ransoms developed is unclear. It may find an echo in Duke William of Normandy's demand to Guy of Ponthieu for the release of Harold in 1064.[52] Conversely, Orderic's description of the fighting at Sainte-Suzanne, 1083–5, and at Chaumont, 1097, where mercenary knights were attracted to these war zones by the profits to be made, strongly suggests that here the knights themselves gained a significant proportion, if not the entirety of ransoms taken. It may well be that conditions in regard to the division of spoil and prisoners varied depending on a knight's status, with vassals being under a greater obligation than mere stipendiary warriors. Certainly John's *routiers* enjoyed special protection of their booty[53] and seem to have kept their own prisoners. When John ordered Robert de Vieuxpont to deliver all captured French to Hugh de Gournay, those taken by Martin Algais were specifically excepted.[54] The presence of the king or lord on campaign may also have affected questions of prescriptive right. William of Malmesbury implies that Stephen's earls felt entitled to the ransoms of those Angevins they had captured at Winchester in 1141, when King Stephen was still imprisoned.[55] Certainly during the minority of Henry III, the king's claim to prisoners, so tangible under John, was waived, with royalist lords keeping the entirety of the ransoms from prisoners such as those taken at Lincoln in 1217.[56] Practice, moreover, varied outside the Anglo-Norman *regnum*, for it seems that the Latin kings of Jerusalem were only entitled to a share of captives, a situation more akin to Celtic custom, where the ruler received a proportion of captives assigned to him by lot.[57]

[49] *GH*, I, p. 121: *HGM*, ll. 11242–64.   [50] *GS*, pp. 182–3.

[51] *Rot. Litt. Pat.*, pp. 15b, 33b; Powicke, *Loss of Normandy*, pp. 245–6.   [52] WP, pp. 100–3.

[53] *Rot. Pat.*, pp. 21b, 24a.   [54] *Ibid.*, p. 15; Powicke, *Loss of Normandy*, pp. 230–1.   [55] *HN*, p. 67.

[56] Holt, *The Northerners*, pp. 246–9; Carpenter, *The Minority of Henry III*, pp. 41, 46–9. The principle that, in this instance, only the captors had a right to ransoms was explicitly stated in regard to William the Marshal (*Rot. Litt. Claus.*, I, p. 600b; Holt, *The Northerners*, p. 246, n. 6).

[57] Zajac, *Captured Property on the First Crusade*, pp. 143–4; Hay, 'The Divisions of the Spoils of War', p. 101; JH, p. 116.

Given the likelihood of capture at some stage in a knight's active career and the heavy financial outlay which ransom might demand, the obligations between lord and man naturally came to encompass the vital issue of ransom. The ransoming of the lord's person was one of the occasions for which a general tax or aid could be levied on a lord's free tenants.[58] In 1125, William fitz Herbert received Norbury from the prior of Tutbury so that 'if the lord of Tutbury shall redeem his body from capture or give his eldest daughter in marriage or redeem his honour, and the prior shall give an aid for these occasions, then William or his heir shall tender a suitable aid to the prior, proportionate to his fee'.[59] Similarly, in a charter of 1183–4, William son of Richard stated that the monks of St Andrew, Northampton, were to have the land granted to them by his vassal Waleran of Sulgrave for the same services, among which 'if the need shall arise they shall help to redeem my body and to make my eldest son a knight, and to give in marriage my eldest daughter'.[60] Magna Carta reiterated this obligation when it stipulated that aids should only be exacted on these occasions and on no other pretext.[61] The levying of such a tax for the purposes of ransom is recorded in the Patent Rolls, where King John ordered the knights and free tenants of Roger, constable of Chester, to provide an aid for their lord's ransom, which had been set at £1,000.[62]

It was naturally considered a vassal's duty to redeem his lord as swiftly as possible. Orderic records how William, son of Giroie, 'voluntarily destroyed his own castle of Montagu to secure the ransom of his lord, Geoffrey of Mayenne, whom William Talvas had captured and would only release on condition that this castle, which was a threat to his power, was demolished'. On his release, Geoffrey rewarded such loyalty by building his vassal a new castle at Saint-Ceneri-sur-Sarthe.[63] Often, however, financial self-interest took precedence over vassalic propriety. William of Malmesbury noted sourly that in 1141 Stephen's earls refused Robert of Gloucester's proposal that he should be exchanged for the captured king on condition that all others taken with him at Winchester should be released. The earls greatly desired the king's release, 'but not if it meant any loss of money to themselves; for Earl Gilbert had taken William of Salisbury at Winchester, William of Ypres, Humphrey de Bohun, and a number of others those whom they could, and they were eager for many marks as their ransom'.[64]

---

[58] For such aids, see Stenton, *English Fuedalism*, pp. 172–5. Stenton stresses that these aids were not simply owed by those holding of the lord for military service, but by all free tenants (*libere tenentes*).
[59] *Ibid.*, p. 175.   [60] Stenton, *English Feudalism*, p. 173.   [61] *MC*, pp. 454–5 (c. 12).
[62] *Rot. Litt. Pat.* p. 41b; for the value of the ransom, *Rot de Lib.*, p. 103.   [63] Orderic, II, pp. 26–9.
[64] *HN*, p. 67.

Similarly, the poem attributed to Richard I while held in captivity in Germany in 1193 complains of the length of his captivity, chides his vassals 'whose swords are sheathed and rust in peace', and reminds his subjects that he would never have allowed any man of his, no matter how humble, to languish thus in an enemy's prison while he had gold to free him.[65] Only the year before he had given proof of this when in October, 1192, before leaving the Holy Land, he redeemed Peter des Préaux, who had sacrificed himself to save the king from capture. To ransom Peter, Richard exchanged ten noble Turkish prisoners, whose ransoms, as Ambroise noted, would have brought the king much wealth.[66]

To aid a loyal vassal to pay his ransom was an important act of good lordship and an overt recognition of service. Such assistance, moreover, must have been crucial to landless household knights or men who lacked extensive estates or tenants from whom they could levy an aid.[67] King John's grant of a prisoner captured at Mirebeau to the archbishop of Canterbury to help him redeem those of his knights taken prisoner at Château Gaillard in 1204 shows this process working at several levels.[68] John similarly paid the ransom of his favoured lieutenant Gerard d'Athée, provided cash for the release of the son of one of his chief men, William Briwerre, and arranged a loan for the ransom of Roger de Lacy.[69] By contrast, though he claimed to have authorized the precipitous surrender of the key fortress of Vaudreuil, there is no evidence that John assisted in ransoming Robert fitz Walter and Saher de Quinci, who were universally branded as cowards and traitors.[70]

THE VALUE OF RANSOMS

The value of ransoms demanded might vary considerably, from the king's ransom of 100,000 marks demanded of Richard by the Emperor Henry VI, to a mere handful of marks, sometimes supplemented by payments in kind, demanded from poor knights.[71] Common sense dictated that the sum demanded by a captor bore a realistic relationship to the captive's means and ability to pay. By the fourteenth century, a reasonable ransom was held

---

[65] A translation is provided by Norgate, *Richard the Lion Heart*, pp. 278–9 and references to the French and Provençal texts (p. 277, n. 6). See also J. K. Archibald, 'La chanson de captivité du roi Richard', *Cahiers d'études médiévales*, 1 (1974), pp. 149–58.   [66] Ambroise, 11. 12263–9; *Itinerarium*, p. 440.

[67] Cf. the case of Gilbert Foliot's relative, below, p. 219, n 76.   [68] *Rot. Pat.*, p. 40b.

[69] *Rot. Litt. Pat.*, p. 65a; *Rot. Ob. et Fin.* p. 271; *Rot. de Lib.*, p. 103; cf. also *Rot. Litt. Pat.*, pp. 41b–42a.

[70] *Rot. Litt. Pat.*, p. 31; Powicke, *Loss of Normandy*, p. 162. Cf. Holt, *The Northerners*, p. 64, for William d'Albini's efforts to help raise Robert fitz Walter's ransom.

[71] For Richard's ransom see Norgate, *Richard the Lion Heart*, pp. 271–84, while for the ransoms of lesser knights see above, p. 189.

– in theory – to be about the equivalent of one year's revenue of the prisoner's lands,[72] or at least a sum that was within the resources of his patrimony. In practice, however, ransom demands were often excessive and many were ruined by the payments.[73] Likewise, greed, expediency and the context of capture seem to have been the predominant factors in determining ransom values in the eleventh and twelfth centuries.[74]

Rebels could naturally expect to be heavily penalized, while personal animosity might account for the severity of ransom demanded. Thus the heavy sum of 10,000 marks charged for the release of the warrior bishop Philip of Beauvais was as much due to Richard's bitter hostility towards him as to the fact that he was kinsman of the king of France.[75] Several of those baronial rebels captured in the war of 1215–17 were crippled by ransom payments, for the amnesty prescribed by the Treaty of Lambeth did not include those taken at Rochester in 1215 nor those who had been released on terms before the treaty. Many were forced to sell or mortgage manors, and the captors were often ruthless in the conditions of repayment they imposed.[76]

If individuals suffered financial hardship as a result of the payment of ransom, the war effort of a king or lord might be seriously hampered by the cumulative losses sustained either directly by him or by his vassals in order to redeem knights taken following a battle or a campaign. Powicke has argued that towards the end of the wars of 1203–4 in Normandy, there was a substantial imbalance in ransom payments to the detriment of John's subjects and his own war chest.[77] This was a marked reversal of the situation a century earlier. Suger had noted that although prisoners were taken on both sides during the clashes between William Rufus and the young Louis the Fat, his far greater wealth allowed Rufus to redeem his men far more quickly: 'King William, concerned at his need to hire more knights, quickly ransomed the English prisoners, while the French wasted away during lengthy captivity'.[78]

---

[72] Cf., in this context, Barrow's observation that the 'ransom' of 10,000 marks paid by William the Lion to Richard I in 1189–90 for the repeal of the Treaty of Falaise 'may be seen as the revenues of the Scottish crown and baronage for one year' (RRS, II, p. 15, n. 64).   [73] Keen, Laws of War, pp. 158–9.

[74] While the Dictum of Kenilworth, 1264, provides a detailed sliding scale of payment for those involved in De Montfort's rebellion to buy back their lands, these are penal fines for participation in revolt rather than ransoms per se (Documents of the Baronial Movement of Reform and Rebellion, 1258–1267, selected by R. F. Threharne and ed. I. J. Sanders (Oxford, 1973), pp. 316–37). Nevertheless, setting these amercements in the context of the later custom of ransom equalling a year's income illustrates the severity of the mulct inflicted on the most prominent rebels.   [75] Howden, IV, p. 78.

[76] For details see Holt, The Northerners, pp. 246–9; Carpenter, The Minority of Henry III, pp. 46–8.

[77] Powicke, Loss of Normandy, p. 298 and n. 91. In 1198, however, Richard had captured over 100 knights in his rout of Philip at Gisors, so that at the start of his reign the balance may well have been tilted in John's favour (Howden, IV, p. 58).

[78] Suger, pp. 10–11; tr. Cusimano and Moorhead, p. 26. Suger adds that 'there was only one way to get free. They had to undertake knightly service for the king of England, bind themselves to him by homage, and swear on oath to attack and make trouble for the kingdom and the [French] king' (ibid., pp. 10–11; p. 27).

By implication, Henry I's victory at Brémule, which led to the ransoming of over one hundred French knights,[79] must have similarly resulted in a severe drain on the finances of Louis VI and his barons, although neither the individual nor the total sums paid are known. In 1139, Henry de Tracy captured 104 of William de Mohun's knights in a cavalry engagement, and though no details of ransoms are available, the financial repercussions for de Mohun must have been disastrous.[80] At Bouvines, 1214, the French took 131 allied knights, including 5 counts and 25 knights banneret,[81] while at the battle of Lincoln in 1217, the royalist forces captured 380 knights, not including sergeants, burghers and lesser folk.[82]

It was perhaps because he could not envisage the loss of such potential wealth that the Young King, whose already precarious finances had been ruined by the war, did not reciprocate his father's act of largesse in remitting the ransoms of his prisoners taken in the war of 1173–4. Despite his reputation for generosity, in this instance he exacted ransom from his hundred or so noble captives, although as Ralph of Diceto admits, this was done 'iure belli'.[83]

Given the potential impoverishment that a ransom could entail, men might go to considerable lengths to avoid capture or to disguise their true rank and hence their financial worth. After the defeat of the French at Brémule in 1119, Peter de Maule and his comrades threw away any means of recognition and mingling with the victors shouted out the war-cry of Henry I's own knights.[84] The *Gesta Stephani* records how, during the rout of Winchester in 1141, knights and even great lords in the army of the Empress 'cast away all the emblems of their knighthood and going on foot in sorry plight, gave false names and denied that they were fugitives'. Some were forced to hide in 'sordid places' until a chance for escape came, while some who were less lucky were taken or received beatings from the local peasantry.[85]

Following the battle of Bourgthéroulde, 1124, William Lovel gave his arms and armour as ransom to his captor, a countryman (*rusticus*), so that he might escape. He then had his hair cut by the man to make him look like a squire and, carrying a staff, he made his way to the Seine, where he had to pay a ferryman with his boots.[86] The surrender of arms and horses was to become a standard form of ransom in tournaments, but it seems that Lovel could only have succeeded in thus ransoming himself in a wartime situation because he was dealing with a rustic – presumably an infantryman

[79] Orderic, vi, pp. 238–9, where the number is given as 140. The *Chronica de Hida* gives the figure as 114.
[80] *GS*, pp. 82–3.   [81] WB, *Gesta*, p. 290; Verbruggen, *Art of Warfare*, p. 236.   [82] WC, ii, pp. 237–8.
[83] Diceto, i, p. 395.   [84] Orderic, vi, pp. 242–3.   [85] *GS*, pp. 134–5.   [86] Orderic, vi, pp. 352–3.

– to whom the value of a knight's equipment must have seemed very great. Had he been taken by a fellow knight who appreciated his value as a captive, it seems unlikely he would have escaped without a far heavier ransom. According to Orderic, Louis VI only avoided having to pay a king's ransom following his signal defeat at Brémule because a peasant who guided him to safety failed to recognize him.[87] David of Scotland was reported to have been captured three successive times after the battle of Winchester in 1141, but each time was fortunate enough to have secured his release by a bribe.[88]

THE TREATMENT OF PRISONERS

In addition to offering a substantial degree of protection against indiscriminate killing of noble opponents in battle, the convention of ransom equally sought also to give security against indefinite incarceration once captured. Conditions afforded to knightly captives taken for ransom, however, might vary widely. Some captives were detained in honourable and open custody either in token of their rank or in recognition of their bravery in war. Orderic says that despite sporting the long hair and beard that was symbolic of a captive, Count Helias of Maine was honourably treated by Rufus. Following Roger de Lacy's heroic but ultimately unsuccessful defence of Château Gaillard, Philip Augustus ordered him to be kept 'sub libera custodia' in recognition of his bravery.[89]

Conversely, personal animosity towards captives might result in harsh conditions of confinement. When, during a bitter local war in 1091, Ascelin Goel captured his own lord William de Breteuil, Roger de Glos and others, he kept them in a dungeon at Bréval, 'and often, in the most severe cold of winter, he would expose them to the north or north west wind in the window of his upper hall, clad only in shirts soaked in water, until the whole garment was frozen stiff around the prisoners' bodies'.[90] In the war between Robert de Bellême and Henry I in 1105, Gunter d'Aunay, Reginald de Warenne and other ducal partisans seized Robert fitz Hamon, one of Henry's leading supporters, and others of his *familia*, 'and kept them in close imprisonment for a long time, both to extort ransoms and to show their contempt and hatred of their lord'.[91] Following his defeat at Lincoln

---

[87] Orderic, VI, pp. 240–1.   [88] GS, pp. 134–5.
[89] Orderic, IV, pp. 238–9, 246–7, and cf. p. 247, n. 6; MP, II, pp. 488–9.
[90] Orderic, IV, pp. 286–7, and cf. pp. 288–9.
[91] *Ibid.*, VI, pp. 60–1. Malmesbury says that Henry I's subsequent burning of Bayeux was in order to gain his release, and that fitz Hamon's wounding and death later in the campaign was just retribution for the sacrilegious combustion of the town's churches (GR, II, p. 475).

in 1141, King Stephen was first kept under honourable custody at Bristol, but was later confined in irons because, noted Malmesbury, of malicious advice and his propensity to stray beyond his allotted bounds.[92] Because of their longstanding enmity, Philip of Beauvais suffered privation at the hands of Richard I when he was taken prisoner in 1197 and was only released after sustained diplomatic pressure from the papacy.[93]

Those taken in the context of rebellion were particularly liable to harsh treatment. At Bouvines in 1214, the leading rebel Renaud de Dammartin had come close to slaying Philip Augustus; as a captive, he was subjected to a very harsh and vindictive confinement, being so loaded down with chains he could hardly move.[94] After his spectacular victory at Mirebeau in 1202, which in Powicke's words 'wiped out the political influence of half a province', John threw away much support by insulting and maltreating many of the prisoners taken there, and may even have had some put to death. The 200 or more lords and knights taken at Mirebeau were sent in chains to their various destinations on carts, a practical if degrading form of transportation.[95] The *Histoire de Guillaume le Maréchal* noted that of these prisoners, those confined at Chinon were treated so badly that those who assisted in the king's cruelty brought shame upon themselves.[96] Hugh de Lusignan was placed in irons in solitary confinement at Caen, the keep being cleared of all other prisoners for the purpose, while his uncle Geoffrey was imprisoned at Falaise.[97] The Margam annalist believed that twenty-two prisoners at Corfe were starved to death, though this act of brutality may have been linked to an attempt by captives to seize the keep.[98]

By the fourteenth century, jurists were arguing that since a prisoner was held essentially as a pledge for the price of his ransom, the captor might take reasonable measures to encourage payment, even keeping the prisoner in irons, but that death threats or any act contrary to law or the prisoner's honour freed the latter from his obligation.[99] From the ill-treatment all too regularly afforded noble captives, it would seem that no such concept troubled the minds of captors in the eleventh or twelfth century. Even outside the context of revolt, the desire to speed ransom payments led to deliberately harsh captivity. After being wounded in the thigh and taken prisoner during a skirmish in Poitou against the Lusignans in 1167, William

[92] *HN*, p. 50.   [93] Above, p. 47 and n. 88.   [94] WB, *Gesta*, p. 292.
[95] Coggeshall, pp. 137–8; MP, II, p. 479; *Histoire des ducs*, pp. 94–6; and Pipe Roll 4 John, pp. xv, xvi, which records the purchase of fetters, and shows that among other castles, prisoners were kept at Newcastle, Lancaster, York, the Peak, Wallingford, Sherbourne and Corfe. Chrétien de Troyes makes the degrading nature of transportation by cart a central theme in his *The Knight of the Cart*, otherwise known as *Lancelot* (Chrétien de Troyes, *Arthurian Romances*, esp. p. 211).   [96] *HGM*, ll. 12507–12.
[97] *Rot. Litt. Pat.*, pp. 16 ff.   [98] *Annales de Margam*, in *Annales Monastici*, I, p. 26; *Rot. Pat.*, pp. 24, 33b.
[99] Keen, *Laws of War*, pp. 157–8.

Marshal's injuries were ignored by his captors in order to speed his efforts to ransom himself. He was forced to bandage his thigh himself with the cords that held up his braies, until a woman smuggled him some linen bandages inside a loaf.[100] When Ascelin Goel captured William de Breteuil, even though he was his lord, he 'cruelly ill treated him in his foul dungeon through the following Lent, forcing him involuntarily to endure the hardship of a lenten penance for his sins'.[101] On the capture of one of Henry I's leading household knights, Ralph the Red de Pont-Echanfray, the king secured his swift release by an exchange for Walo de Trie. Walo's death two weeks later from his wounds and the ill-treatment he had received in captivity indicates the nature of the pressure the king might exert to gain the freedom of a valued warrior.[102]

Above all, it was the desire to extort the surrender of key castles that led to the maltreatment of important lords. The capturing of a lord or castellan presented the captor with an opportunity to gain vital strongholds by intimidation without the need for a costly siege. There was always the possibility that a resolute garrison might refuse to surrender even when the life of their lord was threatened. In 1146, Roger de Berkeley was captured by Walter, brother of Roger, earl of Hereford, and hanged three times in front of Berkeley castle. The castle, however, did not surrender, and the wretched Roger was returned half-dead to his dungeon.[103] Robert fitz Hubert was less fortunate. Threatened by John the Marshal with hanging unless he gave up the castle of Devizes, he refused, as did his garrison. But in this instance, the garrison had been deliberately misled, for John the Marshal had encouraged them to keep resisting with a promise that no harm would befall their lord. As a result, Robert went to the gallows following his two nephews.[104]

If the blackmail succeeded, spectacular gains might be achieved without a blow. Hence Geoffrey Martel, count of Anjou, captured Theobald of Blois at the battle of Nouy, 1044, and as ransom for himself and his men, forced him to surrender the strategically vital city of Tours.[105] Similarly, he was able to gain a large sum of gold, extensive lands and an oath of allegiance from his own lord, William the Great, count of Poitiers and Bordeaux, following his seizure at the battle of Mount Couer in 1033.[106]

Physical maltreatment, torture or death threats, however, might be necessary to ensure compliance to such demands. When, in 1141, Alan of

---

[100] *HGM*, ll. 1717–30.   [101] Orderic, IV, pp. 202–3.
[102] *Ibid.*, VI, pp. 220–1; Chibnall, 'Feudal Society in Orderic Vitalis', p. 45.
[103] *GS*, pp. 190–1.   [104] JW, pp. 62–3; *HN*, p. 44.   [105] *Chroniques des comtes d'Anjou*, pp. 57–8, 235.
[106] WP, pp. 32–3; L. Halphen, *Le comté d'Anjou au XIe siècle* (Paris, 1906), pp. 57–8.

Brittany was captured by Rannulf of Chester, he was 'put in chains and subjected to torment in a filthy dungeon until he assumed the yoke of forced submission and the most degraded servility, did homage to the earl of Chester, and delivered over his castles to his disposal'.[107] The Empress threatened Walter de Pinkeney, the captured castellan of Malmesbury, with torture or death unless he yielded the castle up.[108] William Martel, who was taken prisoner while covering Stephen's flight at Wilton in 1143, was kept 'in very close and harsh confinement' by Robert of Gloucester, and thereby forced to surrender custody of the castle of Sherbourne, 'the master key of the whole kingdom'.[109] King Stephen gained control of the Tower of London, Pleshy and Saffron Walden in 1143 by threatening to hang Geoffrey de Mandeville,. and subsequently regained Saffron Walden from its rebellious new castellan, Turgis of Avranches, by similar means.[110] Stephen had earlier secured the surrender of Devizes, Lincoln, Sleaford, Newark, Ely, Salisbury, Malmesbury, Sherbourne and other castles by starving the bishops of Salisbury and Lincoln, and threatening to hang Roger of Salisbury's son, the chancellor, Roger le Poer.[111]

The recourse to such treatment of important captives was an indirect manifestation of the great strength of castles. In siege warfare, the art of defence so outstripped that of offence that to take such strongholds as the Tower, Malmesbury or Pleshey would have necessitated a prolonged and uncertain investment. To gain such castles at a stroke by the intimidation of an individual, without loss of time, men and money, was an act of expediency that few could afford to ignore if presented with the opportunity. Yet in all such cases, the threat of death or physical suffering was only conditional, not wholly gratuitous. For though the price of ransom might be high, compliance with the captor's demands inevitably brought release. Unsavoury though such conduct might be, it was still far removed from the outright refusal of ransom, which might entail the death, mutilation or perpetual incarceration of prisoners.

To refuse ransom to a prisoner captured in warfare with an external enemy – in contrast to situations of rebellion[112] – was regarded as among the most heinous of atrocities in war, for it negated the crucial assumption that, notwithstanding the price demanded, a captured nobleman could ultimately purchase his freedom. The torturing of prisoners and denial of ransom was one of the principal reasons for the hatred and fear aroused in contemporaries for Robert de Bellême, who seems to have taken sadistic pleasure in maltreating his captives and condemning them to permanent

---

[107] GS, pp. 116–7.   [108] Ibid., pp. 178–9.   [109] Ibid., 148–9.   [110] Ibid., pp. 162–3, 174–7.
[111] GS, pp. 78–80; HN, p. 27; HH, pp. 265–6.   [112] Below pp. 240–7.

incarceration. During Lent, 1098, in a vicious war of attrition conducted against the Manceaux from nine castles with which Bellême had been entrusted by Rufus as his chief commander, Orderic records how 'more than three hundred fettered prisoners perished in Robert's prison. They offered him large ransoms for their release, but were cruelly spurned by him and died of starvation and cold and other sufferings.'[113] On his expulsion from England in 1102, he waged war against those supporting Robert Curthose against him in Normandy: 'He pillaged their estates, burning all behind him, and tortured to death or mutilated the knights and other persons he was able to capture. He was so cruel that he preferred tormenting his prisoners to growing rich on fat ransoms offered for their release.'[114] Not even the men of his own brothers were spared. Of those he took captive after routing the forces of his brother Arnulf at the nunnery of Almenêches, 'some he subjected to the misery of a long and wretched captivity, the remainder he condemned to death or mutilation'.[115]

Such habitual cruelty on a large scale was the exception, standing in isolation with the outrages of a handful of notorious lords.[116] These men apart, breach of the notion of surrender occurred but spasmodically as isolated expressions of personal animosity. Hence in the war of the Breteuil succession, Reginald de Grancy 'resolutely stormed an enemy castle, and as the defenders emerged, he seized every one, plunged his own sword into their entrails, and slaughtered them without mercy like brute beasts. This was the chief act that made him an object of universal hatred.'[117] It is significant that such incidents were generally restricted to conditions of private

---

[113] Orderic, v, pp. 234–5.

[114] *Ibid.*, vi, pp. 30–1; and cf. iv, pp. 159–61, where Bellême is described as a man 'ready in speech and appalling cruel . . . a merciless butcher in the way he tortured men'. Earlier in his *Ecclesiastical History*, Orderic gives a graphic description of Bellême's excesses: 'He thought nothing of mutilating men by putting out their eyes or cutting off their hands or feet, and took delight in devising unheard of punishments for torturing unhappy wretches . . . He tormented those who were thrown into his dungeons for any offence in unspeakable ways, more cruelly even than Nero or Decius or Domitian, boasting of what he had done as he laughed and joked with his sycophants. He took pride in his enjoyments of the torments of his prisoners, and laughed at men's condemnation of the excessive cruelty of his punishments; he greatly preferred inflicting torture on his wretched captives to increasing his wealth with their ransoms' (Orderic, iv, pp. 298–9). Orderic was heavily biased against Robert for his oppression of St Evroul, but his repeated allegations of his sadism and brutality receive corroboration from William of Malmesbury and others (*GR*, ii, pp. 475–6: K. Thompson, 'Robert of Bellême Reconsidered', *Anglo-Norman Studies*, 13 (1990), pp. 263–86, esp. pp. 281–2).

[115] Orderic, vi, pp. 34–5.

[116] Thomas of Marle, for example, ranked alongside Bellême in his excesses, hanging up prisoners by the thumbs or genitals to speed the extortion of ransoms. 'No one can tell', commented Guibert of Nogent in his *De Vita Sua*, 'how many expired in his dungeons and chains from starvation, disease and torture' (*Self and Society in Medieval France; the Memoirs of Abbot Guibert of Nogent*, (Guibert), ed. J. F. Benson (New York, 1970), pp. 184–5). Cf. the conduct ascribed by William of Malmesbury to one of his particular enemies, the Fleming Robert fitz Hubert (*HN*, pp. 43–4).

[117] Orderic, vi, pp. 44–5.

warfare that prevailed in the duchy of Normandy both before the establishment of effective authority by William I and during the ineffectual governance of Robert Curthose. It was within the context of such bitter local feuding that one can place the murder of Robert de Bellême, the paternal uncle of Mabel de Bellême, who was hewn down with axes in a dungeon at Ballon by the sons of Walter Sor, and the mutilation of William son of Giroie by William Talvas.[118]

In warfare between the territorial princes, by contrast, the torture and mutilation of prisoners, or the refusal to ransom them, was far less prevalent. One must take with considerable scepticism William of Poitiers's statement that:

> among many peoples of the Gauls there was an abominable custom utterly contrary to Christian charity, whereby, when the powerful and rich were captured, they were thrown ignominiously into prison, and there maltreated and tortured even to the point of death, and afterwards sold as slaves to some magnate.[119]

This remark, given to contextualize the seizure of Harold by Guy of Ponthieu, was intended as a contrast to Duke William's magnanimity and the proper behaviour of the Normans, as well as heightening the sense of Harold's debt to the duke for his salvation from such a fate. Conversely, Guibert of Nogent is probably equally guilty of exaggeration when he says that William I never ransomed anyone he took captive.[120] For while it is true that internal rebels were sometimes incarceraed for life,[121] there is little evidence to suggest that William extended this piece of harsh but understandable realpolitik to prisoners taken in war; French knights taken at Mortemer, for example, were released.[122]

Though in chansons such as *Lorrains* and *Girart de Rousillon* the mutilation of prisoners appears as a matter-of-fact accompaniment to war,[123] instances afforded by more sober non-literary sources are isolated and sporadic. Significantly, most occur within the context of rebellion, and even here those so punished were frequently non-noble.[124] When, in the first quarter of the eleventh century, Geoffrey of Thouars had the knights (*caballarios*) of Hugh de Lusignan captured in the castle of Mouzeil

---

[118] Orderic, VI, pp. 396–9; *ibid.*, II, pp. 14–15.   [119] WP, pp. 102–3.   [120] Guibert, p. 69 and n. 2.

[121] Thus, for example, William was adamant that although he was to be in comfortable confinement, Roger of Hereford was never to leave his prison alive for the role he had played in the revolt of 1075 (Orderic, II, pp. 318–9; IV, pp. 96–7).   [122] WP, p. 74.

[123] Examples are collected by Luchaire, *Social France at the Time of Philip Augustus*, pp. 258–60.

[124] Below, p. 241. The Alan the Welshman who received compensation for having lost his hand in the king's service was presumably a non-noble auxiliary, and may perhaps have been an archer mutilated on capture by Philip's forces (*Rot. de Liberate*, p. 32).

mutilated by cutting off their hands, it was clear he was in violation of acceptable behaviour. So too in his turn was Hugh when in revenge he refused to ransom forty-three of Geoffrey's warriors whom he had subsequently taken prisoner.[125]

The unacceptability of mutilating knights who were not rebellious vassals is stated explicitly by Orderic. When in 1124, following the suppression of the French-backed rebellion in favour of William Clito, Henry I ordered the blinding of Geoffrey de Tourville, Odard of Le Pin and Luke de La Barre, Charles, count of Flanders objected: 'My lord king, you are doing something contrary to our custom (*nostris ritibus iniustam*) in punishing by mutilation knights captured in war in the service of their lord.'[126] Henry's justification in response was that Geoffrey and Odard had violated their liege homage and were thus being punished for treason. Luke had never done him homage, but had committed lese majesté by scurrilous songs and jokes about the king, and had continued fighting Henry after he had been allowed to go free after his capture at Pont Audemer.[127] Roger of Howden could equally believe that the mutilation of prisoners by Philip Augustus and Richard in their ceaseless conflicts from 1194–9 marked a significant escalation of hostilities in a war that contemporaries agreed was waged with unusual hatred and ferocity.[128]

How conduct might thus degenerate with tit-for-tat reprisals is well illustrated by a letter sent by John to Hubert de Burgh in 1203, ordering him to exchange Peter, a prisoner in his care, for Ferrand the engineer: 'If Ferrand be whole, let Peter be delivered whole also; but if Ferrand be lacking in any limb, Peter must first be deprived of the same limb and then delivered in exchange.'[129] The execution of prisoners, the most extreme manifestation of such conduct, also occurs, but examples such as Richard's treatment of

---

[125] Martindale, 'Conventum inter Guillelmum Aquitanorum comes et Hugonem Chiliarchum', pp. 542–3; Crouch, *The Image of Aristocracy*, pp. 125–6.   [126] Orderic, VI, pp. 352–3.

[127] *Ibid.*, pp. 352–5.

[128] Howden, IV, p. 54, where the blame for such escalation is naturally ascribed to Philip. William le Breton tells in his *Philippidos* how, in reprisal for the killing of a body of Welsh mercenaries, Richard hurled three French prisoners from the rock at Andeli and blinding fifteen others, sent them back to Philip led by a companion who for the purpose had been deprived of only one eye. Philip responded by inflicting exactly the same punishment of precipitation and blinding on an equal number of Richard's men (*Philippidos*, Bk v, ll. 300–28, pp. 136–7). Given Howden's laconic comment about retaliatory mutilations, and Richard's punishment of certain captives in 1183, such actions are not wholly improbable, though coming from the pen of William le Breton, ever anxious to portray Richard in an unfavourable light, the tale inspires little confidence. Though Powicke was right to be suspicious, his belief that William had confused accounts of the Welsh defeat at Pain's castle in 1198 seem less plausible than the tale being William's conscious invention (Powicke, *Loss of Normandy*, pp. 243–4).

[129] *Rot. Litt. Pat.*, p. 25. Here it may be wondered whether fear for Ferrand's safety was based on the fact he was a non-noble *ingeniator*, whose manual skills in building or directing siege weapons might have encouraged an enemy to deprive his erstwhile employer of his future expertise by the loss of sight or touch, a fate that might well befall captured archers and crossbowmen.

certain prisoners during the war of 1183, or Count John's beheading of captured French knights at Evreux in 1194, appear as rare infractions of the convention of ransom.[130]

In contrast to such behaviour, and still more to the actions of lords like Bellême, the ideal of the chivalric virtues of largesse and clemency to captives was epitomized by William Rufus. When, in 1098, Robert de Bellême handed over the captured Helias of Maine, Rufus 'ordered him to be kept in honourable captivity'. 'He at least', adds Orderic in conscious juxtaposition to Bellême's own outrages, 'was not cruel in his treatment of knights, but was gracious and courteous, jovial and at ease'.[131] In 1098, Bellême's garrison of Ballon had sallied out and taken the besieging army of Fulk Rechin and the Manceaux by surprise, taking captive many leading nobles, 140 knights and many footsoldiers. Orderic records how on the arrival of Rufus, who had been summoned to aid the garrison:

> the prisoners all shouted together at the tops of their voices, 'William, noble king, free us.' Hearing the shouts he ordered them to be released at once and given a good meal in the courtyard outside with his own men, releasing them on parole until after dinner.[132]

John of Marmoutier, as we have seen, shared Orderic's view that magnanimity to knightly prisoners was a key chivalric virtue. His tale about Geoffrey le Bel releasing four Poitevin knights without ransom and loaded with gifts sought to portray the Angevin count as the model of *largesse* and *franchise*.[133] Yet the anecdote is equally based on the assumption that prisoners of knightly rank might be detained for considerable periods and in poor conditions as a matter of course.[134] Thus while there were clear ideals of correct or praiseworthy conduct, in reality behaviour towards prisoners was largely dependent on personal volition. At its most pragmatic, the desire to speed ransom payment had to be tempered by ensuring the life, if not the well-being, of the prisoner. In the more intangible matter of honour, most, though not all, lords must have been constrained to some extent by fear of peer disapproval and the desire to embellish, not to sully, their reputation as knights.

---

[130] *GH*, i, p. 293; Rigord, p. 127.   [131] Orderic, v, pp. 238–9.

[132] *Ibid.*, v, pp. 244–5: above, p. 149.   [133] *Chroniques des comtes d'Anjou*, pp. 194–6; above, p. 148.

[134] Such treatment is reflected, for example, in a letter to Geoffrey, prior of Winchester, by Gilbert Foliot thanking him for the aid he has already given his captive kinsman Roger Foliot, and asking him to intercede on Roger's behalf with Henry of Blois. The unfortunate Roger was evidently being straitly confined in chains in the bishop's castle of Merdon, (Hants.), and was gravely ill. Gilbert, who doubtless feared less he might die before being redeemed, was clearly angry at the conditions of his kinsman's captivity: 'Ignominiose enim tenetur in carcere et iam extrema alflictus est egestate' (Foliot, no. 30, p. 70).

8

RESPITE, RESISTANCE AND HONOURABLE SURRENDER: CONVENTIONS OF SIEGE WARFARE

THE ROLE OF THE CASTLE IN WAR

Castles dominated medieval warfare as they dominated the landscape. The lands of the Anglo-Norman and Angevin kings were studded with castles, not simply in vulnerable border areas such as the Vexin or the Welsh and Scottish marches, but throughout the hinterland. Their distribution was less the result of some consciously designed military 'network', but rather the product of localized defensive, tenurial and administrative factors.[1] While their density, location and design fluctuated with changing political and social circumstances, the crucial military and governmental function of castles ensured that they would always be of fundamental importance in contemporary warfare, as would be those conventions designed to regulate the prosecution of siege.

Serving in peacetime as both lordly residences and local centres of administration, castles formed an integral element of both royal and baronial government, controlling most towns of any size as well as forming a vital component of the honorial baron's *caput*.[2] Royal castles in particular constituted 'the bones of the kingdom',[3] in William of Newburgh's famous phrase, guarding as much against actual or potential rebellion as against external invasion. Conversely, it was the castles of disaffected magnates, from which the authority of the king or duke might be defied, which formed the nodal points of such rebellions. Control of major castles was the key to effective power in both peace and war. Recent

---

[1] R. Eales, 'Royal Power and Castles in Norman England', *The Ideals and Practice of Medieval Knighthood*, III, pp. 49–78; *idem.*, 'Castles and Politics in England, 1215–1224', *Thirteenth Century England*, II, ed. P. R. Cross and S. D. Lloyd (Woodbridge, 1988), pp. 23–43; Strickland, 'Securing the North', pp. 179–81; N. J. G. Pounds, *The Medieval Castle in England and Wales. A Social and Political History* (Cambridge, 1990), pp. 54–71.   [2] Pounds, *The Medieval Castle, passim.*   [3] WN, p. 331.

scholarship has urged caution over generalizations concerning royal licensing of castles and the extent of rendability in eleventh- and twelfth-century England,[4] but it is clear that castle construction was the *sine qua non* of *de facto* royal or ducal authority. The Angevin kings in particular expended vast sums on castle building as part of a deliberate policy to increase the ratio of royal to baronial castles, and to achieve and maintain political supremacy by means of a series of stone fortresses which out-matched those of their opponents in scale, cost and sophistication of design.[5]

In war, the castle fulfilled a variety of offensive and defensive func-tions. The castle might act, particularly in areas such as Wales or Ireland, as an offensive instrument of conquest, acting as a forward base for further expansion.[6] Elsewhere, it could serve as a strongpoint from which knights might sally out to lay waste an opponent's lands, to attack enemy forces or simply to patrol and dominate the countryside.[7] In times of emergency or invasion, castle garrisons might be rapidly brought together to form an effective field force.[8] In terms of defence, the castle might give shelter to the garrison and the local populace, and although fortifications might not prevent raiding or the invasion of an enemy army,[9] the ability of garrisons to threaten supply lines and to make dam-aging sallies ensured that an area could not be effectively conquered without first reducing the castles which guarded it. As we have seen, while great set-piece battles such as Tinchebrai, Brémule or Bouvines were rare occurrences, castles were frequently the focus of much bitter fighting between sizeable groups of mounted knights. Castles, then, were the pivotal points of war and the ultimate strategic objective of the majority of campaigns. Skill in the art of siege, and concomitantly in that of defence, was thus a necessary prerequisite for any successful military commander.[10]

---

[4] For a re-evaluation of royal 'licensing' see Eales, 'Royal Power and Castles', pp. 69–78, and for con-cepts of rendability C. Coulson, 'Rendability and Castellation in Medieval France', *Château Gaillard*, 6 (1973), pp. 59–67; *idem.*, 'Fortress Policy in Capetian Tradition and Angevin Practice: Aspects of the Conquest of Normandy by Philip II', *Anglo-Norman Studies*, 6 (1983), pp. 13–38; and *idem.*, 'The Impact of Bouvines upon the Fortress Policy of Philip Augustus', in Harper-Bill, Holdsworth and Nelson (eds.), *Studies in Medieval History*, pp. 71–80.
[5] R. A. Brown, 'Royal Castle-Building in England, 1154–1216', *EHR*, 70 (1955), pp. 353–98; and *idem.*, 'A List of Castles, 1154–1216', *EHR*, 74 (1959), pp. 249–80.
[6] J. Le Patourel, *The Norman Empire* (Oxford, 1976), pp. 65–67, 303–18, 351–53; Pounds, *The Medieval Castle*, pp. 152–83.   [7] Brown, *English Castles*, pp. 198–9.
[8] *Ibid.*, p. 199; M. Chibnall, 'Mercenaries and the *Familia Regis* under Henry I', *History*, 62 (1977), pp. 19–21; Strickland, 'Securing the North', p. 185 and n. 58.
[9] Strickland, 'Securing the North', pp. 180–8.
[10] For siege warfare see P. Warner, *Sieges of the Middle Ages* (London, 1968); Bradbury, *The Medieval Siege*; and R. Rogers, *Latin Siege Warfare in the Twelfth Century* (Oxford, 1992).

10 The castle dominated the warfare of the eleventh and twelfth centuries. Here the
Maciejowski Bible depicts a fierce skirmish beneath the walls of a fortress, while
on the left, an artilleryman prepares to release a traction trebuchet. Many knights
who were otherwise well protected suffered wounds from arrows in the face, as
depicted here, when wearing the simple conical helmet (Pierpont Morgan
Library, M. 638, f. 23v, detail).

If such a commander was fortunate, a castle or fortified town might be
surrendered through fear on his arrival, or be taken by treachery or decep-
tion.[11] If not, a direct assault on the walls or a chance opportunity of
rushing a main gate might gain his objective. Thus, for example, Orderic
recounts how in 1113 the castle of Bellême fell to Henry I's forces after a
sally by the besieged miscarried.[12] Should guile, intimidation or direct
assault fail, however, an attacking commander was faced with the choice of
withdrawing or of settling down to the protracted business of a siege: a

[11] For the surrender of Aumâle to the Flemish in 1173, and that of the great fortress of Vaudreuil to
Philip Augustus in 1203, see below, pp. 225–8. Only widespread collusion can account for the rapidity
with which so many castles fell to Richard and Philip in their campaign of 1189 against Henry II
(*GH*, II, pp. 67–9), and to Philip during his invasion of Normandy, 1203–4 (Powicke, *Loss of
Normandy*, pp. 161–7). Similarly, conflicting loyalties and political pressure caused by Richard's captivity and John's treason led in 1193 to the bloodless surrender to Philip of the vital Norman stronghold
of Gisors and several other border castles (Howden, III, p. 206; Gillingham, *Richard the Lionheart*,
pp. 231–2).   [12] Orderic, VI, pp. 182–3.

blockade might be established, lines of circumvallation drawn or siege-castles constructed, engines set up and trained on vulnerable points of walls or towers, and mines begun. But although siege was the most sustained form of tactical commitment in warfare of the period, it had many disadvantages for the besieger. The increasing use of stone for castle construction from the early twelfth century, and the growing sophistication of design, made the disparity between the science of attack and that of defence still more pronounced. Even the earth and timber defences of the motte and bailey type, which were still widespread, could offer prolonged and effective resistance.[13]

More substantial fortresses with a stone curtain and *donjon* were still harder to take. The strength of the castle of Brionne required an investment of almost three years, c. 1047–50, by William the Conqueror before it fell.[14] The siege by Henry I of France of the castle of Thimert near Dreux, held for William the Conqueror, began in 1058, was still continuing in May 1059 when Philip I was consecrated, and was probably not over by 1060,[15] while Geoffrey Le Bel of Anjou took three years to reduce the fortress of Montreuil, after having built siege-castles of stone to enforce the blockade.[16] Though it is impossible to estimate the cost of the majority of sieges before the end of the twelfth century, such lengthy investment must have been enormously expensive. Ralph of Diceto describes the universal tax levied by Louis VII, and ruthlessly collected throughout his domains irrespective of rank, to enable him to besiege the key Norman stronghold of Verneuil in 1173.[17] The author of the *Gesta Stephani* reckoned that Stephen's three-month siege of Exeter had incurred 'an expenditure on various items of as much as fifteen thousand marks',[18] while that of Rochester, which lasted two months, was estimated by Coggeshall to have cost John 60,000 marks.[19] Roger of Wendover does not specify an amount for Rochester, but notes that its expense was a principal factor in John's wish to execute the garrison on their surrender.[20]

A garrison of only a handful of knights, supported by serjeants and other retainers, might hold off an attacking force numbering in their thousands

---

[13] See, for example, Brown, *English Medieval Castles*, pp. 25–8.   [14] WP, p. 18.

[15] Douglas, *William the Conqueror*, p. 74.   [16] Torigny, pp. 160–1.

[17] Diceto, I, p. 372. According to the *Annals of Dunstaple*, to meet the cost of the siege of Bedford in 1224, Henry III levied a carucage from the lands of the bishops and abbots assessed at half a mark for each demesne carucate and two marks for each tenant's carucate. Two men were to be sent from each hide to work the siege engines (*Annales monastici*, III, p. 86). For the record evidence for this siege, which gives a striking impression of the extensive logistics, and thus the cost, involved in reducing just one powerful stone castle, see G. H. Fowler, 'Munitions in 1224', *Bedfordshire Historical Record Society*, 5 (1920), pp. 117–32.   [18] GS, pp. 38–9.   [19] Coggeshall, p. 176.

[20] MP, II, p. 626. Matthew Paris adds his own assessment of the cost as being 55,060 marks, but it would be unwise to put any great reliance on such uncorroborated estimates of chroniclers.

for weeks, even months.[21] Meanwhile, in addition to the great drain in both men and material, the besiegers faced cumulative difficulties of supply and sanitation. Disease, notably dysentery and typhus, might decimate an attacking force, while the longer the siege, the more difficult it became to live off the countryside. Should a besieger have supply lines, these might be cut by enemy action,[22] while the static deployment of a besieging army invited attack from an opponent's field army. In situations of civil war or rebellion, moreover, the protracted nature of siege gave ample opportunity for dissident elements among the besieging forces to communicate with and supply aid to the besieged, or to apply sustained political pressure upon the ruler to deal leniently with erstwhile vassals under attack.[23]

Such strategic, logistical and political considerations, coupled with the ubiquity of castles and the resulting predominance of siege-based warfare, led to the formation of a body of conventions which attempted to provide a mutually acceptable way of regulating the prosecution of siege. Unlike the circumstances pertaining to battle, the protracted and essentially static nature of siege allowed the conduct of investment to assume a more premeditated and closely defined quality, just as the comparatively safe and regulated nature of the tournament fostered the development of those theatrical and ceremonial aspects of the 'cult of chivalry', such as Arthurian pageant, heraldry and the non-military role of heralds, which of necessity were largely precluded from the battlefield itself.

CONDITIONAL RESPITE: THE FUSION OF HONOUR AND PRAGMATISM

Foremost among these conventions of siege was that which may be labelled 'conditional respite', usually rendered in the Latin sources by the noun 'treuga' or its variants, or in the vernacular as 'terme' or 'respit'.[24] By

[21] The important Norman fortress of Radepont, which resisted Philip's army for three weeks in 1203, had a garrison of twenty knights, one hundred sergeants and thirty crossbowmen (Rigord, p. 159). From this Powicke estimates that in addition to the forty knights known to have been defending Château Gaillard, the rest of the garrison consisted of about two hundred sergeants and sixty crossbowmen or engineers (Powicke, *Loss of Normandy*, p. 256). The efficacy of castles in defence is still more strikingly revealed on the Scottish march, where far smaller garrisons might successfully resist large Scottish forces (Strickland, 'Securing the North', p. 185).
[22] In 1174, for example, Henry II sent his Welsh infantry to harass the French supply columns that had to pass through dense forest on their way to the siege of Rouen. The Welsh ambushed convoys and slew carters, creating terror and panic among the French (*GH*, II, pp. 74–5). A similar guerilla campaign was launched by Wilikin of the Weald and his men against those attempting to supply Prince Louis's forces besieging Dover in 1216–17 (*Histoire de ducs*, p. 181; *HGM*, II. 15785–808, and *HGM*, III, p. 210, n. 6.).   [23] See below, pp. 247–8.
[24] For example Orderic, v, pp. 302–3, 'mutuo treuias'; JF II. 501 and 510, 'quarante jorz de terme'; I. 500, 'triewe'; I. 519, 'le terme'; I. 593, 'terme ne respit'; I. 1425, 'respit'; I. 1638, 'terme'; *HGM* I. 463, 'trieve'.

this, a hard-pressed garrison might apply to a besieging commander for a respite of a set number of days in which to seek aid from their lord, on the understanding that if such aid was not forthcoming within the stipulated period, they would surrender their castle without further resistance. The garrison would thereupon be spared life and limb, and might even be granted honourable egress with their horses and arms. The convention of conditional respite was both geographically and chronologically wide-spread, examples occurring, for instance, in the majority of campaigns in England and North-west France in the later eleventh and twelfth centuries, as well as in Outremer. In some campaigns, notice of the granting of respite appears frequently. Thus in 1173, for example, conditional respite was granted to Drincourt by Philip of Flanders, to Verneuil by Louis VII, and to Wark, Carlisle, and probably Alnwick and Prudhoe, by William the Lion.[25]

As with all established conventions in war, that of conditional respite could only develop and operate where mutual advantage was to be gained by adherence to it. The ubiquity of respites is explained by the fact that in response to the prevalence of castle-based warfare, this usage provided a highly pragmatic solution to the problems raised by siege, going far towards reconciling the conflicting interests of besieger and besieged.

What then had a besieging commander to gain by granting a truce or conditional respite to a beleaguered garrison? Frequently, as with so many elements of behavioural restraint, a profit motive can be readily detected. Hence in 1204, the citizens of Rouen and Verneuil, and the garrison of Arques, had to purchase Philip's assent to a forty-day truce in which to seek John's aid.[26] In 1216, the baronial army launched a fierce attack on York, but accepted a truce until June for a payment of 1,000 marks from the citizens.[27] Doubtless many such payments lay behind the laconic notices of chroniclers of truces granted or respites received.

Yet in marked contrast to the importance of ransom as a control against killing in battle, financial dictates were only of secondary importance in the granting of terms during siege. It was tactical and strategic considerations that were paramount. A besieging commander might grant a garrison respite in the hope that an opponent, in bringing relief to his beleaguered men, might be drawn from a primary objective. Hence in 1142, being hard-pressed by Robert of Gloucester, Stephen's garrison of Wareham sought a

---

[25] Torigny, p. 258; Diceto, I, pp. 374–5; *GH*, I, p. 50; JF II. 508–19, 539–44 and below, pp. 219–21.

[26] Coggeshall, p. 145. He similarly accepted the proffer of 500 marks from both Robert of Leicester and William Marshal for a truce of a year and a day in which to see whether John would hold or lose Normandy (*HGM*, II. 12861–98; above, p. 236).   [27] Coggeshall, p. 180.

respite. 'This proposal was most agreeable to the earl, though he was filled with an impatient longing to possess the castle, because it afforded a hope of bringing the king away from besieging his sister' at Oxford.[28]

The principal function of respite, however, was to facilitate the capture of castles. Direct assault might well be costly in lives and ultimately prove fruitless; lengthy investment was fraught with financial, logistical and sanitary problems, as well as putting the besiegers at a tactical disadvantage vis-à-vis any relieving force. It was often in the best interests of the attackers, therefore, to minimize the length of the siege, and besieging commanders normally considered it a worthwhile gamble to run the risk of the garrison being relieved in order to gain the castle or fortified town at the end of a limited period without further fighting.

This risk of relief, moreover, might often be small, for the successful relief of garrisons who had sought conditional respites seems to have been relatively uncommon. Were a relieving army close at hand and aid readily forthcoming, there would have been little need for a conditional respite in the first instance; the convention only tended to operate in circumstances where garrisons believed themselves to be in dire straits. Indeed, the relative paucity of effective reliefs is largely explained by the fact that in many situations the besieging forces clearly granted conditional respite only because they adjudged it impossible for a garrison to be relieved. Hence Jordan Fantosme hints at the calculation behind William the Lion's acceptance in 1173 of the request of Roger de Stuteville, castellan of Wark, for a conditional respite to seek aid: 'Then King William beheld Roger in the depths of grief, and all Northumberland dolorously troubled: there is none to withstand him and his might. He had no hesitation in granting a respite until the fortieth day.'[29] In the case of Carlisle, which William besieged the following year, Jordan is unequivocal in linking acceptance of respite with assurance of its impossibility. Replying to Robert de Vaux's petition for a truce, William is made to reply, 'I have no apprehension at all about doing that; you will not get any help, that I know for a fact.'[30] Similarly, in 1173 Louis VII granted the citizens of Verneuil the very short respite of three days to seek aid from Henry II, 'because he judged it impossible'.[31]

Yet despite this innate, underlying pragmatism, there were other pressures to urge the acceptance of such terms by a besieging commander. By granting conditional respite, the besieger might enhance his military repu-

---

[28] *HN*, p. 75.
[29] JF, 11. 516–19. According to the *Histoire de Guillaume le Maréchal*, Stephen granted the garrison of Newbury one day's respite to seek aid from their lord, John Marshal (*HGM*, 11. 461–72). In this case, however, the author gives no hint that such a short time span was unreasonable, for John himself was near at hand.   [30] JF, 11. 1634–42.   [31] Diceto, 1, p. 374; above, pp. 126–7.

tation by a display of *franchise* – the greatness of spirit that was expected of a knight and a great lord. In the context of war in revolt, such a display of generosity might also act as a crucial mechanism for the re-establishment of lordship.[32] Despite the calculated nature of his grants of respite, William the Lion was clearly seeking to gain much chivalric kudos from his treatment of the Northumbrian castellans, many of whom he must have known personally.[33]

The benefits of conditional respite for the besieged were obvious. They could seek aid, making their lord aware of their plight, and as a result might be relieved or have their investment raised. Hence at the siege of Wark in 1173, Roger de Stuteville sought a truce of forty days from William the Lion, 'and sought aid so successfully that before the time granted was up he brought back such an army that he was able to tell the king of Scotland that he was free to attack them with his Flemings and that he [Roger] will confidently await them'.[34] The following year, Odinel d'Umfraville was able to raise a relieving army to lift the siege of Prudhoe, which also served indirectly to relieve Carlisle.[35] In 1173, Henry II had come rapidly to the relief of Verneuil when its citizens obtained a brief respite from Louis VII. Though Louis's subsequent duplicity prevented Henry from saving the burgesses from being pillaged, his arrival nevertheless threw the French into a panic, forcing them to lift the siege and to abandon that part of the town which they had taken.[36]

Should a garrison not be relieved, the defenders ensured for themselves both a safe and honourable surrender by the pre-arranged terms of the respite. If, moreover, a lord could not send relief to a garrison who requested it, he invariably granted them permission to surrender, since he himself had failed – albeit unwillingly – to supply his vassals with the protection *in extremis* that was one of the principal obligations of good lordship. This concept is strikingly expressed by Jordan Fantosme in a speech put into the mouth of Roger de Stuteville in 1173. Although Roger's address to the absent Henry II is highly stylized and exaggerated in its emotion, it encapsulates the notion of reciprocity of aid inherent in the bond between lord and vassal:

> Then he thinks sadly of his liege lord, valiant King Henry, his tears course down his cheeks: 'Since you are now powerless, what will it help you that once you were strong? You cannot give any aid to your vassal! I shall go to the king of Scotland and ask him for a truce (*sa triewe*), a breathing space of forty days (*quarante jorz de terme*), so that I can cross the seas. If then I cannot

[32] Below, pp. 249–54.   [33] Below, pp. 219–20.   [34] JF, ll. 526–9.   [35] *Ibid.*, ll. 1705–7.
[36] *GH*, I, pp. 50–5; WN, pp. 174–5; above, pp. 126–7.

procure help, from then on you will certainly *and rightly* (*par raisun*) have lost the whole of Northumberland.'[37]

NO SURRENDER? HEROISM, VASSALIC LOYALTY AND THE LIMITS OF RESISTANCE

Inherent in such statements as that given by Jordan to de Stuteville was the notion that there was a definable limit to which loyalty and the duty to resist extended. Many garrisons did put up a prolonged and heroic resistance, even when their lord was unable to bring aid. Hence the Manceaux garrison of Mayet resisting Rufus in 1099 consisted of 'determined men, loyal to their lord and firmly resolved to fight to the death for him, clearly proving their valour by their praiseworthy example'.[38] When in 1105 Henry I approached Bayeux, the garrison commander, Gunter d'Aunay, handed over Robert fitz Hamon, one of Henry's leading supporters who had been captured by Robert Curthose's forces, in order to win the king's favour. He nevertheless resolutely refused Henry's demands to surrender the city, and was taken prisoner along with his men when the town fell by storm.[39] Despite Henry II's flight from Le Mans in 1189, William de Silli had valorously held out in the citadel, only surrendering after Philip Augustus's men had mined the keep.[40]

Philip's subsequent invasion of Normandy and Anjou in 1203–4 resulted in rapid and widespread capitulation by many garrisons, but several castellans put up a fierce resistance. Although John was unable to bring effective relief and ordered each commander 'to do as seemed best to them',[41] Gerard d'Athée at Loches, Hubert de Burgh at Chinon and Roger de Lacy at Château Gaillard held out valiantly until they were finally compelled to surrender.[42] The defence of Château Gaillard, indeed, which lasted six months from September 1203, to March 1204, is a *locus classicus* both for the nature of siege warfare and for the heroic resistance of a beleaguered garrison.[43] Contrary to the allegations of sloth and indecision made by both his contemporary and modern detractors, John had in fact made a serious effort to relieve this keystone in the defences of Normandy. The bold attempt to break the French blockade, however, was botched, while

---

[37] JF 11. 496–503.   [38] Orderic, v, pp. 258–9.   [39] *Ibid.*, VI, pp. 194–7.
[40] *HGM* 11. 8878–86; *GH*, I, p. 68.   [41] MP, II, p. 498; Coggeshall, pp. 145–6.
[42] MP, II, pp. 488–9; Coggeshall, p. 144; WB, *Philippidos*, VIII, 11. 408–34, pp. 225, 226.
[43] The siege is reconstructed in detail by K. Norgate, *England under the Angevin Kings*, 2 vols. (London, 1887), II, pp. 411–23. The most detailed contemporary account of the great siege is that given by William the Breton, which reflects both the strategic and symbolic significance of its capture by Philip (WB, *Gesta*, pp. 212–20; *Philippidos*, VII, 11. 1–843, pp. 176–209). See also Powicke, *Loss of Normandy*, pp. 253–6.

attempts to draw Philip away by campaigning against his Breton allies in the west proved equally unsuccessful.[44] This failure, coupled with the endemic treason that hampered John's ability to bring further relief, meant that the garrison were on their own. All John could do was to praise the defenders by letter and urge them to continue resistance. If they could no longer hold out, they were to follow the orders which would be conveyed to them by Peter des Préaux, who was in charge of the defence of Rouen, William of Mortemer and the royal clerk Hugh of Wells.[45]

Whether or not Roger de Lacy and his men expected further relief, they put up a prolonged and fierce resistance. In order to conserve supplies, they expelled the many refugees who had sought safety in the castle before the siege. Even when Philip refused to allow the last batch of four hundred through his lines, the garrison resolutely refused to re-admit them. They were determined to preserve their stores for the siege, even though this meant watching friends and relatives die of starvation and exposure between the lines. When finally want of supplies and the efforts of the French miners made further resistance impossible, the defenders sallied out and attacked the besiegers before being overwhelmed.[46]

The siege of Château Gaillard has achieved prominence because of the unusually detailed description furnished by Philip Augustus's encomiast, William le Breton. Such a striking instance of vassals' courage and loyalty, however, does not stand in isolation. Though we know virtually nothing concerning Hubert de Burgh's resistance at Chinon, save that it was vigorous but ultimately doomed, his later defence of Dover in 1216–17 against the persistent attacks of Prince Louis brought him great renown.

In 1216, Dover held out when most of the royal castles in Kent submitted to Louis on his arrival.[47] Hubert de Burgh and the garrison bravely fought off an intensive siege from 22 July–14 October, during which the castle was battered by engines, the great barbican fell and Louis's miners succeeded in bringing down one of the two towers of the 'Norfolk' gate.[48] Finally, however, Hubert and his fellow commander Gerard de Sotengi were forced to seek a respite in which to send to John for aid.[49] The garrison's messenger had found John lying ill in Lindsey, in no position to relieve the garrison himself. It is unclear whether or not John acquiesced to the surrender of Dover or whether the king's death shortly after (19 October)

[44] WB, *Phillipidos*, VII, 11. 140–385, pp. 181–92.
[45] Powicke, *Loss of Normandy*, pp. 255–6, citing a letter preserved in Philip's earliest register.
[46] WB, *Gesta*, pp. 213–20; *Philippidos*, VII, 11. 407–817.   [47] Coggeshall, pp. 181–2.
[48] *Histoire des ducs*, pp. 177–80; Coggeshall, p. 182. For the military and political context of the siege of Dover see Carpenter, *The Minority of Henry III*, pp. 19–49, especially pp. 20–1, 32–3.
[49] *Histoire des ducs*, p. 180; Coggeshall, p. 182; WC, II, p. 232.

convinced Hubert to renew his resistance on behalf of his new lord, the boy-king Henry III.[50]

The exact nature of the terms agreed on 14 October is unclear.[51] At some stage, however, Louis granted the garrison a truce until Easter 1217, a concession motivated both by his need to return to France to gain reinforcements and by the changing political situation following the death of John.[52] On his return from France, Louis had to besiege the castle a second time, but the crushing defeat of the Franco-baronial forces at Lincoln in May 1217 forced him to raise this second investment.

Such instances of resolute resistance should be seen as the result of a personal decision to fight on out of an individual or corporate sense of vassalic loyalty and honour. Garrisons occasionally swore oaths never to yield as a mechanism for strenghtening their resistance. The garrison of Exeter in 1136, for example, were 'bound by fealty and an oath never to yield to the king at all'.[53] Such a pledge might sometimes be demanded by lords from their garrisons. Thus in 1203, Philip Augustus granted the newly captured Norman fortress of Radepont, of great strategic value, to Peter de Moret on condition that anyone residing there must swear that whatever happened, even if this meant death or capture, they would never give Radepont up to anyone except to Philip or to a well-known royal messenger carrying his letters patent.[54]

In reality, however, lords invariably released their men from such undertakings in situations where further resistance was seen to be futile. Hence, according to Orderic, on leaving to fight Henry I at Tinchebrai in 1106, Robert Curthose bound the defenders of Falaise by an oath never to surrender the castle to anyone except himself or his faithful follower William de Ferrières. After his defeat and capture, however, Robert permitted William de Ferrières to go ahead of Henry's army to Falaise and other Norman strongholds as yet unsubdued, to receive their submission on behalf of his victorious brother at the duke's command. Henry thus received the castle of Falaise and the fealty of the burgesses on Robert's

---

[50] The *Histoire des ducs*, p. 180, believed John was angered by the terms agreed with Louis, presumably because of his inability to bring aid before the expiry of the respite.

[51] Given the strategic value of the 'key of England' and his sustained efforts to capture the castle, it would have been very strange had the initial respite not been conditional. Yet Hubert did not yield the castle, but rather replenished its supplies on Louis's first departure, suggesting the extended truce may have been the result of renegotiation following John's death. The later dramatized accounts of Wendover and Paris do not mention a truce, but stress Hubert's heroic resistance and unflinching loyalty in the face of bribery, intimidation and force (MP, III, pp. 3–5).   [52] WC, II, p. 232.

[53] *GS* pp. 34–5. Similarly, when William Fitz Alan fled from Shrewsbury in 1138 on Stephen's arrival, he left behind in the castle men 'qui sibi non reddendo illo fidelitatem iuraverunt' (JW, pp. 50–1).

[54] *Receuil des actes de Philippe Auguste*, II, no. 761; *Cartulaire Normand*, no. 184; Powicke, *Loss of Normandy*, p. 164, n. 228.

orders, while Hugh de Nonant surrendered the citadel of Rouen. 'The other castellans too all over Normandy were released by the duke from their fealty, and, by surrendering all their castles with his consent, were reconciled to the conqueror.'[55]

For a lord to refuse a request to surrender should he be incapable of bringing relief, or to order a garrison never to capitulate, would have exceeded the bounds of expected fidelity. The point is exemplified by the conduct of Robert de Bellême towards his garrison of Arundel, besieged by Henry I in 1102. Hard pressed by the royal investment, the garrison 'humbly petitioned the king for a truce (*inducias*) so that they might apply to their lord either for reinforcements or permission to surrender'. Robert, however, was too occupied in completing his new castle at Bridgnorth to bring relief: 'His heart sank when he heard of the collapse of his men; he absolved them from their allegiance (*a promisso fide . . . absoluit*), since he was powerless to help them, and in bitter grief authorized them to make peace with the king.'[56] In his acceptance of the limits of duty, Bellême, otherwise notorious for his refusal to ransom his captives,[57] was acting with complete propriety towards his vassals.

A garrison might have clear notions as to how far their duty to resist extended. In 1118, Fulk of Anjou besieged the Norman stronghold of La Motte-Gautier-de-Clinchamp with a powerful army. On hearing of the investment, Henry I summoned his host to prepare for battle. Meanwhile, however, the castle fell after eight days of continuous assaults and pounding by engines. The Norman garrison of 140 knights, whose commanders had been hand-picked by the king, were granted safety of life and limb and free egress with their arms. Returning sorrowfully to Henry I at Alençon, they faced the king's wrath with shame, but 'defended their failure on the reasonable grounds (*rationabiliter*) that though they had waited long and had repeatedly sent urgent messages he had delayed too long in bringing the help they needed, and they had been shut in under a ceaseless bombardment from the besiegers'.[58] Henry I might be enraged at the loss of an important fortress, but the garrison clearly felt that his failure to bring relief when his vassals were in need had fully vindicated their capitulation. Their honourable treatment by the Angevins implies that the attackers were of a similar mind.

Similarly, the poet of the *Song of Dermot and the Earl* attached no censure to the action of Hugh Tyrell, constable of Trim, who abandoned his lord's newly built castle in the face of a vastly superior Irish army when it became

---

[55] Orderic, VI, pp. 90–3.   [56] Orderic, VI, pp. 22–3; below, p. 252.   [57] Above, pp. 199–200.
[58] Orderic, VI, pp. 194–7.

clear that Earl Richard could not come to his relief in time.[59] Although the Irish entirely raised this important fortress of Hugh de Lacy to the ground, the *Song* simply notes that subsequently 'Hugh Tyrell went to Trim and re-fortified his fortress; after that he guarded it with great honour until the arrival of his lord'.[60] Examples of castellans abandoning castles deemed to be too weak to withstand a sizeable enemy army are not infrequent.[61] Valour and the duty to resist might clearly be tempered with considerable discretion.

Nevertheless, knights were clearly conscious of an ideal to which they might aspire, and which not a few actually attained. The epitome of expected vassalic conduct is nowhere more forcefully expressed than in the reply put into the mouth of Robert de Vaux, castellan of Carlisle, when faced with a demand to surrender by William the Lion in 1174: 'We here in this castle are loyal men and secure (*bone gent asseure*); cursed be he who sur-renders as long as his food last out!'[62] Jordan Fantosme stresses that Robert only seeks conditional respite when 'neither wine nor wheat can get to him any more, nor will help reach him from Richmond: if he does not get aid quickly, he will be starved out'.[63] That such sentiments were not merely literary exaggeration is suggested by the fact that when the garrison of Wark surrendered to David I in 1138 after a prolonged resistance, they did so only through starvation: the only food found within the walls was one salted horse and another still alive.[64]

Whatever the realities of the situation, however, the discrepancy between the duty to resist and the inability to continue to do so might seri-ously compromise a castellan's honour. Hence Jordan Fantosme was at pains to stress the dilemma in which the Scottish attack on Wark-on-Tweed placed Roger de Stuteville, who was conscious of his duty to resist but lacked sufficient men for an adequate defence; 'It was no wonder if Lord Roger was dismayed!'[65] It is his honour, or rather the risk of it being tar-nished, that forms the keynote of two speeches given to him by Jordan.[66] Roger's solution was to petition William successfully for a conditional respite, which made provision for an honourable capitulation, sanctioned by his lord, should relief not be forthcoming.

---

[59] *Song of Dermot*, 11. 3260–96. For the building of Trim, *ibid.*, 11. 3222 ff.   [60] *Ibid.*, 11. 3337–41.
[61] For examples see Strickland, 'Securing the North', p. 182 and n. 33.   [62] JF, 11. 1411–12.
[63] *Ibid.*, 11. 1587–9. This is confirmed by Howden, *GH*, I, p. 65, who noted that Robert made peace with William the Lion, 'victu sibi et burgensibus, qui intus erant, deficiente'.
[64] JH, p. 118; RH, p. 100.   [65] JF, 11. 481–7.
[66] Thus to the Virgin Mary he prays, 'Give me such guidance as will maintain my honour, for the Scots are waging war mercilessly against me' (JF, 11. 488–90). And in asking for a truce from King William, he says, 'Do not bring dishonour on me! Hold your wrath in check! I am all in favour of improvement of your prospects, so long as my own are not brought to ruin' (*ibid.*, 11. 508–9).

11 The symbolic surrender of a castle, from the Bayeux Tapestry. On the left, Breton knights defend the castle of Dinan, whose ditches, motte, wooden keep and flying-bridge are carefully depicted. The Normans attempt to fire the wooden palisade, while on the right, Count Conan hands the keys of the castle over to Duke William on the end of a lance. The surrender of a fortress involved important rituals, such as the sounding of trumpets and the raising of the victor's banner over the ramparts to symbolize possession (by special permission of the City of Bayeux).

This gaining of a lord's permission to capitulate should he be unable to succour his vassals was of crucial importance. It both legitimized a garrison's surrender and vindicated their honour.[67] With their lord's licence thus granted, the garrison could feel they had fulfilled their vassalic duty, and recognition of this was in turn reflected by the honourable treatment normally proffered to them by the besiegers. When, on the death of Rufus, Helias of Maine besieged the Norman garrison of Le Mans, the defenders, unsure as to which of the Conqueror's two sons was now their lord in Maine, sought and were granted a truce (*mutuo treuias*) to seek aid from both Robert and Henry. Both rulers, however, were too preoccupied to bring relief, but thanked the garrison and gave them licence to negotiate an honourable surrender.[68] Deprived, therefore, of a 'natural lord', the Normans yielded the citadel to Helias in return for a large sum of money, and proclaimed him as count of Maine. Despite the fact that this vital and otherwise impregnable fortress had passed out of Norman hands, and with it effective control of Maine itself, Orderic Vitalis nevertheless felt that the garrison 'had magnificently vindicated their loyalty'. Helias believed so too, permitting them to leave with their arms and all their belongings, and escorting them safely past the hostile citizens.[69]

CLEMENCY, *FRANCHISE* AND REPUTATION: THE TREATMENT OF ENEMY GARRISONS

The generosity of terms granted to a surrendering garrison might vary widely, depending on the volition of the besieging commander and the circumstances of hostilities. Those granted in the context of revolt, for example, naturally tended to be harsher than those granted to garrisons in no way bound by homage or fealty to the besieger.[70] Yet the proffering of acceptable conditions for surrender was the rule rather than the exception, and the enunciation and guarantee of such terms lay at the heart of the convention of conditional respite. If not actually set free, the least a garrison who had entered into such an agreement could expect was 'the safety of life and limb', that is immunity from execution or mutilation. Once captive, they would invariably be ransomed, though, as we have seen, conditions of captivity might vary widely.[71]

A valiant defence might at the very least win honourable captivity, such as that granted by Philip Augustus to Roger de Lacy and the heroic defend-

---

[67] Below, pp. 224–9.   [68] Orderic, v, pp. 302–5.   [69] *Ibid.*, pp. 302–7; above, pp. 137–8.
[70] Below, pp. 241–6.   [71] Above, pp. 196–203.

ers of Château Gaillard in 1204.[72] Frequently, however, a besieger might publicly acknowledge the fortitude and constancy of his erstwhile opponents by bestowing on them the greatest mark of honour in surrender, the freedom to leave with horses, arms and possessions. In 1217, Prince Louis granted this privilege to the garrisons of Hertford and Berkhampstead.[73] After the prolonged siege of Wark in 1138, David I even gave the garrison of Wark fresh mounts on which to depart since starvation had forced them to eat their own horses.[74] It was a convention that might even be observed in situations of rebellion. Thus Henry I, whose ruthlessness has been more often highlighted than his undoubted sense of chivalry, granted free egress to the defenders of Pont-Audemer in 1124, despite the fact that they had been supporting William Clito against him.[75]

This was a symbolic recognition by the besiegers of a valiant and loyal defence. Though defeated, the garrison were considered worthy enough to escape capture and ransom, and to keep their destriers and equipment which represented both the symbols of knighthood as well as a considerable capital investment. Indeed, so costly were horses and arms that their loss might meant ruin for poorer knights.[76] Conversely, for the victorious besiegers such magnanimity represented a very real financial sacrifice. They not only voluntarily gave up the taking of valuable booty in the form of war-horses, hauberks, helmets and weapons which might be re-distributed to vassals, but also a very considerable sum of money in the cumulative ransoms of a garrison. Here then we have a convention the underlying motivation of which, far from being that of financial gain, was that of the much valued qualities of largesse and *franchise*. What the grantor *did* gain was something less tangible but of no less value, the praise and esteem of his contemporaries by which his own knightly reputation was augmented.

In certain instances, moreover, the desire to gain such praise and esteem might even override pragmatic military considerations. Thus, for example, by granting a whole series of conditional respites to Northumbrian castellans in his campaigns of 1173–4, William the Lion did much to hamper seriously his own war effort. In 1173, he misjudged the likelihood that the key

---

[72] MP, II, pp. 488–9. Roger was kept in open custody because of his valour (*sub libera custodia propter probitatem suam*).   [73] MP, III, pp. 5, 8.   [74] JH, p. 118; RH, p. 100.

[75] Orderic, v, pp. 304–7; *ibid.*, VI, pp. 352–5. At least part of the garrison, however, including Luke of La Barre, were French knights who were not Henry's homagers.

[76] Hence in a letter to Henry of Blois, the powerful bishop of Winchester and brother to King Stephen, Gilbert Foliot pleads with the bishop to release his kinsman, Roger Foliot, who his men are holding in captivity: 'For your sanctity should know that his father never had more than half a hide of land: he himself had only what he had acquired by his service as a knight. Till the present time he has served the lord Brian [fitz Count] as a stipendiary (*ad donativum*), and now, despoiled of his horses and arms, he has lost all at once everything he had' (Foliot, no. 29, p. 69; quoted by Cronne, *The Reign of Stephen*, p. 151).

fortress of Wark-on-Tweed would be relieved, and accordingly lost the opportunity to seize one of his principal objectives when it was poorly garrisoned.[77] The reinforced garrison were subsequently able to repel a second and more determined Scottish siege the following year.[78] Likewise, despite the failure to take Carlisle after prolonged investment and hard fighting in 1173, his grant of respite to the garrison in 1174 when they were close to capitulation through want of supplies threw away William's chance to gain this great Cumbrian fortress which he desired so badly.[79] Before marching on Prudhoe in 1174, William sent messengers to warn Odinel de Umfraville that he would be besieged, and despite the king of Scots' deep-seated hostility towards Odinel, he too may have been granted a respite.[80] If so, the final irony was that it was the relieving army mustered by de Umfraville to raise the siege of Prudhoe which defeated and captured William outside Alnwick in 1174.[81]

William the Lion's magnanimity towards the Northumbrian castellans is partly explained by the fact that, prior to becoming king of Scots, he had briefly held the lordship of Tynedale. Several of the men who found them-selves defending their castles against him in 1173–4 had attended first his comital then his royal court, where they attest several charters.[82] Nevertheless, William seems to have taken adherence to convention in the field to an extreme. By contrast, his grandfather, David I, had conducted the siege of Wark in 1138 with a methodical determination, not offering respite and specifically excluding this castle from the truce arranged by the papal legate Alberic.[83] Yet whether William's conduct was a deliberate attempt to distance himself from the excesses of his native Scottish and Galwegian troops,[84] or to appear more Anglo-Norman than his Anglo-Norman knights,[85] his campaigns of 1173–4 furnish a clear instance of chivalric notions being taken to a point where the pragmatic origins of the convention of respite were largely overshadowed by a magnanimity that jeopardized military success.

[77] JF, 11. 508–29.   [78] Ibid., 11. 1185–286.   [79] GH, 1, p. 65; JF, 11. 1637–42.
[80] JF, 11. 1646–7. Jordan insists that Odinel alone left Prudhoe to seek aid, but he is unclear whether this was because of a respite, or because the garrison, knowing of William's animosity towards Odinel, wished their lord to ride to safety (ibid. 11. 1650–7).   [81] Ibid., 11. 1705–806.
[82] RRS, 11, nos. 2–5, pp. 123–25; Strickland, 'Arms and the Men', p. 219, n. 141.
[83] RH, p. 99. David's initial attack on Wark had been by surprise, at dawn and in the depths of mid-winter (ibid., p. 77: JH, p. 115). David also launched a winter campaign in January, 1136 (RH, pp. 71–2; JH, p. 114).   [84] Below, pp. 323–9.
[85] William's court was dominated both politically and linguistically by Anglo-Normans to the exclusion of the native aristocracy, and he delighted in the chivalrous society of North-west France. He was present at Henry II's siege of Toulouse in 1159, and at some of the great tournaments held on the continent (Strickland, 'Arms and the Men', p. 213; JF, 11. 1250–3, which implies William had been with his brother Malcolm at Toulouse; above, p. 150).

William did not stand in isolation in making chivalric gestures which might prove prejudicial to tactical and strategic considerations. We have already noted Stephen's acts of magnanimity which were to cost him dear, and Louis VII's grant of a day's respite to Rouen in 1174 which redounded so unfavourably on him.[86] In 1099, William Rufus granted the Manceaux garrison of Mayet respite from attack because a Sunday was approaching – an intriguing gesture given his alleged impiety – although his knights had been ready to take the castle by storm. The garrison, however, used the respite to strengthen their castle to such effect that Rufus's subsequent assaults failed and he was finally forced to withdraw.[87]

It was to cover just such an eventuality that certain respites were conditional on the besieged not adding to their fortifications during the period of truce. Hence Jordan has William the Lion say of William de Vesci, the castellan of Alnwick, that 'if he will pledge me the same terms as he did the constable of Wark two days ago, not to strengthen his garrison nor add to his fortifications (*senz guarisun atraire e senz rien esforcier*), we shall pass on to Warkworth'.[88] A more exact expression of this convention was stated almost a century earlier in 1088, in one of the clauses of the sworn pact between William of St Calais, bishop of Durham, and Roger de Montgomery, Odo and Alan of Brittany recorded by the *De injusta vexatione Willelmi episcopi*:

> The bishop on his side has pledged his faith to Roger of Poitou that if he is conducted back to his castle and during his absence the castle [Durham] has been strengthened either in its garrison or in its fortification, then the bishop will cause such additional armament to be totally removed lest the bishop should have unfair profit or the king unfair loss.[89]

A good example of such 'unfair loss' is provided by the *Histoire de Guillaume le Maréchal*, which describes how, during Stephen's siege of Newbury, the garrison were granted respite by the king to seek aid from their lord, John Marshal. The Marshal in turn sent to the king for a truce so he could consult his lady, the Empress, which Stephen granted on condition that one of John's sons, William – the poet's hero – should be given as hostage. Seemingly impervious to the fate of his infant son,[90] however, John violated the truce by filling Newbury with good knights, serjeants and archers, and once the truce had expired refused outright to surrender. The king's rage at John's duplicity almost cost young William's life, but Stephen's gentleness prevailed and the boy was spared.[91]

---

[86] Above, pp. 49, n. 94, 127–8.   [87] Orderic, v, pp. 258–61; and above, p. 160.   [88] JF, 11. 541–4.
[89] SD, 1, pp. 177–8; *EHD*, 11, p. 657. On the veracity of the *Injusta Vexatione* see below, p. 279, n. 97.
[90] Cf. Duby, *William Marshal*, pp. 63–7.   [91] *HGM*, 11. 462–538.

Whether Rufus made any such stipulation to the garrison of Mayet which they subsequently violated, or whether, as seems more likely, he mistakenly adjudged one day to make no significant difference to the defenders' chances, is unknown. Nevertheless, in view of the failure of their respective campaigns, both he and William the Lion must, with hindsight, have regretted such costly acts of magnanimity.

THE RIGHT OF STORM

Occasionally, a garrison might choose to ignore terms offered by a besieger and fight on until they were overwhelmed and taken by storm. The repercussions of so stubborn a defence, however, were potentially very grave. Should a town or castle fall by storm (*per vim*) after having rejected reasonable terms offered by a besieging commander, the lives and chattels of the defenders were held to be at the mercy of the besieger. It was this custom that Philip Augustus invoked in 1203 to intimidate the defenders of Normandy. After John's departure from the duchy, Philip sent to each major town and fortress, declaring that they had been deserted by their lord and proposing that henceforth he should be their sole lord. This he offered 'in a friendly manner', but if they refused to accept his overlordship freely, and were taken by force in subsequent hostilities, Philip vowed to have them all hanged or flayed alive. As a result, the Normans gave the French king hostages for a truce of one year, and pledged that if they were not relieved by John within this time, they would surrender the castles and towns and recognize Philip as lord.[92]

Towns caught up in fighting as well as those besieged directly might be plundered by victorious forces. Henry of Huntingdon noted that, in 1141, the city of Lincoln was seized and plundered by the forces of Robert of Gloucester and Rannulf of Chester 'hostili lege' after they had defeated Stephen's army outside the walls.[93] In 1217, Lincoln was again pillaged, this time in the king's name by the triumphant royalists following the rout of the Franco-baronial forces in the streets of the city. With the express permission of the legate Guala, they included churches in the sack, since the clergy had supported the baronial rebels.[94]

This 'right of storm', as it may be termed, had ancient origins, linked from biblical times (if not still earlier) to the treatment of walled cities in particular. The seizure of chattels and the slaying of inhabitants of a town which had refused terms is explicitly sanctioned in the Book of Deuteronomy.[95] Yet if commanders in the Anglo-Norman period were aware of this and other Old Testament exemplars, it is unlikely that they

---

[92] MP, II, pp. 483–4.   [93] HH, p. 275.   [94] MP, III, p. 23.   [95] Deuteronomy 20:1–20.

regarded the legitimacy of their actions in respect of the right of storm to rest directly on biblical precedent, still less on Roman juridical ideas which supported similar measures. Rather it seems they acted according to well-established custom: it is not until Henry V's siege of Harfleur in 1415 that the sources reveal a commander explicitly invoking the law of Deuteronomy, and here it is significant that the *Gesta Henrici Quinti* is at pains to stress that the garrison are contumacious rebels, withholding the king's lawful inheritance from him.[96]

Whatever its legal foundations, however, the convention was one of the greatest importance. It had far-reaching implications not simply for the treatment of the inhabitants but for the division of captured property and the subsequent legal status of the castle or town. The right of storm features prominently in Christian–Muslim relations in Palestine, where, as with the granting of conditional respite, it was clearly a mutually recognized convention.[97] When discussing the crusaders' siege of Acre in 1191, the English author of the *Itinerarium* has the Muslims urge Saladin to allow the garrison to surrender lest they should all be put to death 'jure belli' if the city fell by storm.[98]

In England and North-west France, however, its workings are far less well documented, and its operation has to be pieced together from fragmentary and laconic references. Such a dearth of evidence may reflect sufficient familiarity with the convention that few thought to comment upon it in any detail, but it would rather seem that in warfare between the territorial principalities, the execution of enemy garrisons taken by force was generally eschewed. Count John's order to behead many of the French king's knights when Evreux fell to the Normans in 1194 is an isolated exception and reflects badly on John's character. The act may well have been an attempt by John to ingratiate himself with the brother against whom he had so recently plotted. But Richard would no doubt have agreed with Rigord that the deed was done shamefully (*turpiter*), not least because John had earlier been entrusted with the city by Philip Augustus to hold against Richard.[99] By contrast, when Henry Plantagenet took Stephen's castle of Crowmarsh in 1153, he executed sixty archers but spared the knights,[100] thereby clearly revealing not only the considerations of class that affected the fate of defeated opponents, but also the hostility with which missile-men were often treated.[101]

---

[96] *Gesta Henrici Quinti*, pp. 34, 36, 48, 154; above, p. 35.   [97] See above, p. 45, n. 77.

[98] *Itinerarium*, p. 231. For the nature of such a *ius* see above, pp. 34–6.

[99] Rigord, p. 127; Powicke, *Loss of Normandy*, p. 101. William le Breton later elaborated this story, having John treacherously slay the French after feasting them, then placing their heads on long poles (WB, I, p. 196).   [100] Torigny, pp. 173–4.   [101] Above, pp. 180–1.

Significantly, it is only in the context of revolt that the right of storm achieves any prominence.[102] In 1088, for example, Rufus initially refused terms to Odo's garrison at Rochester, but swore he would take the castle by force (*virtute potenti*) and hang all inside.[103] Stephen was equally adamant that the blockade of the garrison of Exeter in 1136 should be pushed home 'usque ad mortem'.[104] Though, in both these cases, political expediency and baronial pressure forced the king to relent from enforcing the death penalty, it was not always so. In 1138, King Stephen executed ninety-three of the garrison of Shrewsbury when the castle fell by assault, including the commander, Arnulf of Hesdin.[105] Richard refused to accept the surrender of the defenders of Chaluz Chabrol in 1199 and had all but one hanged when the castle fell to him by storm.[106] In such instances, the king was using his prerogative *qua* besieger to dispose of the lives of a garrison taken by assault to reinforce his ability to punish rebels for treason.[107]

Nevertheless, despite the infrequency of its implementation in external warfare between the territorial principalities, the right of storm was clearly recognized as being the ultimate sanction of the besieger. Had it not been, the usages of conditional respite and surrender would have lost much of their validity and force.

FAINT-HEARTED DEFENCE: COWARDICE OR TREACHERY?

If some garrisons resisted to the last until they were overrun or starved out, there were equally those who contrasted unfavourably with such heroic acts of resistance. In 1136, for example, the garrison of Norham earned general opprobrium for surrendering too quickly to the Scots, for although there were only nine knights, some of whom had been wounded, against a far greater Scottish host, it seemed to contemporaries that, given the strength of the castle and its abundant provisions, resistance should have been far more stubborn.[108] Even when a garrison had decided upon a rapid capitulation, some token show of defence might be deemed necessary to attempt to save face. Hence when, in 1102, Vignats, a castle of Robert de Bellême, was invested by Robert Curthose, the garrison hoped to be vigorously attacked so they could then surrender, having been seen to have put up a defence in the face of a sustained assault.[109]

---

[102] Below, pp. 241–6.   [103] Orderic, IV, pp. 128–9.   [104] *GS*, pp. 42–3.

[105] Orderic, VI, pp. 520–3.   [106] Howden, IV, pp. 82–3.   [107] Below, pp. 242–6.

[108] RH, p. 83. These knights were presumably not alone, but accompanied by serjeants or other retainers.

[109] Orderic, VI, pp. 22–3. Similarly, when the castle of Neufmarché was besieged by Henry II's brother Geoffrey and King Louis in 1152, 'redditum est castellum fraude observantium, quasi esset vi praereptum' (Torigny, p. 165).

Failure to put up an adequate resistance might not only draw down upon the garrison the slur of cowardice but also the charge of treason. In 1174, Jordan notes that William the Lion took Appleby 'very speedily': 'Its constable was an old white-headed Englishman, Gospatric son of Orm, and he gave in and begged for mercy at once'.[110] After the war, however, Gospatric was amerced by Henry II, though it is unclear whether for failure adequately to garrison Appleby, for too peremptory surrender or on suspicion of collusion with the Scots.[111] Similar suspicions surrounded the surrender of Aumâle by its count to Philip of Flanders in 1173 after a token siege, these misgivings being confirmed when he also surrendered his other castles.[112] Such acts might bring lasting opprobrium upon their perpetrators. Gilbert de Vascoeuil's surrender of Gisors in 1193 during Richard's captivity in Germany was regarded as heinous enough to merit inclusion in a Norman custumal, while King John could date a charter of 1203 'in the year in which Count Robert of Séez betrayed us at Alençon'.[113]

To surrender a castle without the lord's permission was a fundamental violation of the feudal bond, and in the custumals of the Latin Kingdom of Jerusalem was explicitly cited as treason.[114] Thus the *Livre au roi*, c. 1200, cites as a crime for which perpetual disherison was the punishment the surrender of a castle or town without the lord's permission,[115] while the thirteenth-century tract of Jean d'Ibelin added that it was manifest treason to surrender a castle or fortress while there was suffcent to eat and drink.[116] Nor were such strictures confined to theoretical codification: several

---

[110] JF, 11. 1459–62. He again repeats that it was unprovisioned in 1. 1458.

[111] *The Great Roll of the Pipe for the Twenty-Second year of the reign of Henry II, AD 1175–1176*, ed. J. H. Round (Pipe Roll Society, London 1904), p. 119. Gospatric had to pay 500 marks and twenty others of the garrison lesser fines. The Pipe Roll fully reveals the inadequacy of the garrison, which was comprised only of domestic officials and civilians (see Strickland, 'Securing the North', p. 182 and n. 32).

[112] WN, p. 173. Howden, (*GH*, 1, p. 47), says that Aumâle fell 'sine aliqua difficultate', while Diceto comments on the shame of the event (Diceto, 1, p. 373).

[113] *Coutumiers de Normandie*, ed. J. Tardif, 1, p. 108, and c. lxiv; *Calendar of Documents*, ed. J. H. Round, 1, p. 131, no. 391; F. M. Powicke, 'Roger of Wendover and the Coggeshall Chronicle', *EHR*, 21 (1906), p. 296; and for the context of this surrender see Powicke, *Loss of Normandy*, p. 158.

[114] These custumals are of particular value since the comparatively recent nature of the state's foundation led to the codification of elements of feudal custom, not the least those concerned with military matters. Similar customs were doubtless in force in the West during the eleventh and twelfth centuries, but because of their gradual evolution never received such precise expression.

[115] The relevant chapter (xvi) of the *Livre au roi* reads: 'La dousime raison si est, que c'il avient que aucun home lige vent ou baille por aucun aver son hostel ou sa vile qu'il teneit, as Sarasins, sans congé de son seignor, si juge la raison qu'il det estre deserités à tousjormais' (*RHC, Lois*, 2 vols. (1841–3), 1, p. 617).

[116] 'Qui rent, sanz le congie de son seignor, sa cité ou son chasteau ou sa forterece à son ennemi tant come il ait à mangier et à boivre tant ne quant' (*ibid.*, pp. 304–5, ch. cxc). For a discussion of notions of treason in the Latin kingdom of Jerusalem, see J. La Monte, *Feudal Monarchy in the Latin Kingdom of Jerusalem* (Massachusetts, 1932, repr. New York, 1970), Appendix E, pp. 276–80.

examples from the kingdom of Jerusalem reveal the implementation of the death penalty for peremptory surrender.[117]

While in Outremer the gravity of such a heinous felony and the reproach it incurred must have been immeasurably compounded when a castle was betrayed to the enemies of Christ, the surrender of a lord's castle without adequate reason might also be viewed and punished as treason within the Anglo-Norman realm. In 1191, during Richard's absence on crusade, the castles of Nottingham and Tickhill, which had been entrusted by William Longchamp when justiciar to the care of Roger de Lacy, constable of Chester, 'in fidelitate regis custodienda', were surrendered to Count John by their respective castellans, Robert de Crocston and Eudo de Daiville. Incensed that his officers had yielded these key strongholds 'inconsulte et sine insulto', Roger ordered their arrest. Despairing of pardon, however, they fled, thereby branding themselves, adds Howden, with the name of traitor for eternity.[118]

Nothing daunted, Roger seized two of their subordinates implicated in the surrenders and hanged them, even though one of them, Peter de Bouencourt, had proclaimed his innocence and had offered to purge himself before both Count John and the chancellor.[119] Here is a striking example of a baron condemning and executing his own men for yielding up castles which ultimately had been entrusted to him on the king's behalf. Roger clearly believed the crime had not only tarnished his own honour but was also a beatrayal of both their lord and the king himself. To drive home his point, Roger proceeded to hang the squire of one of the two condemned men, who had dared to drive off birds from his lord's corpse as it hung on the gallows.[120] Vassalic propriety, above all when it concerned the guarding of a lord's castle, was very close to Roger's heart: thirteen years later it was he who won great honour by the resolute defence of Château Gaillard long after all hope of relief by King John had disappeared.[121]

By the time Château Gaillard had fallen in 1204 and with it any hopes of holding Normandy, John had found out by bitter experience how few men were prepared to engage in such conduct on his behalf. In 1203, Philip Augustus laid siege to the great Norman fortress of Vaudreuil, which, as a

[117] Thus William of Tyre relates how the castellan of the fortified cave of Tyre was caught and hanged after colluding in the surrender of the stronghold, which was considered impregnable, to the Muslim leader Shirkuh. The same year, probably 1166, a similar fortified cave 'beyond Jordan on the borders of Arabia', was surrendered to Shirkuh by the Templars who were garrisoning it, even though King Amaury was hurrying with a strong force to its relief. 'Disconcerted and infuriated at the news, the King caused about twelve of the Templars responsible for the surrender to be hanged from a gallows' (WT, Bk 19, c. 11, p. 879; tr. Babcock and Krey, 11, p. 312).   [118] GH, 11, pp. 232–3.
[119] Ibid.
[120] Ibid., 11, p. 233. Count John's reply was to disseize de Lacy of all he held of him and to devastate his lands (ibid., 11, pp. 233–4).   [121] Above, pp. 212–13.

vital lynch-pin in the duchy's defences,[122] had been entrusted by John to Saher de Quincy and Robert fitz Walter with a great quantity of supplies and equipment.[123] But before Philip could even bring his engines into action, the garrison promptly surrendered without any show of resistance.[124] This shameful capitulation earned the two commanders the contempt and opprobrium of both sides.[125] John nevertheless found it expedient in the unstable political climate prevailing to put it about – however implausibly – that he had ordered the castellans to surrender.[126] In contrast, however, to the aid he afforded others taken captive in his service,[127] there is no evidence that the king contributed to the ransom of fitz Walter or de Quincy.[128]

Philip's response was less ambiguous. Despite the ease with which he had gained so vital a fortress, the French king himself was enraged by the cowardice of de Quincy and fitz Walter. He had them straitly confined in chains at Compiègne, where they were kept 'shamefully', and only released on payment of a huge ransom of 5,000 marks sterling.[129] Doubtless Philip felt the need to punish such token resistance lest it set a dangerous precedent for the conduct of his own castellans, but his action is important in revealing a shared concept of the acceptable degree of vassalic loyalty in defence of a lord's castle.

The cowardly surrender of Vaudreuil, and John's seeming acquiescence to it, was a grave psychological blow to the defenders of the Norman duchy,[130] and similar acts of rapid capitulation were soon to follow. Argentan was surrendered, seemingly without resistance, by its Flemish castellan, Roger de Gouy,[131] while the town and great castle of Falaise, despite being entrusted to Louvrecaire, one of John's most prominent mercenary commanders, capitulated after only a week.[132] Caen offered to surrender before Philip was at its gates, and in a chain reaction of

---

[122] Powicke, *Loss of Normandy*, pp. 105, 162.

[123] Coggeshall, p. 143. Boats were being sent laden with supplies down the Seine to Vaudreuil (*Rot. Pat.*, p. 30, a, b; *Rotuli Normanniae in Turri Lundonensi Asservati Johanne et Henrico Quinto Angliae Regibus*, ed. T. D. Hardy, vol. 1 (London, 1835) pp. 69, 75, 80–2), and John himself was close by (Powicke, *Loss of Normandy*, p. 162).   [124] Coggeshall, pp. 143–4; MP, 11, p. 482.

[125] Coggeshall, pp. 143–4; above, p. 119.

[126] *Rot. Pat.*, 1, p. 31. Powicke, 'Roger of Wendover and the Coggeshall Chronicle', p. 296. Though the precipitous surrender of Vaudreuil may have contributed to John's worsening relations with Robert fitz Walter, John's continuing favour to both men suggests he did not suspect treason (Painter, *King John*, pp. 32–4).   [127] Above, p. 193.

[128] Warren, *King John*, p. 86, n. 2. It is perhaps ironic that William d'Albini, who in 1215 was to lead such a heroic defence of Rochester against John after being deserted by his baronial allies including fitz Walter, helped to raise fitz Walter's ransom in 1203 (Holt, *The Northerners*, p. 64).

[129] Coggeshall, p. 144; MP, 11, p. 482.

[130] Powicke, *Loss of Normandy*, p. 162; Holt, *The Northerners*, p. 152; Warren, *King John*, p. 86.

[131] Powicke, *Loss of Normandy*, p. 257 and n. 33.

[132] WB, *Philippidos*, VII, 11. 9–21, p. 211; Powicke, *Loss of Normandy*, p. 257.

capitulation, Bayeux and other strongholds of the Bessin followed suit.[133] It is notable that those garrisons who offered a sustained resistance, such as Verneuil, Château Gaillard and, further south, Chinon, were led by and largely composed of Englishmen who had little stake in Normandy, whereas treachery among the Norman baronage seems to have been endemic.[134]

Not all mercenaries, however, were as fickle as Louvrecaire had been at Falaise. Gerard d'Athée had put up a stiff resistance at Loches in 1205,[135] while Waleran the German and Fawkes de Bréauté distinguished themselves by their loyal defence of English castles in the face of Louis's invasion in 1216–17.[136] The name of Mercadier, Richard's devoted captain, was a byword for loyalty, while Philip Augustus was well served by his counterpart, Cadoc.[137] Indeed, given that their livelihood ultimately depended on their reliability, mercenaries prided themselves in their loyalty. This is nowhere more sharply revealed than in Orderic's account of the siege of Robert de Bellême's castle of Bridgnorth by Henry I in 1102. The feudal element of the garrison, threatened by the king with hanging unless they surrendered within three days, agreed to yield and sent word of their capitulation to their lord. But, notes Orderic, the mercenary knights (*milites stipendarii*) in the castle

> knew nothing about the peace, which all the feudal garrison (*oppidani*) and the burgesses had made without consulting them, to save their skins. When they heard the unwelcome news they were outraged and, snatching up their arms, tried to put a stop to the peace-making. Therefore, the feudal garrison shut them up by force in a part of the castle, and welcomed the king's troops with the royal standard, amid general rejoicing. The king allowed the mercenary knights to leave freely with their horses and arms, because they had served their master as was right (*ut decuit*). As they rode out through the besieging forces they bewailed their fate, loudly complaining that they had been unfairly let down by the deceit of the garrison and their masters, and called the whole army to witness the tricks of these plotters, so that their downfall might not bring down contempt upon other mercenaries.[138]

Nothing could illustrate more clearly the professional pride of these stipendiary knights, and their great desire both to avoid being personally branded with cowardice and to maintain the good name of their profession.

---

[133] *Ibid.*   [134] *Ibid.*, p. 254 and n. 19; Warren, *King John*, pp. 87–91.   [135] Coggeshall, p. 152.
[136] MP, III, p. 5, 6, 8; Carpenter, *The Minority of Henry III*, pp. 20–21.
[137] Powicke, *Loss of Normandy*, pp. 231–2, and for the *routiers* in general see below, pp. 291ff. Cf. D. Brown, 'The Mercenary and his Master: Military Service and Monetary Reward in the Eleventh and Twelfth Century', *History*, 74 (1989), pp. 20–38.   [138] Orderic, VI, pp. 28–9.

The incident at Bridgnorth equally highlights the dichotomy facing feudal vassals of a lord in rebellion against the king. So strong was the conviction that vassals should put up a resolute resistance in defence of their lord's castle that even when the besieger was the king himself, rebel garrisons might gain the censure of contemporaries for too peremptory a surrender. Thus the author of the *Gesta Stephani*, a firm upholder of royal authority, nevertheless criticized the rebel garrison of Plympton for a feeble resistance and betrayal of their lord, Baldwin de Redvers, during his revolt in 1136.[139] Similarly, the *Histoire de Guillaume le Maréchal* did not hesitate in labelling the garrison of Carrickfergus traitors (*li traitor*) for surrendering their ward to King John in 1210; the castle was strong and had been well provisioned (*fortz et garniz*), yet it had been yielded up 'par menace e par peor'.[140]

Yet set against such a duty was an often profound reluctance to resist the person of the king, the Lord's anointed, to whom many sub-vassals had performed liege homage.[141] To scruples against taking up arms against a consecrated ruler was added the fear of punishment, not simply by imprisonment, mulct or disseisin, but by mutilation and even execution.[142] Such tensions reflected the often uneasy and contradictory relationship between royal power and feudal custom. It is to the effects of the context of rebellion on conventions and conduct in war that we now must turn.

---

[139] *GS*, pp. 34–7, and cf. *ibid.*, pp. 36–7, where the *Gesta* notes that Stephen's men 'at length received the surrender of the castle from the traitors themselves, on the pretext that they were too weak to stand a siege'.   [140] *HGM*, ll. 14276–8.

[141] M. J. Strickland, 'Against the Lord's Anointed: Aspects of Warfare and Baronial Rebellion in England and Normandy, 1075–1265', *Law and Government*, pp. 56–79, esp. p. 57.

[142] Below, pp. 240–7.

9

REBELLION, TREASON AND THE PUNISHMENT OF REVOLT

Hostilities arising from baronial insurrection accounted for a high proportion of the warfare waged in England, Normandy and the other continental lands of the Norman and Angevin kings between 1066 and 1217. In England itself, for example, the king or his representatives were forced to fight major campaigns against discontented factions of the aristocracy or rebellious royal cadets in 1075, 1078–9, 1088, 1095, 1101, 1102, 1155, 1173–4, 1183, 1194 and 1215–17, to list but the more prominent conflicts, while during Stephen's reign a combination of civil war and baronial insurgency demanded constant military action from the king. Normandy was riven with baronial feuding during the reign of Robert Curthose, and even after the restoration of centralized authority from 1106, Henry I found himself preoccupied with the threat of internal revolt in favour of his nephew William Clito. Henry II's tireless military efforts were involved as much with the maintenance of authority in the constituent elements of his empire as with the safeguarding or expansion of his frontiers. Likewise, Richard's rule as count of Poitou and duke of Aquitaine was marked by frequent hostilities against turbulent elements of the baronage such as the Lusignans, the Taillefer lords of Angoulême and Geoffrey de Rancogne.

If the funding of war was the central dynamic behind administrative and governmental developments,[1] then much of this warfare was directed against rebellious vassals, often themselves leagued with the external enemies of the Anglo-Norman *regnum*. Rulers consistently expended enormous sums both on stipendiary troops and on the building and maintenance of fortresses whose *raison d'être* was as a defence as much against internal unrest

---

[1] Prestwich, 'War and Finance in the Anglo-Norman State', pp. 59–83.

as external invasion.[2] The nature of warfare itself could be significantly altered by the context of rebellion. Rulers might proffer battle far more readily against baronial rebels than against the armies of other suzerains in order to exploit the widespread reluctance to bear arms directly against the person of the king or duke.[3] The resulting tendency for rebels to fight a more defensive form of castle-based war led to a still greater emphasis on siege, but such a strategy normally favoured the king who, in addition to controlling numerous royal castles, could command an effective siege train, professional engineers and seasoned mercenary troops.[4] Unless in receipt of substantial aid from external allies, as for example in 1216–17, the forces of baronial rebels were almost always at a financial, logistical and military disadvantage.[5]

Here, however, we can only concern ourselves with one central facet of warfare in the context of rebellion, the treatment of those in arms against the ruler. Did the conventions of surrender, respite and ransom hitherto examined continue to be observed? Or did the need for kings forcefully to suppress and chastise rebellious vassals lead to a partial or total rejection of such customs? How, in short, might rebellion be punished, and what political, military or ethical considerations served to limit the *ira et malevolentia* of the king or duke?

TREASON, REBELLION AND DIVIDED ALLEGIANCE

While certain crimes against the king or lord were unequivocally regarded as *proditio* or treason,[6] the legal status of baronial rebellion has been disputed. Pollock and Maitland believed that until the 1352 Statute of Treason, levying arms against the king or lord did not constitute treason because homage was both contractual and revocable by the defiance or *diffidatio*. Men no longer the lord's homagers could not therefore commit treason.[7]

---

[2] Brown, 'Royal Castle-Building, 1154–1216', pp. 353–98.

[3] These themes are explored more fully in Strickland, 'Against the Lord's Anointed', pp. 56–79.

[4] Painter, *King John*, p. 352; Brown, 'Royal Castle-Building, 1154–1216', pp. 369–74; Prestwich, 'The Military Household of the Norman Kings', pp. 93–127; and Chibnall, 'Mercenaries and the *Familia Regis* under Henry I', pp. 84–92.   [5] Cf. the comments of Painter, *King John*, pp. 349–53.

[6] Such as, for example, privy plotting against the king's life or failing to reveal such a plot, aiding the lord's enemies, 'imagining' or 'compassing' his death by word as much as deed, and default of duty by flight from battle or the surrender of a lord's castles (*Leges Henrici Primi*, 10.1, 12.1a, 13.1, 75.1; *Glanvill*, pp. 3, 171–3; Orderic, II, pp. 320–1, VI, pp. 178–9; SD, I, p. 174).

[7] Pollock and Maitland, *The History of the English Law*, II, p. 505. For the explicit statement that to levy arms against the king was treason see 25 Edward III Statute 5, cap. 2, *Statutes of the Realm (1101–1713)*, ed. A. Luders, T. E. Tomlins, J. Raithby *et al.*, 11 vols. (Record Commission, 1810–28), I, p. 319. In fact, the novelty of the 1352 Statute is deceptive. Among other charges, for example, William Wallace was condemned for 'displaying a banner in mortal war against the king his legitimate lord' – an unequivocal statement that armed rebellion was treason – while Edward I responded to Bruce's rebellion of 1306 with a spate of executions (*Year Book 11–12 Edward III*, ed. and trans. A. J. Horwood and L. O. Pike (Rolls Series, 1883), pp. 170–1; G. W. S. Barrow, *Robert the Bruce* (3rd edn, Edinburgh, 1988), pp. 153–9, 161–2).

Such a view, however, is highly questionable, and John Gillingham has recently argued that rebellion was always treason'.[8] Certainly, if *proditio* might be committed by default of duty which injured the lord, or by plotting (and all rebellions needed to be planned), it is hard to see how bearing arms against him could not but be regarded as a worse form of betrayal. The charges brought against John and his supporters by Richard in March 1194 strongly suggest that resisting the king by force was treason.[9]

Contemporaries, moreover, repeatedly stress that rebellion was a violation of sworn fealty and homage. 'How can I be unfaithful to such a lord', Orderic has Waltheof say of William I in 1075, 'unless I utterly desecrate my faith?' To do so would earn him the label of a *proditor sacrilegus*.[10] The *Leges Henrici* consistently link together 'proditio et infidelitas'.[11] Those who had aided Robert Curthose against Henry I in 1101 were fined, disinherited or banished after being charged 'with the offence of violating their pledged faith in many ways', while the rebels in 1124 were blinded 'pro periurii reatu'.[12] William of Malmesbury recorded that as Henry hurled the rebel Conan from the keep of Rouen in 1090, he averred to his companions that no respite was due to a traitor, and 'that the injuries of a stranger might be endured in some manner or other, but that the punishment of a man who with an oath had done homage, when once convicted of perfidy, should never be deferred'.[13]

That rebellion was regarded as the violation of sworn allegiance is clearly

---

[8] Gillingham, 'The Introduction of Chivalry', p. 47. The scope of this book unfortunately does not permit here a detailed examination of this important issue, but I intend to explore it further in a study of baronial rebellion currently in preparation.

[9] John, 'contrary to the faith which he had sworn him [Richard], had occupied his castles, destroyed his lands on both sides of the sea, and had entered into an alliance with his enemy the king of France'. Similarly, Gerard de Camville was charged with aiding John and other of the king's enemies 'vi et adjutorio' in the seizure of Nottingham and Tickhill. Jolland, brother of Henry de Pomeroy, fled on being appealed for being treasonously (*proditiose*) involved in the capture of St Michael's Mount (Howden, III, pp. 241, 243, 249). Compare the speech Orderic puts into the mouth of Robert, count of Meulan, concerning those magnates who had abandoned Henry I in favour of Robert Curthose in 1101: 'There is no doubt that anyone who chooses to desert his lord in an hour of deadly danger and seek another lord for greed of gain, or insists on payment for the military service that he ought to offer freely to his king for the defence of the realm, and attempts to deprive him of his own demesne will be judged a traitor (*proditor*) by a just and equitable judgement, and will rightly be deprived of his inheritance and forced to flee the country' (Orderic, v, pp. 316–7).

[10] Orderic, II, pp. 314–5, and cf. VI, pp. 94–5. Cf. *The Letters of Lanfranc, Archbishop of Canterbury*, ed. and trans. H. Clover and M. Gibson (Oxford, 1979), no. 32, pp. 120–1, where Lanfranc tells Roger of Hereford that 'It would not be right that a son of Earl William ... should be called faithless (*infidelis*) and be exposed to the slur of perjury or any kind of deceit.' The rebels of 1075 are 'perjurii', and Earl Ralph a 'traditor' (*ibid.*, pp. 124–5).

[11] *Leges Henrici Primi*, 10.1, 12.1a, 13.1. The *Anglo-Saxon Chronicle*, 'E', *s.a.* 1088, remarked that in rebelling against Rufus in 1088, Odo 'thought to treat him just as Judas Iscariot did our Lord'.

[12] Orderic, VI, pp. 12–13, and cf. pp. 178–9, where in opposing Henry I in 1112, Robert de Bellême 'breaking his oath of fealty ... openly committed perjury'; *ibid.*, VI, pp. 352–3, and cf., VI, pp. 276–7.

[13] *GR*, II, p. 469.

revealed in the careful distinction made by kings between those who had violated their homage and fealty and those among their opponents who had not performed homage. When, in 1136, Stephen's barons pleaded with him not to execute Baldwin de Redvers's garrison in Exeter, one of their most cogent arguments was that 'the besieged had not sworn allegiance to the king's majesty (*non in regiam maiestatem iurasse*), and had taken up arms only in fealty to their lord (*nec nisi in fidelitatem domini sui arma movisse*); indeed could not show they were dealing directly with the king except by handing over to him what was his by right'.[14] It was similar considerations that compelled Orderic to justify Henry I's blinding of Luke de La Barre in 1124, for unlike Odard of Le Pin and Geoffrey de Tourville who had violated their faith to him, Luke had not sworn the king homage. As Henry is made to say:

Luke . . . never did homage to me (*homagium michi nunquam fecit*), but he recently fought against me in the castle of Pont Audemer. In the end, when peace had been made, I pardoned his guilt and allowed him to go away freely with his horses and baggage. But he straightaway gave suport to my enemies, united with them to stir up fresh trouble against me and went from bad to worse.[15]

When, in 1216, John accepted the negotiated surrender of a mixed force of baronial rebels and French at Colchester castle, he allowed the French to go free but imprisoned the English contingent straitly in chains.[16] As external enemies who did not owe him homage or fealty, the French were felt by the king to deserve the chivalric gesture of free egress with horses and arms, while the English were to be punished as traitors.[17] If Wendover is to be believed, the strained relations between Louis's forces and the barons had as a principal cause the fact that the French despised the English as traitors to their lord (*ut proditores domini sui*).[18]

Such sentiments weigh heavily against the idea that rebellion might be placed on some form of legal footing by the act of *diffidatio*. Feudal custom, embodied in the *Leges Henrici* and echoed in the Leicester–Chester *conventio*, assumed that nobles in a relationship of homage might legitimately defy one another.[19] But could a man defy a liege lord who was also an anointed king? William of Malmesbury complained that it was 'unfair' (*iniquum*)

[14] GS, pp. 42–3. In 1224, the garrison of Bedford had refused to yield to Henry III on similar grounds, but such a plea did not in this instance prevent their execution (MP, III, pp. 86, 89).
[15] Orderic, VI, pp. 352–5.   [16] Coggeshall, p. 179.
[17] According to Coggeshall, however, the French released by John came close to being hanged by the barons in London, who, angered by the fate of their fellows, accused them of treachery (Coggeshall, pp. 179–80).
[18] MP, II, pp. 666–7; and cf. ibid., III, pp. 21–2, for the similar insult which cost the count of Perche his life at Lincoln.   [19] Leges Henrici Primi, 43.8, 43.9; Stenton, English Feudalism, pp. 287, 251–2.

when Stephen failed to defy Rannulf of Chester before attacking him in 1141.[20] But his very words betray the fact that Stephen felt no obligation so to do. Instances of other Anglo-Norman kings accepting or reciprocating the defiance of vassals are rare indeed. There is no evidence that Henry II, Richard or John ever defied their rebellious vassals, although John was himself defied by the barons in 1215.[21] Furthermore, in each of the seemingly exceptional instances where a sovereign defied rebellious vassals, rather than vice versa, he did so in order to sanction extreme measures against his erstwhile subjects.

By revoking his obligations of lordship, a lord could place his rebellious vassals both outside his protection and outside the law. Thus following John's condemnation by the Capetian king's court in 1202 as a contumacious vassal, Philip Augustus defied John before commencing his invasion of Normandy.[22] In a like manner, he had defied Richard in 1193 while the latter was in captivity in Germany,[23] in order to justify his invasion of his erstwhile vassal's lands. In 1204, Philip was thus using both the condemnation of his court and his renunciation of homage as an excuse to refuse John all further treaties for peace and as a justification for blatant aggression.

Similar motives underlay Henry III's defiance in 1233 of Richard Marshal, the leader of the baronial opposition, before the king marched against his lands and castles on the Welsh border. It was only after being defied by the king that Richard was forced, very unwillingly, to issue a reciprocal defiance.[24] Likewise, just prior to the battle of Lewes, Richard of Cornwall and the Lord Edward defied Simon de Montfort, Gilbert de Clare and the other rebels in the king's name.[25] The mutilation of Simon de Montfort's body and the slaying of many of the rebel lords with him following their subsequent defeat at Evesham showed what the removal of such restraints might mean in practice.[26]

In general, however, both in the situations of revolt within a kingdom, or in war between two rulers where feudal ties were involved, such as between Plantagenet and Capetian, the renunciation of feudal homage was very

---

[20] Above, pp. 40–1.
[21] WC, II, p. 219. John had been defied in 1201 by Ralph, count of Eu, who in so doing presumably did not stand alone among Norman magnates (*Rot. Litt. Pat.*, p. 2a).
[22] For discussion of John's trial see Warren, *King John*, pp. 74–5 and Appendix A, pp. 263–4 for earlier bibliography and historical debate on the issue. The defiance is mentioned by Innocent III in a letter to John (*Selected Letters of Pope Innocent III*, pp. 60–1). Cf. *Recueil des actes de Philippe Auguste*, ed. H. F. Delaborde, Ch. Petit-Dutaillis, J. Boussard, and M. Nortier, 4 vols. (Paris, 1916–1979), II, p. 293.
[23] Howden, III, p. 205.   [24] MP, III, pp. 249, 258.
[25] *Flores Historiarum*, ed. H. Luard, 2 vols. (London, 1890), II, p. 493.
[26] Powicke, *Henry III and the Lord Edward*, p. 502; D. Carpenter, *The Battles of Lewes and Evesham, 1264–65* (University of Keele, 1987), pp. 64–6.

rarely employed. Despite intermittent warfare with the man who was tech-nically his feudal suzerain, Henry II seems never to have defied Louis VII, nor vice versa, and it was only utter exasperation at Philip's repeated and unprovoked aggression that in 1188 goaded Henry to the extreme measure of renouncing his homage.[27] Similary, in situations of revolt, defiance of the king was far from universal, precisely because of the vulnerability which such an action brought upon rebel lords. But if opponents of Rufus, Henry I or Stephen, indeed, believed that the prior performance of homage and fealty to Robert Curthose or Matilda abrogated the need for such a defi-ance, Anglo-Norman kings nonetheless regarded their insurrections as violations of subsequent homage and fealty.[28] These rulers, moreover, were also highly conscious of being heirs to a monarchy which had dealt sum-marily with rebels. At the siege of Rochester in 1088, it was the Anglo-Saxon elements in Rufus's army that urged the king to hang Odo and his garrison on their capitulation.[29]

In certain cases, the convention of the *diffidatio* was used by a vassal faced with the invidious position of having two men who were both his lords being at war with each other. This was the problem which confronted William the Lion in 1173, and one which he attempted to solve by renounc-ing his allegiance to Henry II in favour of the Young King.[30] Earlier, in 1138, the Anglo-Norman lord Robert de Brus, who held lands of both King Stephen and David of Scotland, was forced to decide where his loyal-ties lay when the Scots and English armies confronted one another at Northallerton. Though a close friend of the Scots king,[31] Robert realized his first loyalty and own best interests lay with Stephen. He therefore renounced his homage to David just prior to the battle,[32] in which he and his Anglo-Norman colleagues inflicted a crushing defeat on the Scots. On the same occasion, Bernard de Balliol likewise renounced the fealty he had once been made to swear to David when formerly a captive.[33] The immi-nence of a major engagement had forced both Brus and Baliol to clarify their feudal status before giving battle to the forces of their erstwhile lord.

Defiance, however, was both a drastic measure and one not always applicable to the prevailing political or military circumstances. To seek the

---

[27] Henry had threatened to revoke his homage in 1188 (*GH*, II, p. 46). That he finally did so is revealed by the humiliating terms forced on the dying king by Philip and Richard in July 1189, when Henry 'iterum fecit homagium regi Franciae, quia ipse . . . reddiderat regem Franciae dominum suum' (*ibid.*, II, p. 70).   [28] Cf. Orderic, v, pp. 314–15.   [29] Orderic, IV, pp. 134–5; below, p. 246.

[30] JF, 11. 276–83, 295–9, 334–7.

[31] *Relatio*, pp. 192–5. For a good discussion of the general context of such divided loyalties see J. Green, 'Aristocratic Loyalties on the Northern Frontier of England, c. 1100–1174', in *England in the Twelfth Century. Proceedings of the 1988 Harlaxton Symposium*, ed. D. Williams (Woodbridge, 1990), pp. 83–100.

[32] RH, p. 88; *Relatio*, p. 195; 'vinculum fidei, quo eatenus regi astrictus fuerat, patrio more dissolvens, ad suos non sine magno dolore revertitur'.   [33] RH, p. 88.

suspension of hostilities for a limited period might prove a far more politic and appropriate solution to the problems of divided allegiance. When Rufus invaded Maine in 1098, Ralph de Beaumont, Geoffrey de Mayenne, Rotrou de Montfort and other Manceaux commanders, in a grave dilemma since their lord Count Helias was a prisoner of the Normans, successfully petitioned the king for a truce until they received orders from the regency council.[34] Following Stephen's capture in 1141, Robert, earl of Leicester, negotiated a similar truce with Geoffrey of Anjou on behalf of his brother Waleran, whose absence in England prevented him from defending his lands threatened by the successful Angevin invasion.[35] When confronted in 1204 by the choice of having to swear homage to Philip Augustus or lose their extensive lands in Normandy, both William the Marshal and Robert, earl of Leicester, paid Philip Augustus 500 marks each for a truce of a year in which to see whether King John, their lord, would hold or lose the duchy.[36] Here, as with the closely analogous respites granted in the context of siege, pragmatism combined with the dictates of loyalty and honour to create an important mechanism for both the postponement of actual fighting and the safeguarding of vassalic propriety.

Given its fundamental importance, it is not surprising to find the question of vassalic obligation in situations of conflicting loyalties to the fore in documents such as the indentures between the king of England and the count of Flanders, and the *conventiones* of Stephen's reign. Thus in the two agreements between Henry I and Robert of Flanders, by which the king hired first 1,000 then 500 Flemish knights, it was stipulated that if the king of France wished to invade England, then Count Robert was to do all in his power by counsel and by entreaty to dissuade him, provided it was in good faith and did not involve the payment of money. If, however, the king should invade, 'and he shall bring Count Robert with him, Count Robert shall bring with him so small a force of men as he shall be able, so that, however, he shall not forfeit his fief thereby on account of the king of France'. Robert was thus to provide his feudal service, thereby fulfilling the military obligation which technically justified the holding of his fiefs from the king of France, but no more forces in addition. In such an instance, moreover, the count was still to send Henry the force of knights agreed by the indentures within the forty days between being summoned to the king of France's host and the actual muster. If the French king was to attack Henry in Normandy, the count was only to furnish his Capetian overlord

---

[34] Orderic, v, pp. 240–1; and cf. above, p. 123.
[35] Orderic, vi, pp. 546–50; Crouch, 'A Norman "conventio"', p. 304.   [36] *HGM*, 11. 12863–98.

with a token force of knights – twenty in the 1101 treaty, ten in that of 1110.[37]

Similarly, the Leicester–Chester *conventio* asserts the right strictly to limit the support each earl should give his liege lord to twenty knights in the event of the two earls being forced to fight against each other by rival claimants to the throne. 'And', continues one of the reciprocal clauses,

> if the earl of Leicester or those twenty knights shall take anything of the goods of the earl of Chester, he will return the whole. Neither the earl of Leicester's liege lord nor any other may attack the earl of Chester or his men from the earl of Leicester's castles or his land.[38]

Such an explicit circumscription of the power of the liege lord in war is remarkable, limiting his base of operations and strictly capping the extent of military aid on which he might draw. Twenty knights was obviously considered too small a force to alter the military balance significantly. We learn from William of Malmesbury that a similar arrangement was entered into with the Empress by Henry of Blois, bishop of Winchester and papal legate, following his brother Stephen's capture at Lincoln in 1141. During the Council of Winchester that same year,

> there was one layman, an envoy from the Empress, who publicly forbade the legate, by the pledge he had given to the Empress, to make any decision in that council to the prejudice of her position, saying he had given her this pledge, not to aid his brother in any way, unless perchance he sent him twenty knights and no more.[39]

This division of service was seen as a means of technically fulfilling conflicting obligations. Yet what is striking is that in the indentures with the count of Flanders, the Leicester–Chester *conventio* and Henry of Blois's agreement with the Empress, it is the interests of the liege lord, who had prior claim on a vassal's loyalty, which were marginalized and subordinated to those of the contracting parties. Thus the knight service quotas owed to the king by the honours of Chester, Leicester and the great bishopric of Winchester were greatly in excess of twenty knights.[40] It is all the more remarkable, therefore, to find such arrangements endorsed by 'Glanvill':

---

[37] *Diplomatic Documents*, I, pp. 1–3, 5–7.   [38] Stenton, *English Feudalism*, pp. 286–7, 251.

[39] *HN*, p. 63.

[40] No *carta* is recorded for the honour of Leicester in the returns of 1166 and other evidence is surprisingly scarce for such a great earldom, but quotas for comparible baronies strongly suggest it comprised c. 125 knights fees (Crouch, *The Beaumont Twins*, p. 102; cf. Round, 'King Stephen and the Earl of Chester', pp. 253–4; I. J. Sanders, *English Baronies* (Oxford, 1960), p. 61, n. 2). The returns for 1210 x 1212, which list only the Montfort share of the earldom when it was split in two on the death of Robert IV, alone lists over eighty knights fees (Crouch, *The Beaumont Twins*, p. 102; *Red Book of the Exchequer*, ed. H. Hall, 3 vols. (Rolls Series, 1896), II, pp. 552–3). For Rannulf of Chester's landed

The general rule is that he may not, without breach of the faith of homage, do anything which works to the disinheritance or bodily dishonour of his lord. If anyone has done several homages for different fees to different lords who are attacking each other, and his liege lord (*capitalis dominus*) commands him to go personally with him against another of his lords, he must obey his command in this matter, but saving to that other lord the service for the fee which he holds of him.[41]

Marjorie Chibnall has suggested that 'Glanvill's' ruling may have been directly influenced by cases arising during the turmoil of Stephen's reign.[42] Certainly, outside this anomalous context, it is hard to envisage monarchs like Henry I or Henry II tolerating such a division of loyalty which so blatantly compromised their interests. Only his position as a powerful territorial prince allowed the count of Flanders the prerogative of limiting service to his Capetian overlord in contracts with the kings of England with relative impunity.

A more realistic gauge of Angevin feelings is provided by John's reaction to the compromise reached by William Marshal with Philip Augustus in 1205 in order to maintain his cross-Channel estates. On learning that William had sworn 'liege homage on this [the French] side of the sea (*hominagium ligantium citra mare*)' to King Philip, John bitterly accused him of treason. The quarrel was exacerbated the following year when William refused to follow John to Poitou on account of his oath to Philip, and John demanded the Marshal's eldest son as a hostage.[43] It would seem that, deprived of an effective royal arbiter for much of Stephen's reign, the baronage had resorted to expedients more germane to an earlier period of political centrifugality in France, but ones which could scarcely outlive the restoration of effective power by Henry Plantagenet.

One instance from Stephen's reign itself, which created numerous problems of divided allegiance, serves to indicate that honorial lords might share such an insistence on uncompromised loyalty. Following Earl Henry of Scotland's forfeiture of the honour of Huntingdon in 1138, David Olifard, who had held the fief of Sawtry and was David I's godson, now

---

wealth, amounting perhaps to some 198 fees, see Cronne, 'Ranulf de Gernons', pp. 103 ff., 174–6, and *idem.*, *The Reign of King Stephen*, pp. 174–6; White, 'King Stephen, Duke Henry and Ranulf de Gernons', pp. 555–65; Sanders, *English Baronies*, p. 32, n. 2. The quota owed from Winchester was sixty knights (J. H. Round, *Feudal England* (London, 1909), p. 249).

[41] *Glanvill*, IX:1, p. 104. Bracton similarly admits that a man who holds land in England and France may be bound to aid both kings if they wage war against one another, serving his liege lord in person and sending his service due to the other (Bracton, *On the Laws and Customs of England*, ed. and tr. S. E. Thorne and G. Woodbine, 4 vols., (Cambridge, Mass., 1968–77), IV, p. 329).

[42] M. Chibnall, *Anglo-Norman England, 1066–1166* (Oxford, 1986), p. 98.

[43] *Layettes du Trésor des Chartes*, ed. M. A. Teulet and M. J. De Laborde, 3 vols. (Paris, 1863–75), I, no. 1397; *HGM*, ll. 12875–900, 12944–13256; Painter, *William Marshal*, pp. 139–42.

found himself in the service of the new earl, Simon de Senlis II, who was a firm supporter of Stephen. In 1141, Olifard accompanied Earl Simon in the attack on the Empress's forces at Winchester, which included King David and his retinue. During the rout of the Angevins, however, Olifard changed sides, covering David I's escape and saving him from capture.[44] Simon confiscated David Olifard's fief of Sawtry and, by founding upon it a Cistercian house for monks from Warden abbey, ensured that this part of his honour remained inalienable and in friendly, or at least neutral, hands.[45]

In certain instances, however, lords might recognize the dilemma of divided loyalty in war caused by ties of multiple vassalage, and mitigate their behaviour accordingly. During the battle of Mortemer in 1054, for example, one of Duke William's leading commanders, Roger de Mortemer, allowed the escape of Count Ralph of Montdidier 'on account of the fealty he had formerly sworn to him'. Orderic puts the following comment in the mouth of William:

> So, in his lord's hour of need, he performed a just and seemly service by protecting him in his own castle [of Mortemer] for three days and then escorting him back to his lands. I banished Roger from Normandy for this offence, but became reconciled with him soon afterwards and restored the rest of his honour to him. I withheld from him, however, the castle of Mortemer in which he had preserved my enemy, acting – I believe – rightly; and gave it to his kinsman, William of Warenne, a loyal knight.[46]

Whether such sentiments were a valid reflection of those of the duke or merely Orderic's own opinion, Roger had clearly chosen to risk the wrath of one lord to satisfy his vassalic obligation to another, even in a situation where lord and man were opposed in battle. In 1208, William the Marshal used the letter of feudal propriety to protect the fugitive William de Braose in Ireland, by claiming that he had merely been giving refuge to his lord and had no knowledge of the king's anger against Braose. Though John proceeded to destroy Braose, no further action was taken against the Marshal, who was careful to obey John's summons to the host mustered for an expedition to Ireland in 1210.[47]

If, following Mortemer, Duke William had blended a recognition of divided loyalty with a degree of condign punishment, other rulers could react to the question of divided vassalic loyalty by more magnanimous gestures. Following his signal yet unbloody victory over Louis VI at Brémule in

---

[44] JH, p. 138.
[45] K. Stringer, 'A Cistercian Achive: The earliest Charters of Sawtry Abbey', *Journal of the Society of Archivists*, 6 (1980), pp. 325–34, at pp. 327–8. David Olifard retired to Scotland, where he was subsequently handsomely endowed with the lordship of Bothwell and holdings in Lothian and Roxburghshire (*ibid.*, pp. 329–30).   [46] Orderic, IV, pp. 88–9.   [47] Painter, *King John*, pp. 245–7.

1119, Henry I 'freely pardoned Burchard and Hervey de Gisors and some others because they were vassals of both kings, released them from imprisonment, and allowed them to depart'.[48] Similarly, the Anonymous of Bethune recounts how at Bouvines, 1214, the Flemish lord Arnoul of Audenarde was taken by the French, but Philip Augustus directly turned him over to the count of Soissons whose cousin he was and to Roger of Rassoi whose daughter he had wed. The Anonymous explains the reason:

> In the evening, the Duke of Burgundy mentioned this and said to the King: 'You have the right to ransom him because if it were not for him you would have 200 more knights in your prisons.' And the King answered the duke, 'Duke of Burgundy, I am well aware of this! But he never did like war and he always advised his lord against it; he had never wanted to do homage to the king of England when the others did so; if he has done me wrong in order loyally to serve his lord, I hold no ill will toward him on that account.' Thus the King did honour to Arnoul of Audenarde.[49]

Such princely *franchise*, made in the full flush of victory, epitomized both good lordship and the chivalric ideal. Nevertheless, while in these instances recognition of divided loyalties might mitigate royal *ira et malevolentia*, the deeply held conviction that rebellion was a heinous felony ensured that kings sought to inflict more severe chastisement upon on the majority of their rebellious vassals.

THE PUNISHMENT OF REBELLION

How then was rebellion punished? Mulct, disseisin, banishment and imprisonment were the most common and politically expedient means by which Anglo-Norman rulers brought recalcitrant nobles to heel.[50] Though as Roger of Hereford, Robert de Mowbray and Robert de Bellême discovered, imprisonment for rebellion was often for life,[51] the great merit of such mechanisms was their flexibility. Banishment might be revoked, prisoners released, and the hope of partial or complete restoration of lands skilfully manipulated as an instrument of political control.[52]

---

[48] Orderic, VI, pp. 240–3.   [49] RHF, XXIV, pp. 769–70; tr. in Duby, *The Legend of Bouvines*, p. 196–7.

[50] Cf. C. W. Hollister, *Monarchy, Magnates and Institutions in the Anglo-Norman World* (London, 1986), pp. 102–8, 117–27.

[51] Orderic, II, pp. 318–19 (Roger of Hereford); *ibid.*, IV, 282–3 (Mowbray); FW, II, p. 66: HH, p. 238; *ASC*, 'E', *s.a.* 1112; Orderic, VI, 178–9 (Bellême). Similarly, following Tinchebrai in 1106, Henry I condemned William of Mortain, Robert de Stuteville and others to perpetual imprisonment, and refused all pleas for their release (*ibid.*, VI, 94–5). Cf. the honourable captivity for life of Robert Curthose at Corfe, Devizes, then Cardiff (VI, pp. 98–9, and p. 98, n. 2).

[52] Hollister, *Monarchy, Magnates and Institutions*, pp. 117–27, 134–6, 181–2, 176–7; J. C. Holt, 'Politics and Property in Early Medieval England', *Past and Present*, 67 (1972), pp. 31–2.

Rulers nevertheless consistently claimed the right to execute or mutilate rebels. Orderic, for example, noted that Henry I was justified in punishing the rebel nobles of 1124 'by death or mutilation' (*nece seu privatione membrorum*), though he only resorted to the latter option,[53] and the recurrent formula of granting of 'life and limb' to vanquished garrisons in situations of revolt stressed the king's ultimate power to deprive insurgents of both.[54]

Such power was at times exercised. Those defeated by William I's commanders at the battle of 'Fagaduna' in 1075 were condemned, irrespective of rank, each to lose his right foot. Others were blinded.[55] On the fall of Robert de Bellême's castle of Saint-Céneri to Robert Curthose in 1088, the castellan was blinded on the spot and many who 'had contumaciously resisted' were subsequently mutilated by sentence of the duke's court.[56] Here, at least, punishment was the result of a judicial sentence, not simply a besieger's right of storm. To intimidate the remaining defenders of Rochester in 1215, John had many of those expelled by the rebel garrison in order to conserve their supplies mutilated by the loss of hands of feet.[57]

The majority of victims in such instances were probably non-noble. But as the blinding and castration of William of Eu in 1096 revealed, mutilation was a fate that could befall even the greatest lords.[58] Robert de Bellême's garrison at Arundel only surrendered to Henry I in 1102 'with this remarkable condition; that its lord, with safety of limb (*integra membrorum*), should be suffered to retire to Normandy'.[59] Even though Bellême was not present in the castle, Robert's men clearly believed it lay within both Henry's power and volition to mutilate, if not execute, their lord. They were not prepared to yield without securing a guarantee – which was honoured – concerning his safety.[60] Not that Henry eschewed such methods. Though in 1124 the most important insurgents were only imprisoned, he had Geoffrey de Tourville, Odard of Le Pin and Luke de La Barre blinded.[61]

Execution was uncommon, though more so than many kings might have wished. Of nobles executed following formal trial in the *curia regis* and not on campaign, the case of William of Eu's steward, William de Alderie, stands in virtual isolation. In 1096, he was hanged and others 'taken to London and there destroyed', a fate which may well have been connected to

---

[53] Orderic, VI, pp. 352–3; cf. WP, pp. 18–20.
[54] *The Letters of Lanfranc*, no. 35, pp. 124–5; WN, p. 176; *GH*, I, p. 73; Howden, III, p. 237; *Documents of the Baronial Movement*, pp. 320–1, and cf., p. 334, n. 47.   [55] Orderic, II, pp. 316–17; *ASC*, 'D', s.a. 1075.
[56] Orderic, IV, pp. 154–5.   [57] WC, II, p. 227.
[58] William was mutilated following his defeat by Geoffrey Baynard, having been 'publicly found guilty of treason' (*ASC*, 'E', s.a. 1096; Orderic, IV, pp. 284–5).   [59] *GR*, II, p. 472.
[60] Orderic, VI, pp. 30–1.   [61] *Ibid.*, VI, pp. 352–5.

the fact that the 1095 rebellion had involved a plot on Rufus's life.[62] The explicit statement of both Malmesbury and Orderic that Henry refused to spare Conan, ringleader of the rebel citizens of Rouen in 1090, because he was a traitor, and the fact that his body was dragged through the streets of Rouen tied to a horse's tail, weigh heavily against Jean Foyer's view that his precipitation by Henry from Rouen keep was an act of war, not a judicial sentence for treason.[63] There are, moreover, no parallels for precipitation nor the degradation of corpses in external warfare in England or France.[64] While Conan may well have owed his fate to his non-noble status, it should be noted that of the twenty-eight or so men precipitated from the keep at Bruges following their implicated in the murder of Charles the Good in 1127, several were knights.[65] The close analogy between these executions has led to the suggestion that precipitation was a Norman punishment, and that its employment at Bruges owed much to the presence of the new count, the Norman William Clito.[66]

In the majority of cases, however, the act of coming to the king's court and pleading guilt appears to have circumvented death or mutilation.[67] Significantly, almost all executions within the Anglo-Norman *regnum* occur in situations of actual warfare between a suzerain and rebel forces. Stephen hanged Arnulf of Hesdin and ninety-three others of the garrison following the capture of Shrewsbury castle in 1138.[68] Earlier, at the start of his reign, Stephen had hanged one of Henry I's former 'janitors', who was waging private warfare against his neighbours, and executed and imprisoned some of his men.[69] It was only with the greatest difficulty that baronial pressure prevented William Rufus from hanging the rebel garrison of Rochester in 1088, and Stephen from executing the defenders of Exeter in 1136.[70] John was moved to spare William d'Albini and the garrison of

____

[62] *ASC*, 'E', *s.a.* 1096; Orderic, IV, pp. 280–1. Certainly the *Anglo-Saxon Chronicle* directly equated the mutilation or execution of many of the Bretons following the 1075 revolt with their attendance at the marriage feast of Ralph de Gael and Earl Roger of Hereford's daughter, where the plot had been hatched (*ASC*, 'E', *s.a.* 1075).

[63] *GR*, II, p. 469; Orderic, IV, pp. 224–7; J. le Foyer, *Exposé du droit pénal normand au XIIIe siècle* (Paris, 1931), pp. 114, 231.

[64] The same is not true, however, for conduct between Franks and Muslims in Outremer. Richard's men, for example, threw about sixty of the Turkish defenders of Darum from the walls on taking the fortress by storm in 1192 (Ambroise, II. 9327–8; *Itinerarium*, p. 355). The mutilation of corpses by both sides was a commonplace.   [65] Galbert of Bruges, pp. 250–2.   [66] *Ibid.*, p. 47.

[67] See, for example, the case of Roger of Hereford; Orderic, II, pp. 318–19; *The Letters of Lanfranc*, nos, 32, 33, pp. 120–3.

[68] Orderic, VI, pp. 520–3. Of the varying accounts of the executions, Orderic is the most detailed and Chibnall believes his figures in all probability to be accurate (*ibid.*, p. 522, n. 2). Huntingdon says only 'some' were hanged (HH, p. 261), John of Worcester that 'five of the more noble men' went to the gallows (JW, p. 51).

[69] *GS*, pp. 8–9. R. H. C. Davis suggests Osbert 'hostiarius', John 'hostiarius', or Geoffrey Purcell as possible identifications for this man (*ibid.*, p. 7, n. 2).   [70] Orderic, IV, pp. 128–9; *GS*, pp. 40–3.

12 The execution of the garrison of Bedford, 1224, from Matthew Paris's *Chronica majora*. The royal banner flies triumphantly from the keep whilst that of Fawkes de Bréauté is placed over the gallows from which his men swing. Though rarely implemented even in situations of rebellion, the death penalty remained the ultimate sanction of a victorious besieger (Corpus Christi College, Cambridge, MS 16, f. 60r).

Rochester from hanging in 1215, but a more secure position allowed Henry III to execute William de Bréauté and the garrison of Bedford to a man when the castle fell in 1224.[71] In all these instances, the defenders had been taken by force, rather than surrendering on terms, suggesting that the king or duke might reinforce his *de jure* power to inflict the death sentence on rebels by invoking a successful besieger's right of storm. By summary execution in the field, the king, desirous of making an example, may have been trying to circumvent a more formal judicial process that would militate against the death penalty.

It is true that death threats were frequently uttered by besiegers against

[71] MP, II, p. 626.

garrisons of an opposing suzerain, where a breach of homage and fealty had not occurred. Thus William the Lion threatened to hang Robert de Vaux during both his abortive attempts to take Carlisle in 1173 and 1174, while Prince Louis had recourse to such intimidation during his fruitless siege of Dover in 1217.[72] When in 1209 King John could not take the castle of Roche-au-Moine by force, he set up gallows outside the walls to frighten its defenders.[73] On a larger scale, Philip Augustus sent to each city and castle in Normandy in 1203, offering the choice between accepting his lordship, or being hanged or flayed alive should they be captured resisting him.[74]

Yet in external warfare, such threats were often no more than the last gambit of a desperate besieger, resorting to psychological warfare when confronted with impregnable defences. They were rarely if ever implemented. Once the tactical objective of gaining a castle had been achieved, there was little to gain by punitive action save to create dangerous precedents. Indeed, the very efficacy of such intimidation rested on the garrison's knowledge that if they complied with the terms offered as an alternative to death, they would on surrender be assured of safety of life and limb. Despite his prolonged and fierce resistance, William the Lion actually granted Robert de Vaux respite to seek relief during the second siege in 1174, an agreement which must almost certainly have guaranteed life and limb to Robert and his men should they be forced to surrender.[75] For all Philip's threats against the Norman garrisons in 1203, those which held out were not so punished, but were often honourably treated in recognition of their loyal defence.[76] Similarly, though Louis never took Dover, it seems most unlikely that he would have stained his honour by executing Hubert de Burgh and his men for so brave a resistance. Indeed, he too granted respites to Hubert and his fellow commander Gerard de Sotegni to seek relief from King John, while he treated all other English garrisons that capitulated to him with magnanimity.[77] Even during Stephen's reign, in which the tenor of warfare was marked by a frequent

---

[72] JF, 11. 613–20, 1359–1366; MP, II, p. 664; *ibid.*, III, pp. 3–4.

[73] *Chroniques des comtes d'Anjou*, p. 253; WB, *Gesta*, p. 262.   [74] MP, II, p. 483.

[75] *GH*, I, p. 65; cf. above, pp. 210, 220.

[76] Hence, for example, Roger de Lacy was honourably treated after his valiant defence of Château Gaillard, being kept in open custody (above, pp. 218–19). Both Hubert de Burgh and Gerard d'Athée lived to serve John again after Philip had taken their respective castles of Chinon and Loches after prolonged resistance (Coggeshall, pp. 152, 154–5). Their treatment should be compared to Philip's harsh treatment of Renaud of Boulogne following the battle of Bouvines (WB, *Gesta*, pp. 292–3).

[77] *Histoire des ducs*, p. 180; Coggeshall, p. 182; WC, II, p. 232. For the respite granted to Hubert see above, pp. 213–14, and for his treatment of the garrisons of Hertford and Berkhamstead, above, p. 219.

reversion to death threats against captured castellans to secure the surrender of their castles, actual execution was most uncommon.[78]

By contrast, in situations of rebellion defenders could be far less certain of clemency. Sufficient precedents of mutilation or execution existed to convince rebel garrisons that the king was quite capable of implementing such threats. Rulers were swift to exploit both this fear and the deep-seated reluctance that many felt in resisting their liege lord and still more an anointed king.[79] In 1101, for example, Henry I swore to hang the defenders of Robert de Bellême's castle of Bridgnorth unless they surrendered within three days.[80] Stephen similarly gained the surrender of one of Earl Gilbert de Clare's castles in 1147 'by constraint and intimidation of the garrison'.[81] Examples might be made 'pour encourager les autres' and to speed surrender. William the Conqueror blinded a hostage before the walls of Exeter in 1068, while at Rochester in 1215, John mutilated those expelled by the garrison to conserve supplies.[82] In 1136, Stephen's men captured one of the garrison of Robert of Bampton's castle and 'hanged him on high in the sight of all his comrades, the king saying that all should be punished by a similar death if they did not speedily submit to his command'.[83] Similarly, Richard hanged some of the sergeants who had been captured outside Nottingham castle, which held out for John in 1194.[84] Nevertheless, in all these cases, the inherent assumption was that instant capitulation would save the defenders from a similar fate.

It was imperative, however, that a garrison which felt itself incapable of further resistance should agree surrender terms with the king before he succeeded in taking them by force. It was with this fear in mind that, in 1173, the garrison of Dol, who had resisted Henry II's Brabançons, capitulated once the king had arrived in person and set up his siege engines.[85] In a letter to England reporting his successes in Poitou in 1214, King John noted how he had laid siege to Geoffrey de Lusignan's castle at Vouvant

> in which he himself and two of his sons had shut themselves, and when, after a continual battering for three days from our engines the opportunity for assault was approaching, the count of La Marche came up and induced Geoffrey to put himself at our mercy, together with his two sons, his castle and everything in it.[86]

Both Hugh and Geoffrey clearly feared that once in a position to press home a successful assault, John might not show any mercy but execute or

---

[78] Above, pp. 198–9.   [79] Cf. Strickland, 'Against the Lord's Anointed', pp. 62–6, 69–71.
[80] Orderic, VI, pp. 26–7.   [81] GS, pp. 202–3. The castle was probably Tonbridge (ibid., p. 202, n. 2).
[82] WC, II, p. 227.   [83] GS, pp. 30–1.   [84] Howden, III, p. 239.   [85] GH, I, p. 57.
[86] MP, II, p. 573.

mutilate the garrison as would be his right as a victorious besieger. In such circumstances, the besieged were clearly not in a position to bargain. In 1194, Richard refused the surrender of Tickhill unless the garrison placed themselves in his mercy 'without any exception'. The defenders of Nottingham likewise put themselves in mercy for life, limb and possessions.[87] At Rochester in 1088, it was Odo's presumption in demanding very favourable terms, despite the fact that his garrison was beset by starvation and disease, that led the infuriated William Rufus wholly to refuse the rebels' surrender. The king 'would not yield an inch to the requests of the intermediaries, but swore that the perjured traitors (*perfidos traditores*) in the town must be captured by force (*virtute potenti*) and instantly hung on gibbets, or by some other form of execution utterly removed from the face of the earth'.[88]

In the event, however, Odo and his men secured their release. The execution or mutilation of a rebel garrison, even when carried by force, was anything but automatic,[89] and actual refusal to accept surrender was a most extreme measure. Few shared the fate of the garrison of Chaluz-Chabrol, whose entreaties to surrender to Richard I in 1199 were spurned by him. After taking the castle by storm, the king hanged all inside, save for the crossbowman who had given him his death wound.[90] By strictly applying the right of storm, the king was forcing rebels to resist as their only option, so that they would meet death either by fighting or by execution when taken. Uncommon even in situations of revolt, such implacable treatment of an enemy garrison was almost wholly absent in warfare between the teritorial principalities.[91] The execution of rebel garrisons such as those of Shrewsbury or Bedford cannot therefore have simply been in accordance with the customs of war. Rather, their fate reflected the king's insistence that in certain circumstances, rebellion could be punished by death. Nevertheless, it is perhaps unwise to draw too sharp or legalistic a distinction in such circumstances between the king's powers *qua* suzerain and those *qua* besieger. Execution was but an extreme expression of *vis et voluntas*. And in reality, the fate of a rebel garrison depended less on

---

[87] Howden, III, pp. 238, 240.   [88] Orderic, IV, pp. 128–9.
[89] Thus, for example, the defenders of Tonbridge and Pevensey, taken by storm in 1088, appear not to have been harmed, nor seemingly were the garrisons of Mowbray's castles of Newcastle and Morpeth stormed in 1095 (*ASC*, 'E', *s.a.* 1088, 1095). John's own letters close make no mention of execution or mutilation following his successful storming of Geoffrey de Lusignan's castle of Mervant in 1214 (*MP*, II, p. 573).   [90] Howden, IV, pp. 82–3.
[91] Significantly, however, Richard could deal this harshly with Muslim opponents, refusing offers of surrender on terms to the Turkish defenders at Acre in 1191 and at Darum, 1192. In carrying the defenders by force, he thereby ensured full rights over their lives and property, unqualified by any conditional surrender (*Itinerarium*, pp. 228–30; Ambroise, p. 213, n. 33, p. 217, n. 36, and p. 226 n. 47, collects the divergent accounts of the surrender terms of Acre. For Darum, Ambroise, 11.9267–86).

the king's personal volition than the strength of his position in regard to his nobles.

CLEMENCY OR EXPEDIENCY? THE LIMITATIONS OF ROYAL ACTION

In the suppression of rebellion, a ruler's actions were frequently circumscribed by a number of potent factors. Extensive ties of kinship between the Anglo-Norman nobility meant that there was frequently a strong pressure group within the king's own supporters urging clemency for defeated friends or relatives, as at Rochester in 1088 and Exeter in 1136.[92] In situations of civil war, moreover, many of the king's erstwhile supporters might harbour sympathies for his opponents. Describing Henry I's campaigns of 1118 against those Norman rebels who were in support of his nephew William Clito, Orderic noted:

> At that time King Henry could not support a long siege, because in the general confusion that always occurs in conflicts between kinsmen he was unable to trust his own men. Men who ate with him favoured the cause of his nephew, and, by prying into his secrets, greatly helped these men.[93]

The protracted nature of siege offered a perfect and recurrent opportunity for such collusion. Simeon of Durham believed that at the siege of Pont Audemer in 1123, Henry I feared the treachery of his own men more than the strength of rebel forces.[94] During Rufus's siege of Rochester in 1088, Roger de Montgomery and many others 'dared not raise arms openly against the king' but had secretly aided Odo as far as they could.[95] There were again fifth-column elements among Rufus's forces during his suppression of Robert de Mowbray's revolt in 1095. But unlike in 1088, the king's more powerful position left them helpless to assist their beleaguered allies in Bamburgh castle.[96]

Baronial pressure on the king to act with leniency was motivated not simply by dictates of kinship. The execution of members of the nobility for rebellion set a dangerous precedent in a political society in which the recourse to armed opposition was the primary and near-automatic method of expressing grievances against the suzerain. When in 1102 Henry I had brought Robert de Bellême to bay at Bridgnorth, Orderic has the magnates

[92] Orderic, IV, pp. 128–33; GS, pp. 41–3. Similarly, in the quarrels between Robert Curthose and his father, magnates such as Roger de Montgomery, Hugh of Chester, Hugh de Gournay, Roger de Beaumont and Hugh de Grandmesnil found sons or cadet members of their families leagued with Robert, and were consequently in the forefront to obtain peace and the king's clemency toward these hothead *juvenes* (Orderic, III, pp. 110–13)   [93] *Ibid.*, VI, pp. 200–1.
[94] SD, II, p. 274; cf. Orderic, VI, pp. 340–1.   [95] Orderic, IV, pp. 126–9.   [96] *Ibid.*, IV, pp. 282–3.

urge restraint, fearing that if the king broke so mighty a lord, they too would be trodden underfoot by royal power.[97] Over-severity, moreover, ran the risk of escalating violence and upsetting those conventions of surrender, capture and ransom that might otherwise considerably reduce the physical danger to members of the aristocracy. Even in the context of rebellion, warfare in the later eleventh and twelfth centuries was still far removed from the bloody proscriptions and slaughters following defeats in the English civil wars of the fifteenth century. The butchery of Simon de Montfort and his supporters at Evesham in 1265 had been unprecedented since Hastings, and was to mark the inception of a significant escalation in the severity with which rebels were punished. Prior to this, however, kings who in the heat of the moment attempted to override the boundaries of restraint were quickly reminded of such limitations by men acutely conscious of an aristocratic community of interest. Thus Wendover has Savaric de Mauleon urge John not to hang William d'Albini and the rebel garrison of Rochester in 1215;

> My lord king, our war is not yet over. Therefore you ought carefully to consider how the fortunes of war may turn; for if you now order us to hang these men, the barons, our enemies (*barones adversarii nostri*) will perhaps by a like event take me or other nobles of your army, and following your example, hang us; therefore do not let this happen, for in such a case no one will fight in your cause.[98]

Such were powerful sentiments, equally if not more forceful in warfare between rulers, where a punitive dimension was generally considered inappropriate.[99] Suzerains, however, while no doubt acutely aware of these considerations, had their own pragmatic reasons for leniency; restraint eased the suppression of rebellion.

Most rulers operated on the principle that the innate reluctance to take up arms against the king or duke was exploited far better by clemency than by brutality. A judicious balance had to be struck between calculated severity and magnanimity, lest mercy was mistaken for weakness. In putting down the habitual spate of lawlessness and localized insurrection that accompanied a change of ruler, initial ruthlessness was imperative. While Rufus in 1088 and Henry I in 1100–2 were careful not to alienate support by

---

[97] *Ibid.*, VI, pp. 26–33.   [98] MP, II, p. 626.

[99] These very arguments were put by Sir Walter Manny to Edward III when pleading for the lives of the citizens of Calais in 1337 (Froissart, *Chronicles*, ed. and tr. G. Brereton (Harmondsworth, 1968), p. 106): "'My lord, you may well be mistaken, and you are setting a bad example for us. Suppose one day you send us to defend one of your fortresses, we should go less cheerfully if you have these people put to death, for then they would do the same to us if they had the chance." This argument did much to soften the King's heart, especially when most of his barons supported it.'

execution or mutilation, they were swift to disseize and banish opponents. By contrast, Stephen's magnanimity at Exeter may have set a dangerous precedent. His execution of the garrison of Shrewsbury in 1138 was 'because unruly men regarded his gentleness with contempt and many great lords scorned to come to his court when summoned'.[100]

Terror had its place, and the fate of one garrison might quickly induce the surrender of others. Thus in 1051, following the mutilation of the garrison of the castle at Alençon by Duke William, the townsfolk 'dismayed at such severity, fearful lest similar penalties should be inflicted upon them, threw open their gates and surrendered the town to him'.[101] The great fortress of Domfront which he was currently investing also capitulated immediately. As part of his campaign to conquer the duchy of Normandy, Henry I burnt Bayeux in 1105 as a deliberate and successful act of intimidation. 'When the other castellans heard of the destruction of this great city', noted Orderic, 'they were thoroughly alarmed and dared not put up much resistance to the king'. The men of Caen, 'hearing of the massacre of those of Bayeux and fearing they might suffer a similar fate', surrendered at once and 'made peace with him on his own terms'.[102] At Bridgnorth in 1102, Henry used a combination of terror and inducement. Summoning the three castellans, he vowed to hang the whole garrison unless they surrendered within three days. The fear thus engendered was exploited by sending William Pantulf, one of Bellême's former vassals who had gone over to Henry after being disinherited by his erstwhile lord, to offer favourable terms to the garrison, including gifts of land.[103]

Conversely, refusal to show clemency might stiffen resistance from men who had nothing more to lose. It was the boldness born from despair as much as a desire for personal vengeance that led one of the defenders of Chaluz-Chabrol to wound Richard I mortally after his refusal to allow the garrison to surrender.[104] When, at Exeter in 1068, William I countered continued resistance by blinding one of the hostages in full sight of the city, the act failed 'to shake the resolution of the angry citizens; instead their obstinate determination to defend themselves and their homes grew all the stronger'.[105] Similarly in 1224, after Henry III had vowed 'by the soul of his

[100] Orderic, VI, pp. 522–3. Speaking of general policy rather than specifically about revolt, William of Malmesbury noted that whereas in his later years Henry I was increasingly content to punish by mulct, earlier in his reign he had favoured mutilation in order to set an example (*GR*, II, p. 487).

[101] WJ, pp. 124–7. Likewise, when in 1088 the garrisons of Alençon, Bellême and other castles heard that Robert Curthose had mutilated Robert Quarrel and the defenders of St Céneri, 'their nerve gave way and they began to discuss surrendering the fortresses entrusted to them when the duke arrived' (Orderic, IV, pp. 156–7).   [102] Orderic, VI, pp. 78–9.   [103] *Ibid.*, VI, pp. 24–9.

[104] Howden, IV, p. 82; Coggeshall, pp. 94–5; Cf. Gillingham, 'The Unromantic Death of Richard', pp. 18–41.   [105] Orderic, II, pp. 212–3; above, p. 2.

'father' to hang all the defenders of Bedford, the garrison 'being provoked to do further wrong by the king's threats, forbade the messengers of the king to speak to them again on the subject of giving up the castle'.[106] As a result of Henry III's ordinance in September 1265, disseizing all rebels following Evesham, resistance stiffened at Kenilworth and in the isles of Ely and Axholme until wiser council led to a general indemnity and oblivion embodied in the Dictum of Kenilworth.[107] By contrast, the general amnesty granted in 1217 had succeeded in bringing the war with Louis to a rapid end.

The dividends of clemency are well illustrated by Henry II's actions during the 'great war' of 1173–4. Of those rebels captured at Dol in 1173, some were imprisoned, but many leading nobles, including his old enemy Ralph de Fougères, were released on receipt of sureties and renewal of homage and fealty.[108] William of Newburgh was indignant that these men 'were treated by him much more mercifully than they deserved', yet an element of calculation augmented Henry's innate sense of restraint.[109] Dol was his first major victory in the war over the rebels in his own domains, and his treatment of them would set a crucial precedent for the rest of the war. Fresh from his rout of Louis VII's army at Verneuil, his position was strong and he could afford to be magnanimous. Conversely, he well knew that the war was far from won, and he had no wish to stiffen support for the Young King's position or swell his son's ranks by acts of brutality.

That Henry II was astute in his judgement of the political climate was shown by the series of chain reactions of surrender that followed his personal arrival in areas of disaffection. Thus his entry into Anjou in November 1173 brought about the rapid surrender of the castle of Haye, followed shortly afterwards by Pruilli and Campenni.[110] Still more striking was the total collapse of resistance in England following Henry's landing and the capture of William the Lion at Alnwick. Within two weeks of his march from London in July 1174, Henry had received the submission of Huntingdon from Earl David, William's brother, Framlingham and Bungay from Hugh Bigod, Norham, Durham and Northallerton from Hugh de Puiset, Leicester, Groby and Mountsorrel from the castellans of the captive earl of Leicester, Thirsk from Roger de Mowbray, and Tutbury and Duffield from Earl Ferrers.[111] All these capitulations had at their core the

---

[106] MP, III, p. 86.
[107] Powicke, *Henry III and the Lord Edward*, pp. 505–8; *Documents of the Baronial Movement*, pp. 316–37.
[108] WN, p. 176; JF, II. 227–31.
[109] WN, p. 176: 'the magnanimity of this great monarch in this affair towards these most disloyal traitors and his most bitter enemies is beyond doubt justly worthy of admiration and applause' (cf. JF, II. 227–31).   [110] *GH*, I, p. 62.   [111] *Ibid.*, I, pp. 72–3.

assumption of royal clemency. The same phenomenon can be observed in John's campaigns following the fall of Rochester. Between December 1215 and April 1216, almost every baronial castle had capitulated to John or his commanders, and it was only the arrival of Louis that saved the baronial opposition from extinction.[112] Had John executed the garrison of Rochester, he would have undoubtedly met with stiffer resistance.

It would be misleading to suggest that pragmatism alone dictated the ruler's response to the treatment of rebels. In most cases, there was recognition of degrees of resistance by those involved in rebellion. Passive defence of a castle was not the same as attacking the king in a pitched battle.[113] Where rebels were executed, it was often as the result of antagonizing the king or duke either by persistent refusal to surrender or by some personal insult. The garrison of the fortress at Alençon in 1051 were mutilated by Duke William for mocking at his bastardy and his mother's lowly status.[114] Similarly, Stephen hanged a number of the garrison of Shrewsbury because Arnulf of Hesdin had 'proudly rejected repeated offers of peace made by the king, and besides this presumed to speak contemptuously of the king and stubbornly forced others who wished to surrender to persist in their rebellion'.[115] At Bedford in 1224, Henry III believed the defenders to have merited death by their persistent refusal to surrender, the heavy losses they had inflicted on the royal army, the cost and duration of the siege, their excommunication immediately prior to the siege (though they were absolved before execution) and, above all, the cause of the hostilities – their seizure of a royal justice, Henry de Braibroc, who was in the process of impleading their lord, Fawkes de Bréauté.[116]

It was appreciated, moreover, that despite an often profound reluctance to resist the king or duke, occasioned not least by the fear of punishment, the garrisons of rebel lords were constrained by their own sense of honour and vassalic obligations. Any suzerain knew that it was on just such bonds of homage and fidelity that his own political authority rested. The force of these ties had to be acknowledged to a degree in the context of rebellion, just as in external warfare commanders might punish cowardice or treachery among the enemy, even if they had been beneficiaries of such acts, lest they set a damaging example to their own men and undermined standards

---

[112] MP, II, pp. 636–42; Painter, *King John*, pp. 364–71, provides a detailed account of this campaign.
[113] Strickland, 'Against the Lord's Anointed', pp. 64–6.
[114] The incident is recorded by Orderic in his interpolations in William of Jumièges (WJ, p. 171); cf. above, p. 161.
[115] Orderic, VI, pp. 520–3. At Roche-au-Moine, it was only after one of the defending crossbowmen had slain John's shield-bearer as the king reconnoitred the walls that John ordered gallows to be erected before the castle (*Chroniques des comtes d'Anjou*, p. 253: WB, *Gesta*, p. 262).
[116] MP, III, pp. 86, 89.

of courage and loyalty.[117] Even in war against the king, contemporaries might expect more than a token degree of resistance.[118] Hence the garrison of Robert de Bellême's castle of Vignats, besieged in 1102 by Robert Curthose, 'were hoping to be stormed in battle, for they were ready to surrender the castle in the face of a strong assault' but 'could not honourably surrender without a fight for fear of earning condemnation as faithless deserters'.[119] It is sigificant in this context that during Henry I's campaign of 1102 against Robert de Bellême, Arundel and Bridgnorth resisted Henry, but, if we may believe Orderic, at Tickhill the garrison immediately came out to meet him 'acclaiming him as their natural lord (*naturalem dominum*), and received him jubilantly'.[120] Chibnall has plausibly suggested that this disparity reflected the differing feudal status of the respective garrisons, for unlike Bridgnorth and Arundel, Bellême may only have held Tickhill as the king's castellan and not in fee.[121]

This same campaign reveals the crucial importance of conditional respite as a mechanism to resolve the dilemma of divided loyalty. Thus Henry I allowed the garrison of Arundel to seek relief from Robert de Bellême or his permission to surrender. Unable to assist them, he granted them leave to capitulate, on which 'the castellans thankfully surrendered the castle to the king who received them kindly and loaded them with gifts'.[122] The garrison of Bridgnorth were similarly permitted to inform Robert that further resistance was impossible.[123] Once given their lord's licence, the garrison could feel that they had vindicated their honour without jeopardizing life or limb. In granting gifts to the garrisons of Arundel and Bridgnorth, Henry both acknowledged the constancy of their defence while seeking to transfer their ultimate loyalty to himself. Similar motives prompted him to grant free egress with horses and arms to Bellême's garrison of Alençon in 1112.[124] Robert himself had received the same privilege on his capitulation at Shrewsbury in 1102, together with a safe conduct out of England, although he and the vassals who had supported him were disseised.[125] Criticism of Henry I's ruthlessness should be set against such actions, which reveal a highly developed sense of chivalric propriety.[126] Political severity and magnanimous gestures were not necessarily incompatable.

Nevertheless, there were limits. In every theatre of war, successful sieges

[117] Above, p. 227.   [118] Above, p. 229.   [119] Orderic, vi, pp. 22–3.
[120] *Ibid.*, vi, pp. 22–3.   [121] *Ibid.*, vi, p. 22, n. 2.
[122] *Ibid.* For a general study of this campaign see C. W. Hollister, 'The Campaign of 1102 against Robert of Bellême', pp. 193–202.   [123] Orderic, vi, pp. 28–9.   [124] *Ibid.*, vi, pp. 178–9.
[125] *Ibid.*, vi, pp. 30–1; *GR*, ii, p. 472.
[126] C. W. Hollister, 'Royal Acts of Mutilation: The Case Against Henry I', in idem. *Monarchy, Magnates and Institutions*, pp. 291–302.

were concluded by highly symbolic rituals of victory. The transference of power was marked by the surrender of the keys to a fortress, the planting of the victor's banners on the walls as a sign of conquest and ownership, and the departure of the defeated garrison.[127] As we have seen, garrisons might often be permitted to leave with honour in token of a brave defence,[128] but particularly in situations of rebellion, it was important that acts of clemency were not seen to undermine the impact of the ruler's triumph. Thus despite granting life and limb or even free egress, a suzerain might choose to emphasize the humiliation of defeat. Though Henry I granted Robert de Bellême freedom to leave Shrewsbury in 1102, it was not before Robert had personally handed over the keys to the town, surrendered unconditionally, and confessed his treachery (*crimen proditionis*).[129] Orderic's description of the siege of Rochester in 1088 reveals how important such gestures might be. Despite being granted freedom to leave with horses and arms in 1088, Odo tried to win 'the concession that the trumpeters should not sound their trumpets' as the men came out, 'as is customary when an enemy is defeated and a stronghold captured by force (*sicut moris est dum hostes vincuntur et per vim oppidum capitur*)'.[130] Rufus, however, utterly refused, proclaiming that 'he would not grant it even for a thousand marks in gold' and the garrison were forced to leave in shame and sorrow to the blaring of the royal trumpets.[131] Yet Odo and his men were fortunate. For others the price of reconciliation might be far higher. Duke Robert the Magnificent had forced William de Bellême to sue to peace carrying a saddle on his shoulders following the fall of Alençon, while in 1233, Henry III vowed only to pardon Richard Marshal if he submitted with a halter around his neck.[132]

Yet here again, such conduct was limited by the need to re-assert lordship without irreparably alienating those punished and so further fanning the flames of discontent. That men both spared punishment and treated honourably would serve the king loyally in the future was an argument consistently adduced by baronial elements lobbying for clemency. Though he had originally intended to execute the garrison of Exeter in 1136, it was in order 'that he might win their closer attachment' that Stephen granted them the concession 'to go forth in freedom but also to take away their possessions and be the followers of any lord they willed'.[133] Orderic has the

---

[127] See, for example, the raising of banners by the Franks on the walls of Messina, 1190, Acre, 1191 and Darum, 1192 (Ambroise, ll. 824–48, 9311–26; *Itinerarium*, pp. 164, 233–4). Orderic recounts how when the Norman advance guard under Robert de Montfort took possession of the citadel of Le Mans for Rufus in 1098, they 'raised the king's standard with great ceremony from the main tower' (Orderic, v, pp. 246–7). The *Bayeux Tapestry* shows the keys of Dinan being handed to Duke William on the end of a lance in 1064 (*BT*, pl. 23).   [128] Above, pp. 218–19.   [129] Orderic, vi, pp. 30–1.
[130] *Ibid.*   [131] *Ibid.*, iv, pp. 132–4.   [132] WJ, p. 101; MP, iii, p. 265.   [133] *GS*, pp. 42–3.

magnates tell Rufus at Rochester in 1088 that if he restores the rebels to their former positions or even allows them to leave unharmed from the castle,

> you will earn their gratitude and service on many future occasions . . .
> Among these men are many distinguished knights, ready to offer their
> service to you, and you ought not, great king, to underrate its worth.[134]

Under such pressure, Rufus turned political necessity to advantage by a display of magnanimity, allowing the rebels not only life and limb but safe conduct with horses and arms.[135]

In addition to its rewards, mercy was urged as a chivalric and kingly virtue.[136] Was not clemency in strength the attribute of the king of beasts? Bertran de Born, who himself was restored to Richard's favour following the suppression of the revolt of 1183 which he had helped to foment, remarked: 'The lion's custom appeals to me, who is not cruel to a creature once overcome, but who is proud in the face of pride.'[137] In an important article, John Gillingham has argued that such notions of clemency towards political opponents were essentially imported into England by the Normans. Though their transition from Norman dukes to Anglo-Norman kings increased their *de facto* power, rulers were now constrained, as they had earlier been in Normandy, by a powerful climate of opinion which eschewed the violent removal of dynastic rivals and the punishment of rebellion by death. Kings might occasionally act contrary to such opinion, but no longer could they indulge in the mutilations, executions and political assassinations which had been characteristic of the late Anglo-Saxon polity and continued to be commonplace in the 'barbarian' Celtic lands.[138]

Certainly there is much in this view, which correlates closely with the shift from the habitual slaughter to the frequent sparing of noble opponents, which equally set Anglo-Scandinavian and Celtic custom apart from that of the Normans and French. Anglo-Norman kings were forced to display a marked degree of restraint towards their dynastic opponents. Thus Edgar Aetheling enjoyed a clemency throughout his chequered career

---

[134] Orderic, IV, pp. 132–3.

[135] *Ibid.*, IV, pp. 128–33. Rufus did, however, disseize them and 'absolutely refused to give them any hope of recovering their inheritances or lands in his kingdom so long as he reigned'.

[136] At Rochester, the magnates tell Rufus 'that just as you conquered them in their pride and folly by your strength, you should by your graciousness spare them now they are humble and penitent. Temper your royal rigour with mercy, and let the fact of your victory proclaim the triumph of your might' (*ibid.*, IV, pp. 130–1).

[137] *Ar ve la coindeta sazos*, *TLP*, PP. 166–7; *L'amour et la guerre*, II, pp. 716–70. Similarly, citing the *De mirabilibus mundi*, Orderic has the barons tell Rufus in 1088 that 'The noble lion's wrath can spare the vanquished; do likewise all who govern on this earth' (Orderic, IV, pp. 130–1, and 130, n. 2).

[138] Gillingham, 'The Introduction of Chivalry', pp. 31–55.

that he would certainly have been denied under Cnut. Henry I could be severely criticized for keeping his brother Robert Curthose imprisoned, and felt unable to remove the certain threat posed by the young William Clito by similar means.[139] Equally, while Stephen may have been foolish not to seize Matilda at Arundel in 1139, her life was never seriously in danger, nor was his own following his capture after Lincoln in 1141.

In the treatment of rebellious vassals rather than royal kinsmen, the king might act with greater severity, given that he was punishing treason and breach of faith. Yet even here, as we have seen, a ruler's actions were circumscribed by a complex amalgam of factors. It might be argued, however, that vengeance against rebels was contrainted more by the dictates of *realpolitik* than by the quality of mercy itself. In 1096, Rufus could imprison Mowbray and execute William de Alderie but he nevertheless had to refrain from bringing others to trial 'for fear of fomenting their discontent still more, and goading them to another unlawful insurrection against the state'.[140] Henry I felt able to blind Odard of Le Pin, Geoffrey de Tourville and Luke de La Barre in 1124, but even then, the care taken by Orderic to justify these measures suggests distinct unease at such a punishment.[141]

Nevertheless, while chivalric leniency was always far more than a substitute for effective action, we should not overemphasize its operation in situations of revolt or civil war. It may well be argued that it was the anomalous conditions of his troubled reign, which undoubtedly witnessed a distinct degeneration of the political climate, that reduced the otherwise chivalrous Stephen to seizing rivals in violation of the peace of the court and to gaining control of the castles of Geoffrey de Mandeville, Turgis d'Avranches and Rannulf of Chester by threatening to hang these captured lords unless their garrisons capitulated.[142] Yet how exceptional really was such conduct? Rufus, a still greater paragon of chivalry, gained the surrender of Bamburgh from Roger Mowbray's wife and nephew by threatening to put out the captured earl's eyes.[143] And both his father at Alençon in 1051 and his elder brother and St Ceneri in 1088 had resorted to mutilation.

The Angevins displayed an equal readiness to resort to extreme measures in situations of revolt and to exploit ties of lordship with utter ruthlessness. Significantly, however, their favoured method of coercion or even

---

[139] Instead, he entrusted him to Helias de Saint-Saens, 'for fear that it might be held against him if the boy came to any harm while in his hands (Orderic, IV, 92–3).   [140] Orderic, IV, pp. 284–5.

[141] Orderic, VI, pp. 352–5.

[142] *GS*, pp. 162–3, 176–7, 196. The inviolacy of the court, which enjoyed the king's peace, had been overtly stated by Henry I when Reginald de Bailleul had come to defy him at Falaise in 1119, 'You have come to my court and I will not arrest you, but you will regret having defied me.' The king waited till Reginald had left before sending his men to burn his castle (Orderic, VI, pp. 214–16).

[143] *ASC*, 'E', *s.a.* 1095.

termination was starvation. Thus in December 1215, John procured the surrender of the important castle of Belvoir from Nicholas d'Albini after threatening to starve his father, William, who had been taken at Rochester and was then in prison at Corfe.[144] The subsequent submission of Gilbert fitz Renfrey cannot have been dissociated from the fact that his son William of Lancaster had also been taken prisoner at Rochester.[145] On capturing Oliver d'Argentan during the skirmish on the Medway bridge immediately prior to the siege of Rochester, John denied him food until his brother, a prominent baronial supporter, came over to the king and gave hostages for his future loyalty.[146] While Richard had won men's loyalty by example and largesse, much of John's political failure was due to the delusion that fidelity could be maintained by fear and coercion.

Such acts of intimidation might be regarded merely as further examples of the particular cruelty of the man capable of having Matilda de Braose and her eldest son William starved to death.[147] Yet John was not alone in employing such methods. In 1174, Henry refused the request of Robert of Leicester's castellans to consult with their lord, who since his capture at Fornham had languished in prison, and vowed that no food or drink would pass the lips of Earl Robert until the castle was handed over.[148] Still more strikingly, Ralph of Coggeshall noted laconically that on the fall of Nottingham in 1194, Richard ordered Robert Brito to be starved to death in prison.[149] John may only have been following a family example. The Angevins' resort to starvation perhaps acknowledged the strong feeling among the political community that the bodies of nobles should remain inviolate. Less immediate, less public, it removed an opponent more by default than by the overtly brutal act of mutilation or hanging. How far opinion militated against the open mutilation or killing of leading enemies is shown by the secrecy and confusion surrounding John's removal of Arthur. His 'disappearance', rather than punishment following a formal trial, allowed Philip Augustus to make great capital out at John's expense and to condemn him in the French court.[150]

Yet while the nobility naturally resisted the corporal or capital punishment of rebellion, there was nevertheless a powerful notion that rebels had

---

[144] MP, ii, p. 638.   [145] Rot. Ob. et Fin., p. 570.
[146] Coggeshall, p. 175. Cf. GH, i, pp. 77–9; Rot. Lit. Claus., i, pp. 241, 241b; Rot.. Lit. Pat., p. 163, for John's concern to re-establish the loyalty of disaffected barons.
[147] For Matilda de Briouse see Painter, King John, pp. 242–50.   [148] WN, pp. 194–5.
[149] Coggeshall, p. 63. Little is known about the circumstances of such alleged severity, except that his fate was clearly linked to John's insurrection and probably to the siege of Nottingham. The Pipe Roll for 1194 records that Robert Brito 'dissaisitus fuit de hereditate sua per Regem' (The Great Roll of the Pipe for the Sixth Year of the Reign of King Richard I, ed. D. M. Stenton (London, 1928), p. 175).
[150] Powicke, The Loss of Normandy, pp. 309–26.

violated the sacrosanct bond of fidelity to their lord, and deserved fitting retribution. Even in the case of Arthur, while many were shocked by John's actions, others were conscious that Arthur had received a condign punishment for treason. The Barnwell annalist regarded the anonymity of Arthur's grave to be a just reward for his pride.[151] But most striking of all were the words Wendover believed to have been those of Innocent III:

> Arthur was no innocent victim. He was captured at Mirebeau, a traitor to his lord and uncle to whom he had sworn homage and allegiance, and he could be rightly condemned without judgement to die even the most shameful of deaths.[152]

---

[151] WC, II, p. 196; cf. J. C. Holt, 'King John', *Historical Association General Ser.*, 53 (1963), repr. in *idem.*, *Magna Carta and Medieval Government* (London, 1985), at pp. 100–1.   [152] MP, II, p. 659.

WAR AGAINST THE LAND: RAVAGING AND ATTRITION

I will not seize bulls, cows, pigs, sheep, lambs, goats, asses or the burden they bear, mares, or their untamed colts. I will not seize villeins of either sex, or sergeants or merchants, or their coins, or hold them for ransom, or ruin them with exactions on account of their lord's war (*propter werram senioris*), or whip them for their possessions ... I will not burn or destroy houses unless I find an enemy horseman or thief (*nisi inimicum caballarium aut latronem*) within, and unless they are joined to a real castle. I will not cut down or uproot the vineyards of another, or harvest them for reasons of war (*propter werram*), unless it is on my own land ... I will not destroy a mill or seize the grain that is in it, unless I am on a cavalcade or with the host (*nisi cavallicata aut in hoste*), or it is on my land ... I will not attack merchants or pilgrims or take their possessions unless they commit crimes. I will not kill the animals of villeins except for my consumption and that of my men.[1]

So runs but part of the peace oath proposed by Bishop Warin of Beauvais to the Capetian king, Robert the Pious, in 1023. Intended as part of the Peace of God to curb the depredations of the castellans and their *milites*, its clerical drafters presupposed that pillaging, theft, kidnap and extortion

---

[1] The full text is printed in C. Pfister, *Etudes sur le règne de Robert le Pieux, 996–1031* (Paris, 1885), pp. lx–lxi; and translated in Head and Landes, *The Peace of God*, pp. 332–4. *Cavallicata* or *cavalacata*, here rendered 'cavalcade', was synonymous with the *equitatio* or *expeditio* of Anglo-Norman texts, 'not military service but the duty of escorting an immediate lord or the king from place to place' (Stenton, *English Feudalism*, pp. 176–8). Such service was performed armed, and might clearly entail the requisitioning of supplies. Further on in the oath the *cavalacata militium* is listed along with other conditions of service to which the restraints of the oath did not apply; 'except when besieging or building a castle, or when I am in the host of the king or our bishops, or on cavalcade of knights (*excepto per bastimentum et obsidionem castelli ac per hostem regis atque episcoporum nostrorum et excepta cavalcata militium*)'.

were the habitual activity of the knighthood of the Beauvasis, with the peasantry as their principal victims. Yet the oath by no means represents a total ban on such violence. A lord's rights of justice and distraint are safeguarded. Still more significantly, the legitimacy of seizing livestock and grain, and of house and mill burning is readily conceded if the knights are fulfilling their service in the royal or episcopal host or are on an expedition for their lord. And when adding a postscript to the oath, Bishop Warin was careful to add that all the conditions of the oath did not apply to the king's war (*nisi de werra regis*).

The ravaging of the enemy's countryside was the most common manifestation of medieval warfare, and arguably the most fundamental of all its forms. The importance of ravaging lies not only in the extent of its application, but also in the methods of its implementation. For unlike the other principal expressions of aggression in war, namely siege, skirmish or battle, ravaging did not necessarily entail direct conflict between members of the warrior aristocracy. Rather, it consisted of an assault on the material and psychological basis of an opponent's lordship, achieved by the seizure or destruction of the central components of his landed wealth – his chattels, crops, livestock and peasantry. As a consequence, ravaging reveals the phenomenon of a professional warrior elite directing much of its efforts in war against a largely defenceless peasantry or against the inhabitants of towns. It highlights aspects of knightly behaviour which stand in marked contrast – though in contemporary eyes not necessarily in contradiction – to the extensive and relatively sophisticated conventions of conduct in operation between members of their own class. A study of ravaging is therefore essential to place any assessment of 'chivalric' notions of behavioural restraint in a wider social context.

The importance of this form of economic warfare and of the great harrying raid or *chevauchée* by which it was frequently implemented has long been recognized by historians of the fourteenth and fifteenth centuries, particularly in connection with the Hundred Years War.[2] Yet despite its equal ubiquity and significance in earlier medieval warfare, ravaging has not, with the notable exception of John Gillingham's recent work,[3] received the attention from eleventh- and twelfth-century historians that it both deserves and which would have been assigned to it by contemporary commanders. What then were the aims and mechanisms of ravaging? Can

---

[2] The best account of ravaging in relation to the Hundred Years War is furnished by H. J. Hewitt, *The Organization of War under Edward III, 1338–62* (Manchester, 1966), pp. 99 ff., while for a detailed study of a great chevauchée in action see *idem.*, *The Black Prince's Expedition of 1355–57* (Manchester, 1958).

[3] Gillingham, 'Richard I and the Science of War', pp. 83–5; *idem.*, 'War and Chivalry in the *History of William the Marshal*', pp. 4–6; *idem.*, 'William the Bastard at War', pp. 148–52.

we perceive varying degrees to which this economic warfare could be implemented, and is it possible to gauge contemporary attitudes to the forms of conduct which it frequently involved?

FORAGING: THE COMMAND OF LOCAL RESOURCES

One of the most basic elements of ravaging in war was the foraging for food and fodder for men and horses. Even in time of peace, the problems of supplying and housing an often sizeable and invariably itinerant royal or ducal household might result in sporadic violence and scenes little different from the ravaging by an external enemy. The *Anglo-Saxon Chronicle* complained that while Rufus was waiting for good weather to cross to Normandy in 1097, 'his court did the greatest damage in the districts in which they stayed that ever court or army was reported to have done in a land at peace', and that similarly, following the treaty of Alton in 1101, men of Robert Curthose 'always did much damage wherever they went while the court was staying in this country'.[4] The behaviour of Henry I's court in 1104 was scarcely better: 'and always wherever the king went there was complete ravaging of his wretched people caused by his court, and in the course of it [there were] often burnings and killings'.[5] Such incidents caused Henry I to legislate for the provisioning of his court in an attempt to eradicate this longstanding source of unpopularity.[6]

In a like manner, monastic chroniclers frequently bemoaned the inordinate expense of forced hospitality to baronial or episcopal households. Orderic, for example, records how Mabel of Bellême attempted to strike vicariously at

---

[4] *ASC* 'E', s.a. 1097, 1101.

[5] *ASC* 'E', s.a. 1104. Orderic similarly noted of Hugh, earl of Chester, that his hunting with his men resembled 'a daily devastation of his lands' (Orderic, II, pp. 262–3). The problem raised by the need to supply an itinerant court and royal officials, and the resulting grievances of those who bore the brunt of such requisitions, was far from new. In a tract specifically on this issue, Archbishop Hincmar of Reims complained to Charles the Bald that 'when the impending arrival of the royal entourage is announced in any given place, there is a reaction as if the army of Antichrist was coming, an army that is always accompanied by evils'. This tract, 'To Control Military Requisitions', is translated in Head and Landes, *The Peace of God*, pp. 343–6.

[6] *GR*, II, p. 487: '[Henry] made a regulation for the followers of his court at whichever of his possessions he might be resident, stating what they should accept without payment from the country folk; and how much and at what price they should purchase, punishing the transgressors by a heavy pecuniary fine or loss of life.' That royal agents nonetheless continued to requisition supplies in a manner felt to be little different from licensed robbery, not least in times of war, is reflected in the grievances expressed in clauses 30 and 31 of Magna Carta. Tallages and prises were later to be among the principal grievances underlying the political crisis of 1297–8, prominent in both the *Confirmatio Cartarum* and its earlier draft, the *De Tallagio* (*MC*, pp. 324–5; M. Prestwich, *Edward I* (London, 1988), pp. 427–8. For examples of food prises in 1297 see *Documents Illustrating the Crisis of 1297–8 in England*, ed. M. Prestwich, Camden 4th series, vol. 24 (London, 1980), pp. 12–13, while for the burdens of purveyance see J. R. Maddicott, 'The English Peasantry and the Demands of the Crown, 1294–1341', *Past and Present Supplement*, 1, (1975), pp. 15–34).

her enemies, the sons of Giroie, by demanding from the monastery of St Evroul hospitality for herself and a great retinue of knights; 'in this way, she brought the monks, who were struggling to wring a living from the barren soil, to the verge of ruin'.[7] Similarly, William of Newburgh complained bitterly of how, in the name of his legatine authority, William Longchamp demanded hospitality from the larger monasteries in England for his vast household, which descended 'like locusts', and forced smaller houses to fine with him to avoid the economic ruin such billeting might bring.[8]

Though monasteries might offer lords a tempting, cheap and no doubt comfortable solution to the problem of billeting, monastic hospitality was neither boundless nor ubiquitous. Other sources of food and shelter had to be sought, often with explosive results. Despite its enormous political repercussions, the great crisis of 1051 between Edward the Confessor and the house of Godwine was initially sparked off by a quarrel over billeting between the retinue of Eustace of Boulogne and the townspeople of Dover, during which several people were killed.[9] Well over a century later, Peter of Blois could note sourly how men of Henry II's court often drew swords over possession of a hovel not fit for pigs, and it was in just such a quarrel that in John's reign, Geoffrey de Mandeville was alleged to have killed a serjeant of William Briwerre.[10]

In war itself, in addition to the plundering of valuables as booty, the seizure of grain and livestock from an opponent's territory served concurrently both to provision an invading army and to inflict severe economic damage upon the enemy. This duality of function was clearly recognized by Orderic Vitalis when noting how on his retreat from the unsuccessful siege of Mayet in 1099, William Rufus was advised by his councillors to lay waste the land: 'In this way he would wisely provide for the welfare of his own men and the ultimate destruction of the enemy.'[11] Hence the Angevin army that invaded Normandy in 1136 fed itself upon captured livestock and, to maximize their economic gain, sent the hides of the slaughtered animals back to Anjou in carts,[12] while in 1181, the Brabançon mercenaries in the

---

[7] Orderic, II, pp. 54–5.
[8] WN, p. 334. One wonders whether Newburgh's animus against Lonchamp had been sharpened by his own priory of Newburgh having falling victim to this form of blackmail.
[9] ASC 'D' and 'E', s.a. 1051.
[10] Peter of Blois, *Opera Omnia*, I, letter 14, p. 51; *PL*, CCVII, letter 14, pp. 48–9; *Histoire des ducs*, pp. 116–19. Cf. the quarrel over lodgings between Hugh de Puiset, bishop of Durham, and William the Lion at Brackley in 1194, when both were attending Richard at Silverstone (Howden, III, pp. 246–7).
[11] Orderic, V, pp. 260–1.
[12] *Ibid.*, VI, pp. 472–3. Similarly, when Geoffrey de Mandeville was forced into revolt against King Stephen in 1143, 'he devoted himself with insatiable greed to the plundering of flocks and herds; everything belonging to adherents of the king's party he took away and used up, stripped and destroyed' (*GS*, pp. 164–5).

13 From their beach-head at Pevensey and Hastings, Norman soldiers forage for food and slaughter captured livestock. Living off an opponent's land inflicted economic and pyschological damage while provisioning one's own army. The struggle for control of local supplies lay at the heart of much medieval warfare (by special permission of the City of Bayeux).

pay of Henry II's sons took a huge number of oxen as booty from the lands of the count of Sancerre.[13] It was little wonder that when, sometime after 1149, Osbert de Wanci, a minor knight holding land in the area of Banbury, came to draw up a charter in favour of the abbey of St Mary at Biddlesden, he automatically associated war with the seizure of livestock:

> If there shall be so great war that we cannot keep our animals in peace, they [the monks] shall keep them with their own, without cost to themselves and saving their order, that is, they shall not pledge their faith or take any oath on this account if anyone wishes to take the animals away by force. If, moreover, the animals shall be taken away by theft or lost through any other mischance or shall die or be killed or be seized by beasts, the monks shall not make good the loss. If moreover, I or my wife or son shall be captured, the monks shall send one of their breathren to help us by mediation but not with money.[14]

Osbert was clearly well aware that placing his cattle in the care of religious offered precious little safeguard to a determined aggressor.

The law itself recognized that in *tempus werrae* plundering and the seizure of livestock were the inevitable consequence of war and as such might be pardoned. Thus referring to the war of 1173–4, the Assize of Northampton, 1176, stated that 'cases of petty thefts and robberies, which have been committed in time of war, as of horses and oxen and lesser things', were exempt from its remit.[15] The stipulation that, by contrast, more serious pleas such as murder, treason and arson were generally to be answered for is a reminder that the general amnesty for acts committed *tempus discordiae* embodied in Magna Carta was an anomaly, resulting from immediate political circumstance and the need to establish peace.[16] Pleas of deeds committed *tempus werrae* resumed their former degree of circumscription following the establishment of peace more favourable to the king in 1217 and 1265.[17]

---

[13] Diceto, II, p. 9. The figure of 5,000 pairs of oxen given by Diceto is undoubtedly an exaggeration, but the method of economic attrition is clear enough. The provision of grain was equally as important as livestock. Orderic notes how, as a prelude to the campaign that culminated in Brémule, Henry I 'had the crops around Etrepagny cut by his rapacious foragers, and ordered the great sheaves to be taken to the castle of Lyons on the backs of their horses' (Orderic, VI, pp. 234–5).

[14] The charter is printed by Stenton, *English Feudalism*, pp. 284–5 and translated on p. 247.

[15] *GH*, I, p. 108; *EHD*, II, p. 444.   [16] *MC*, c. 62, pp. 472–3.

[17] In the aftermath of the war of 1215–17, for example, Henry III's assize judges noted that one Nicholas of Barston, a murderer, 'was not in frankpledge because it was in the war (*in guerra*)', and was accordingly exacted and outlawed (*Rolls of the Justices in Eyre for Gloucestershire, Warwickshire and Staffordshire, 1221–1222*, ed. D. M. Stenton (*Seldon Society*, 59, 1940), no. 880). Those breaking gaol having been imprisoned for murder were similarly convicted, whilst those who released such felons might be placed in mercy (*ibid.*, no. 879, 760). In the case of Robert of Thurlaston, however, the accused was outlawed for suspected murder, but the men appealed as his accomplices were not convicted as 'the deed was done in the war (*in guerra*) and therefore there is nothing to be done' (*ibid.*, no. 925). Acts of disseisin occurring during time of war were almost always revoked following a writ of novel disseisin (*ibid.*, nos. 1131, 1016, 1017). See also Powicke, *Henry III and the Lord Edward*, pp. 23–26 and for the war of 1264–5, pp. 507, 555 and n. 1.

Foraging and the seizure of livestock were necessitated by the frequent, though far from universal absence of adequate logistical organization before the thirteenth century.[18] Yet the essentially ad hoc nature of the procurement of supplies by living off the land that resulted from this lack of regular provision had far-reaching and detrimental consequences on the military effectiveness of an army in the field. First, it exacerbated the ever-present problems of health and sanitation. Orderic recounts with some satisfaction how a shortage of cooks among the invading Angevin army of 1136 led to a severe outbreak of dysentery after many men had eaten unsalted or poorly cooked meat.[19] William of Poitiers similarly records how, at Dover in 1066, the Conqueror's army ate newly slaughtered meat and drank water, so that many died of dysentery.[20] The need to drink only wine or beer to avoid such illness from contaminated water must have greatly exacerbated the problem of logistics on the march; the great wine vats portrayed in the Bayeux Tapestry being loaded on to William I's ships were not a luxury but a necessity.[21]

Secondly, campaigns might be hampered or even frustrated if an attack was launched at the wrong time in the agricultural year. Thus Orderic, probably drawing on the now lost portion of William of Poitiers's *Gesta Guillelmi*, speaks of the privations suffered during William I's forced march to Chester in midwinter 1069–70, when 'sometimes all were obliged to feed on horses which had perished in the bogs'.[22] In June 1098, Rufus was forced to withdraw from Le Mans, for although he had ravaged the countryside he was unable to undertake a prolonged siege because of a shortage of food and the ruinously high price of oats, vital to keep the war-horses in good condition.[23]

Reliance on the procuring of supplies by ravaging might be such that an invading army could be forced to retreat if the defending forces succeeded in depriving it of the crops, livestock and victuals in the vicinity. In 1173, Ralph de Fougères had ordered his men to herd their horses and livestock into the local forest with the intention both of protecting them and of denying food to the Brabançon mercenaries sent against him by Henry II.[24] In 1233, Henry III was forced to raise the siege of Richard Marshal's castle

---

[18] A notable exception was Duke William's invasion preparations in 1066, the extent and sophistication of which have been discussed in detail by Bachrach, 'Some Observations on the Military Administration of the Norman Conquest', pp. 1–25. It was only this efficiency in victualling an army encamped for weeks in one spot that enabled William to issue and effectively enforce a prohibition against pillaging the local countryside (above, p. 38).   [19] Orderic, VI, pp. 472–3.
[20] WP, p. 212.   [21] BT, pl. 38.   [22] Orderic, II, pp. 236–7.
[23] Orderic, V, pp. 242–5. The destruction by storm of many of Rufus's supply ships during his campaign against Malcolm III in September 1091, led to many of his army perishing by cold and starvation (FW, II, p. 28).   [24] Torigny, p. 259.

of Usk because of the failure of supplies, while later the same year he was again forced to withdraw after the Marshal, 'that cautious soldier', had removed all livestock and provisions from the path of the royal army.[25]

As a logical extension of this process, defending forces might implement a scorched-earth policy against their own lands. Hence in 1085, when faced with the prospect of an imminent Danish invasion, William I 'had the land near the sea laid waste, so that if his enemies landed, they should have nothing to seize on so quickly'.[26] In an attempt to frustrate Rufus's invasion of Maine in 1099, Count Helias 'began hostilities again after Easter, and with the consent of the inhabitants quietly set about scorching the earth in the frontier regions and harassing the king's forces'.[27] Similarly, the baronial opponents of King John laid waste their own estates in the face of the king's advance into the North early in 1216.[28]

Towns were frequently fired in the face of enemy attack. This might be for tactical purposes. When its Breton garrison fired Lisieux in 1136, the besieging Angevins were prevented from approaching the citadel or from storming it in any way due to the violence of the flames, and were forced to withdraw.[29] In 1189, Henry II fired the suburbs of Le Mans to cover his retreat from the forces of Richard and Philip Augustus.[30] John likewise attempted to fire Winchester as he withdrew on the approach of Prince Louis's army in 1216.[31]

Firing a town, however, equally aimed at denying the enemy shelter, defence, booty and supplies. It was for this reason that Ecouché and Le Sap were also burned by the Normans in the face of the Angevin invasion of 1136.[32] Orderic records how as they watched Lisieux burn the Angevins 'grew angry and frustrated, because they had been cheated of the loot on which they had counted, and bewailed the loss of the rich booty which was being consumed by fire'.[33] Orderic's comment is far more than the spiteful rhetoric of an aggrieved Norman cleric. Behind it lies a clear appreciation of how crucial a factor the regular availability of booty was in maintaining cohesion in an army in the field and in preventing desertion by the hope of further gain. If men who had joined an army principally in the expectation of material gain were repeatedly denied plunder by its deliberate destruc-

---

[25] *Annales Monastici*, I, p. 90; MP, III, pp. 249, 253.

[26] *ASC* 'E', *s.a.* 1085. In striking contrast, William had actually given the Viking army in Yorkshire in 1069–70 permission to obtain supplies from coastal regions by plundering, so anxious was he to be rid of them and deprive the northern rebels of their support (FW, II, p. 4).

[27] Orderic, V, pp. 254–5, and cf. *ibid.*, V, pp. 258–9.   [28] *Chronicle of Melrose*, p. 62.

[29] Orderic, VI, pp. 468–71.

[30] *GH*, II, p. 67; Gerald of Wales, *De Vita Galfridi, Opera*, IV, ed. J. S. Brewer (Rolls Series, 1873), Bk I, c. iv, p. 369; *idem.*, *De Principis Instructione Liber*, p. 283.

[31] Coggeshall, p. 182. The citizens, however, succeeded in putting out the fire and welcomed in Louis.

[32] Orderic, VI, pp. 466–71.   [33] *Ibid.*, pp. 468–9.

tion, their morale would be seriously undermined and their desire to continue campaigning greatly reduced. Although Orderic uses the burning of
Lisieux to indulge in shameless propagation of the 'Norman myth', his
words nevertheless highlight the important psychological element present
in scorched-earth policy:

> In this way they [the Angevins] learnt to their cost how brave at heart the
> Normans were, and marvelled at the determination they showed in their
> implacable hatred, for it was plain that they would rather allow their wealth
> to be burnt than save their treasures by bowing their necks to the yoke of
> foreign dominion.[34]

Supply and mastery over available local resources, moreover, was the key
to siege warfare. For if want of supplies might hamper the efforts of an
attacking force, starvation was equally one of the most potent weapons
available to the besieger. Starvation, if one may invert Macbeth's comment
on the safety of Dunsinane, might laugh a castle's strength to scorn. It was
only starvation that brought about the capitulation of Wark-on-Tweed in
1138 and of Rochester in 1215, only thirst that compelled the surrender of
Exeter in 1136.[35] As well as establishing a blockade with lines of
circumvallation and pickets, a besieging army might ravage the countryside
around enemy fortresses in an attempt to deprive the defenders of potential supplies by destroying foodstuffs or seizing them for their own use.
Thus before laying siege to the castle of Pont Audemer in 1123, Henry I
laid waste the countryside around for more than twenty miles.[36] In preparation for his investment of the reputedly impregnable fortress of
Taillebourg in 1178, Richard, then count of Poitou,

> carried off the wealth of the farms, he cut down the vines, he fired the vil-
> lages and having pulled down everything else laid it waste; then at the
> approaches of the fortress he pitched his tents close to the walls, to the great
> alarm of the townsmen who had expected nothing of the kind.[37]

This intimate connection between siege and ravaging was fully recognized
by Jordan Fantosme in a speech he creates for Count Philip of Flanders,
advising Louis VII on how William the Lion should wage war against
Henry II in 1173:

---

[34] *Ibid.* Cf. R.H.C. Davis, *The Normans and their Myth* (London, 1976).
[35] RH, p. 80; MP, II, p. 621; *GS*, pp. 38–43. Similarly, it was want of food that led to the surrender of
Saint-Céneri to Robert Curthose in 1088 (Orderic, IV, p. 154–5), and of Oxford to Stephen in 1142
(*GS*, pp. 142–5).
[36] SD, II, p. 274. On taking Baldwin de Redvers's castle of Plympton in 1136, Stephen's forces 'stripped
bare, by frightful ravages, all Baldwin's land, which in those districts is extensive and pleasant and rich
in all good things, and returned to the king at Exeter with many thousands of sheep and cattle' (*GS*,
pp. 36–7, and cf. *ibid.*, pp. 66–7, 144–5, 200–1).   [37] Diceto, I, p. 431.

Let him destroy your enemies and lay waste their land: let all be consumed in fire and flames! Let him not leave them, outside their castles, in wood or meadow, as much as will furnish them a meal on the morrow. Then let him assemble his men and lay siege to their castles. They will not get succour or help for thirteen leagues around them.[38]

Naturally, the besieged themselves might also resort to plundering the locality in order to provision their castles in readiness for siege. Hence in 1088, on taking up arms against his nephew William Rufus, Odo ravaged his own earldom of Kent, and 'utterly laid waste the king's land and the archbishop's and he carried all the goods into his castle at Rochester'.[39] When, in 1106, William de Mortain came to the relief of his castle of Tinchebrai, he was so successful in keeping Henry I's besieging force at bay that 'he even had the green corn cut down in the fields and supplied to his garrison as fodder for their horses'.[40]

Towns adjacent to or containing a castle might be plundered by their would-be defenders in order to provision the garrison. Thus the *Gesta Stephani* linked Baldwin de Redvers's victualling of Exeter castle before his atempt to defy King Stephen in 1136 with the imposition of his lordship on the citizens of the town and neighbouring villages.[41] In 1137–8, Miles de Beauchamp, preparing to resist the king from Bedford castle, 'forcibly took from everyone and carried away with him any food on which he could lay his hands, and shamelessly robbing the townsmen and their neighbours, whom hitherto he had humanely spared as his own dependants, he gathered everything into the castle that met his eyes'.[42] In this respect, it is significant that, during the troubles of Stephen's reign, contemporaries consistently linked baronial demands for supplies, tax and forced labour known under the general term of *tenserie* to the construction or refurbishment of fortresses.[43]

Failure to requisition such supplies prior to a siege could prove fatal. In 1215, the baronial forces under William d'Albini occupied the castle of Rochester but found it completely unprovisioned. As there was not sufficient time to collect enough supplies 'by plundering in the province or by other means' for the large garrison of 140 knights and their retainers, they had to make do with what they could find in the town of Rochester itself. Despite a valiant resistance, it was this deficiency of victuals which finally

---

[38] JF, 11. 443–8.
[39] *ASC* 'E', *s.a.* 1088. The same annal records how his fellow rebels Geoffrey de Coutances and Robert de Mowbray 'went to Bristol and ravaged it and carried the plunder to the castle, and then went out of the castle and ravaged Bath and all the surrounding area, and laid waste all the district of Berkeley'.
[40] Orderic, VI, pp. 84–5; cf. *ibid.*, pp. 348–9.   [41] *GS*, pp. 30–3.   [42] *Ibid.*, pp. 48–9.
[43] See below, pp. 84–6.

compelled them to surrender to John.[44] The following year, the castellan of
Dover, Hubert de Burgh, avoided a similar fate by taking advantage of a
temporary withdrawal of the besieging forces of Prince Louis to sally out,
burn the houses and buildings erected by the enemy and to procure a
plentiful supply of food by ravaging the Kentish countryside.[45]

WAR AGAINST THE LAND: ECONOMIC ATTRITION

Though the provisioning of an army was a prerequisite for a successful
campaign, the ravaging of an opponent's territory might consist of far more
than merely foraging for supplies. The fundamental objective was the
destruction, or at the very least the temporary dislocation, of the enemy's
economic resources. The burning of crops was a principal element of ravaging, both in local private warfare and in major campaigns. As the *Histoire de
Guillaume le Maréchal* astutely recognized, 'when the poor can no longer reap
a harvest from their fields, then they can no longer pay their rents and this, in
turn, impoverishes their lords'.[46] Orderic noted that it was for waging
private war and burning his neighbours' crops that Henry I heavily amerced
Ivo de Grandmesnil in 1102.[47] On a larger scale, John burned the granaries
of Bury and Crowland during his punitive campaign in East Anglia in 1216,
both to deprive actual or potential rebels of supplies and to strike a financial
blow at the religious houses felt to be in sympathy with the king's enemies.[48]

Closely associated with the desire to disrupt an opponent's supply of
victuals was the destruction of mills, which at once both hit at the chief
means of converting cereal products into foodstuffs and deprived a lord of
valuable fiscal dues. Mill burning was prohibited by the Norman
Consuetudines of 1091 as a major manifestation of private warfare in the
duchy.[49] Other forms of ravaging aimed at still more basic disruption of
the agriculture by the preventing of ploughing. When the Young King's
routiers removed great numbers of oxen from the lands of the count of
Sancerre,[50] it was not simply to provision their own army but to deprive the
count's peasantry of the draught animals that pulled their ploughs. This
measure must have severely disrupted the agricultural cycle of that year and
presented the count and his men with both the problem of restocking and a
concomitantly heavy financial outlay. The ruin that could result from such
measures was fully recognized by the ecclesiastical Council of Rouen in

---

[44] MP, II, p. 621.   [45] Ibid., III, p. 5.   [46] *HGM*, 11. 659–69.   [47] Orderic, VI, pp. 18–19.
[48] MP, II, p. 667; MP, *Historia Anglorum*, pp. 189–90; above, pp. 90–1.
[49] Haskins, *Norman Institutions*, p. 283, c. 6. Equally, the Norman Exchequer made allowance for 'waste'
'in defectu molendinorum vastorum per guerram per Comitem Johannem' at Gavrai, presumably
referring to John's insurrection in 1193–4 (*Rot. Scacc.*, II, p. 292).   [50] Diceto, II, p. 9.

1096 which decreed that 'oxen and horses at the plough, and men leading the plough, and men harrowing and the horses with which they harrow' were to be 'in peace at all times, so that no one shall ever presume to attack or seize them, or rob or molest them in any way'.[51]

Not merely beasts of burden but ploughs themselves, or other agricultural tools such as hoes, might be removed or destroyed. The *Très ancien coutoumier* placed the plough and the ploughman under the ducal peace and protection, while similarly the Council of Rouen appears to have regarded the plough as providing a place of sanctuary, stating the inviolacy of 'men who fly to the plough'.[52] Such protection had its roots in Scandinavian custom,[53] but the very need for either custumal or canonical pronouncement against the destruction of the plough strongly suggests its importance as a target in warfare.

The disruption of agriculture was not limited to the methods of cereal production. Vines, olives and fruit-bearing trees were frequently burnt or uprooted. In 1098, as part of his efforts to suppress the county of Maine on behalf of Willam Rufus, Robert de Bellême 'vented his wrath on the people of the province who resisted him and punished them cruelly by ravaging their lands. With a great force of soldiers he tore up their vines, trampled down their corn, and laid waste the province all around.'[54] Nor were such methods peculiar to Bellême. Retreating from his unsuccessful siege of Mayet in 1099, the forces under Rufus himself 'used all kind of implements to devastate the hostile country. They tore up the vines, cut down the fruit trees, smashed fences and walls, and laid waste the whole of that most fertile region with fire and sword.'[55] In 1174, the Scots army besieging Prudhoe castle devastated the land and stripped the bark from the fruit trees.[56]

Such destruction, employed in campaigns where hostilities had become particularly bitter,[57] represented a more extreme manifestation of war than

---

[51] Mansi, xx, col. 924, canon 2; Orderic, v, pp. 20–1.

[52] *Très ancien coutoumier de Normandie*, ed. E. J. Tardif (Rouen, 1881), 1, p. 17; Orderic, v, pp. 20–1; Mansi, xx, col. 924. In addition to ploughs, hoes were placed under the Peace of God by the Council of Toulouges in 1041 (*RHF*, xi, p. 511).

[53] Cf. Dudo of St Quentin, *De moribus et actis primorum Normanniae ducum*, ed. J. Lair (Caen, 1865), pp. 171–2; Haskins, *Norman Institutions*, pp. 28, 65.

[54] Orderic, v, pp. 242–3. This campaign also included the destruction of the property and land of Hildebert, bishop of Le Mans, one of Rufus's chief opponents in Maine, the author of the *Gesta domni Hildiberti episcopi* relating how the king's men burned the episcopal vill of Coulaines, near Le Mans 'and cruelly devastated everything which the bishop had there' (*Actus pontificum Cenommanis in urbe degentium*, ed. G. Busson and A. Ledru (Le Mans, 1901), pp. 400–1). Cf. Migne, *PL*, clxxi, cols. 215–16, for Hildebert's own comments in a letter excusing his presence at a papal council.

[55] Orderic, v, pp. 260–1.   [56] JF, 11. 1676–79.

[57] Such destruction was employed, for example, as a prelude to William I's attack on Mantes in 1087 and in 1181 during Philip of Flanders's attempt to oust the young Philip Augustus (Orderic, iv, pp. 78–9; Diceto, ii, p. 8).

merely foraging or the destruction of crops. Its long-term economic
implications were far more serious, for to regrow olive trees or vines, particularly for an acceptable vintage, might take many years, depriving the locality of an essential source of supply, crippling their trade capability and
striking at profits from tolls and other duties. William of Tyre recorded
how Baldwin II ensured the capitulation of the otherwise impregnable
trans-Jordan citadel of 'the valley of Moses' by starting to uproot the olive
trees that formed the economic mainstay of the inhabitants.[58] It was thus
for good reason that the Peace of God promulgated at Toulouges in 1041
proscribed the burning of the peasants' olive groves.[59] The council of
Narbonne, 1054, repeated this prohibition, adding by way of justification
that the olive had been a token of God's peace brought to Noah after the
Flood, that the olive was used for the oil of chrism, and that altars were lit
by lamps burning olive oil.[60]

KILLING OF THE PEASANTRY

Attacks on the peasantry formed the logical extension of such economic
warfare. By burning their dwellings or even slaying the husbandmen themselves, an opponent sought to disrupt the labour supply of an enemy lord
and deprive him of his workforce. Villages, seldom if ever fortified, were
easy targets and a principal object of attack. A typical instance of private
warfare in Normandy serves to illustrate how the peasantry bore the brunt
of the hostilities between feuding lords. In 1136, Waleran of Meulan burnt
the town of Acquiny during his war against Roger de Tosny. Roger replied
by burning three of the Beaumont villages, probably La Croix-Saint-
Leufroi, Caillé and Ecardeville-sur-Eure.[61] Later the same year, Waleran
and his brother Robert allied with Count Theobald of Blois, and invading
Ralph's lands 'burnt the cottages of many poor people in three hamlets',
and fired the church of Bougy-sur-Risle with the men and women in it.[62]
The vicious cycle of this local war was continued when Roger devastated
Waleran's lands in the diocese of Evreux, 'burning and massacring everywhere'. At Vaudreuil he 'laid waste the rich province in an orgy of slaying,
plundering and burning without respect of persons, and left many people
destitute after he and his confederates had carried off their possessions'.[63]

Orderic viewed these acts as 'unexpected excesses', largely due to
Roger's plundering of the monastery at La Mary Magdalene at Vaudreuil.[64]

---

[58] WT, II, 16: 6, p. 722; tr. Babcock and Krey, II, p. 145.   [59] *RHF*, XI, p. 511.   [60] *Ibid.*, p. 515, c. 11.
[61] Orderic, VI, pp. 458–9. The identifications are those suggested by Dr Chibnall (*ibid.*, p. 458, n. 2).
[62] Orderic, VI, pp. 464–5.   [63] *Ibid.*, pp. 474–5.   [64] *Ibid.*

Yet in such conduct Roger merely typified the behaviour of the Anglo-Norman aristocracy. In describing the internal strife that racked Normandy in 1104, Orderic portrayed Robert de Bellême as being exceptional in the degree of his brutality, but he readily acknowledged that many of the nobility waged war against the countryside with considerable ruthlessness. 'It is impossible', he lamented, 'to describe the destruction wrought by vicious men of the region; they scarred the whole province with slaughter, rapine and, after carrying off booty and butchering men, they burnt down houses everywhere'.[65]

In its most extreme forms, ravaging aimed at the total deprivation of shelter and food to a local populace. William the Conqueror's 'harrying of the North' had as its deliberate aim the creation of an artificial famine, intended to kill off the peasantry of the northern Anglo-Saxon lords and thereby break once and for all the power of this separatist region.[66] Orderic recounts how William

> continued to comb forests and remote mountain places, stopping at nothing to hunt out the enemy hidden there. His camps were spread over an area of a hundred miles. He cut down many in his vengeance; destroyed the lairs of others; harried the land and burned homes to ashes. Nowhere else had William shown such cruelty. Shamefully he succumbed to this vice, for he made no effort to restrain his fury and punished the innocent with the guilty. In his anger he commanded that all crops and herds, chattels and food of every kind should be brought together and burned to ashes with consuming fire, so that the whole region north of the Humber might be stripped of all means of sustenance. In consequence, so serious a scarcity was felt in England, and so terrible a famine fell upon the humble and defenceless populace, that more than 100,000 Christian folk of both sexes, young and old, perished by hunger.[67]

The *Gesta Stephani* reveals that King Stephen, faced with the growing influence of Duke Henry, considered implementing a similar policy on a smaller scale in 1149 in order to break the strategic deadlock existing between his Angevin opponents and his own supporters:

> . . . at last it seemed to him sound and judicious to attack the enemy everywhere, plunder and destroy all that was in their possession, set fire to the crops and other means of supporting human life, and let nothing remain

---

[65] *Ibid.*, pp. 58–9.   [66] FW, II, p. 4; SD, II, p. 188.

[67] Orderic, II, pp. 230–3, and cf. the death-bed speech Orderic puts in William's mouth: 'In mad fury I descended on the English of the north like a raging lion, and ordered that their homes and crops with all their equipment and furnishings should be burnt at once, and their great flocks and herds of sheep and cattle slaughtered everywhere' (*ibid.*, IV, pp. 94–5).

14 The pity of war distilled. A woman and her child flee from a house torched by
Norman troops, from the Bayeux Tapestry. As with Duke William's devastation
of Harold's estates on the Sussex coast in early October, 1066, a chief object of
the raid or chevauchée was to undermine an opponent's lordship by highlighting
his impotence to protect his own subjects. In such warfare, 'non-combatants'
enjoyed scant protection despite the strictures of the Church (by special permission of the City of Bayeux).

anywhere, that under this duress, reduced to the extremity of want, they might at last be compelled to yield and surrender.[68]

If we are to lend any credence to the chroniclers' reports, such measures were the closest that medieval society approached to 'total war': it was not until the advent of aerial bombing that a 'civilian' population could experience suffering greater in scale and degree than that inflicted by such systematic, regionalized harrying. Men equated William's devastation of the north with the onset of a severe famine.[69] 'Florence' of Worcester noted that men were forced to eat the flesh of humans, horses, dogs and cats; Others were forced to seek exile, or even to sell themselves into slavery to gain sustenance.[70] Houses, heaths and roads were littered with decaying bodies, which gave off a pestilential stench, since there was no one left to bury them. Between York and Durham there were no inhabited villages, and the land remained a desert for years.[71] William of Malmesbury, indulging in similar exaggeration, believed that the land around York still lay uncultivated for more than a sixty-mile radius at the time he was writing.[72]

THE EFFECTS OF RAVAGING: PROBLEMS OF EVIDENCE

Descriptions of ravaging by writers such as Orderic or 'Florence' raise the central problem that the vast majority of our evidence for such activities in the eleventh and twelfth centuries is literary and anecdotal. As such, it suffers from all the associated shortcomings of this type of material. Chroniclers were notoriously prone to hyperbole, as Orderic's estimation of 100,000 fatalities incurred during the 'harrying of the North' amply demonstrates. Not only might the severity of local conditions first be exaggerated, but these in turn might then be inflated into broad generalities. The lamentation of the *Anglo-Saxon Chronicle* over the enormities occurring during the 'anarchy' is a famous instance,[73] as is the picture painted by the *Gesta Stephani* of the general condition suffered by Englishmen in 1143:

> Some, putting together humble cottages around the churches in hope of protection, lived in fear and suffering; some, from lack of food (for a terrible famine prevailed all over England), ate the forbidden and unaccustomed flesh of dogs or horses, others to relieve their hunger, fed unsatisfied on raw and filthy herbs or roots; some, in every county, because the affliction of the

---

[68] *GS*, pp. 218–19, and cf. *ibid.*, pp. 220–1, where the *Gesta* describes the implementation of this policy in the district of Marlbrough and Devizes.   [69] *ASC* 'D', *s.a.* 1069, pp. 150–1.   [70] *FW*, II, p. 4.
[71] *SD*, II, pp. 188.   [72] *GR*, II, pp. 308–9.   [73] *ASC*, 'E', *s.a.* 1137.

famine was more than they could bear, wasted away and died in droves . . .
You could have seen villages extremely well known standing lonely and
almost empty, because the peasants of both sexes and all ages were dead . . .
and all England wearing an aspect of sorrow and misfortune, an aspect of
wretchedness and oppression.[74]

Clearly such generalities invite scepticism, not only for their lack of sub-
stantive detail, but also for their recurrence as *topoi*. Yet one should not be
completely dismissive. First, extended ravaging in a rural, subsistence
economy must *a priori* have occasioned localized dearth and famine. And
while one can point, for example, to the resilience of peasant agriculture, or
the ease with which wattle and daub or wooden structures could be rebuilt,
there is a tendency to overlook the sheer human suffering which devastation, on whatever scale, must have caused – the plight of the individuals
involved, the shortage of food, lack of shelter and fatalities by fire or the
sword.[75]

Second, not all chronicle evidence is vague and inflated. In describing
how his own house of St Evroul had suffered from the ravaging of its
estates by Robert de Bellême during his feud with the monks, Orderic was
clearly drawing on a vivid, and none too distant tradition which commands
far greater respect than the generalized observations of the *Gesta Stephani*.
As a result of Bellême's depredations, 'the monks suffered acutely from
want, and Abbot Roger was obliged to seek supplies from King William in
England for the use of the needy who had lost all their means of sustenance through the tyrant's ravages'.[76]

Equally if not more compelling is the uniquely detailed and localized
account of the refugees from the 'harrying of the North' provided by the
eleventh-century life of Aethelwig, abbot of Evesham. Incorporated into
the later *Chronicon de Evesham*, this records how William's army laid waste
not only Yorkshire but also Cheshire, Shropshire, Staffordshire and
Derbyshire. Of those caught up in this maelstrom and the ensuing famine,
some managed to struggle as far south as the abbey of Evesham in search
of charity. The town of Evesham, notes the abbot's biographer, was
crowded with a vast number of men, young and old, and women with children fleeing from the famine. They lay in and outside houses and throughout the town, some in the cemetery where they had been overtaken by

[74] *GS*, pp. 152–5.
[75] Cronne, *The Reign of King Stephen*, p. 183, while expressing reservations as to the nature of the descriptions, accepts the reality of the sufferings portrayed by the chroniclers of Stephen's reign. For a critical analysis of the possible extent of damage caused to the Midland shires by warfare during
Stephen's reign see G. White, 'Were the Midlands "Wasted" in Stephen's Reign?', *Midland History*, 10
(1985), pp. 26–46.   [76] Orderic, IV, pp. 296–7; cf. *ibid.*, pp. 159–61 and VI, pp. 58–9.

hunger before they could reach the abbey. Some, who had gone without food for so long, died on being given sustenance, while the mortality was such that the prior had to bury five or six people every day. In an attempt to provide food and shelter for the numerous children, Aethelwig assigned one to each of the monastic servants and even to the brothers, and further commanded that all pilgrims and poor people should be received and supplied with victuals.[77]

Yet even such accounts are but isolated vignettes, allowing only an impressionistic view of the nature and extent of damage inflicted by ravaging. Given this, it is unsurprising that in order to assess the extent of destruction more accurately, much has been made of the existing record material, in particular Domesday Book and the Pipe Rolls for the early years of Henry II's reign. Thus the significant decline in the values of land between 1066 and 1086 recorded by Domesday have been used to plot the destructive march of William I's army from the coast to Berkhampstead in 1066 – in effect a minor chevauchée intended to intimidate the capital into surrender.[78] Likewise, the numerous entries of 'waste' (*wasta*) in the great survey for the northern and midland counties have been taken as eloquent testimony to the effectiveness of William's 'harrying of the North'.[79] Similar entries of 'waste' in the Pipe Roll of 1156 have equally been regarded as revealing the attrition wrought by the 'anarchy' of Stephen's reign.[80]

Such interpretations, however, have been questioned. Rather than representing tax liability written off as the results of physical devastation, it has been suggested that the term 'waste' in the 1156 Pipe Roll reflected rather the difficulties encountered in levying a geld 'in the aftermath of war and

[77] *Chronicon abbatiae de Evesham*, ed. W. D. Macray (Rolls Series, 1863), p. 90. The importance of this life of Aethelwig and its early date of composition are discussed by R. R. Darlington, 'Aethelwig, Abbot of Evesham', *EHR*, 47 (1933), pp. 1–22 (especially pp. 1–10) and pp. 177–98. In the latter section, he reproduces the relevant passage concerning the refugees to Evesham (pp. 178–9) and examines the Domesday evidence for the damage inflicted in Cheshire, Shropshire, Staffordshire and Derbyshire (pp. 177–85).

[78] The route of William's army in 1066 has been plotted from Domesday Book by calculating the fall in value from manors *tunc-post*. For a summary of these calculations and a map of William's suggested route, see R. W. Finn, *The Norman Conquest and Its Effect on the Economy, 1066–86* (London, 1971), pp. 19–23. Among the more detailed studies are F. H. Baring, 'The Conqueror's Footsteps in Domesday Book', *EHR*, 13 (1898), pp. 17–25, reprinted in his *Domesday Tables* (London, 1909), pp. 207–16; G. H. Fowler, 'The Devastation of Bedfordshire and the Neighbouring Counties in 1065 and 1066', *Archaeologia*, 72 (1922), pp. 41–50; and C. H. Lemmon, 'The Campaign of 1066', *The Norman Conquest*, ed. D. Whitelock *et al.* (London, 1966), pp. 116–22.

[79] For the record of Domesday Book for the 'harrying of the North' and a discussion of the nature of 'waste', see Finn, *The Norman Conquest*, pp. 27, 123–4, 127–8 and T. A. M. Bishop, 'The Norman Settlement of Yorkshire', *Studies in Medieval History presented to Frederick Maurice Powicke*, ed. R. W. Hunt, W. A. Pantin and R. W. Southern (Oxford, 1948), pp. 1–14.

[80] White, 'Were the Midlands "Wasted" in Stephen's Reign?', pp. 26–27 and n. 5; E. M. Amt, 'The Meaning of Waste in the Early Pipe Rolls of Henry II' *Economic History Review*, 44 (1991), pp. 240–8.

following a period in which danegeld had not been levied in much of the country for at least seventeen years'.[81] As a result of widespread tenurial upheaval and disputed claims, there was frequently a shortfall between the amounts the sheriffs were able to collect and the liabilities as indicated by pre-1135 assessments. 'Waste' was thus a term of administrative convenience applied to these fiscal discrepancies, and was not necessarily, or even primarily, indicative of war damage.[82] The same argument has been applied to waste in Domesday Book, though recently a strong case has been made to re-emphasize the devastation of William's forces as the principal cause of waste recorded in the northern shires in 1086.[83]

If, however, the term 'waste' in Domesday and the Pipe Rolls remains equivocal, more specific, abundant and unambiguous evidence from the later thirteenth century makes plain the economic destruction that might be caused by systematic and repeated ravaging. Using manorial rent rolls and tithe records, Scammell has mapped the economic consequences of the repeated Scottish raids from 1311 against the north of England, which fully exploited the complete inability of Edward II to protect his own border shires. The value of manors rapidly declined till many were yielding no revenue, while flight or mortality occasioned the widespread disappearance of serfs or poorer tenantry.[84]

Such sustained devastation, which prohibited recovery and therefore was cumulative in its impact, was the exception in Britain. It was the result of the

---

[81] *Ibid.*, p. 28.

[82] *Ibid.*, p. 33: 'To the exchequer, the land was waste if danegeld could be neither collected nor formally pardoned – regardless of its physical condition and whatever the reasons the decision not to pursue the tax might be'. As a result, 'the value of the term as an indicator of physical devastation under Stephen is seriously diminished' (*ibid.*).

[83] W. E. Wightmam, *The Lacy Family in England and Normandy* (Oxford, 1966), p. 53; *idem.*, 'The Significance of "Waste" in the Yorkshire Domesday', *Northern History*, 10 (1975), pp. 55–71; D. M. Palliser, 'Domesday Book and the Harrying of the North', *Northern History*, 29 (1993), pp. 1–23, which provides the most detailed and critical examination of the Domesday material. Despite significant doubts on the validity of mapping the devastation by entries of Domesday 'waste', Palliser nevertheless remarks that 'it would be wrong to conclude that William's punitive actions in 1069–70 were not catastrophic', and that the harrying 'shocked men of the twelfth century and struck them as beyond normal or acceptable limits' (*ibid.*, p. 20). This revisionism, however, is challenged by J. Palmer, 'War and Domesday Waste', in *War and Chivalry. The Proceedings of the Twelfth Harlaxton Symposium*, ed. M. J. Strickland (Stamford, forthcoming).

[84] J. Scammell, 'Robert I and the North of England', *EHR*, 188 (1958), pp. 385–403. The accounts for the estates of Alnwick castle, for example, show a decline from a deficit of 4.1 per cent of their normal value in 1315 to 28.6 per cent by 1317, while by 1318 no rents could be collected at Whitsun and few at Michaelmas. By 1319 several manors had been completely abandoned. In 1322, lands around Bamburgh could furnish no rent, and as late as 1328 were only yielding 61 per cent of their normal revenue. It was the same story with ecclesiastical income. By 1319, the monastery of Durham was unable to collect the tithes of any but one of its dependent churches, which in 1313–14 had yielded £412, while in 1316 the archiepiscopal manor of Hexham recorded a 98 per cent loss of rent (*ibid.*, pp. 387–8). The entirety of Scammel's article is an invaluable study of the effects of sustained raiding against a locality.

extreme vulnerability of the northern English shires caused by a military and political vacuum at the centre of English government, and as such was far more analogous to the destruction suffered by many areas in France during the Hundred Years War.[85] The impact of William Wallace's invasion of England in 1297 is more representative of the damage caused by a single incursion by a sizeable enemy force.[86] As a result of Wallace's activities between October and December 1297, record evidence reveals a dramatic drop in income from tithes, altarage and rents, the destruction of towns, mills and churches, and the slaying of bondmen.[87] With a precision which suggests access to some form of documentary record, the St Edmundsbury Chronicle noted that in 1297, the Scots destroyed 715 vills, compared to the 120 vills burnt in the more limited border raiding the year previously.[88] Although record evidence of the type employed by McNamee or Scammell is lacking for the twelfth century, it would seem probable that earlier Scottish incursions, such as those of David I into Northumbria in 1138, or of William the Lion in 1173–4 caused a similar level of destruction.[89]

RAVAGING AS INTIMIDATION AND POLITICAL CONTROL

Given the enormous potential destruction that could be inflicted by unleashing an army against the countryside and its inhabitants, it is not surprising to find that in addition to the practical aspects of gaining or denying supplies, ravaging might be employed in war as a highly effective form of intimidation. In 1141, for example, Stephen's queen used ravaging to pressurize the Londoners to abandon their support for the Empress.[90] The unfortunate Londoners had earlier been subjected to a similar experience when William I, faced in 1066 with continuing resistance from London despite his victory at Hastings, chose not to attempt to take the city by storm, but instead to cow its citizens into submission by an encircling march, harrying as he went.[91] The intimidation had its desired effect, and at

---

[85] See, for example, R. Boutrouche, 'The Devastation of Rural Areas during the Hundred Years War and the Agricultural Recovery of France', *The Recovery of France in the Fifteenth Century*, ed. P. S. Lewis (New York, London, 1972), pp. 23–59; and L. Carolus-Barré, *Benoît XII et la mission charitable de Bertrand Carit* (Mélanges d'Archéologie et d'Histoire publiés par L'Ecole française de Rome, 1950), which studies the destruction inflicted by Edward III in the Cambrésis in 1339.

[86] C. J. McNamee, 'William Wallace's Invasion of Northern England in 1297', *Northern History*, 26 (1991), pp. 40–58.   [87] *Ibid., passim.*   [88] *Ibid.*, p. 40, n. 1.

[89] For these raids see Strickland, 'Securing the North', pp. 183–7.   [90] *GS*, pp. 122–3.

[91] While a Norman detachment routed a force of Londoners close to the city and fired Southwark, his main army divided into units and left a trail of devastation through Sussex, the regions around both Canterbury and Southampton, Surrey, Hampshire, Berkshire, Oxfordshire, Buckinghamshire, Bedfordshire, Cambridgeshire, Hertfordshire and Middlesex (WP, pp. 214–16; FW, I, p. 228; *ASC* 'D', *s.a.* 1066; cf. Douglas, *William the Conqueror*, pp. 205–6; Brown, *The Normans and the Norman Conquest*, p. 179).

Berkhampstead he received the submission of the leading Anglo-Saxon clergy and magnates.

Earlier that year, before the battle of Hastings, William had ravaged lands on the south coast, and it may well be that this was a deliberate attempt to provoke Harold into an early confrontation by inflicting both material and psychological damage to an area under his personal lordship.[92] This ravaging is graphically depicted in the Bayeux Tapestry, which shows soldiers seizing and slaughtering livestock, and burning a house while a woman and child flee from it (Plates 13 and 14).[93]

Ravaging and the conduct it frequently entailed must, moreover, be seen in a wider perspective than merely a method of waging war between principalities. If, as we have seen, the difficulties posed by provisioning and billeting itinerant households might result in sporadic and unpremeditated violence, a king or prince might deliberately employ any or all of the constituent elements of harrying against his erstwhile subjects who offered resistance to his authority, be they individuals, institutions, or, in times of armed rebellion, whole regions implicated in rebel activity.

Quite apart from situations of revolt, Anglo-Saxon kings had harried towns or localities for civil misdemeanours such as resistance to taxation, the maltreatment of merchants or foreigners under the king's protection or the slaying of important individuals.[94] The political crisis of 1051 had ostensibly as its catalyst the refusal by Earl Godwine to implement Edward the Confessor's orders to ravage his town of Dover in reprisal for the townsmen's attack on the men of Eustace of Boulogne.[95] Doubtless only the paucity of the sources prevents us from seeing the implementation of such fundamental mechanisms of control in earlier Anglo-Saxon periods.

The Conquest saw not simply the continuation of such methods of government, but arguably their intensification. It has long been recognized that distraint and the denial of access to the machinery of justice were an

[92] WP pp. 168, 180; Douglas, *William the Conqueror*, pp. 196–7. Cf. C. J. Turner, 'William the Conqueror's March to London', *EHR*, 106 (1912), pp. 209–25. For Harold's estates see A. Williams, 'Land and Power in the Eleventh Century: The Estates of Harold Godwineson', *Proceedings of the Battle Conference*, 3 (1980), pp. 171–87.
[93] *BT*, pls. 44–5, 'et hinc milites festinaverunt Hestinga ut cibum raperentur', and pls. 50–1, 'hic domus incenditur'.
[94] In 1041, Harthacnut had Worcestershire ravaged in reprisal for the killing of two of his housecarls who had attempted to collect the severe tax levied the previous year (*ASC* 'C', s.a. 1041). Eadred, in 952, 'ordered a great slaughter to be made in the borough of Thetford in vengeance for the abbot Eadhelm, whom they had slain', while in 969, Edgar 'ordered all Thanet to be ravaged' for maltreating some merchants from the Danelaw (*ASC* 'D', s.a. 952. 969). In 986 Aethelred II 'laid waste the diocese of Rochester' because Bishop Aelfstan had ejected one of the king's thegns from an episcopal vill, unaware that the king had granted it to this man (*ASC* 'C', s.a. 986; and for a full discussion of the incident, S. Keynes, *The Diplomas of King Aethelred the Unready, 978–1016* (Cambridge, 1980), pp. 178–9).   [95] *ASC* 'E', s.a. 1051.

integral element in the process of Anglo-Norman and Angevin government. The ravaging of a subject's lands was but an extension of such coercion, the most extreme manifestation of royal 'Ira et malevolentia'.[96]
Nowhere is the use of harrying as a means of political coercion more
graphically revealed than in the tract *De injusta vexatione Willelmi episcopi*,
which relates the systematic plundering and devastation of the lands of
William of St Calais, bishop of Durham, by agents of William Rufus after
he had been accused of complicity in the revolt of 1088.[97] On his refusal to
plead in the *curia regis* as a secular baron, his lands and goods were apportioned to lay lords, his livestock seized, his men held to ransom and some,
presumably villeins, were even sold off. Finally, Rufus sent a force to burn
and pillage those estates which remained in the bishop's hands.[98]

Although unusually well documented, the fate of William of St Calais
was by no means untypical. Thomas Becket and Geoffrey Plantagenet,
Archbishop of York, were but two of the most prominent political opponents to suffer violent disseisin at the hands of the Angevin kings.[99]
Refinement of such intimidation reached its height in 1208 with the case of
William de Braose, who, having fallen foul of King John and suffered
attack from a force of 500 infantry and 25 mounted serjeants under the
mercenary captain Gerard d'Athée, was even ordered to pay 1,000 marks to
meet the cost of the expedition against him.[100]

The description provided by the 'De injusta vexatione' highlights once
more the essentially vicarious nature of this form of warfare. It was the
tenants, townsfolk or men at the soil who ultimately paid the price for their
lord's misdemeanours. This phenomenon was still more pronounced when
the king took action against rebellious lords in times of revolt. Whole communities might suffer because of real or suspected affinities with political
opponents, and here again, the Norman and Angevin kings merely continued pre-existing practice. Following Cnut's withdrawal from Lindsey in
1014, for example, Aethelred II had laid waste this area and killed all the
men he caught as punishment for supporting the Danish invaders.[101]

Though William I's 'harrying of the North' in 1069–70 represents an

---

[96] J. E. A. Jolliffe, *Angevin Kingship* (London, 1955), pp. 87–109.

[97] SD, I, p. 172, *EHD*, II, p. 654. The text used is that printed in Simeon of Durham, *Opera Omnia* (SD, I, pp. 170–95). It is translated in full in *EHD*, II, no. 84, pp. 652–68, and is discussed by C. W. David, 'A Tract Attributed to Simeon of Durham', *EHR*, 32 (1917), pp. 382–7. Its authenticity was questioned by H. S. Offler, 'The Tractate *De injusta vexatione Willelmi episcopi primi*', *EHR*, 66 (1951), pp. 32–41, who assigned to it a date somewhere in the second quarter of the twelfth century. This redat-
ing, however, was rejected by both R. W. Southern (*St Anselm and his Biographer* (Cambridge, 1963), p. 148) and D. C. Douglas, (*EHD*, II, p. 652).   [98] SD, I, pp. 173–80, *EHD*, II, pp. 653–9.

[99] F. Barlow, *Thomas Becket* (London, 1986), pp. 124–7; Howden, IV, pp. 139–40.

[100] *Rot. Pat.*, p. 81. For a detailed discussion of John's actions against William, see Painter, *King John*, pp. 242–45.   [101] *ASC 'C'*, *s.a.* 1014.

extreme instance of such behaviour and was anomalous in the extent of its destruction, John's attempt to crush baronial resistance in 1215–16 brought fire and sword to a large number of counties. During his punitive campaign against the northern rebels in early 1216, John's *routiers* laid waste the lands of his baronial opponents, burning crops, seizing livestock and destroying their woods and orchards, while John's second army under Fawkes de Bréauté, Savaric de Mauleon and other captains conducted a great harrying raid through the eastern and home counties.[102] The granaries of Bury St Edmunds and Crowland were burned, and it was only by good fortune that the monasteries themselves, along with Ely, escaped being put to the torch.[103] Towns and vills were fired, or were forced to fine with the king to escape similar punishment.[104]

John's acceptance of these proffers demonstrates how the fate of a town or locality in situations of revolt might be mitigated by the desire of the king to win support by a display of clemency. The fear of provoking further resistance in a volatile political climate almost certainly lay behind William I's leniency towards Exeter in 1068,[105] while there must have been an awareness that, in some cases, townsmen could have done little to oppose the insurrection of a powerful local lord. Hence in 1173, when the justiciar Richard de Lucy took the town of Leicester by force, he demolished the town gates and part of the walls, but on payment of a fine allowed the citizens to leave unharmed with their chattels. They could go anywhere they wished in the king's lands until there should be peace, when they would be allowed to return to their property.[106] De Lucy's actions were designed to strike a severe financial and psychological blow against Robert of Leicester, one of the leading rebels against Henry II, effectively to halt the economic potential of the town for the duration of the *tempus werrae*, but at the same time to show leniency in order to encourage further capitulation of rebel towns. In situations of revolt, the sacking of a rebel-held town might assume the status of a judicial act of punishment. In 1199, for example, John had seized Le Mans, pulled down its walls, demolished the castle and the houses in the town and took many of its citizens captive because they had received Arthur as their lord.[107] The sack of Lincoln following the defeat of the combined French and baronial forces in 1217 was not a spontaneous act resulting from indiscipline, but a calculated act of chastisement carried out in the king's name and, with the sanction of the legate,

---

[102] MP, II, pp. 635–9, 641, 645–6; Coggeshall, pp. 177–9.   [103] Above, pp. 90–1; below, p. 319.
[104] *Chronicle of Melrose*, p. 62; *Rot. Ob. et Fin.*, pp. 574, 596.
[105] Orderic, II, pp. 212–15. Cf. above, p. 2.   [106] Diceto, I, p. 376; *GH*, I, p. 58.
[107] Howden, IV, p. 87.

extending even to ecclesiastical property. Unlike the sack of the same city in 1141, the royalists appear to have refrained from insensate killing, and the looting was brought to an orderly and official conclusion by proclaiming the king's peace throughout the city.[108]

In situations of rebellion or civil war, indeed, it was inevitable that, as political and economic centres, towns should be caught up in hostilities and suffer severely. At Rouen in 1090, following their hard-won victory over the pro-Rufus faction led by Conan, son of Gilbert Pilatus, the men of Robert Curthose finally gained the upper hand and proceeded to indulge in 'a ferocious slaughter of the townsmen' who had supported Rufus. Those who escaped the carnage were divided up for ransom by the ducal supporters and carried off in chains 'as if they had been foreign enemies'.[109] The feud between Robert of Gloucester and Waleran of Meulan led to the pillaging and partial destruction of Worcester and Tewkesbury,[110] and such examples could be greatly multiplied. The real or imagined wealth of towns meant that the right of storm, enjoyed by victors over the lives and property of a town or castle taken by force, was more often than not fully exercised by troops eager for booty with scant regard to the lives of the burgesses.

THE ANTITHESIS OF CHIVALRY?

Such, then, were the aims, mechanisms and context of ravaging. But how far is it possible to gauge the attitudes of either the knights themselves or contemporary observers to the forms of behaviour which ravaging necessarily entailed? The question is one of cardinal importance, for there has been a tendency, particularly among historians of the Hundred Years War, to assume that the killing of defenceless peasantry and the burning of crops and dwellings was essentially 'unchivalric'. Such behaviour could be seen to stand in antithesis to the behavioural norms in operation between members of the knighthood, and thus to suggest a fundamental dichotomy in the nature of knightly conduct.

From this, it is but a small step to the conclusion reached by Huizinga and others, acutely aware of the extensive and repeated devastation caused by the widespread employment of the chevauchée in the fourteenth and fifteenth centuries, that chivalry itself had become but a veneer, serving only to gloss over *de facto* knightly brutality and the real horrors of war. Such a view was derived in no small part from the criticism of late medieval writers like Honoré Bonet:

---

[108] MP, III, pp. 23–4. For the brutal sack of Lincoln in 1141 see Orderic, VI, pp. 544–7; *GS*, pp. 112–13; *HN*, p. 49.   [109] Orderic, IV, pp. 220–3, 224–7.   [110] JW, pp. 57, 60.

... in these days, all wars are directed against the poor labouring people and against their goods and chattels. I do not call that war, but it seems to me to be pillage and robbery. Further, that way of warfare does not follow the worthy ordinances of chivalry or of the ancient custom of noble warriors who upheld justice, the orphan and the poor. And nowadays it is the opposite that they do everywhere, and the man who does not know how to set places on fire, to rob churches and to usurp their rights and to imprison priests is not fit to carry on war. And for these reasons the knights of today have not the glory and the praise of the old champions of former times, and their deeds can never come to great perfection of virtue.[111]

Bonet's contrast between a golden age of knighthood and the moral decadence of contemporary warriors was completely fallacious.[112] As we have seen, knights of the eleventh and twelfth centuries were just as prone to arson, the despoliation of churches and the slaying of peasantry. Ravaging and the chevauchée was no innovation in the fourteenth century but an integral aspect of warfare throughout the Middle Ages. Yet given this, does the fundamental criticism that ravaging marked the antithesis of chivalry hold just as true for the Anglo-Norman period as for the supposed 'Indian summer' of late medieval chivalry? Is it valid to posit a dichotomy between chivalric conduct and the conduct ravaging entailed towards the *inermes*? Or is this rather an anachronistic and subjective judgement based on modern, rather than contemporary perceptions of the nature of chivalry?

The Church's thinking on the legitimacy of ravaging was to be most cogently expressed by Honoré Bonet in his *Tree of Battles*, where he argued that attacking the peasantry was a violation of the fundamental interdependence of the 'three orders':

Ox-herds, and all husbandmen, and ploughmen with their oxen, when they are carrying on their buisness, and equally when they are going to it or returning from it, are secure, according to the written law. And in truth that this should be so is not without good reason, because it is expedient and convenient for all sorts of people, since those whose cultivate the soil plough and work for all men and for everybody, and all manner of folk live of their labour. Therefore, right reason does not permit that they should receive any ill or annoyance, seeing as they have no concern with war or with harming anyone.[113]

Though a gloss on conditions in the fourteenth century, the standpoint encapsulated by Bonet was long-established. From the late tenth century, ecclesiastical criticism of ravaging had been implicit in the legislation of the

[111] Bonet, *The Tree of Battles*, p. 189.   [112] Above, pp. 18–19.   [113] Bonet, *The Tree of Battles*, p. 188.

Peace and Truce of God, which sought to shield both clergy and peasantry
– the *inermes* – from knightly aggression. Yet it is these very decrees that so
eloquently reveal the extent to which the peasantry and their agricultural
implements were a primary target for the warriors.[114]

Ecclesiastics were acutely aware that in time of war or political dis-
turbance they were the principal victims of spoliation at the hands of
the warriors. The Peace and Truce legislation was conceived to defend
the Church's landed and material wealth just as much as to protect the
ordo of labourers. If such vulnerability coloured clerical conceptions
of the morality of ravaging, then attacks on their own foundations
naturally provoked vociferous indignation from monastic writers.
Orderic, as we have seen, was predictably outspoken in his criticism of
the men of Robert Blouet who attacked St Evroul and 'instead of over-
running the lands of warlike knights, tried to carry off without warning
the herds that were peacefully grazing in the fields belonging to the
monks'.[115] It seems clear, however, that Orderic disapproved of the
seizure of livestock not so much as a method of war *per se*, but because in
this instance the victim had been a defenceless monastery, and his own at
that.

The implication here that lands of knights at war were a legitimate
target for their fellow warriors highlights something of a discrepancy in
contemporary clerical attitudes. On the one hand, ecclesiastics such as
Orderic or the author of the *Gesta Stephani* were clearly moved by the
human suffering that ravaging caused. Even though not a contemporary
of the 'harrying of the North', the anger and bitterness Orderic felt
towards William I for this slaughter still rings from his pages. Yet on the
other, even these men were aware that though the Church attempted to
shield the peasantry from aristocratic violence by the Peace and Truce of
God, such measures could in reality do little to prevent what were essentially unavoidable aspects of war. It was possible, for instance, for the penitential of Ermenfrid of Sion, issued in the aftermath of the battle of
Hastings and very much concerned to stress the just war doctrine of right
intent, to draw a distinction between mere plunder and needful – and
hence legitimate – foraging:

> Whoever before the consecration of the king killed anyone offering resis-
> tance as he moved through the kingdom in search of supplies is to do one
> year's penance for each person so slain. Anyone, however, who killed not in

---

[114] See, for example, the Council of Toulouges, 1041 (*RHF*, XI, pp. 510–11, cc. 4, 5 and 6), and the
Council of Narbonne, 1054 (*RHF*, XI, p. 515, cc. 9 and 10).

[115] Above, p. 15; Orderic, VI, pp. 459–61.

search of supplies but in looting is to do three years' penance for each person so slain.[116]

Equally, ravaging and its ensuing brutality was so habitual, so integral an element of contemporary warfare that even the hagiographers of Thomas Becket did not scruple to impute such behaviour to the saint, when, in his worldly years as chancellor, he had been a prominent and aggressive commander on Henry II's great Toulouse campaign of 1159.[117]

There was, however, a fine dividing line between ravaging in war and mere brigandage which might proliferate in times of internal disorder or lawlessness. Thus the troubadour Giraut de Borneil, himself the victim of brigands following his return from the court of Castile, bitterly castigated the unworthiness of mere pillage;

> You once saw tourneys proclaimed and well equipped men following them, and then for a time [you heard] talk of the best exploits; now it is merit to steal and snatch sheep from the fold! Shame on the knight who proceeds to pay court [to a lady] after he lays his hands on bleating sheep, and robs churches and travellers on the road![118]

Such a view was shared by Richard I, who in 1190 hanged William de Chisi, a Gascon castellan preying on the pilgrims *en route* for Compostela.[119]

Nevertheless, there were those knights who regarded plundering as a way of life. Such a man was Warin de Walcote, an 'honest itinerant knight who fought in the war' during Stephen's reign who, falling on hard times because under Henry II's peace he could not rob and plunder as he used to, resorted to his old ways of brigandage before being finally overtaken by the law.[120] Others were driven to plundering by economic necessity. In a letter to Henry of Blois, Brian fitz Count angrily countered the bishop's protests that he had robbed travellers going to the great St Giles fair at Winchester by reminding him that for supporting the Empress, at the behest of Henry himself, Brian had lost his fief and livelihood, and now had to feed his knights by any means he could.[121]

---

[116] Brown, *The Norman Conquest*, p. 157. The *terminus ante quem* of William's coronation is significant. Prior to Christmas Day 1066, acts of foraging would be regarded as the necessary activity of an invading army. Thereafter, however, unauthorized despoliation would be viewed as a breach of the king's peace and as an act of private war which might be severely punished.

[117] Edward Grim, *Vita Sancti Thomae, Materials for the History of Thomas Becket, Archbishop of Canterbury*, ed. J. C. Robertson, 7 vols. (Rolls Series, 1875–85), II, p. 365; William fitz Stephen, *Vita sancti Thomae, Materials for the History of Thomas Becket*, III, pp. 34–5.

[118] Stanza 3 of *Per solatz revelhar, TLP*, pp. 146–7.   [119] Howden, III, p. 35.

[120] *Rolls of the Justices in Eyre for Gloucestershire, Worcestershire and Staffordshire, 1221–1222*, ed. D. M. Stenton (Selden Society, 49, 1940), no. 390.

[121] See the correspondence printed in H. W. C. Davis, 'Henry of Blois and Brian FitzCount', *EHR*, 25 (1910), pp. 297–303, at pp. 301–2.

Many, however, did not need such an excuse. The list of depredations suffered by the nuns of Holy Trinity, Caen, during the weak rule of Robert Curthose reveal a roll call of Norman lords involved in cattle rustling, petty agricultural theft and localized incidents of violence during an earlier period of political destabilization.[122] In wartime, pillaging became both easier and endemic. Bertran de Born, with aggressive contempt for the merchant class, looked forward to the renewal of hostilities as a time for enrichment:

> Trumpets, tabors, banners and pennants, and ensigns, and black and white horses we shall see soon, and life will be good, when one takes from the usurers their wealth, and no pack-horse goes on the roads even by day in safety, nor townsmen without fear, nor any merchant coming from France; rather will he be rich who is ready to plunder.[123]

If some lords may not have shared Bertran de Born's view of brigandage, the attitude of the knights themselves to ravaging in war itself appears unequivocal. Harrying was an essential element in the effective prosecution of the warfare. Its practice was seen as a basic facet of the warrior's *metier*, and one which bore no stigma concerning its means of execution. Indeed, Gillingham has rightly pointed out that the *Histoire de Guillaume le Maréchal* not only portrays the chevauchée as 'the normal business of war', but regards the counselling of such ravaging as completely compatible with knightly behaviour. When the Marshal suggested to Henry II at Gisors in 1188 that his forces should enter Philip's lands by surprise and devastate the area, the king thanked him, saying that William was 'most courteous (*molt corteis*)'.[124] Similarly, Jordan Fantosme has Philip of Flanders, 'le noble guerreur', advise ravaging as a principal means of waging war and Louis VII 'approves and welcomes' this counsel.[125]

It might be objected, however, that the realities of ravaging sat uneasily with the ideal of the knight as the protector of the *inermes* – the poor, the widows, orphans and, of course, the clergy. Such a duty had long been inherent in the authority wielded by the warrior aristocracy, but the twelfth century witnessed increasingly explicit expression and conscious clerical sponsorship of the concept that knighthood constituted a discrete *ordo*, entry into which conferred not simply distinction but a defined set of moral responsibilities.[126] Such notions, most clearly visible, for example, in the writings of John of Salisbury,[127] achieved a more concrete manifesta-

[122] Haskins, *Norman Institutions*, pp. 63–4.
[123] *Miei-sirventes vuolh far dels reis amdos*, stanza 3, *TLP*, pp. 168–9; Gouiran, *L'amour et la guerre*, II, pp. 652–3.
[124] *HGM*, II. 7782–7802; Gillingham, 'War and Chivalry in the *History of William the Marshal*', pp. 5–6.
[125] *JF*, II. 137–54; above, pp. 266–7
[126] On these developments see Morris, '*Equestris Ordo*', pp. 87–96.   [127] Below, pp. 55–6, 56 n. 4.

tion in the ceremony of belting to knighthood: the girding on of the sword-belt not only admitted the young warrior into this secular vocation, but, in a distant echo of earlier royal investiture, conferred upon him both the authority and the duty to protect the defenceless.[128] When in Chrétien's *Perceval*, the hero is knighted by his tutor Gornement, he is admonished not only to spare defeated opponents, but also to protect ladies and to pray to be kept a true Christian.[129]

The apparent discrepancy between such ideals and the violence towards the *inermes* inherent in ravaging did not go unnoticed by clerical observers.[130] Certain chroniclers, for example, felt obliged to attribute a sense of reluctance or regret to lords involved in the implementation of extensive harrying. Thus in describing the war between Geoffrey de Mortagne and Robert de Bellême, Orderic noted how Robert's avoidance of open battle through fear of the treachery of his own men left Geoffrey no option but to strike at him through attacks on his lands and peasantry:

> Though it distressed him to injure defenceless and innocent people, he could not force the public enemy to meet him in open battle and so punish him as he deserved . . . So a protracted struggle dragged on between the two powerful border lords and caused severe losses and casualties to their subjects.[131]

Similarly, the author of the *Gesta Stephani* was quick to exonerate King Stephen's decision to implement extreme measures against his opponents in 1149:

> It was evil indeed, he thought, to take away the sustenance of human life that God vouchsafed, yet far worse for the kingdom to be constantly disturbed by the enemy's raiding and impoverished by daily pillage; it was more endurable to put up for a time with whatever troubles cruel fate might offer than bear so much continually from each one of the enemy. And no wonder, either, if he must rage with such cruelty against the enemy, as many opponents cannot be wiped out without much slaughter.[132]

Such a plea of necessity seems to have been reinforced by the concept that the duty to defend the weak and defenceless was not a univeral injunction, but one which applied only to one's own dependants. To his own and Holy Church, a man must be a munificent protector, but to his enemies he might be terrible in time of war. This profound duality inherent in good lordship is encapsulated in Orderic's praise for Count Geoffrey de Mortagne:

---

[128] Keen, *Chivalry*, pp. 64–73.
[129] *Le Conte du Graal*, 11. 1637–45; *Chrétien de Troyes: Arthurian Romances*, p. 402; cf. above, pp. 154–5.
[130] Below, pp. 55, 282.   [131] Orderic, IV, pp. 160–3.   [132] *GS*, pp. 218–21.

he was a distinguished count, handsome and brave, God-fearing and devoted to the church, a staunch defender of the clergy and God's poor; in time of peace he was gentle and loveable and conspicuous for his good manners: in time of war, harsh and successful, formidable to the rulers who were his neighbours, and an enemy to all.[133]

Thus to Orderic, ruthlessness in war – at least in the case of Geoffrey, sworn enemy of Orderic's *bête noire* Robert de Bellême – was not only legitimized, but became a lordly virtue. He expresses the same idea in describing the sons of Giroie: 'All these brothers were valiant and courtly; in war, nimble and cunning, to their enemies a scourge, to their friends gracious and gentle.'[134] Perceived thus, a lord, one of whose most essential functions was the provision of protection for his own men, became in war an instrument of destruction to those of any opponent without tarnishing his knightly reputation. Hence the virtues of knighthood and good lordship could be reconciled with the often brutal methods of warfare itself. Had this attitude not been preponderant, it is hard to see how warriors such as William Rufus or William Marshal, still less commanders of a later age such as Edward III, the Black Prince or Henry V who made extensive use of the chevauchée, could have enjoyed the glittering chivalric reputations bestowed on them by their contemporaries.

A striking example of the potential polarity between the munificent lord and the uncompromising warrior is furnished by the Beaumont twins. Both Waleran and Robert de Beaumont were lords pre-eminent in their wealth and position, regarded as generous, well-educated patrons.[135] They had received schooling in philosophy and theology from Abbot Faritus of Abingdon, and as young favourites in the court of Henry I, were capable of arguing precociously with the cardinals who had accompanied Calixtus II to Gisors in 1119.[136] They were benefactors to religious houses, and fully indulged in contemporary expressions of religious piety.[137] Yet in war both were capable of acts of no little brutality. In 1136, during a war against Roger de Tosny, Robert ordered the church of St Mary Magdalene at Bougy-sur-Risle to be burnt along with the men and women who had taken refuge in it.[138] According to Orderic, a not impartial witness due to his man-

[133] Orderic IV, pp. 160–1.   [134] *Ibid.*, II, pp. 24–5.

[135] For a detailed study of Waleran and Robert de Beaumont see Crouch, *The Beaumont Twins*, and E. King, 'Waleran, Count of Meulan, Earl of Worcester, 1104–1166', in *Tradition and Change: Essays in Honour of Marjorie Chibnall*, ed. D. Greenway, C. Holdsworth and J. Sayers (Cambridge, 1985), pp. 165–76.   [136] *GR*, II, p. 482. For their education, Crouch, *The Beaumont Twins*, p. 7 and n. 19.

[137] See, for example, S. Mesmin, 'Waleran, Count of Meulan and the Leper Hospital of St Gilles at Pont Audemer', *Annales de Normandie*, 32, pp. 3–19. A letter of 1145, written by Waleran to William Beauchamp, refers to his imminent departure on pilgrimage to Jerusalem (H. W. C. Davis, 'Some Documents of the Anarchy', in *Essays in History Presented to Reginald Lane Poole*, ed. H. W. C. Davis (Oxford, 1927; reprinted 1969), pp. 170–1).   [138] Orderic, VI, pp. 464–5.

ifest condemnation of Waleran's rebellion against Henry I, just prior to the battle of Bourgthéroulde in 1124, Waleran entered the forest of Brotonne, took prisoner many of the peasants he found cutting wood in the thickets, and crippled them by cutting off their feet' as punishment for aiding the king's forces.[139] Such an act of savagery, felt Orderic, violated the feast of the Annunciation, and Waleran's subsequent defeat in battle at Bourgthéroulde was clearly the result of divine retribution.[140]

Yet neither Waleran or Robert was a sadistic butcher in the mould of Robert de Bellême. Indeed, they were regarded as exponents rather than violators of chivalry. John of Worcester, for example, records how, in 1140, Waleran attacked Tewkesbury and burnt Robert of Gloucester's magnificent house in the town. Nevertheless, he spared the goods of the abbey on the supplication of the abbot, and although he took much booty from the town, 'he mercifully commanded that the prisoners be speedily released from their fetters and returned to their own houses'.[141]

In this mixture of cruelty and magnanimity, the Beaumonts seem to have been representative of the majority of the warrior aristocracy.[142] While Orderic regarded Robert de Bellême's notorious cruelty towards the peasantry as exceptional in both its degree and its extent,[143] it seems that the nobility had little compunction about ill-treating the peasantry or townsfolk in times of war. Just as a sense of professional and class solidarity helped to formulate and enforce usages of behavioural constraint between the knights themselves, so disdain for the lesser orders must have seriously compromised any sense of restraint and sanctioned much of the harsh treatment meted out to them. As we have seen, the butchery of defeated infantry, too poor to merit ransom, was regarded as a commonplace which did not even merit the effort of estimating the number of non-noble casualties.[144] If, before the battle of Bourgthéroulde in 1124, Waleran de Meulan could speak contemptuously of the stipendiary knights of Henry I's own *familia regis* as 'country bumpkins and mercenaries (*pagenses et gregarii*)', it is not hard to imagine his feelings towards the peasantry.[145] Similarly, Robert of Rhuddlan's treatment of the Welsh shows what a famous and respected Norman lord was capable of – even though in his own mind the fact that his enemies were Celtic *untermenschen* may well have fully justified his harsh behaviour.[146]

---

[139] *Ibid.*, VI, pp. 348–9.   [140] *Ibid.*   [141] JW, p. 60.

[142] Hence, for example, during the local war between Robert de Bellême and Rotrou de Mortagne, the two lords 'plundered poor and helpless people, constantly made them suffer loss or live in fear of losses, and brought distress to their dependants, knights and peasants alike, who endured many disasters' (Orderic, VI, pp. 396–7), Cf. *ibid.*, VI, pp. 58–9.

[143] Orderic, IV, pp. 298–9; and cf. above, pp. 199–200.   [144] Above, p. 176.

[145] Orderic, VI, pp. 350–1.   [146] Orderic, IV, pp. 138–9.

An incident recorded by Guibert of Nogent illustrates the aggressive disdain shown for the lives of the peasantry by a lord such as Thomas of Marle, lord of Coucy:

> It is certain that two years ago, when he had gone to Le Mont de Soissons to give aid to someone against some peasants, three of these men hid in a cave, and when he came to the entrance of the cave with his lance, he drove his weapon into the mouth of one of them with so hard a thrust that the blade of the lance tore through his entrails and passed out through his anus. Why go on with instances that have no end? The two left in the cave both perished by his hand.[147]

The extreme brutality of men such as Thomas de Marle and Robert de Bellême towards the peasantry cannot be taken as representative of the aristocracy as a whole, but sufficient examples of excessive cruelty exist to make one question the extent to which they stand wholly in isolation. Peter of Vaux-de-Cernay, for instance, noted of a local lord in Perigord, Bernard of Cahuzac, that 'it pleases him especially to mutilate the innocent. In a single monastery, that of the black monks at Sarlat, one hundred and fifty men and women were found whose hands and feet had been cut off, or whose eyes had been put out by him.'[148] Though it would be a grave injustice to Waleran of Meulan to compare him in most respects with the notorious Thomas de Marle, one of the deeds of the lord of Coucy recorded by Guibert of Nogent is reminiscent of Waleran's alleged behaviour towards his own peasantry in the forest of Brotonne. According to Guibert,

> one of his prisoners was wounded and could not march. He asked the man why he did not go faster. He replied that he could not. 'Stop', said he, 'I'll fix things so you'll make speed with real trouble'. Leaping down from his horse he cut off both the man's feet, and of that he died.[149]

Modern sensibilities may be offended at such a discrepancy between the treatment which knights afforded each other as members of a warrior elite, and that which they meted out to the peasantry, whether working in the fields or fighting as footsoldiers. But to conclude as a result that the process of ravaging was somehow 'unchivalric' is to impose an anachronistic value-judgement on the actions of contemporary warriors. In the eyes of the knights, the mechanisms of ravaging did not undermine the validity of 'chivalry', because the actions and gestures that comprised 'chivalrous' behaviour were never intended to be applied to the lesser orders; they were the strict preserve of members of the warrior aristocracy. If knights violated the strictures of the Peace of God in attacking unarmed peasants this

---

[147] Guibert, p. 185.   [148] *RHF*, xix, p. 98.   [149] Guibert, p. 185.

was because they were breaking regulations of conduct not of their own making and which in important respects were contradictory to the practical dictates of their own profession.

This said, there was equally a sense in which the burning of fields or attacks on peasantry gained the warrior more material profit than martial glory. Bertrand de Born's paean of the joys of war, 'Be.m platz lo gais temps de pascor', for instance, is concerned primarily with valiant feats of arms, with bravery and skill in combat between knights themselves. The *Histoire de Guillaume le Maréchal* might well stress the Marshal's grasp of strategy concerning raids, his military pragmatism, and the acclaim he thereby won from his royal masters and noble colleagues. But his greatest renown is won in the saddle against fellow knights either in the tourney or, still more important, in combat in the field. Likewise, Jordan Fantosme fully recognized the importance of ravaging, but his most fulsome praise for both English and Scottish knights alike is for their courage and prowess in pitched battle or in hard-fought siege.[150] One is left with the impression that while the harrying of the countryside was a crucial, highly profitable and totally commonplace element of war with which the knighthood was occupied for a greater proportion of time than with sieges or open engagement, this form of conflict was not where the highest honour or the greatest praise of one's brothers in arms was to be won.

By its very nature, ravaging entailed a degree of brutality towards the peasantry in war. This in turn raises the question of the nature of 'atrocity' and of what in the eyes of contemporaries *did* constitute unacceptable behaviour in time of war. To examine these vital issues, and thereby to set the mechanisms of ravaging in a broader ethical context, we must turn to the conduct of two non-knightly groups of warriors, both consistently denounced by Anglo-Norman observers as habitual perpetrators of atrocity: the Scots and the mercenary *routiers*.

---

[150] Compare Jordan's brief approbation of Humphrey de Bohun's ravaging of Lothian (11. 796–804) which causes 'nuisance', to his praise of the protagonists at the first siege of Wark, 1173, (11. 650–7, 661–8), at the battle of Fornham, 1173, (11. 1008–53, 1076–9), the second siege of Wark, 1174, (11. 1191–233) and the battle of Alnwick (11. 1758–892).

I I

TOTAL WAR? THE SCOTS AND THE *ROUTIERS*

Any examination of conduct of war must of necessity confront the question of extremes of conduct, of 'atrocities' perpetrated during hostilities. For though the conduct inherent in ravaging stood in sharp contrast to conventions of behavioural restraint in operation amongst the knighthood, these mechanisms of harrying must in turn be set against the behaviour of two groups of combatants vilified by hostile contemporaries as the epitome of cruelty and brutality. These men were the native Scots and Galwegian warriors, who formed the bulk of twelfth-century Scottish armies, and the bands of itinerant European mercenaries, prominent from the mid-twelfth century, known collectively as *routiers* or *ruptarii*.[1] Though some of these mercenaries received more specific racial designation, such as Brabançons, Biscayans or Navarrese, contemporaries regarded them as a specific class of man, normally of humble origin, who was both warrior and social outcast. The term *ruptarii*, rendered here as *routiers*, conveyed this duality and distinguished these men, spurned as sacrilegious brigands, from other more socially acceptable categories of stipendary troops.[2]

---

[1] General studies of the *routiers* are provided by H. Géraud, 'Les routiers au XIIe siècle', *Bibliothèque de l'Ecole des Chartes*, 3 (1841–2), pp. 125–47; *idem.*, 'Mercardier: les routiers au XIIIe siècle', *Bibliothèque de l'Ecole des Chartes*, 3 (1841–2), pp. 417–43; H. Grundmann, 'Rotten und Brabazonen. Sölner-Heere im 12 Jahrhundert', *Deutsches Archiv für Erforschung des Mittlealters*, 5 (1942), pp. 419–92; J. Boussard, 'Les mercenaires au XIIe siècle: Henri II Plantagenet et les origines de l'armée de metier', *Bibliothèque de l'Ecole des Chartes*, 106 (1945–6), pp. 189–224; A. Mens, 'De "Brabanciones" of bloeddorstige en plunderzieke avonturiers (XIIe–XIIIe eeuw)', *Miscellanea historica in honorem Alberti de Meyer* (Louvain and Brussels, 1946), I, pp. 558–70. These *routiers* were the twelfth-century equivalent of the free companies of the fourteenth and fifteenth centuries (Contamine, *War in the Middle Ages*, pp. 243–9).

[2] For the etymology of the term '*ruptarii*' see Ducange, VII, pp. 237–8, under '*rumpere*'; Grundmann, 'Rotten und Brabazonen', pp. 424–36 and the references there cited; Mens, 'De "Brabanciones"', p. 563, nn. 3 and 4. The English Exchequer clerks knew them as *coterelli* (*The Great Roll of the Pipe for the Eleventh Year of the Reign of King Henry II, 1164–5* (Pipe Roll Society, London 1887), p. 31). For stipendiary service of an honourable nature see Chibnall, 'Mercenaries and the "Familia Regis" under Henry I',

To Anglo-Norman observers, the Galwegian levies who formed a significant element in the hybrid armies of the Scottish kings[3] were regarded with a potent mixture of fear and contempt as scarcely human savages, set apart by their extreme barbarity in war.[4] The exact identity of the Galwegians was a source of some confusion to these Anglo-Norman writers.[5] By the twelfth century, they were in fact the remnants of the once powerful British kingdom of Strathclyde, which at its height had stretched from above Loch Lomond to Rere Cross on Stainmore.[6] Racially, the Galwegians were a blend of indigenous British with Scottish and Norse settlers, but seem to have spoken Gaelic, adding a further dimension to their perceived 'otherness'.[7] Among the Scots, they were renowned as

pp. 84–92; Prestwich, 'The Military Household of the Norman Kings', pp. 93–127; S. D. B. Brown, 'The Mercenary and his Master: Military Service and Monetary Reward in the Eleventh and Twelfth Century', *History* 74 (1989), pp. 20–38.

[3] Scottish armies of this period comprised principally of a native levy, strengthened by a far smaller number of enfeoffed or mercenary knights and other stipendaries. For the national levy and its organization see *RRS*, II, pp. 56–8. The hybrid nature of the Scottish forces is clearly indicated by descriptions of David I's battle order at the Standard in 1138 (*Relatio*, pp. 190–1; cf. RH, p. 79). No equivalent detail survives for the composition of William the Lion's forces in 1173–4, but despite a developing policy of enfeoffing Anglo-Norman vassals, the levy still formed the mainstay of his forces. In addition to contingents from Ross, Moray, Buchan and Angus, forces were led by Duncan II, earl of Fife, and Waltheof, earl of Dunbar (JF, II. 300, 385, 471–6; *GH*, I, p. 66). Cf. G. W. S. Barrow, 'The Army of Alexander III's Scotland', *Scotland in the Age of Alexander III*, ed. N. Reid (Edinburgh, 1981), pp. 132–47.

[4] Thus the *Gesta Stephani* could describe *Scotia* 'which is also called Albany' as a fertile land 'but it has inhabitants that are barbarous and filthy ... among foreigners they surpass all in cruelty' (*GS*, pp. 54–5). Walter Daniel, speaking of Ailred's visit to Rievaulx's daughter house of Dundrennan in Galloway, noted 'it is a wild country, where the inhabitants are like beasts, and is altogether barbarous' (Walter Daniel, *The Life of Ailred of Rievaulx* (*Vita Aelredi*), ed. and tr. F. M. Powicke (London, 1950), p. 45).

[5] Most Anglo-Norman writers make a clear distinction between the Galwegians and the 'Scots', a name usually given as a blanket term for the whole of David I's or William the Lion's forces. Thus Howden could note how 'David per Scottos et Galwegenses suos execrabiliter egit' (*GH*, I, p. 65). 'Scots' also denoted more precisely those dwelling north of the Forth–Clyde estuaries. Hence Jordan speaks of 'that miserable race, upon whom be God's curse, the Gallovidians (*les Galvens*), who covet wealth, and the Scots who dwell north of the Forth (*li Escot qui sunt en Albanie*) who have no faith in God, the son of Mary' (JF, II. 684–7). The chroniclers confuse the issue, however, by calling the Galwegians 'Picts' and by using the two terms synonymously. John of Hexham refers to the '*acies Scottorum et Pictorum*', and Richard of Hexham to '*Pictis, qui vulgo Galleweienses dicuntur*' (JH, p. 120; RH, p. 79). The Galwegians were not, of course, Picts, that is the people formerly inhabiting northern and central Scotland whose kingdom had by the tenth century become amalgamated with that of the Scots.

[6] D. P. Kirby, 'Strathclyde and Cumbria', *TCWAAS*, 62 (1962), pp. 77–94. Cf. A. A. M. Duncan, *Scotland: The Making of the Kingdom* (Edinburgh, 1975), pp. 87–9, 163–4; A. Smyth, *Warlords and Holy Men: Scotland, AD 80–1000* (Edinburgh, 1984), pp. 227–31. The kingdom lost its independence in 1018, and was incorporated into Scotland until 1092, when Rufus annexed its southern part below the Solway Firth, creating a Norman enclave at Carlisle and fixing the boundary with Scotland at the river Sark (*ASC* 'E', *s.a.* 1092; Kapelle, *The Norman Conquest of the North*, p. 227; cf. G. W. S. Barrow, 'The Anglo-Scottish Border', in *idem.*, *The Kingdom of the Scots* (1973), pp. 142–8, for an excellent summary of the subsequent fluctuations of the border). This southern part of Cumbria once again fell into Scottish hands in 1136, when David regained Carlisle and re-established the Scottish border to the west of Stainmore.

[7] Cumbria and Strathclyde may once have been synonymous terms for the same political and racial entity (P. A. Wilson, 'On the Terms "Strathclyde" and "Cumbria"', *TCWAACS*, 66 (1966), pp. 57–92; Smyth, *Warlords and Holy Men*, pp. 229–31). It seems clear, however, that by the early twelfth century,

fighters, and claimed the right of forming the front rank of the army in order to inflame others by the example of their wild bravery.[8]

The native elements of Scottish armies, whether Galwegians or Scots, were viewed by the Anglo-Normans with unrestrained loathing and contempt. To Richard of Hexham, they were 'more atrocious than the whole race of pagans, neither fearing God nor regarding man', acting 'in the manner of beasts'.[9] His fellow monk John expressed horror at 'the wicked, infamous and blasphemous doings of that army of the Scots against God, and their abuses of humanity itself', while Jordan Fantosme refers to the earls of Scotland leading 'the detestable people whom pity never made refrain from devilries'.[10] The essentially derivative nature of contemporary historical writing inevitably led to the cumulative elaboration of such invective. Hence though William of Newburgh utilized Jordan's poem, he added his own diatribe against the Scots:

> Everything was consumed by the Scots, to whom no kind of food is too filthy to be devoured, even that which is fit only for dogs; and while they were grasping their prey, it was a delight to that inhuman nation, more savage than wild beasts, to cut the throats of old men, to slaughter children, to disembowel women and to do everything of this kind that is horrible to mention.[11]

The summation of this odium is achieved by Ailred of Rievaulx. The English at the battle of the Standard fight not against men 'but against beasts, in whom there is no humanity, no piety'. The Galwegians are a 'nefarious race of men', and in a speech put into the mouth of Walter Espec, he urges their extirpation from the face of the earth.[12]

At the root of such invective was a hatred and fear born of repeated allegations of habitual acts of savagery in war. Almost every account of Scottish incursions, and in particular those of the campaigns of 1070, 1138 and 1173–4, contains a more or less detailed description of Scottish atrocities perpetrated on the inhabitants of northern England. Similarly, accusations of barbarity consistently accompany contemporary Angevin or Capetian references to the Brabançons, Coterells or other such groups of mercenary troops.

English writers regarded the Cumbrians, that is those dwelling south of the Solway, as distinct from the Galwegians, the dwellers in Galloway. The two best-informed writers, Richard of Hexham and Ailred, who seems to have used the former's work, distinguish between the Cumbrians, the Galwegians, the men of Lothian and the men of Teviotdale, these last providing a rough easterly boundary to the Galwegians (*Relatio*, p. 191: RH, p. 79). For a valuable collection of essays on early Galloway see *Galloway: Land and Lordship*, ed. R. D. Oran and G. P. Stell (Edinburgh, 1991).

[8] *Relatio*, pp. 189–90, 193; HH, p. 263. This prerogative can scarcely have been an innovation in 1138.
[9] RH, pp. 78, 83.   [10] JH, p. 116; JF, ll. 1342–3.   [11] WN, pp. 182–3.   [12] *Relatio*, p. 188.

The nature of these alleged acts and their reportage raises several important considerations. To what extent, if at all, did such reports approach the actuality of the behaviour of these groups in war? What aspects of the conduct of the *routiers* or the Scots were felt in the minds of Anglo-Norman or French observers to violate acceptable bounds of behaviour? How far in reality was their conduct distinct from that of the warrior aristocracy and the methods of ravaging employed by the knights themselves? Were there any discernible differences between the behaviour of the Scots and that of the *routiers*? Finally, if such atrocities were more than the xenophobic exaggerations of writers south of the Tweed or the embittered invective of aggrieved clerics, to what extent were such actions the result of indiscipline or of direct policy on behalf of those who led or employed such troops?

THE REPORTING OF ATROCITY: PROPAGANDA OR TRUTH?

Any attempt to answer such questions in relation to the Scots is immediately confronted by source-related problems closely analogous to those involved in any critical assessment of the behaviour of Viking warriors.[13] In both instances, there is scant native written evidence to act as a corrective. One is therefore dependent on the unfavourable observations of predominantly monastic chroniclers, who were often only superficially informed and had a marked tendency to indulge in hyperbole. Similarly, in sharp contrast to the abundance of material concerning the later *condottieri*, no material sympathetic or at the very least neutral to the position of the *routiers*, such as conditions of hire, regulations for internal discipline, details of composition or command structure, has survived. They too can only be glimpsed through the eyes of hostile ecclesiastics, not through those of the kings or lords who employed them and recognized their enormous military worth. In both cases, the direct involvement of the religious houses of many of the writers, suffering destruction of their property and raids threatening the lives of the brethren themselves, precluded any objective reporting and labelled the attackers sacrilegious enemies of God.

---

[13] See, for example, P. Sawyer, *The Age of the Vikings* (2nd edn, London, 1971), pp. 120–2, 138–47; *idem.*, *Kings and Vikings* (London and New York, 1982), pp. 93–7. Cf. J. M. Wallace-Hadrill, 'The Vikings in Francia', in his *Early Medieval History* (Oxford, 1975), pp. 217–36 and S. Coupland, 'The Rod of God's Wrath or the People of God's Wrath? The Carolingian Theology of the Viking Invasions', *Journal of Ecclesiastical History*, 42 (1991), pp. 535–54. For a valuable summary of views concerning the problem of whether Viking behaviour, particularly in regard to churches, stemmed from militant paganism or mere economic pragmatism, see C. P. Wormald, 'Viking Studies: Whence and Whither?' *The Vikings*, ed. R. T. Farrell (London, 1982), pp. 128–56, esp. pp. 137–41.

In the case of Scottish atrocities, description becomes increasingly stereotyped and imitative. Thus Roger of Howden borrowed, in a slightly abridged form but otherwise verbatim, Henry of Huntingdon's account of Scottish barbarities, and subsequently re-used the same when he came to expand his *Gesta Henrici Secundi* into the *Chronica*.[14] Likewise, Ailred of Rievaulx took the story of the Scots drinking water mixed with blood from Richard of Hexham, elaborating it into an extended description of Scottish brutalities, while he too borrowed from Huntingdon for references to detruncated priests.[15]

Ailred's whole treatment of Scottish atrocities, indeed, is a reflection of contemporary attitudes to historical narrative. Although he had personally been to Galloway, and had been at Rievaulx in 1138 when the battle of the Standard was fought at nearby Northallerton,[16] Ailred chose rather to indulge in literary imitation than provide his own reflections on Scottish outrages. His elaborations of standard *topoi* put into the mouths of Walter Espec and Robert de Brus add little save affronted rhetoric and pious exhortation to vengeance.[17] Through his close personal ties to both David I and leading Anglo-Norman lords such as Brus and Espec, Ailred was in a position to provide much detailed information, as his description of the battle of the Standard reveals. Yet his attempts to describe the Scots and Galwegians in the worst possible terms redound unfavourably on his credibility as to their conduct. Ailred alone accuses them of eating the flesh of their victims.[18]

Of the various descriptions of Scottish barbarities, those of Huntingdon and Richard of Hexham appear the most independent, and between them they supply the standard elements of what were taken to be Scottish atrocities. Huntingdon's account is the more succinct, although it is sensationalist, formulaic, and vague in terms of person and place to the point of abstraction:

They ripped open pregnant women and drew out the expectant foetuses. They threw children onto the points of lances, beheaded priests on the altars and, cutting off the heads from the images of crucifixes, placed them on the bodies of the slain, while in exchange they fixed on the crucifixes the heads of their victims. Wherever the Scots came there was the same scene of horror and cruelty; women shrieking, old men lamenting, amid the groans of the dying and the despair of the living.[19]

[14] Compare *GH*, I, pp. 64, 66 with Howden, II, p. 60 and HH, p. 261.
[15] *Relatio*, pp. 187, 188; RH, p. 78; HH, p. 261.
[16] *Vita Ailredi*, pp. xxxvi, xliv, xlvi and n. 1, xcii, xciv; pp. 45–6.   [17] *Relatio*, pp. 187–9, 193–4.
[18] *Ibid.*, pp. 187, 189.   [19] HH, p. 261.

Huntingdon was writing with the edification of a wide audience in mind. By contrast, Richard of Hexham probably composed his work for the more limited readership of his own community at Hexham.[20] Historiographically retrospective, it is more overtly didactic, although the most detailed of all the northern accounts. Richard describes Scottish outrages in several places, but the main account stands apart as providing the most extensive catalogue of barbarities:

> They murdered everywhere persons of both sexes, of every age and rank, and overthrew, plundered and burnt towns, churches and houses. For the sick on their couches, women pregnant and in childbed, infants in the womb, innocents at the breast, or on the mother's knee with the mothers themselves, decrepit old men and worn out old women, and persons debilitated by whatever cause, wherever they met with them they put to the edge of the sword and transfixed by their spears; and by how much more a horrible a death they could dispatch them, so much the more did they rejoice . . . It is said that in one place they slew a multitude of children together, and having collected their blood in a brook which they had previously dammed back, they drank the mixture, the greater part of which was pure blood. It is said also that in the church, they shattered crucifixes with every mark of dishonour, in contempt of Christ and to their own infamy; they dug up the altars, and near them, yea upon them, they slaughtered the clergy and the innocent children.[21]

Many of these details have the ring of hearsay, and Richard's addition of the qualifying phrase 'it is said' suggests a degree of unease concerning the authority of such claims. The bizarre story related by Huntingdon of exchanging the heads of corpses and those of crucifixes is either (most likely) the product of a lurid imagination, or an isolated incident blown up into a generalization. The most far-fetched tales such as the drinking of blood or the eating of flesh – which seem to form standard features of hysterical accusations of atrocity[22] – can be summarily dismissed, though

---

[20] A. Gransden, *Historical Writing in England, c. 550–1307* (London, 1974), p. 216. Richard may well have known Ailred of Rievaulx personally, while he seems to have been echoing certain passages from Henry of Huntingdon. From the latter, however, he appears to have borrowed nothing concerning the Scots. His own narrative is fuller, more detailed and reflects his geographical proximity to the events described. His *De gestis regis Stephani et de bello de Standardo* was probably written shortly after the events it narrates, perhaps in 1139 when the piece ends. If so, Richard could not have drawn on Ailred's *Relatio de Standardo*, composed according to Powicke between 1155 and 1157 (*Vita Aelredi*, p. xcix). Indeed, it seems Ailred used the prior of Hexham's work (Gransden, *Historical Writing in England*, p. 216).   [21] RH, pp. 78–9.

[22] Acts of cannibalism were, for example, attributed to the Mongols. See the letter of Ivo of Narbonne recorded and graphically illustrated by Matthew Paris (MP, IV, p. 273). Earlier, charges of cannibalism had been levied against the 'Tafurs', the warlike band of ragged paupers attached to the First Crusade. The *Chanson d'Antioche* has the Tafurs, 'not Franks but living devils', strike terror into the Muslims by feasting on the bodies of the enemy dead and roasting the meat (*Chanson d'Antioche*, ed. S.

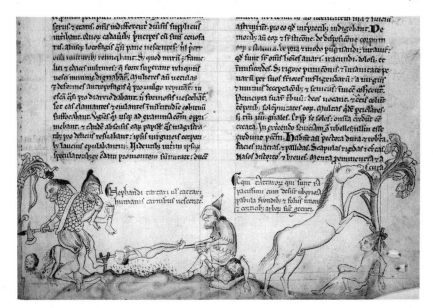

15 Medieval accusations of atrocity, born from a potent mixture of fear and ignorance, feature cannibalism as a stock charge. Here Tartars (i.e. Mongols) roast and eat their victims, from Matthew Paris's *Chronica majora* (Corpus Christi College, Cambridge, MS 16, f. 44r).

Ailred's authorship of these is a sobering reminder of the credulity inspired by fear even among the most learned of men.

As for the *routiers*, the nature of their conduct was summarized by the Third Lateran Council in 1179. It decreed that not only the Albigensian heretics were to be smitten with the sword of anathema but also all groups of

> Brabançons, Aragonese, Navarrese, Biscayans, Coterells and *Triaverdini*, who exercise such enormous cruelties against Christians as not to pay any respect to either churches or monasteries or to spare widows or orphans, young or old, or any age or sex, but who, after the manner of pagans, lay waste and ravage in every direction.[23]

Duparc-Quiroc (Paris, 1976), CLXXV, ll. 4042–75). On the Tafurs see L. A. M. Sumberg, 'The "Tafurs" and the First Crusade', *Medieval Studies*, 21 (1959). Whatever the behaviour of the semi-legendary Tafurs, it seems certain that in 1098, some crusaders were reduced by famine to feeding on Muslim corpses (Riley-Smith, *The First Crusade*, p. 68 and n. 45).

[23] *Ecumenical Councils*, I, pp. 224–5; *GH*, I, p. 228; Howden, II, p. 178; WN, p. 209; cf. *Councils and Synods*, I, pp. 1011–14. The 'Triaverdini' seems to have been a generic name like 'Cotterels'. Ducange suggests an alternative reading of 'Trialemellinis', defining a *trialemellum* as a three-edged dagger (Ducange, VII, p. 175 and the references there cited). The chronicler of Laon refers to the 'importuna lues Ruthariorum, Arragonensium, Basculorum, Brabanciorum et aliorum conductorum' (*Chronicon universale anonymi Laudunensis* (*Chronicon universale*), ed. A. Cartellieri and W. Stechele (Leipzig and Paris 1909), p. 37), while Basques numbered among the *routiers* led by Raymond Brennus, defeated at

This laconic statement receives ample elaboration from the pens of chroniclers, of whom Roger of Wendover may be taken as typical. He describes how, early in 1216, John's army of *routiers* marched north against the king's opponents

> burning the buildings belonging to the barons, making booty of their cattle, plundering them of their goods and destroying everything they came to with the sword . . . they ransacked towns, houses, cemeteries and churches, robbing every one and sparing neither women or children; the king's enemies wherever they were found were captured and confined in chains and compelled to pay a heavy ransom. Even the priests while standing at the very altars . . . were seized, tortured, robbed and ill-treated . . . They inflicted similar tortures on knights and others of every condition for monetary gain . . . Markets and traffic ceased, and goods were exposed for sale only in churchyards; agriculture was at a standstill and no one dared go beyond the limits of the churches.[24]

The similarity in style and content between this form of account and those concerning the native Scots is readily apparent. As with the Scots, the nature of description of the *routiers'* conduct demands caution and measured scepticism. For though chroniclers sometimes furnish specific details of people or places that fell victim to the *routiers*, the majority of accounts likewise consist merely of vague, exaggerated generalities. The allegations of atrocities of John's army in the north of England in 1216 have been soberingly contrasted with a jury statement in 1228 that John and his men took nothing from the fee or liberty of the chapter of Ripon.[25] In contrast to the Scots, moreover, the ravaging inflicted by the *routiers* in 1216 was not indiscriminate, but restricted to the lands of John's baronial enemies and their tenants. That one soldier had his hand cut off for stealing a cow from a cemetery suggests that the royalist commanders were attempting to enforce discipline aimed at protecting to some degree those not labelled as *inimici regis*.[26]

The constituents of atrocity imputed to the *routiers* suggest another important distinction between their conduct and that of the Scots. The *routiers'* primary concern was ransom, not the systematic slaying of the local

---

Gorre in 1183 by Richard (Vigeois, *RHF*, XVIII, p. 213). The *routiers* hired by John in 1215–16 consisted of Brabançons, Poitevins, Flemish, men from Louvain, and Gascons (MP, II, p. 622), while men from Hainault were numbered among those in the pay of Philip Augustus (Boussard, 'Les mercenaires au XIIe siècle', p. 217 and n. 2).

[24] MP, II, pp. 639–40. Wendover supplies a long catalogue of the tortures inflicted by the *routiers* on the local populace.

[25] Holt, *The Northerners*, p. 134, n. 1; *Memorials of the Church of SS Peter and Wilfrid, Ripon*, ed. J. T. Fowler (Surtees Society, 74, 1882), p. 59.

[26] *Rolls of the Justices in Eyre for Yorkshire, 1218–19*, no. 851, pp. 310–11. Cf. above, p. 38.

populace that seems to have set apart the Scottish method of warfare.[27] As a result, it seems no coincidence that while full of graphic accounts of torture and extortion for ransom, the descriptions of the excesses of the *routiers* rarely if ever contain the elements of hysterical fantasy such as the drinking of blood and eating of flesh associated with the Scots.

Descriptions of the behaviour of native Scots are pervaded by a sense of fear and racial hatred stemming from ignorance and misunderstanding of the habits of men considered to be worse than pagans and little more than beasts. The *routiers*, hated as they were, were less on the fringes of men's knowledge. They might be placed outside the bounds of Holy Church, and be linked in the same breath with Albigensian heretics, but as the Third Lateran's decree reveals, the constituent elements of their hybrid forces, drawn from a number of nationalities, were easily distinguishable and readily comprehensible. Hence Jordan Fantosme could graphically convey the contempt and loathing felt by the Anglo-Norman baronage towards the Flemish mercenaries in 1173–4, but assigns to them none of the fear and revulsion he displays towards the native Scots.[28]

To Matthew Paris, John's *routiers* were 'Satan's minions, ministers of the Devil', 'murderers bloodied with human slaughter, night-prowlers, arsonists, the sons of Belial'.[29] But for all such vituperative rhetoric, such mercenaries were anything but an unknown quantity. They were a commonplace, not simply in war but in daily aspects of royal government. Many of their captains were prominent in the governance of the Angevin lands as castellans, army leaders and royal confidants.[30] The real grievance of the St Albans chroniclers, writing as they did in a growing sense of insularity and resentment of foreign influence at court, was that such men were invariably 'alienigenae' – foreigners.[31] In this they were merely echoing the sentiments of clauses 50 and 51 of Magna Carta which not only demanded the dismissal from office of the relatives of Gerard d'Athée, Engelard de Cigogné, Geoffrey de Martigny, Philip Marc and others, with the pledge that henceforth they were to have no office in England, but also the immediate expulsion of 'all foreign knights, crossbowmen, serjeants

[27] Below, pp. 304–9.
[28] Compare JF, ll. 991–9, 1031–1 and 1053–63 with ll. 630–6, 684–8, 1175–8, 1687–90, 1741, 1896–901.
[29] MP, II, pp. 639, 637. The majority of these perjorative epithets are additions by Paris to Wendover's more restrained, though still hostile, phraseology.
[30] Powicke, *The Loss of Normandy*, pp. 228–9; W. S. Mckechnie, *Magna Carta. A Commentary on the Great Charter of King John* (2nd edn, New York, 1958), pp. 444–7; Warren, *King John*, pp. 91, 188–9.
[31] MP, II, pp. 622, 639. Interpolating Wendover, Paris tells how John was turned away from the advice of his 'natural councillors' by the taunts of the 'abhorrent routiers' (*ibid.*, II, pp. 610–11). For a comparative discussion of such nationalistic sentiments, and of the notion of 'evil counsellors' see Strickland, 'Arms and the Men', pp. 209 ff.

and stipendiaries, who have come with horses and arms to the harm of the kingdom'.[32] The leaders of the *routiers* and their men were hated not simply because of their conduct in the field but because of the recognition by the baronial opposition to John that they formed one of the principal means for the enforcement of the royal will.

Such, then, was the form and nature of reported atrocities. But were such allegations simply hostile propaganda, or were they based on a degree of fact? Accusations of atrocity were, as we have seen, formulaic, rhetorical and imitative with clear elements of hysteria and hyperbole. Nevertheless, a kernel of truth underlay these reports. Though fragmentary, sufficient evidence exists to suggest that acts of brutality were indeed perpetrated by both the Scots and the *routiers*.

Though ecclesiastical decrees concerning the limitation of warfare were frequently idealistic and removed from pressing military practicalities, the canon of the Third Lateran Council concerning the *routiers* indicates that a significant number of leading ecclesiastics considered that there were valid and urgent reasons for the promulgation of extensive measures for the eradication of such men. More compelling witness to the reality of the *routiers'* excesses is furnished by the treaty drawn up, probably in the mid 1160s, between Louis VII and Frederick Barbarossa explicitly for the expulsion of the Brabançons and Coterells from their respective domains. Both rulers pledged on pain of excommunication and secular distraint that niether they nor their men would in future employ 'maleficos illos homines' in the area bounded by the Rhine, Alps and Paris.[33] Though the value of the *routiers* as troops led to a consistent disregard for both the terms of this pact and the subsequent canonical prohibition of their employment in 1179, the fact that two leading European monarchs concluded a specific agreement concerning the *routiers* strongly indicates the exceptional nature of the problem posed by these marauding bands of mercenaries. Similarly, though the confederation of the *Capuciati* aimed at preserving the general peace of the region against all aggressors, it, and similar peace leagues, had been created primarily as a response to the depredations of the Brabançons who 'mercilessly pillaged everyone resisting them without respect of condition, rank or age, nor spared churches.'[34]

It is difficult, moreover, to dissociate the malpractices attributed to the

---

[32] *MC*, pp. 464–5.

[33] *RHF*, xvi, p. 697. For the date of the treaty see Geraud, 'Les routiers au XIIe siècle', pp. 129–30.

[34] For the *Capuciati* see Vigeois, *RHF*, xviii, p. 219; Gervase, i, pp. 300–1, who notes that the peace confederations were formed against the Brabançons who were the 'especial enemies of peace'; *Chronicon universale*, pp. 37–40.

routiers from the ferocity with which they were treated by both knights and peasantry following defeat in battle. In 1173, the Flemish mercenaries in the pay of the earl of Leicester were ruthlessly cut down during the battle of Fornham, while many of those taken prisoner died of starvation in captivity.[35] The Flemings accompanying William the Lion at Alnwick in 1174 were similarly shown no quarter.[36] Following his victory at Gorre in 1183 over the rebel army of Aimar of Limoges, which had been composed predominantly of *routiers* under Raymond 'Brennus', Richard had some of the prisoners beheaded, some mutilated and others drowned in the Vienne.[37] Large numbers of *routiers*, including womenfolk, were massacred when their stronghold of Beaufort in the Limousin fell to the army of Viscount Aimar V and Bishop Gerald of Limoges in 1177, and in 1183 the sworn peace confederations of Berry, the Limousin and the Auvergne defeated and slew many thousands of *routiers* outside the walls of Charentan.[38] Such extremes of retaliation are only adequately explained by the hatred born of fear and vengeance.

Some more concrete instances of atrocities are available. Archbishop Henry of Reims noted that the *routiers* who laid waste his diocese in 1162 had burned thirty-six people alive in a church.[39] In 1166, the *routiers* sent by Count William of Chalons against the monks of Cluny massacred the unarmed townsmen who had accompanied the brethren processing out to confront the mercenaries with relics and images.[40] The sack of Ely in 1216 by the troops of Walter Buc, Fawkes de Bréauté and Savaric de Mauleon was accompanied by the capture and torture of many refugees to extract ransoms.[41] According to Coggeshall, the mercenaries carried out a 'terrible extermination', sparing neither age, sex, condition nor religion.[42] A degree of support for this is supplied by the near-contemporary Barnwell chronicler's suggestive comment that of the great number of nobles, knights,

---

[35] Diceto, I, p. 378; *GH*, I, p. 62; Howden, II, p. 55; JF, II. 1051–2, 1080–5; WN, p. 179; above, pp. 179–80. Gervase, who puts the number of Flemings slain at three thousand, says that this was only right, since the Flemish wolves had abandoned their peaceful skills of weaving and, envious of the wealth of England, had boasted of its capture (Gervase, I, p. 246).   [36] JF, II. 1796–8, 1808–10.

[37] Vigeois, *RHF*, XVIII, p. 213. Henry II's Brabançon and Welsh mercenaries suffered heavily at the hands of the combined forces of Richard and Philip Augustus during the rout at Le Mans in 1189 (*GH*, II, p. 68).

[38] Vigeois, *RHF*, XII, p. 446, where the doubtless inflated number of 2,000 slain is given; *ibid.*, *RHF*, XVIII, p. 219; Rigord, I, p. 36 says at Charentan 7,000 were slain, the *Chronicon universale* by the anonymous of Laon a more implausible 17,000 (*Chronicon universale*, p. 40). The latter, however, gives details of the ruse by which the lord of Charentan, Ebbe VII, brought about the destruction of the *routiers* (*ibid.*, pp. 39–40). Soon after this massacre, the prominent *routier* captain Curbaran was captured and hanged with 500 of his men (Vigeois, *RHF*, XVIII, p. 219, but cf. the *Chronicon universale*, p. 40, for a differing account of the demise of Curbaran).   [39] Géraud, 'Les routiers au XIIe siècle', p. 178.

[40] *Historia gloriosi regis Ludovici*, *RHF*, XVII, p. 131.   [41] MP, II, pp. 645–6; Coggeshall, pp. 178–9.

[42] Coggeshall, p. 178.

women and children who had fled to the island for refuge, some of the knights were saved by escaping across the frozen marshes, while many of the women were protected by order of the earl of Salisbury who was in overall command.[43] The earl clearly had good reason to issue such protection. Though John's mercenary force was hybrid, consisting of Poitevins, Flemish, Normans and Brabançons, Coggeshall noted that it was the men of Walter Buc – the Brabançons – who were foremost in acts of extortion and torture at Ely.[44]

With regard to the Scots, Simeon of Durham records that during his ravaging of Northumbria in 1070, Malcolm executed a number of Anglo-Saxon nobles at Hunderthwaite, and personally supervised the burning of St Peter's at Wearmouth, as well as other unspecified churches along with the people who had fled inside them.[45] Richard of Hexham tells of the massacre in 1138 of a large group of civilians by a Scottish raiding party south of the Tyne, and in this is corroborated by John of Hexham who, seemingly drawing on an independent source for the incident, specifies Tanfield as the location.[46]

There is corroborative evidence that in 1174, the Scots slaughtered the inhabitants of Warkworth. Jordan Fantosme notes how 'the Scots burned and laid waste the countryside, and on that day St Lawrence's church was desecrated, three priests in the church were brutally castrated, and three hundred people, without any exaggeration were slain, never again to see parents or any of their kinsfolk'.[47] It is probable that Jordan was in the border counties himself during 1174, and may well have been with the English force that seized William the Lion at Alnwick, shortly after the incident at Warkworth.[48] Jordan was deeply moved by the massacre, referring to it on several occasions. Indeed, it colours his whole treatment of King William, and it was to this that Jordan assigns the principal and most immediate cause of William's defeat and capture.[49] Jordan fortunately receives confirmation from the more sober and laconic Roger of Howden, who himself had been sent to Scotland in 1174 to deal with attempts at Galwegian separatism following the capture of the Scottish king.[50]

That acts of brutality actually occurred seems certain, that they were widespread probable. But the crucial question is what specific aspects of behaviour by the Scots or *routiers* so differed from excesses in war of the Anglo-Norman aristocracy themselves that they incurred such odium and

---

[43] WC, II, p. 229.
[44] Coggeshall, p. 179. For the composition of John's army, *ibid.*, p. 177, and MP, II, pp. 622, 635–6.
[45] SD, II, pp. 190–1.   [46] RH, p. 79; JH, pp. 116–17.   [47] JF, ll. 1700–4.
[48] Strickland, 'Arms and the Men', pp. 189 and n. 7, 218–20.   [49] JF, ll. 1893–903.
[50] *GH*, I, pp. 66, 80.

sweeping condemnation. For if northern oral tradition had forgotten the walls of Durham being decorated by Earl Uhtred with the severed heads of the Scots, washed and groomed by local women for payment in cattle,[51] the effects of the Conqueror's most bloody act, the ravaging of the North in 1069–70, must have been vividly printed in the minds of those who could still witness its effects a generation later. Similarly, such vociferous complaints against the Scots and *routiers* came from the same milieu in which Abbot Suger could write approvingly of the appalling tortures inflicted upon rebel vassals by Louis VI, and which witnessed the barbarities perpetrated by Simon de Montfort and his companions in the Albigensian crusade.[52]

Indeed, in war against the heretic or the infidel, where religious zeal exercised a profound effect on men's conduct, the Franks had shown themselves capable of extremes of barbarity. On the First Crusade, for example, the fall of Jerusalem in 1099 resulted in a wholesale massacre of the city's Muslim and Jewish communities while the *Gesta Francorum* blithely relates how, at Antioch, Muslim corpses were dug up, mutilated and their heads collected.[53] The taking of severed heads of enemies as trophies was still commonplace by the Third Crusade, and Richard I personally indulged in the practice in order to demonstrate his commitment to war against the Turks.[54]

Though so acute a religious dimension was absent from most of the contemporary hostilities in the West, such incidents are important to demonstrate the *potential* for such behaviour. They reinforce the contention that for all their manifest shortcomings, Anglo-Norman accounts of Scottish 'atrocities' are not in themselves inherently implausible. Problems of bias, propaganda and literary *topoi* invite measured scepticism, yet comparable descriptions of acts of barbarity in war or conquest can be adduced from almost every period or theatre of conflict. The twentieth century alone provides such recurrent and ubiquitous instances of atrocity, many of which are more fully sustantiated (not the least by film footage), that one must conclude that, in situations of war, the darker side of the

---

[51] The incident is recorded in the tract *De obsidione Dunelmi* (SD, 1, p. 216). Following a later siege in 1040, the heads of slain Scots were placed on stakes (SD, 1, pp. 90–1). Cf. Kapelle, *The Norman Conquest of the North*, p. 16 and n. 32.

[52] Suger, pp. 120–1; *Historia Albigensium, RHF*, XIX, pp. 30, 87, for some of the atrocities committed by Simon de Montfort.

[53] S. Runciman, *A History of the Crusades*, 3 vols. (Cambridge, 1951–54), 1, pp. 286–7 and 287, n. 1; *GFr*, p. 42. At the siege of Nicea, heads of Turks were catapulted into the city 'in order to cause more terror among the Turkish garrison', while Muslim prisoners were beheaded outside a gate at Antioch (*ibid.*, pp. 15, 29). After defeating the Turkish relief force outside Antioch, the Franks similarly despatched a hundred heads to the city gate in the sight of the ambassadors from the Egyptian caliph (*ibid.*, p. 37).   [54] *Itinerarium*, p. 297; above, p. 101.

human psyche renders acts of corporate barbarity as the near-inevitable consequence of war. The question is less whether acts of brutality by such as the Galweglans or *routiers* actually occurred, but how such acts were perceived by contemporaries.

Even to those aggrieved religious whose houses experienced the depredations about which they wrote with such bitterness, the ravaging of lands and the pillaging of chattels could not in itself be regarded as an act exceeding the bounds of tolerable behaviour in war. As has been shown, devastation was such an integral element of hostilities that it was only to be expected in all theatres of war. The response of Louis VII to the ravaging of Cluny's lands by the *routiers* of William of Chalons was in turn to lay waste the count's land as far as the Saone.[55] As count of Poitou, Richard was eager to eradicate the mercenaries who represented a standing threat to the internal stability of his county, but, just as his father had done, he automatically employed ravaging as a means of bringing to heel his rebellious vassals.[56] Similarly, the English undertook reprisal ravaging of the Scottish lowlands on each available occasion when the Scots were driven back across the border. In 1138, for example, Stephen forced David's retreat and burnt the area north of the Tweed up to Roxburgh, ordering his men 'to slaughter and make havoc on the land of the king of Scotland'.[57] Having forced William the Lion to raise the siege of Carlisle in 1173, Humphrey de Bohun and the barons of Northumberland burnt Berwick and devastated the surrounding area 'like cruel lions', while in 1216 John ravaged as far as Dunbar.[58]

If, however, ravaging itself was regarded as a commonplace, the Scots and *routiers* were consistently accused of actions which were felt to exceed the normal means of harrying. Three constituent elements dominate the chroniclers' allegations – the indiscriminate killing of the population, the ill-treatment or enslavement of prisoners, and the destruction of churches.

THE CONSTITUENTS OF ATROCITY

Indiscriminate slaughter

From the comments of Anglo-Norman observers, wholesale killing of local inhabitants regardless of whether they were combatants or not appears to have been the hallmark of Scottish raiding. Richard of Hexham comments:

---

[55] *RHF*, XII, p. 131.   [56] See, for example, Diceto, I, p. 431; Vigeois, *RHF*, XVIII, p. 223.
[57] RH, p. 81; JH, p. 117.
[58] JF, ll. 802–3; *Chronicle of Melrose*, p. 62. William of Newburgh similarly records that, in 1173, the English devastated the whole of Lothian with fire and sword, pillaging everything that lay outside the protection of walls (WN, p. 376).

Sparing no rank, no sex, no condition, they first massacred in the most barbarous manner possible children and kindred in the sight of their relatives, masters in the sight of their servants, and servants in the sight of their masters, and husbands before the eyes of their wives.[59]

Jordan Fantosme suggests less rhetorically that the English knew only too well what to expect of the Scots:

King William rides off with his barons, but before they get back to their own wild country they will have inflicted such grievous losses on the English that a thousand will leave their own heads in hostage; for they are terrible in war, and of the direst courage, as those well know whom they find in their path. Those who are caught up with in the open country or in the forest will never live to tell the tale to any of their kinsfolk.[60]

Richard of Hexham states that the papal legate Alberic, sent to establish a peace settlement in the closing months of 1138, made the Galwegians 'and all the others' swear firmly that in future they would spare children, the female sex and those debilitated by age or infirmity, and that they would only slay those resisting them.[61] If Richard's statement is to be believed, and there seems little reason to doubt its accuracy, Alberic recognized the killing of non-combatants to be an actuality, not simply the exaggerated reportage, of Scottish conduct in war.

Only a profit motive mitigated the Scots' prosecution of what amounted by contemporary standards to total war. Whereas menfolk were peremptorily slain, women seem to have rather been enslaved.[62] This in part may have been due to the practical difficulties of guarding and feeding large numbers of adult males, or in creating too large a proportion of potentially rebellious slaves once they had returned to their homelands. Principally, however, the killing of men must be seen as a deliberate attempt to weaken the agricultural and military manpower of the enemy. It has been suggested, moreover, that this extreme manifestation of warfare reflects a basic anthropological phenonenon, namely the clash between highland tribesmen, dependent chiefly on the grazing of livestock, and lowland farmers. Kapelle regards such atrocities as 'the usual result of contact between agriculturalists and a semi-pastoral folk given to plundering and slaving'.[63] In support of this theory, it is worth noting that when chroniclers specify the perpertrators of such acts of savagery in more than blanket terminology, it is rarely if ever the men of Lothian, predominantly

---

[59] RH, pp. 82–3.   [60] JF, 11. 629–36.   [61] RH, pp. 99–100; cf. JH, p. 121.
[62] JH, p. 116: 'Having slain all the males, they next drove off in gangs to Scotland . . . all the virgins and widows.'   [63] Kapelle, *The Norman Conquest of the North*, p. 227.

English-speaking and with a substantial degree of arable farming, but
rather the Galwegians or the *Scotti*, that is the men of central Scotland
north of the Forth–Clyde line, both peoples from predominantly pastoral
areas.

Still more significant, however, was the fact that the killing of able-
bodied men and the enslaving of women was a time-honoured facet of
Celtic warfare, equally visible in Wales and Ireland. As early as 697 at the
synod of Birr, Adomnan had promulgated the *Lex innocentium*, whereby
the monastery of Iona took under its protection women, children and
clerics.[64] As Smyth notes, such a striking attempt to protect non-combatants bears a close resemblance to the later Peace of God in France, but,
like the Peace, its efficacy must be doubted.[65] The description furnished
by the Annals of Ulster, for example, of the sacking of Limerick in 967 by
Mathgamain, king of Munster, reveals the reality of Celtic warfare. The
Irish first rounded up their Scandinavian captives, then 'every one of
them that was fit for war was killed, and every one that was fit for a slave
was enslaved'. The latter category consisted principally of 'soft, youthful,
bright, matchless girls' and 'blooming, silk-clad young women'.[66] Such
behaviour correlates closely with John of Hexham's insistence that, in
the raids of 1136–8, the Scots slaughtered the menfolk and enslaved
women.

On other occasions, all might be put to the sword, irrespective of
sex. In 1188, Henry II's Welshmen raided into French territory – though,
Howden is careful to add, without the king's knowledge – burnt the
castle of Danville and several villages, and slew all they found, sparing
no one.[67] When Richard the Fleming's castle of Slane had fallen to
Melaghlin, son of Mac Loughlin, king of the Kenel-Owen, in 1176, the
entire garrison was killed 'besides women, children and horses ... and not
one individual escaped with his life from the castle'.[68] The taking of
enemy heads symbolized the fate of any defeated warrior. After
FitzStephen and his Normans had defeated the men of Ossory in their
first major engagement in 1169, Diarmait MacMurchada was presented
by his native troops with the severed heads of eleven score of the

---

[64] Anyone slaying or wounding such persons was to pay compensation to the protecting institution.
   The Law was reissued in Ireland in 727, and by 929 there was still a *procurator* for the Law of Adomnan
   at the monastery of Derry (Smyth, *Warlords and Holy Men*, pp. 133–5).   [65] *Ibid.*

[66] *Annala Uladh: Annals of Ulster, otherwise Annala Senait, Annals of Senat, a Chronicle of Irish Affairs from
   A.D. 431–1540*, ed. W. M. Hennessy and B. MacCarthy, 4 vols. (Dublin, 1887–1901), I, pp. 482–3; and
   quoted by A. P. Smyth, *Scandinavian Kings in the British Isles* (Oxford, 1977), p. 156.

[67] *GH*, II, pp. 46–7.

[68] *Annals of the Four Masters*, s.a. 1176, quoted by Orpen, *Song of Dermot and the Earl*, pp. 316–17. The
   number of men slain is here given as the improbable 500, an inflation from the '100 or more' given by
   the *Annals of Ulster* on which it was based (*ibid.*).

enemy.[69] Gerald of Wales noted that in the battle, the knights had scat-tered the enemy infantry, after which 'groups of Irish foot soldiers immediately beheaded with their large axes those who had been thrown to the ground by the horsemen'.[70]

The taking of heads had long been an integral element of Celtic battle ritual, and the kudos attached to the possession of the head of a valorous opponent goes far to explaining the habitual killing of enemy warriors.[71] Though by the eleventh century the practice had no doubt lost much of the religious symbolism attached to the 'exaltation of the head' in pre-Christian Celtic culture, the collection and display of heads as trophies was clearly still prevalent in Ireland as late as the last quarter of the twelfth century. The Welsh who slew Robert of Rhuddlan in 1088 cut off his head and fixed it to the mast of one of their ships, while decapitation remained a common fate of prisoners taken by the Welsh well into the thirteenth century.[72]

There is little comparative evidence for Scotland, but the so-called Sveno stone, dating possibly to the tenth century, graphically records the execu-tion of enemy prisoners. Amid a complex battle scene, six headless corpses with their hands tied lie beside a pile of severed heads, while an executioner holds the head of a seventh. Below this, more severed heads are piled up with one, presumably that of a king or chief, surrounded by a square frame.[73] Given that Franks and Muslims freely indulged in similar practices in Outremer, it is hard to believe that the practice was unknown to the Scots and Galwegians of the eleventh and twelfth centuries.

Anglo-Norman observers were acutely aware of the essential disparity

---

[69] *Song of Dermot and the Earl*, 11. 776–83. Gerald of Wales elaborates this incident in an attempt to portray Dairmait as an uncouth barbarian: 'When he had turned each one over and recognized it, out of an excess of joy he jumped three times into the air with arms clasped over his head, and joyfully gave thanks to the Supreme Creator as he revelled in his triumph. He lifted up to his mouth the head of one he particularly loathed, and taking it by the ears and hair, gnawed at the nose and cheeks – a cruel and most inhuman act' (*Expugnatio*, pp. 36–7, and cf. p. 37, n. 41).   [70] *Expugnatio*, pp. 36–7.

[71] Material concerning the taking of heads by Celtic warriors is collected and discussed by Ellis Davidson, *Myths and Symbols in Pagan Europe*, pp. 71–8. The practice was also prevalent among the early Germanic peoples. See also F. C. Suppe, 'The Cultural Significance of Decapitation in High Medieval Wales and the Marches', *Bulletin of the Board of Celtic Studies*, 36 (1989), pp. 147–60, esp. pp. 149–50, 158.

[72] Orderic, IV, pp. 141–3. According to Wendover, for example, the Welsh beheaded all the garrisons of the castles fell to them in 1212, while in 1220, Llewelyn ap Iorwerth beheaded the defenders of two castles belonging to William Marshal the younger (MP, II, p. 534; *ibid.*, III, p. 76). In 1245, in retaliation for the execution of Welsh nobles, four knights and one hundred serjeants taken prisoner on the Degannwy campaign were hanged, then beheaded and their bodies hacked to pieces (MP, V, pp. 481–3, and cf. p. 664). The Welsh evidence is discussed in detail by Suppe, 'The Cultural Significance of Decapitation', pp. 147–60.

[73] The Sveno stone is illustrated in A. Ritchie, *Picts* (Edinburgh, 1989), p. 63. It has been suggested by A. A. Duncan, 'The Kingdom of the Scots', *The Making of Britain: The Dark Ages* (London, 1984), pp. 131–4, at pp. 139–40, that the stone depicts the death of King Dubh at Forres, under the bridge at Kinloss, in 966.

16 The Celtic way in warfare? Whether the great tenth-century Sveno stone at
Forres, Moray, commemorates a triumph of the Scots over the Picts, or of the
men of Moray over an invading force is uncertain. The fate of those captured,
however, is unequivocally depicted. Amid a complex battle scene, rows of decapitated bodies, their hands bound, lie by what may be a broch (in the second panel
from the top), and beneath a bridge (bottom panel). Of the pile of severed heads,
one – presumably that of a king or chief – is marked out by a square frame,
perhaps lending weight to the suggestion that the stone represents the death of
the Scottish king Dubh at the hands of the men of Moray at the bridge of
Kinloss in 966. Far from being the preserve of hostile allegations of 'atrocity', the
beheading of enemy warriors is here vaunted in a vivid celebration of a great
victory (T. E. Gray).

in both methods of fighting and conduct in war between themselves and the Celtic peoples. Gerald of Wales regarded the automatic slaying of the enemy instead of ransoming them as a hallmark of Welsh and Irish behaviour.[74] As late as the 1390s, Froissart had been told by an English squire, Henry Crystede, who had accompanied Richard II on his expedition to Ireland in 1394–5 and had first-hand experience of Irish customs, that they 'take no man for ransom' and 'never leave a man for dead until they have cut his throat like a sheep'.[75]

But to what extend did such conduct mark a radical departure from the customary behaviour in war of the Anglo-Norman nobility? The Normans did occasionally execute prisoners, yet instances are almost wholly confined either to situations of feud or rebellion, or to warfare against Celtic 'barbarians'.[76] To a contempt for peoples whose language, dress and method of warfare proclaimed them as savages was added the strong sense that in executing Celtic prisoners, the Anglo-Normans were only repaying these enemies in kind.[77] When, following their first victory on Irish soil at Baginburn in 1170, the Normans debated whether to spare or slay their captives, Gerald of Wales makes Hervey de Montmorency urge execution on the grounds that such ruthlessness would aid conquest and that the Irish themselves would have slain not ransomed any Normans they took.[78] In 1220, William the Marshal the younger beheaded Welsh prisoners after the garrisons of two of his castles had been decapitated by the Welsh.[79] Some instances of executions of captives by Normans appear to have had a judicial flavour. The Normans executed Murtough O'Brien because, noted *Song of Dermot and the Earl*, 'he had betrayed Dermot, his rightful lord', while at Dublin in 1171 they beheaded the Norse leader Hasculf – 'the traitor' (*li trechur*) – 'in the presence of the sea folk'.[80]

More often, however, the slaying of Celtic captives must be seen as a

---

[74] Gerald of Wales, *Descriptio Kambriae, Opera*, IV, ed. J. F. Dimock (Rolls Series, 1868), p. 220.

[75] Froissart, *Chronicles*, ed. G. Brereton (Harmondsworth, 1968), p. 410. Henry had been captured whilst in the service of the earl of Ormonde – a fact which itself reveals not all prisoners were slain – and lived for seven years with the Irish, marrying a daughter of his captor (*ibid.* pp. 409–17). Despite the value of Henry's eye-witness observations, dubious elements of sensationalism are introduced into his account, one suspects more by Froissart than by his informant. Not only do the Irish slit the throat of an enemy but they 'slit open his belly to remove the heart, which they take away. Some, who know their ways, say that they eat it with great relish' (*ibid.*, p. 410). Here again is the motif of cannibalism, with its source as mere hearsay.

[76] Suppe, 'The Cultural Significance of Decapitation' pp. 147–60; Gillingham, 'Conquering the Barbarians', pp. 67–84.   [77] Cf. Robert of Rhuddlan's enslavement of Welsh captives, below, p. 000.

[78] *Expugnatio*, pp. 60–5.   [79] MP, III, p. 76.

[80] *The Song of Dermot*, ll. 2165–80, 2465–80. Similar instances in Wales, such as the execution of Trahaearn Fychan of Brcheiniog by William de Braose in 1197, occur 'in contexts which seem more judicial than martial' (Suppe, 'The Cultural Significance of Decapitation', p. 148).

deliberate act of terrorism to deter raiding or to weaken resistance. Suppe has argued convincingly that the hanging or beheading of Welsh prisoners was the response of marcher lords exasperated by incursions they were unable to prevent.[81] Such executions were one way to strike back at an enemy who refused to be brought to pitched battle, but who waged guerilla warfare and melted into the hills on the arrival of any powerful Anglo-Norman force. Thus in 1231, for example, Hubert de Burgh ordered prisoners taken by the garrison of Montgomery to be beheaded and their heads sent to Henry III, while in 1233, a Richard de Muneton received a bounty of fifty-seven shillings from the Exchequer for the heads of fifty-seven Welshmen killed in Strattondale.[82] These tactics, however, were not always successful.[83] Anglo-Welsh warfare strikingly demonstrates how the tenor of war could degenerate as prisoners were executed by both sides in an escalating series of revenge killings.[84]

Nor was such behaviour universally condoned. Gerald of Wales condemned the execution of the Irish prisoners at Baginburn in 1170 as 'deplorable and inhuman brutality', and has Raymond le Gros urge clemency on the grounds that mercy in victory was noble and honourable. The Irish, he argued, were neither rebels nor traitors but men defending their homeland, and as such should be treated humanely. By ransoming them, the Normans would both benefit financially and set an example of good conduct.[85] Whether Raymond actually shared the views given him by Gerald, their articulation in the *Expugnatio Hibernica* is nevertheless an important indication of the thinking of a highly educated product of the twelfth-century renaissance whose own part-Celtic background made him highly conscious of such issues of conduct. That the Normans proceeded to behead their captives, however, suggests that such sentiments carried less weight in the field than the more pragmatic arguments of Hervey de Montmorency.

If the execution of prisoners by the Normans was largely confined to Celtic enemies, what of their indiscriminate killing of non-combatants? Examples of the slaying of husbandmen and the burning of non-combatants by knights can be readily adduced.[86] Yet such deeds emerge from the sources as isolated instances, common enough, but not inevitable. The

---

[81] F. C. Suppe, *Military Institutions on the Welsh Marches: Shropshire, A.D. 1066–1300* (Woodbridge, 1994), pp. 21–2.   [82] MP, III, pp. 202; Suppe, 'The Cultural Significance of Decapitation', p. 146.
[83] Suppe, *Military Institutions on the Welsh Marches*, p. 22.
[84] Suppe, 'The Cultural Significance of Decapitation', pp. 154–6.   [85] *Expugnatio*, pp. 58–61.
[86] Above, pp. 270–3; and cf. the descriptions of Geoffrey de Mandeville's ravaging in Cambridgeshire in 1143–4, or of the excesses committed by John's forces in Flanders against the French in 1214 (GS, pp. 164–7; MP, II, pp. 577–8). Wendover attributes much of this latter brutality to Hugh de Boves, who significantly was in command of the Brabançons at Bouvines (*ibid.*, p. 579).

difference was essentially one of scale and calculation rather than method. Whereas Scottish incursions were automatically associated with indiscriminate slaughter, Anglo-Norman campaigns could vary considerably in the severity of their execution. Only William the Conqueror's harrying of the North approached and indeed surpassed the Scots' form of warfare in the extent and calculated nature of the killing involved.[87] But though revealing the behaviour of which a Franco-Norman army was ultimately capable, the devastation of 1069–70 was an act *sui generis*, born of desperation and the failure of statesmanship, designed finally to break the power of a turbulent and separatist region that threatened the security of the conquest itself.[88]

The harrying of the North finds few parallels in Anglo-Norman warfare, and the obloquy which it brought upon William, even from erstwhile admirers, is in itself testimony to the exceptional nature of these measures. Thus Orderic Vitalis, departing from his hitherto close following of a now lost portion of William of Poitiers's *Gesta Guillelmi*, was moved roundly to censure both King William and his sycophantic biographer:

> My narrative has frequently had occasion to praise William, but for this act which condemned the innocent and the guilty alike to die by slow starvation, I cannot commend him. For when I think of helpless children, young men in the prime of life and hoary greybeards perishing alike with hunger I am so moved to pity that I would rather lament the griefs and sufferings of the wretched people than make a vain attempt to flatter the perpetrator of such infamy. Moreover, I declare most assuredly that such brutal slaughter cannot remain unpunished. For the almighty Judge watches over high and low alike; he will weigh the deeds of all men in a fair balance, and as a just avenger he will punish wrongdoing, as the eternal law makes clear to all men.[89]

The slaughter of non-combatants regardless of age and sex was also attributed to the *routiers*. Yet even the most sensationalist and generalized reports of their conduct lack the repeated insistance on wholesale killing found in accounts of Scottish raids. When sources note that the *routiers* did not 'spare' women, the clergy and the poor, they meant not that such civilians were put to the sword but rather were not spared from being seized, and frequently tortured, for ransom. In his account of a raid on the Northumbrian town of Belford by a group of William the Lion's knights

---

[87] Kapelle, *The Norman Conquest of the North*, p. 123, argues convincingly that Malcolm III's invasion of Northumbria in 1070 can be seen as a direct parallel to William the Conqueror's operations against Yorkshire, intended to produce the same economic devastation in the more northerly province.

[88] Kapelle, *The Norman Conquest of the North*, pp. 115–21; above, pp. 271–5.

[89] Orderic, II, pp. 232–3. Cf. the lengths taken by the *Gesta Stephani* to excuse a similar, though more limited act of destruction by Stephen in the West Country in 1149 (*GS*, pp. 218–221, above, pp. 271–3, 286).

and Flemish mercenaries in 1174, Jordan Fantosme makes the clear distinction between the conduct of the *routiers* and that of the native Scots, absent from this particular foray. The Flemings take booty and prisoners, 'leading them off roped together like heathens', and violate sanctuary to seize women.[90] At least, however, these prisoners were not slaughtered, but kept alive for ransom. Jordan is swift to make the parallel:

> ... but God showed his love for these goodly peasants who had no protection, in that their mortal enemies (*lur mortel enemi*), the Scots, were not there, for *they* would have beaten and killed and ill-treated them.[91]

Whereas the Scots seem to have slain those they did not enslave as a conscious, deliberate means of waging war, the cruelty of the *routiers* was not an end in itself, but only a means to financial gain. Indeed, the extortion by torture from people regardless of rank, sex or vocation appeared to contemporaries as the hallmark of *routier* conduct. The tortures so luridly recorded in the *Anglo-Saxon Chronicle*'s account of the evils of Stephen's reign were inflicted by the mercenary garrisons of castles on 'those people who they thought had any goods' in order to 'extort gold and silver'.[92] Malmesbury, who agreed with the *Chronicle* that such behaviour was closely linked to the exaction of *tenserie*,[93] similarly noted that:

> under-tenants (*vavassores*), peasants, any who were thought welathy, they kidnapped and compelled to promise anything by the severity of their tortures. After pillaging the dwellings of the wretched countrymen to the very straw they bound the owners and imprisoned them, and did not let them go until they had spent for their ransom all they possessed or could in any way obtain.[94]

Roger of Wendover likewise records how during their punitive march through Essex, Hertfordshire, Middlessex, Cambridgeshire and Huntingdonshire in 1215, John's *routiers* held villages to ransom and took men captive,[95] while Walter Buc's harrying of Ely was also marked by the extraction of heavy ransoms by torture.[96] In John's northern campaign in 1216, his mercenaries allegedly tortured knights and men of rank 'pecuniae causa', their torturers being satisfied with 'nothing but their money'. The Melrose chronicler even believed that the *routiers* who sacked Berwick in 1216 had taken along Jews to instruct them in such tortures.[97] One set of social outcasts, worse than heathens, were being abbetted by another, the Jews, frequently portrayed in contemporary anti-semitic propaganda not

---

[90] JF, 11. 1163–84.   [91] *Ibid.*, 11. 1175–8.   [92] *ASC*, 'E', *s.a.* 1137.   [93] Below, pp. 84–6.
[94] *HN*, p. 41.   [95] MP, 11, p. 637.   [96] *Ibid.*, p. 640, 645; Coggeshall, p. 178.
[97] *Chronicle of Melrose*, p. 62.

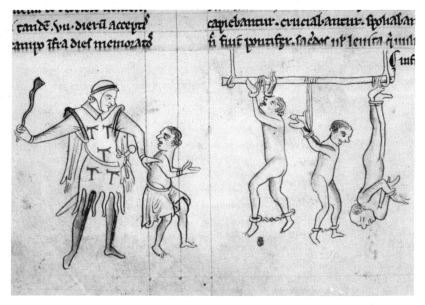

17 The *routiers* were consistently accused of torturing captives to extract ransoms. Here Matthew Paris depicts similar acts, perpetrated by King John's hired soldiery upon his subjects (Corpus Christi College, Cambridge, MS 16, f. 44r).

only as grasping usurers, but as cruel torturers of Christian children in the ritual child-murder blood-libels.

The enslavement of prisoners

The fact that the *routiers* extorted ransom, albeit by brutal methods, highlights a second major difference between their conduct and that of the native Scots. For ransom, however obtained, implied release once payment was met. What observers felt to be so horrific about the Scots was that instead of returning their prisoners for cash, they sold them into slavery. Some captives were destined for the home market while others were traded with the Norse slavers via the Scandinavian settlements in the north of Scotland and the Isles.[98] If the story related by the biography of Gruffudd ap Cynan can be believed, Scandinavian raiders were carrying out slaving raids on the north English and Welsh coasts as late as the time of Earl

---

[98] For a discussion of the Viking slave trade at its height during the late ninth and tenth centuries, see Smyth, *Scandinavian Kings in the British Isles*, pp. 155–68, and for later activities B. E. Crawford, *Scandinavian Scotland* (Leicester University Press, 1987), pp. 210–11. For slavery in Scandinavian society in general see R. M. Karras, *Slavery and Society in Medieval Scandinavia* (Yale University Press, 1988).

Hugh of Chester, who died in 1101.[99] Well into the twelfth century, Ireland served as a ready slave market, while the threat of slave-raiding by Irish pirates was still a very real danger until the Anglo-Norman invasion of Ireland.[100]

Anglo-Norman observers regarded such enslavement as wholly intolerable. Richard of Hexham, amid his moral outrage, specifically notes that enslavement was an outstanding feature of the invasion of 1138:

> then, horrible to relate, they carried off like so much booty, the noble matrons and chaste virgins, together with other women. These, naked, fettered, herded together by whips and thongs, they drove before them, goading them with their spears and other weapons. This took place in other wars, but in this to a far greater extent . . . Finally, these brutal men, making no account of adultery, incest or such crimes, when tired of abusing these poor wretches like animals, made them their slaves or sold them for cattle to other barbarians.[101]

Earlier, Simeon of Durham had noted that the incursions of Malcolm III had led to enslavement on a large scale: 'Scotland was filled with slaves of the English race, so that even to this day cannot be found I say not a hamlet, not even a hut without them.'[102] While there is no doubt a substantial element of exaggeration in these statements, their general validity is suggested by a revealing passage in the *Life of St Margaret*, composed c. 1100–7. Describing the pious works of this Anglo-Saxon princess, sister of Edgar Atheling, who had become the queen of Malcolm III, the author of the *Life* noted that in the mid 1090s, Margaret had ransomed countless English 'whom the ferocity of their enemies had led away captive from the nation of the Angles and reduced to slavery'. She even sent her agents throughout the country to find out which captives were being treated the most harshly, and strove to purchase their release.[103]

Captives seized by the Scots were pooled then apportioned at the end of a given raid, along with other plunder, a customary division which even applied to the Scots King.[104] John of Hexham noted that in 1138, David restored those captives who fell to him by lot to Robert, prior of Hexham, 'in token of their freedom'.[105] While the Scots and Galwegians 'carried off

---

[99] D. Pelteret, 'Slave Raiding and Slave Trading in Early England', *Anglo-Saxon England*, 9 (1981), p. 110 and n. 92.

[100] *Ibid.*, pp. 113–14; see also P. Holm, 'The Slave Trade of Dublin', *Peritia*, 5 (1986), pp. 317–45.

[101] RH, p. 83.

[102] SD, 1, p. 192. The *ASC*, 'E', *s.a.* 1079, noted that Malcolm 'ravaged Northumberland as far as the Tyne, and killed many hundreds of people, and took home much money and treasure and people in captivity'.

[103] *Vita sanctae Margaretae reginae*, in *Symeonis Dunelmensis opera et collectanea*, ed. H. Hinde (Surtees Society, 51, 1868), 1, Appendix III, p. 247. For a discussion of the authorship of this tract, *ibid.*, pp. lvii–lx.

[104] RH, p. 83.   [105] JH, p. 116.

those who fell to their share to their own country', others followed the king's example and restored their captives to freedom at the church of St Mary at Carlisle.[106] It is uncertain whether these fortunate souls had to purchase their liberty, or whether their captors were motivated solely by the urgings of pity somewhat implausibly suggested by the chroniclers. It is possible, however, that David, with his campaign ended, may have been attempting to dissociate himself from the grosser excesses of his native troops. Although the king could not wholly abjure responsibility for the behaviour of the Scots, his upbringing as an Anglo-Norman knight would have made him acutely aware that south of the Tweed enslavement of captives was regarded as a violation of acceptable conduct of the highest magnitude.

In England prior to the Conquest, the enslavement of prisoners of war had been a commonplace. Earl Godwine sold some of the companions of the *aetheling* Alfred in 1036, while it is possible that the men seized by Harold in his raiding of 1052 were similarly enslaved.[107] The *Anglo-Saxon Chronicle* is unambiguous in its statement that the Northumbrians travelling south to demand Morcar as their earl in 1065 'captured many hundreds of people and took them north with them, so that the shire and other neighbouring shires were the worst for it for many years'.[108] Servitude was undoubtedly still in existence by the end of the eleventh century, for the Domesday survey records varying degrees of the unfree, the lowest of which was the class of *servi*.[109] The ruling attributed to William I, moreover, that no one should be sold outside the kingdom, carried with it the implication that the selling of men was permissible within it.[110]

Yet the Norman invasion marked a sea-change in both attitudes to and the practice of enslaving. Canon law strictly forbade the selling of fellow Christians into slavery,[111] and that the Anglo-Saxons were already beginning to move into conformity with this directive is suggested by the fervent

---

[106] Carlisle was a natural choice to send released English captives, for although it was in David's hands from 1136, it had been developed by Rufus as an important Anglo-Norman settlement (Barlow, *William Rufus*, pp. 297–8). Cf. Pelteret, 'Slave Raiding and Slave Trading', pp. 108–9, where he notes that in the early eleventh century, Corbridge seems to have been an important meeting place for Scots, Scandinavians and Northumbrians, where slaves were traded.

[107] *ASC*, 'C', *s.a.*, 1036; *ASC*, 'E', *s.a.*, 1052; Pelteret, 'Slave Raiding and Slave Trading', p. 111, and cf. *idem*. 'Late Anglo-Saxon Slavery: An Interdisciplinary Approach to the Various Forms of Evidence' (unpublished PhD dissertation, University of Toronto, 1976), pp. 384–90.

[108] *ASC*, 'D', 'E', *s.a.*, 1065.   [109] Chibnall, *Anglo-Norman England*, pp. 187–9.

[110] *Willelmi I articuli*, c. 9, in Liebermann, *Die Gesetze der Angelsachsen*, i, p. 488.

[111] Pelteret, 'Slave Raiding and Slave Trading', pp. 111–14, from which the following references are taken. Ecclesiastics had not condemned slavery *per se*, but the sale of Christians abroad, where they might be pruchased by pagans. As early as 732, Pope Gregory III had prescribed a penance for selling Christians abroad equal to that of homicide, while these strictures were taken up by Wulfstan of York in his legislation (*ibid.*, p. 112 and references there cited).

and successful preaching by Bishop Wulfstan of Worcester against the sale of captives to Ireland from Bristol, a major slave market.[112] He or Lanfranc persuaded William I to prohibit the Anglo-Irish slave trade, while the slave trade in England was outlawed by canon 28 of the Westminster Council.[113]

There is equally little or no evidence to suggest that in practice prisoners of war were sold into slavery in the Anglo-Norman *regnum*. Significantly, as Chibnall has noted, 'the Norman conquest was the first conquest that did not lead to an increase in the number of slaves. Between 1066 and 1086 the number of *servi* declined in some places.'[114] Though the *De injusta vexatione* explicitly says that Rufus's followers not only took captive some of the bishop of Durham's men in 1088 but sold off others, the context of this action was forceable distraint not war, and it seems likely that those sold were serfs, not freemen.[115] Orderic Vitalis could accuse Robert of Bellême of torturing or starving prisoners to death, but he never imputed to him the selling of his captives into servitude. Orderic, indeed, sharply censured Robert of Rhuddlan, towards whom he was otherwise very favourable, for the enslavement of his Welsh prisoners:

> For fifteen years he harried the Welsh mercilessly, invaded the lands of men who when they still enjoyed their liberty had owed nothing to the Normans, pursued them through woods and marshes and over steep mountains and found different ways of securing their submission. Some he slaughtered mercilessly on the spot like cattle; others he kept for years in fetters, or forced into a harsh and unlawful slavery. It is not right that Christians should so oppress their brothers, who have been reborn in the faith of Christ by holy baptism.[116]

Robert may well have felt that the nature of his enemy – mere Celtic tribesmen – permitted such behaviour, or that he was only matching like with like; the Worcester chronicle accuses the Welsh of selling English prisoners into captivity in foreign lands.[117] It is significant in Anglo-Scottish warfare, however, that for all the contempt and loathing expressed towards the native Scots, there is no reference to the Anglo-Normans seizing

---

[112] The *Vita Wulfstani of William of Malmesbury*, ed. R. R. Darlington (Camden Society, 3rd ser., 40, London 1928), pp. 43–4.   [113] *GR*, II, p. 329; Eadmer, p. 143.

[114] Chibnall, *Anglo-Norman England*, pp. 187–8. See also H. R. Loyn, *Anglo-Saxon England and the Norman Conquest* (London, 1962), pp. 326, 349–51.   [115] SD, I, p. 173.

[116] Orderic, VI, pp. 138–9. Orderic's reproof should be compared with his otherwise fulsome praise for Robert, a generous patron to Saint-Evroul. Though he was slain in Wales, he was buried at Saint-Evroul where Orderic himself wrote his epitaph (*ibid.*, IV, pp. 138–9; VI, pp. 144–7).

[117] FW, II, p. 97. In 1055, Griffith ap Llewelyn, in league with Earl Aelfgar, had raided Hereford and carried off some of the townsfolk, while in 1081 a Norman army operating in Wales 'there liberated many hundreds of men' (*ASC*, 'C', *s.a.* 1055; *ASC*, 'E', *s.a.* 1081; Pelteret, 'Slave Raiding and Slave Trading', p. 111. Cf. E. I. Bromburg, 'Wales and the Mediaeval Slave Trade', *Speculum*, 17 (1942), pp. 263–9).

Scottish captives for sale. Scots infantry might be ruthlessly cut down in battles such as the Standard, and doubtless English harrying into Scotland involved much slaying, but it seems the local populace were not enslaved. When, in its bid to stamp out the bands of *routiers*, the Third Lateran Council of 1179 decreed that any such mercenaries who were captured could be legitimately enslaved, it was because they had been placed by anathema outside the community of the Catholic church.[118] Ransom, it is true, was little more than forcing a man to purchase his liberty, but such a mechanism was far removed from deportation and sale on a foreign slave-market. It was this aspect of Celtic warfare that provoked so much outrage from the English chroniclers.

Nor were they alone in such condemnation. An attempt to enforce the canonical prohibition of enslavement upon the Scots formed an important element in the mission of the papal legate Alberic in 1138. Having obtained a temporary cessation of hostilities, he made the Galwegians pledge to restore 'all the girls and women' whom they held captive to Carlisle before 11 November.[119] How such a restoration was effected, and whether it involved any form of monetary compensation or merely coercion from the king, is unknown. Nevertheless, combined with his injunction against the slaying of non-combatants, there could be no clearer indication of the gulf in conception between a leading European ecclesiastic and Celtic warriors concerning the ethics of war. It is doubtful whether his strictures were of great effect. By the war of 1173–4, Jordan Fantosme could still regard acts of barbarism as the natural conduct of the Scots and Galwegians.[120]

Sacrilege

The desecration of holy places was naturally very much to the fore in the accounts of ecclesiastical chroniclers, but that churches and their posses-sions were repeatedly plundered by the *routiers* and the Scots is beyond doubt. There was frequently a direct correlation between the spoliation of churches and the need to provide cash for mercenaries.[121] The destruction of churches had been high on Alberic's list of 'war crimes' with which he confronted David I in 1138. The Galwegians and Scots were made to swear to abstain in future from such acts of sacrilege, while the king himself promised recompense for damage inflicted, a promise which Richard of Hexham states he in large part honoured.[122] It was outrage at such deeds that lent the resistance of the English to the Scottish invasion of 1138 the

[118] *GH*, I,. pp. 228–9. [119] RH, p. 99; JH, p. 121. [120] JF, 11. 630–6, 681–8, 1687–90, 1894–901.
[121] Below, pp. 81–3. [122] RH, p. 99; JH, p. 121.

flavour of a holy war.[123] Similarly, the Third Lateran Council assigned lengthy indulgences to those taking up arms to extirpate the *routiers*.[124]

Yet undoubtedly ecclesiastical writers misinterpreted the nature of both mercenary and Scottish attacks on religous foundations, much in the same way that earlier chroniclers had misconstrued the real motive behind the raids of the Vikings. Like the Norsemen, the Scots were seen as purposefully anti-Christian, digging up altars, smashing crucifixes in an iconoclastic fury, deliberately polluting sanctified ground by the shedding of blood, and profaning altars by beheading priests upon them.[125] The *routiers* were likewise portrayed as deliberately profaning the host, mocking and abusing clergymen, and desecrating holy statues.[126] Both groups were seen as worse than the pagans, because they were nominally Christian yet acted as barbarous apostates against a fellow Christian people.[127] The opprobrium directed towards the *routiers* was further fuelled by their employment by lords accused of complicity with the Albigensian heretics.[128]

In reality, of course, such troops were neither apostates nor the enemies of religion *per se*, even if they showed scant respect for the conventions of sanctuary and for the persons and property of the clergy. The Galwegians themselves could boast the thriving cults of Ninian and Kentigern,[129] while Orderic could praise the piety of the Scots. Anglo-Norman accusations of sacrilege should be contrasted with his approving statement concerning Malcolm III's resumption of peace in the 1070s that 'the Scottish people, though fierce in war, prefer ease and peace, seek no quarrel with their neighbours and give more thought to the religion of Christ than the pursuit of arms'.[130] He further noted that under David I, 'the kingdom of Scotland became famous for its religious zeal and learning'.[131]

When the Scots and *routiers* raided monasteries and churches, they did so primarily for the basic motive that led knights to commit similar sacrilege – plunder. Altars were broken up and images destroyed not out of deliberate acts of blasphemy, but to obtain the precious metals and gems with which

---

[123] RH, pp. 86–92; JH, pp. 118–20. Ailred noted that Archbishop Thurstan summoned the army '*ecclesiam Christi contra barbaros defensuri*' (*Relatio*, p. 182). See also the sentiments expressed in the speech Ailred gives to Walter Espec (*ibid.*, pp. 187–9).   [124] *GH*, I, pp. 228–9.

[125] RH, p. 78; *Relatio*, pp. 188–9; HH, p. 261.

[126] See, for example, the accusations of sacrilege committed by *routiers* made by the synod of Lavaur to both the king of Aragon and the Pope in 1213 (*Historia Albigensium*, RHF, XIX, pp. 73, 75). Cf. Vigeois, *RHF*, XVIII, pp. 214–5. Rigord, pp. 36–7, similarly inveighs against the robbing of churches and the profaning of the host.

[127] Richard of Hexham, for example, calls the Scots 'more atrocious than all the races of pagans' (RH, p. 78).   [128] *Historia Albigensium*, RHF, XIX, pp. 73, 75.

[129] G. W. S. Barrow, *Kingship and Unity* (London, 1981), pp. 63–83. See also *Lives of S Ninian and S Kentigern*, ed. A. P. Forbes (Edinburgh, 1874), esp. pp. lxiii–cv, and K. H. Jackson, 'Sources for the Life of St Kentigern', *Studies in the Early British Church*, ed. H. N. K. Chadwick *et al.* (Cambridge, 1958), pp. 273–357.   [130] Orderic, II, pp. 218–19.   [131] *Ibid.*, IV, pp. 276–9.

they were frequently covered. Behind the accusations against the *routiers* of profaning the host was merely the seizure of pyxes made of precious metals.[132] To Rigord, it might appear blasphemous for a *routier* to give an altar cloth to his concubine, but to the mercenaries church ornaments and vestments were simply another form of moveable wealth.[133] The *Chronicle of Melrose* noted that when, in 1216, Alexander II invaded Cumbria, the Scots pillaged Holmcultram 'of everything they could lay their hands upon – holy books, vestments, chalices, horses and cattle, utensils and garments; so that they even stripped to the skin a monk who was lying at last gasp in the infirmary'.[134]

That financial gain was the overriding reason for the attack on religious foundations is shown by the readiness of the Scots or *routiers* to be bought off. David I's forces, for example, spared the monastery at Tynemouth for 27 marks of silver, and Hexham gained charters of protection.[135] Savaric de Mauleon spared Crowland for a bribe of 50 marks, Fawkes de Bréauté was bought off several times from firing the abbey and town of St Albans.[136] When these two commanders jointly ravaged Ely in 1216, they demanded a bribe of 209 marks to prevent the burning of the cathedral.[137]

It is only perhaps in the treatment of the clergy themselves that one can perceive a distinction between the conduct of the Scots and that of the *routiers*. The Scots are frequently accused of killing or mutilating clergy. Henry of Huntingdon portrays them as beheading clergy, while Fantosme claimed that at Warkworth in 1174, the Scots castrated three priests.[138] If these allegations have any validity, the slaying of priests must be seen simply as an extension of the Scots' refusal to recognize the immunity of non-combatants. In contrast, while the *routiers* are frequently accused of maltreating priests and clergy, instances of them killing clerics or religious are much less common. When the *routiers* of the count of Chalons attacked Cluny, they slew many of the unarmed burghers who had accompanied the monks in a procession against their aggressors, but spared the monks themselves.[139] For all his vociferous complaints about the robbing or striking of clergy by mercenaries, William of Malmesbury seldom if ever records the slaying of any of them. Behind the aggrieved rhetoric, the

---

[132] Rigord, p. 37; *Historia Albigensium*, RHF, xix, p. 73.

[133] Rigord, p. 37. Cf. the tale of demoniac possession befalling two Galwegians who had plundered the oratory of St Michael on the Tyne near Hexham and had 'carried off what they found' (JH, p. 116; RH, p. 80).   [134] *Chronicle of Melrose*, p. 63.

[135] RH, pp. 79–81; JH, p. 116. The charter of immunity for Hexham is lost, but that granted to Tynemouth is extant and printed in A. C. Lawrie, *Early Scottish Charters* (Glasgow, 1905), pp. 91–2. The charter, given in June 1138, while David was besieging Norham, was addressed to '*Francis et Anglis et Scotis et Galwensibus*'.   [136] Above, p. 84.

[137] MP, *Historia Anglorum*, ii, p. 189; MP, iii, p. 12; *ibid.*, ii, p. 645.

[138] HH, p. 261; JF, ll. 1701–2, 1899.   [139] *RHF*, xii, p. 131.

financial motive behind this conduct is again apparent. Malmesbury records how mercenaries from Flanders and Brittany in King Stephen's employ plundered churches and dragged off clergy to captivity.[140] Similarly, it was extortion for cash, not an innate desire to kill, that underlay the treatment of religious houses by John's mercenaries.[141]

   Excepting the possible slaying or mutilation of clergy, the conduct of the Scots and *routiers* towards churches differed little from that of the Anglo-Norman knighthood. As we have seen, attacks on churches for financial or tactical reasons formed an integral element of the warrior aristocracy's methods of waging war.[142] It was thus quite unrealistic of the English chroniclers to believe the Scots and Galwegians should respect the rights of Holy Church in wars fuelled by racial hatred, when their own nobility repeatedly violated the Church's property and ignored ecclesiastical strictures. Still less could mercenaries who depended on such plunder for their livelihood be expected to behave differently when the lords who were their employers fully indulged in similar conduct.

THE EXTENT OF ROYAL COMPLICITY

One of the most crucial questions concerning atrocities, real or alleged, is the degree of responsibility attributable to the kings who hired the *routiers* or levied the native Scottish tribesmen. Here the case of the *routiers* differs considerably from that of the Scots. For unlike the northern levies, the Brabançons were highly disciplined and professional in battle. Though not extant (and probably never committed to writing), a rudimentary set of regulations concerning such crucial issues as command structure and division of spoil must have underpinned their effectiveness and cohesion as a fighting force. It was, moreover, in the interests of the kings who employed *routiers* to control and direct their depredations strictly. Henry II was careful to bring his Brabançons to England only once, in a critical situation during the war of 1173–4, when he needed to be sure of a force whose loyalty was total.[143] That he kept this unit under tight rein is suggested by the complete absence of criticism of their conduct by chroniclers, in marked contrast to the vociferous complaints against the Flemings employed during the civil war of Stephen's reign. Indeed, one of Henry's first acts as king, and one that no doubt won him much political capital, had been the expulsion of the numerous foreign

---

[140] *HN*, pp. 17, 40–1, 43–4. Cf. Vigeois, *RHF*, XVIII, pp. 214–15, where he records the mockery and abuse of two monks from Pierre-Buffiere by Curbaran's *routiers*. The monks were not slain, however, but 'sold', i.e. ransomed, for 18 *solidi* each.   [141] MP, II, pp. 645–6; *ibid.*, III, p. 12.
[142] Above, pp. 75–91.   [143] *GH*, I, p. 72; Diceto, I, p. 382; WN, p. 181.

mercenaries.[144] During the establishment of peace in 1174 he was similarly eager to remove from the kingdom as swiftly as possible the various
units of Flemings who had been in rebel employ.[145] Even in his punitive
campaign of 1216, John was careful to unleash his mercenaries only
against the lands of his baronial opponents and their Scottish allies.
Depredation of church property appears to have been forbidden and
punished if discovered.[146]

Conversely, princes were fully aware of the conduct of which such
bands were capable, and did not hesitate to set them upon their enemies
both foreign and domestic when the need arose. The attitude of employers
to the excesses of the *routiers* was thus twofold. On the one hand, political
sagacity dictated that the *routier* units be strictly controlled in friendly territory to avoid alienating support – a consideration particularly to the fore in
times of revolt such as 1173–4 and 1215–17. On the other, they fully sanctioned the use of extreme measures against opponents. Over and above
their excellence as troops, the willingness of the *routiers* to indulge in behavioural excesses must have been a principal reason for royal employment of
such mercenaries.

Kings were to some extent distanced from the opprobrium felt towards
the *routiers* by the nature of these troops. For unlike the Scots and
Galwegians who formed the bulk of the infantry available to the Scottish
monarchs, the *routier* bands were neither an indigenous part of the armies
of the Angevin or Capetian kings, nor usually the 'natural' subjects of these
lords. Their bands were essentially small, independent standing armies of
hybrid racial and social composition – very similar to the notorious Free
Companies of the fourteenth century – employed frequently but not
permanently. Though certain captains like Mercadier, Cadoc and Fawkes
de Bréauté might serve consistently in the service of either the Angevin or
Capetian kings, the *routiers* as a whole were regarded as aliens, set apart from
subjects in arms and other forms of stipendiaries such as household
knights. While they performed the unsavoury work of kings and lords, they
could not be said to be the deliberate creation of such rulers, even if the
constant hiring of such groups did nothing to discourage the growth of
their numbers.

In addition, there was a sense – at least from chroniclers not directly

---

[144] WN, pp. 101–2; Gervase, I, p. 161. William fitz Stephen assigns the credit for this decision to Becket, *Materials for the History of Thomas Becket*, III, pp. 18–19.

[145] Gervase, I, p. 246; Diceto, I, p. 385; *GH*, I, pp. 67, 73.

[146] Above, p. 298. Aubrey de Trois Fontaines believed, perhaps somewhat implausibly, that Philip Augustus's mercenaries paid due regard to the property of his subjects (*RHF*, XVII, p. 767; Boussard (1945–6), p. 193 n. 6).

hostile to the kings concerned – that the employment of these *routiers* was a very necessary evil when faced with baronial rebellion. For the cardinal value of such stipendaries was that provided their wages were forthcoming, their loyalty was assured and uncompromising.[147] In situations of revolt, where the king frequently had cause to mistrust many of his great lords, the *routiers* provided a military force that was not only formidable in the field but of unequivocal reliability. Henry owed much of his success in 1173–4 to the *routiers*, as did Richard in his near-incessant campaigns in Aquitaine, and contemporaries knew it. Although men such as Geoffrey of Vigeois were naturally embittered against the type of mercenaries who had plundered their own foundations, it is not until the reign of John that English chroniclers begin to treat the *routiers* in royal service with unreserved hostility. The kings themselves were often on intimate terms with *routier* captains, many of whom, despite the prejudice of the chroniclers, were far more than mere brigands.[148]

Furthermore, though rulers did not scruple to use the terror inspired by the behaviour of the *routiers* as a real or potential weapon against their enemies, contemporaries regarded the greatest threat from the *routiers* to be when they had been discharged from the service of a prince. Once deprived of regular pay, the *routier* groups roamed at will, being forced to live by pillage and brigandage. Thus, ironically, the establishment of peace between kings or the great territorial lords might entail great suffering to areas in the path of mercenary bands. It was no coincidence that both the formation of the peace confraternities and the majority of attempts to extirpate the *routiers* came at a time when they were not in royal employment but ravaging at large throughout the Midi. In contrast to their lawless behaviour during these periods of unemployment, kings appeared as a regulating and controlling influence. Despite frequently hiring *routiers* himself, Philip Augustus was capable of falling upon a large band of *routiers* in 1183 and exterminating them.[149]

Indeed, in comparison to the verdicts passed by Anglo-Norman writers on the Scottish kings concerning their employment of the Scots and Galwegians, it is remarkable how little direct criticism accrued to monarchs such as Henry II, Richard or Philip Augustus for hiring the *routiers*. Nor, despite the Third Lateran's prohibition in 1179, did the Church make a serious attempt to excommunicate those monarchs who repeatedly employed these mercenaries. In 1181, the pope had even given the command of a large company of Brabançons to Hugh, duke of Bar, in

---

[147] WN, pp. 172, 277.   [148] Powicke, *The Loss of Normandy*, pp. 338–43; Warren, *King John*, p. 91.
[149] Rigord, p. 37.

order for him to wage war against the infidel in Spain, thereby attempting to set one scourge against another.[150]

Only John earned sustained condemnation for his widespread use of *routiers* against his own rebellious vassals in 1215–16, and even he was criticized less for their deployment in war than for their political influence and use in government. Hiring such crack troops for war against an external enemy, or holding them in reserve to counter the potential disaffection of elements of the baronage was understandable, but using them to coerce one's native populace as a standard feature of administration was quite another matter. The *Histoire de Guillaume Le Maréchal* asked rhetorically why King John was unable to keep the love of his people. His answer was because the *routier* captain Louvrecaire maltreated them, and pillaged them as though he were in enemy territory, shaming their wives and daughters and giving not a penny in compensation.[151] Similar disaffection was created in John's other continental lands by the employment of *routier* captains as agents of government.[152] Whereas his father and brother had reserved the employment of units of *routiers* for specific short-term military and political crises, John's constant fear and mistrust of his own baronage led to the use of hired captains as a permanent feature of his rule, an unwise policy that might highlight the reliability of such men but which, by the deep resentment it fomented amongst the nobility, served instead to undermine the stability of the regime that it had sought to safeguard.

But what of the Scottish kings and their native troops? The question of complicity in atrocities affected the Scottish kings more profoundly than it did those rulers who employed the Brabançons, largely because the Scottish and Galwegian tribesmen were both the kings' subjects and the mainstay of their armies. To what extent, then, did David I and William the Lion, Anglo-Norman knights by training, nourished on chivalric notions of conduct, patrons of the church and arts, either condone or actively encourage the excesses of the native infantry? The difficulty of answering such a question was recognized by contemporaries. Richard of Hexham condemns David for his complicity, Ailred seeks to exonerate him. Jordan Fantosme even contradicts himself in his assessment of the culpability of William the Lion. Was ravaging and the perpetration of brutalities royal policy, or simply the result of indiscipline?

INDISCIPLINE AND THE CONTROL OF RAVAGING

The question of discipline, always a problem in medieval armies, was still more acute in the racially hybrid Scottish armies of the twelfth century. In

---

[150] *GH*, I, p. 276.   [151] *HGM*, II. 12595–606.   [152] Powicke, *The Loss of Normandy*, p. 339.

particular, the king had only limited control over the Galwegians, while the native elements and the Anglo-Norman knights of the royal *familia* were constantly at odds. David's own life was put in danger by a Galwegian mutiny at Durham in 1138,[153] while the fierce dispute over precedence in battle immediately prior to the Standard further revealed David's inability to overrule the Galwegians without the fear of mass desertion or inter-necine fighting.[154] During the rout following the Standard, his native troops started fighting among themselves, David being as powerless to prevent this as he had been to stem their precipitous flight from the field. Once back in his own kingdom he amerced the Scots and Galwegians for both these offences.[155]

Kings might on occasion forbid looting, but such prohibitions might be difficult or impossible to enforce. Jordan specifically states that in 1173 William the Lion 'orders that peace be kept with regard to Holy Church, and metes out stern justice to those who break it'. Nevertheless, 'that does him not the slightest bit of good', for the Scots and Galwegians still 'destroy churches and indulge in wholesale robbery'.[156] When David granted immunity to Hexham in 1138, he felt obliged to send five Scots, presumably men of some rank, to ensure his wishes were obeyed and to protect the place from his own troops.[157]

Strict control over the perpetration of atrocities, particularly by far-flung raiding groups, would have been equally problematic. Yet Anglo-Norman observers regarded Scottish acts of brutality not as isolated incidents stem-ming from the breakdown of authority, but rather as a behavioural com-monplace habitually associated with their incursions. Evidence suggests, moreover, a substantial and consistent degree of acceptance of such conduct by army leaders. Simeon of Durham believed that Malcolm III personally supervised the burning of St Peter's chuch at Wearmouth in 1070, and on hearing of Cospatric's raid into Cumbria, explicitly sanctioned the slaying or enslavement of the local populace.[158] Richard of Hexham could similarly note that in both his incursions of January and April 1138, David 'destroyed, together with the husbandmen, many farms of the monks who served God and St Cuthbert'.[159]

William the Lion was held equally responsible. According to Howden, William the Lion divided up his army outside Alnwick in 1174, keeping his *familia* as one division to blockade the castle, and sending the other two divi-

---

[153] RH, p. 82.   [154] *Relatio*, pp. 189–90; above, p. 114.   [155] RH, p. 94; JH, p. 120. Cf. RH, p. 95.
[156] JF, 11. 681–88.   [157] JH, p. 116.   [158] SD, 11, pp. 190–2.
[159] RH, pp. 79, 82. The *Gesta Stephani* believed that giving the Scots 'free licence', David 'commanded them to commit against the English, without pity, the most savage and cruel deeds they could invent' (*GS*, pp. 53–4).

sions out raiding under Earl Duncan, Richard de Moreville and the Earl of Angus, 'giving them orders to lay waste the neighbouring provinces in all directions, slaughter the people and carry off the spoil'.[160] Having stated earlier that William the Lion had given orders for the protection of churches in the 1173 campaign, Jordan subsequently accuses him directly of ordering the killing of men and the destruction of religious buildings – an escalation of hostilities that may have been linked to his deep-seated animosity towards Odinel de Umfraville. He has the king say:

> We shall not go out of the country without capturing it. Let us set our Scots to harrying the sea coast, leaving not a house or a church standing. Also we shall let the men of Galloway go in the other direction into the heart of Odinel's country killing off all the men.[161]

Though anxious to censure William's prosecution of the war, Jordan was by no means hostile in all respects to the Scottish king.[162] Yet he repeatedly equates the killing of menfolk as royal policy, and twice contrasts William's complicity in sacrilege with the honourable conduct of his younger brother, Earl David of Huntingdon, in regard to churches and the religious: 'Holy Church was never robbed by him, nor was any abbey, and no one under his orders would do any wrong to a priest.'[163]

Ravaging might be carefully directed by commanders, selecting specific areas for attack and reserving others for when the army was in need of fresh supplies and booty. Richard of Hexham noted how, during January 1138, David's army laid waste 'almost all Northumberland as far as the river Tyne, excepting the towns on the sea coast which lies on the eastern side, but this they designed to devastate on their return'.[164] The initial Scottish incursion was repulsed by the arrival of King Stephen, but by April David had once again crossed the border, the Scots returned and devastated this coastal strip and any areas, including the lands of St Cuthbert 'on the eastern side between Durham and the sea' which had remained unharmed.[165]

In the light of this, the problems stemming from indiscipline should perhaps not be overstressed. Raiders, under high-ranking leaders, seem to have had clear objectives. The commander of David's foraging vanguard was none other than his nephew, William son of Duncan, who had sufficient authority to prevent the destruction of Hexham when he so chose.[166] His raid into Lancashire seems to have had a specific objective, possibly the

---

[160] *GH*, I, p. 66.   [161] JF, II. 1686–90.   [162] Strickland, 'Arms and the Men', pp. 208–13.   [163] JF, II. 1098–9; cf. II. 1135–8; above, pp. 155–6.   [164] RH, p. 79.   [165] *Ibid.*, pp. 81–2.   [166] JH, pp. 115–16.

destruction of a concentration of local English forces, which was subsequently achieved by a battle at Clitheroe.[167] Jordan describes an attack
launched in 1174 by a party led by knights on Belford and the region around
Bamburgh.[168] In such circumstances it is hard to see how army leaders
could not but be involved should acts of atrocity occur. Following the split-
ting of William's army into three units outside Alnwick, Earl Duncan then
further divided his force into three more units. He retained one and sent the
other two, according to Howden, to burn and plunder in neighbouring villages, and to kill the men of all conditions:

> And he himself, with the part of the army which he had chosen for himself,
> entered the village of Warkworth, and burnt it, and killed within it all he
> found, men and women, great and small; he had his followers break into the
> church of St Lawrence which was there and kill in it, and in the dwelling of
> the priest of the village, more than a hundred men, as well as women and
> children.[169]

Here then is an explicit statement of the direct involvement of one of
the foremost native earls, and it is difficult to believe that Duncan was an
isolated case.

Whatever the reality of the sanctioning of atrocities by the Scottish
kings, the behaviour of native elements gravely compromised the attempts
of David and William to cut the figure of chivalric Anglo-Norman knights.
Even if they had been personally in opposition to the perpetration of
atrocities, which seems at best uncertain, English writers imputed ultimate
responsibility to them. Jordan Fantosme regarded William's capture at
Alnwick as just retribution for the outrages of the Scots. When the king is
trapped under his slain horse, Jordan notes that it is more than his mount
that prevents his escape – 'The sins of the Scots weigh him down.'[170] More
specifically, it had been the massacre at Warkworth which had brought
down divine vengeance on William:

> My lords, do not marvel if they are routed. On that day the Scots cruelly ill-
> treated more than a thousand, and death has separated sons from their
> fathers. When you think of the grief, the tears and the lamentations of those
> unhappy people in St Lawrence's church, some of them with their bodies
> and their breasts slashed open, and even tonsured priests not guaranteed
> from harm, you have no need to ask if God is angered and roused to hatred
> of King William. Misfortune has come on many because of his sin, and he
> himself was that day overthrown.[171]

---

[167] JH, p. 117; RH, p. 82; and cf. *Relatio*, p. 190.   [168] JF, ll. 1149–62.   [169] *GH*, I, p. 66.
[170] JF, l. 1785.   [171] *Ibid.*, ll. 1893–1903.

Howden equally regarded the surprise at Alnwick as God's vengeance for the injury to his martyr.[172]

Ailred's treatment of David I was considerably more ambiguous. In his *Relatio de Standardo*, Ailred puts a speech into the mouth of Robert de Brus addressed to David prior to the battle, saying that Robert knows the king to have been horrified at the behaviour of the Scots, weeping and beating his breast at acts carried out against his 'precept, wish or decree'.[173] Ailred clearly wanted to believe this was so, but even he entertains an element of doubt. For Brus is made to challenge David to prove his non-involvement by prohibiting the Scots from further iniquity and by calling off battle at Northallerton. David, as Ailred well knew, did neither. Ailred's reluctant acceptance that David had ultimately to bear censure because of his position of supreme authority is revealed by Brus's warning to David lest the sins of the impious are brought upon himself.[174]

Ailred's hesitation was very natural. Before taking the habit at Rievaulx around 1134, he had spent his formative years at the Scottish court, becoming a close companion to the king's son, Earl Henry, and serving as a royal *dapifer*.[175] His lament for David, who died in 1153, portrays him as a humble, just and pious ruler, a shield to the poor and oppressed, a munificent benefactor to the Church, a model king like his biblical namesake.[176] Yet, admits Ailred, like the scriptural David, David had sinned greatly, because he had unleashed against England the Scots, who

> raged beyond the manner of men, and wrought cruel dooms upon the Church and the priests, upon either sex and every age. And all these things were done, although against his will, yea, even against his command; yet he might have refrained from leading them, might, having had experience of them once, not have led them again. He might perchance have restrained them more, and we confess with tears that he sinned. May others excuse him ... for he himself preferred to accuse rather than to excuse himself ...[177]

There were those, he notes, who had justified the king's actions by claiming he was upholding his oath to Henry I, and that his invasion supported his niece against a perjured usurper. But David had acknowledged his guilt, and

---

[172] *GH*, I, p. 66.   [173] *Relatio*, p. 194.   [174] *Ibid.*

[175] *Vita Aelredi*, pp. 2–5. On Ailred and his background see also F. M. Powicke, 'Ailred of Rievaulx', in his *Ways of Medieval Life and Thought* (London, 1949), pp. 7–26, the second part of this article being from his introduction to the *Vita Aelredi*; and A. Squire, *Aelred of Rievaulx* (London, 1969), esp. 72–97 for his historical writing.

[176] The full text of the *Eulogium Davidis* is given in W. M. Metcalfe, *Pinkerton's Lives of the Scottish Saints*, 2 vols. (Paisley, 1889), II, pp. 269–85. A partial translation, taken from Twysden's substantially abridged text (reprinted in Migne, *PL*, CVC, cols. 711–38) is given by A. O. Anderson, *Scottish Annals from English Chroniclers, AD 500 to 1286* (London, 1908), pp. 232–6.

[177] *Eulogium Davidis*, p. 275; Anderson, *Scottish Annals from English Chroniclers*, p. 179, n. 3.

had sought to atone by generous alms and frequent masses and psalms; only the counsel of churchmen, the tears of paupers and the groans of widows had prevented him from taking the cross.[178] God, moreover, as an avenging but just father, had chosen to scourge him in this life by political dissention and the premature death of his son Henry.[179] The intercessory note of Ailred's eulogy is striking. He clearly believed that responsibility for the actions of the Scots would endanger David's soul, and his consistent emphasis on the king's justice and piety were intended to redress the balance.

The kings themselves must have been acutely conscious of such criticism, aware also how starkly the conduct of the Scots clashed with their own accepted notions of knightly behaviour.[180] Yet they had little choice but to employ the Scots and Galwegians, forming as they did the bulk of available fighting men. It was, moreover, unrealistic to attempt to reform the conduct in war that was an integral part of the lifestyle and mentality of these peoples. On the contrary, kings must have clearly appreciated the great psychological impact such troops had on the English. If the forces south of the Tweed could not be defeated in pitched battle,[181] bereft as the Scottish kings were of a powerful cavalry arm, then the threat of Scottish raids with their concomitant acts of brutality might act as a diplomatic bargaining counter or as a military deterrent. The price they paid for exploiting such calculated terror was a substantial qualification of their chivalric reputations.

Significantly, the Scots for whom both Ailred and Jordan reserve their most fulsome and unqualified priase are not the kings, implicated in atrocity, but the royal cadets, Earl Henry, son of David I, and Earl David of Huntingdon, brother of William the Lion, who are seen to be free of this taint to their honour. In his *Relatio de Standardo*, written after Henry's premature death in 1152, Ailred describes his boyhood companion in glowing terms as the perfect prince, handsome, humble, devout, generous to the poor, obedient to the religious, a wise soldier and 'of such bravery that none in that army was like him, either in attacking the enemy or in courageously receiving his attack; bolder than the rest in pursuit, keener for the repulse, unreadier to flee'.[182] Both Ailred and Henry of Huntingdon describe Earl Henry's cavalry charge against the Anglo-Norman flank, at a time when the bulk of the Scots infantry were turning in flight, with unrestrained admiration.[183] Despite the Scots' defeat, he is portrayed as one of

---

[178] *Eulogium Davidis*, pp. 275–6.   [179] *Ibid.*, pp. 276–7.   [180] Above, pp. 121, 150, 155, 219–20.
[181] Strickland, 'Securing the North', pp. 187–94.   [182] *Relatio*, pp. 190–1.
[183] *Relatio*, pp. 196–7; HH, p. 264, where Huntingdon notes, 'The king's most vigorous son paid no heed to what he saw being done by his side, but yearned solely after glory and valour; and while the others fled, he assailed with great bravery the enemy's line, and smote it with a wonderful onslaught.'

the heroes of the day, unvanquished and resourceful in defeat, his honour untarnished.[184] Similarly, Jordan Fantosme portrays Earl David as a model of chivalric propriety, a mirror to reflect the shortcomings of both his erring elder brother and, by extension, the rebellious Young King.[185] Despite being in arms against Henry II, David is a valiant warrior whose deeds of prowess in 1174 are described with considerable enthusiasm.[186]

Nor did Scottish atrocities ever completely blacken the fame of either David I or William the Lion in the eyes of Anglo-Norman observers. This was partly due to the visible contrast between native Scot and Anglo-Norman in the Scottish armies and the manifest tensions existing between the two.[187] Several observers, particularly those who had considerable knowledge of Scottish affairs such as Ailred or Jordan Fantosme, showed some appreciation of the military and moral dilemma confronting the Scottish kings. In this, Jordan Fantosme can perhaps be seen as representative of the attitude of the Anglo-Norman warriors who fought the Scots. Personally, William was, as his grandfather had been, a fine warrior – 'pruz, merveillus et hardi', 'un chevalier bon et de grand vasslage'.[188] As a knight, brave, chivalrous and surrounded by a *familia* of esteemed knights, he readily complied with knightly conventions and notions of honourable conduct. But as king, he had employed the Scots and Galwegians against them and the inhabitants of northern England, and for this he must incur censure, not only from the English, but from God.

---

[184] Even though the main battle is lost, Ailred gives Earl Henry, 'that pride of youths, glory of knights, joy of old men' a rousing speech vindicating his knights' honourable withdrawal. He then leads them to safety through the English ranks by pretending to join in the pursuit, having first ordered them to cast away any banners by which they might be distinguished. Even in flight, Henry is a magnanimous prince, enduring the weight of his hauberk until he finds a poor cottager to whom he gives it as a source of great wealth (*Relatio*, pp. 196–7).

[185] Above, pp. 155–6; Strickland, 'Arms and the Men', pp. 206–8.   [186] JF, 11. 1096–9, 1131–38.

[187] *Relatio*, pp. 191–3.   [188] JF, 11. 1766, 709.

CONCLUSION

Chivalry, with its idealization of the freelance fighting man, could not be a force effective in limiting the horrors of war: by prompting men to seek wars and praising those who did so, its tendency, for all its idealism and because of it, was rather to make these horrors endemic.[1]

In important respects, Keen's sobering verdict is surely correct. A study of the *Histoire de Guillaume le Maréchal* or the career of Arnold of Ardres[2] reveals 'the idealization of freelance fighting man' to be as much a phenomenon of the twelfth as of the fourteenth and fifteenth centuries. Such ideals doubtless added a chivalric lustre to the ruthless acquisitiveness of Franco-Norman adventurers in Italy, Sicily, Spain, as well as in Wales and Ireland, whose feats of conquest were proudly invoked by the Anglo-Normans.[3] Equally, the inflammatory poems of Bertrand de Born, castigating the making of peace and urging the renewal of hostilities, could provide no clearer example of 'prompting men to seek wars and praising those who did so'.[4] Thus his famous *sirventes*, *Be.m platz lo gais temps de pascor*, contains the exhortation, 'Barons! Put into pawn your castles and towns and cities sooner than not wage war among yourselves!'[5] Chansons and other forms

---

[1] Keen, 'Chivalry, Nobility and the Man-at-Arms', p. 45.
[2] Duby, 'Youth in Aristocratic Society', pp. 112–22. [3] Davis, *The Normans and Their Myth*, pp. 63–8.
[4] Thus, for instance, the whole of the *sirventes*, *Puois als baros enoia e lor pesa*, fulminates against the peace of Châteauroux, 1187, between Henry II and Philip Augustus, with the poet vowing: 'I'll compose such a song that, when it is known of, each of them [the kings] will long to be at war' (*TLP*, pp. 162–70; Gouiran, *L'amour et la guerre*, II, pp. 602–5; and cf. *TLP*, pp. 158–9; Gouiran, *L'amour et la guerre*, I, pp. 20–1).
[5] The poem concludes with the taunt; 'Papiol, with good heart go quickly to my lord Yes-and-No [Richard], and tell him that he stands too long in peace'; *TLP*, pp. 162–3; Gouiran, *L'amour et la guerre*, II, pp. 734–5, 742–3.

of secular literature sought to create a milieu of martial fortitude and daring, a thought-world of the boast and feats of arms to which knights were exposed from boyhood, in which bravery, physical prowess, loyalty and largesse were lauded as the greatest of virtues. In a society where honour and reputation might be as important as material wealth or status – witness the rise of William Marshal – the fear of shame and reproach, mirrored by a desire for honour and glory, acted as a powerful stimulus not only to stand firm in war but to outmatch one's fellow warriors in deeds of valour.

Yet it might be argued that in creating models of courage and fidelity one of the principal functions of chivalric literature was to offset the natural fear experienced by men confronted with the realities of combat. When one moves from the chansons' epic world of ideals to eye-witness accounts of actual experience in war such as those of Ambroise or Joinville, the terrors of battle are often recounted with considerable candour.[6] Despite Bertran de Born's aggressive paeans on the joys of war, there can in reality have been few knights who would not have preferred the relative safety of the tournament to the battlefield as a means for attaining wealth and honour.

As a result, the existence of a martial milieu, where honour was fiercely competitive and reputation required constant replenishing, did not necessarily preclude attempts by the warriors to control the nature of hostilities and to lessen the extent of risk to themselves in fulfilling their *raison d'être*. If it is legitimate to label customs such as respite, ransom and the honourable treatment of opponents as 'chivalric', then we must qualify Keen's statement by stressing that such conventions had as their principal purpose to regulate and minimize the 'horrors of war' as they affected members of the knighthood.

Indeed, the emphasis on the suspension, delay and circumscription of hostilities is one of the most striking features of warfare in the later eleventh and twelfth centuries. The inception of war was often carefully regulated by defiance or notification of impending attack, which might allow diplomatic efforts to avert fighting. Frequently, the drawing up of forces in battle array was intended to do no more than call an enemy's bluff. The exchange of embassies, in which churchmen were often to the fore, was an almost ritual preamble to open battle,[7] which due to its enormous risks was generally shunned unless conditions were either exceptionally

---

[6] Verbruggen, *The Art of Warfare*, pp. 42–52.
[7] See, for example, Orderic, VI, pp. 86–7 (Tinchebrai, 1106); GH, I, pp. 51–4 (Verneuil, 1173); *ibid.*, II, pp. 6–7 (Châteauroux, 1187).

favourable or so desperate as to admit no other option.[8] Challenges to single or group combat which might form part of such negotiations were similarly intended to delay rather than speed the clash of armies. Even when a suzerain desired a major engagement, he might be constrained from joining battle by elements of his nobility as much in conflicts between rulers as in situations of civil war.[9]

Once commenced, moreover, hostilities might be punctuated by a series of truces granted on a local, regional or national basis; to suspend fighting along a given border or within a specified war zone for fiscal or strategic advantage; to consult absent suzerains on questions of defence or surrender; to abstain from a commitment to war until a political or military situation had been clarified; or to negotiate if a pitched battle seemed imminent.[10] The clerically sponsored Truce of God may have been unrealistic in its attempts to prohibit warfare between certain days of the week and on religious festivals, but it nonetheless could draw its name and the basic concept of temporary suspension of hostilities from secular practice.

During siege, conditional respite sought both to obviate the risks and expense of investment, and to preclude the dangers of assault with the concomitant fear of vengeful reprisal on fallen garrisons. The besieger gained his tactical objective with no further wastage in men, materials or time, the besieged ensured bodily safety or even freedom of egress while vindicating their honour and vassalic duty. Offering a rational and mutually beneficial solution to siege, a ubiquitous and potentially sanguinary form of conflict, such 'bons usages de guerre' encapsulate the pragmatism and capacity for restraint of which the warrior aristocracy was capable. If one of the major themes of recent medieval military historiography has been an increasing appreciation of the relative sophistication of the 'science of war', involving a re-evaluation of tactics, generalship and military thinking, then the study of conventions and customs in warfare only serves to reinforce this recognition of the complexity and subtlety of contemporary concepts concerning the prosecution of war.

Many of the most significant customs regulating war were visible in

---

[8] Cf. the letter of Richard I noting that he had placed both his life and his kingdom in peril in attacking Philip Augustus near Gisors in 1198, though his tactical judgement was sound and he had routed and nearly captured Philip (Howden, IV, p. 58).

[9] Thus Henry I and Robert Curthose were prevented from fighting at Alton in 1101, while Henry Plantagenet and Stephen were forced to negotiate a settlement at Crowmarsh in 1153 (Hollister, *Monarchy, Magnates and Institutions*, p. 90; HH, pp. 287–8). In 1214, John was prevented from attacking the forces of Prince Louis during the Bouvines campaign, with ultimately disastrous results, when the Poitevin barons refused to commit themselves to a pitched battle (MP, II, p. 577).

[10] The extent of truces is well illustrated by the war of 1173–4, for although hostilities spanned two years, the course of warfare itself was subject to repeated interruptions for significant periods of time by numerous respites (Diceto, I, pp. 376; 378; GH, I, pp. 53–4, 59, 63–4, 75–7, 376).

northern France by the time Duke William led his Franco-Norman army of invasion to England in 1066. Had William of Poitiers written in the vernacular, or had even couched his panegyric in a less stylized and inflated Latin, the similarities between his *Gesta Guillelmi* and the *Histoire de Guillaume le Maréchal* concerning images of knighthood and perceptions of war would have been more striking than their inherent differences. Neither codified nor judicially enforceable, the development and continued application of customs and conventions regulating war depended largely both on the pragmatic military benefits they bestowed and on their adoption, following repeated usage, into the currency of honourable behaviour. Adherence to them was ultimately a matter of personal volition, which might admit a polarity of response epitomized, for example, by the divergent treatment of captives by William Rufus and Robert de Bellême. In situations of mutual advantage, resort to mechanisms such as conditional respite might be automatic. But where one protagonist might be disadvantaged, there was no compulsion to offer or accept respite, truce or similar conventions.[11] Equally, the majority of chivalric acts of largesse, such as the granting of respite, freedom of egress with horses and arms or the magnanimous treatment of prisoners were granted from a position of real or supposed military superiority.

Yet to recognize an innate pragmatism behind the inception and application of many chivalric conventions is not to be cynical about the notions of honour that accompanied them or about the nature of chivalry itself. That many knightly gestures were granted from a position of power or security does not detract from their inherent validity. For in such situations the victors might have behaved very differently towards a vanquished opponent. Rather, the fact that a significant proportion of such acts accrued little or no tactical or financial gain emphasizes their essential quality as expressions of professional empathy, respect and magnanimity among the warrior class. Some, like King Stephen or William the Lion, might even hamper their war effort by observance of such conventions. Concepts of chivalric behaviour could clearly create a momentum of their own which might override pragmatism.

This is not, however, to deny a very real potential for massacre, mutilation or execution. Ultimate provision for such extremes of conduct was supplied by the right of storm in siege, and was inherent in the *de jure* power of the king or duke to deprive rebellious subjects of life and limb. Yet while

---

[11] Thus in 1138, David I specifically excluded the castle of Wark from a general truce in order to reduce it by starvation, while Jordan Fantosme believed that it was only ignorance of the earl of Leicester's invasion of East Anglia in 1173 that led William the Lion to grant the truce sought from him by Henry II's justiciar Richard de Lucy (RH, p. 99; JF, 11. 791–4).

recognized as a final recourse, instances of execution in warfare between rival suzerains remained rare in the extreme. Execution or mutilation occurred more frequently within the context of revolt, but even here a combination of the desire to facilitate surrender of rebel garrisons coupled with strong baronial pressure to spare kin, friends or political allies ensured that such treatment was never commonplace. Nevertheless, knowledge and fear of the possibilities of such penalties served as an important dynamic in enforcing conventions such as summonses, respites and the granting of life and limb which served to moderate the prosecution of war even in situations of rebellion.

In combat itself, the operation of behavioural restraint was perforce more circumscribed. Ransom acted as an important control on killing, but it was far from mandatory. Vendetta, personal animosity or simply the heat of battle might lead knights intentionally to slay their opponents, and in such instances, armour was no proof against the charge with the couched lance. In the context of feud, such as in the Norman duchy in the 1030s or 1090s, dictates of vengeance and family hatreds could lead to deliberate slaying in the field and the mutilation or killing or captured opponents. In sharp contrast, there was a marked absence of fatalities in many battles such as Tinchebrai, 1106, Bourgthéroulde, 1124, Mirebeau, 1202, or Lincoln, 1217, fought in situations of more generalized civil war between rival claimants for England, Normandy or constituent elements of the Angevin empire.

Anglo-French warfare might vary markedly in the restraint or bitterness with which it was prosecuted. While a brotherhood in arms was certainly a potent concept, all forms of engagement in this theatre, whether siege, skirmish or pitched battle, could result in numerous fatalities. The large number of knights slain at Bouvines in 1214 appears more representative of the realities of battle than the almost bloodless engagement at Brémule in 1119 cited by Orderic as the forceful expression of a *notitia contubernii*. In battle, the effectiveness of missile weapons and infantry polearms, the sheer difficulty of surrender in the confusion of a mêlée and the dangers of accidental death in flight ensured that, irrespective of any volition to take noble captives for ransom, casualties remained high. Once taken captive, prisoners might experience a range of treatment from honourable custody to harsh confinement. Though it may have been considered dishonourable to maltreat a noble captive or even to threaten to execute him in order to extort ransom or the surrender of strategic sites, there were many who did not scruple to resort to such expedients.

Nevertheless, warfare waged within the Anglo-Norman *regnum* and northern France between the later eleventh and thirteenth centuries stands in marked contrast to earlier and later conflicts. Thus Anglo-Saxon and Viking warfare had been epitomized by the deliberate slaying of noble opponents, the general absence of the custom of ransoming high-status warriors, and the enslavement of prisoners, forms of conduct which continued in Celtic countries well beyond the twelfth century. Equally, warfare of the later Middle Ages was distinguished from that of the Anglo-Norman period by two significant trends. First, whereas in situations of civil war within the Anglo-Norman and Angevin realms both hostilities in war and the treatment of defeated enemies had been remarkably unbloody, the butchery of Simon de Montfort and his supporters at Evesham in 1265 was to mark a degeneration of notions of restraint which culminated in the bitterly fought civil wars of the mid-fifteenth century. Not only were casualties often very high in battles between the Yorkists and Lancastrians, such as at Towton, 1461, but victory was almost automatically followed by the execution of leading opponents.

Second, though the bitter aristocratic feuds which fuelled these vendettas were largely absent from external warfare in the later Middle Ages, battles from the early fourteenth century witnessed markedly higher casualty rates due to the increasing size of armies and the changing nature of tactics. The massed spear formations of the Flemish militias, the Scots and later the Swiss led to large numbers of knights being slain in battles such as Courtrai, 1302, Bannockburn, 1314, Sempach, 1386, and in the engagements of the Burgundian wars like Morat, 1476 and Nancy, 1477.[12] Similarly, the combined use of dismounted knights and large numbers of longbowmen, the hallmark of English tactics in the Hundred Years War, resulted in an appallingly high death rate among the enemy. At Crécy, about 1,500 French men at arms, together with several thousand infantry, perished, while at Agincourt numbers of noble dead were still higher, estimated at 3 dukes, around 90 lords and 1,560 knights.[13] Even when the greater numbers involved in these later battles is taken into account, the tally of 163 knights slain at Bouvines pales by comparison.

In both periods, however, lesser ranks were habitually slaughtered on defeat. Even the numbers of plebian dead were frequently regarded as unworthy of record. That the peasantry, whether in battle or in the fields, might be cut down with little compunction points to perhaps the most significant limitation of chivalry as a mechanism for limiting the miseries of

[12] Verbruggen, *The Art of Warfare in Western Europe*, pp. 166–73; Barrow, *Robert the Bruce*, pp. 228–30; Oman, *The Art of War in the Middle Ages*, ii, pp. 247–52, 268–72.
[13] Casualty figures at Crécy from varying sources are tabulated by H. de Wailly, *Crécy, 1346: The Anatomy of a Battle* (Poole, 1987), p. 90. For Agincourt, see H. Nicholas, *History of the Battle of Agincourt* (London, 1833), pp. 276–85.

war. Secular conventions of warfare extended only to the knighthood; it
was left to the Church to attempt to establish some form of protection to
the *inermes* by means of the Peace and Truce of God. If ravaging might not
be wholly indiscriminate, its mechanisms nevertheless deliberately struck at
the most vulnerable sections of society, attacking enemy lords vicariously
through the disruption of their economic base and the destruction of their
peasantry. 'We can only guess', wrote Powicke, 'at the amount of beggary,
prostitution and starvation produced by feudal warfare. All we can know
with certainty is that those who suffered must have been very numerous.'[14]

As one of the most fundamental forms of large-scale violence, moreover, ravaging was as integral to political coercion as it was to open warfare.
War was an instrument of power that could be unleashed as much within a
country as across its borders against an external enemy. Edward the
Confessor could order Godwine 'to bring war into Kent to Dover'
in 1051,[15] while John's attempted suppression of rebellion from 1215 could
be consistently regarded as 'tempus werrae'. And if ravaging formed the
ultimate means of enforcing royal authority, its mechanisms might equally
be employed by baronial insurgents.[16] The habitual use of harrying by the
representatives of authority within their own territories served to blur
overall distinctions between conditions of war and peace. To the inhabitants of the Anglo-Norman *regnum*, there can have been little differentia-
tion between the destruction wrought by their own king or duke against
recalcitrant subjects and that inflicted by an invading army from France or
Anjou. Still less of a distinction must have been made by the Norman populace during the duchy's recurrent periods of anarchy, when feuding lords
automatically resorted to war to settle every political problem – land disputes, quarrels with the religious, suppression of the peasantry and resistance to ducal authority.

Yet while one may find the discrepancy between the treatment of nobles
and non-nobles in war disturbing, it would nonetheless be anachronistic to
label ravaging and the chevauchée as 'unchivalric', and still more mistaken
to deduce from this disparity that chivalry was merely an elaborate veneer
for aristocratic brutality and profiteering. For the chivalric code of conduct
was the creation of the warrior aristocracy itself and it was assumed
without question that it should only apply to those who bore the arms of
knighthood. Nor, given the nature of medieval warfare, would it have been

[14] Powicke, *Loss of Normandy*, p. 242.   [15] *ASC* 'E', *s.a.* 1051.
[16] Thus, for example, in 1215, the magnates ranged against John had claimed the right, embodied in
clause 61 of Magna Carta, forcibly to 'distrain and distress' (*distringere et gravare*) the king himself 'by
seizing castles, lands and possessions' should he fail to implement the reforms promised in the
charter (*MC*, pp. 334–5).

realistic to grant the kind of immunity to non-combatants urged by the Church. Not only were armies often forced to live off the land, but the chevauchée itself remained one of the most basic and time-honoured forms of warfare known. If the Hundred Years War witnessed far greater destruction than the Angevin–Capetian wars of the later twelfth and early thirteenth centuries, it was because earlier armies were smaller and operations were conducted on a far more restricted scale,[17] not because, as men like Honoré Bonet believed, the mechanisms of ravaging and scorching the land marked the debasement of war from an earlier golden age of true chivalry.

The nature of conduct in war, and hence the essence of chivalry, is thrown into clearest relief by a series of comparisons. In the East, the Franks encountered opponents as militarily sophisticated as themselves, if not more so, who might employ different tactics, but who, unlike Celtic enemies, waged war by siege, raid and pitched battle. The Muslims too possessed a well-equipped, equestrian warrior aristocracy and a concomitant set of 'chivalric' values, including notions of ransom. Franks and Turks could respect the military worth of their enemy, and on occasion acknowledge this by gift-giving, the bestowal of arms and magnanimous gestures in war. Yet these shared military and social factors that encouraged the limitation of war were crucially offset by the religious dimension of hostilities between Christian and Muslim. Concepts of holy war fostered a powerful, and often overriding, hatred of the infidel that could result in the enslavement or execution of prisoners, the collecting of heads and the mutilation of corpses.

By contrast, the fact that the Welsh, Irish and Scots were co-religionists had virtually no positive effect on their treatment at the hands of the Anglo-Normans. Here, behaviour was determined by racial animosity that stemmed from pronounced cultural and linguistic differences, reinforced by the Celtic methods of war. Lacking heavy cavalry and advanced siege equipment, the Welsh and Irish generally eschewed pitched battle and utilized hills, woods and bogs for defence more than fortifications.[18] Such highly mobile guerilla warfare denied the Anglo-Normans the chance of decisive combat, but at the same time removed any sense that they were fighting honourable equals who would engage in close combat with lance and sword. Unlike William the Lion of Scotland and his Franco-Norman *mesnie*, Welsh princes and their war-bands were not to be found fighting in the twelfth century tournaments in northern France, an absence symptomatic of the failure of the native Celtic aristocracies to integrate with the

---

[17] Cf. Powicke, *Loss of Normandy*, pp. 223 ff.   [18] Lloyd, *A History of Wales*, II, pp. 606–79.

chivalric milieu of continental Europe.[19] That the Anglo-Normans recognized the military value of such troops is shown by their employment not only in Ireland and Wales but in France, yet they despised the lightly equipped, often bare-shod warriors as barbarians.

The Celts' habitual killing or enslaving of men, women and children only confirmed these assumptions. In both retaliation and frustration at being unable to bring such opponents to bay by regular methods of war, the Anglo-Normans might resort to equally ruthless measures, including the beheading or hanging of prisoners and killing by guile. When, in 1175, the marcher lord William de Braose lured Seisyll ap Dyfnwal to Abergavenny castle, treacherously slew him and his men then ravaged Seisyll's lands, killed his son and abducted his wife, he was resorting to the kind of conduct that had occurred in the bitter aristocratic feuding in the Norman duchy in the 1030s, but which Braose's contemporaries would have regarded as wholly intolerable had the victims been Anglo-Normans.[20]

Nowhere were such cultural and military determinants on the workings of chivalry more visible than in Anglo-Scottish warfare. For here the clash of Celtic and Frankish cultures was reflected in the hybrid composition of the Scottish armies themselves. A profound disparity, and hostility, existed between the mailed Anglo-Norman knights of the king of Scotland's *familia* and the unarmoured, semi-naked Galwegian and Scottish troops with shaven heads, armed only with spears and light shields. Behaviour in war was equally polarized. Even as their troops indulged in the wholesale massacre of the local populace, David or William the Lion might grant truces, conditional respite or freedom of egress with horses and arms to beleaguered garrisons. Conversely, their Anglo-Norman opponents might ruthlessly cut down the Scots and Galwegians, but as at Alnwick in 1174, capture William and his retinue unharmed for ransom. Such were these opposing assumptions that contemporaries could regard the battle of the Standard in 1138 as a holy war fought with the blessing of God and his saints against the sacrilegious Scots, yet at the same time regard David I's son Earl Henry as a model of chivalry and praise his feats of arms in this battle against the English.

The behaviour of the twelfth-century Scottish kings, and their cadets such as Earl Henry and Earl David, is of first importance in revealing the process of absorption by a Celtic kingdom of Anglo-Norman concepts of

---

[19] Gillingham, 'Conquering the Barbarians', pp. 83–4.
[20] Lloyd, *A History of Wales*, II, pp. 547–8. William was avenging the death of his uncle Henry, but even against the Welsh, such conduct could be severely criticized. Though Gerald of Wales attempted to exonerate William himself from the deed, he remained circumspect about detailing this 'inhuman slaughter' (Gerald of Wales, *Itinerarium Kambriae, Opera*, VI, pp. 49–53).

chivalric behaviour in war. Yet if by virtue of marriage and the plantation of a Franco-Norman aristocracy, the dynasty of Malcolm Canmore had, in William of Malmesbury's words, 'rubbed off all the tarnish of Scottish barbarism'[21] and entered a chivalric world whose epicentre was France, their Anglo-Norman contemporaries were still highly conscious that they led armies largely composed of troops who were not bound by any such concepts.

The expressions of total war as practised by the native Scots and Galwegians serve as a bench-mark for the conduct of the Anglo-Norman knighthood. Clerical outrage at the violation of behavioural norms by the Welsh or Scots tended to disguise the fact that their own aristocracy were hardly less guilty in some aspects of their own conduct. Ravaging and the devastation of the countryside were integral to the warfare of both groups of warriors. Similarly, churches and religious houses suffered despoliation by knights as much as by the Scots, though the former were more restrained in their treatment of ecclesiastics. There were nevertheless essential differences in conduct. The enslavement of prisoners was effectively alien to post-Conquest warfare south of the Tweed. When it did occur, for example in Wales in the first stages of Norman penetration, it met with the outspoken condemnation of ecclesiastics. Ransom was an essential element in the knighthood's perception of war, but behind it lay the fundamental assumption that an individual could gain his liberty on payment of a required sum. The belief that the greater a man's nobility, the greater was his safety from death or mutilation, marked a complete reversal of Celtic and Anglo-Saxon concepts of war, which saw aristocratic enemies as noble and worthy opponents, but sought their deaths for precisely this reason. Ransom might act as a dynamic for war, but it was far less socially disruptive than the permanent mass depopulation of an area by slaving. Knights often indulged in localized violence against the peasantry of an opponent, but the calculated, wholesale massacre of a region's inhabitants was an anomaly, exceptional enough to incur the obloquy of chroniclers.

Anglo-Norman observers were acutely aware of the disparity between their own methods of fighting and conduct in war and those of their Celtic enemies. This was most succinctly expressed by a man intimately acquainted not with the Scots, but with the Welsh and Irish, and whose own mixed Welsh and Norman lineage made him a uniquely qualified observer. Speaking here as a Welshman, Gerald of Wales encapsulates these fundamental distinctions:

---

[21] *GR*, ii, p. 477, referring to David I.

In their own countries, the Flemings, Normans, French *routiers* and
Brabançon mercenaries are bonny fighters and make well-disciplined soldiers, but the tactics of French troops are no good at all in Ireland or Wales.
They are used to fighting on the level, whereas here the terrain is rough; their
battles take place in open fields, but here the country is heavily wooded; with
them, the army is an honourable profession but with us it is a matter of dire
necessity; their victories are won by stubborn resistance, ours by constant
movement; they take prisoners, we cut off their heads; they ransom their
captives, we massacre them.[22]

Taken as a code of conduct that sought to restrain and regulate the full
violence of war, chivalry indeed had serious limitations. Its workings were
largely restricted to a warrior elite. And of this elite, some, perhaps many,
fell short of ideals whose binding power lay in a precarious fusion of
honour and pragmatism. Yet even if not adhered to by all, the development
and articulation of such ideals was of profound significance. No longer
was the automatic killing of vanquished warriors, the indiscriminate
slaughter of an enemy populace and the enslavement of captives regarded
as the norm of behaviour in warfare. The emphasis on sparing a defeated
or disadvantaged opponent, on ransom and honourable captivity, on the
qualities of mercy, magnanimity and *franchise* as constituents of noble
conduct befitting a knight went beyond the raw warrior virtues of courage,
prowess and largesse, and marked the crucial transition from a heroic to a
chivalric ethos.

[22] Gerald of Wales, *Descriptio Kambriae, Opera*, IV, p. 220. The translation is that of L. Thorpe, *Gerald of Wales: The Journey through Wales/The Description of Wales* (Harmondsworth, 1978), p. 269. The passage is reworked from Gerald's observations in his earlier *Expugnatio Hibernica* (pp. 246–7). Gerald here is describing the customary conduct of the native Welsh, not *pace* Suppe, 'The Cultural Significance of Decapitation', p. 146, 'the practice by which Marcher troops [i.e. Anglo-Normans] were decapitating their Welsh prisoners'.

BIBLIOGRAPHY

I PRIMARY SOURCES

Abu Shamah, *Le Livre des Deux Jardins, RHF Or*, iv.

Actus pontificum Cennomanis in urbe degentium, ed. G. Busson and A. Ledru (Le Mans, 1901).

Ailred of Rievaulx: *Relatio venerabilis Aelredi, abbatis Rievallensis, de Standardo*, ed. R. Howlett in *Chronicles and Memorials*, iii (Rolls Series, 1886), pp. 181–99.

    Eulogium Davidis, in W. M. Metcalfe, *Pinkerton's Lives of the Scottish Saints*, 2 vols. (Paisley, 1889), ii, pp. 269–85.

Albert of Aachen: *Alberti Aquensis historia Hierosolynitana, RHC Occ.*, iv, pp. 271–713.

The Alexiad of Anna Comnena, tr. E. R. A. Sewter (Harmondsworth, 1969).

Alphonso X The Wise, *Las Siete Partidas*, ed. G. Lopez (Paris, 1861): tr. S. Parsons Scott, *Las Siete Partidas of Alphonso the Wise* (Chicago, 1931).

Ambroise, *L'Estoire de la Guerre Sainte*, ed. G. Paris (1897); tr. M. J. Hubert and J. L. La Monte as *The Crusade of Richard the Lion-Heart by Ambroise* (Columbia, 1941, repr. New York, 1976).

Anderson, A. O., *Scottish Annals from English Chroniclers, A.D. 500–1286* (London, 1908).

Anglo-Saxon Chronicle, tr. in *English Historical Documents*, i *(500–1042)*, ed. D. Whitelock (2nd edn, London, 1979) for annals up to 1042, and *English Historical Documents*, ii *(1042–1189)*, ed. D. C. Douglas (2nd edn, London, 1981) for annals 1042–1144.

Annales monastici, ed. H. R. Luard, 5 vols. (Rolls Series, 1864–9).

Annales Uladh: Annals of Ulster, otherwise Annala Senait, a Chronicle of Irish Affairs from A.D. 431–1540, ed. W. M. Hennessy and B. MacCarthy, 4 vols. (Dublin, 1887–1901).

Anthology of Troubadour Lyric Poetry, ed. and tr. A. R. Press (Edinburgh, 1971).

Arab Historians of the Crusades, ed. and tr. F. Gabrieli (London, 1969).

The Bayeux Tapestry. The Complete Tapestry in Colour with an Introduction and Commentary, ed. D. M. Wilson (London, 1985).

Beha-ad-din (Ibn Shaddad), *The Life of Saladin*, tr. C. L. Conder (Palestine Pilgrims' Text Society, xiii, London, 1897).

Beowulf, ed. and tr. M. Swanton (Manchester, 1978).

St Bernard: *Sancti Bernardi opera*, iii: *Tractatus et opuscula*, ed. J. Leclercq and H. M. Rochais (Rome 1963).

Bertran de Born: *L'Amour et la Guerre. L'Ouevre de Bertan de Born*, ed. and tr. G. Gouiran, 2 vols. (Aix-en-Provence, 1985).

Bracton, *On The Laws and Customs of England*, ed. and tr. S. E. Thorne and G. Woodbine, 4 vols. (Cambridge, Mass., 1968–77).

Calendar of Documents Preserved in France Illustrative of the History of Great Britain and Ireland, ed. J. H. Round (London, 1899).

The Carmen de Hastingae Proelio of Guy, Bishop of Amiens, ed. and tr. C. Morton and H. Muntz (Oxford, 1972).

Cartulary of St John of Pontefract (c. 1090–1258), ed. R. Holmes, 2 vols. (Yorkshire Archaeological Society Record Series, 25, 1899; 30, 1902).

Chanson d'Antioche, ed. S. Duparc-Quiroc (Paris, 1976).

La Chanson de Roland, ed. F. Whitehead (Oxford, 2nd edn, 1946); tr. G. Burgess, *The Song of Roland* (Harmondsworth, 1990).

Charters of the Honour of Mowbray, ed. D. E. Greenway (London, 1972).

Chrétien de Troyes: *Erec et Enide*, ed. M. Roques (Paris, 1953).

  Cligés, ed. A. Micha (Paris, 1957).

  Le conte du Graal (Perceval), ed. F. Lecoy, 2 vols. (Paris, 1972).

Chronica de Hida, in *Liber monasterii de Hyda*, ed. E. Edwards (Rolls Series, 1886).

Chronica monasterii de Abingdon, ed. J. Stevenson (Rolls Series, 1858).

The Chronicle of Ernoul and the Continuations of William of Tyre, ed. M. R. Morgan (Oxford, 1973).

  La Continuation de Guillaume de Tyre (1184–1197), ed. M. R. Morgan (Paris, 1982).

The Chronicle of Melrose, ed. A. O. and M. O. Anderson (Studies in Economics and Political Science, London 1936).

Chronicles and Memorials of the Reigns of Stephen, Henry II, and Richard I, ed. R. Howlett, 4 vols. (Rolls Series, 1884–90).

Chronicon abbatiae de Evesham, ed. W. D. Macray (Rolls Series, 1863).

Chronicon abbatiae Ramesiensis, ed. D. Macray (Rolls Series, 1886).

Chronicon universale anonymi Laudenensis, ed. A. Cartellieri and W. Stechele (Leipzig and Paris, 1909).

Chroniques des comtes d'Anjou et des seigneurs d'Ambroise, ed. L. Halphen and R. Pourpardin (Paris, 1913).

Chroniques des Eglises d'Anjou, ed. P. Marchegay and E. Mabile (Société de l'histoire de France, 1869).

Chronique d'Ernoul et de Bernard le Tresorier, ed. M. L. De Mas Latrie (Société de l'histoire de France, 1871).

Codex Manesse. Die Miniaturen der Grosser Heidelberger Liederhandschrift, ed. I. F. Walther and G. Siebert (Frankfurt, 1988).

Cosmas of Prague: *Chronica Boemorum*, ed. B. Bretholz, *Die Chronik der Bohmen des Cosmas von Prag, MGH, SS*, n.s., II (Berlin, 1923).

Councils and Synods and other Documents Relating to the English Church, I (871–1204), ed. D. Whitelock, M. Brett and C. N. L. Brooke, 2 vols. (Oxford, 1981).

De expugnatione Lyxbonensis; The Conquest of Lisbon, ed. and tr. C. W. David (New York, 1936).

De injusta vexatione Willelmi episcopi, ed. T. Arnold, in *Symeonis monachi opera omnia*, 2 vols. (Rolls Series, 1882–5), I, pp. 170–90.

De obsessione Dunelmi, ed. T. Arnold, in *Symeonis monachi opera omnia*, 2 vols. (Rolls Series, 1882–5), I, pp. 215–20.

De rebus gestis Roberti Guiscardi, ducis Calabriae et Rogerii, comitis Siciliae, in *Thesaurus antiquitatum et historiarum Siciliae*, ed. J. G. Graevius (Lugduni Batavorum, 1723), IV.

Diplomatic Documents Preserved in the Public Record Office, I (1101–1272), ed. P. Chaplais (London, 1964).

Documents of the Baronial Movement of Reform and Rebellion 1258–1267, collected by R. E. Treharne and ed. I. J. Saunders (Oxford, 1973).

Documents Illustrating the Crisis of 1297–8 in England, ed. M. Prestwich (Camden 4th ser., XXIV, London, 1984).

Documents Illustrative of the Social and Economic History of the Danelaw, ed. F. M. Stenton (London, 1920).

Ducange, *Glossarium mediae et infimae latinitatis*, ed. L. Favre, 10 vols. (Niort, 1883–7).

Dudo of Saint-Quentin, *De moribus et actis primorum Normanniae ducum*, ed. J. Lair (Société des Antiquaires de Normandie, 1865).

Eadmer: *Eadmeri historia novorum in Anglia et opuscula duo de vita sancti Anselmi et quibsdam miraculis ejus*, ed. M. Rule (Rolls Series, 1884); tr. G. Bosanquet, *Eadmer's History of Recent Events in England* (London, 1964).

Earldom of Gloucester Charters, ed. R. Patterson (Oxford, 1973).

Early Scottish Charters, ed. A. C. Lawrie (Glasgow, 1905).

Early Sources for Scottish History, tr. A. O. Anderson, 2 vols. (Edinburgh, 1922; repr. Stamford, 1990).

Ecumenical Councils: *Decrees of the Ecumenical Councils*, ed. N. P. Tanner from the text of G. Alberigo *et al.*, 2 vols. (Georgetown, 1990).

English Historical Documents

    I (c. 500–1042), ed. D. Whitelock (2nd edn, London, 1979).

    II (1042–1189), ed. D. C. Douglas (2nd edn, London, 1981).

    III (1189–1327), ed. H. Rothwell (London, 1975).

'Florence' of Worcester: *Chronicon ex chronicis*, ed. B. Thorpe, 2 vols. (London, 1848–9).

Foedera, conventiones, litterae et cujuscunque generis acta publica, ed. T. Rymer, new edn, vol. I, part I, ed. A. Clarke and F. Holbrooke (Record Commission, 1816).

Froissart, *Chronicles*, ed. G. Brereton (Harmondsworth, 1968).

Fulcher of Chartres: *Fulcheri Cartonensis Historia Hierosolymitana, 1095–1127*, ed. H. Hagenmeyer (Heidelberg, 1913); tr. F. R. Ryan and ed. H. S. Fink, *Fulcher of Chartres: A History of the Expedition to Jerusalem, 1095–1127* (University of Tennessee Press, 1969).

Galbert of Bruges: *The Murder of Charles the Good*, tr. J. B. Ross (New York, 1960). *De vita et martyrio beati Caroli boni Flandriae comitis; vita altera*, Migne, *PL*, CLXVI, cols. 943–1046.

Geoffrey de Charny: *Livre de Chevalerie*, ed. K. de Lettenhove, *Oeuvres de Froissart*, 28 vols. (Brussels, 1867–77), I, pt iii, pp. 463–533.

Geoffrey Gaimar: *L'Estoire des Engles*, ed. T. D. Harris and C. T. Martin, 2 vols. (Rolls Series, 1888).

Geoffrey of Monmouth: *The Historia regum Britanniae of Geoffrey of Monmouth*, ed. A. Griscom (London, 1929).

Geoffrey of Vigeois: *Chronicon Gaufredi coenobitae monasterii sancti Martialis Lemovicensis ac prioris Vosiensis coenobii*, *RHF*, XXII (1060–1182), pp. 412–50; XVIII (1183–4), pp. 211–23.

Gerald of Wales: *Giraldi Cambrensis opera*, ed. J. S. Brewer, J. F. Dimock, and G. F. Warner, 8 vols. (Rolls Series, 1861–91).

    Expugnatio Hibernica, ed. and tr. A. B. Scott and F. X. Martin (Dublin, 1978).

Gervase of Canterbury: *The Historical Works of Gervase of Canterbury*, ed. W. Stubbs, 2 vols. (Rolls Series, 1879–80).

Gesta abbatum monasterii sancti Albani, ed. H. T. Riley, 3 vols. (Rolls Series, 1867).

Gesta domni Hilberti episcopi, in *Actus pontificum Cenommanis in urbe degentium*, ed. G. Busson and F. Ledru (Le Mans, 1901).

Gesta Francorum et aliorum Hierosolimitanorum, ed. R. Hill (London, 1962).

Gesta Henrici Quinti, ed. and tr. F. Taylor and J. S. Roskell (Oxford, 1975).

Gesta Herewardi incliti exulis et militis, in *Geoffrey Gaimar, L'Estoire des Engles*, ed. T. D. Harris and C. T. Martin, 2 vols. (Rolls Series, 1888), I, pp. 339–404.

Gesta regis Henrici secundi Benedicti Abbatis, ed. W. Stubbs, 2 vols. (Rolls Series, 1867).

Gesta Stephani, ed. and tr. K. R. Potter with an introduction by R. H. C. Davis (Oxford, 1973).

Gilbert Foliot: *The Letters and Charters of Gilbert Foliot*, ed. A. Morey and C. N. L. Brooke (Cambridge, 1967).

'Glanvill': *Tractatus de legibus et consuetudinis regni Anglie qui Glanvilla vocatur*, ed. G. D. G. Hall (Edinburgh, 1965).

Guibert of Nogent: *Self and Society in Medieval France: The Memoirs of Abbot Guibert of Nogent*, tr. J. F. Benton (New York, 1972).

Henry of Grosmont: *Le Livre de Seyntz Medicines*, ed. J. Arnould (Oxford, 1940).

Henry of Huntingdon: *Historia Anglorum*, ed. T. Arnold, (Rolls Series, 1879).

Histoire des ducs de Normandie et des rois d'Angleterre, ed. F. Michel (Société de l'histoire de France, Paris, 1840).

L'Histoire de Guillaume le Maréchal, ed, P. Meyer, 3 vols. (Société de l'histoire de France, Paris, 1891–1901).

Historia Albigensium, RHF, XIX, pp. 1–113.

Historia et cartularium monasterii sancti Petri Gloucestriae, ed. W. H. Hart, 2 vols. (Rolls Series, 1863).

Historia gloriosi regis Ludovici, RHF, XII, pp. 124–33.

Historia Ramesiensis, ed. W. D. Macray in *Chronicon abbatiae Ramesiensis* (Rolls Series, 1886).

Historia sancti Florentii Salmurensis, in *Chroniques des Eglises d'Anjou*, ed. P. Marchegay and E. Mabille (Paris, 1896).

Honoré Bonet: *L'arbre de batailles*, ed. E. Nys (Brussels, 1883); tr. G. W. Coopland, *The Tree of Battles of Honoré Bonet* (Liverpool, 1975).

Innocent III: *Selected Letters of Pope Innocent III Concerning England, 1198–1216*, ed. C. R. Cheney and W. H. Semple (London, 1953).

Itinerarium perigrinorum et gesta regis Ricardi, ed. W. Stubbs, *Chronicles and Memorials of the Reign of Richard I*, I (Rolls Series, 1864).

Das Itinerarium Perigrinorum. Eine zeitgenossiche englische Chronik zum dritten Kreuzzug in ursprunglischer Gestalt, ed. H. E. Meyer, *MGH Shriften*, 18 (Stuttgart, 1962).

Jean de Bueil, *Le Jouvencel*, ed. C. Favre and L. Lecestre, 2 vols. (Paris, 1887–9).

Jocelin of Brakelond: *The Chronicle of Jocelin of Brakelond*, ed. and tr. H. E. Butler (London, 1949).

John of Hexham: *Historia Johannis, prioris Haugustadensis ecclesiae*, ed. J. Raine, *The Priory of Hexham, its Chroniclers, Endowments and Annals*, 2 vols. (Surtees Society, 44, Durham, 1868), I, pp. 107–72.

John of Legnano, *Tractatus de bello, represaliis et de duello*, ed. T. E. Holland, tr. J. L. Brierly (Oxford, 1917).

John of Salisbury: *Ioannis Saresberiensis episcopi Cartonensis policratici sive de nugis curialium et vestigiis philosophorum libri VIII*, ed. C. C. J. Webb (Oxford, 1909); tr. J. Dickinson as *The Statesman's Book of John of Salisbury* (New York, 1927).

John of Worcester: *The Chronicle of John of Worcester, 118–40*, ed. J. R. H. Weaver (Oxford, 1908).

Joinville: *Jean, sire de Joinville, Histoire de Saint Louis*, ed. N. N. de Wailly (Société de l'histoire de France, 1868); tr. M. R. B. Shaw, *The Life of St Louis, Joinville and Villehardouin: Chronicles of the Crusades* (Harmondsworth, 1963).

Jomsvikinga Saga, ed. and tr. N. F. Blake (London, 1962).

Jordan Fantosme's Chronicle, ed. and tr. R. C. Johnston (Oxford, 1981).

Layettes des Trésor des Chartes, 3 vols., ed. M. A. Teulet and M. J. De Laborde (Paris, 1863–75).

Leges Henrici Primi, ed. L. J. Downer (Oxford, 1972).

The Letters of Lanfranc, Archbishop of Canterbury, ed. and tr. H. Clover and M. Gibson (Oxford, 1979).

Liber Eliensis, ed. E. O. Blake (Camden Third Series, 92, London, 1962).

Lives of S Ninian and S Kentigern, ed. A. P. Forbes (Edinburgh, 1874).

Magna Carta, ed. and tr. J. C. Holt, *Magna Carta* (Cambridge, 2nd edn, 1992), pp. 448–73.

Magni rotuli scaccarii Normaniae sub regibus Angliae, ed. T. Stapleton, 2 vols. (Society of Antiquaries of London, 1840–4).

Materials for the History of Thomas Becket, Archbishop of Canterbury, ed. J. C. Robertson and J. B. Sheppard, 7 vols. (Rolls Series, 1875–85).

Matthew Paris: *Matthaei Parisiensis, monachi sancti Albani, chronica majora*, ed. H. R. Luard, 7 vols. (Rolls Series, 1872–3).

   Historia Anglorum, sive, ut vulgo dicitur, historia minor, ed. F. J. Madden, 3 vols. (Rolls Series, 1866).

Mediae Latinitatis Lexicon Minus, ed. J. F. Niermeyer (Leiden, 1976).

Memorials of the Church of SS Peter and Wilfrid, Ripon, ed. J. T. Fowler (Surtees Society, 74, 1882).

Odo of Deuil: *De profectione Ludovici VII in Orientem*, ed. and tr. V. G. Berry (Columbia University Press, 1948).

Orderic Vitalis: *The Ecclesiastical History of Orderic Vitalis*, ed. and tr. M. Chibnall, 6 vols. (Oxford, 1969–80).

Otto of Freising: *Ottonis et Rahewini gesta Friderici imperatoris*, ed. G. Waitz, *MGH, SS*, XLVI (Hannover, 1922); tr. C. C. Mierow, *The Deeds of Frederick Barbarossa by Otto of Freising and his continuator, Rahewin* (New York, 1953).

Patrologia cursus completus, series latina, ed. J. P. Migne *et al.*, 221 vols. in 222, with supplements (Paris, 1878–1974).

Peter of Blois: *Petri Blesensis Archidiaconi opera omnia*, ed. J. A. Giles, 4 vols. (Oxford, 1846–7).

Phillipe de Novarre: *Les Quatres Ages de l'Homme*, ed. M. de Freville (Société des Anciens Textes Français, Paris, 1988).

Pipe Rolls: *The Great Roll of the Pipe for the Eleventh Year of the Reign of Henry II, AD 1164–5*, (Pipe Roll Society, London, 1887).

   The Great Roll of the Pipe for the Twenty Second Year of the Reign of Henry II, AD 1175–76, ed. J. H. Round (Pipe Roll Society, London, 1904).

   The Great Roll of the Pipe for the Sixth Year of the Reign of Richard I, ed. D. M. Stenton (Pipe Roll Society, London, 1904).

Ralph of Coggeshall: *Radulphi de Coggeshall chronicon Anglicanum*, ed. J. Stevenson (Rolls Series, 1875).

Ralph of Diceto: *Radulphi de Diceto decani Lundoniensis opera historica*, ed. W. Stubbs, 2 vols. (Rolls Series, 1876).

Raoul de Cambrai, ed. and tr. S. Kay (Oxford, 1992).

Raymond d'Aguilliers: *Historia Francorum qui ceperunt Iherusalem*, ed. J. Hill (Philadelphia, 1968).

Recueil des actes des ducs de Normandie de 911 à 1066, ed. M. Fauroux (Mémoires de la Société des antiquaires de Normandie, 36, Caen, 1961).

Recueil des actes de Philippe Auguste, ed. H. F. Delaborde, C. Petit-Dutaillis, J. Bousard and M. Nortier, 4 vols. (Paris, 1916–79).

Recueil des historiens des croisades, 16 vols. (Paris, 1841–1906):
    Lois, 2 vols. (1841–3).
    Historiens orientaux, 5 vols. (1872–1906).
    Historiens occidentaux, 5 vols. (1844–95).

Recueil des historiens des Gaules et de la France, ed. M. Bouquet *et al.*, nouv. édn, ed. L. Delisle, 24 vols. (Paris, 1869–1904).

Red Book of the Exchequer, ed. H. Hall, 3 vols. (Rolls Series, 1896).

Regesta regum Anglo-Normannorum, 1066–1154:
    I. *1066–1100*, ed. H. W. C. Davis, with the assistance of J. R. Whitwell (Oxford, 1913).
    II. *1100–1135*, ed. C. J. Johnson and H. A. Cronne (Oxford, 1956).
    III. *1135–1154*, ed. H. A. Cronne and R. H. C. Davis (Oxford, 1968).
    IV. *Facsimiles of Original Charters and Writs of King Stephen, the Empress Matilda and Dukes Geoffrey and Henry*, ed. H. A. Cronne and R. H. C. Davis (Oxford, 1968).

Regesta Regum Scottorum:
    I. *The Acts of Malcolm IV, King of Scots 1153–1165*, ed. G. W. S. Barrow (Edinburgh, 1960).
    II. *The Acts of William the Lion, King of Scots 1165–1214*, ed. G. W. S. Barrow (Edinburgh, 1971).

La Règle du Temple, ed. H. de Curzon (Paris, 1886); tr. J. Upton Ward, *The Rule of the Templars* (Woodbridge, 1992).

Richard of Devizes: *Chronicon Ricardi Divisensis de tempore regis Ricardi*, ed. and tr. J. Appleby (London, 1963).

Richard of Hexham: *De gestis regis Stephani et de bello Standardii*, ed. J. H. Raine, *The Priory of Hexham, its Chroniclers, Endowments and Annals*, 2 vols. (Surtees Society, 44, Durham, 1868), I, pp. 63–106.

Richer: *Histoire de France*, ed. R. Latouche, 2 vols. (Paris, 1937).

Rigord: *Gesta Philippi Augusti*, ed. H.-F. Delaborde in *Oeuvres de Rigord et Guillaume le Breton, historiens de Philippe Auguste*, 2 vols. (Paris, 1882–5), I, pp. 1–167.

Robert of Gloucester: *The Metrical Chronicle of Robert of Gloucester*, ed. W. A. Wright, 2 vols. (Rolls Series, 1887).

Robert of Torigny: *The Chronicle of Robert of Torigni*, ed. R. Howlett, *Chronicles of the Reigns of Stephen, Henry II and Richard I*, vol. IV.

Roger of Howden: *Chronica Rogeri de Hovedene*, ed. W. Stubbs, 4 vols. (Rolls Series, 1868–71).

Roger of Wendover: *Chronica Rogeri de Wendover liber qui dicitur flores historiarum*, ed. H. G. Hewlett, 3 vols. (Rolls Series, 1886–9).

Rolls of the Justices in Eyre for Gloucestershire, Warwickshire and Staffordshire (1221–2), ed. D. M. Stenton (Selden Society, 59, 1940).

Rolls of the Justices in Eyre for Yorkshire, 1218–19, ed. D. M. Stenton (Selden Society, 56, 1937).

Rolls Series: *Rerum Britannicarum Medii Aevi Scriptores, or Chronicles and Memorials of Great Britain and Ireland during the Middle Ages, published under the authority of the Master of the Rolls* (London, 1858–97).

Rotuli de liberate ac de missis et praestitis, ed. T. Duffus Hardy (Record Commission, 1844).

Rotuli litterarum clausarum in turri Londinensi asservati, ed. T. Duffus Hardy (Record Commission, 1833–4).

Rotuli litterarum patentium in turri Londinensi asservati, ed. T. Duffus Hardy, vol. 1 (Record Commission, 1835).

Rotuli Normanniae in turri Londiniensis asservati ed. T. Duffus Hardy, vol. 1 (Record Commission, 1835).

Rotuli de oblatis et finibus in turri Londinensi asservati, ed. T. Duffus Hardy, 2 vols. (Record Commission, 1835).

The Rules, Statutes and Customs of the Hospitallers, 1099–1310, tr. E. J. King (London, 1934).

Sacrorum conciliorum nova et amplissima collectio, ed. J. D. Mansi, continued by J. B. Martin and L. Petit (Florence, Venice, Paris and Leipzig, 1759–1927).

Saxo Grammaticus, ed. K. Christianson (British Archaeological Reports, International Ser., 84).

Scriptores Rerum Germanicarum in usum scholarum ex Monumentis Germanicae Historicis seperatim editi (repr. Hannover, 1922).

Select Charters and other Illustrations of English Constitutional History from the Earliest Times to the Reign of Edward the First, ed. W. Stubbs (Oxford, 9th edn, revised by H. W. C. Davis).

Serlo of Bayeux: *De capta Bajocensium civitate*, ed. T. Wright, *The Anglo-Latin Satirical Poets and Epigrammatists*, 2 vols. (London, 1892), II, pp. 241–51.

Simeon of Durham: *Symeonis monachi opera omnia*, ed. T. Arnold, 2 vols. (Rolls Series, 1885).

The Song of Dermot and the Earl, ed. and tr. G. H. Orpen (Oxford, 1892).

The Song of Roland: An Analytical Edition, ed. G. J. Brault, 2 vols. (University Park, Pennsylvania and London, 1978).

Statutes of the Realm (1101–1713), ed. A. Luders, T. E. Tomlins, J. Raithby *et al.*, 11 vols. (Record Commission, 1810–28).

Stephen of Fougères: *Livre des Manières*, ed. R. A. Lodge (Geneva, 1979).

Suger: *Vita Ludovici grossi regis*, ed. H. Waquet (Paris, 1929); tr. R. Cusimano and J. Moorhead, *Suger, The Deeds of Louis the Fat* (Washington, 1992).

Thomas Agnellus, *De morte et sepultura Henrici regis junioris*, ed. J. Stevenson, in *Radulphi de Coggeshall chronicon Anglicanum* (Rolls Series, 1875).

Très ancien coutoumier de Normandie, ed. E. J. Tardiff (Rouen, 1881).

Usamah: *An Arab-Syrian Gentleman and Warrior in the Period of the Crusades: Memoirs of Usamah Ibn-Munqidh*, tr. P. K. Hitti (New York, 1924).

Vita beati Simonis, Migne, *PL*, CLVI.

Vita domni Herluini abbatis Beccensis, ed. J. A. Robinson, in *Gilbert Crispin, Abbot of Westminster: A Study of the Abbey under Norman Rule* (Cambridge, 1911).

Vita sancti Margaretae reginae, in *Symeonis Dunelmensis opera et collectanea*, ed. H. Hinde (Surtees Society, 51, 1868), I, Appendix III.

Wace: *Le Roman de Rou de Wace*, ed. A. J. Holden, 3 vols. (Société des anciens textes français, Paris, 1970–3).

Walter of Coventry: *Memoriale fratris Walteri de Coventria*, ed. W. Stubbs, 2 vols. (Rolls Series, 1872–3).

Walter Daniel: *The Life of Ailred of Rievaulx*, ed. and tr. F. M. Powicke (London, 1950).

Walter Map: *De nugis curialium*, ed. and tr. M. R. James (Oxford, 1983).

The Waltham Chronicle, ed. and tr. L. Watkiss and M. Chibnall (Oxford, 1994).

William le Breton: *Gesta Philippi Augusti*, ed. H.-F. Delaborde, in *Oeuvres de Rigord et Guillaume le Breton, historiens de Philippe Auguste*, 2 vols. (Paris, 1882–5), I, pp. 168–333; *Philippidos*, II, pp. 1–385.

William of Jumièges: *Guillaume de Jumièges, Gesta Normannorum ducum*, ed. J. Marx (Société de l'histoire de Normandie, 1914).

The Gesta Normannorum Ducum of William of Jumièges, Orderic Vitalis and Robert of Torigny, ed. and tr. E. M. C. van Houts, 2 vols. (Oxford, 1992–95).

William of Malmesbury: *De gestis regum Anglorum*, ed. W. Stubbs, 2 vols. (Rolls Series, 1887–9).

De gestis pontificum Anglorum, ed. N. Hamilton (Rolls Series, 1870).

The Vita Wulfstani of William of Malmesbury, ed. R. R. Darlington (Camden Society, 3rd ser., 40, London, 1928).

Historia Novella, ed. K. R. Potter (London, 1955).

William of Newburgh: *Historia rerum Anglicarum*, ed. R. Howlett, *Chronicles and Memorials of the Reigns of Stephen, Henry II and Richard I* (Rolls Series, 1884), I, pp. 1–408; II, pp. 409–53.

William of Orange: J. Walthelet-Willem, *Recherches sur la chanson de Guillaume. Etudes accompagnés d'une édition*, 2 vols. (Paris, 1975); tr. G. Price, *William Count of Orange. Four Old French Epics* (London, 1975).

William of Poitiers: *Guillaume de Poitiers: Histoire de Guillaume le Conquérant*, ed. R. Foreville (Paris, 1952).

William of Tyre: *Willelmi Tyrensis archiepiscopi chronicon*, ed. R. B. C. Huygens (*Corpus Christianorum Continuatio Medievalis*, LXIII, 1986); tr. E. A. Babcock and A. C. Krey, *William of Tyre, A History of Deeds Done Beyond the Sea* (New York, 1943).

Year Book 11–12 Edward III, ed. and tr. A. J. Horwood and L. O. Pike (Rolls Series, 1883).

2 SECONDARY SOURCES

Abels, R., *Lordship and Military Obligation in Anglo-Saxon England* (Berkley, 1988).

'English Tactics, Strategy and Military Organization in the Late Tenth Century', *The Battle of Maldon, 991*, ed. D. Scragg (Oxford, 1991), pp. 143–55.

Ailes, A., 'Heraldry in Twelfth-Century England', *England in the Twelfth Century. Proceedings of the 1988 Harlaxton Symposium*, ed. D. Williams (Woodbridge, 1990), pp. 1–16.

'The Knight, Heraldry and Armour. The Role of Recognition and the Origins of Heraldry', *Medieval Knighthood, IV. Papers from the Fifth Strawberry Hill Conference*, ed. C. Harper-Bill and R. Harvey (Woodbridge, 1992), pp. 1–21.

Alexander, J. J. G. 'Ideological Representation of Combat in Anglo-Norman Art', *Anglo-Norman Studies*, 15 (1992), pp. 1–24.

Allmand, C. T., 'The Aftermath of War in Fifteenth Century France', *History*, 61 (1976), pp. 344–67.

Amt, E. M., 'The Meaning of Waste in the Early Pipe Rolls of Henry II', *Economic History Review*, 44 (1991), pp. 240–8.

Anderson, M. O., 'Lothian and the Early Scottish Kings', *Scottish Historical Review*, 39 (1960), pp. 98–112.

Archibald, J. K., 'La chanson de captivité du roi Richard', *Cahiers d'études médiévales*, 1 (1974), pp. 149–58.

Arnold, B., *German Knighthood, 1050–1300* (Oxford, 1985).

Bachrach, B. S., 'Fortifications and Military Tactics: Fulk Nerra's Strongholds circa 1000', *Technology and Culture*, 20 (1979), pp. 531–49.

'The Angevin Strategy of Castle-building in the Reign of Fulk Nerra, 987–1040', *American Historical Review*, 88 (1983), pp. 533–60.

'Some Observations on the Military Administration of the Norman Conquest', *Anglo-Norman Studies*, 8 (1985), pp. 1–26.

'The Practical Use of Vegetius' *De Re Militari* in the Early Middle Ages', *The Historian*, 47 (1985), pp. 239–55.

'Angevin Campaign Forces in the Reign of Fulk Nerra, count of the Angevins, 987–1040', *Francia*, 16 (1), (1989), pp. 67–84.

Baker, D. (ed.), *Religious Motivation: Biographical and Sociological Problems for the Church Historian*, (Studies in Church History, 25, Oxford, 1978).

'Ailred of Rievaulx and Walter Espec', *The Haskins Society Journal*, 1 (1989), pp. 91–8.

Barber, R., *The Knight and Chivalry* (London, 1970).

Barber, R. and Barker, J. R. V., *Tournaments. Jousts, Chivalry and Pageants in the Middle Ages* (Woodbridge, 1989).

Barbier, P., *La France féodal, I: Chateaux forts et églises fortifiées du midi de la France* (Paris, 1968).

Baring, F. H., 'The Conqueror's Footsteps in Domesday Book', *EHR*, 13 (1898), pp. 17–25; repr. in *idem.*, *Domesday Tables* (London, 1909), pp. 207–16.

Barker, J. R. V., *The Tournament in England, 1100–1400* (Woodbridge, 1986).

Barker, J. R. V. and Keen, M., 'The Medieval English Kings and the Tournament', *Das ritterliche Turnier im Mittlealter*, ed. J. Fleckenstein (Gottingen, 1985), pp. 212–8.

Barlow, F., *Edward the Confessor* (2nd edn, 1979).

William Rufus (London, 1983).

Thomas Becket (London, 1986).

Barnie, J., *War in Medieval Society. Social Values and the Hundred Years War, 1337–99* (London, 1974).

Barrow, G. W. S., *The Kingdom of the Scots* (London, 1973).

The Anglo-Norman Era in Scottish History (Oxford, 1980).

Kingship and Unity: Scotland 1000–1306 (London, 1981).

'The Army of Alexander III's Scotland', *Scotland in the Age of Alexander III*, ed. N. Reid (Edinburgh, 1981), pp. 132–47.

David of Scotland (1124–1153): the Balance of New and Old (The Stenton Lecture, Reading, 1985).

Robert the Bruce (3rd edn, Edinburgh, 1988).

Bartlett, R., *Trial by Fire and Water* (Oxford, 1986).

'Technique militaire et pouvoir politique, 900–1300', *Annales: économies, sociétés, civilizations*, 41 (1986), pp. 1135–59.

The Making of Europe. Conquest, Colonization and Cultural Change, 950–1350 (London, 1993).

Bates, D., *Normandy Before 1066* (London, 1982).

William the Conqueror (London, 1989).

Bédier, J., *La Chanson de Roland commentée* (Paris, 1927).

Bedoz Rezak, B., 'The Social Implications of the Art of Chivalry: The Sigillographic Evidence (France, 1050–1250)', *The Medieval Court of Europe*, ed. E. R. Haymes (Munich, 1986), pp. 142–75.

'Medieval Seals and the Structure of Chivalric Society', *The Study of Chivalry: Resources and Approaches*, ed. H. H. D. Chickering and T. H. Seiler (Michigan, 1988), pp. 313–72.

Beeler, J. H., 'Castles and Strategy in Norman and Early Angevin England', *Speculum*, 21 (1956), pp. 581–601.

'Towards a Re-Evaluation of Medieval English Generalship', *The Journal of British Studies*, 3 (1963), pp. 1–10.

'The Composition of Anglo-Norman Armies', *Speculum*, 39 (1965), pp. 398–414.

Warfare in England, 1066–1189 (Ithaca and New York, 1966).

Bennet, M., 'Poetry as History? The *Roman de Rou* of Wace as a Source for the Norman Conquest', *Anglo-Norman Studies*, 5 (1982), pp. 1–39.

'Wace and Warfare', *Anglo-Norman Studies*, 11 (1988), pp. 37–58, reprinted in Strickland, *Anglo-Norman Warfare*, pp. 230–50.

'La Règle du Temple; or, How to Deliver a Cavalry Charge', *Studies in Medieval History Presented to R. Allen Brown*, ed. C. Harper-Bill, C. Holdsworth and J. Nelson (Woodbridge, 1989), pp. 7–20, reprinted as an appendix to J. M. Upton Ward, *The Rule of the Temple* (Woodbridge, 1992).

Benson, L. D., 'The Tournament in the Romances of Chrétien de Troyes and *L'Histoire de Guillaume le Maréchal*', *Chivalric Literature: Essays on Relations between Literature and Life in the Middle Ages*, ed. L. D. Benson and J. Leyerle (Kalamazoo, 1981), pp. 1–24.

Benton, J., '"*Nostre Franceis n'unt talent de fuir*": The *Song of Roland* and the Enculturation of a Warrior Class', *Olifant*, 6 (1979), pp. 237–58.

Bernstein, D. J., 'The Blinding of Harold and the Meaning of the Bayeux Tapestry', *Anglo-Norman Studies*, 5 (1982), pp. 40–64.

The Mystery of the Bayeux Tapestry (London, 1986).

Biddle, M., 'Towns', *The Archaeology of Anglo-Saxon England*, ed. D. M. Wilson (London, 1976), pp. 99–150.

'Wolvesey: the *domus quasi palatium* of Henry de Blois in Winchester', *Château Gaillard*, 3 (1966), pp. 28–36.

Biddle, M. and Hill, D., 'Late Saxon Planned Towns', *Antiquaries Journal*, 51 (1971), pp. 70–85.

Bishop, T. A. M., 'The Norman Settlement of Yorkshire', *Studies in Medieval History presented to Frederick Maurice Powicke*, ed. R. W. Hunt, W. A. Pantin and R. W. Southern (Oxford, 1948), pp. 1–14.

Blair, C., *European Armour, c. 1066–1700* (London, 1958).

Bleise, J., 'Ailred of Rievaulx's Rhetoric and Morale at the Battle of the Standard, 1138', *The Haskins Society Journal*, 1 (1989), pp. 99–107.

'Rhetoric and Morale: A Study of Battle Orations from the Central Middle Ages', *Journal of Medieval History*, 15 (1989), pp. 201–26.

Bloch, M., *La Sociéte Féodale*, tr. L. A. Manyon as *Feudal Society* (2nd edn, 1962).

Bloomfield, M. W., 'Beowulf, Byrhtnoth and the Judgement of God: Trial by Combat in Anglo-Saxon England', *Speculum*, 44 (1969), pp. 545–59.

de Bouard, M., 'Sur les origines de la trêve de Dieu', *Annales de Normandie*, 9 (1957), pp. 179–89.

Boulton, D. J. d'A., *The Knights of the Crown. The Monarchical Orders of Knighthood in Later Medieval Europe* (Woodbridge, 1987).

Boussard, J., 'Les mercenaires au XIIe siècle. Henri II Plantagenet et les origines de l'armée de metier', *Bibliothèque de l'École des Chartes*, 106 (1945–6), pp. 189–224.

Le gouvernment d'Henri II Plantagenet (Paris, 1961).

Boutrouche, R., 'The Devastation of Rural Areas During the Hundred Years War and the Agricultural Recovery of France', *The Recovery of France in the Fifteenth Century*, ed. P. S. Lewis (New York and London, 1972), pp. 23–59.

Bowlus, C. R., and Schwatz, G. M., 'Warfare and Society in the Carolingian Ostmark', *Austrian History Yearbook*, 14 (1978), pp. 3–30.

Bradbury, J. 'Battles in England and Normandy, 1066–1154', *Anglo-Norman Studies*, 6 (1983), pp. 1–12; repr. in Strickland, *Anglo-Norman Warfare*, pp. 182–93.

The Medieval Archer (Woodbridge, 1985).

'Geoffrey V of Anjou, Count and Knight', *The Ideals and Practice of Medieval Knighthood, III*, ed. C. Harper-Bill and R. Harvey (Woodbridge, 1990), pp. 21–38.

The Medieval Siege (Woodbridge, 1992).

Bradley-Cromey, N., 'The *Recreantise* Episode in Chrétien's *Erec and Enide*', *The Study of Chivalry: Resources and Approaches*, ed. H. H. D. Chickering and T. H. Seiler (Michigan, 1988), pp. 449–71.

Bridney, E., *La condition juridique des croisés et le privilège de la croix* (Paris, 1900).

Bromberg, E. I., 'Wales and the Mediaeval Slave Trade', *Speculum*, 17 (1942), pp. 263–9.

Brooke, C. N. L., and Morey, A., *Gilbert Foliot and His Letters* (Cambridge, 1965).

Brooke, Z. N. and Brooke, C. N. L., 'Hereford Cathedral Dignitaries in the Twelfth Century – Supplement', *Cambridge Historical Journal*, 8 (1944–6), pp. 179–85.

Brooks, N. P., 'Arms, Status and Warfare in Late Anglo-Saxon England', *Ethelred the Unready*, ed. D. Hill (British Archaeological Reports, British Series, 59 Oxford, 1978), pp. 81–103.

Brooks, N. P. and Walker, H. E., 'The Authority and Interpretation of the Bayeux Tapestry', *Proceedings of the Battle Conference (Anglo-Norman Studies)*, 1 (1978), pp. 1–34.

Brown, R. A., 'Framlingham Castle and Bigod, 1154–1216', *Proceedings of the Suffolk Institute of Archaeology*, 25 (1951), pp. 127–48; repr. in *idem.*, *Castles, Conquest and Charters. Collected Papers* (Woodbridge, 1989), pp. 187–208.

English Medieval Castles (London, 1954).

'Royal Castle-Building in England, 1154–1216', *EHR*, 70 (1955), pp. 353–98.

'A List of Castles, 1154–1216', *EHR*, 74 (1959), pp. 249–80.

The Normans and the Norman Conquest, (London, 1969).

Origins of English Feudalism (London, 1973).

'The Battle of Hastings', *Proceedings of the Battle Conference*, 3 (1980), pp. 1–21, repr. in Strickland, *Anglo-Norman Warfare*, pp. 161–81.

The Norman Conquest (London, 1984).

'The Status of the Norman Knight', *War and Government*, pp. 18–32, repr. in Strickland, *Anglo-Norman Warfare*, pp. 128–42.

Brown, S., 'The Mercenary and His Master: Military Service and Monetary Reward in the Eleventh and Twelfth Century', *History*, 74 (1989), pp. 20–38.

Brundage, J. A., 'An Errant Crusader: Stephen of Blois', *Traditio*, 16 (1960), pp. 380–95.

'The Crusade of Richard I: Two Canonical *Quaestiones*', *Speculum*, 38 (1963), pp. 443–52.

Medieval Canon Law and the Crusader (Wisconsin, 1969).

'Holy War and the Medieval Lawyers', *The Holy War*, ed. T. Murphy (Columbus, Ohio, 1976), pp. 99–140.

'The Limits of the War-Making Power: The Contribution of Medieval Canonists', *Peace in a Nuclear Age: The Bishop's Pastoral Letter in Perspective*, ed. C. J. Reid, Jr (Washington, 1986), pp. 69–85.

The Crusades, Holy War and Canon Law (Aldershot, 1991), which reprints all Brundage's articles cited above.

Bull, M., *Knightly Piety and the Lay Response to the First Crusade. The Limousin and Gascony, c. 970–1130* (Oxford, 1993).

Bumke, J., *Studien zum Ritterbegriff im 12. und 13. Jahrhundert* (Heidelberg, 1977), tr. W. H. T. and E. Jackson as *The Concept of Knighthood in the Middle Ages* (New York, 1982).

Bur, M., *La formation du comté du Champagne* (Nancy, 1977).

Burgess, G. S., *Chrétien de Troyes: Erec and Enide* (London, 1984).

Caerwyn Williams, J. E., 'The Court Poet in Medieval Ireland', *Proceedings of the British Academy*, 57 (1971), pp. 85–135.

Carolus-Barré, L., 'Benôit XII et la mission charitable de Betrand Carit dans le pays dévastés du nord de la France, Cambrésis, Vermandois, Thiérache, 1340', *Mélanges d'archéologie et d'histoire publiés par l'école française de Rome*, 62 (1950), pp. 165–232.

Carpenter, D., *The Battles of Lewes and Evesham 1264/5* (University of Keele, 1987).
  The Minority of Henry III (London, 1990).

Cessford, C. 'Cavalry in Early Bernicia: A Reply', *Northern History*, 29 (1993), pp. 185–7.

Chadwick, H. M., *The Heroic Age* (Cambridge, 1912).

Chaytor, H. J., *Savaric de Mauleon, Baron and Troubadour* (Cambridge, 1939).

Cheney, C. R., *English Bishop's Chanceries, 1100–1250* (Manchester, 1950).

Cherniss, M. D., *Ingeld and Christ: Heroic Concepts and Values in Old English Poetry* (Mouton, 1972).

Chibnall, M., 'Mercenaries and the "Familia Regis" under Henry I', *History*, 62 (1977), pp. 15–23; repr. in Strickland, *Anglo-Norman Warfare*, pp. 84–92.
  'Feudal Society in Orderic Vitalis', *Anglo-Norman Studies*, 1 (1978), pp. 35–48.
  The World of Orderic Vitalis (London, 1984).
  Anglo-Norman England, 1066–1166 (Oxford, 1986).
  'Castles in Orderic Vitalis', *Studies in Medieval History Presented to R. Allen Brown* (Boydell, 1989), pp. 43–56.

Chickering, H. H. D. and Seiler, T. H. (eds.), *The Study of Chivalry: Resources and Approaches*, (W. Michigan University, 1988).

Ciklamini, M., 'The Old Icelandic Duel', *Scandinavian Studies*, 35 (1963), pp. 175–94.

Clark, C., 'Byrhtnoth and Roland: A Comparison', *Neophilologus*, 51 (1967), pp. 288–93.

Clark, G., 'The Hero of Maldon: *Vir pius et strenuus*', *Speculum*, 54 (1979), pp. 257–82.

Cleary, T., *The Japanese Art of War* (Boston and London, 1992).

van Cleve, T. M., *The Emperor Frederick II of Hohenstaufen* (Oxford, 1972).

Cline, R. H., 'The Influences of Romances on Tournaments of the Middle Ages, *Speculum*, 20 (1945), pp. 204–11.

Colvin, H. M., 'Holme Lacy: An Episcopal Manor and its Tenants in the Twelfth and Thirteenth Century', *Medieval Studies presented to Rose Graham*, ed. V. Ruffer and A. J. Taylor (Oxford, 1950).

The Complete Peerage, ed. G. E. Cokayne, revised by V. Gibbs, H. E. Doubleday and Lord Howard de Walden, 12 vols. in 13 (London, 1910–57).

Contamine, P., *Guerre, état et société à la fin du Moyen Age. Etudes sur les armées des rois de France, 1337–1494* (Paris, 1972).
  La Guerre au Moyen Age, (Paris, 1980); tr. M. Jones, *War in the Middle Ages* (Oxford, 1984).

Cook, D. R., 'The Norman Military Revolution in England', *Proceedings of the Battle Conference*, 1 (1978), pp. 94–102.

Coss, P., *The Knight in Medieval England, 1000–1400* (Stroud, 1993).

Coulson, C., 'Rendability and Castellation in Medieval France', *Château Gaillard*, 6 (1973), pp. 59–67.
  'Fortress Policy in Capetian Tradition and Angevin Practice: Aspects of the conquest of Normandy by Philip II', *Anglo-Norman Studies*, 6 (1983), pp. 13–38.
  'The Impact of Bouvines upon the Fortress Policy of Philip Augustus', *Studies in Medieval History Presented to R. A. Brown*, ed. C. Harper-Bill, C. Holdsworth and J. Nelson (Boydell, 1989), pp. 71–80.

Coupland, S., 'Carolingian Arms and Armour in the Ninth Century', *Viator*, 21 (1990), pp. 29–50.

'The Rod of God's Wrath or the People of God's Wrath?', *Journal of Ecclesiastical History*, 42 (1991), pp. 535–54.

Cowdrey, H. E. J., 'Bishop Ermenfrid of Sion and the Penitential Ordinance Following the Battle of Hastings', *Journal of Ecclesiastical History*, 20 (1969), pp. 225–42.

'The Peace and Truce of God in the Eleventh Century', *Past and Present*, 46 (1970), pp. 42–67.

Crawford, B. E., *Scandinavian Scotland* (Leicester, 1987).

Crist, L. S., 'A propos de la desmesure dans la Chanson de Roland: quelques propos (démesurés?)', *Olifant*, 4 (1974), pp. 10–20.

Cronne, H. A., 'Ranulf de Gernons, Earl of Chester, 1129–53', *TRHS*, 4th ser., 20 (1937), pp. 103–34.

The Reign of King Stephen. Anarchy in England 1135–54 (London, 1970).

Cross, J. E., 'Oswald and Byrhtnoth: A Christian Saint and a Hero who is Christian', *English Studies*, 44 (1965), pp. 93–109.

'The Ethic of War in Old English', *England Before the Conquest*, ed. P. Clemoes and K. Hughes (Cambridge, 1971), pp. 269–82.

Crouch, D., 'Robert, Earl of Gloucester and the Daughter of Zelophehad', *Journal of Medieval History*, 11 (1985), pp. 227–43.

The Beaumont Twins. The Roots and Branches of Power in the Twelfth Century (Cambridge, 1986).

William Marshal: Court, Career and Chivalry in the Angevin Empire, 1147–1219 (London and New York, 1990).

The Image of Aristocracy in Britain, 1000–1300 (London and New York, 1992).

'A Norman "Conventio" and Bonds of Lordship in the Middle Ages', *Law and Government in Medieval England and Normandy. Essays in Honour of Sir James Holt*, ed. G. Garnett and J. Hudson (Cambridge, 1994), pp. 299–324.

Dalton, P., 'Aiming at the Impossible: Rannulf II, Earl of Chester and Lincolnshire in the Reign of King Stephen', *The Earldom of Chester and Its Charters: A Tribute to Geoffrey Barraclough*, ed. A. T. Thatcher (*Journal of the Chester Archaeological Society*, 7 (1991)), pp. 109–34.

'In Neutro Latere: The Armed Neutrality of Rannulf II Earl of Chester in King Stephen's Reign', *Anglo-Norman Studies*, 14 (1991), pp. 39–60.

Darlington, R. R., 'Aethelwig, Abbot of Evesham', *EHR* 47 (1933), pp. 1–22.

David, C. W., 'A Tract Attributed to Simeon of Durham', *EHR*, 32 (1917), pp. 382–7.

Robert Curthose, Duke of Normandy (Harvard, 1920).

Davis, H. W. C., 'A Contemporary Account of the Battle of Tinchebrai', *EHR*, 24 (1909), pp. 728–32.

'Henry of Blois and Brian fitzCount', *EHR*, 25 (1910), pp. 297–303.

'Waldric, the Chancellor of Henry I', *EHR*, 26 (1911), pp. 84–9.

'Some Documents of the Anarchy', *Essays in History Presented to Reginald Lane Poole*, ed. H. W. C. Davis (Oxford, 1927, repr. 1969), pp. 168–89.

Davis, R. H. C., 'King Stephen and the Earl of Chester Revisited', *EHR*, 75 (1960), pp. 654–60.

'The Treaty between William, Earl of Gloucester, and Roger, Earl of Hereford', *A Medieval Miscellany for Doris Stenton*, ed. P. M. Barnes and C. F. Slade (Pipe Roll Society, new ser., xxxvi, 1962), pp. 139–46.

The Normans and Their Myth (London, 1976).

'Did the Anglo-Saxons have Warhorses?', *Weapons and Warfare in Anglo-Saxon England*, ed. S. C. Hawkes (Oxford University Committee for Archaeology Monograph no. 21, Oxford, 1989), pp. 141–4.

King Stephen (London, 3rd edn, 1990).

Davis, W. and Fouracre, P. (eds.), *The Settlement of Disputes in Early Medieval Europe* (Cambridge, 1986).

Debord, A., 'The Castellan Revolution and the Peace of God in Aquitaine', *The Peace of God. Social Violence and Religious Response in France around the Year 1000*, ed. T. Head and R. Landes (Ithaca and London, 1992).

Delumeau, J., *La péché et la peur* (Paris, 1983), tr. E. Nicholson as *Sin and Fear: The Emergence of a Western Guilt Culture, 13th–18th Centuries* (New York, 1990).

Denholm-Young, N., 'The Tournament in the Thirteenth Century', *Studies Presented to F. Powicke*, ed. R. W. Hunt, W. A. Pantin and R. W. Southern (Oxford, 1948), pp. 204–68.

Dodwell, C. R., 'The Bayeux Tapestry and French Secular Epic', *The Burlington Magazine*, 107 (1966), pp. 549–60.

Anglo-Saxon Art; A New Perspective (Manchester, 1982).

Douglas, D. C., 'The Song of Roland and the Norman Conquest of England', *French Studies*, 14 (1960), pp. 99–116.

William the Conqueror (London, 1964).

Drew, K. F., 'The Carolingian Military Frontier in Italy', *Traditio*, 20 (1964), pp. 437–47.

Duby, G., *La Société aux XIe et XIIe siècles dans la région mâconnaise* (2nd edn, 1971, repr. Ecole des Hautes Etudes, 1982).

Le dimanche de Bouvines (Paris, 1973), tr. C. Tihanyi as *The Legend of Bouvines. War, Religion and Culture in the Middle Ages* (Cambridge, 1990).

'La diffusion du titre chevaleresque sur le versant méditerranéen de la Chrétienté latine', *La Noblesse au Moyen Age*, ed. P. Contamine (Paris, 1976), pp. 39–70.

Le trois ordres ou l'imaginaire du féodalisme (Paris, 1978), tr. A. Goldhammer as *The Three Orders. Feudal Society Imagined* (Chicago and London, 1980).

The Chivalrous Society, tr. C. Postan (London, 1977).

'The Culture of the Knightly Class: Audience and Patronage', *Renaissance and Renewal in the Twelfth Century*, ed. R. L. Benson and G. Constable (Oxford, 1982), pp. 248–62.

Guillaume le Marechal ou le meilleur chevalier du monde (Paris, 1984), tr. R. Howard as *William Marshal: The Flower of Chivalry* (London, 1985).

Le Moyen Age, 987–1460 (Paris, 1987), tr. J. Vale as *France in the Middle Ages* (London, 1991).

Duggan, A., 'The Cult of St Thomas Becket in the Thirteenth Century', *St Thomas Cantilupe, Bishop of Hereford. Essays in His Honour*, ed. M. Jancey (Hereford, 1982).

Dumezil, G., *The Stakes of a Warrior* (Berkley, 1983).

Dunbabin, J., *France in the Making, 843–1180* (Oxford, 1985).

Duncan, A. A. M., *Scotland. The Making of the Kingdom* (Edinburgh, 1975).

'The Kingdom of the Scots', *The Making of Britain: The Dark Ages* (London, 1984), pp. 131–44.

Dyer, J., 'Earthworks of the Danelaw Frontier', *Archaeology and the Landscape*, ed. P. J. Fowler (London, 1972), pp. 222–36.

Eales, R., 'Royal Power and Castles in Norman England', *The Ideals and Practice of Medieval Knighthood III*, ed. C. Harper-Bill and R. Harvey (Woodbridge, 1990), pp. 49–78.

'Castles and Politics in England, 1215–1224', *Thirteenth-Century England, II*, ed. P. R. Coss and S. D. Lloyd (Woodbridge, 1988), pp. 23–43.

Edbury, P. W. (ed.), *Crusade and Settlement: Papers Read at the First Conference of the Society for the Study of the Crusades and the Latin East* (Cardiff, 1985).

Edwards, J. G., 'The *Itinerarium Regis Ricardi* and the *Estoire de la Guerre Sainte*', *Historical Essays in Honour of James Tait*, ed. J. G. Edwards, V. H. Galbriath and E. F. Jacob (Manchester, 1933), pp. 59–77.

Eeles, 'The Monymusk Reliquary of Diechbennoch of St Columba', *Proceedings of the Society of Antiquaries of Scotland*, 68 (1934), pp. 433–8.

Ellis Davidson, H. R., *Myths and Symbols in Pagan Europe* (Syracuse, 1988).

Erdmann, C., *Die Entstehung des Kreuzzugsgedankens* (Darmstadt, 1955), tr. M. W. Baldwin and W. Goffart, *The Origin of the Idea of Crusade* (Princetown, 1977).

Evans, D., 'Old English and Old French Epics: Some Analogues', *Guillaume d'Orange and the Chanson de Geste*, ed. W. van Emden and P. E. Bennet (Reading, 1984), pp. 23–31.

Faral, E., *Les jongleurs en France au Moyen Age* (1971).

Ferguson, A. B., *The Indian Summer of English Chivalry. Studies in the Decline and Transformation of Chivalric Idealism* (Durham, N. C., 1960).

Finn, R. W., *The Norman Conquest and Its Effect on the Economy, 1066–86* (London, 1971).

Fino, J. F., 'Le feu et ses usages militaires', *Gladius*, 8 (1970), pp. 15–30.

Fleming, D. F., 'Landholding by Milites in Domesday Book', *Anglo-Norman Studies*, 13 (1990), pp. 83–98.

Flori, J., 'La notion de chevalerie dans les chansons de geste du XIIe siècle. Étude historique du vocabulaire', *Le Moyen Age*, 81 (1975), pp. 211–44, 407–45.

Sémantique et société médiévale: le verb *adouber* et son évolution au XIIe siècle', *Annales*, 31 (1976), pp. 915–40.

'Chevalerie et liturgie. Remise des armes et vocabulaire "chevaleresque" dans les sources liturgiques du IXe au XIVe siècle', *Le Moyen Age*, 84 (1978), pp. 147–78.

'L'idéologie politique de l'Eglise au XIIe siècle: Bernard de Clairvaux, Jean de Salisbury, Géroh de Reichersberg', *Conscience et Liberté*, 1 (1978), pp. 29–37.

'Les origines de l'adoubment chevaleresque; étude des remises d'armes dans les croniques et annales latines du IXe au XIIIe siècle', *Traditio*, 35 (1979), pp. 209–72.

'Pour une histoire de la chevalerie: l'adoubment chez Chrétien de Troyes', *Romania*, 100 (1979), pp. 21–53.

'La chevalerie selon Jean de Salisbury', *Revue d'Histoire Ecclésiastique*, 77 (1982), pp. 35–77.

L'essor de la chevalerie, XIe–XIIe siècles (Geneva, 1986).

'Encore la lance . . . La technique du combat chevaleresque vers l'an 1100', *Cahiers de civilization médiévale*, 31 (1988), pp. 213–40.

Foote, P. and Wilson, D. M., *The Viking Achievement: The Society and Culture of Early Medieval Scandinavia* (London, 1972).

Forey, A., *The Military Orders from the Twelfth to the Early Fourteenth Century* (London, 1992).

Fowler, G. H., 'The Devastation of Bedfordshire and the Neighbouring Counties in 1065 and 1066', *Archaeologia*, 72 (1922), pp. 41–50.

Fowler, K., *The King's Lieutenant: Henry of Grosmont, First Duke of Lancaster, 1310–1361* (London, 1969).

Le Foyer, J., *Exposé du droit penal normand au XIIIe siècle* (Paris, 1931).

France, J., 'La guerre dans la France féodal à la fin du IXe et au Xe siècle', *Revue belge d'histoire militaire*, 33 (1979), pp. 177–98.

Frank, R., 'The Ideal of Men Dying with their Lord in *The Battle of Maldon*: Anachronism or *Nouvelle Vague*', in *People and Places in Northern Europe, 500–1600*, ed. I. Wood (Woodbridge, 1991), pp. 95–106.

'*The Battle of Maldon* and Heroic Literature', *The Battle of Maldon, AD 991*, ed. D. Scragg (Oxford, 1991), pp. 196–207.

Frappier, J., *Les chansons de geste du cycle de Guillaume d'Orange*, 2 vols. (Paris, vol. I, 1955; vol. II, 1964, 2nd edn 1967).

Freeman, E. A., *A History of the Norman Conquest of England*, 6 vols. (Oxford, 1870–9). *William Rufus* (Oxford, 1882).

Fournier, G., *Le château dans le France médiévale. Essai de sociologie et monumentale* (Paris, 1978).

Fournier, P., 'La prohibition par la deuxieme concile de Latran d'armes jugées trop meutrieres', *Revue générale de droit international public*, 33 (1916), pp. 471–9.

Ganshof, F. L., 'A propos de la cavalerie dans les armées de Charlemagne', *Academie des Inscriptions et Belles-Lettres. Comptes rendus des séances* (1952), pp. 531–6.

'Note sur le premier traité Anglo-Flamand de Douvres', *Revue du Nord*, 40 (1958), pp. 245–57.

'L'armée sous les Carolingiens', *Ormanmenti militari in Occidente nell'alto Medievo*, 2 vols. (Settimane di Studio del Centro Italiano di studi sull'alto Medeovo, Spoleto, 1968), I, pp. 109–30.

Garmonsway, G. N., 'Anglo-Saxon Heroic Attitudes', *Franciplegius: Medieval and Linguistic Studies in Honour of F. P. Magoun*, ed. J. B. Bessinger, Jr and R. P. Creed (New York and London, 1965), pp. 139–46.

Gautier, L., *Chevalerie* (2nd edn, Paris, 1900), ed. J. Levron and tr. C. D. Dunning as *Chivalry* (London, 1965, repr. 1989).

Gem, R., 'Lincoln Minster: *Ecclesia Pulchra Ecclesia* Fortis', *Medieval Art and Architecture at Lincoln Cathedral* (*British Archaeological Association Conference Transactions*, 8, 1986 for 1982), pp. 9–28.

Genicot, L., 'La noblesse au moyen age dans l'ancienne Francie; continuité, rupture ou évolution?', *Comparative Studies in Society and History*, 5 (1962), pp. 52–9.

'Recent Research on the Medieval Nobility', *The Medieval Nobility*, ed. T. Reuter (New York, Oxford and Amsterdam, 1978), pp. 17–36.

Gneuss, H., 'The Battle of Maldon 89: Byrhtnoth's *Ofermod* Once Again', *Studies in Philology*, 73 (1976), pp. 117–37.

Géraud, H., 'Les routiers au XIIe siècle', *Bibliothèque de l'Ecole des Chartes*, 3 (1841–2), pp. 125–47.

'Mercardier. Les routiers au XIIIe siècle', *Bibliothèque de l'Ecole des Chartes*, 3 (1841–2), pp. 417–43.

Gillingham, J., 'The Unromantic Death of Richard I', *Speculum*, 54 (1979), pp. 18–41. *Richard the Lionheart* (2nd edn, London, 1989).

'Richard I and the Science of War in the Middle Ages', *War and Government in the Middle Ages. Essays in Honour of J. O. Prestwich*, ed. J. Gillingham and J. C. Holt (Woodbridge, 1984), pp. 78–91.

'War and Chivalry in the History of William the Marshal', *Thirteenth Century England II. Proceedings of the Newcastle upon Tyne Conference, 1987*, ed. P. R. Coss and S. D. Lloyd (Woodbridge, 1988), pp. 1–13.

'William the Bastard at War', in *Studies in Medieval History Presented to R. Allen Brown*, ed. C. Harper-Bill, C. J. Holdsworth and J. L. Nelson (Woodbridge, 1989), pp. 157–8.

'The Context and Purposes of Geoffrey of Monmouth's *History of the Kings of Britain*', *Anglo-Norman Studies*, 13 (1991), pp. 99–118.

'Conquering the Barbarians: War and Chivalry in Twelfth Century Britain', *Hasksins Society Journal*, 4 (1993), pp. 57–84.

'1066 and the Introduction of Chivalry into England', *Law and Government in Medieval*

England and Normandy. Essays in Honour of Sir James Holt, ed. G. Garnett and J. Hudson (Cambridge, 1994), pp. 31–55.

Grabois, A., 'De la trêve de Dieu à la paix du roi. Etude sur la transformation du mouvement du paix au XIIe siècle', *Melanges offert à René Crozet*, 2 vols. (Poitiers, 1966), 1, pp. 585–96.

Graham-Campbell, J., 'Anglo-Scandinavian Equestrian Equipment in Eleventh-Century England', *Anglo-Norman Studies*, 14 (1991), pp. 77–90.

Gransden, A., *Historical Writing in England, c. 550–1307* (London, 1974).

Gras, P., 'Aux origines de l'héraldique' *Bibliothèque de l'Ecole des Chartes*, 109 (1951), pp. 198–208.

Graus, F., 'Der Heilige als Schlactenhelfer', *Festschrift für Helmut Beumann*, ed. K.-U. Jaschke and R. Wenskus (Sigmaringen, 1977), pp. 330–48.

Green, J., 'Aristocratic Loyalties on the Northern Frontier of England, c. 1100–1174', *England in the Twelfth Century. Proceedings of the 1988 Harlaxton Symposium*, ed. D. Williams (Woodbridge, 1990), pp. 83–100.

Grundmann, H., 'Rotten und Brabanzonen. Sölner-Heere im 12. Jahrhundert', *Deutsches Archiv für Erforschung des Mittlealters* (1942), pp. 419–92.

Hackett, W. M., 'Knights and Knighthood in *Girart de Roussillon*', *The Ideals and Practice of Medieval Knighthood II. Papers of the Third Strawberry Hill Conference, 1986*, ed. C. Harper-Bill and R. Harvey (Boydell, 1988), pp. 40–5.

Hallam, E. M., *Capetian France* (London, 1980).

Hallam, H. E., 'The New Lands of Elloe: A Study of Early Reclamation in Lincolnshire', *University of Leicester: Department of English Local History, Occasional Papers*, 6 (1954), pp. 1–42.

Halphen, L., *Le comté d'Anjou au XIe siècle* (Paris, 1906).

Hardy, R., *Longbow. A Social and Military History* (revised edn, London, 1986).

Harmuth, E., 'Die Armbrustbilder des Haimo von Auxerre', *Waffen- und Kostumekunde*, 22 (1970), pp. 127–30.

Harper-Bill, C., 'The Piety of the Anglo-Norman Knightly Class', *Anglo-Norman Studies*, 2 (1979), pp. 63–77.

Harvey, S., 'The Knight and the Knight's Fee in England', *Past and Present*, 49 (1970), pp. 133–73.

Haskins, C. H., 'The Norman "Consuetudines et Justicie" of William the Conqueror', *EHR*, 1st ser., 89 (1908), pp. 502–8.

Norman Institutions (New York, 1918).

Hay, D., 'The Division of Spoils of War in Fourteenth Century England', *TRHS*, 5th ser., 4 (1954), pp. 91–109.

'Booty in Border Warfare', *Transactions of the Dumfreisshire and Galloway Natural History and Antiquarian Society*, 3rd ser., 31 (1952–3), pp. 148–66.

Head, T. and Landes, R. (eds.), *The Peace of God. Social Violence and Religious Response in France Around the Year 1000* (Ithaca and London, 1992).

Hehl, E., *Kirche und Krieg im 12. Jahrhundert. Studien zu kanonischem Recht und politischer Wirklichkeit* (Stuttgart, 1980).

Hewitt, H. J., *The Black Prince's Expedition of 1355–57* (Manchester, 1958).

The Organization of War under Edward III, 1338–62 (Manchester, 1966).

Higham, N. J., 'Cavalry in Early Bernicia?', *Northern History*, 27 (1991), pp. 236–41.

Holdsworth, C., 'Ideas and Reality: Some Attempts to Control and Diffuse War in the Twelfth Century', *The Church and War*, ed. W. J. Sheils (*Studies in Church History*, xx, Oxford, 1983), pp. 59–78.

'War and Peace in the Twelfth Century. The Reign of Stephen Reconsidered', *War and Peace in the Middle Ages*, ed. B. P. McGuire (Copenhagen, 1987), pp. 67–93.

Hollister, C. W., *Anglo-Saxon Military Institutions on the Eve of the Norman Conquest* (Oxford, 1962).

The Military Organisation of Norman England (Oxford, 1965).

Monarchs, Magnates and Institutions in the Anglo-Norman World (London, 1986).

'The Campaign of Henry I against Robert of Bellême', *Studies in Medieval History Presented to R. A. Brown*, ed. C. Harper-Bill, C. J. Holdsworth and J. L. Nelson (Woodbridge, 1992), pp. 193–202.

Holm, P., 'The Slave Trade of Dublin', *Peritia*, 5 (1986), pp. 317–45.

Holmes, U. T., Jr, 'The Arthurian Tradition and Lambert d'Ardres', *Speculum*, 25 (1950), pp. 100–3.

Holt, J. C., 'Politics and Property in Early Medieval England', *Past and Present*, 67 (1972), pp. 3–52.

Magna Carta and Medieval Government (London, 1985).

The Northerners (revised edn, Oxford, 1992).

Magna Carta (2nd edn, Cambridge, 1992).

Holtzmann, W., *Papsturkunden in England* (Abhandlung der Gesellschaft der Wissenschaften zu Gottingen, Philologisch-Historische Klasse, Dritte Folge, no. 14, Berlin, 1935).

Hooper, N., 'The Housecarls in England in the Eleventh Century', *Anglo-Norman Studies*, 7 (1984), pp. 161–76, reprinted in Strickland, *Anglo-Norman Warfare*, pp. 1–16.

'The Aberlemno Stone and Cavalry in Anglo-Saxon England', *Northern History*, 29 (1993), pp. 188–96.

Housely, 'Crusades Against Christians: Their Origins and Early Development', *Crusade and Settlement*, ed. P. W. Edbury (Cardiff, 1985), pp. 17–36.

van Houts, E. M. C., 'Latin Poetry and the Anglo-Norman Court, 1066–1135: the Carmen de Hastingae Proelio', *Journal of Medieval History*, 15 (1989), pp. 39–62.

Huizinga, J., *The Waning of the Middle Ages* (London, 1927, repr. 1985).

Hunt, T., 'The Emergence of the Knight in France and England, 1000–1200', in *Knighthood in Medieval Literature*, ed. W. H. Jackson (Woodbridge, 1981), pp. 1–22.

Jackson, K. H., 'Sources for the Life of St Kentigern', *Studies in the Early British Church*, ed. H. N. K. Chadwick *et al.* (Cambridge, 1958), pp. 273–357.

Jackson, W. H., 'Aspects of Knighthood in Hartmann's Adaptations of Chrétien's Romances and in the Social Context', *Chrétien de Troyes and the German Middle Ages*, ed. M. H. Jones and R. Wiseby (Cambridge and London, 1993), pp. 37–55.

Johnston, R. C., *The Versification of Jordan Fantosme* (Oxford, 1974).

'The Historicity of Jordan Fantosme's Chronicle', *Journal of Medieval History*, 2 (1976), pp. 159–68.

Joliffe, J. E. A., *Angevin Kingship* (London, 1955).

Jones, G., 'Some Characteristics of the Icelandic *Holmganga*', *Journal of English and Germanic Philology*, 32 (1933), pp. 203–24.

Jones, G. F., *The Ethos of the Song of Roland* (Baltimore, 1963).

Jones, M.H., 'Chrétien, Hartmann and the Knight as Fighting Man: On Hartmann's Chivalric Adaptation of *Eric and Enide*', in *Chrétien de Troyes and the German Middle Ages*, ed. M. H. Jones and R. Wiseby (Cambridge and London, 1993), pp. 85–109.

Kapelle, W. E., *The Norman Conquest of the North* (London, 1979).

Karras, R. M., *Slavery and Society in Medieval Scandinavia* (Yale, 1988).

Kaufman, C. M., *Romanesque Manuscripts, 1066–1190* (London, 1975).

Keegan, J., *The Face of Battle* (Harmondsworth, 1976, repr. 1983).

Keen, M. H., 'Brotherhood in Arms', *History*, 47 (1962), pp. 1–17.

The Laws of War in the Late Middle Ages (London, 1965).

'Chivalry, Nobility and the Man at Arms', *War, Literature and Politics in the Late Middle Ages. Essays in Honour of G. W. Coopland*, ed. C. T. Allmand (Liverpool, 1976).

'Huizinga, Kilgour and the Decline of Chivalry', *Medievalia et Humanistica*, new ser., 8 (1977), pp. 1–20.

'Chaucer's Knight, the Aristocracy and the Crusades', *English Court and Culture in the Late Middle Ages*, ed. V. J. Scattergood (London, 1983), pp. 47–61.

Chivalry (Yale, 1984).

Keynes, S. D., *The Diplomas of Aethelred the Unready, 978–1016* (Cambridge, 1980).

Kibler, W. W., 'Roland's Pride', *Symposium*, 26 (1972), pp. 147–60.

Kilgour, R. L., *The Decline of Chivalry* (Cambridge, Mass., 1937).

King, E., 'King Stephen and the Anglo-Norman Aristocracy', *History*, 59 (1974), pp. 180–94.

'Mountsorrel and its Region in King Stephen's Reign', *Huntington Library Quarterly*, 44 (1980), pp. 1–10.

'The Anarchy of Stephen's Reign', *TRHS*, 34 (1984), pp. 133–53.

'Waleran, Count of Meulan, Earl of Worcester, 1104–1166', *Tradition and Change: Essays in Honour of Marjorie Chibnall*, ed. D. Greenway, C. Holdsworth and J. Sayers (Cambridge, 1985), pp. 165–82.

'Dispute Settlement in Anglo-Norman England', *Anglo-Norman Studies*, 14 (1991), pp. 115–30.

Kingsford, C. L., 'Some Political Poems of the Twelfth Century', *EHR*, 5 (1890), pp. 311–26.

Kirby, D. P., 'Strathclyde and Cumbria', *TCWAAS*, 62 (1962), pp. 77–94.

La Monte, J., *Feudal Monarchy in the Latin Kingdom of Jerusalem* (Massachusetts, 1932; repr. New York, 1970).

Lane Poole, S., *Saladin and the Fall of the Latin Kingdom of Jerusalem* (London, 1901).

Larson, L. M., *The King's Household in England before the Norman Conquest* (Madison, 1904).

Lebecq, S., 'Francs contre Frisons (VIe–VIIIe siècles)', *Actes du CIe Congrès national des Sociétés savantes, Lille, 1976: Section de philologie et d'histoire jusqu'a 1610: La Guerre et la Paix* (Paris, 1978), pp. 53–71.

Leedom, J. W., 'William of Malmesbury and Robert of Gloucester Reconsidered', *Albion*, 6 (1974), pp. 251–62.

Lees, B. A., 'The Letters of Queen Eleanor to Pope Celestine', *EHR*, 21 (1906), pp. 78–93.

Legge, '"Osbercs Dublez". The Description of Armour in Twelfth-century Chansons de Geste', *Société Rencevals. Proceedings of the Fifth International Conference* (Oxford, 1970), pp. 132–42

Lemmon, C. H., 'The Campaign of 1066', *The Norman Conquest*, ed. D. Whitelock *et al.* (London, 1966), pp. 116–22.

Le Patourel, J., 'Normandy and England, 1066–1144' (Stenton Lecture 1970, Reading, 1971).

The Norman Empire (Oxford, 1976).

Lewis, S., *The Art of Matthew Paris in the Chronica Majora* (University of California and Aldershot, 1987).

Leyser, K., 'The Battle of the Lech, 955', History, 50 (1965), pp. 1–25; repr. in *idem.*, *Medieval Germany and its Neighbours* (London, 1982), pp. 43–68.

'Henry I and the Beginnings of the Saxon Empire' *EHR*, 83 (1968), pp. 1–32; repr. in *idem.*, *Medieval Germany and its Neighbours* (London, 1982), pp. 11–42.

Communications and Power in Medieval Europe: The Carolingian and Ottonian Centuries, ed. T. Reuter (London, 1994).

Lloyd, J. E., *A History of Wales From the Earliest Times to the Edwardian Conquest*, 2 vols. (3rd edn, London, 1939).

Lloyd, S., '"Political Crusades" in England c. 1215–17 and c. 1263–5', *Crusade and Settlement*, ed. P. Edbury (Cardiff, 1985), pp. 113–20.

Lodge, A., 'Literature and History in the *Chronicle* of Jordan Fantosme', *French Studies*, 44 (1990), pp. 257–70.

Loomis, R. S., 'Chivalric and Dramatic Imitation of Arthurian Romance', *Medieval Studies in Memory of A. K. Porter*, ed. W. W. Koelher (Cambridge, Mass., 1939), pp. 79–97.

Loyn, H. R., *Anglo-Saxon England and the Norman Conquest* (London, 1962).

Lucas, A. T., 'The Plundering and Burning of Churches in Ireland, 7th to 16th Century', *North Munster Studies* (1967), pp. 172–229.

Luchaire, A., *Social France at the time of Philip Augustus*, tr. E. B. Krehbiel, (London, 1912).

van Luyn, P., 'Les *milites* de la France du XIe siècle', *Le Moyen Age* (1971), pp. 1–51, 193–238.

McKechnie, W. D., *Magna Carta. A Commentary on the Great Charter of King John* (2nd edn, New York, 1958).

McNamee, C. J., 'William Wallace's Invasion of Northern England in 1297', *Northern History*, 26 (1991), pp. 40–58.

Maddicott, J. R., 'The English Peasantry and the Demand of the Crown, 1294–1341', *Past and Present Supplement*, 1 (1975), pp. 15–34.

Magnusson, M., *Vikings!* (London, 1980).

Major, K., 'Conan the son of Eliis, An Early Inhabitant of Holbeach', *Associated Architectural Societies Reports and Papers*, 42 (1934), pp. 1–28.

Mallet, M., *Mercenaries and their Masters. Warfare in Renaissance Italy* (London, 1974).

Mann, J., *European Arms and Armour*, 2 vols. (Wallace Collection Catalogues, London, 1962).

Marshal, C., *Warfare in the Latin East, 1192–1291* (Cambridge, 1992).

Martindale, J., '*Conventum inter Guillelmum Aquitanorum comes et Hugonem Chiliarchum*', *EHR*, 84 (1969), pp. 528–48.

'The French Aristocracy in the Early Middle Ages: A Reappraisal', *Past and Present*, 75 (1977), pp. 5–45.

Mason, E., 'Timeo Barones et Donas Ferentes', *Religious Motivation: Biographical and Sociological Problems for the Church Historian*, ed. D. Baker (*Studies in Church History*, xv, Oxford, 1978), pp. 61–75.

'The Hero's Invincible Weapon: An Aspect of Angevin Propaganda', *The Ideals and Practice of Medieval Knighthood, III*, ed. C. Harper-Bill and R. Harvey (Boydell, 1990).

Matthew, D. J. A., *Norman Monasteries and their English Possessions* (Oxford, 1962).

Mens, A., 'De "Brabanciones" of bloeddorstige en plunderzieke avonturiers (XIIe–XIIe eeuw)', *Miscellanea historica in honorem Alberti de Meyer* (Louvain and Brussels, 1946), I, pp. 558–70.

Mesmin, S., 'Waleran, Count of Meulan and the Leper Hospital of St Gilles at Pont Audemer', *Annales de Normandie*, 32 (1982), pp. 3–19.

Miller, W. I., *Blood-Taking and Peace Making: Feud, Law and Society in Saga Iceland* (Chicago and London, 1990).

Moriss, C., 'Equestris Ordo: Chivalry as a Vocation in the Twelfth Century', in *Religious Motivation: Biographical and Sociological Problems for the Church Historian*, ed. D. Baker (Studies in Church History 15, Oxford, 1978), pp. 89–98.

'Policy and Visions: The Case of the Holy Lance at Antioch', *War and Government in the*

Middle Ages. Essays Presented to J. O. Prestwich, ed. J. Gillingham and J. C. Holt (Woodbridge, 1984), pp. 33–45.

Mortimer, R., 'Religious and Secular Motives for Some English Monastic Foundations', in *Religious Motivation: Biographical and Sociological Problems for the Church Historian*, ed. D. Baker (Studies in Church History 15, Oxford, 1978), pp. 77–86.

Musset, L., 'Cimiterium ad refugium tantum vivorum non ad sepulturam mortuorum', *Revue du Moyen Age Latin*, 4 (1948), pp. 56–60.

'L'aristocratie normande au XIe siècle', in *La Noblesse au Moyen Age, XIe–XVe siècles: essais à la memoire de Robert Boutrouche*, ed. P. Contamine (Paris, 1976), pp. 85–94.

Mutherich, F. and Gaede, J. E., *Carolingian Painting* (London, 1977).

Nelson, J., 'Ninth-century Knighthood: the Evidence of Nithard', *Studies in Medieval History. Presented to R. A. Brown*, ed. C. Harper-Bill, C. Holdsworth and J. Nelson (Woodbridge, 1989), pp. 235–66.

Nicolle, D., *Arms and Armour of the Crusading Era, 1050–1350*, 2 vols. (New York, 1988).

Norgate, K., *England Under the Angevin Kings*, 2 vols. (London, 1887).

Richard the Lion-Heart (London, 1924).

North, S., 'The Ideal Knight as Presented in Some French Narrative Poems, c. 1090–c. 1240: An Outline Sketch', *The Ideals and Practice of Medieval Knighthood. Papers from the First and Second Strawberry Hill Conferences*, ed. C. Harper-Bill and R. Harvey (Woodbridge, 1986), pp. 111–32.

Oakeshott, R. E., *The Archaeology of Weapons. Arms and Armour from Prehistory to the Age of Chivalry* (London, 1960).

The Sword in the Age of Chivalry (revised edn, London, 1981).

Records of the Medieval Sword (Woodbridge, 1991).

Offler, H. S., 'The Tractate *De inusta vexatione Willelmi episcopi primi*', *EHR*, 66 (1951), pp. 32–41.

O'Keefe, K. O., 'Heroic values and Christian Ethics', *The Cambridge Companion to Old English Literature*, ed. M. Godden and M. Lapidge (Cambridge, 1991), pp. 107–25.

Oman, C. W. C., *A History of the Art of War in the Middle Ages, 378–1485*, 2 vols. (2nd edn, London, 1924).

Oran, R. D. and Stell, G. P. (eds.), *Galloway: Land and Lordship* (Edinburgh, 1991).

Owen-Crocker, G. R., 'Hawks and Horse-Trappings: the Insignia of Rank', *The Battle of Maldon, AD 991*, ed. D. Scragg (Oxford, 1991), pp. 220–37.

Painter, S., *William Marshal, Knight-Errant, Baron and Regent of England* (Johns Hopkins Press, 1933).

French Chivalry (Baltimore, 1940).

'The Ideals of Chivalry', *Feudalism and Liberty*, ed. F. A. Cazel, Jr (Baltimore, 1961), pp. 90–104.

Palliser, D. M., 'Domesday Book and the Harrying of the North', *Northern History*, 39 (1993), pp. 1–23.

Parisse, M., 'Le tournoi en France, des origines à la fin du XIIIe siècle', in *Das ritterliche Turnier im Mittelalter*, ed. J. Fleckenstein (Gottingen, 1985), pp. 175–211.

Parker, M. A., *Beowulf and Christianity* (New York, 1897).

Partner, N. F., *Serious Entertainments: The Writing of History in Twelfth Century England* (Chicago and London, 1977).

Paterson, L., 'Knights and the Concept of Knighthood in Twelfth-century Occitan Epic', *Forum for Modern Language Studies*, 17 (1981), pp. 115–30, and reprinted in *Knighthood in Medieval Literature*, ed. W. H. Jackson (Woodbridge, 1981), pp. 23–38.

Patterson, R. B., 'William of Malmesbury's Robert of Gloucester: A Reevaluation of the *Historia Novella*', *American Historical Review*, 70 (1964–5), pp. 983–7.

Prinno, J., 'The Knight his Arms and Armour in the Eleventh and Twelfth Centuries', *The Ideals and Practice of Medieval Knighthood. Papers from the First and Second Strawberry Hill Conferences*, ed. C. Harper-Bill and R. Harvey (Woodbridge, 1986), pp. 152–64.

'Arms, Armour and Warfare in the Eleventh Century', *Anglo-Norman Studies*, 10 (1987), pp. 237–57.

'The Development of the Medieval Sword, c. 850–1300', *The Ideals and Practice of Medieval Knighthood, III*, ed. C. Harper-Bill and R. Harvey (Boydell, 1990), pp. 139–58.

'The Knight, His Arms and Armour, c. 1150–1250', *Anglo-Norman Studies* 15 (1992), pp. 251–74.

Pfister, C., *Etudes sur le règne de Robert le Pieux, 996–1031* (Paris, 1885).

Pitt-Rivers, J., 'Honour and Social Status', *Honour and Shame. The Values of Mediterranean Society*, ed. J. G. Peristiany (London, 1965), pp. 19–77.

Pollock, F. and Maitland, F. M., *The History of the English Law Before the Time of Edward I*, 2 vols. (2nd edn, Cambridge, 1898).

Poly, J. P. and Bournazel, E., *The Feudal Transformation, 900–1200* (New York, 1991).

Pounds, N. J. G., *The Medieval Castle in England and Wales* (Cambridge, 1990).

Powicke, F. M., 'Roger of Wendover and the Coggeshall Chronicle', *EHR*, 21 (1906), pp. 286–96.

The Loss of Normandy (Oxford, 1913).

King Henry III and the Lord Edward. The Community of the Realm in the Thirteenth Century (Oxford, 1947).

'Ailred of Rievaulx', in *idem.*, *Ways of Medieval Life and Thought* (London, 1949), pp. 7–26.

Prestwich, J. O., 'The Military Household of the Norman Kings', *EHR*, 96 (1981), reprinted in Strickland, *Anglo-Norman Warfare*, pp. 93–127.

'Richard Coeur de Lion: Rex Bellicosus', *Riccardo Cuor di Leone Nella Storia et Nella Legenda* (Accademia Nazionale dei Lincei, Rome, 1981), pp. 1–15.

'Military Intelligence under the Norman and Angevin Kings', *Law and Government in Medieval England and Normandy. Essays in Honour of Sir James Holt*, ed. G. Garnett and John Hudson (Cambridge, 1994).

Prestwich, M., *Documents Illustrating the Baronial Crisis of 1297–8 in England* (Camden, 4th ser., London, 1980).

Edward I (London, 1988).

Radford, C. A. R., 'The Later Pre-Conquest Boroughs and Their Defences', *Medieval Archaeology*, 14 (1970), pp. 83–103.

'The Pre-Conquest Boroughs of England, 9th–11th Centuries', *Proceedings of the British Academy*, 64 (1980 for 1978), pp. 131–53.

Ray, R. D., 'Orderic Vitalis on Henry I: Theocratic Ideology and Didactic Narrative', in *Contemporary Reflections on the Medieval Tradition: Essays in Honour of Ray C. Petry*, ed. G. H. Shriver (Durham, N. C., 1974), pp. 119–34.

Renn, D., *Norman Castles in Britain* (2nd edn, London, 1973).

'Burghgeat and Gonfanon: Two Sidelights from the Bayeux Tapestry', Anglo-Norman Studies, 16 (1993), pp. 177–98.

Reuter, T., 'Plunder and Tribute in the Carolingian Empire', *TRHS*, 35 (1985), pp. 75–94.

'The End of Carolingian Military Expansion', in *Charlemagne's Heir: New Perspectives on the Reign of Louis the Pious*, ed. P. Godman and R. Collins (Oxford, 1990), pp. 391–405.

Rey, R., *Les vielles églises fortifiées du midi de la France* (Paris, 1925).

Reynolds, S., *Kingdoms and Communities in Western Europe, 900–1300* (Oxford, 1984).

Riley-Smith, J., *The First Crusade and the Idea of Crusading* (London, 1986).

Riley-Smith, I., and J., *The Crusades: Idea and Reality* (London, 1981).

Ritchie, R. L. G., *The Normans in Scotland* (Edinburgh, 1953).

Robinson, I. S., 'Gregory VII and the Soldiers of Christ', *History*, 58 (1973), pp. 169–92.

    The Papacy, 1073–1198 (Cambridge, 1990).

Rogers, R., *Latin Siege Warfare in the Middle Ages* (Oxford, 1992).

Rosenwein, B. H., 'Feudal War and Monastic Peace: Cluniac Liturgy as Ritual Aggression', *Viator*, 2 (1971), pp. 129–57.

Ross, D. J. A., 'L'originalité de "Turoldus": le maniement de la lance', *Cahiers de civilization médiévale*, 6 (1963), pp. 127–38.

Round, J. H., *Geoffrey de Mandeville* (London, 1892).

    Feudal England: Historical Studies on the Eleventh and Twelfth Centuries (London, 1895).

    'King Stephen and the Earl of Chester', *EHR*, 10 (1895), pp. 87–91.

Rousset, P., 'La description du monde chevaleresque chez Orderic Vital', *Le Moyen Age*, 75 (1969), pp. 427–44.

Runciman, S., 'The Holy Lance Found at Antioch', *Analecta Bollandiana*, 68 (1950), pp. 197–209.

    A History of the Crusades, 3 vols. (Cambridge, 1951–54).

Russell, F. H., *The Just War in the Middle Ages* (Cambridge, 1975).

Rychner, J., *La chanson de geste. Essai sur l'art épique des jongleurs* (Geneva and Lille, 1955).

Salet, M. F., 'Verneuil', *Congrès Archéologique de France*, 111 (1953), pp. 407–58.

Sanders, I. J., *English Baronies* (Oxford, 1960).

Sawyer, P., *The Age of the Vikings* (2nd edn, London, 1971).

    Kings and Vikings (London and New York, 1982).

Searle, E., *Predatory Kinship and the Creation of Norman Power, 840–1066* (Berkeley, Los Angeles and London, 1988).

von See, K., 'Hastings, Stiklastadir und Langemarck; Zur Uberlierung vom Vortrag heroischer Lieder auf dem Schlachtenfeld', *Germanisch-romanische Monatschrift*, 57 (1976), pp. 1–13, reprinted in *idem., Edda, Saga, Skaldendichtung: Aufsatze zur skaninavischen Literatur des Mittlealters* (Heidelberg, 1981), pp. 259–71.

Shippey, T. A., *Old English Verse* (London, 1972).

Short, I., 'Patrons and Polyglots: French Literature in Twelfth Century England', *Anglo-Norman Studies*, 14 (1991), pp. 229–49.

Smail, R. C., *Crusading Warfare, 1097–1193* (Cambridge, 1956).

Smyth, A. P., *Scandinavian Kings in the British Isles* (Oxford, 1977).

    Warlords and Holy Men: Scotland, AD 80–1000 (Edinburgh, 1984).

Southern, R. W., *St Anselm and his Biographer* (Cambridge, 1963).

    'Peter of Blois. A Twelfth Century Humanist?' in *idem., Medieval Humanism and Other Essays* (Oxford, 1970), pp. 105–32.

Spiegel, 'The Cult of St Denis and Capetian Kingship', *Journal of Medieval History*, 1 (1975), pp. 43–69.

Squibb, G. D., *The High Court of Chivalry* (Oxford, 1959).

Squire, A., *Aelred of Rievaulx* (London, 1969).

Stein, P., 'Vacarius and the Civil Law', *Church and Government in the Middle Ages*, ed. C. N. L. Brooke, D. E. Luscombe *et al.*, (Cambridge, 1976).

Stenton, F. M., *The First Century of English Feudalism* (2nd edn, Oxford, 1961).

Stevens, S. D., *Music in Honour of St Thomas* (Sevenoaks, 1973).

Strickland, M. J., 'Securing the North. Invasion and the Strategy of Defence in Twelfth-century Anglo-Scottish Warfare', *Anglo-Norman Studies*, 12 (1989), pp. 177–98, reprinted in Strickland, *Anglo-Norman Warfare*, pp. 208–29.

'Arms and the Men: War, Loyalty and Lordship in Jordan Fantosme's *Chronicle*, in *Medieval Knighthood IV. Papers from the Fifth Strawberry Hill Conference*, ed. C. Harper-Bill and R. Harvey (Woodbridge, 1992), pp. 187–220.

'Slaughter, Slavery or Ransom? The Impact of the Conquest on Conduct in Warfare', *England in the Eleventh Century. Proceedings of the 1990 Harlaxton Symposium*, ed. C. Hicks (Harlaxton Medieval Studies, Vol. II, Stamford, 1992), pp. 41–59.

(ed.), *Anglo-Norman Warfare* (Woodbridge, 1992).

'Against the Lord's Anointed: Aspects of Warfare and Baronial Rebellion in England and Normandy, 1066–1265', *Law and Government in Medieval England. Essays in Honour of Sir James Holt*, ed. G. Garnett and J. Hudson (Cambridge, 1994), pp. 56–79.

Storry, R., *The Way of the Samurai* (1978).

Stringer, K., 'A Cistercian Archive: The Earliest Charters of Sawtry Abbey', *Journal of the Society of Archivists*, 6 (1980), pp. 325–34.

David, Earl of Huntingdon, 1152–1219 (Edinburgh, 1985).

Sumberg, L. A. M., 'The "Tafurs" and the Third Crusade', *Medieval Studies*, 21 (1959), pp. 224–46.

Suppe, F. C., 'The Cultural Significance of Decapitation in High Medieval Wales and the Marches', *Bulletin of the Board of Celtic Studies*, 37 (1989), pp. 147–60.

Military Institutions on the Welsh Marches: Shropshire, A.D. 1066–1300 (Woodbridge, 1994).

Switten, M., '*Chevalier* in Twelfth Century French and Occitan Vernacular Literature', *The Study of Chivalry: Resources and Approaches*, ed. H. H. D. Chickering and T. H. Seiler (W. Michigan University, 1988), pp. 403–47.

Thompson, K., 'Robert of Bellême Reconsidered', *Anglo-Norman Studies*, 13 (1990), pp. 263–86.

'Orderic Vitalis and Robert of Bellême', *Journal of Medieval History*, 20 (1992), pp. 131–8.

Thomson, R. M., *William of Malmesbury* (Woodbridge, 1987).

Thordemann, B., *Armour from the Battle of Wisby, 1361*, 2 vols. (Stockholm, 1939).

Tolkein, J. R. R., 'Homecoming of Beortnoth Beorhthelm's Son', *Essays and Studies*, n.s., 6 (1953), pp. 1–18.

Topsfield, L. T., *Chrétien de Troyes* (Cambridge, 1984).

Tout, 'The Fair of Lincoln and the "Histoire de Guillaume le Maréchal"', *EHR*, 17 (1903), pp. 240–65.

Turner, C. J., 'William the Conqueror's March to London', *EHR*, 106 (1912), pp. 209–25.

Tweddle, D., *The Coppergate Helmet* (York, 1984).

Tyerman, C., *England and the Crusades, 1095–1588* (Chicago, 1988).

Ullman, W., *Law and Politics in the Middle Ages. An Introduction to the Sources of Medieval Political Ideas* (London, 1975).

Vale, M., *War and Chivalry. Warfare and Aristocratic Culture in England, France and Burgundy at the End of the Middle Ages* (London, 1981).

Verbruggen, F., *De Krijgskunst in West-Europa in de Middeleeuwen (IXe tot begin XIVe eeuw)* (Brussels, 1954), tr. S. C. M. Southern and S. Willard as *The Art of Warfare in Western Europe During the Middle Ages, From the Eighth Century to 1340* (Amsterdam and New York, 1976).

'L'armée et la strategie de Charlemagne', *Karl der Grosse. Lebenswerk und Nachleben, I: Personlichkeit und Geschichte* (Dusseldorf, 1965), pp. 420–36.

'L'art militaire dans l'Empire carolingien', *Revue belge d'histoire militaire* (1979), pp. 299–310 and (1980), pp. 343–412.

Wallace-Hadrill, J. M., 'The Vikings in Francia', in *idem.*, *Early Medieval History* (Oxford, 1975), pp. 217–36.

Warner, P., *Sieges of the Middle Ages* (London, 1968).

Warren, W. L., *King John* (London, 1964).

   Henry II (London, 1973).

White, G., 'King Stephen, Duke Henry and Ranulf de Gernons, Earl of Chester', *EHR*, 91 (1976), pp. 555–65.

   'Were the Midlands "Wasted" in Stephen's Reign?', *Midland History*, 10 (1985), pp. 26–46.

White, S. D., 'Feuding and Peace-Making in the Touraine Around the Year 1100', *Traditio*, 42 (1986), pp. 195–263.

Whitehead, F., '*Ofermod* et desmesure', *Cahiers de civilisation médiévale*, 3 (1960), pp. 115–17.

Wightman, W. E., *The Lacy Family in England and Normandy, 1066–1194* (Oxford, 1966).

   'The Significance of "Waste" in the Yorkshire Domesday', *Northern History*, 10 (1975), pp. 55–71.

Williams, A., 'A Bell-house and a Burgh-geat: Lordly Residences in England Before the Norman Conquest', in *Ideals and Practice of Medieval Knighthood, IV*, ed. C. Harper-Bill and Ruth Harvey (Boydell, 1992), pp. 221–40.

Wilson, P. A., 'On the Terms "Strathclyde" and "Cumbria"', *TCWAAS*, 66 (1966), pp. 57–92.

Woolf, R., 'The Ideal of Men Dying with their Lord in the *Germania*, and in *The Battle of Maldon*', *Anglo-Saxon England*, 5 (1976), pp. 63–81.

Wormald, P., 'Viking Studies: Whence and Wither?', *The Vikings*, ed. R. T. Farrell (London, 1982), pp. 128–56.

Wright, N. A. R., 'The Tree of Battles of Honoré Bouvet and the Laws of War', *War, Literature and Politics in the Late Middle Ages*, ed. C. T. Allmand (Liverpool, 1976), pp. 12–31.

Yver, J., 'L'interdiction de la guerre privée dans les très ancien droit normand', *Travaux de la Semaine de droit normand* (Caen, 1928).

   'Les châteaux forts en Normandie jusqu'au milieu du XIIe siècle. Contribution a l'étude du pouvoir ducal', *Bulletin de la Société des Antiquaires de Normandie*, 53 (1955–6), pp. 28–115.

Zajac, W. G., 'Captured Property on the First Crusade: A Study on the late Eleventh Century Laws of War' (unpublished M.A. thesis, University of Milwaukee, 1986).

Zarnecki, G., Holt, J. and Holland, T. (eds.), *English Romanesque Art* (London, 1984).

INDEX

Aachen (Aix), 110
    Albert of, 44 n. 71
Abingdon, 85
Acquiny, 270
Acre, 26
    siege of (1191), 9, 36, 100, 102, 157, 162, 223, 246 n.91, 253 n.127
Adomnan, 306
Aelfgar, earl of Mercia, 67
Aelfwine, son of Aelfric, thegn at Maldon, 111, 124
Aethelred II, king of England (978–1016), 278 n.94, 279
Agincourt, battle of (1415), 28 n.116, 335
Aimar V, viscount of Limoges, 52, 71 n.77, 301
Aixe, 52
aketon, 170, 177
Al-Adil, brother of Saladin, 26, 101
    son knighted by Richard I, 26–7
    sends gift of horses to Richard at Jaffa, 26
    al-Kamil, his son, 27 n.112
Alberic, cardinal bishop of Ostia and papal legate, 220, 305, 317
Albi, cathedral of, 88
Albigensians, 299, 303
d'Albini, William, of Belvoir, 120, 193 n.70, 242, 248, 256, 267
    Nicholas, his son, 256
Alderie, William de, 241, 255
Alençon, 2, 161, 215, 225, 249 and n.101, 251, 252, 253, 255
    battle of (1118), 179
Alexander II, king of Scots (1214–49), 319
Alfred, brother of Edward the Confessor, 25, 315
Alfred the Great, king of Wessex (871–99), 146
Algais, Martin, 191
Almenèches, 200
Alnwick, 65, 117, 209, 276, 326
    ambush of William the Lion at (1174), 150, 179, 180, 220, 250, 290 n.150, 301, 302, 326

Alton, treaty of (1101), 260, 332 n.9
Amadour, St, 83
Amaury (Amalric), king of Jerusalem (1162–74), 226 n.117
Ambroise, Norman trouvère, 10–11, 99, 100–2, 111, 116 n.95, 331
Andely, 79 n.123, 130, 202 n.128
Anet, 48, 150 n.95 and 96, 151
Anglo-Saxon Chronicle, 59 n.23, 104, 118, 242 n.62, 260, 273, 312
Anglo-Saxons, Norman treatment of in war, 1–2, 4
    use of burghs, 3
    habitual slaying of noble opponents in battle, 3, 133, 334
    enslaving of prisoners, 315
    view defeat at Hastings as providential, 59
    churches plundered post-Conquest, 83
    urge Rufus to hang rebels at Rochester (1088), 235
Angoulême, Taillefer lords of, 230
Angus, earl of, 325
Anjou, counts of, 123
    Fulk III Nerra, (987–1040); victory at Pontlevoy (1016), 59; takes Saumur on terms, 36 n.26; vows to rebuild church of St Florent, Saumur, 94; acts of sacrilege, 94 n.198; pilgrimages of, 95 n.205; castle-building of, 134
    Fulk IV le Rechin (1067–1109), 138, 203
    Fulk V (1109–42), 215
    Geoffrey II Martel (1040–60), 43, 198
    Geoffrey V le Bel (1142–51); invests Montreuil for three years, 207; invasion of Normandy (1136), 14, 261, 264, 265–6; forbids army to seize church goods, 38, 81; takes protection money from Norman churches, 84; chivalry towards captured Poitevin knights, 148, 203; grants truce to Robert of Leicester (1141), 236
Annals of Dunstable, 207 n.17

366

Annals of Ulster, 306
Antioch, 44, 62, 303 and n.53
    Holy Lance found at, 67
    'rope dancers' of, 177
    chanson d'Antioche, 296 n.22
Appelby, 225
Aquitaine, dukes of, William V (995–1029), 134
    William VI (1029–38), 198
    William X (1126–37), 95 n.203
    Eleanor, duchess of, 50 n.97
    see also Richard I Coeur de Lion
Arbroath, abbey of, 65, 67 n.59
d'Arcelles, Louis, 151 n.101
archers, 72, 141 and n.45, 174–5, 180–1, 223
    see also crossbowmen
Ardres, Arnold of, 330
Argences, 84
Argentan, 227
d'Argentan, Oliver, 256
armiger, 25
    see also squire
armour, 168–76
arms, bestowal of, 5, 147 and n.80
    between warriors of different cultures, 25–7
    religious inscriptions on, 62–4
    see also, knighthood, belting to
Arques, 209
Arsuf, battle of (1191), 9, 102 n.28, 112, 115–16,
    117, 119, 179
Arthur, duke of Brittany, son of Geoffrey
    Plantagenet, 256–7, 280
Arthurian romances, 17, 29, 149
    see also Troyes, Chrétien de
Artois, count of, 117 n.98
Arundel, 49 n. 94, 241, 252, 255
    William I, earl of, 67 n.56
Ascalon, 117 n.98
Ascelin, son of Andrew, 130
Ascelin Goel, 174, 184, 196, 198
Ashingdon, battle of (1016), 173 n.86
Assize of Arms, (1181) 39, 145
    (1242), 39
Atheé, Gerard de, 184, 193, 212, 228, 244 n.76,
    279, 299
atrocities, 12, 30 n.123, 291–329 *passim*
    see also routiers; and Scots
d'Aubigny, Nigel, 95 n.200
Audenarde, Arnoul of, 240
Aumâle, castle of, 206 n.11, 225
    William, count of, 93
    Stephen, count of, 162
    Hawise, his wife, 162
d'Aunay, Gunter, 196, 212
Auxerre, 66
    Haimo of, 72 n.82
Avars, 29, 135
Avesnes, James de, 102, 119, 151 n.101
d'Avranches, Hugh, *see* Chester, earls of
    Turgis, 199, 255
axes, 170, 171, 172, 173

Axholme, island of, 250
Axspoele, battle of (1128), 62, 168

Baginburn, battle of (1170), 180, 309, 310
Bailleul, 40 n.47
    Reginald of, 255 n.142
Baldwin II, king of Jerusalem (1118–31), 270
Balliol, Bernard de, 117, 235
Ballon, 149, 153, 190, 201, 203
Bamburgh, 119, 161, 162, 247, 276 n.84
Bampton, Robert of, 245
Banbury, 263
banishment, 239, 240
banners, 43
    hallowed, 56, 57, 60 n.30, 62, 65–7
    French and English royal standards, 66
    papal, at Hastings, 4 and n.11, 29
    of Fakhr-ad-Din, bearing arms of Frederick
        II, 27 n.112
    treason to raise against king, 231 n.7
    as symbol of ownership, 253 and n.127
    see also Oriflamme; Mountjoie
Bannockburn, battle of (1314), 179, 335
Bar, Hugh, duke of, 322–3
Barnard Castle, 175 n.98
Barnwell chronicler, 257, 301
Barres, William II des, 48, 52, 101, 102, 151, 170
    n.76
Barston, Nicholas of, 263 n.17
Basil, St, 64 n.36
Basques, 53, 82, 297 n.23
Bath, 267 n.39
battle,
    avoidance of, 43–4, 59
    outcome seen as judgement of God, 59–60
    restraint from killing in, 132–4
    less sanguinary than in later Middle Ages,
        335
    factors affecting extent of casualties in,
        163–9
    difficulty of escape from when dismounted,
        167–9
    at sea, 69, 175 and n.103
    trial by, 44, 59
    see also tactics
Battle, abbey of, 5 n.18
Bayeux, 89, 212, 228, 249
    Odo, bishop of, 73 n.88, 83 n.140, 221, 224,
        232 n.12, 246, 247, 253, 267
Bayeux Tapestry, 4 nn.11–12, 5, *6*, 137 n.26, 145,
        170, 172, *178*, 184, *217*, *262*, 264, *272*
Baynard, Geoffrey, 241 n.58
Bazoches-au-Houlme, 84
Beauchamp, William, 76 n.101, 85 n.154, 86
    Miles de, 267
Beaufort, 301
Beaumont, Ralph, viscount of, 123
Beaumont, Roger de, 139
    see also Leicester, earls of
    and Waleran, count of Meulan

Beauvais, Philip, bishop of, 47 and n.88, 188,
    194, 196, 176
    Warin, bishop of, 258–9
Bec, 14
    Herluin, abbot of, 42, 143–4
Becket, Thomas, St, archbishop of Canterbury,
    65, 95 and nn.202 and 204, 279, 284
Bedford, abbey of, 86
    castle, siege of (1137–8), 36, 267
    siege of (1224), 68 n.67, 175, 207 n.17, 233,
    243, 246, 250, 251
Beha-ad-Din, 157
beheading, 52–3, 189, 180, 181, 301
Belford, 311, 326
bellatores, 22, 29, 55–6, 71
    see also milites
Bellême, castle of, 206, 249 n.101
    Robert de, son of Roger de Montgomery, 64,
        180, 181 n.124, 196, 224, 228, 232 n.12, 241,
        247, 249, 252, 271, 286, 316
    bias of Orderic against, 200 n.114, 287
    oppresses St Evroul, 274
    fights Geoffrey and Rotrou of Mortagne,
        286–7, 288 n.142
    besieges Courcy (1091), 139, 186
    besieges Exmes, 139
    defeated by Helias of Maine, 186
    captures Helias (1098), 188
    brutal campaigns against Maine (1098), 160,
        200, 269
    Henry I's campaign against (1102), 252
    authorises surrender of Arundel (1102), 215,
        252
    capitulates to Henry I at Shrewsbury (1102),
        252–3
    imprisoned for life, 240
    imposes tenserie and castle-work, 85, 186
    church burning, 89
    military expertise, 125
    cruelty towards prisoners, 199–200, 288–9,
        333
    propriety towards vassals, 215
    their loyalty, 241, 252
    Robert de, uncle of Mabel, 201
    Mabel de, 201, 260–1
    William Talvas, 192, 201, 253
Belvoir, 256
Berkeley, 198, 267 n.39
    Roger de, 198
Berkhampstead, 189, 219, 244 n.77, 275, 278
Bernard, St, 117
Berwick, 304, 312
Beorn, nephew of Godwine, 118 n.104
Beowulf, 8, 23, 28, 64, 146
Bessin, 228
Béthune, anonymous of, 240
Beugy, siege castle of, 185
Beverley, St John of, 65
Bhuddism, Zen, 29
Biddlesden, abbey of St Mary's, 263

Biet-Nuba, 116 n.95
Bigod, Hugh, earl of Norfolk, 250
billetting, 260–1
Birr, synod of (697), 306
Biscayans, see routiers
Bjarkamal, 111 n.74
Black Prince, Edward the, son of Edward III,
    301
blinding, 2, 53, 189, 202 and n.128, 249 and
    n.101, 301
Blois, counts of
    Odo II, 59
    Stephen II, father of King Stephen, 107 n.53,
        122
    Theobald III, 198
    Theobald IV, 88, 167, 270
    Theobald V, 151 n.101
    see also Stephen, king of England
    and Winchester, Henry of Blois, bishop of
    Peter of, 55, 57, 75, 261
Blouet, Robert, 15, 283
boasting, 110–12
Bohemond, 122
Bohun, Humphrey de, 192, 290 n.150, 304
Bonet, Honoré, L'arbre des batailles of, 32–3, 46,
    53, 281–2, 337
booty, 1,2, 34, 39, 183–4, 185, 261
    division of, 37 n.33, 187–8, 189 n.41
    destruction of, 264–5
    changing patterns of aquisition, 135–6
    as catalyst for development of 'laws of war',
        32–3, 48
    privileges of routiers, 191
    see also ransom
Borleng, Odo, 107, 141, 168
Born, Betran de, 71 n.77, 103 n.32, 254
    castle of Hautefort besieged (1183), 35
    laments for Young King, 108–9
    extols plunder of merchants, 285
    in praise of war, 290, 330 and nn.4 and 5, 331
Borneil, Giraut de, 284
Bothwell, 239 n.45
Bouencourt, Peter de, 226
Bougy-sur-Risle, 89, 270
Boulogne, counts of,
    Eustace II, 103, 261, 278
    Matthew, 175
    Renaud de Dammartin, 104, 105, 166, 180,
        197, 244 n.76
Bourgthéroulde, battle of (1124), 23, 107, 156,
    166, 167 n.57, 168, 169 n.63, 180, 189, 195,
    288, 334
Bouvines, battle of (1214), 17, 66, 68, 104, 105,
    112, 119, 164–6, 169, 170 n.70, 179, 180,
    195, 197, 205, 240, 244 n.77, 310 n.86, 332
    n.9, 334, 335
Boves, Hugh de, 105, 119, 310 n.86
bows, 174–5
    see also crossbows
Brabançons, see routiers

Brackley, 261 n.10
Braibroc, Henry de, 251
Brakelond, Jocelin of, 83 n.142, 122
Braose, William de, 12 n.43, 42, 239, 279, 309
   n.80, 338
   Matilda, wife of, 256
   William, son of, 256
Bray, 44
Bréauté, Fawkes de, 68 n.67, 141 n.48, 228, 251,
   280, 321
   extortions from St Albans, 76 n.101, 84, 319
   sacks Ely, 90, 301, 319
   commands crossbowmen at Lincoln (1217),
   141
   William de, his brother, 68 n.67, 243
Brechbennoch, reliquary of St Columba, 67
Brémule, battle of (1119), 13, 14, 23, 130–1, 132,
   142, 162, 163, 164, 166, 167 n.57, 169 and
   n.63, 171 n.78, 175, 180, 181, 195, 205, 239,
   263 n.13, 334
Brennus, Raymond, *routier* captain, 52, 297 n.23,
   301
Breteuil, 103 n.31, 110, 163, 183
   William de, 196, 198, 174, 184
Breton, Hervey le, 163
Breton, William le, 66, 72 n.82, 169, 170 n.76,
   202 n.128, 212 n.43, 213, 223 n.99
Bréval, 60 n.30, 196
Bridgnorth, siege of (1102), 228–9, 245, 247,
   249, 252
Bridlington, priory of, 93
brigandage, 284–5
Brionne, 139, 207
   Gilbert de, 442
Bristol, 49 n. 94, 188, 267 n.39
Brittany, Alan IV Fergant, count of, 221
   Alan of Dinan, count of, 198–9
Briwerre, William, 261
   William the younger, 184, 193
Brotonne, forest of, 288, 289
Bruce, Robert, king of Scots (1306–29), 231 n.7
Bruges, 242
   Galbert of, 62, 136
   Robert de, 116 n.95
Brunanburgh, battle of (937), 100 n.8
Brus, Robert I de, 235, 295, 327
Bruyère, Guy de la, 153
Buc, Walter, *routier* captain, 301–302, 312
Bueil, Jean de, 28
Bungay, 250
Burgh, Hubert de, 79 n.122, 120, 202, 212,
   213–4, 244 and n.76, 268, 310
Burgundy, duke of, 119, 240
Buridan, Baldwin de, 112
Burwell, 171
Bury St Edmunds, 67, 83, 86 n.158, 90, 268, 280
   St Edmundsbury Chronicle, 277
Byrhtnoth, ealdorman of Essex, 24 and nn.
   97–8, 111 and n.71, 124, 146
bushido, 29

Cadoc, *routier* captain, 175 n.102, 228, 321
Caen, 197, 227, 249
   abbey of Holy Trinity, 285
Cahagnes, William de, 188
Cahuzac, Bernard de, 289
Caillé, 270
Calais, 248 n.99
Caldret, Henry de, 86 n.155
   Ralph de, 86 n.155
Campenni, 250
Camville, Gerard de, 232 n.9
canon law, *see* law, canon
Canterbury, 277 n.91
   Anselm, archbishop of, 141 n.42
   Lanfranc, archbishop of, 232 n.9, 316
   Gervase of, 301, n.35
   Theobald, archbishop of, 80, 85 n.149. 167
Capuciati, 300
Cardiff, 240 n.51
Carentan, 62, 78
Carlisle, 121, 209, 210, 211, 292 n.6, 304, 315
   n.106, 317
   St Mary's, 315
Carmen de Haestingae Proelio, 5 nn.16 and 18, 103
Carrickfergus, 229
carrochio, 65
Carron, Baldwin de, 104, 116–17
cartae baronum, 21
Cassel, battle of (1071), 130
Castile, 284
castles, *passim*
   proliferation affects warfare, 134–5
   role in war, 204–8
   conventions governing, *see* truce
   and respite
   see also siege
cavalacata (*cavallicata*), 258 and n.1
Celestine III, pope, 47 n.88, 50 nn.96 and 97
Celtic warfare,
   conduct in, 30, 292–7, 302–29 *passim*, 337–40
   see also Scots; slavery; heads, taking of
challenge, 42–4, 332
Chalons, William, lord of, 301, 304, 319
Chaluz Chabrol, castle of, 101, 224, 246, 249
Champagne, Theobald II, count of, 88
   see also Blois, counts of, Theobald IV
chansons,
   difficulties as sources, 9–10
   see also *Song of Roland*
   and William, count of Orange
Charentan, 301 and n.38
   Ebbe VII, lord of, 301 n.38
Charlemagne, king of the Franks (768–814) and
   Emperor, 104, 110, 113, 114, 123
Charles the Bald, king of the West Franks
   (843–77), 145, 260 n.5
Charny, Geoffrey de, 99 and n.7
   Demandes of, 33
   Livre de Chevalerie of, 99
Chartres, Fulcher of, 44 n.71

Château Gaillard, 193, 208 n.21, 212–13, 219, 226, 228, 244 n.76
Châteauneuf-en-Thimerais, Hugh de, 169 n.63
Châti... ...uf our Fpre 167
Châtillon, Guy de, 151 n.101
Chaumont, William de, 130, 184 n.6
    siege of (1098), 132, 139, 141 n.48, 142, 153, 162, 180, 191
Chauvigni, Andrew de, 102
Chesney, Robert de, bishop of Lincoln, 49
    William de, 92
Chester, 264
    earls of
        Hugh d'Avranches, 7 n.19, 171, 247 n.92, 260 n.5, 314
        Rannulf 'de Gernons', besieged by Stephen at Lincoln (1141), 40–1, 88, 234; in battle of Lincoln, 167; sacks city, 222; captures Alan of Brittany, 199; conventio with Robert of Leicester, 11 n.43, 41, 49, 233, 237; seized by Stephen, 41, 255; restitution to churches, 93 and n.195
        Rannulf 'de Blundeville', 114
    knight service of honour, 237 n.40
    constable of, see Lacy, Roger de
chevauchée, 19, 86, 258–90 passim
Chinon, 197, 212, 213, 228, 244 n.76
Chisi, William de, 284
chivalry, passim
    definitions of, 19–30, 330–40
    Christian dimension of, 55–70
    confessional and cultural factors, 135–8
    tensions between clerical ideals and secular realities, 70–97
    strategic and tactical factors affecting, 135–7
    supposed decline in later Middle Ages, 18–19, 281–2
    certain values universal to warrior elites, 23–28
    chivalric gestures between Christians and Muslims, 25–7
    and mutual recognition of prowess, 157–8
    features peculiar to Western Europe, 28–30
    importance of ransom in Frankish chivalry, 30, 134–8
    and of mercy to vanquished, 148–9, 154–5, 253–4
    recognition of enemy's bravery by gifts and freedom of egress, 218–9, 137–8
    nature and limitations of chivalric custom, 31–54
    restricted to warrior aristocracy, 176–81, 281–90
Chivalry, High Court of, 46, 186
Chronica de gestis consulum Andegavorum, 36 n.26
Chronicle of Melrose, 319
Chronicon de Evesham, 274
churches,
    knightly violence towards, 15, 18, 55–7, 75–91
    as repository for goods in time of war, 78–9

violation of sanctuary and despoliation, 75–83, 280–31, 317–20
    fortified, 87–8
    use as temporary castles, 76–7, 82, 87–8
    protection money extorted from, 83, 84, 319–20
    burdened with tenserie, 84–6
    enforced hospitality, 260–1
    damaged or burned in warfare, 86–91
    deliberately fired, 89–91, 270, 302
    targeted as symbols of lordship, 90–1
    violation of used as clerical propaganda, 75–7
    lands ravaged, 276 and n.84, 274, 279, 280
    grants of restoration to, 90–7
Cigogné, Engelard de, 84, 299
Citeux, 57
Claivaux, Bernard of, 57, 74
    In Praise of the New Chivalry, 74–5
Clare, Gilbert de, 245
    Richard de, 8, 216
Clements, Alberic, French marshal, 102
clergy,
    clerical bias of Latin sources, 8, 12–16
    ambiguity towards role of knights, 8, 12, 18, 29, 92
    concepts of Christian knighthood, 55–7, 74–5
    alleged slaying by Scots, 295–6, 302
    clerical abuse of sanctuary, 79
    as guarantors of conventiones, 49
    intercession during war, 2, 56, 60–2, 65–8, 91
    aiding victims of war, 274–5
    as castle builders, 73
    as warriors, 73
    efforts to protect inermes, 70–1
    see also Lateran councils
        Peace of God
        Truce of God
        churches
Clermont, council of (1095), 29, 57, 70 n.74; (1130) 73
    Raoul, count of, 147
Clitheroe, battle of (1138), 326
Close Rolls, 11, 184, 187
Clovis, king of the Franks (481–511), 29
Cluny, 301, 304, 319
    Hugh, abbot of, 145
cnihtas, 20
Cnut, king of England and Denmark (1016–35), 3, 36, 82, 118, 255, 279
Coggeshall, 76 n.101, 82
    Ralph of, 76 n.101, 207, 256, 301, 302
Colchester, 233
Coleshill, battle of (1157), 122
Cologne, 74
Columba, St, 67
comitatus, see household, military
Compiègne, 227
compositio amoris, 41, 42
    see also conventiones

Compostela, 51, 284
Conan II, duke of Brittany, 25, *217*
Conan, son of Ellis, 91 and n.184
Conan, son of Gilbert Pilatus, citizen of Rouen, 232, 242, 281
Conan, son of Guiomarc'h, 184, 191
Conches, 139
  Ralph III de, 60
  see also Tosny
Confirmatio Cartarum (1297), 260 n.6
Conques, church of Sainte Foi, tympanum of, *93*
constable, 37 n.31
  court of, 38, 46–7
Consuetudines et judicie (1091), 39, 43, 184 and n.4, 268
conventiones, 11 and n.43, 41–2, 49, 233, 236–7
conversi, 58, 95
Corbridge, 315 n.106
Corfe, 197 and n.95, 240 n.51, 256
Cornwall, Reginald, earl of, 49
Corpus iuris civilis, 35
Cospatric, 324
Coterells, 293, 297 and n.23, 300
  see also routiers
Coucy, 139
  Raoul de, 117 n.98
  see also Marle, Thomas de
Coulaines, 269 n.54
Courcy, 186
Courtenai, Peter de, 147
courtly love, 17
Courtrai, battle of (1302), 179, 335
Coutances, Geoffrey, bishop of, 73 n.88, 267 n.39
Coventry, 76 n.101, 88
Crécy, battle of (1346), 335 and n.13
Crema, siege of (1159), 36 n.25
Crépy, Simon de, 144 n.64
Crispin, Gilbert, 42, 143, 184 n.6
  William, 132, 141 n.42, 166, 171 n.78
Croc, Reginald, 141 n.48, 154 n.114, 166
Crocston, Robert de, 226
crossbow,
  effectiveness against armour, 72, 152, 175, 180
  use by Richard I, 72 and n.85, 100
  and Philip II, 72 and n.85
  canonical prohibition of, 72, 181
  this widely ignored, 34, 56, 71 and n.80
  used at Lincoln (1217) against horses not riders, 141 and n.47
crossbowmen, 299
  executed, 180
Crowland, abbey of, 86 n.158, 90–1, 268, 270, 319
Crowmarsh, 181, 223, 332 n.9
crusade,
  First, 29, 55, 83, 149, 303
  Second, 66

Third, 9, 26, 66, 115–16, 120, 303
  against Christians, 68, 137 n.24
Crystede, Henry, 309 and n.75
cuir-bouilli, 179 n.76
culvertagium, 118 and n.103
Cumbria, 292 nn.6–7
Curbaran, *routier* captain, 301 n.38, 320 n.140
custom, 33–46, 48–54
custumals, 225
Cuthbert, St, 65
Cyprus, 67

Daiville, Eudo de, 226
Damietta, 116 n.95, 117 n.98
Danes, 36, 265
  see also Vikings
Daneville, 306
Dartmouth, 37 n.31
Darum, 242 n.64, 246 n.91, 253 n.127.
David, St, 65
David, I, king of Scots (1124–53), 49 n.94, 168, 291–329 *passim*, 338
  raised as an Anglo-Norman baron, 121
  raids northern England, 277, 324–5
  defied by Robert de Brus before the Standard, 235
  besieges Wark (1138), 216, 220
  difficulty controlling feuds within army, 114, 324
  nature of army, 292 n.3
  protection to monasteries, 84, 319, 324
  releases captives, 314–5
  blamed for excesses of troops, 327–8
  promises war reparations, 317
  escapes from rout of Winchester (1141), 196
  saved by David Olifard, 239
  his chivalry, 219
  and piety, 318
David, earl of Huntingdon, brother of William the Lion, praised for chivalry, 156, 159, 325, 328–9, 338
  surrenders Huntingdon to Henry II (1174), 250
defiance, see *diffidatio*
Degannwy, 307 n.72
De injusta vexatione Willelmi episcopi, 40 n.47, 279 and n.97, 316; see *also* Durham
demesure, 24
Derby, earls of
  Robert II de Ferrières, 41
  William de Ferrières, 161, 250
De re militari, see Vegetius
Deuteronomy, book of, 35, 222
Devizes, 79 n.122, 198, 199, 240 n.51, 273 n.68
  Richard of, 37, 118
Diceto, Ralph of, 35, 50, 77, 108, 195, 207, 261 n.13
diffidatio, 40–1, 42, 231–5
Dinan, *217*, 253 n.127

discipline, 298, 320–6
    legislation governing, 36–9, 118
    tensions between honour and, 24, 113–17
    see also *Lex castrensis*; and Templars, *Rule* of
Dives, 160
Dol, siege of (1076), 135
    siege of (1173), 176, 245, 250
Domesday Book (1086), 21, 275–6, 315
Domfront, 43, 249
Dorylaeum, battle of (1098), 157
Dover, 118
    Anglo-Saxon burgh of, 261, 264, 278, 336
    taken by William the Conqueror, 1, 31, 45
    Anglo-Flemish treaty of, (1101), 11 n.43
    siege of (1216–17), 120, 208 n.22, 213–14, 268
    William of, 95 n.203, 199
Dream of the Rood, 25 n.103
Dreux, 184
    count of, 119
Drincourt, 175, 209
droit d'armes, 32, 33; *see also* 'law of arms'
dubbing, *see* knighthood
Dubh, king of Scots (d. 966), 307 n.73, 308
Dublin, 170 and n.75, 309
Duffield, 250
Dunbar, 304
Duncan II, earl of Fife, 292 n.3, 325, 326
Duncan, William son of, 325
Dundrennan, abbey of, 292 n.4
Durendal, Roland's sword, 64 and n.36
Durham, 65, 250, 273, 276 n.84, 303
    'lands of St Cuthbert' ravaged by Scots, 324, 325
    Simeon of, 40 n.47, 247, 302, 314, 324
    William of St Calais, bishop of; prevented from coming to court, 40 n.47; lands plundered by king, 279, 316; pact with Roger de Montgomery, 221

Eadhelm, abbot of Thetford, 278 n.94
Eadmer, 59, 141 n.42
Eadred, king of Wessex (946–55), 278 n.94
d'Earley, John, 11, 113
Ecardeville-sur-Eure, 270
d'Echauffour, Arnold, 60
Ecouché, 265
Edgar, king of England (959–75), 278 n.94
Edgar Aetheling, 254
Edith 'Swan-neck', mistress of Harold II, 5 n.18
Edmund, St, 66, 67, 83 n. 142
Edward, the Black Prince, son of Edward III, 287
Edward the Confessor, king of England (1042–66), 2, 4 n.12, 25, 261, 278, 336
Edward I, king of England (1272–1307), 231 n.7
Edward II, king of England (1307–27), 276
Edward, III, king of England (1330–77), 47, 248 n.99, 277 n.85, 287
Elie de Saint-Gilles, 117
Elne, 70 n.74

Ely, 83, 85 n.149, 199, 250, 301, 312
equitatio, 258 n.1
Ermenfrid of Sion, legate, 34, 283; *see also* penance
Ernoul, continuator of William of Tyre, 27 n.114
Espec, Walter, 66, 293, 295
Estoire d'Eracles, 27 n.114
Estoire de la Guerre Sainte, see Ambroise
Etheldreda, St, 79
Etrepagny, 263 n.13
Eu, 152
    Ralph, count of, 234 n.21
    William, count of, 241 and n.58
Eugenius III, pope, 85 n.154, 87 n.162
Eustace the Monk, 69, 167 n.53
Everard, serjeant of Hubert Walter, 102
Evesham, abbey of, 80, 274–5
    Aethelwig, abbot of, 274–5
    battle of (1265), 5 n.16, 248, 250, 335
Evreux, 162, 270
    burnt by Henry I, 47, 89, 94, 161, 173
    Audoin, bishop of, 47, 94
    church of St Taurin, 90
    garrison of executed by John (1194), 53, 190, 223
Exeter, siege of (1068), 2, 31, 45, 245, 249, 280
    siege of (1136), 49 n.94, 86, 160, 207, 224, 233, 247, 249, 253, 266 and n.36, 267
expeditio, 258 n.1
Expugnatio Hibernica, 310

'Fagaduna' (? Fawdon in Whaddon, Cambs.), battle of (1075), 241
Fakhr-ad-Din, ambassador of al-Kamil, 27
Falaise, 40 n.47, 163, 175 n.98, 194 n.72, 197, 214, 227, 228, 255 n.142
    treaty of (1174), 194 n.72
familia regis, see households, military
Fantosme, Jordan, 8, 11, 67, 99, 107, 111, 117, 119, 120–1, 129, 179, 211, 212, 216, 225, 266, 285, 290, 291–329 *passim*
Faringdon, siege of (1145), 186, 191
fasting, before battle, 60, 62 n.31
Fécamp, 84
    priest of, 140, 176
Ferrand the engineer, 202
Ferrières (Ferrars), William de, 141 n.42, 186, 214
    see also Derby, earls of
feud, 70, 138–40
Fine Rolls, 11, 187
fitz Count, Brian, 87, 219 n.76, 284
fitz Ernis, Oliver, 52
fitz Gilbert, John, *see* Marshal, John
fitz Hamon, Robert, 173, 196, 212
fitz Henry, Melier, 65
fitz Herbert, William, 192
fitz Hildebrand, Robert, 81 n.131
fitz Hubert, Robert, 76 n.101, 198, 200 n.116

fitz Gilbert, Baldwin, 167
fitz Gilbert, John, 85, 129, 139–40
fitz Goubert, Richard, 186
fitz Osbern, William, see Hereford, earls of
fitz Richard, Roger, 166
fitz Richard, William, 192
fitz Renfrey, Gilbert, 187, 256
fitz Stephen, Robert, 306
fitz Walter, Robert, 68, 193 and n.70, 227 and nn.126, 128
fitz Walter, Simon, 189
Flanders, counts of
  indentures with kings of England, 11, 46, 236–7
  Baldwin V (1035–67), 144 n.63
  Baldwin VII (1111–19), 171 n.78, 173
  Charles the Good (1119–27), 136, 202, 242
  Philip of Alsace (1163–91), 151 n.101, 269 n.57; grants respite to Drincourt (1173), 209; takes Aumale (1173), 225; advises Louis to take Rouen by guile, 127–8; use of ruses in tournaments, 128; chivalric patron of Young King, 129; patron of Chrétien, 129, 149 n.92; attacks Baldwin of Hainault, 151; advice on ravaging, 266–7, 285
  Robert I Le Frison (1070–93), 130
  Robert II (1093–1111), 167, 236
Flemings, 81 n.131, 179–80; 155, 299, 301 and n.35, 312, 320–1; see also mercenaries; routiers
Florent, St, 94
Foliot, Gilbert, bishop of Hereford and London, 42, 76 n.101, 80–1, 85, 87 nn.162 and 164, 92, 96, 203 n.134, 219 n.76
  Roger, his kinsman, 219 n.76
Fontaine-Milon, 148
foraging, 260–8
Forham, battle of (1173), 67, 179, 180, 189 n.37, 290 n.150, 301
Fougerès, Ralph de, 176, 250, 264
  Stephen of, 13 n.47, 14, 55, 75
Framlingham, 181 n.125
franchise, 99, 103, 203, 210, 219, 240
Frederick I Barbarossa, German emperor (1155–90), 35 n.25, 300
Frederick II, German emperor (1220–50), 27 n.112
Frederick, son of Leopold of Austria, 50 n.97
Fréteval, engagement at (1194), 43, 166, 177
Froissart, Jean, 31–2, 53, 309 and n.75
Fulk, see counts of Anjou
Furnival, Gerard de, 191

Gacé, 79
Gael, Ralph de, 103, 183, 242 n.62
Gaillon, 175 n.102
Gaimar, Geoffrey, 40 n.47
Galloway, 292 nn.4–7, 295
Galwegians, 155, 291, 291–329 passim
  identity of, 292 and nn.5–7

demand right to attack first at Standard, 114, 293
  see also Scots
gambeson, 170, 177
Ganelon, 103 n.31, 104, 114
Gant, Gilbert de, 92
Garlande, Anselm de, 174
Gasny, 130, 162 n.20
Gaugi, Roger de, 152
Gavrai, 268 n.49
Geoffrey, brother of Henry II, 224 n.109
Geoffrey, count of Brittany, son of Henry II, 52, 83 n.138, 110
Geoffrey Plantagenet, natural son of Henry II, archbishop of York, 279
Gerald of Wales, 174, 307 and n.69, 309, 310, 339–40
Gerberoi, battle of (1079), 104, 135
Germain, St, 66
Germania, of Tacitus, 23
Germans, 67
Gerold, chaplain to Hugh d'Avranches, 7 n.19
Gesta domni Hildeberti episcopi, 269 n.54
Gesta Francorum, 157, 303
Gesta Friderici, 35 n.25
Gesta Henrici quinti, 35, 223
Gesta Henrici secundi, 189
Gesta Herewardi, 25 n.103
Gesta Stephani, 36, 49, 76 and n.101, 77, 79, 82, 83, 195, 207, 229, 271, 273, 274, 283, 286, 292 n.4, 311 n.89
Girart de Rousillon, 159, 160, 201
Giroie, 85, 261
  sons of, 287
  William, son of, 192, 201
Gisors, 44, 51, 130, 150 n.96, 153, 167, 194 n.77, 206 n.11, 225, 285, 332 n.8
  Hervey and Burchard de, 190, 240
Givervilla, 60
'Glanvill', Tractatus de Legibus, 38, 118–19, 237–8
Glanville, Rannulf de, 155
Glos, Roger de, 196
Gloucester, abbey of, 85–6, 86 n.155
  Robert, earl of, 12 n.43; 66 n.52, 78, 175, 192; defeats Stephen at Lincoln (1141), 167; sacks city, 222; besieges Wareham (1142) 40, 209; harshly confines William Martel (1143), 199; conventio with Rannulf of Chester, 41; with Miles of Hereford, 42; war with Waleran of Meulan, 281, 288; conduct towards churches, 76, 79, 89
  Philip, his son, 49
  Roger of, 163
  William, earl of, 12 n.43
Godwine, earl of Wessex, 261, 278, 315, 336
Gornemant of Gohort, Perceval's tutor, 149, 154–5, 286
Gorre, engagement at (1183), 52, 297 n.23, 301

Gospatric, son of Orm, 225 and n.111
Gotland, 173 n.83
Gournay, 151
　Hugh de, 191, 247 n.92
Gouy, Roger de, 22)
Grancy, Reginald de, 200
Grandcourt, William de, 156, 166, 189
Grandmesnil, Hugh de, 186, 247 n.92
　Ivo de, 186, 268
　John de, 189
　Robert de, 139
Grandmont, 83
Gregory III, pope, 315 n.111
Gregory VII, pope, 75
　see also papacy, Gregorian
Groby, 250
Gruffyd ap Cynan, 313
Guala, legate, 68, 222
Guisnes, Baldwin of, 152, 175 n.98
Guy, count of Ponthieu, 191, 201
Gwynedd, Owain of, 189 n.35
Gyrth, brother of Harold II, 4
Gytha, mother of Harold II, 5 n. 18

Hainault, Baldwin, count of, 151
Harding, Stephen, 137 n.26
Hardraada, Harald, king of Norway (1047–66), 3
Harfleur, 223
Harold, II, son of Godwine, king of England
　(1066), 4, 60, 278
　sells captives (1052), 315
　seized by Guy of Ponthieu, 201
　receives arms from Duke William, 25
　victory at Stamford Bridge, 3
　slain at Hastings, 4–5, 6
　fate of body, 4–5, 5 nn. 16–18
'harrying of the North', 271 and n.67, 273,
　274–5, 279–80, 283, 303, 311
　see also ravaging
Harthacnut, king of England (1035/40–42), 278
　n.94
Harwarden, 122
Hasculf, leader of Dublin Norse, 309
Hastings, 262
　battle of (1066), 1, 3–7, 179, 248, 277, 283
　papal banner at, 4, 29
　size of Norman force at, 135 and n.16
　Norman victory seen as judgement of God,
　59
　'feigned flight' at, 130
Hattin, battle of (1187), 67, 157
hauberk, 43, 168–75
Hautefort, castle of, 35
Haye, 250
heads, taking of, 101, 303 and nn.51 and 53,
　306–10
Helias, count of Maine, 64, 236
　jokes with Norman garrison of Le Mans,
　137–8, 160
　protects them on surrender (1100), 218

war against Rufus as a crusade (1096), 137
　n.24
　defeats Robert of Bellême, 186
　in honourable captivity, 196
　[... by anointed earth (1090), 265
　at Tinchebrai (1106), 141 n.43
helmets, 62–3, 171 and n.78, 172, 206
Henry I, king of England (1100–35), 121, 131,
　140, 141, 163, 176, 230, 235, 238, 267, 327
　Orderic as apologist for, 13–14, 77
　hurls Conan from keep of Rouen (1090), 232,
　242
　exacts castle-work, 85
　punishes depredations of court, 260 and n.6
　indentures with count of Flanders, 236–7
　reduces Bellême's castles (1102), 245, 252
　Bellême surrenders to, 253
　amerces Ivo de Grandmesnil, 268
　burns Bayeux (1105), 89, 212, 249
　hair shorn as penance, 62
　vows of restoration before Tinchebrai (1106),
　60
　releases captives, 190
　struck by William Crispin at Tinchebrai, 132,
　171 n.78
　informs Anselm of victory, 141 n.42
　accepts surrender of Norman castles (1106),
　214–15
　imprisons Robert Curthose, 188, 240 n.51
　criticized for this, 255
　seizure of Normandy challenged at council of
　Reims (1119), 34
　takes Bellême (1113), 206
　enraged at surrender of La-Motte-Gautier-
　du-Clinchamp (1118), 215
　defied by Reginald of Bailleul, 40 n.47
　burns Evreux, 89, 161
　hampered by treachery, 247
　tricked into abandoning siege of Laigle
　(1118), 130
　rewards loyalty of Ralph the Red, 103, 198
　punishment of rebels, 189, 202, 232–3, 240–1,
　248–9, 255
　his chivalry, 219, 233, 252
Henry I, king of France (1031–60), 144, 207
Henry II Plantagenet, king of England (1154–89),
　41, 49 n.94, 147, 148, 155, 168 n.59,
　189 n.35, 211, 230, 238, 261, 266, 271, 275,
　280, 284
　executes archers at Crowmarsh (1153), 181,
　223
　Toulouse expedition (1159), 121, 284
　spares Henry of Essex, 122–3
　relieves Verneuil (1173), 126–7, 211
　peace terms with sons (1173–4), 42, 45–6
　penance at Becket's tomb, 65
　drives Richard from Saintes (1174), 77
　secures rapid capitulation of rebels, 245
　amerces Gospatric, son of Orm, for
　surrender of Appelby (1174), 225

threatens earl of Leicester with starvation, 256
clemency towards rebels, 250 and n.109
releases prisoners without ransom, 190
honours Richard by grant of prisoners (1176), 190
loyalty of vassals, 161
household knights seized, 51
shot at by men of Limoges (1183), 52, 174
peace of Chateauroux (1187), 330 n.4
renounces homage to Philip (1188), 51, 235 and n.27
surprise chevauchée, 129–30, 153
fires Le Mans (1189), 154, 265
Henry, son of Henry II, the Young King (1170–83), 35, 250
knighted by William Marshal (1173), 146–8
at siege of Rouen (1174), 127
peace terms with father, 42
ransoms captives, 195
adopts Philip of Flanders as chivalric patron, 129
patronage of tournaments, 107–9
cosmopolitan household in tourneys, 150
attacks count of Sancerre (1181), 261–2, 268
violates safe conduct (1183) 52
allows men of Limoges to shoot at father, 52
plunders monasteries, 64 n.36, 76 n.101, 82–3
repentance and death, 95
chivalric reputation, 108–9
Henry III, king of England (1216–72), 191, 214
besieges Bedford (1224), 207 n.17
executes garrison, 243, 249–50
receives heads of Welsh (1231), 310
withdraws from siege of Usk (1233), 264–5
raises banner of mortal war, 66
'excommunicated' by rebels at Kenilworth, 161
defies rebels, 234
punishment of rebels (1265), 250
Henry V, king of England (1413–22), 35, 223, 287
Henry VI, emperor of Germany (1190–7), 47, 50 n.97
Henry, earl of Northumberland, son of David I, boyhood companion of Ailred of Rievaulx, 327
saved from capture by Stephen at Ludlow, 49 n.94
chivalric reputation of, 121, 328–9
escapes from battle of Standard by ruse, 131 n.182
gives armour to peasant, 168 n.60
forfeits honour of Huntingdon, 238
Henry of Essex, Henry II's standard bearer, 122–3
heraldry, 17, 137 and n.26

heralds, 34, 48, 150, 208
Hereford, 67, 244 n.77
earls of,
William fitz Osbern, 136, 168 n.58
Roger, his son, 201 n.121, 232 n.10, 240, 242 n.62
Miles of Gloucester, convenio with Robert of Gloucester, 12 n.43, 42; relieves Wallingford, 77; desecrates convent at Wilton, 76
Roger, his son, convenio with William of Gloucester, 12 n.43, 41; with William de Braose, 41–2; alleged violations of sanctuary, 80–1; assumes the habit, 96; Walter, his brother, 198
Hereward, 25 n.103
heriot, 25 n.103
Hertford, 219
Hesdin, Arnulf of, 224, 242, 251
Hexham, abbey of, 276 n.84
granted immunity by David I (1138), 84, 319, 324
protected by William son of Duncan, 325
John of, 60, 65, 291–329 passim
Richard of, 60, 65, 291–329 passim
Robert, prior of, 314
hird, 30
Histoire des ducs de Normandie, 9
Histoire de Guillaume le Maréchal, 7, 8, 10–11, 27, 48, 98, 99, 100, 106, 114, 128, 129, 147, 150–1, 197, 210 n.29, 221, 229, 268, 285, 290, 323, 330, 333
Holland, William, count of, 37
Holmcultram, abbey, 319
homines ad arma (hommes d'armes), 22, 33
horses,
symbols of nobility, 19–20, 23
in battle, 23, 111–16
provision of remounts by vassals, 103–4
seizure as booty, 39, 183
as prizes in tournaments, 48
as ransom, 184, 189
as gifts between warriors, 27, 103 n.31, 106 n.45
defeated garrisons retain as token of valour, 219
Hospitallers, 19, 39 n.42, 115, 116, 157
master of, 115, 116 and n.95
marshal of, 116, 117
households, military, 11 n.43, 22, 30, 146, 183
of Hugh d'Avranches, 7 n.19
pre-Conquest, 25 n.103
comitatus, 30, 147
regulations governing Anglo-Danish, 36–7
chivalric values within, 30, 48, 146–8
knights of, 51, 75, 193, 321
familia regis, 107, 141, 168, 189, 196, 288
of kings of Scots, 324, 329, 338
role in training, 145–6
composition in tourneys, 150–1

Howden, Roger of, 35, 37, 72 n.85, 120, 147, 170
    n.70, 176 n.104, 189 nn.37 and 41, 202, 226,
    295, 302
Hubert, lord of St Suzanne, vicomte of Maine,
    163, 185–6
Hugh of Tiberias, 26
Huizinga, Jan, 18–19, 24, 28, 33 n.3, 281
Humphrey of Toron, 26
Hunderthwaite, 302
Hundred Years War, 31–2, 259, 277, 281, 335, 337
Huntingdon, Henry of, 35, 76, 121, 222, 295–6,
    319, 328
    see also David, earl of Huntingdon
huskarlesteffne, 36, 118 n.104

d'Ibelin, Jean, 225
Ibn al-Athir, 68 n.65, 157
Imad al-Din, 68 n.65
indentures, 11
infantry, 22
    treatment in battle, 141 and nn.42–3, 175–9
    see also archers
    crossbowmen
Innocent III, pope, 72 n.85, 234 n.22, 257
ira et malevolentia, 240, 279
Irish, 306–7, 309, 310, 314
Isaac, ruler of Cyprus, 67
Itinerarium perigrinorum, 10, 26 n.109, 27 n.113, 35,
    64, 66 104, 116, 119, 157, 223
ius ad bellum, 34, 68; see also just war
ius armorum, 31–3, 47, 52; see also 'laws of war'
ius belli, 31–3; see also 'laws of war'
ius divinum, 32
ius gentium, 32–3
ius in bello, 34, 56, 73
ius militare, 33; see also 'laws of war'
ius naturale, 32

Jaffa, battle of (1192), 9, 27, 101
James, St, of Compostela, 51
Jerusalem, 36 n.25, 45, 68, 119, 303
    kings of, 191, 226 n.117
    kingdom of, 225–6
    custumals of, 225 and nn.114–16
Jews, 312
John, king of England (1199–1216), 206 n.11,
    226–9, 268
    Nottingham and Tickhill surrendered to
        (1191), 226
    executes garrison of Evreux (1194), 53, 90,
        203, 223
    charged with treason (1194), 232 and n.9
    captures Philip of Beauvais (1197), 176, 188
    razes Le Mans (1199), 280
    failure to relieve Norman garrisons (1203–4),
        212–13
    supposed dalliance with wife, 106
    mocked for military failures, 110
    accuses William Marshal of treason (1205),
        238

attacks William de Braose, 279
threatens garrison of Roche-au-Moine (1208)
    244
takes Vouvant (1214), 245
deserted by Poitevins (1214), 33
mutilates those expelled from Rochester
    (1215), 241, 245
desires to execute garrison, 242–3
but is prevented, 248, 251
hangs crossbowmen, 181
punitive campaigns against rebels (1216), 280,
    298, 321
met in north by scorched earth, 265
baronial castles surrender en masse to
    (1215–16), 251
burns granaries of Crowland and Bury St
    Edmunds, 86 n.158, 90–1, 268
grants free egress to French at Colchester,
    233
garrison of Dover seeks relief from (1216),
    213
attempts to fire Winchester (1216), 265
use of starvation, 256
murder of Arthur, 256–7
defied, 234
cruelty towards prisoners, 197, 202
grants out profits of war and ransoms, 188,
    191, 193
aids payment of ransoms to loyal men, 192,
    193
use of routier captains in government, 321–3
John II, the Good, king of France (1350–64), 33
John 'the Mad', leader of the Ostmen, 170
Joigny, 149 n.92
Joinville, Jean, sire de, 9, 112, 119, 123, 331
Jomsvikinga Saga, 36 n.28
Josephus, 36 n.25
Josselin de Tours, seneschal of Anjou, 148
Le Jouvencel, 28
Julian, St, 64
Jumièges, William of, 141 n.45
just war, 14, 18, 34–5, 50, 181
Justinian, code of, 35
juvenes, 48, 106–7, 108–9, 247 n.92

Kafartab, 170 n.70
Kenilworth, 160, 250
    Dictum of, 194 n.74, 250
Kentigern, St, 318
Kinloss, 307 n.73, 708
knighthood, deprivation of belt of, 4, 37
    dubbing and belting to, 17, 25, 57, 74
    symbolism of belting, 147
    as admission into the militia, 146–8
    ordo of, 285
    see also militia
knight service, limitation of, 236–8

La Barre, Luke de, 110, 202, 219 n.75, 233, 241,
    255

La Couronne, monastery of, 83
La Couture, monastery of, 186
La-Croix-St-Leufroi, 82, 270
Lacy, Gilbert de, 41, 42, 76 n.101, 80
    Henry de, 92–3
    Hugh de, 216
    Roger de, constable of Chester; hangs deputy
        castellans of Nottingham and Tickhill
        (1191), 226 and n.120; defends Château-
        Gaillard, 212–13, 226; ransom of, 184, 192;
        kept in honourable custody, 196, 218–19,
        244 n.76
Laigle, 15, 171 n.78
    Gilbert de, 139, 140
    Gilbert, his nephew, 140
    Nicholas de, *Quaestiones* of, 47
    Richer, son of Engenulf de, 163
    Richer de, 15, 76 n.101, 79, 171
Lambeth, treaty of (1217), 190, 194
lamellar, 170 n.75
La-Motte-Gautier-du-Clinchamp, 215
Lancaster, 197 n.95
    Henry of Grosmont, duke of, 110 n. 66
    John of Gaunt, duke of, 31
lance, couched, 23, 144–6, 171, 174
    thrown, 140
    Holy Lance, 67
    of St Maurice, 67
Laon, anonymous of, 297, 301 n.38
L'arbre des batailles, see Bonet, Honoré
Lateran councils, Second (1139)
    72, 95 n.204
    Third (1179), 70 n.71, 72, 297, 299, 300, 317,
        318, 322
    Fourth (1215), 78 n.114
Laval, John de, 144
Lavaur, synod of (1213), 318 n.126
'law of arms', 'laws of war', 31–54, 222–4
    paucity of evidence for pre-Conquest, 3
    application by William I in England, 1–3, 31
    profits of war as catalyst for development,
        32–3
    as uncodified body of military custom, 34–41
    between Franks and Muslims, 45
    problems of enforceablity, 46–54
    use of terms *lex* and *ius*, 34–6
    fourteenth century codification, 31–3
    see also ius belli
law, canon, 34, 47
    see also ius in bello, ius ad bellum
    and just war
    Roman, 35–6, 38, 39, 222
Lawrence, St, 120 n.115, 126, 127
Lech, battle of the (955), 67
Leges Henrici Primi, 118, 232, 233
Legnano, John of, *Tractatus de bello, de represaliis et
    de duello*, 32–3. 35, 39, 46, 53
Le Goulet, 110
Leicester, 250, 280
    earls of

Robert de Beaumont, count of Meulan, 232
    n.9, 247 n.92
Robert II, 89; *conventio* with Rannulf of
    Chester, 12 n.43, 41, 46 n. 80, 49, 233, 237,
    270; truce with Geoffrey of Anjou (1141),
    236; burns churches, 287; restitution to
    Lincoln cathedral, 93 n.195
Robert III, 67, 250, 256, 280, 301, 333 n.11;
    invokes aid of St Thomas (1173), 65
Robert IV, 102, 103 n.36, 104, 236, 237 n.40
    knight service of honour, 237 n.40
Le Mans, 64, 88, 168 n.59, 180, 189, 212, 253
    n.127, 264, 265, 280, 301 n.37
    siege of (1100), 137–8, 149, 160, 218
    Hildebert, bishop of, 269 n.54
Leofwine, brother of Harold II, 4
Leominster, 81 n.128
Leopold, duke of Austria, 47, 50 n.97
Le Pin, Gilbert of, 139
    Odard of, 202, 233, 241, 255
Le Puiset, 174
    Hugh of, 174
Le Sap, 81, 265
Leschans, Peter de, 150 n.96
Lex castrensis,
    of Anglo-Danish households, 36, 118 n.104
    of Frederick Barbarossa, 37, 38
lex deditionis, 36 n.26
Lex innocentium (697), of Adomnan, 306 and n.64
lex pacis, 37 n.31
Liberate Rolls, 184
Lillebonne, council of (1080), 78, 79 n.119
Limerick, 65, 306
Limoges, 31, 52 n.106, 53, 76 n.101, 82, 86 n.159
    Gerald, bishop of, 301
    abbey of St Martial, 76 n.101, 82
    see also Aimar, count of
Lincoln, battle of (1141), 23, 35, 76, 107, 119,
    137, 167, 179 and n.110, 180, 196, 255
    battle of (1217), 68, 98, 114, 119, 141 an n.48,
        167, 184, 195, 213, 334
    sack of (1141), 35, 222, 281
    sack of (1217), 83, 222, 280
    cathedral, 76, 88 and n.167, 93 n.195
    castle of, 199
    Robert de Chesney, bishop of, 49
Lindsey, 213, 279
Lisbon, 37 n. 31
Lisieux, 265, 266
Livre au roi, 225 and nn.115–16
Llewelyn ap Griffith, 67
Llewelyn ap Iorwerth, 307 n.72
Loches, 212, 244 n.76
Loch Lomond, 292
Lombards, 135
London, 170 n.75, 241, 277
London, Tower of, 199
Longchamp, Stephen de, 165
    William, 226, 261 and n.8
loricati, 169

Lorrains, 201

Lothian, 304 n.58, 305

Louis VI, king of France (1108–37), 165, 195
inability to ransom knights through poverty, 194
tortures rebels, 303
appeals to pope against Henry I's seizure of Normandy, 34 n.18
escapes capture at Brémule (1119), 196
challenges Henry I to single combat, 44
respects sanctuary at Andeli, 79 n.123
besieges Chateauneuf-sur-Epte, 163
Philip and Florus, sons of, 163

Louis VII, king of France (1137–80), 177, 250, 266, 285
takes Neufmarché by collusion (1152), 224 n.109
treaty with Barbarossa expelling *routiers* (1160s), 300
ravages lands of count of Chalons (1166), 304
prevents peace between Henry II and sons (1173), 42
besieges Verneuil (1173), 43, 207
violates respite to citizens, 35, 120, 126–7, 209, 210
guile at Rouen (1174), 127–8

Louis VIII, king of France (1223–6), 7, 98, 113, 190, 233, 250, 265
besieges Dover (1216–17), 120, 208 n.22, 268
grants respite, 213–14, 244
allows garrisons of Hertford and Berkhampstead free egress (1217), 219, 244
fleet destroyed at Sandwich, 69
extortions from St Albans, 76 n.101, 84 and n.148

Louis IX, king of France (1226–70), 115

Louis the German, Frankish king (825–76), 145

Louvrecaire, *routier* captain, 227, 228, 323

Lovel, William, 195

loyalty, 24, 30, 99, 102–4, 251–4

Lucca, Anselm of, 75

Lucius II, pope, 85 n.149

Lucy, Richard de, 121, 179, 280, 333 n.11

Ludgershall, 140

Ludlow, 49 n.94

Lusignan,
family of, 140 n.37, 197, 230
Hugh 'Chiliarchus', 134, 201–2
Hugh 'le Brun', 245
Geoffrey de, 197, 245

Lyons-la-Foret, 263 n.13

Maciejowski Bible, *172*, 173 n. 84, *177*, *206*

Macmurchada, Dairmait, king of Leinster, 306, 307 n.69, 309

Mâconnais, 20 n.75, 21

Magna Carta, 46 n.81, 192, 260 n.6, 263, 299–300, 336 n.16

Magnus III Bareleg, king of Norway, 171

Magyars, 29

Maine, 64, 123, 160, 185
see also Helias, count of; *and* Le Mans

Malcolm III, king of Scots (1057–93), 302, 311 n.87, 314, 318, 324, 339

Malcolm IV, king of Scots (1153–65), 121, 220 n.85

Maldon, battle of (991), 23, 28, 111, 124

Malet, William, 5 n.18

Malmesbury, abbey of, 87 n.162
castle of, 199
William of, 4 and n.12,5 and n.18, 10, 37, 46, 81, 191, 192, 197, 200 nn.114 and 116, 232, 233, 237, 242, 249 n.100, 273, 319
as apologist of Robert of Gloucester, 40–1, 76–7
on *diffidatio*, 40–1

Maluvel, Richard, 155 nn.122 and 125

Mandeville, Geoffrey de, 76, 78 n.112, 81, 88, 92 n.189, 95, 171, 199, 255, 261 n.12, 310 n.86
Arnulf, son of, 76 n.101
Geoffrey, son of, 95 n.202, 174, 261

Manny, Sir Walter, 248 n.99

Mansourah, battle of (1250), 112, 117 n.98, 119, 123

Mantes, 52, 88, 269 n.57

Marc, Philip, 299

Marches, 188, 204, 208 n.21
law of the, 44
Warden of the, 46

Margam, Annales de, 197

Margaret, St, wife of Malcolm III, 314

Marlborough, 273 n.69

Marle, Thomas de, lord of Coucy, 125, 200 n.116, 289

Marmion, Robert de, 76, 88

Marmoutier, John of, 148, 203

Marshal, John (fitz Gilbert), 198, 210 n.29, 221
William, his son, 11, 22, 68, 113, 287, 331
life endangered as hostage, 221
and tournaments; generosity at, 151, 152 n.106; prowess in, 152, 171 and n.78; profits from, 152; redress for stolen horses, 48; emulates guile of Philip of Flanders in, 128–9; early reputation based largely on, 109
in skirmish at Drincourt (1167), 109 n.59
wounded and captured in Poitou (1168), 109 n.59, 197–8
tutor in arms to Young King, 109 n.59
knights Young King (1173), 147
fulfils Young King's vow of pilgrimage, 95
advises Henry II on surprise chevauchée, 129–30, 285
reconnoitres, 168 n.59
unhorses Count Richard (1189), 154, 174
captures castellan of Milli (1197), 153–4
seeks respite from Philip (1204), 236

swears liege homage to him for French lands (1205), 238
refuses to follow John to Poitou (1206), 238
protects William de Braose (1208), 239
exhortation to royalists before Lincoln (1217), 98
grief at death of count of Perche, 154
takes Nicholas de Stuteville for ransom, 185, 191 n.56
assumes mantle of the Templars, 74, 96
piety of, 74–5, 96
as epitome of chivalry, 124–5
presents prisoners to Henry II and Richard I, 189
see also *Histoire de Guillaume le Maréchal*
his sons
William the younger, 114, 307 n.72, 309
Richard, 152, 175 n.98, 253, 264–5
Gilbert, 123 n.139
marshals, 37 n.31, 38, 46
'of the Army of God', 68
Martel, William, 85 n.154, 142, 199
Martigny, 299
mass, before battle, 60, 61
before tournaments, 74
'Mategriffon', Richard I's portable castle, 162
Mathgamain, king of Munster, 306
Matilda, Empress, daughter of Henry I, 40, 49, 77, 87, 89, 139, 195, 221, 235, 237, 255, 277, 284
Matilda, queen of England, wife of King Stephen, 277
Matthew Paris, 69, 84, 119, 171, 207 n.20, 296 n.22, 299 and nn.29 and 31
Chronica Majora 105, 243, 313
Gesta abbatum of, 84
Maule, knights of, 58
Peter de, 131, 195
Mauleon, Savaric de,
urges clemency for garrison of Rochester (1215), 248
punitive chevauchée in eastern counties (1216), 280, 301
plunders Tilty and Coggeshall, 76 n.101, 82
attempts to burn Ely, 90 n.183, 280
spares Crowland, 91, 319
Maurice, St, 64 n.37, 67
Mayenne, Geoffrey de, 192
Mayet, siege of (1099), 160, 212, 261, 269
Melaghlin, son of Mac Loughlin, king of the Kenel Owen, 306
Mercadier, Richard's general and mercenary captain, 72, 188, 228, 321
mercenaries, 81 and n. 131, 228, 230–1, 312, 320, 340
see also Flemings; *milites, gregarii; routiers*
Merdon, 203 n.134
Mervant, 246 n.89
mesnie, 22, 30
see also household, military

Messina, 37, 50 n.96, 52 n.106, 72 n.85, 118, 130, 162, 253 n.127
military orders, 19
see also Templars; *and* Hospitallers
milites, 178, 258
humble origins as a class and social advancement of, 20–2
title *miles* adopted by aristocracy, 20–2, 142–4
social status of, 21–2, 143–5
sancti Petri, 29
united with noblity by function, 22, 143–4
gregarii milites, 81, 288
militia, 8, 22, 75, 143
militia saecularis, 8, 58, 75, 139, 149
clerical reservations concerning, 8, 55–6
growth of notions of, 137
mill burning, 259, 268 and n.49, 277
Milli, castle of, 47, 153, 189
Mirebeau, battle of (1202), 110, 164, 184, 193, 197, 257, 334
Mohun, William de, 195
monasteries,
aristocratic benefaction of, 57–8
quit-claims to before expedition or battle, 60
entry to by knights *ad succurendum*, 58, 95–6
atonement by knights for violence towards, 91–6
as spirtual castles, 58
see also churches; *and* clergy
Mongols, 296 n.22, *297*
Monmouth, 175 n.98
Montagu, 192
Mont Coeur, battle of (1033), 198
Montdidier, Ralph, count of, 239
Montfort (l'Aumary),
Amaury de, 174
Richard de, 139
Amaury de, count of Evreux, 47, 89, 107, 156, 161, 163, 166, 168, 189
Simon de, Albigensian crusader, 303
Simon de, earl of Leicester, 66, 194 n.74, 248; defied by Henry III, 234; mutilation of corpse, 5 n. 16, 234, 335; see also Evesham, battle of (1265)
Montfort (-sur-Risle),
Robert de, William Rufus's *magister militum*, 253 n.127
Hugh IV de, 169 n.63
Robert de, 122
Montgomery, 310
see Shrewsbury, earls of
see also Bellême, Robert de
Montmorency, Hervey de, 309, 310
Montreuil, 207
Jerome de, 52 n.106
Morat, battle of (1476), 335
Moray, men of, 292 n.3, 308
Morcar, earl of Northumbria, 315
Moret, Peter de, 214
Moreville, Richard de, 325

Morgarten, battle of (1315), 179
Morpeth, 246 n.89
Mortagne,
    Rotrou, count of, 99
    Geoffrey, count of, 140, 285–6
    Juliana, daughter of, 140
Mortain, William, count of, 141 n.42, 189, 240
    n.51, 267
Mortemer, battle of (1054), 161, 163 and n.26,
    165, 201, 239
    William de, 213
Mortimer, Roger de, 5 n.16, 239
    William de, 155 nn.122
Moulins-la-Marche, 140
Mountjoie, French royal banner, 66
    see also war-cries
Mountsorrel, 250
Mouzeil, 201
Mowbray, Robert de, earl of Northumberland,
    162, 240, 247, 255, 267 n.39
    Roger de, 156 and n.128, 250, 255
Muneton, Richard de, 310
Murtough O'Brien, 309
mutilation, 2, 5 n.16, 37, 134, 200–2, 233, 241,
    249 and nn. 100 and 101, 254–5, 288, 301,
    303, 307 n.72
    guarantees of safety from, 218
    see also heads, taking of

Nancy, battle of (1477), 355
Nantes, count of, 168
Narbonne, council of (1054), 70 n.74, 270, 283
    n.114
    Ivo of, 296 n.22
Navarre, Philip de, 106
Navarrese, see routiers
Neufmarché, 224 n. 109
Newark, 199
Newburgh, Robert of, 103
    William of, 35, 47 n.88, 50 n.97., 74, 93, 127–8,
    204, 250, 261 and n.8, 293, 304
Newbury, 210 n.29, 221
Newcastle, 197 n.95, 246 n.89
Nicaea, 303 n.53
Nicholas II, pope, 78 n.117
Ninian, St, 318
Nithard, 145
nithing, 37, 118
Nogent, Guibert de, 200 n.116, 201
Nonant, Hugh de, 215
Norbury, 192
Norham, 224, 250, 319 n.135
Normandy, dukes of, see Robert 'the
    Magnificent'; William I; Robert Curthose;
    William II
Norreis, Henry le, herald, 109
Northallerton, 250
    battle of (1138), see Standard, battle of
Northampton,
    St Andrew's priory, 192

    Assize of (1176), 263
Norwich, priory of, 93
Nottingham, 89, 226, 232 n.9, 245, 246, 256
Noyt, battle of (1044), 108
Nutley, abbey of, 96

Odart, Heimeri, 189
ofermod, 24
Offa, Byrhtnoth's thegn, 111 n.71
Olaf, St, king of Norway, 25 n. 103
Olifard, David, 238–9 and 239 n.45
Oliver, companion of Roland, 10, 102, 120
Ordene de chevalerie, 25, 74
Orderic Vitalis, passim
    value and limitations as a source for chivalry,
        12– 16
    ideals concerning Christian warfare, 12–16, 56
        n.5, 132–3
    as apologist for Henry I, 13–14, 77, 94, 132,
        181–2
    condemns 'harrying of the North', 271, 283,
        311
    views on ravaging, 283
    criticizes Norman conduct towards Welsh,
        316
Oriflamme, 66
Origny, 90, 91
Orreby, John of, 189
Osbert, 'hostarius', 242 n.69
Ossory, men of, 306
Oswald, St, king of Northumbria (633–42), 66
    n.52
Otto, I, German emperor (962–73), 67
Otto, IV, German emperor (1198–1212)
    coronation sword of, 64 n.37
    banner of, 66 n.54
    at Bouvines, 166, 170 n.70
Ottobuono, legate, 161
Outremer, 45, 67, 115, 226
    see also Jersusalem; and crusades
Oxford, 87, 210

Pantulf, William, 249
papacy, 29, 47, 50
Paris, 42
    Parlement of, 186
parole, 52, 187 and n.22, 190, 194 n.78, 203
Paschal, pope, 122 n.130
Patent Rolls, 11, 184, 187, 192
patria, 3, 24, 57, 165, 180
    see also just war
Paynell, Ralph, sheriff of Yorkshire, 40 n.47
Peace of God, 34–5, 56, 70, 77, 139, 258, 268–9,
    270, 283, 289, 306, 336; see also Truce of
    God
Peak, castle of the, 197 n.95
pedites, see infantry
penance, before battle 60–2
    penitential edict after Hastings, 34, 283–4 and
    n.116

Perche, count of, 141 n.48, 154 and n.114
Percy, Alan de, 114
Peter the Hermit, 122
Peter, St, 64 n.36, 65
Peterborough, Brand, abbot of, 25 n.103
Pevensey, 246 n.89, 262
Philip I, king of France (1060–1108), 60 n.30,
    207
Philip II, Augustus, king of France (1180–1223),
    119, 164, 177, 206 n.11, 269 n.57, 321 n.146
  attacks *routiers* (1183), 322
  exploits war between Richard and Raymond
    of Toulouse (1188), 51
  cuts down elm tree at Gisors, 51
  takes Le Mans (1189), 212, 265
  departs prematurely from crusade (1191),
    120
  breaks vow not to attack Richard's lands, 41,
    50 n.96
  prevented by nobility from attacking
    Normandy (1192), 50
  defies Richard (1193), 234
  uses challenge to cover retreat, 43
  defeat at Fréteval (1194), 43
  burns Evreux (1194), 90
  escapes drowning at Gisors (1198), 167
  conquest of Normandy, 212
  punishes hasty surrender of Vaudreuil (1203),
    226–7
  summons Norman garrisons to surrender on
    pain of death, 222, 244
  sells respite to Arques, Rouen and, Verneuil
    (1204), 209
  besieges Chateau Gaillard (1203–4), 212–13
  recognizes bravery of castellan, 196, 218–19
  entrusts Radepont to Peter de Moret, 214
  exploits death of Arthur, 256
  nearly killed at Bouvines (1214), 166
  orders annihilation of Flemish mercenaries at
    Bouvines, 179–80
  use of Oriflamme, 66
  offerings to St Denis, 67
  mutilates prisoners, 202 and n.128
Picts, 292 n.5, 308
Pierre-Buffiere, 320 n.140
piety, knightly, 18, 56–70, 91–7
  see also banners; war-cries; fasting; mass;
    churches
pilgrimages, 95
Pinkeney, Walter de, 199
Pipe Rolls, 11, 225 n.111, 275–6
Pisan, Christine de, *Livre des Fays d'Armes et de
    Chevalerie* of, 33
Pleshy, 199
Pleurs, 151 n.101, 171 n.78
Plympton, 229, 266 n.36
poets, as recorders of feats of arms, 111–12
Poitiers, William of, 1, 3, 38, 43, 44, 134, 144, 168
    n.58, 201, 264, 311, 333
Poitou, Roger of, 221

Pomeroy, Henry de, 232 n.9
  Jolland de, his brother, 232 n.9
Pont Audemer, 202, 219, 233, 247, 266
Pontefract, priory of, 92
Pontlevoy, battle of (1016), 59
Port, Adam de, 156 and n.128
Préaux, William des, 102
  Peter des, 93, 213
Prendergast, Maurice de, 65 n.45
prisoners, execution of, 52–3, 164, 189
  maltreatment of, 125, 196–202
  magnanimity towards, 124, 188, 196, 203,
    218–9
  division of, 187–91
  lists of captured knights (1173–4), 189 and
    n.37
  see also ransom
proditio, see treason
Prudhoe, 209, 220 and n.80, 269
prudhomme, 99 and n.5
Pruilli, 250
Psalterium Aureum, 145
Puiset, Hugh de, 250, 261 n.10
Purcell, Geoffrey, 242 n.69
pyx, 65, 83

quaestiones, 47 nn.87, 88
Quincy, Saher de, 193, 227

Radepont, 188, 208 n.21, 214
Rahewin, see *Gesta Friderici*
Ralph Archer, 188
Ralph de Gael, earl of Norfolk, 232 n.10
Ralph the Red, 103, 110, 198
Ramlah, 103 n.36, 122
Ramsey, abbey of, 85, 86 n.155, 88, 92 n.189, 95
Rancogne, Geoffrey de, 230
ransom, 183–203 *passim*
  earlier Frankish precedents, 31, 134
  operation in France pre-1066, 134–7
  absence at Hastings, 4
  introduction into England, 30
  aids development of customs of war, 32–4
  incentive to spare opponents, 185
  but catalyst for escalation of war, 185–6
  values of, 184, 193–6
  refusal of, 189–90, 199–201
  lord's rights concerning, 187–9
  vassals obligations concerning, 192–3
Raoul de Cambrai, 90, 91, 139, 160
Rassoi, Roger de, 240
Raymond Le Gros, 310
ravaging,
  evidence for extent of destruction, 273–7
  destruction by itinerant courts, 260 and nn. 5,
    6
  seizure of livestock, 258, 261–5, 262, 266 n.36,
    271
  burning of towns, 265–6
  destruction of crops, 266–70, 271

ravaging (*cont.*)
  of agricultural implements, 269
  of vines and olive groves, 266, 269–70
  slaying of husbandmen, 270–3, 281
  creation of artificial famine, 271, 273
  used to punish subjects, 278–9
  against rebels, 268, 271, 279–81
  criticized as unchivalric, 281–2, 289–90
  but recognized by contemporaries as
    essentially legitimate form of war, 285–7
  see also 'harrying of the North'
  and 'waste'
rebellion, legal status of, 231–40
  as violation of fealty, 232–3
  renunciation of homage, 233–5
  defiance of rebellious vassals by lords, 234
  problems of divided lordship, 235–40
  role of castles in, 204–5
  humiliation of rebels, 253
  punishment of, 240–7; imprisonment, 240;
    mutilation, 241, 245–6, 249, 255 starvation,
    256; precipitation, 242; hanging, 241–3,
    245–6, 248–51, 255
  right of storm pressed home against rebels,
    245–6
  severity as result of provocation, 251
  limitations on royal vengeance, 247–8
  suppression aided by judicious clemency,
    248–55
  recognition of vassals' obligations to
    rebellious lords, 229, 251–2
  see also mutilation; treason
Redvers, Baldwin de, 86, 229, 233, 266 n.36, 267
Reims, council of (1119), 34, 47, 94 n.197
  Henry, archbishop of, 301
  Hincmar, archbishop of, 260 n.5
  cathedral of, interior of west front, *61*
Reivers, Richard de, 144
relics, in weapons, 62–3 and n. 36
  use in war, 65–8
  stripping of 82–3
  True Cross, 67
  see also lance
  and banners
Remelard, 167 n.53
respite, granted to besieged garrisons, 40,
    208–29 *passim*
  chivalric kudos gained by granting of, 210–11,
    218–19
  but might hamper war effort, 219–22
  as mechanism for safeguarding honour of
    defenders, 211–18, 252
  as period of notification before attack, 41, 45
  see also truce
Resson le Mals, 151
Rhuddlan, Robert of, 25, 288, 307, 309 n.77, 316
Riblard, Walter, 163
Richard I Coeur de Lion, king of England
    (1189–99), 12, 124, 170 n.76, 180, 206 n.11,
    225, 230, 256, 261 n.10, 330 n.4
  fortifies church at Saintes (1174), 77
  sends captured Aquitainian barons to father,
    188
  takes Taillebourg (1178), 266
  victory at Gorre (1183), 297 n.23
  takes Bertran de Born's castle of Hautefort,
    35
  war against Raymond of Toulouse (1188),
    50–1
  captures William des Barres (1188), 52, 155
    n.111
  pursues father from Le Mans (1189), 168
    nn.59–60, 265, 301 n.37
  unhorsed by William Marshal, 154, 174
  golden spurs in coronation, 147
  repeals Treaty of Falaise, 194 n.72
  hangs William de Chisi, 284
  promulgates regulations for crusade army, 37
  prowess on crusade, 100–1
  fights with William des Barres, 101, 152 n.108
  sends Isaac's banner to Bury St Edmunds, 67
  executes Muslim garrison of Acre (1191),
    158, 189
  maintains cohesion at Arsuf (1191), 115–16
  use of Standard as rallying point, 66 n.50
  saved from capture by William des Préaux,
    103
  later redeems him (1192), 193
  knights son of Al-Adil, 26–7
  receives gift of horses from Al-Adil at Jaffa
    (1192), 27
  composes derisory ballads against French,
    119
  precipitates Muslim garrison of Darum
    (1192), 242 n.64
  captivity and ransom, 193
  defied by Philip (1193), 234
  appeals to pope, 47, 50 n.97
  claims of just war against Philip, 50
  suppression of John's castles (1194), 246
  hangs John's sergeants at Nottingham, 245
  punishment of John and supporters (1194),
    232
  starves Robert Brito, 256
  wounded at Gaillon (1196), 175 n.102
  imprisons Philip of Beauvais, 47, 188, 194,
    197
  grants ransoms to William Marshal, 190–1
  burns St Valéry, 67
  victory at Gisors (1198), 167, 194 n.77, 332
    n.8
  refuses surrender of garrison of Chaluz
    Chabrol (1199), 224, 246, 249
  fatally wounded by crossbow bolt, 175
  licenses tournaments, 109 n.62, 152
  use of ravaging, 266, 304
  use of *routiers*, 322
  military skill, 100, 115–6
  martial reputation, 101, 108–9, 146
  seen as superior to Roland, 10, 100

loyalty to his men, 104, 193
war-cry on crusade, 64
mutilates prisoners, 202 and n.120
executes prisoners, 52, 164, 189, 203
Richard, natural son of Henry I, 103
Richard the Fleming, 306
Richmond, 216
Ridefort, Gerard de, Grand Master of the
Temple, 117 n.98
Rievaulx, 292 n.4, 295
Ailred, abbot of, 65, 66, 114, 121, 168, 292
nn.4 and 7, 293–7 passim, 318 n.123
praise and censure of David I, 327–9
Rigord, chronicler of St Denis, 53, 223, 318
n.126, 319
Ripon, 65, 298
Robert, I, 'the Magnificent', duke of Normandy
(1027–35), 42, 138, 143, 253
Robert II the Pious, king of France (996–1031),
258
Robert Brito, 256
Robert the Burgundian, 186
Robert Curthose, duke of Normandy
(1087–1106), 82, 83, 138, 139, 201, 230, 232
and n.9, 235, 247 n.92, 266 n.35, 281, 285
mutilates defenders of Saint-Céneri (1088),
181
n.124, 241, 249 n.101
devastations caused by his court (1101), 260
storms Vignats (1102), 224, 252
failure to protect churches, 77–8
captured at Tinchebrai (1106), 188
authorises surrender of castles to Henry I,
214–15
captivity, 240 n.51, 255
Robert Quarrel, castellan of St Céneri, 181
n.124, 249 n.101
Roche-au-Moine, 244
Rochester, siege of (1088), 40, 224, 235, 246,
247, 253, 267
siege of (1215), 120, 175, 181, 187, 194, 207,
241, 245, 251, 256, 266, 267–8
Aelfstan, bishop of, 278 n.94
Gundulf, bishop of, 73
Roland, cantilena sung at Hastings about, 10,
111
see also Song of Roland
Rollo, duke of Normandy (911–33), 134
Rolls of the Justices in Eyre, 263 n.17, 284
Rotuli de oblatis et finibus, 189
Rouen, 209, 213, 214, 242, 281
La-Trinité-du-Mont, 60
council of (1096), 70 n.74, 71 n.79, 268–9
siege of (1174), 127–8, 208 n.22
Roumare, William de, 93
routiers (ruptarii), 12, 16, 34, 261–3, 264, 268, 290,
291–329 passim
canonical prohibition of (1179), 297, 299,
300, 317, 318, 322
widely disregarded, 56, 71–2

peace leagues against, 300–1, 322
mixed racial composition, 291, 297 and n.23
employment against rebels, 72, 243, 252,
320–2
royal control of, 320–3
political prominence of captains, 299–300,
321, 323
special rights to booty and ransoms, 191
excellence as troops, 179, 320, 322
animosity of knights towards, 179–80
cut down in battle, 153, 155, 179–80, 301
executed on capture, 52–3
charges of atrocities, 297–300
extortion and torture by, 312–13
sacrilege, 318–20
but refrain from killing clergy, 91
Roxburgh, 121
Rufus, see William II, king of England
Rupierre, William de, 186
ruptarii, see routiers

Saint-Aubin-le-Cauf, battle of (1052/3), 130
Saint-Ceneri-sur-Sarthe, 181 n.124, 192, 241, 249
n.101, 255, 266 n.35
Saint-Evroul, 14 n.51, 15, 60, 76 n.101, 261, 274,
283
Roger, abbot of, 274; see also Orderic Vitalis
Saint-Jamme, 150 n.94
Saint-Laurent, William, son of Roger of, 164
Saint-Pierre-sur-Dives, 60, 82, 190
Saint-Saens, Helias de, 255 n.139
Sainte-Suzanne, siege of (c. 1084), 135, 163, 171,
185–6, 191
St Albans, abbey of, 76 n.101, 84 and nn.147–8,
299
William of Trumpington, abbot of, 84
St Davids, 65
St Denis, 64, 66, 67
Suger, abbot of, 44, 165, 194, 303
St Michael's Mount, 232 n.9
St Pol, count of, 104
St Valéry, 38, 67
Thomas de, 180
Safadin, see Al-Adil
safe conduct, 40, 49, 52
Saffron Walden, 199
Saintes, 77, 88
saints, 64–66, 186, military, 7 n. 19, 57
see also banners; war-cries; relics
Saladin, 26, 35, 67, 223
in the Ordene de Chevalerie, 26
possibly knighted by Humphrey of Toron,
26
Salisbury, castle of, 199
John of, 13, 14, 55–6, 285
Patrick, earl of, 129, 140, 154
Roger, bishop of, 73 n.87, 87 n.162, 199
Roger le Poer, his son, 199
William, earl of, 192, 302
Sancerre, count of, 263

sanctuary, 78–80
    violation of 76–80
    of the plough, 260
Sandwich, sea battle off (1217), 69, 167 n.53,
    176
Sarlat, 289
Saumur, church of St Florent, 94
Sawtry, 238–9
scorched earth, 265–6
    see also ravaging
Scots, 12, 16, 62, 66, 119, 161, 269, 290, 291–329
    passim, 337–9
    chroniclers' terms of reference, 292 and
        nn.5–7
    composition of armies, 114, 292 n.3
    infantry cut down in defeat, 180
    familiarity of Anglo-Normans with Scottish
        knights, 150, 155
    their prowess at Alnwick, 155 n.122
    numerical inferiority in cavalry, 121
    tactics, 114, 121–2
    strategies of ravaging, 324–6
    disputes between elements of army, 114
    discipline and royal control of, 323–9
    later devastations of northern England, 276
        and n.84, 277
    hostility of Anglo-Norman writers towards,
        291–7
    alleged 'atrocities', 293–7
    indiscriminate killing, 302–9
    enslaving, 313–17
    see also David I; William I, the Lion
Séez, Serlo, bishop of, 62, 78, 89
    Robert, count of, 225
Seillan, Peter, 51
Seisyll ap Dyfnwal, 338
Sempach, battle of (1386), 335
Senlis, Simon II de, earl of Northampton, 41,
    239
Sherbourne, 197 n.95, 199
Shirkuh, 226 n.117
Shrewsbury, 224, 242, 246, 249, 251
    earls of, Roger de Montgomery, 60, 136, 167
        n.53, 221, 247 and n.92
    Hugh de Montgomery, 171
    see also Bellême, Robert de
Sicily, 170 n.75
siege, passim
    military role of castles, 204–5
    methods of siege, 205–8
    conventions governing, 208–29 passim
    extent of resistance expected from garrisons,
        212–18, 224–9
    right of storm, 222–4
    see also respite; and truce
Siete Partidas, of Alphonso X the Wise of Castile,
    39
Sigismund, German emperor (1410–37), 35
Sigvat, skald, 25 n.103
Silli, William de, 212

Silverstone, 261 n.10
Siverey, Erard de, 123
Slane, 306
slavery, 30, 304, 305, 313–17
Sleaford, 199
squires, 25, 52, 195, 226
Soissons, count of, 112, 240
Song of Dermot and the Earl, 8, 64–5, 170, 215, 309
Song of Roland, 9, 24, 28, 57, 64, 100, 102, 110,
    113, 114, 120, 123, 120, 123, 157 and n.133,
    187 n.22
Sorrel-Moussel, 48, 150 n.95, 151
Sotengi, Gerard de, 213, 244
Southampton, 277 n.91
Southwark, 277 n.91
Stainmore, 292
Stamford Bridge, battle of (1066), 3, 173 n.86
Standard (or Northallerton), battle of the (1138),
    23, 49 n.94, 60, 114, 119 n.109, 131 n.182,
    167 n.57, 168, 179, 180, 235, 292, 295, 324,
    327, 328–9, 338
Standard, wheeled flagpole used on Third
    Crusade, 66 n.50
Stephen, king of England (1135–54), 40, 119,
    128, 191, 229 n.139, 235, 236, 238, 244, 261
    n.12, 266 n.35, 267, 284, 320, 333
    executes former 'janitor' of Henry I, 242
    ravages lands of Baldwin de Redvers (1136),
        266 n.36
    desires to execute garrison of Exeter (1136),
        224, 233, 242
    but spares them, 249, 253
    saves Earl Henry from capture at Ludlow,
        49
    executes garrison of Shrewsbury (1138), 224,
        242, 249
    ravages Lothian (1138), 304
    besieges Lincoln castle (1141), 40
    refuses to avoid battle, 107 and n.53
    prowess in battle of Lincoln, 167
    imprisonment, 188, 196–7, 255
    negotiations for ransom, 192
    spares life of William Marshal as hostage, 221
    violates peace of the court, 41, 255
    use of systematic devastation (1149), 271–3,
        286, 311 n.89
    fortifies churches, 76–7
    use of intimidation to gain castles, 199, 245,
        255
    his chivalry, 49 n.94, 221
    grants Matilda safe conduct, 40, 49 n.94,
        255
    angered at violation of truce, 49
    pays Henry Plantagenet's passage home, 49
        n.94
Stiklestadir, battle of (1030), 111 n.74
storm, right of, 1, 36, 222–4, 242–7
Strathclyde, kingdom of, 292 and nn.6–7
Strathearn, Malisse, earl of, 114
Strattondale, 310

Stuteville, Roger de, castellan of Wark,
    gains respite from William the Lion (1173),
        46, 218–12, 218 and n.88
    forbids men to taunt retreating Scots, 161
    Nicholas de, 184
    Robert de, imprisoned after Tinchebrai
        (1106), 141 n.42, 240 n.51
Sulgrave, Waleran of, 192
surcoats, 171
Sutri, Bonzino of, 75
Sutton, Saher of, 189
Svein, son of Godwine, 118 and n.104
Sveno, Danish chronicler, 36, 118 n.104
Sveno stone, 307, *308*
Swabia, Philip of, 50
swords, 62–4, *63*, 170, 171, 172, 173

Tacitus, 23
tactics,
    fighting dismounted, 23, 167 n.57, 167–9
    'feigned flight', 130
    in the tournament, 128
    Turkish, 115
    at Arsuf (1191), 115–16
    see also battle
Tafurs, 296 n.22
Taillebourg, 266
Talbot, Geoffrey, 88
De Tallagio, 260 n.6
Tancarville, William de, chamberlain, 130, 183
Tancred, 122
Tanfield, 302
Templars, 19, 26, 29, 74, 115, 116 and n.95, 117
    and
        nn.96–8, 157, 226 n.117
    master of, 184
    Rule of the Temple, 39, 117 and n.96, 120,
        169–70
tempus werrae, 263
tenserie, 84–6, 267, 311
terme, see truce
Tewkesbury, 281, 288
Thanet, 278 n.94
Thetford, 278 n.94
Thimert, 207
Thirsk, 250
Thouars, Geoffrey de, 134, 201–2
three orders, 16, 70–1
Thurlaston, Robert of, 263 n.17
Tickhill, 226, 232 n.9, 246, 252
Tillières, 130, 184 n.6
Tilty, 82
Tinchebrai, castle of, 267
    battle of (1106), 14, 23, 60, 140–1 and
        nn.42–3, 167 n.57, 169, 176, 188, 189, 190,
        205, 214, 334
Tofi the Proud, 25 n.103
Tonbridge, 245 n.81, 246 n.89
Torigny, Robert of, 141 n.45, 176
Tosny (Conches), Ralph III de, 60, 184

Roger III de, 82, 89, 270–1
Roger I de, 139
    and sons Elbert and Elinant, 139
Toulouges (Elne), council of (1027), 70 n.74,
    270, 283 n.114
Toulouse, 50,
    Raymond V, count of, 51–2
tournament, 17, 208
    earlier forms of cavalry exercises, 145–6
    value for knightly training, 73–4, 152 and
        n.108
    role in development of chivalry, 149–53
    furthers creation of brotherhood of arms,
        149–51
    regional composition of teams, 150 and
        nn.94–5
    as source of glory and profit, 73–4, 108–9
    Arthurian influences on, 11, 149 and n.92, 20
    taking of ransom and horses in, 48, 151–2
    rules of conduct in, 48
    forbidden by canon law, 73–4
    licensed in England by Richard I, 109 n.62
    participation in by Henry II's sons, 108, 109
        and n.62
Tournay, church of, 89
Tours, 198
Tourville, Geoffrey de, 202, 233, 241, 255
Towton, battle of (1461), 335
Tractatus de bello, de represaliis et de duello, see
    Legnano, John of
Tracy, Henry de, 195
Trahearn Fychan, of Brycheiniog, 309 n.80
treason, 37, 118 n.103, 231–57 *passim*, 309
    crimes incurring charges of, 231 and n.6
    surrendering castles without lord's
        permission, 225, 226
    surrendering without adequate resistance, 225
    punished by enforcing right of storm, 224
    Statute of Treason (1352), 231 and n.7
    baronial rebels regarded as traitors by French
        allies (1216–17), 233 and n.18
Trés ancien coutoumier de Normandie, 269
Triaverdini, 297 and n.23
Trie, Enguerrand de, 173
    Walo de, 103, 198
Trim, 215–16
Trois Fontaines, Aubrey de, 321 n.146
Troyes, Chrétien de, 10, 11, 129, 149 and n.92,
    154–5
    Cligés, 106
    Conte du Graal (Perceval), 129, 149, 286
    Erec, 106 and n.45
    Lancelot (The Knight of the Cart), 197 n.95
    Yvain, 106 n.45
truce, 41–2, 45, 52, 331–2, 208–9, 236; *see also*
    respite
Truce of God, 34, 56, 70–1, 139, 283, 332, 336
    see also Peace of God
    and clergy
Truie, Gerard de, 170 n.70

Tutbury, 192, 250
Tynedale, 220
Tynemouth, abbey of, 84, 210 and n.115
Tyre, 226 n.117
  William of, 226 n.117, 270
Tyrell, Hugh, 215–16

Uhtred, earl of Northumbria, 303
Umfraville, Odinel de, 117, 211, 220 and n.80, 325
Urban II, pope, 29, 57
Usamah ibn Munqidh, 27, 45 n.77, 102, 170 n.70, 174
Usk, 265
d'Ussy, Robert, 163

Val-es-Dunes, battle of (1047), 163, 167
Valennes, 150 n.94
Valognes, Philip de, 150
Varaville, battle of (1057), 163 and n.26
Vascoeuil, Gilbert de, 225
Vaudreuil, 89, 119, 192, 206 n.11, 226–7, 270
  monastery of St Mary Magdalene, 270
Vaux, Robert de, castellan of Carlisle, 210, 216, 244
Vaux-de-Cernay, Peter de, 289
Vegetius, Epitoma rei militari, 14, 38, 55
Vendôme, 43
Verneuil, 228
  siege of (1173), 35, 43, 50, 120, 126–7, 250, 177
Vesci, Eustace de, 175 n.98
  William de, castellan of Wark, 221
Vexin, 132, 185, 204
Vichiers, Renaud de, 116 n.95
Vieuxpont, Robert de, 163, 191
Vigeois, Geoffrey of, 35, 52, 82, 322
Vignats, 224, 252
Vikings, 3, 28, 265 and n.26, 279
  bias of sources against, 294, 318
  habitually slay opponents in battle, 133
  slave-trading, 313–14
  mobility in war, 134
  religious dimension of war against, 136–7, 294 n.13
Villerai, Aymer de, 167 n.53
vis et voluntas, 246
Vitot, Matthew de, 163
Vitry, 88
  Jacques de, 56 n.3
Vivien, nephew of William of Orange, 57
Vouvant, 245

Wace, 5 n.18, 11
Walcote, Warin de, 284
Waldric, chancellor to Henry I, 188 and n.29
Waleran de Beaumont, count of Meulan, 89, 107, 137 n.26, 236, 270, 281, 287–9
  at Bourgthéroulde (1124), 141, 288
  war with Robert of Gloucester, 281, 288

his cruelty, 288
his chivalry, 288
  see also Leicester, earls of
Waleran the German, 228
Wales, see Welsh
Walincourt, Matthew de, 152 n.106
Wallingford, 77, 87, 197 n.95
Walter Daniel, 292 n.4
Walter Sor, sons of, 201
Waltham,
  abbey, 5 n.18
  Chronicle, 5 n.18, 25 n.103
  Holy Rood of, 25 n.103
Waltheof, earl of Dunbar, 292 n.3
Waltheof, earl of Huntingdon, 232
Wanci, Osbert de, 263
war cries, 64, 130–1
  Anglo-Saxon, 4 n.12
  as religious invocations, 56
  Norman, 29, 64
  French, 64, 66, 130
Warden, abbey of, 239
Wareham, seige of (1142), 40, 209
Warenne, Reginald de, 190
  William de, 239
Wark-on-Tweed, 48, 209, 219, 220 and n.83, 221, 266, 290 n.150, 333 n.11
Warkworth, 221, 302, 319
  St Lawrence's church, 302, 326
'waste', 275–6
Waterford, 180
Weald, forest of, 181
Wearmouth, St Peter's abbey, 302, 324
Weid, George, count of, 37 n.31
Wells, Hugh of, 213
Welsh, 66, 122, 179 n.103, 208 n.22, 288, 301 n.37, 306, 307, 309, 310, 316, 338, 339–40
Wenceslas, St, helmet of, 62
Wendover, Roger of, 119 and n.109, 141 n.48, 207, 233, 248, 257, 298 and n.24, 307 n.72, 312
Westminster, 66, 316
Wherewell, abbey of, 77 and n.108, 139–40
Wigain, clerk to Young King, 152
Wilfrid, St, 65
William, duke of Normandy, king of England (1066–87), 59, 60, 134, 136, 137, 138, 184, 232
  invests Brionne (1047–50), 207
  takes knights for ransom, 134
  mutilates garrison of Alençon (c. 1051), 2, 161, 249, 251
  defends Domfront, 43
  portrayed as flower of knighthood, 144
  taunts French with defeat at Mortemer (1054), 161
  banishes Roger de Mortemer, 239
  demands Harold's release by Guy of Ponthieu (1064), 191, 201

accepts surrender of Dinan (1064), *217*, 253
n.127
bestows arms on Harold (1064), 5, 25
forbids army at St Valéry to loot, 38, 264 n.18
ravages Harold's estates, 272, 278
supposed offer of single combat to Harold,
44
at Hastings, 3
with relics and papal banner, 29, 67
given new mounts in battle, 103, 104
treatment of Harold's body, 5 n.18
accepts surrender of Dover (1066), 1
destructive march to subdue London, 275 and
n.78, 277–8
problems of supply, 264 and n.18
blinds hostage at Exeter (1068), 245
but spares citizens, 2, 280
'harrying of the North', 271 and n.67, 273,
283, 303, 311
unsuccessfully besieges Sainte-Suzanne
(1083–5), 185–6
scorches English coast (1085), 265
burns Mantes, 88, 269 n.57
makes restitution, 95
imprisonment of enemies, 201
prohibits slave-trade, 315–16
William II Rufus, king of England (1087–1100),
83, 118, 124, 125, 235, 267, 281, 287
refuses surrender of garrison of Rochester
(1088), 224, 235, 242, 246
relents, 253–4
insists on royal fanfare, 40, 253
treatment of rebels, 241–2, 254 and nn.135–7
quarrel with William of St Calais, 40 n.47,
279
attacks Chaumont (1098), 132–3
grants truce to Manceaux lords, 123, 236
grants respite to garrison of Mayet (1099),
160, 221–2
logistical problems, 264 and n.23
damage inflicted by his court (1097), 260
ravages Maine (1099), 160, 261, 265, 269
repentence on sick-bed, 95 n.200
as epitome of chivalry, 146
wealth enables him to ransom his knights
quickly, 194
honourable treatment of prisoners, 149, 188,
190, 203, 333
William I the Lion, king of Scots (1165–1214),
266, 277, 291–329 *passim*, 333
tourneys in France, 150, 220 n.85
at siege of Toulouse (1159), 220 n.85
self-perception as Anglo-Norman knight,
219–20
proposes duel to settle claim to
Northumberland (1173), 44

defies Henry II, 235
urged to war by the *juvenes*, 107
mocked for avoiding battle, 128–2
threatens Robert de Vaux, 244
grants respites to Northumbrian castles
(1173–4), 46, 209, 210–11, 221, 244
hampers own war effort thereby, 219–20
unsuccessful sieges of Carlisle, 216, 220
takes Appleby (1174), 225
repulsed fom Wark (1174), 161, 220
notifies Odinel d'Umfraville he will besiege
Prudhoe, 220 and n.80
captured at Alnwick (1174), 65, 122, 150, 155,
220, 301, 302
attempts to distance himself from excesses of
troops, 220, 323–9
but blamed for their atrocities, 302, 305,
324–6
forbids sacrilege, 324
orders slayings, 325–6
dedicates Arbroath abbey to St Thomas, 65
quarrel with Hugh de Puiset over billetting
(1194), 261 n.10
William the Carpenter, 122
William Clito, son of Robert Curthose, 62, 130,
141, 202, 219, 242, 247, 255
William, count of Orange, 5, 7 n.19
chanson de Guillaume, 5–6, 7 n.19, 57, 110–11
William Talvas, *see* Bellême
William Wallace, 231, 277
Willikin of the Weald, 208 n.22
Wilton, 76, 78, 81, 139, 142, 199
Winchester, 77 n.108, 89, 142, 265, 284
rout of (1141), 191, 192, 195, 196, 239
Henry of Blois, bishop of, 73 nn.87 and 88;
promises Matilda to restrict aid to Stephen
(1141), 237; burns Winchester (1141), 76,
89; hires mercenary knights, 82; and Brian
fitz Count, 284; imprisons kinsman of
Gilbert Foliot, 203 n.134, 219 n.76
Geoffrey, prior of, 203 n.134
Peter des Roches, bishop, 141 n.47
knight service of bishopric, 237 and n.40
fair of St Giles at, 284
Wisby, battle of (1361), 173 and nn.85–7
Worcester, 66, 78, 281
John of, 66 n.52, 78, 273, 288, 316
Ralph of, 80
Simon, bishop of, 85, 87 n.164
Wulfstan, St, bishop of, 66 n.52, 316

York, 65, 209, 273
Thurstan, archbishop of, 318 n.123
Wulfstan, archbishop of, 315 n.111

Ypres, William of, 77, 140, 192

DATE DUE
